THE ACTS OF THE APOSTLES

A SHORTER COMMENTARY

THE ACTS OF THE APOSTLES

A SHORTER COMMENTARY

C. K. BARRETT

Emeritus Professor of Divinity, Durham University

2002'

T&T CLARK LTD

A Continuum imprint

59 George Street
Edinburgh EH2 2LQ
Scotland

www.tandtclark.co.uk

470 Lexington Avenue
New York 10017–6504
USA

www.continuumbooks.com

First published 2002

ISBN 0 567 08817 0

British Library Cataloguing-in-Publication Data
A catalogue record for this book is available from the British Library

Typeset by Waverley Typesetters, Galashiels
Printed and bound in Great Britain by MPG Books, Bodmin

CONTENTS

PREFACE

This book, made at the Publisher's request, is a shortened and simplified version of my commentary on the Acts of the Apostles in the International Critical Commentary (two volumes, 1994, 1998). I hope it may be useful to some who have found the larger book unsuited to their needs. In this shorter book the reader is not asked to deal with quotations in Latin, Greek, Hebrew, Aramaic, German and French. This, with other economies, will mean that sometimes – not always – conclusions are presented without the arguments, or at least without a full statement of the arguments, that may be supposed to justify them. This will inevitably, I fear, give the book a dogmatic flavour, which I should prefer to avoid. I hope that the reason for it will be understood.

My gratitude to those mentioned in the Preface to the large edition remains undiminished.

C. K. Barrett

COMMENTARIES

Readers of this commentary will wish to compare the views expressed in it with those of other writers. A list of commentaries available in English follows, with a few notes that may help readers to choose what they may find most useful.

BRUCE, F. F., *The Book of the Acts* (New International Commentary on the NT), Grand Rapids, 3rd edition 1990

CALVIN, J., *The Acts of the Apostles*, translated by J. N. Fraser and W. J. C. McDonald. Two volumes, Edinburgh/London, 1965, 1966

CONZELMANN, H., *The Acts of the Apostles* (Hermeneia), Philadelphia, 1987

DUNN, J. D. G., *The Acts of the Apostles* (Epworth Commentaries), London, 1996

FITZMYER, J. A., *The Acts of the Apostles* (Anchor Bible), New York/London/Toronto/Sydney/Auckland, 1998

HAENCHEN, E., *The Acts of the Apostles*, Oxford, 1971

HANSON, R. P. C., *The Acts* (New Clarendon Bible), Oxford, 1967

JACKSON, F. J. F. and LAKE, K., *The Beginnings of Christianity*, Part I: The Acts of the Apostles. Five volumes (Vol. IV contains the Commentary), London, 1920–33

JOHNSON, L. T., *The Acts of the Apostles* (Sacra Pagina 5), Collegeville, 1992

LÜDEMANN, G., *Early Christianity according to the Traditions in Acts: a Commentary*, London, 1989

MARSHALL, I. H., *The Acts of the Apostles* (Tyndale NT Commentaries), Leicester, 1980

PACKER, J. W., *The Acts of the Apostles* (Cambridge Bible Commentaries), Cambridge, 1975

WALASKAY, P. W., *Acts* (Westminster Bible Commentaries), Louisville, Kentucky, 1998

WILLIAMS, C. S. C., *The Acts of the Apostles* (Black's NT Commentaries), London, 1957

WITHERINGTON, B., *The Acts of the Apostles. A Socio-rhetorical Commentary*, Grand Rapids/Cambridge (UK)/Carlisle, 1998

Calvin's commentary is the work of a theologian who was also a classical scholar and historian. This work is in many ways surprisingly up to date.

The following are all fairly small commentaries, but written by scholars of distinction with views of Acts that should be kept in mind: Dunn, Hanson, Marshall, Packer, and Walaskay.

Bruce, Johnson, Williams are somewhat longer, have more detail, and use a little Greek. Lüdemann may be put in this group, but the book is not a commentary in the ordinary sense; see pp. xlvf.

Among longer and more detailed commentaries it is unfortunate that the English translation of Haenchen's was made before a number of changes were introduced into the original German. Some of Haenchen's views are open to challenge but the book remains an important one. Witherington's is a large book, not (despite its title) one-sidedly devoted to sociological and rhetorical studies but a good guide to modern work on Acts. Fitzmyer's commentary, by one of the most learned and thoughtful of living NT scholars, is not too demanding in style and can by used by anyone with time and determination sufficient to face its 860 pages. Conzelmann's is short, but by no means easy.

ABBREVIATIONS

B	Babylonian Talmud
Background	C. K. Barrett, *The NT Background: Selected Documents*, London, 2nd edition, 1987
Barth, *CD*	*Church Dogmatics*, 13 volumes, Edinburgh, 1936–69
Begs.	See Commentaries, s.v. Jackson and Lake
BGBE	Beiträge zur Geschichte der biblischen Exegese
CIL	*Corpus Inscriptionum Latinarum*
CMS	C. K. Barrett, *Church, Ministry, and Sacraments in the NT*, Exeter, 1985
1 Corinthians	C. K. Barrett, *A Commentary on the First Epistle to the Corinthians*, London, 2nd edition, 1992
2 Corinthians	C. K. Barrett, *A Commentary on the Second Epistle to the Corinthians*, London, 1973
Dalman, G. *SSW*	G. Dalman, *Sacred Sites and Ways*, London, 1935
Danby	H. Danby, *The Mishnah*, London, 1933
Dibelius	M. Dibelius, *Studies in the Acts of the Apostles*, ed. H. Greeven, London, 1956
Dinkler	E. Dinkler, *Signum Crucis*, Tübingen, 1967
EThL	*Ephemerides Theologicae Lovanienses*

Eusebius, *HE*	Eusebius, *Historia Ecclesiastica*
Praep. Ev.	Eusebius, *Praeparatio Evangelica*
FS Corsani	*Protestantesimo* 48.3 (1994), *I Metodi dellè indagine sul Nuevo Testamento*. Omaggio per B. Corsani. Ed. S. Rostagno, Rome, 1994
FS Jervell	*Mighty Minorities?* Essays in Honour of J. Jervell. Ed. D. Hellholm, H. Moxnes, and T. K. Seim. Oslo/Copenhagen/Stockholm/ Boston, 1995
FS Neirynck	*The Four Gospels*, Ed. F. Van Segbroeck, C. M. Tuckett, G. Van Belle, J. Verheyden. Leuven, 1992
FS Schweizer	*Die Mitte des Neuen Testaments. Einheit und Vielfalt Neutestamentlicher Theologie.* Ed U. Luz and H. Weder. Göttingen, 1983
FS Smit Sibinga	*Novum Testamentum* 38.2 (1996). Special number in Honour of J. Smit Sibinga. Ed. P. Borgen and others. Leiden, 1996
Hatch, *Essays*	E. Hatch, *Essays in Biblical Greek*, Oxford, 1889
Hemer	C. J. Hemer, *The Book of Acts in the Setting of Hellenistic History*, ed. C. H. Gempf (Wissenschaftliche Untersuchungen zum Neuen Testament 49), Tübingen, 1989
Hort	F. J. A. Hort, *The Christian Ecclesia*, London, 1914 (first edition, 1897)
Jeremias, *Jerusalem*	J. Jeremias, *Jerusalem in the Time of Jesus*, ET London, 1969
Josephus, *War*	*History of the Jewish War against the Romans*
Ant.	*Jewish Antiquities*
Apion	*Against Apion*
JSNTSupps	Journal for the Study of the NT, Supplements
LCL	Loeb Classical Library

LS	*A Greek–English Lexicon*, compiled by H. G. Liddell and R. Scott, New edition by H. S. Jones and R. McKenzie, Oxford [1940]. Supplement ed. E. A. Baker, Oxford, 1968. Revised Supplement ed. P. G. W. Glare and A. A. Thompson, Oxford, 1996
Lüdemann	G. Lüdemann; see Commentaries
LXX	Septuagint
M.	Mishnah
Moule, *Idiom Book*	C. F. D. Moule, *An Idiom Book of NT Greek*, Cambridge, 1953
MT	Masoretic text
Murphy-O'Connor	*Holy Land*, J. Murphy-O'Connor, *The Holy Land*, Oxford, 1981, and several subsequent editions
	St Paul's Corinth, J. Murphy-O'Connor, *St Paul's Corinth: Texts and Archaeology*, Wilmington, 1983
NS	*The History of the Jewish People in the Age of Jesus Christ (175 BC–AD 135)*, by E. Schürer. Revised and edited by G. Vermes, F. Millar, P. Vermes, and M. Black. Vols I–III.2, Edinburgh, 1973–87
NTS	*New Testament Studies*
OCD	*The Oxford Classical Dictionary*, ed. N. G. L. Hammond and H. H. Scullard, 2nd edition 1978
OCT	Oxford Classical Texts
P	Palestinian Talmud
Qumran 1 QS	Community Rule
CD	Damascus Document
1 QM	War Scroll

1 QH	Hymns
1 QpHab	Habakkuk Pesher
1 QapGen	Genesis Apocryphon
4 QExod	Fragments of Exodus found in Cave 4
4 QFlor	Florilegium found in Cave 4
4 QTest	Testimonies found in Cave 4
4 QpIs[a]	Pesher on Isaiah, fragment a, found in Cave 4

Romans	C. K. Barrett, *A Commentary on the Epistle to the Romans*, London, 2nd edition, 1991
Schwarz	D. R. Schwarz, *Agrippa 1*, TSAJ 23, Tübingen, 1990
SNTSMS	Society for NT Study, Monograph Series
Taylor, J.	J. Taylor, *Les Actes des deux Apôtres.* Commentaire Historique V (Act. 9.1 – 18.22), Études Bibliques, Nouvelle Série 23, Paris, 1992; VI (Act. 18.23 – 28.31), Études Bibliques, Nouvelle Série 30, Paris, 1996
TDNT	G. Kittel and G. Friedrich, *Theological Dictionary of the NT*, 10 volumes, ET Grand Rapids, 1964–76
T	Tosephta
Trebilco	P. R. Trebilco, *Jewish Communities in Asia Minor*, SNTSMS 69, Cambridge, 1991
Wilson, *Gentiles*	S. G. Wilson, *The Gentiles and the Gentile Mission in Luke–Acts*, SNTSMS 23, Cambridge, 1973

ADRIATIC
ROME
Three Taverns
Appii Forum
ITALY
Puteoli
THR
MACEDONIA
Philippi
Neapolis
Amphipolis
THESSALONICA
Beroea
Samoth
AEGEAN
ACHAEA
Rhegium
Cephallenia
CORINTH
Cenchreae
ATHENS
SYRACUSE
Melita
Crete
Phoenix
Fair
MEDI
CYRENE
SYRTIS
CYRENE
LIBYA
0
100
200
300 km

BLACK SEA
ACE
BITHYNIA
GALATIA
PONTUS
Byzantium
Ancyra
race
MYSIA
Troas
Assos
Adramyttium
ASIA
GALATIA
Mitylene
Thyatira
PHRYGIA
CAESAREA - MAZACA
Chios
LYCAONIA
CAPPADOCIA
Iconium
EPHESUS
Samos
Lystra
Derbe
PISIDIA
Miletus
PAMPHYLIA
Perge
Attalia
TARSUS
Cos
LYCIA
CILICIA
Cnidus
Patara
Myra
Antioch
Seleucia
Rhodes
SYRIA
Salmone
Salamis
Paphos
Cyprus
Havens
TERRANEAN
DAMASCUS
Sidon
Tyre
Ptolemais
GALILEE
CAESAREA
Sharon
Samaria
Joppa
Lydda
JERUSALEM
JUDAEA
Gaza
ALEXANDRIA
ARABIA
EGYPT

INTRODUCTION

I. TEXT

The text of Acts is to be recovered from a large number of Greek MSS, written at many different periods of Christian history; from a number of ancient versions; and from quotations made by ancient writers. Detailed study of all these sources, which is manifestly impossible here, shows that the earliest of them fall into two main groups, giving two distinguishable[1] types of text. It will not often, in this commentary, be necessary to refer to these variant types; they will be referred to as the Old Uncial text and the Western text.[2] Even less frequently will it be necessary to mention particular MSS, but a few examples of the textual sources may be given here.

P[45], Chester Beatty Papyrus. This MS originally contained the four gospels and Acts. It is now fragmentary, but parts of all the gospels remain, with Acts 4.27 – 17.17. It constitutes an exception to what was written above, for its text is neither simply of the Old Uncial kind nor Western. It may represent an independent (Caesarean?) text type, perhaps more probably it is a combination of readings from Old Uncial and Western sources. The papyrus dates from about AD 300, and is in the Chester Beatty collection in Dublin.

[1] This must not be misunderstood. In all essentials the two groups tell the same story; the variants are interesting and in themselves important, but they affect details rather than the substance of the book.

[2] This text got its name from the fact that it was first recognized in sources of (geographically) Western origin. It is now apparent that it was known in all parts of the ancient world, but the name Western (often placed within inverted commas) is retained.

B, Codex Vaticanus, so called because it has been in the Vatican Library since at latest 1475. It was written in the fourth century, and is the primary witness to the Old Uncial text. It was originally a complete Bible but has lost the beginning and the end. Acts is preserved entire.

D, Codex Bezae Cantabrigiensis, a bilingual MS (Greek on the left hand page, Latin on the right). It was given by the Reformer Theodore Beza to Cambridge University (in whose library it now is) in 1581. It is known to have been in Lyons in 1562, but its place of origin is not known. There are numerous conjectures. The probable date of writing is *c.* AD 400. Codex Bezae is the most important witness to the Western text. Unfortunately it has been damaged and 8.29 – 10.14; 21.2–10, 16–18; 22.10–20; 22.29 – 28.31 are wanting.

Latin Versions. The Latin Vulgate was made towards the end of the fourth century. Whether Jerome, to whom the work as a whole was entrusted, himself made the translation of Acts is disputed. It represents a reaction towards the Old Uncial (or Alexandrian) type of text and away from the earlier (Old Latin) versions which, with a good deal of variety, are predominantly Western.

Syriac Versions. The early history of Acts in Syriac is not known, but it seems that Ephrem Syrus (died AD 373) had a Syriac text. No MS of Acts is extant corresponding to the Old Syriac gospels. Of interest are certain marginal notes and readings (of a Western kind) in the Harclean Syriac (AD 616).

Coptic Versions. The Sahidic (variously dated in second, third and fourth centuries) has some Western elements, the Bohairic (probably about AD 400) fewer. Of great interest is a Middle Egyptian MS, clearly Western in text. This too (so far the MS has been available only on microfilm) has been variously dated (fourth, fifth, sixth centuries). It ends at Acts 15.3, not through damage but of intention – a fascinating problem.

Patristic Quotations. The first extant Christian writer who quotes Acts explicitly is Irenaeus (Bishop of Lyons, *c.* AD 130–200). His text is akin to that of Codex Bezae, and demonstrates the antiquity of the Western text.

The student of Acts will for the most part adopt the 'eclectic method'; that is, each variant will be assessed on its own merits, and neither adopted nor rejected because it belongs to a particular family of readings (Old Uncial or Western). It is, however, impossible to escape the wider textual problem. We possess Acts in what are virtually two recensions, the Old Uncial and the Western.[3] The critic naturally wishes to know the history of these two texts and the relation between them. The ground has been fought over for many years, and both text forms have been defended as the earlier and as representing best what Luke wrote.

Even a sketch of this debate would occupy more space than is available in this commentary. It must suffice to mention a few outstanding names. In 1895 F. Blass[4] developed the view that both forms of the text were written by Luke himself. The Western text, a first draft with a number of literary roughnesses in it, was written in Rome; later Luke travelled to Antioch, where he gained fresh information and also had leisure to improve his style, producing the Old Uncial text. On the whole this suggestion did not gain acceptance; but see below. In 1926 J. H. Ropes[5] edited and printed the texts of both B (Codex Vaticanus) and D (Codex Bezae), and concluded that the Old Uncial text (of B and others) was the older and better form, though in a few places D (and other Western authorities) had preserved a primitive reading. In 1933 A. C. Clark[6] argued that the longer text (of D) was primitive; the shorter Old Uncial text had been formed for the most part by dropping whole lines. Ropes probably had a majority of followers, but more and more it was recognized that the eclectic method must be adopted – in principle no reputable critic would have denied this.

But the question of the origin of the two recensions remains. In 1984 M. E. Boismard and A. Lamouille[7] returned to something not unlike the theory of Blass. In essence, their method was first to establish the original form of the Western text, then to isolate the material which it contained in excess of the Old Uncial text. When this material was examined it was seen to be marked by features of Lucan style and vocabulary, which showed, they thought, that it

[3] The later 'Antiochian' text is essentially a conflation in varying proportions of the two earlier (Old Uncial and Western) texts.

[4] *Acta Apostolorum sive Lucae ad Theophilum liber alter* (Göttingen, 1895).

[5] *The Beginnings of Christianity, Part I: The Acts of the Apostles, Vol. III, The Text of Acts* (London, 1926).

[6] *The Acts of the Apostles* (Oxford, 1933).

[7] *Texte Occidental des Actes des Apôtres* (Paris, 1984).

had been written by Luke himself. Thus both text forms came from the same author.[8]

In 1986 Professor B. Aland published a paper,[9] critical of Boismard and Lamouille and agreeing to some extent with Ropes; she placed the origin of the Western text, however, much later than Ropes had done. For Ropes it was already in existence by about AD 150. Dr Aland, using the evidence of some papyri, argued that it could not be earlier than about 250. For this date the main difficulty is caused by Irenaeus (on whose text see p. xviii). If Irenaeus is a witness to the Western text, that text was in existence long before 250. But, in Dr Aland's view, Irenaeus was not a representative but a forerunner of the Western text. His was an early text with a tendency to paraphrase.

It will be observed that Boismard and Lamouille set out to establish the original form of the Western text; Ropes believes that there was a Western reviser who made a Western revision not later than 150; Dr Aland places this process somewhat later. All have made important contributions to the study of the text of Acts, but it may be that the point on which all agree is mistaken. Was there ever *a* Western reviser who produced *a* (or *the*) Western text of Acts? The facts suggest that it was not so. The various authorities that contain readings of a characteristically Western kind – Codex Bezae and some other Greek MSS, the various Old Latin MSS, the Coptic versions, Irenaeus and many other church fathers – are all different. What we call the Western text is not so much a text as a tendency, expressed on similar lines but with differences in detail. The Western process (if this term may be used) did not begin from unity, or uniformity, subsequently scattered and diversified in a variety of forms. It began with variety, when many writers edited and 'improved' the text as they saw fit. The results of their work were ultimately co-ordinated in such a MS as Codex Bezae. The Old Uncial text was a conservative product, edited here and there with a view to giving a more formal and classical touch to Luke's Greek.

If this view of the text of Acts is correct it has a bearing on the place of Acts in the Canon of the NT. Its wording can hardly have attained the sanctity attributed to sacred and inspired Scripture at the time when editors were so free with it. This leads to the next section.

[8] On Boismard and Lamouille see further pp. xxxiiif.

[9] *EThL* 62 (1986), 5–65.

II. THE BOOK AND ITS AUTHOR

The textual history of Acts suggests that although the book, where it was known, was regarded as a good Christian book, it was not thought of as a sacred and authoritative work, whose every word was inspired and must be preserved without deviation from its original form. Editors felt free to 'improve' the wording, enliven the narrative, and make the language more obviously pious (for example, by expanding 'Jesus' into 'the Lord Jesus Christ'). This freedom suggests that Acts was thought a good book but hardly a canonical book. This is confirmed by the few references to the book and its author made by early Christian writers.

In the NT itself 2 Tim. 3.11 and Mk 16.15 may possibly show awareness of material contained in Acts, but nothing can be built on these passages; they may be based on traditions parallel to Acts.

In the Apostolic Fathers the only passages worthy of note are in the *Epistle of Polycarp*, see 1.2; 2.1, 3; 3.2; 6.3; 12.2. These all fall within what may be regarded as probably the later of the two epistles combined in the so-called *Epistle*. Many would date this to about AD 135, some to 120.

Neither Papias nor Hegesippus can be shown to have known Acts. There is a parallel in the *Epistle to Diognetus* (second half of the second century) to Acts 17.24f., but the argument of these verses is familiar and the parallel does not prove literary contact.

Of similar date is the *Epistle of the Apostles*. On the whole it seems probable that the author of this work knew Acts, though in every passage that can be adduced there are differences from Acts, some of them substantial, so that one must infer either considerable editorial freedom or the use of different (though related) traditions.

Justin, who died a martyr in *c.* AD 165, is a key figure in the second-century story of Acts. Did he know and use Acts? If he knew it, what did he think of it? The evidence is not easy to assess. Much has been made of Justin's emphasis (*1 Apology* 39.3) on the role of the Twelve as missionaries sent out from Jerusalem into all the world, and the correspondence of this with Acts 1.8. There is force in this observation, but there would be a good deal more if Acts went on to describe a world-wide mission on the part of the Twelve. It does not. It rather gives first place as a world missionary to Paul; and Justin completely – or very nearly completely – ignores Paul. We cannot suppose that Justin had not heard of Paul; it may be (the matter cannot be discussed here) that he ignored him because of the misuse (as he no doubt deemed it) of Paul by Marcion. Marcion, though Luke was 'his' gospel, seems to have rejected, certainly he did not use, Acts. His *Antitheses* may have been, in part, a replacement for Acts, serving as an introduction to his NT.

There is much room here for speculation; what is reasonably clear is that in the first three-quarters of the second century there is little evidence of the use of Acts, and when it appears, or its presence may be suspected, it appears as a useful and respected but scarcely as a canonical work.

The position changes with the work of **Irenaeus** (see p. xviii), who frequently refers to Acts and quotes the book at length. It was of great value to him in his controversies with Marcion and other gnostics. It was probably its usefulness for this purpose that gave to Acts the full canonical status that from this time it enjoyed. Roughly contemporary with Irenaeus was the **Muratorian Canon**, which lists the recognized NT books. After mentioning the four gospels, including Luke, written by Luke the Physician, companion of Paul, it later deals with Acts.

> The Acts of all[10] the apostles were written in one book. Luke compiled for 'Most Excellent[11] Theophilus' the several things that were done in his presence, as he plainly shows by the omission of the passion of Peter and the departure of Paul from the city[12] when he left for Spain.

From this time the canonical authority of Acts, and its authorship by Luke, the Beloved Physician (Col. 4.14), are unquestioned. Patristic material could be, but need not be, collected at length. It will suffice to quote Eusebius (*c.* AD 263–339).

> But now that we have reached this point, it is reasonable to sum up the writings of the NT already mentioned. Well then, we must set in the first place the holy quaternion of the Gospels, which are followed by the Book of the Acts of the Apostles (*HE* 3.25.1; cf. 3.4.1).

For Eusebius, Acts is one of the acknowledged books, not one of either the disputed or the spurious.

[10] This exaggeration reflects an interest, shared by Irenaeus, in the unity of the whole apostolic group.

[11] The adjective is used in Lk. 1.3, not in Acts.

[12] Rome is meant.

This, however, does not mean that Acts was widely read and often quoted. It was not. The only continuous commentary on the Greek text that we possess is by Chrysostom (who died in AD 407); he complains of the lack of attention given to Acts. It is probably true that though Acts had achieved canonical status, many in the church were still not sure how this book, neither gospel nor apostolic epistle, should be used.

What can be deduced from such ancient testimonies regarding the origin of the book? Very little. No one ascribes it to any author other than Luke, the beloved physician and companion of Paul (Col. 4.14; 2 Tim. 4.11; Philemon 24). So much for external evidence of authorship. Internal evidence is not so clear. The argument that the use of medical language in the book confirms its authorship by a physician must be abandoned. The author does use some words that are found also in the books of Greek doctors, but these lose their significance because they are found also in non-medical books. There was no technical vocabulary peculiar to Greek medical schools; doctors and laymen described diseases and their symptoms using the same terminology, though of course doctors used it more frequently.

For the rest, Luke (here and generally throughout this book the name is used to mean 'the author of Acts' – whoever he may have been) writes as a popular historian, in a bright, interesting style, describing circumstances and narrating incidents better than he strings them together on a connected thread. He was an educated man, capable of a good Greek style – of more styles than one, for he can write a plain businesslike style, an 'OT' style, and a finer style that he uses for special occasions and for special speakers. Attempts to show that he sometimes translated Aramaic sources seem to have failed. He was familiar with the Roman world as it bordered the Mediterranean, and with Roman administration. There were not a few such men in the first-century world; there is no reason why the Luke of the NT should not have been one of them.

There is, however, a further aspect of internal evidence that must be considered. In a number of passages the narrative is written in the first person plural ('*We* did this or that'). These are[13] 16.10–(14)–17; 20.5–8, 13–15; 21.1–8, 11, 12, 14–18; 27.1–8, 15, 16, 18, 20, 27, 29, 37; 28.1, 2, 7, 10–16. On each of these the notes should be consulted.

[13] See also 11.28; 13.2; 16.8, with the notes.

They have been understood in different ways. There are three main views.

(1) The traditional understanding of the We-passages is that the author of Acts as a whole was an eye-witness of the events concerned, moving into first person narration at those points at which he was himself a member of Paul's party.

(2) It was the writer not of the whole book but of a source of it who used the 'we' and was present; his first person narration was retained by the author of the book though it was no longer appropriate.

(3) The 'we' is fictitious, included in the text for some editorial purpose, perhaps simply in order to add to the verisimilitude of the narrative.

The evidence of ancient literary practice in general[14] suggests that the use of the first person plural points to eye-witness authorship, but it does not decide whether the authorship is of the book or only of one source of the book. The latter seems the more probable alternative when the relation to Paul of Acts as a whole is considered. It is difficult to believe that all parts of the book were written by an intimate companion and fellow traveller of Paul's. The reference to justification in 13.38f. lacks a Pauline note; the natural theology of the Areopagus speech (17.22–31) hardly came from the pen that wrote Romans 1. The greatest difficulty is to be found in Luke's report of the Council in Acts 15. Would one who was on intimate terms with Paul have believed that he approved of the Decree promulgated in 15.29 and delivered it to the Gentile churches for them to observe (16.4)? In his extant epistles Paul never mentions the Decree and gives advice which seems to contradict it. There is no doubt that Luke admired Paul and thought him the outstanding missionary to the Gentile world; he seems however to have failed to distinguish between Paul's mission and that which sprang from the work and martyrdom of Stephen.

This means that it is very difficult to ascribe Acts to one who was on close terms with Paul, but it may well be that such a person – who could have been the physician Luke – provided material that the author used.[15]

[14] The best account is by C.-J. Thornton, *Der Zeuge des Zeugen* (Tübingen, 1991).

[15] For the sources of Acts see pp. xxvi–xxxiv.

In regard to the date of Acts much turns on the question why the book ends where it does.[16] If the author stops at 28.31 because he has now brought the story up to date the book will have been completed in about AD 58, or a little later.[17] This seems very unlikely. Acts is the second volume of a work that included also the Third Gospel. This, as almost all would agree, included material drawn from Mark, which was probably written about AD 70. It is reasonable therefore to think that Luke's first volume was written not much earlier than, say, AD 80, the second volume correspondingly later. External evidence does not suggest a date much earlier than AD 150, but internal evidence will take us much earlier. The fierce conflicts to which Paul's letters bear witness have so far subsided that Luke, it seems, has not grasped how serious and divisive they were; but heresy (probably gnosticism) is little more than a cloud on the horizon (cf. Acts 20.21–31). For the church it was a time of relative internal peace; externally there is an impression that Roman officials may be trusted for at least a fair hearing and a recognition that Roman courts are not places for (Jewish) heresy trials. The persecutions of the later years of Domitian (AD 81–96) have not begun. Allusions to Roman provincial administration are consistent with a date in the late 80s or early 90s. This is a quite probable period for the writing of Acts, but it leaves one unanswered question: Why does Luke show no acquaintance with Paul's letters?

We do not know where Acts was written. Rome, Antioch, Ephesus, somewhere in Macedonia, or Achaea, or Asia, have all been suggested. None of the suggestions can be proved, or, for that matter, disproved.

Luke's reason for writing poses a question that will be considered again later in this Introduction (see pp. xxxv–xl). Here it may be said that Luke had grasped the fact that the only legitimacy that the Christian movement could claim was its origin in the life, teaching, death, and resurrection of Jesus of Nazareth, understood as the fulfilment of the OT. The continuity between Jesus and the church was both historical and theological. Luke found it natural to concentrate on the historical side of this double strand, though from time to time he shows awareness of the theological. In both respects, moral–historical and theological, he would recall the church of his own day to the example of the earliest times.

[16] For a fuller discussion of this question see pp. 427f.

[17] For this and other dates in Acts see pp. xlf.

III. SOURCES AND PLAN

These two themes are taken together because they are bound up with each other and neither can be dealt with satisfactorily on its own. To some extent the plan of the book was determined by the sources available to its author, as well as by the story he had to tell. The book is a unity, but there is a caesura at its arithmetical middle point, between ch. 14 and ch. 15.

The first part ends (14.28) in Antioch, where Paul and Barnabas report to the local Christians, themselves a mixed group of Jews and Gentiles, the success of their missionary tour among the partly Gentile communities of Asia Minor. God had opened a door of faith to the Gentiles. There can be little doubt (and this is confirmed in various ways by chs. 15–28) that it was Luke's intention in these opening chapters to describe a decisive step by which the faith of a group of Jews, and the Gospel that had been committed to them, were communicated to men who were of a different religious and racial background. This fact, sufficiently evident in itself, is made explicit in 1.8, where Jesus sends his witnesses from Jerusalem to Judaea, Samaria, and to the end of the earth. A quick reading of the text confirms the picture of progressive expansion. The Gospel is preached in Jerusalem; by 5.16 it had become known in the surrounding cities (that is, the cities of Judaea); in 8.5 it has reached the (or, a) city of Samaria. In the latter part of ch. 8 a devout Ethiopian, in ch. 10 a devout Roman, are converted. The former event passes without comment, though it is made clear that it is the direct consequence of the direction of the Holy Spirit; the latter leads to the conclusion on the part of the Christians of Jerusalem, Why then, to the Gentiles also God has granted the repentance that leads to life (11.18). Almost immediately (11.20) we hear of the evangelization in Antioch of Greeks – non-Jews, a proceeding which receives the approval and participation of Barnabas, the representative of the mother church in Jerusalem.

The question of the relation of Gentiles to the Gospel, and through the Gospel to the Jewish people, is discussed in ch. 15, and thereafter the Gentile mission continues without hindrance, though the Decree that emanates from the Council in 15.29 is repeated in 21.25. This Decree is of fundamental importance for an understanding of Luke's view of the Gospel and the church, but it is not to be discussed here.

It suffices to observe that in chs. 1–14 Luke has established the Gentile mission as a fact; it is not without problems and calls for regulation, but it is never called in question except by those whose opinion can be virtually ignored, and after deliberation by the apostles and elders it is energetically pursued and in the end reaches Rome itself. The dominant actor in chs. 15–28 is Paul.

When, however, the first fourteen chapters are read with greater care problems and difficulties appear. Who were the Hellenists (6.1; cf. 9.29; 11.20)? Does the use of this term in 6.1 imply that the Gospel had already been preached to Gentiles? What of the Ethiopian? He was not a Jew; he was not a proselyte; if he could be converted and baptized what becomes of the importance of Cornelius? In the Cornelius story, what is the meaning of Peter's vision? Does it refer to food, or to people? If it does refer to food, does it not contradict the Decree, since it sets no limits to permitted food? If it refers to people, how far does it go? Does it permit preaching to Gentiles (who, if converted, must subsequently obey certain rules), or unrestricted intercourse with them? If the conclusion of the discussion that follows (11.18) means what it says, does it not make the debate arising out of 15.1, 5 pointless?

No sooner is Paul introduced in 9.15 as one who will bear Christ's name before the Gentiles, and, from ch. 13 onwards, will be described as the leading missionary to the Gentiles, than he is supplanted by Peter, whom Luke evidently regards as the first if not the greatest missionary to the Gentiles (15.7).

These questions are raised here because they bear on both the plan and the sources of Acts. Many attempts have been made to present literary and historical analyses of Acts, whose author may be supposed to have planned his book in terms either of artistic literary criteria or of historical development – or of a combination of both. All such attempts run into difficulty when confronted by the questions that have been mentioned, and others like them. The following facts must be borne in mind. (1) The author was not present at the events narrated in chs. 1–14. If he was Luke, the companion of Paul, he first, on his own showing, enters the story at 16.10, the first occurrence in narrative of the second person plural.[18] Reports of earlier events must have come to him second-hand (at best). If he was not one of Paul's travelling companions, he stands at an even greater distance from the

[18] On 'We' in 11.28 see the note.

earlier events. (2) The entry of Gentiles into the church was accompanied by severe problems and bitter controversy. This is clearly proved by the Pauline epistles, but there is little sign of it in Acts. (3) It is *a priori* improbable that the development of the Gentile mission proceeded everywhere at the same speed and through the same stages. It is equally improbable that anyone in Jerusalem, or in other Christian centres, was aware of what was happening in all the other Christian centres.

The question of Luke's plan and the question of Luke's sources must be considered in relation to each other. There is no doubt that one of his primary interests was the extension of the Gospel to the Gentiles. It is a hypothesis worth pursuing that he made it his business to collect stories of early contacts with Gentiles wherever he could find them. He had four main sources of supply.

(1) Whatever we make of the historical value of 21.8, the verse claims, on the author's part, some contact with Philip the Evangelist. Even if the contact was less direct than a surface reading of the verse suggests, the author had access to traditions about, perhaps emanating from, Philip – we may again add, so as not to claim too much, whatever their historical value. These provided him with the stories of the Samaritan city (8.4–8)[19] and of the Ethiopian (8.26–40). The Samaritans were at best not full Jews; the Ethiopian was no Jew at all.

(2) The reference to Philip in 21.8 is also a reference to Caesarea; and Caesarea, as a place where Philip is found, is mentioned also at 8.40.[20] The author so wrote as to claim contact with Caesarea; he had been there. It does not seem a wild guess that (even if his contact was something less than that of a travelling companion in Acts 21) he should have asked the Christians there how their church (certainly, at the time when he was in contact with it, a mixed Jewish and Gentile church) had come into being, and that they told him about Cornelius – perhaps a very much shorter and simpler story than that which he tells in ch. 10, but with enough of Peter in it to lead him to

[19] Possibly also 8.9–25, but the story about Simon Magus may come from a different source.

[20] Further references to Caesarea at 9.30; 10.1, 24; 11.11; 12.19; 18.22; 21.16; 23.23, 33; 25.1, 4, 6, 13 indicate Luke's interest.

introduce the story of a vision of clean and unclean beasts, which he had picked up elsewhere.

(3) Ancient tradition made Luke a native of Antioch; this may or may not be true; it is clear from his book that he was aware of Antioch as an important Christian centre, and in particular that it was one of the bases from which Paul conducted his missions. The whole of the tour described in chs. 13 and 14 was carried out under the auspices of the church of Antioch, which both commissioned the missionaries and received their report (13.3; 14.27f.), and subsequently sent them to Jerusalem to discuss the position of Gentiles (15.2). It is certain that Luke received traditional material from Antioch, and that the account that the Antiochenes gave of the origin of their church included the claim that almost from the beginning the Gentiles had been included.

(4) The author of Acts either was a companion of Paul, or represented himself as one, or drew on the memories of one. It is even more certain that he was an admirer of Paul, and that his admiration included the belief that Paul was a notable missionary to the Gentile world. Whether his connection with Paul was close or remote, immediate or second- or third-hand, he clearly used what information he could get from Pauline sources, and, though he seems not to have used the epistles, we may conclude from them that Pauline information must have included information bearing on the inclusion of the Gentiles and perhaps on the problems that arose from this step.

These were sources of information,[21] and their use provided not only information but at the same time the broad outline of the first part of Acts. Luke's first task was to lay a foundation in Jerusalem,[22] showing as well as he could what the apostles had had to say to their fellow Jews, how the church was constituted, and how it fulfilled the Lord's precept of love. After this he proceeded to give various examples – possibly all the examples he knew – of ways in which the Gospel was taken to the heathen. It was natural to begin with the Samaritans, who stood closest to Judaism, and one story about Philip carried the

[21] Not necessarily literary sources.

[22] For this see pp. xxxf.

other with it. Next, in view of 15.7, the story of Peter and Cornelius had to be placed. It was a pity that the Roman centurion had to be preceded by the Ethiopian chancellor, but not so great a pity as to lead Luke to separate the two Philip stories. After that came the story of Antioch, and, arising out of it, the story of the first Pauline mission. They were neither artistic nor chronological considerations that determined Luke's plan; he simply presents a handful of sallies into the pagan world.

This does not cover the whole of Luke's story. What of the conversion of Paul and the immediately following events (9.1–30)? It is clear that the conversion of Paul was to Luke, who narrates it three times, an event of very great importance. He places it where he does because he wishes to represent Paul as the successor of Stephen (cf. 22.20) and perhaps as the colleague of Philip, but he does not in ch. 9 give any serious account of missionary work conducted by Paul because he knows the tradition (15.7) that it was Peter who began the mission outside Judaism, as well as other independent stories about Peter (9.32–43; 12.3–19).

There is also a connecting line that runs back from the founding of the church in Antioch (11.19f.) to the persecution over Stephen (8.1–3) and the appointment of the Seven (6.1). It is probable that this was part of Antiochene tradition. The earliest churches founded outside Jerusalem would wish to show that they had valid contacts with the original Jerusalem church. Samaria had Philip, but (it may be) thought it well to supplement that contact by the account of a visit from Peter and John. Caesarea could appeal to Peter himself, and so perhaps did Lydda and Joppa. Antioch made the most it could of a somewhat remote connection with the first martyr, adding Barnabas and Saul too, though he may have fallen out of favour and been replaced by Peter (Gal. 2.13).

In Acts 1–14 it is probably better to think of traditions, without specifying their form, than of written or even of oral sources, if oral sources are understood as verbally fixed. Two theories of written sources should however be briefly considered.

The first is based on observations made in chs. 2–5 which, it is maintained, contain doublets. Two blocks of material, 3.1 – 5.16 and 2.1–41 + 5.17–42, tell similar stories. In each a supernatural event (the gift of tongues; a miracle of healing) is followed by a speech made by Peter. Apostles (Peter and John only; all) are brought before the Jewish Council, but they are eventually released and continue their work. Here, it is suggested, we have parallel accounts, in parallel sources, of the same sequence of events. There are now few who maintain this theory, or anything like it. It is improbable that the church of the earliest days kept written records of its work, and the proceedings of the Council are sequential rather than parallel. Unlettered laymen (4.13) such as Peter and John could not be punished for a first offence that was an act not specifically forbidden in Torah; only after a warning (4.17f.) could they be punished (5.28, 40).

The second source theory is based not on parallelism and doublets but on persons, places, and continuity of narration. If we begin at 6.1 we read of a division between Hebrews and Hellenists and of the appointment of Stephen and his six colleagues. After the martyrdom of Stephen a general persecution arises. All (except the apostles) are scattered (8.1). This statement is picked up in 8.4, but then dropped, a long digression is inserted and the theme returns at 11.19. This introduces the work of evangelism in Antioch, and Antioch remains the centre of the narrative till 15.35. No one suggests that the whole of this block comes from one source. A reasonable suggestion will put together 6.1 – 8.4; [perhaps 9.1–30]; 11.19–30; 12.25 – 14.28. Whether the source is in any way continued in ch. 15 is a nice question that need not be considered here. Some think of a written source, others of collected traditions.

This leaves us with chs. 16–28, the whole of which may without exaggeration be regarded as a missionary biography of Paul, for which no doubt various sources were used. Of these the most easily identifiable is that which is written in the first person plural. Some regard the 'we' in these passages as fictional, others as showing the hand of the author of Acts as a whole; it is probably better to think of a source derived from an eye-witness. This source covers a good deal of ground. 'We' appears first at 16.10, when Paul, in Troas, is summoned by a dream vision to extend his mission to Macedonia. Accordingly, *we* sought to leave for Macedonia. The person, real or fictional, who says this is in Paul's company; it is reasonable to think that he joined Paul if not at Troas itself at least in that area. It seems unreasonable to think (though it has been suggested) that he himself was the man of Macedonia, in his narrative transforming himself into a vision. He accompanies Paul to Macedonia, reaching Philippi at v. 12. The first person continues up to v. 17 (its absence from v. 16 is insignificant), the point at which Paul exorcises the Python spirit, and with Silas is thrown into prison. *We* appears no more in the chapter. This could mean that the person responsible for it had left Paul's circle, but a much more probable cause is that whereas, up to this point, all the party have been involved in the events described, henceforth the story is focused on Paul and Silas, who are arrested, beaten, imprisoned, delivered by the earthquake, cared for by the converted gaoler, and as Roman citizens set free by the apologetic magistrates. The 'first person' was out of the story and was therefore not mentioned. Did he, when Paul moved on, remain in Philippi? The question is proper whether we are thinking in terms of history or of fiction. He does not appear in the rest of Paul's Macedonian ministry (17.1–12) or in the mission to Athens (17.13–34). Throughout ch. 18 the story is told in the third person, and so it is in ch. 19 (Corinth, Ephesus). Sopater and others (20.4f.) waited for *us* in Troas; *we* sailed away from Philippi and joined them at Troas. Had the 'first person' been in Philippi all this time? It may be so; it may be that the author wishes us to think so; it may be that as a writer of fiction he thinks that variety would be pleasant and reintroduces his alternative reporting style. *We* continues up to the Christian supper in v. 8, drops out in the story of Eutychus, and is resumed when the story is taken up again in v. 13. Does this mean that the miracle story of the raising of Eutychus was drawn from a different source, perhaps not an eyewitness source, a less trustworthy source? It may be so. *We* continues in vv. 13–15, then stops. This may mean that not only the speech of 20.18–35 but the whole Miletus episode is from a different source. This again seems quite probable, though it cannot be proved.

The journey is resumed in 22.1, and *we* returns, found in every verse up to v. 8. Its absence from v. 9, which simply tells objectively of Philip's four daughters (who could well be there because they were known to *us*) is not significant (though the contact between *us* and Philip may be). It is implied in v. 10 and continues to v. 18, where Paul meets James and the elders, with an unimportant omission in v. 13. *We* thus sees Paul through to his destination; it then disappears. Did the 'first person' leave Jerusalem, so that information about Paul's adventures there and in Caesarea had to be drawn from another source? This could well be so, but we remember 16.19–40, where the Philippian troubles are described in the third person, perhaps for no other reason than that they concerned only Paul and Silas.

We returns in ch. 27, in the account of the voyage and shipwreck, again with possibly significant intermissions. It runs without a break up to v. 8, the arrival of the ship at Fair Havens. It is not resumed till after the breaking of the storm in v. 15. The intervening passage records the disagreement between Paul and the nautical authorities on the propriety of continuing the voyage; was this interpolated into narrative that did not originally contain it? Or does the absence of the first person simply mean that this part of the story is about Paul and not about *us*? *We* continues from v. 15 to v. 18. Its absence from vv. 19, 20 does not seem to be significant, but vv. 21–26 are a possibly independent story about Paul, comparable with vv. 9–14. *We* occurs in vv. 27, 29, but after that virtually disappears, since the count of the ship's company in v. 37 could stand on its own.

In ch. 28 *we* is found in vv. 1, 2, 7, 10, that is, in the bare account of the residence in Malta; it is not found in the stories of Paul's snake bite and his cure of the father of Publius. These could be drawn from a different source. Verses 11–16 bring Paul to Rome, and from this point the story is focused on him, and the first person plural disappears.

One can only add to this that Luke evidently sought further information where he could get it. Some would come from members of the Pauline circle, some at least of whom must still have been accessible when the book was written, some he would obtain from local memory persisting in the towns in which Paul had worked.

A note should be added on the elaborate source hypothesis put forward by M. E. Boismard and A. Lamouille, whose work on the text of Acts was noted above, pp. xixf. This hypothesis is contained in three volumes, *Les Actes des deux Apôtres* (Paris, 1990). It is being followed by a historical commentary on Acts by J. Taylor.[23] The authors' work on the text is presupposed in their account of the sources.

The reconstituted Western text of Acts is the nearest approach we have to the original text of Acts, the work of Luke himself. The Alexandrian text is a revision of the original text made by another hand. There are thus two editions of Acts. They contain also many non-Lucan revisions, additions and redactions. Luke had not only a reviser but a precursor, a document which already had the form of a life, passion, and resurrection of Jesus followed by the story of the earliest church. This Boismard and Lamouille call Act I; Act II is the work of Luke himself; Act III is the work of the Lucan reviser. But Act I also made use of a yet more ancient work, already of the same pattern, and centred on the work of Peter. This is DocP

[23] See p. xiii.

(= Document Pétrinien). What we have here is not so much a theory of sources as of several levels of composition. It is possible to go further still and to distinguish a Journal de Voyage (JV), comprising most of the We-passages, and a document Johannique, emanating from a group of disciples of John the Baptist who took John to be the Messiah.

The present writer can only say that he finds this elaborate hypothesis not incredible, for it is quite possible, but incapable of proof or of disproof, and therefore beyond serious discussion. It must of course be added that there is in the work of these three authors much that is of great exegetical and historical importance.

IV. ACTS AS A HISTORICAL SOURCE

Acts cannot be evaluated as a historical source without some consideration of the author's purpose in writing. A sketch of the author himself was given above (p. xxiii). He was a competent writer who, if he was not (as a minority think) himself a Jew, had made himself familiar with the OT in its Greek form, and was able, when it suited his purpose, to write in a style that suggested the continuity of his theme with the OT. In telling the unit stories, or episodes, of which his book is composed, he had great skill; Peter's visit to Cornelius (10.1–48), for example, and Paul's conversion (9.1–19), are complicated stories but they are told not only with clarity and effectiveness but with compelling interest. He shows less skill in planning the whole, but here allowance must be made for the fact that he was dependent on sources, often a matter of distant and imprecise recollection. It is probable that he wrote by the light of nature rather than under the control of accepted rhetorical principles – if indeed there were such principles for the writing of history. He gave picture after picture of things he had discovered to have happened in the generation before his own until he came to the ministry of Paul which he was able to tell as a connected whole, though here too the story is constructed in the form of a series of vivid scenes, and we move from one city to another, and then from one courtroom to another, and it is seldom that the connecting links are given in much detail.

If we ask why Luke wrote, secular motivation is not to be set aside entirely. Luke was born to write this kind of book and it is impossible to doubt that he enjoyed writing it. The enjoyment was partly a Christian enjoyment: it was good to enjoy fellowship with Christians of the past as well as with Christians of the present. But it was only partly a Christian enjoyment – though there is nothing un-Christian in getting pleasure from telling a good story. Or in reading one; and we may suppose that Luke was pleased that readers should enjoy reading his book.[24] That Luke wrote for pleasure, his own and his readers', is a motivation not to be overlooked and not to be ashamed of; but alone it is not adequate as an account of the origin of Acts.

[24] See R. I. Pervo, *Profit With Delight: The Literary Genre of the Acts of the Apostles* (Philadelphia, 1987).

The book has been described as apologetic, and that in various senses. That it is in the most general sense of the word a piece of apologetic is undoubtedly true; in this sense apologetic shades into evangelism, and there can be no question that Luke wished to commend the Christian faith as true, and as truth that all should, for their own good as well as simply because it was true, accept. The reader could not miss the injunction to save himself from the perverse generation by which he was surrounded (2.40), and the instruction, 'Believe in the Lord Jesus and you will be saved' (16.31); nor could he fail to note the repeated assertion that the crucified Jesus had been raised by God from the dead, an assertion which, if true, must constitute the greatest possible claim on his attention and belief. In this general sense, of statement and commendation, the book (following as it does upon an account of the life and teaching of Jesus) may be described as apologetic. Here and there it goes further than this, notably in 14.15–17 and 17.22–31, where Christian belief is set over against the religion of paganism. Polytheism and idolatry are refuted, and the Christian doctrine of God is defended by reference to his forbearance; if his justice is impugned it may be defended in terms of his patience in the past and his intention in the future, and presumably the near future, to carry out a universal judgement.[25] Jewish religion is not treated in the same way as pagan religion, because Judaism, resting as it does on the OT, is true religion. But true Judaism, that is, Judaism as understood by Christians, is defended over against Judaism which so far misunderstands itself as to resist and persecute Christians. Paul repeatedly insists that he is simply a Jew who sees the fulfilment of Judaism and the OT in the life, death, and resurrection of Jesus (e.g. 24.14; 26.22f.). It follows that there is both an affirmation of Judaism and an apologetic directed against its abuse and misinterpretation (e.g. 13.45–47).

It is not incorrect to describe Acts as a work of apologetic, but this is not an adequate description. In particular the view, sometimes held, that Acts is an apology addressed to the Roman judiciary and intended to show that Christianity is a movement which right-thinking Roman officials will view with tolerance is unconvincing. It is true that, according to Acts, Roman courts, when correctly informed, show no disposition to persecute Christians: the proconsul in Cyprus, Sergius Paulus, actually becomes a Christian (13.12); the magistrates

[25] Luke has successors in Justin and other apologists of the second century.

in Philippi, when they learn that Paul and Silas are Roman citizens, immediately release them (16.38, 39); the proconsul Gallio in Corinth is not interested in the case brought against Paul (18.15); the town clerk in Ephesus defends him (19.37, 38); and from the time when Paul is rescued by Roman soldiers from the Temple mob (21.31, 32) the Roman tribune and the provincial governors treat him decently and protect him from Jewish violence up to the moment when Agrippa and Festus agree, 'He could have been released if he had not appealed to Caesar' (26.32). Luke would no doubt have been pleased to hear that a Christian on trial had been able to use some of these precedents, but the book as a whole is not to be thought of as serving such a purpose; no Roman court could be expected to wade through so much Jewish religious nonsense in order to find half-a-dozen fragments of legally significant material. The same argument proves even more conclusively that the book was not written as a brief for the defence at Paul's trial; what would be the use of chs. 1–12 for such a purpose?

The theme of apologetic has been inverted in the suggestion[26] that Acts was an apology addressed to the church on behalf of the Empire. Christians (such would be its theme) have no need to fear and ought not to oppose the Roman administration. When Roman officials are informed of the facts they will give a fair trial and will not believe calumnies. The church may settle down to live in confidence whatever time is left before the End. Again, there is something to be said for this as a subordinate interest of Luke's, but it will not account for more than a relatively small part of the book.

An important observation to be made here is that Luke had provided his church (wherever that may have been) with its NT. It probably had no more. We cannot suppose that Luke wrote his gospel with the notion that it should be published in one of four parallel columns in a Synopsis. He used Mk and collected what other material he could find;[27] he included what he thought should be included and this meant that Mk was no longer needed and could fall out of use. The Third Gospel would provide what Luke's fellow Christians (locally) needed to know about the life and teaching of Jesus. The second volume, Acts, correspondingly contained what the church (in the 80s or early 90s) needed to know about the apostles and their teaching. The disuse of Paul's epistles in Acts is a familiar and often

[26] See P. W. Walaskay, *And so we came to Rome*, SNTSMS 49 (Cambridge, 1983).
[27] See my essay in *FS* Smit Sibinga, 96.

discussed fact. Whether this was due to ignorance or to deliberate omission, Acts was there to serve as Apostle supplementing Gospel. It was what Luke's contemporaries needed to know about the apostles – and Paul. This leads to two observations.

The first was made by W. C. van Unnik,[28] who wrote of Acts as the confirmation of the Gospel. The record of the life and expansion of the church confirms that the claims made in the Gospel for the person of Jesus and the effect of his work were true. The two books thus form a unit, and the purpose of the second must be viewed in the light of the first.

This presupposes (what Luke no doubt took for granted) that the earliest period of Christianity was an exemplary and classical period; this conviction supplies perhaps the strongest because the most practical reason for the writing of Acts. Luke wished to hold up before his readers a set of Christian ideals which would show them what their own Christian life should be and at the same time supply them with a strong motivation for following the example. He probably wrote primarily for church leaders, who are given especially in Paul's Miletus speech (20.18–35) a clear account of their pastoral responsibilities. The nearly contemporary (perhaps somewhat later) Pastoral Epistles encouraged the ministers to whom they are addressed to preach: Preach the word, keep at it in season, out of season, reprove, rebuke, exhort (2 Tim. 4.2). Christian leaders towards the end of the century might reply to such exhortations, Yes, but what must we say? Luke replies, You will find no better examples, no clearer instruction, than in the sermons of Peter and Paul that I am providing.[29] He might similarly claim that he had provided an outline of the kind of behaviour to be expected of the Christian rank and file: They continued steadfastly in the teaching of the apostles and the fellowship, in the breaking of bread and the prayers (2.42).

Beyond these matters one may inquire whether there were any specific theological truths that Luke wished to communicate. For his theology as a whole and in some detail see below, pp. li–lxxvi. One theological point merges with a historical; it is not mentioned by Luke, probably because it seemed to him part of the nature of things, but it was fundamental to his work. For the view that Jesus foretold

[28] *NovT* 4 (1960–1), 26–39, 'The "Book of Acts" – the Confirmation of the Gospel', see also my exploration of the converse of this in *FS* Neirynck 1451–66.

[29] Cf. Dibelius 165: 'This is how the gospel is preached and ought to be preached!'

his suffering and that after his suffering he would be vindicated by God, but did not in this vindication differentiate between resurrection and a coming of the Son of man in glory I may refer to *Jesus and the Gospel Tradition* (London, 1967), pp. 77–83. After his crucifixion Jesus appeared to his disciples, raised from death; but there was no coming with the clouds of heaven. One may guess with some probability, but cannot prove, that the disciples, compelled by events to differentiate where Jesus himself had not done so, believed that the second act, which would complete the first, would follow quickly. It did not do so. Had it done so, there would have been no church history. It was the 'delay of the parousia' that made it possible for the church to have a history, and for the church's historian to write it. It does not seem that the delay, though it must have puzzled many, led to a crisis of belief. Luke did not write to assuage apocalyptic enthusiasm, or to comfort those who were disappointed in their hopes. When he wrote, some measure of delay had been accepted, and Luke himself sets out what were probably widely acknowledged terms of acceptance. After the crucifixion, Jesus had been raised up by God; he had ascended into heaven; he had sent to his followers (and continued to send as more followers were added) the gift of the Holy Spirit. Empowered and directed by the Spirit, the believers would act as witnesses to Jesus till their testimony had reached the end of the earth (1.8). This goal Luke probably saw as representatively achieved in the arrival of Paul at Rome, but there is no hint in his writing that the End could now be expected at any moment. He knew that some thirty years had elapsed between Paul's arrival in Rome and the point at which he was writing; and if God could wait thirty years, he could no doubt wait a good deal longer. This was probably the accepted position; there was no need to argue for it. Luke does however (without saying explicitly that he is doing so) show how the various features of Christian truth cohere with one another. This was something that a gospel alone could not do; his two-volume work was needed. There is an end, including a judgement, to look forward to, and not only Areopagites but all must prepare for it by repentance. For those who repent there is forgiveness and the gift of the Spirit, manifested in such gifts as prophecy and speaking with tongues. The believers live in unity and godly love, and bear witness to Jesus.

This is in fact Luke's theology and he does not see fit to expand it, though there are many points that invite expansion. Who was Jesus, who plays such an important part in the history of God's dealings with men? How did his death effect forgiveness and release from sin? How is the Holy Spirit related to Father and Son? What is the proper constitution of the church, and what happens when it immerses converts in water, and when its members assemble 'to break bread'? Luke gives only the barest hints towards answers to these questions. The basic theology of Judaism he accepts but scarcely develops. He believes as the apostles did, and does not seek to go beyond their pronouncements. To do so indeed would cut across his purpose, which is to record what they said and did, not to point out what they ought to have said and done. On the theology of Acts see further below, pp. li–lxxvi.

All that has been said here about the characteristics, interests, and intentions of Luke as an author bear on the question of the historical value of his book. For details on a number of specific points see the appended note on *Dates and Places*. On such matters, Luke on the whole does fairly well. He is not unfamiliar with the roads and shipping routes that he describes; his references to secular history are usually in reasonably close agreement with the facts as otherwise known. He comes down badly over Judas and Theudas (5.36, 37), but is probably not far out in his references to Claudius, Sergius Paulus, Agrippa I and II, Gallio, Felix and Festus. Oddly it is on Christian matters that he is most open to criticism. His account of Hebrews and Hellenists, of Paul and the Council, is distorted by the refracting medium of continuing church life through which he views the past.

Dates and Places

It will save space if a list is given here of passages which are of interest and importance in the fields of chronology and topography, together with references to those pages of the book on which the passages and the questions they raise are dealt with.

1. The dates of Annas and Caiaphas. See p. 56.
2. The dates of Theudas and Judas. These names do not relate to events in Acts itself but they bear on Luke's accuracy as a historian. See pp. 79f.
3. Saul's conversion. This can only be dated by reckoning back from the Council (7 below).
4. Universal famine under the Emperor Claudius. See p. 177.

5. Herod Agrippa I: persecutor; relation with Tyre and Sidon; death. There are important and ascertainable dates here. See pp. 181f., 186.
6. Sergius Paulus. Epigraphical evidence: see p. 195.
7. The Council (ch. 15). A very important and difficult question, central for the history of Acts. See p. 227.
8. Corinth: Paul, Aquila, Priscilla. Important and ascertainable dates. See p. 276.
9. Gallio, proconsul of Achaea. The dates of his proconsulship can be ascertained with some precision. See p. 279.
10. Ephesus, where Paul spent three years. See pp. 291f.
11. Troas. On this place is based a theory for fixing the date of Paul's voyage. See p. 307.
12. Dates of Ananias the High Priest. See p. 350.
13. Dates of the two procurators; there are some doubtful points. See p. 372.
14. Herod Agrippa II; Bernice. See pp. 379f.
15. The Fast; some think this reference can be used to date Paul's voyage to Rome. See pp. 400f.
16. Date of sailing from Malta. See p. 416.
17. Paul spends two years in Rome; from when to when? And what next? See pp. 428f.

Of these, only 5, 8, 9, 13, 14 give us anything like firm dates which could form fixed points in an Acts chronology. 1, 4, 6, 12 give us wide approximations. The rest are worthless except that they do help to locate the Acts narrative in the first century; they also relate it to the data contained in Paul's letters and provide some relative, though not absolute, chronology.

V. USE AND INTERPRETATION

In Chapter II of this Introduction the use of Acts in the period up to Irenaeus was sketched. For Irenaeus the book showed, against Gnostics, that God the Creator was also God the Redeemer, so that matter was not intrinsically evil; it also showed, against Marcion, that Paul was in agreement and acted in harmony with those who were apostles before him. The book thus served useful purposes, but it was scantily used, and the textual tradition shows (see p. xx) that it was used with some freedom. After the time of Irenaeus it continued to stand a little apart from the other books of the NT. The canon was not thought of as supplying an authorized history of Christian origins; it existed primarily as a basis, and yardstick, for Christian preaching,[30] and there is little to suggest that Acts was frequently preached on. It remained something of a puzzle, neither a gospel, stamped with the authority of the Lord himself, nor an epistle bearing an apostolic signature. And what could a theologian make of stories? The theologians of the early centuries did not see that there might be a positive answer to this question.

There is little material available for writing a history of the use of Acts in the early centuries. There are scattered quotations and exegetical fragments. The only works of which we can read a continuous text are the Homilies of Chrysostom, of which there is no satisfactory critical Greek text, and the exposition of Bede. It is perhaps worthwhile to mention also Arator (sixth century), whose long poetical work may be thought of as a paraphrase of Acts giving special attention to baptism, or as a work on baptism with special reference to Acts.

Chrysostom's Homilies are practical sermons from which we learn as much about life in Antioch in Chrysostom's time as about the times of the apostles, but there is a good deal of plain practical exposition and application of the text. It is notable that the infelicities that trouble modern readers of the Greek text of Acts and lead to hypotheses such as that of an Aramaic original seem to give the Greek orator little or no trouble. Perhaps we are too sensitive. Bede also was a writer of common sense and practical interest – and good at apt quotation, especially from Jerome and Gregory the Great.

[30] See my essay in *FS* Schweizer 5–21, reprinted in *Jesus and the Word* (Allison Park, 1995), 259–76.

Luther saw Acts as essentially a reproduction of Pauline theology. It was not simply a piece of history and an example of good works, expressed in the sharing of property and in mutual concern. 'With this book St Luke means to teach the whole of Christendom, up to the world's end how we must become righteous through faith alone in Jesus Christ, without any contribution from the Law or help of our works.'[31] It is hard to acquit Luther of reading Acts through spectacles more Pauline than Luke himself used. Luke did have an interest in history, and his one reference to justification, though put on Paul's lips, is not cast in quite the Pauline mould (see on 13.38f.). Luke does however insist on faith as the primary Christian requirement (e.g. 15.9). Calvin with a full dress commentary on Acts[32] is able to take exegesis more seriously than many subsequent expositors – sometimes more seriously than even Luke himself.[33] He also takes historical questions seriously, and is perhaps the first of modern commentators, occasionally, and surprisingly, anticipating Enlightenment and post-Enlightenment writers.

It is impossible here to give a full account of more recent work on Acts, and to some extent unnecessary since much of the work has been done. The reader may consult, for earlier work, contributions by A. C. McGiffert and J. W. Hunkin to *Begs.* 2.363–95 and 2.396–435 respectively. Later work is dealt with by W. Gasque, *A History of the Criticism of the Acts of the Apostles*, BGBE 17 (Tübingen, 1975), and 'A Fruitful Field' (*Interpretation* 42 (1988), 117–31). Most recent commentaries, notably that of Haenchen, give some account of further work on Acts.

Modern study of Acts may be said to begin with F. C. Baur. Logically if not chronologically Baur's work began with the observation that our two main sources for the earliest period of Christian history do not tell the same story. The contemporary (though for the most part only allusive) accounts in the Pauline epistles, show a church torn by controversy and discord. Galatians especially (but not alone) depicts Christians who hold that all believers must be circumcised and obey the Law of Moses; for Paul, if a Gentile accepts circumcision he forfeits any benefit that he might receive from Christ (Gal. 5.2). Paul and Peter find themselves on opposite sides of the dispute. In

[31] Preface to the Acts of the Apostles in the 1545 edition.

[32] See the translation by J. W. Fraser and W. J. G. McDonald, two volumes, 1965 and 1966.

[33] See my essay on Calvin as exegete of Acts in *FS* Corsani, 312–26.

contrast with this, Acts represents a church at peace. It is true that in Acts 15.1, 5 there are those who affirm that all must be circumcised and keep the Law, but their opinion is not even voiced in the Council that follows and is never repeated. Here then are two different accounts of early Christianity. They are to be explained by a different tendency (an important word for Baur) on the part of each writer. Baur took the view that the peaceful picture of Acts was derived from a later period when attitudes had changed. As a result he placed much of the NT as late as the second century.

It is this dating, not Baur's initial observation, that has been revised by later generations of students of the NT. J. B. Lightfoot, for example, described the conflicts of Paul's own age in language as strong as Baur's, but was able to show that the literature of reconciliation was earlier than Baur thought. It remains Baur's great contribution to the study of Acts that we must not fail to ask, Why did the author write as he did? And it must not be forgotten (though it often is) that Baur wrote that 'Acts is a source of the highest importance for the history of the apostolic age, though a source from which a truly historical picture of the persons and circumstances described in it can be derived only by strict historical criticism'.[34]

The question of the intention of Acts, made inescapable by Baur, led to the development of hypotheses regarding the sources used by Luke. This is an investigation that preceded Baur and, as is shown above (pp. xxvi–xxxiv), has certainly not come to an end. There is no need to discuss this aspect of the study of Acts further.

The next name of outstanding importance in the study of Acts is that of M. Dibelius, whose pioneering articles were collected in a German publication in 1951 which five years later appeared in English.[35] Dibelius sought to distinguish between and to separate out the traditional material used by Luke and his editorial redaction of it – the process is now known as redaction criticism, though this term was not, it seems, used by Dibelius. A clear (though not in fact convincing – see pp. 152–4) example is provided by Dibelius' treatment of the conversion of Cornelius in ch. 10. At the root of this episode (according to Dibelius) there was a simple pious story of a conversion; this was taken up and used as an important step in Luke's account of the expansion of the Gospel into the Gentile world. Not

[34] *Paulus*, p. 13; reprinted in the second edition (ed. E. Zeller, 1866), p. 17.

[35] ET, *Studies in the Acts of the Apostles* (London, 1956).

only was Peter's short statement of the Gospel added but also the story of Peter's vision, and the setting was constructed so as to bring out the radical step involved in Peter's visit to and, in the end, baptism of a Gentile household.

The total effect of Dibelius' important work was to move the historian's use of Acts a stage or two further back. It is impossible to give an immediate general estimate of the whole book, or even to distinguish between more and less trustworthy sources. The contents of the book must be analysed and classified: speeches distinguished from the narratives that contain them, summaries from particular episodes. In regard to each unit the attempt must be made to distinguish between a traditional basis and the editorial use that has been made of the tradition. This is a more problematical process than some have recognized. It is not necessarily guesswork, but great control has to be exercised in order to prevent criticism from descending into guessing. In the Third Gospel Luke's work can be detected by a comparison with Mk, less confidently by comparison with Mt. In Acts the only comparative material is provided by the Pauline epistles, and this material is narrowly limited in extent. Some control is provided by study of Lucan interests (but may not Luke's interests be based on, derived from, his knowledge of tradition?) and Lucan style (but the variety of styles that Luke could command has often been noted). Also to be noted is the editor's arrangement of his material.

It follows that redaction criticism, though a valuable method, must be practised with a measure of scepticism; in Acts it often has nothing to depend on but subjective judgement. A notable exponent of the method is G. Lüdemann, who attempts through Acts to distinguish between tradition and redaction, and on this basis to assess its value as a historical source. In his Introduction (pp. 10–12) he takes as an example of the method the account in Acts 18 of Paul's visit to Corinth. Redactional features stand out at once: Paul's Sabbath preaching in the synagogue and the favourable picture of Gallio. Perhaps; but the synagogue did afford a ready-made audience, and untrue stories about proconsuls would have the reverse of an apologetic effect. Traditional material also is to be found: Paul's work with Aquila and Priscilla, and their recent arrival in Corinth as a result of Claudius' expulsion of the Jews from Rome; the arrival of Silas and Timothy from Macedonia; Paul's use of the house of Titius Justus; the conversion of the ruler of the synagogue, Crispus, the 'trial' before Gallio; the reference to the ruler of the synagogue,

Sosthenes. 'It is not linguistic reasons which lead us to suppose that Luke is using traditions but the concrete character of the above information and – more important – the evidence . . . that a by no means inconsiderable part of the information is at least partially confirmed by Paul's letters' (p. 10). Later however (p. 195) linguistic evidence is adduced to support the attribution of some parts of the paragraph to redaction. Lüdemann in his Introduction (p. 17) sums up: 'Alongside the letters of Paul Acts remains an important source for the history of early Christianity.'

From redaction criticism it is natural to move by way of a book described by its author, P. F. Esler,[36] as socio-redaction criticism, to the sociological study of Acts. Sociological study is not unrelated to historical criticism, for historical study if it is to be complete must always include a social element; the best historians have always known that they must inquire into the way in which men and women – not only kings and queens and their ministers but ordinary folk – conducted their lives, and that even power struggles on the largest scale were conducted by means of personal and administrative agencies. It is however undoubtedly true that in recent years greater stress has been laid upon investigation of the personal lives of Christians in NT times and that the methods of sociology have been employed. Esler looked back to pioneering work by G. Theissen, W. A. Meeks, and others, but developed his sociological observations in the light of Lucan theology. Much of his book is social history, and his observations on the Law, the Temple, the Poor and the Rich, and Rome are of great value. What calls for attention here is Esler's debate with the ancient historian E. A. Judge (who has also made very valuable contributions to the study of early Christian social history) about the applicability of the methods of sociology in NT history, and indeed to ancient history in general. Unfortunately it is impossible to follow the debate in detail here. 'Reading between the lines of Judge's article,[37] one senses that his real worry with sociological exegesis is that its exponents will attempt to plug holes in first-century data by drawing upon relevant features of the comparative materials they apply to the New Testament text' (Esler, p. 14). Esler and Judge are in fact not so far apart as might at first appear.

[36] *Community and Gospel in Luke–Acts*, SNTSMS 57, 1987, see also *The First Christians in their Social Worlds*, 1994.

[37] *Journal of Religious History* 11 (1980), 201–17.

Esler's reply to Judge's 'worry' is in essence that models and types should be more accurately defined and more carefully used than they are by some sociological practitioners who turn to ancient history, and his own observations in ancient social history as it concerns the NT are, as was noted above, of considerable value. The NT (like e.g. the *Histories* and *Annals* of Tacitus) is an old book, and there are no easy transitions (beyond the basic facts of human nature) between its world, and its forms of society, and our own. Sociological procedures can help to open up and sharpen questions for us, but the answers are to be found in the patient observation and collection of data found in ancient texts, literary and non-literary, and in the results of archaeological exploration, and it must not be expected that answers will be found by sociological analogy, if indeed answers are to be found anywhere.

More recent years have seen the development of methods of literary study, developed first, for the most part, in the realms of secular literature and applied to the NT as a whole. These have more to do with hermeneutics than with history[38] and find more scope in other parts of the NT than in a matter-of-fact work such as Acts. This is not to say that they are of no value, though the thought of Acts lies on the surface and does not require elaborate hermenutical arts to draw it out.

Not that there are no literary questions to ask about Acts. One may ask, for example, to what class of literature it belongs. This is a question that was raised above (pp. xxxv–xxxvii) and here it must suffice simply to mention a few terms, all of which cover part of the truth, none the whole truth. It looks like history, biographical history, the historical monograph. It has been described as an apology, and that in several senses, and like a Hellenistic romance. Luke had found his own way of communicating the Gospel and bearing witness to Christ; that is perhaps as near as we can get to a characterization of Acts. To say that the book is *sui generis* may seem like running away from a difficult and disputed problem of classification, but it is in fact true. No Christian wrote a book like it; the apocryphal Acts are at best like a Western text run even wilder.

[38] See R. C. Morgan and J. Barton, *Biblical Interpretation* (1988), where they are dealt with in ch. 7 (pp. 203–68). 'Some of the different ways that interpreters read a work of art today may prove more suggestive for theological interpretation than a historical scholarship which is less interested in the aesthetic and moral significance of great literature' (p. 203).

Also to be briefly mentioned here is the literary analysis of narrative, in relation not only to the narrator but also to the reader. It is possible to distinguish between the actual author of a piece of literature and the implied author, between the actual readers and the implied readers. The actual author of the Sherlock Holmes stories is Conan Doyle, a historical figure, about whom a good deal is known (far more than about most ancient authors). The implied author, implied by the form and content of the stories, is Dr Watson, a person known only from the stories themselves, though from them quite well; we know something of his medical training, his military service, his marriage, his loyal though not always highly intelligent assistance to his friend. In some kinds of literature this distinction is illuminating; hardly so in Acts, where the actual author is known, if at all, only by identification with the implied author, who shows his hand only in the *We*-passages (if indeed there). Of the actual readers of Acts, again we know little. Some of the evidence has been set out above (pp. xxi–xxiii). There may have been earlier readers, indeed it is highly probable that there were, but we can hardly give a name to one before Irenaeus. There is an excellent discussion of the implied readers in J. B. Tyson, *Images of Judaism in Luke–Acts* (Columbia, South Carolina, 1992). We may infer the characteristics of the implied readership from the extraneous pieces of information[39] which the author thinks it necessary to supply, and from those facts which the author assumes that the reader will know. Tyson's conclusions (pp. 35f.) are worth quoting.

1. Our reader is generally a well-educated person with a rudimentary knowledge of eastern Mediterranean geography and a familiarity with the larger and more significant Roman provinces.
2. The implied reader is familiar with some public figures, especially Roman emperors. He has some knowledge about James and his position within the primitive Christian community . . .
3. The implied reader is not expected to know any language other than Greek . . .
4. The implied reader is knowledgeable about public affairs . . .

[39] See S. M. Sheeley, *Narrative Asides in Luke–Acts*, JSNTSupps 72 (1992) R. Tannehill, *The Narrative Unity of Luke–Acts* (Philadelphia, I 1986, II 1990).

5. . . . has a working knowledge of common Greek and Roman measurements and coinage.
6. . . . has a working knowledge of both pagan and Jewish religions, an aversion to some pagan practices, and an attraction to Jewish religious life. But he is probably not Jewish and is not well informed about certain significant aspects of Jewish religious life.
7. . . . is familiar with the Hebrew Scriptures in their Greek translation and acknowledges their authoritative status but is not familiar with those methods of interpretation that find the fulfilment of the scriptures in Jesus.

From these observations Tyson infers that the implied reader 'is similar to those characters in Acts that are called "Godfearers"' (p. 36).[40] The two centurions (of Luke 7 and Acts 10; 11) serve as good examples.

This sort of observation is interesting and helpful in the study of Acts. It is however fairly described as a further development of historical study, an aspect of historical criticism little noticed in the past and now profitably brought to the fore.

The same comment may be made on the use, of which much is now being made, of the rhetorical principles taught and practised in antiquity. The works of the orators are an important part of ancient literature, and instruction in oratory was an important part of ancient education. These facts are not a new discovery, but the focusing of attention on them is new, and has borne a good deal of fruit in the study of the NT. Not so much fruit however in the study of Acts. As we have seen, Luke writes in such a way as to cause his work to be counted along with and judged alongside the work of ancient historians. His history is a very readable work, clear, fascinating, illuminating and not inaccurate. But this is not because Luke follows the rules of the rhetoricians. On the whole his manner corresponds closely with the words of Shakespeare's Mark Antony: 'I am no orator, as Brutus is . . . I only speak right on.' Special attention has been given to the speeches recorded in Acts, e.g. to the speech of Tertullus (24.2–9), which has been described as a masterpiece of forensic oratory, and Paul's reply (24.10–21). These, however, like

[40] For the problems arising out of this term, which are not discussed by Tyson, see pp. 154f.

most of the speeches in Acts, are too short to make the rules of rhetoric applicable. Rules that are suitable to (e.g.) Demosthenes' *De Corona* (112 pages in OCT), cannot be reasonably adapted to speeches, or summaries of speeches, only a few lines in length.

VI. THE THEOLOGY OF ACTS

So far as Acts makes a specific contribution to the theology of the NT this is to be found not so much in the treatment of particular doctrines as in an understanding of the possibility and course of Christian history and especially of the Christian mission. It may nevertheless be worth while to collect some of Luke's views in relation to a number of important themes before attempting to sum up the general convictions that underlie his presentation of Christian origins.[41]

(a) *Eschatology.* To the modern student of theology biblical eschatology is a problem. It was not a problem to Luke; he knew what to make of it and had already established a position which was, at the end of the first century, quite satisfying. It had long been necessary to recognize the existence of an interval between resurrection and parousia. In the beginning this may not have been expected or, when it happened, understood. The crucifixion (it was believed) would be followed by the vindication of Jesus, and this might be expressed in terms of Daniel 7 (a coming with the clouds) or of Daniel 12 (a rising up of those who sleep in the dust). Luke saw a clear distinction; it appears both in the Third Gospel and in Acts. Jesus was raised from death by God; after a period of forty days during which he appeared to various disciples he went up into heaven, his ascent modelled on Daniel's picture of the coming of the Son of man put into reverse; thence at the right moment he would return. All these events might be described as eschatological in the sense that they belonged to the winding up of God's purpose for the world. God himself had determined that the last act of the play should be a complex one, and had already declared this in the OT. The basic text is given a prominent place in the account of the gift of the Spirit on the Day of Pentecost. Altering the text of Joel 3.1–5 (LXX) Luke writes of the last days, which cover all Christian history. They are initiated by the gift of the Spirit, described by Luke before the text is quoted, and their end will be heralded by cosmic phenomena (the darkening of the sun, and so forth) which have manifestly not yet happened; the great and glorious day of the Lord has not yet arrived. The church

[41] For much fuller analyses of Lucan theology see F. Bovon, *Luke the Theologian: Thirty-three years of Research (1950–1983)* (ET Allison Park, 1987), J. A. Fitzmyer, *Luke the Theologian: Aspects of his Teaching* (London, 1989).

exists in the intervening period, its life determined by what has already happened and by what is still to come. The period is provided by God so that witness may be borne to Jesus (Acts 1.8); Luke describes the record of this witness from Jerusalem as far as Rome, but there is no hint, as his book draws to a close, that the end may be expected soon. That there will be an end, which will include the return of Jesus and judgement carried out by him, is plainly assumed. It is categorically affirmed at the beginning of the book (1.11) and several times repeated, especially in the earlier chapters (2.19–21; 3.20, 21; 10.42; 17.31; (26.6)); it is implied also by some of the passages that refer to salvation, for this is in part salvation from the judgement that will fall upon the sinful human race. The coming of the Messiah waits upon repentance and faith (3.20, 21), which Luke hopes to encourage, but it is clear that his interest is in the present and he makes little use of eschatological threats to encourage response. In this respect Acts is to be contrasted with Luke's gospel; on this see especially Wilson (*Gentiles* 67–80: 'The two strands in Luke's eschatology'). His conclusion is correct. 'In Acts we have a further development of one of the two strands we found in Luke's Gospel to the exclusion of the other. Luke has moved away from belief in an imminent end. One of his methods of doing this is to schematize and objectify the eschatological timetable. Another is to substitute Ascension theology, the present activity of the exalted Lord in his Church, for belief in an imminent end. This is done not so much by dogmatic statement as by the concentration on this element in Acts. The time-scheme of Acts allows for a hiatus between the Resurrection and the Parousia in which the Church can exist and grow' (p. 80). See also the excellent observations of E. Grässer in Kremer, *Actes* 99–127, especially his conclusion on p. 127. Consideration of Luke's eschatology leads immediately to a second theme.

(b) *The Holy Spirit.* According to 2.17, 18 the gift of the Holy Spirit is (after the resurrection and ascension of Jesus) the first part of the fulfilment of the eschatological hope; it initiates the period in which (see above) the church can 'exist and grow'. References to the Spirit are as frequent as references to the parousia are few. The book has been described as the Acts not so much of the apostles as of the Holy Spirit. This is already made clear in 1.6–8 (it is not for disciples to know God's eschatological programme but they will be empowered for witness by the gift of the Spirit) and confirmed in 2.1–4 (after a period of waiting the church receives its full active being in the gift of the Spirit at Pentecost). It is not strictly consistent with this definitive, founding gift of the Spirit that from time to time afterwards Christians are said to be, on special occasions, filled with the Spirit – 4.8, 31; 6.3, 5; 7.55; 9.17; 11.24; 13.9, 52. In addition people are said to be baptized with the Holy Spirit; the Holy Spirit comes upon them, or falls upon them. It is only Luke's mode of expression that is open to logical criticism; his thought is clear and consistent. Believers receive the Holy Spirit as the basic constituent of their believing life, and in times of special need they receive special gifts of the Spirit that enable them to speak or act appropriately. The Holy Spirit has already been at work in the OT (e.g. 1.16; 4.25; 7.51; 28.25), but is now (as prophesied by Joel – 2.17, 18) given generally, so that the possession of the Spirit by Gentiles is a proof that they are rightly included in the church's mission (10.44, 45, 47; 11.15, 16; 15.8). In other ways also the Spirit directs the mission, directing Philip to meet the Ethiopian (8.29) and subsequently conveying him to Azotus (8.39f.), telling Peter to go with Cornelius' messengers (10.19f.; 11.12), forbidding Paul to speak in Asia and to travel to Bithynia (16.6, 7), and ordering him to return to Asia (19.1 – if the Western text is followed). If in 21.4 the Spirit seems to get the directions wrong this is no doubt to be put down to a piece of careless writing by Luke. The Spirit is offered as a gift to those who repent and believe. The offer is explicit on the Day of Pentecost (2.38); cf. 9.17; 13.52. The gift is often but by no means always associated with baptism, sometimes with the laying on of hands; on this see below, pp. lx–lxii. The Spirit, present as a guiding principle in the Christian fellowship, is abused when Christians practise deceit; so Ananias and Sapphira deceive the Holy Spirit and lie to God (5.3, 4); it goes too far to deduce from this text the deity of the Holy Spirit, though it is unlikely that Luke would have wished to deny the proposition had it been made to him. The Spirit is associated with the Father and the Son at 2.33, a verse that is not without ambiguity. Jesus has been exalted to (or by) the right hand of God; he has received the gift of the Holy Spirit; on the precise meaning of this see pp. lx–lxii. Having received the promise of the Spirit (the promised Spirit?) he pours out (the verb points back to the quotation from Joel in 2.17) the Spirit whose presence you can detect in observable phenomena. The Spirit is at least a third form of divine activity.

What was observed (heard rather than seen) was the miraculous speaking with tongues of 2.4, 5–12; it is not clear whether the phenomena of 2.2, 3 were observable outside the house or room in which the disciples were assembled. Speech is in Acts the characteristic mark of the Spirit's presence, sometimes in glossolalia (2.4; 10.46; 19.6), sometimes in prophecy (2.17, 18; 11.27; 13.1–3; 21.(4), (9), 10, 11), sometimes in proclamation (e.g. 4.31). It is striking that Luke (unlike Paul) does not see the work of the Spirit in the moral renovation of human life. This does not mean that he did not believe in the power of God to change human behaviour; it does however mean that he was impressed by what may be regarded as the shallower and showier aspects of Christian life – mainly no doubt because they were easy to describe and likely to impress the reader as they had impressed him.

(c) *Christology*. As truly as the Third Gospel, though in a different manner, Acts is an account of the works of Jesus the Messiah. The opening verse refers back to the contents of the former treatise as concerned with all that Jesus began to do and to teach. It is a probable though less than certain implication that the new treatise is about all that Jesus continued to do and to teach; even if he did not intend it Luke would not have disagreed. The disciples are to be his witnesses (1.8; for their continuing witness cf. 1.22; 2.32; 3.15; 5.22; 10.39, 41; 13.31; 22.15, 20; 26.16, for the word *witness*) and he is the foundation of their testimony (2.22; 3.13; 4.2, 10, 33; 5.42; 8.12, 35; 9.20, 27; 10.38; 11.20; 13.32f.; 16.31; 17.3, 18; 18.5, 28; 20.21; 24.24; 28.23, 31). He is the agent of miracles (e.g. 3.6; 4.10; 9.34). Sometimes he acts indirectly, through the Spirit (who may be called the Spirit of Jesus, 16.7); angels also play their part (8.26; 12.7; 27.23); but Jesus also speaks and acts in his own person, and on specially notable occasions, confronting Saul (9.5; 22.8; 26.15), and encouraging him (18.9; 23.11). He is a supernatural person, able at will to participate in historical events.

To this it is necessary to add that what he does he does as the agent of God the Father. In the healing of the lame man at the Temple gate it may be the intention of 3.13 to suggest that God has glorified his servant Jesus by using him as the agent of cure; in 4.30 the disciples pray to God that he will stretch out his hand for healing and that signs and portents may be done through the name of his servant Jesus. Jesus is the agent not only of healing in a physical sense but of the salvation that means belonging to the elect people who will be brought safely through the perils of the last days (4.12).

Jesus is described by a number of titles, some of them widely used elsewhere in the NT. He is of course the Christ, the Messiah, the Lord's anointed king. Or should we say, he will be the Christ? This question is raised with reference to 3.20; see the notes on this verse on p. 48. It is not likely that the verse refers to an appointment lying still in the future; Luke undoubtedly believed that Jesus was the Christ from his birth onwards; see especially Lk. 2.11. It is not impossible that a source used by Luke took a different view, but it is improbable. It does however seem likely that Acts 2.36 meant originally that Jesus became Christ at the time of his resurrection, though Luke himself must have been able to accommodate the verse to his own view. *Lord*, also occurring in 2.36, is a word that interprets Christ for the Hellenistic world. It is not correct to say that since in the LXX *Lord* renders the name YHWH the use of the word in Acts (and in the NT generally) in itself implies the divinity of Jesus. At least it does not imply that Jesus is to be identified with, or placed on the same level as, the God of the OT. Luke, quoting Ps. 110.1 (The Lord said to my Lord) in 2.34, shows himself to be fully aware that the word Lord could be used in two senses, and he took Jesus to be the second Lord to whom the first Lord speaks. The word is at once an identification of Jesus with the Davidic king and an approach to the Gentile world with its gods many and lords many (1 Cor. 8.5). *Lord* undoubtedly means that Jesus was, and was understood by the Christians to be, one who enjoyed absolute authority, to whom they owed absolute obedience. He himself however stands under the absolute authority of God the Father: it is he who has made Jesus Lord and Christ. There is thus in Acts, as in much of the NT, an element of subordinationism, but it is the subordination of an obedient Son, active in the Father's service. Jesus is the Son of God in only two passages. It may not be a coincidence that it is Paul who proclaims Jesus as the Son of God (9.20) and quotes Ps. 2.7 at 13.33. It would be wrong to read a metaphysical relation into Luke's reporting, whatever Paul himself may have believed. Only in chs. 3 and 4 (3.13, 26; 4.27, 30) is Jesus spoken of as the Servant of God; this may reflect the use by Luke of a source. It is mistaken to suppose that there is a reference here to the Servant of the Lord in Deutero-Isaiah. In 4.25 the word *servant* is applied to David, and in the OT it is used of kings, prophets, and other outstanding figures. There may however be an allusion to Isaiah 52.13 in 3.13 – to the glorification rather than the suffering of the Servant. Luke is here using traditional material;

when, in 8.32, 33 he quotes Isaiah 53 the word 'servant' does not occur.

Other Christological terms occur infrequently. One is *archegos* (3.15; 5.31), which may mean *prince*, *leader*, *author*, *origin*. See the discussion on pp. 46, 79. At 5.31 this word is coupled with *saviour*, which occurs again at 13.23. At 3.14 Jesus is *the holy and righteous one*, at 7.52; 22.14 *the righteous one*. It is uncertain whether these adjectives are titles or simple descriptions. *Nazoraean* (2.22; 3.6; 4.10; 6.14; 22.8; 26.9; cf. 24.5, where it is used in the plural to mean Christians) probably means *coming from Nazareth*, but has been thought to be a title; see p. 25. The expression Son of man, so common in the gospels, is used once only, by Stephen, at 7.56; it was probably chosen as one suitable to denote a person now in heaven but waiting to come with the clouds at some future time.[42] At 2.22; 17.31 the word *man* is used of Jesus; in the latter verse, where the *man* is to be the judge of mankind, it recalls part of the connotation of Son of man.

There is in Acts no profound Christological thought; yet it is clear that Jesus Christ of Nazareth is the person who initiated and will conclude the whole story and directs the whole course of it. His career, marked by portents, signs, and mighty works, was sufficient to show that God was with him, not merely as he had been with, for example, the prophets, but in a unique (though undefined) sense. He was killed through an ignorant error on the part of the Jews, both rulers and people, who handed him over to the Romans, but God soon put the mistake right by raising him from death, thereby confirming – or creating – his status as Messiah (a term meaningful to Jews) and Lord (which would make sense to Gentiles). The risen Jesus continued long enough on earth to prove that he was truly alive and then ascended to his rightful place at the right hand of God. This proved that he belonged essentially to the same order of being as the Creator, the Lord of the OT, though within that order secondary. The sense in which a second being might be said to share the throne of God would have constituted a problem, and engendered disputes, for some Jews; not, apparently, for Luke. Jesus had now sent the Spirit so as to bring into being a renewed Israel, soon to be enriched by the addition of Gentiles. Jesus, crucified and risen, thus brought salvation to the mixed

[42] In Stephen's speech note also words that might have been used in Christology but are in fact used of Moses: *ruler*, *judge*, *redeemer* (7.35).

community: the forgiveness of sins, the inspiring and sanctifying of the Spirit, and the pledge of safety in the eschatological troubles that still lay ahead.

(d) *The Church.* The community just mentioned was an eschatological entity, living within the period of fulfilment initiated by the gift of the Spirit and awaiting its end in the portents described by Joel (Acts 2.17–21). It was also however a historical phenomenon, manifested in a number of groups of believers scattered through various parts of the Mediterranean world. These groups came into being through the preaching of apostles and others. As their hearers accepted the word that they heard they found themselves gathered into believing companies and shared a common life. There was little by way of outward organization to mark this common life;[43] fellowship was constituted by a shared belief that Jesus in truth was what the preachers had declared him to be, offered salvation, and claimed obedience. The Spirit generated speech and no doubt enthusiasm; and Jesus' command of mutual love was expressed in the sharing of goods (2.44, 45; 4.32, 34, 35, 36, 37; 5.1–11; 6.1). How far this practice, which according to Luke resulted in the absence of poverty in the community, resembled and was related to similar customs observed at Qumran is disputed; see pp. 34f., 87.

At first there was one such community, in Jerusalem. At 5.11; 8.1, 3; 11.22; 12.5; 15.4, 22; and perhaps 18.22, it is denoted by the word *ekklēsia.* As the Gospel was taken out from Jerusalem into the world this word came to be applied to other local Christian groups: to the Christians of Antioch at 11.26; 13.1; 14.27; 15.3; to the Christians of Ephesus at 20.17. The word is used of the groups of converts made in Paul's first missionary journey: 14.23; 16.5; of those in Syria and Cilicia at 15.41. An *ekklēsia* thus appears to be a local group of Christians. There are two passages that may suggest a wider meaning. It is often maintained that this is so at 9.31, which refers to the church through the whole of Judaea and Galilee and Samaria. This may be the beginning of such a use, but the geographical designation may be taken to indicate a 'local' church residing in more than one town (see p. 143). More significant is the reference (20.28) to the church of God which he acquired by his own blood, a strange expression in that it appears to refer to the blood of God. However it is interpreted the verse speaks of a single body of all Christians which God has

[43] See however below, sections (e) and (f).

redeemed and constituted through the bloody, that is, sacrificial, death of Christ. *ekklēsia*, then, is here the world-wide company of the redeemed. It is important that the same word is used for both purposes. Luke may not have seen deeply into the meaning of his own language, but it implies (and this is borne out elsewhere in the NT) that each local group of Christians is not merely related to the total church but in fact is the total church in the place in which it exists. It is also important that the word *ekklēsia* is used in the LXX as a rendering of the Hebrew *qāhāl*, the people of God, living (sometimes rebelliously) under his direction. In Acts, see e.g. 7.38. Luke was familiar with the LXX and there can be no doubt that this use of *ekklēsia* would be in his mind. In the OT the Lord had acquired a people by the mighty acts that he performed in Egypt; he had now acquired a people, racially mixed, by the shedding of Christ's blood. Why the death of Jesus should be regarded as a sacrifice and how the sacrifice could have the effect of constituting a people are questions that Luke did not address. For questions that did concern him see below, especially (h) the Jews and (j) Gentiles and the Gentile Mission. For the constitution and actions of the church see (e), (f) and (g).

(e) *Apostles and Ministers.* Luke's account of the church is given for the most part in terms not of its rank and file but of its leading members. Continuity between the earthly life of Jesus of Nazareth and the church after the time of the resurrection is provided by twelve men. Eleven of these (1.13) had belonged to the group of twelve chosen by Jesus (Lk. 6.13–16); from this group Judas Iscariot was removed by defection and death (Acts 1.16–20) and Matthias was added to it (1.21–26), the use of the lot being taken to demonstrate that he equally with the rest had been chosen by Jesus (1.24). These Twelve are referred to again under that title at 6.2, and the title is implied at 2.14, where Peter stood up 'with the Eleven' (cf. 1.26). They are thus responsible for the initial proclamation of the Christian message and are still regarded in ch. 6 as responsible for it, since they profess the intention to give themselves to prayer and the ministry of the word, leaving the administration of charity to Stephen and his colleagues (6.2–6), whom, on the nomination of the people, they appoint.

The Eleven when they are joined by Matthias are described as apostles, a term that accords with Lk. 6.13 and is used much more frequently than the numeral, though not after 16.4. It is sometimes but not always suggested fairly definitely that the Apostles are identical with the Twelve, and there are only two verses (14.4, 14; on both see the notes) where persons not belonging to the Twelve are called apostles. Only in these verses is Paul (and Barnabas with him) called an apostle, and it is clear that Paul (and presumably Barnabas also) did not fulfil the conditions laid down in 1.21, 22 for appointment. The rest of the NT makes it clear that the word *apostle* was used in more senses than one,[44] it is probably best to suppose that the (Antiochene?) source by Luke in ch. 14 referred to Paul and Barnabas as apostles, that is, envoys, or missionaries, of the church of Antioch, and that Luke omitted to bring the reference into line with his use elsewhere.

Luke has some notable stories about Peter. In chs. 3, 4 and 8 John accompanies Peter. In ch. 12 we read of the execution of James, John's brother. Luke has nothing else to tell us of the Twelve Apostles and it is clear that for him their main significance as a group is simply that they exist, and by their existence witness to and (so far as this could be done) guarantee the continuity between Jesus and the post-resurrection church. Only Peter (so far as Luke's narrative goes) makes any other contribution to the life of the church. Their function is important (note the contrast in 13.31, 32; and cf. 10.39) but it neither could nor needed to be repeated. There are no more apostles; the word as used in the sense of 2 Cor. 8.23 (and perhaps Acts 14.4, 14) dropped out of use. Paul, as was noted above, does not meet with the requirements of apostleship as Luke sets them out, yet he was, for Luke and no doubt in fact, the outstanding missionary of the first generation. He also exemplified, for Luke, Luke's understanding of Judaism as the heir of the OT people of God, who nevertheless must now understand both the OT and their own vocation in the light of the Gospel. How is he to be described? Luke has no category for him; he is a *chosen vessel* (9.15), a tool selected by God for a special purpose, a man who would bear Christ's name before Gentiles and kings and the children of Israel. He is not subordinated to the Twelve; the only passage that suggests this is 13.32, and this is a matter not of subordination but of distinction. His address to the Ephesian elders in 20.18–35 is important both as showing his understanding of pastoral ministry, as exercised by himself and expected of the elders, and as indicating the origin of the elders' ministry. They have been appointed

[44] See C. K. Barrett, *The Signs of an Apostle* (London, 1970; Carlisle, 1996), with the summary on pp. 71–3.

neither by the church in which they ministered nor by Paul but by the Holy Spirit (20.28). No provision for future ministers is suggested here; they will come from the same source. To say this is not to deny human participation in the process; especially in the earliest days Paul must himself have played a leading part in making appointments (14.23), but 13.1–3 pictures as 20.28 does appointment not so much to an office as to a task by the Holy Spirit, working, one may suppose, through the prophets of 13.1. The task of prophets and teachers was to prophesy and to teach, to utter messages communicated by the Holy Spirit and to maintain and apply the basic traditions of the faith. Elders would like Paul himself declare the counsel of God (20.27) and maintain discipline in the community. Working for their own living they would out of their own as well as out of the church's resources aid those who were in need. This task elsewhere is the work of deacons, but the word deacon does not occur in Acts. Elders, called *episkopoi* as well as *presbyteroi*, perform all the tasks of ministers; Acts 6 is not intended to be an account of the origin of the diaconate as an order of ministers (see p. 86).

(f) *Baptism and the Christian Meal.* These twin topics (they seem to us to be twins; it is by no means certain that they would have seemed so to Luke – like other NT writers he had no word *sacrament* to unite them) give rise to a number of puzzles. If one concentrates on certain parts of Acts (chs. 1, 2, 8, 9–11, 16, 18, 19 and 22), or rather on parts of these chapters, baptism seems to be the normal and universal way into the Christian church. What are we to do? ask the crowd on the Day of Pentecost. Repent, and let each of you be baptized, Peter replies (2.37, 38). The converted Samaritans respond in the same way; Cornelius and his friends, the Philippian gaoler and his household, many of the Corinthians, are baptized. If however we turn to the other chapters (and to parts of those listed above) there is silence. The Temple crowd are urged to repent and have their sins blotted out; they are not told to be baptized. There are no baptisms in Luke's account of the 'first missionary journey', though churches are established (14.23). Apart from Lydia and the Philippian gaoler there are no baptisms in Macedonia or in the main account (apart, that is, from 19.5) of Paul's work in Ephesus. No baptisms take place after ch. 19, even in Malta, where Paul made so deep an impression. Again, if we ask, Does the gift of the Spirit precede, accompany, or follow the rite of water-baptism? we get different answers in different parts of Acts. If we ask, Must baptism be complemented by the laying on of hands? there is no consistent answer. What is meant by baptism in (or with) the Spirit? Is it a consequence of water-baptism or is it independent of water-baptism? Who are the proper recipients of water-baptism? Adult believers only, or infants also? None of these questions can be answered with any confidence on the basis of Acts. There is quite enough of baptism in Acts to make it clear that Luke was familiar with the practice; we can hardly fail to conclude that baptism was not, as is commonly supposed, a universal custom in the early church, or at least that some of Luke's sources (such as that based on Antioch) were not interested in baptism.

When baptism is mentioned, and if it is specified (and since a good deal of baptizing was going on in the first century it must have been specified – Our baptism is . . .), it is said to be in or into the name of Jesus.[45] Behind this no doubt lies a Hebrew expression which here would mean 'so as to come under the authority of'. Taken into Greek the expression gains a financial connotation: 'so as to be added to the account of', that is, 'so as to become the property of'. This seems to be the primary thought in Luke's mind. The converts (one may say, whether baptized or not) become Christ's men or women. From this consequences follow. They become members of Christ's people. Christ bestows upon them the gift of the Spirit. Their sins are forgiven. These units form in Luke's mind a single whole and he is not concerned to specify an order in which they occur. At 2.38 it is not quite stated but it is implied that the gift of the Spirit follows upon baptism: Let each of you be baptized . . . and you will receive . . . The opposite order occurs at 10.44–48. The Spirit fell upon Cornelius and his friends and to this Peter's response was, 'Can we fail to baptize these people who have received the Holy Spirit just as we did?' There is a further complication in ch. 8 (cf. 19.6) when Philip baptizes the Samaritans and it is not said that they received the Holy Spirit; Peter and John arrive, impose their hands and pray, and the Spirit is given. Is the imposition of hands necessary? It is not mentioned in the other stories we have considered. Is it a rite that only an apostle can execute? We do not know the answers to these questions; see the notes on the various passages. We cannot fail to conclude that Luke gives an unclear account of baptism. He had no fixed principles about its practice, or perhaps its meaning. For Paul baptism meant crucifixion and burial with Christ, and he seems to

[45] There is no hint of a Trinitarian formula such as that of Mt. 28.19.

assume that this is a common Christian understanding (Rom. 6.3). In fact, what Luke says about baptism matches his Christology. He knows quite well that Jesus was crucified and that his resurrection implies his previous death. But for him Christ *crucified* is not his central theme, the theme of all themes that it was for Paul (1 Cor. 2.2); therefore the Christ to whom the converts came to belong was not so specifically and exclusively Christ crucified as he was for Paul. Inevitably, crucifixion dropped out of baptism.

Did Luke's church have a eucharist? He does not say so. Acts contains several references to meals taken by Christians. The description of the Christian fellowship that resulted from Peter's preaching on the Day of Pentecost includes 2.42, 'They continued in the teaching of the apostles and the fellowship, in the breaking of bread and the prayers'; 2.46, 'continuing with one accord in the Temple and breaking bread at home they partook of food with gladness and simplicity of heart'. At 20.7 it is said that Paul and his companions with the church at Troas met to break bread; at v. 11, after the incident of the young man who fell out of the window, Paul went up, broke the bread and ate, and continued his address. At 27.34–36 Paul urged his fellow seafarers to partake of food; this would be for their welfare (*sōtēria*, which in other contexts might be translated *Salvation*); when he had said this and taken the loaf he broke it before them all and began to eat; and they all cheered up and themselves partook of food. On all these passages see the notes. It is striking that all of them refer to the breaking of bread, the last is expressed in language that is particularly close to that of Lk. 22.19, 20 (the Last Supper) and 9.16, 17 (the feeding miracle); see also Lk. 24.30, 35. There is however no reference, as there is in the account of the Last Supper (in 1 Cor. 11.23–26 as well as in the gospels), to the drinking of wine. J. Jeremias is probably right in taking the *breaking of bread* to be a Christian use, describing a specifically Christian meal, wrong in taking Luke's intention to be the concealment from non-Christian readers of a secret Christian rite confined to believers. Luke had already given an account of the meal including explanatory words ('This is my body', etc.) not only for the bread but for the wine; and he goes out of his way in 27.35 to say that what Paul did he did before them all. The four passages in Acts describe a Christian fellowship meal which derived its special significance not from what was eaten and drunk but from the fellowship of Christians who, as they ate and drank, would not forget the Lord who had given himself for them, and in giving himself for them was giving himself to them. If others were present they would get out of the meal what they could – and this might prove, even in the midst of the storm, to be more than physical sustenance. Whether there was wine to drink or not might well depend on circumstances. There is no indication that the meals referred to in Acts were in any way connected with the Passover, at which the drinking of four cups of wine was obligatory. A more difficult problem is raised by the fact that Paul's account of the Christian meal (1 Cor. 10.16, 21 as well as 11.23–26) includes specific reference to wine. It is natural – and correct – to say that there was probably a great deal of variety in Christian observance in the first century, but Luke (whatever we make of the We-passages) was some sort of Paulinist. It is probably best to suppose that though 'the breaking of bread' was not a cypher designed to keep the proceedings secret it had become a formula that pointed to a whole meal and made no attempt to specify all the substances consumed.

It is hardly open to doubt that what was important to Luke was not the symbolic significance of what was done, of what was eaten and drunk, but the shared life that commensality represented. In 2.42 the breaking of bread appears in a context determined by the teaching of the apostles and prayers and by fellowship which in part at least receives its definition from the fact that those taking part had their property in common, and used their resources for the relief of the poor.

(g) '*Primitive Catholicism*' (*Frühkatholizismus*). Some of the features of Acts that have now been considered have led some students of the book to the view that it marks an important stage in the development of Christianity from the simplicity of the apostolic age to the catholicism of the second century. Stated in this way the conclusion is one that requires careful definition of the terms in which it is cast, and of these catholicism itself is notoriously difficult to express precisely. The contrasts drawn by earlier theologians between Spirit and Office, Inspiration and Tradition, have been for the most part abandoned, in the recognition that it is the word of the inspired speaker that becomes the authoritative word of order and tradition. Any body of human beings that persists through several generations will produce traditions; if it increases in numbers it will need institutions. Those who in its earliest days took the lead and at least to that extent exercised authority will wish to see their work continued, and to that end will seek out suitable successors and train them in their own ways. A point of fundamental importance lies in the contrast between a condition in which the Gospel is the only criterion of the church, and one in which the church is thought to legitimize the Gospel and the apostolic origin of church office is the guarantee of legitimate proclamation. This contrast is sharply made and provides a useful tool for critical theology, but this does not mean that it can in itself serve as a valid judgement on Acts – or indeed on any book or any period of the Christian church. This involves also a critical historical question.

The following have been alleged as features of the narrative in Acts that point in the direction of developing catholicism. (1) The emphasis on the importance of the apostles, and (2) the notion of a succession from the apostles as constituting the being of the church and providing its ministry; (3) the notion of a ministry which is essential to the being of the church, and (4) stress on the importance of the sacraments as means by which the ministry nourishes the life of the church.

To some extent these matters have already been discussed. For the apostles, on whom Luke does lay considerable stress, see (e) above. It was they who, led by Peter, spoke to the assembled crowds on the Day of Pentecost. Those who accepted their message on that day continued steadfastly in their teaching. They may be said to exercise authority only in Peter's rebuke to Ananias and Sapphira and in their resolution of the problem of the neglected widows; they appoint the Seven. James is killed with the sword, and Peter departs to 'another place'. They are present at the Council in ch. 15, but only Peter speaks. We hear no more of them, and it seems probable that Luke had no further information. They were important because they had accompanied Jesus in his ministry and thus served as a guarantee – or perhaps rather as a symbol – of the fact that the actions of the post-resurrection church were a valid continuation of the work of Jesus. For this they were important, indeed indispensable, but their importance was unique to themselves; it could not be transmitted to successors because it was they and they alone who bridged the gap between the time of Jesus and the time of the church. Others of course could and did take up the message they had heard (1 Cor. 15.3). It was this that constituted the being of the church and its integrity.

For ministers see also (e). There were in Ephesus those designated both *presbyteroi* and *episkopoi*, *elders* and *bishops*, but of course these words, like the Greek words they represent, require careful definition. At Antioch we do not encounter these words but hear of *prophets* and *teachers*. Paul leaves to these ministers his task of proclaiming the kingdom of God and the Gospel of the grace of God, and preaching repentance and faith (20.21, 24). He has not appointed them (though he did appoint elders, 14.23); the Holy Spirit has made them the bishops that they are; no doubt the same Spirit will make further ministers when they are needed – no other provision for appointment is made.

For 'sacraments' (the word is nowhere used in the NT), see (f). Baptism may have been a universally required rite of admission to the church, but Acts does not say so and does not provide evidence on which such a conclusion might be based. No language that could be described as specifically 'sacramental' is used of the Christians' common meal.

The most that can be said is that there are some hints of what may be regarded as elements in a developing 'catholic' structure of the church, but they are not combined in such a way as themselves to constitute a catholic structure. The existence of leaders, whom we may describe as ministers, the existence of a tradition of belief passed on from one to another, the practice of certain customs, such as fellowship meals, when these features are not regarded as constitutive of the church, do not amount to such a structure. In Acts the vital principle that creates the church is the word that is committed by Jesus to those who follow him and the Spirit of God by which this message is received and activated.

'Primitive Catholicism' is not a good characterization of the church of Acts.

(h) *The Jews.* Acts begins with the converse of Jesus, a Jew, with his Jewish disciples in the weeks immediately after his resurrection. His ascension follows, and soon afterwards the gift of the Holy Spirit. The disciples preach to a large and mixed company of people, many of whom accept their message. They have come from many lands but they have come to Jerusalem and most if not all of them must be thought of as Jews. The Jewish atmosphere persists through the next chapters, so that in ch. 8 Philip's conversion of Samaritans and of an Ethiopian is presented as a new step into a strange world. So is Peter's visit to Cornelius, and Cornelius' baptism. From this point the movement into Gentile world (see (j) below) gathers speed; it is led by Paul and his colleagues, and at the end of the book Paul quotes Isa. 6.9, 10 to the Roman Jews and adds, 'Be it known to you that this salvation of God has been sent to the Gentiles; they will listen' (28.26–28). A superficial reading of this story suggests that the mission to Jews is now over; Christians are leaving them to their own devices and concentrating on the mission to Gentiles. This inference from Acts is not without plausibility, and the book has been understood to be a substantial contribution to Christian anti-Semitism.

This it certainly is not. A book whose main actors – Peter, Stephen, Paul, James, not to mention Jesus (mainly off stage) – are all Jews cannot easily be judged anti-Jewish (still less anti-Semitic – Acts shows no interest in race as such). Most of the leaders of the church have to be pushed very hard, by argument, by vision, by divine intervention through the Holy Spirit, to accept uncircumcised Gentiles as fellow believers. Surely, salvation is for Jews, to whom it was promised. The verse quoted above (28.28) does not stand alone. There are parallels in 13.46 ('Since you thrust [the word of God] from you and consider yourselves unworthy of eternal life, see! we are turning to the Gentiles') and 18.6 ('Your blood be upon your own head, I am clean; henceforth I shall go to the Gentiles'); and in each case Paul's first step in the next place he visits (14.1; 18.19) is to enter the synagogue and pursue his mission there. There is no reason why 28.28, though it stands at the end of the book, should be read in a completely different way.

This does not mean that there are no questions to be asked. It is clear (and in this there is no reason to doubt the accuracy of Acts) that large numbers of Jews were rejecting the belief that Jesus was their, Jewish, Messiah. Stephen's accusation is hard and bitter (7.51–53). Does it mean that the Jewish people have forfeited their special place in the purpose of God? That they have now been replaced by the multi-racial company of believers in Jesus? The questions what role the Jewish people may be expected to have in God's plan, and what is their ultimate hope of salvation, are discussed by Paul at great depth in Romans 9–11. Luke was not capable of this kind of discussion and was probably less aware of the questions than most theologians are today. We may see a pointer, which resembles those that we have seen in 14.1 and 18.19, by returning to the end of Stephen's speech. 'You constantly resist the Holy Spirit; as your fathers did so do you' (7.53). Stephen has described several notable failures on the part of earlier generations of Jews. His brothers sold Joseph into Egypt; his people rejected Moses; they made and worshipped the golden calf; they desired and built a temple, which God did not desire. On each of these occasions God might well have washed his hands of them, but he did not do so. True, Jesus was in a sense his last word, but a misjudgement by the Sanhedrin on a particular occasion could not be regarded as the last word of Israel's reply to God. In comparison with the Romans the Jews come badly out of Luke's account of Paul's suffering, but his first act on reaching Rome is to send for the leading Jews (28.17), and Luke (rightly or wrongly) asserts that his message was nothing but what the prophets and Moses said should happen (26.22), and this he was ready to proclaim to both the people and the Gentiles (26.23).

Here however was the crux of the matter. Did Paul rightly understand what Moses and the prophets had said? Most Jews said no, and that on two fundamental points. According to Paul the Scriptures prophesied the death and resurrection of the Messiah, and this was fulfilled in Jesus. According to Luke they also foretold that God would take out of the Gentiles a people for his name (15.14–18). On this interpretation, Jesus was the Messiah and the church, including uncircumcised Gentiles, was the people of God, with the nation of Israel alongside in an undefined position, waiting till it should return by faith into the divine purpose. This is perhaps not a very satisfactory, or a very clear, position from the point of view of theology, but it was a practical one and probably satisfied Luke and most of his contemporaries. The same must probably be said of the Apostolic Decree (15.29); on this see below and the notes on 15.20, 29. The crucial issue was the Law; see the next section.

(i) *The Law.* 'By three things is the world sustained: by the Law, by the [Temple] service, and by deeds of loving-kindness' (Aboth 1.2 (Danby)). No NT writer, certainly not Luke, raises any objection to the doing of kindnesses. The attitude to the Temple that is revealed in Acts is not simple. The first Christians are represented as continuing to use the Temple. The scene of the Pentecost event (2.1–4) is not specified; it may have been the Temple. In Acts 3 we see Peter and John on their way to the Temple at the time of prayer; they heal a lame man at the Beautiful gate, the party proceeds into the Temple, and there Peter and John address the assembled crowd. In ch. 5 the apostles are preaching in the Temple when they are arrested. In 6.13, 14 Stephen is accused of threatening the Temple with destruction and in ch. 7 he launches the most violent attack on the Temple found outside the OT. From this point in Acts the scene begins to shift from

Jerusalem, but when Paul returns he accepts the challenge to demonstrate his faithfulness to Judaism by taking part in Temple rites (21.23, 24, 26) and thereby affirms that he accepted its discipline (21.24). This double attitude to the Temple reflects the attitude of Acts to Judaism in general. Judaism is good if it is understood in the Christian way. The Temple is an aid to prayer; and participation in the resolution of a Nazirite vow included sacrifice so that Paul's visit to the Temple in ch. 21 must be understood to be for the purpose of sacrifice as well as prayer. But any attempt to confine God within a dwelling of human construction is to be rejected, so that the very existence of a Temple was a peril to true religion, whether in Jerusalem or in Athens (17.24). This is a different attitude from that of the Qumran sect, which did not disapprove of the Temple on principle but only of the way in which it was being administered and of those who controlled it.

It is notable that Stephen, who attacks the Temple with such vehemence, does not attack the Law. Moses received living oracles to give to us (7.38). The Israelites received the Law at the ordinance of angels (a thought that Paul uses in a different way – Gal. 3.19). That they had a Law was a good thing; their fault was that they did not observe it. It cannot be said on the basis of Acts that Stephen initiated a law-free Gospel. There is indeed no law-free Gospel in Acts but a compromise between those who wanted to keep the whole Law in operation and those who as a condition of salvation wanted no law at all. This compromise is expressed in the Decree of Acts 15.29. The Decree undoubtedly inclines markedly in the law-free direction. Circumcision is not demanded, but Gentile converts are required ('these necessary things' in 15.28) to abstain from food offered to idols, from blood, from strangled meat, and from fornication – requirements that combine the moral with the ceremonial.[46] This is presumably the result of years of controversy between Paul and his allies and various groups of Judaizers. It is essentially a practical rather than a theological compromise, and though it is set forth as containing conditions of salvation its main practical effect, in addition to establishing peace within the church, was probably that it made it possible for Jewish Christians and Gentile Christians to share together in the church's common meal. It was, however, based[47] on those

[46] See the Commentary on ch. 15.
[47] See p. 234.

elements of Judaism that a Jew could not give up even in the extremity of persecution – Judaism reduced to an absolute minimum so as to impose as little strain as possible on Gentiles.

Luke's grounds for so far dispensing with the Law are given in ch. 15. The fundamental reasons are put, probably for reasons of policy, in Peter's mouth. First, the pragmatic reason: God called Peter to speak the word to Gentiles; they received it by faith (not by works of Law), and God gave to them the same gift of the Spirit that he had given at the beginning to (Jewish) apostles (15.7f.). The next emphasizes that God made no distinction between the circumcised and the uncircumcised; the latter, unclean Gentiles that they were, were cleansed by God by faith, without any legal device. Finally Peter asserts that Jews themselves were unable to bear the yoke of the Law and should therefore not seek to impose it on Gentiles – an assertion that can hardly be maintained unless observing the Law is understood to include the practice of perfect love to one's neighbours. Barnabas and Paul support the argument by recounting the signs and portents that God had performed in the course of their mission to the Gentiles; these surely he would not have done had he disapproved of what was going on. Finally James points out that Peter's action had been in accordance with Scripture which manifests God's intention to find a people among the Gentiles. James' further, not too clear, point (15.21) may be intended to cut both ways: Moses is so widely read that his Law cannot be simply ignored; but he has enough people to preach him without our joining them.

This is very different from the Pauline argument, not least in the fact that Christ is nowhere mentioned (unless, obscurely, in the reference to the 'tent of David' in 15.16). For it is Christ who is the end of the Law (Rom. 10.4). The precise meaning of these words is disputed, but it is beyond dispute that the whole treatment of the subject turns on the figure of Christ. This is perhaps the clearest indication that Luke did not have a profound understanding of Christian – and especially of Pauline – theology. He was a loyal Christian believer but he did not see all the implications of his faith. Nor was he able to bring out of the various sources that he used a consistent view of the Law. Stephen is accused of speaking against the Law and of saying that Jesus would change the Mosaic customs (6.13, 14). In his speech Stephen speaks highly of the Law and alleges that his accusers break it. The Cornelius episode is full of difficulties. In Mk (though not in Lk.) Jesus declares all foods clean, but Peter has to be convinced by a vision that he must not count common what God makes clean. This vision itself seems to have to do with clean and unclean foods, but it is interpreted with regard to human beings and the legitimacy of dealings with Gentiles. Peter further recognizes that there is no respect of persons with God (10.34). The next verse is difficult to interpret precisely. On the surface it seems to mean that anyone who 'does the right thing' is accepted by God, and that this is as possible for Gentiles as for Jews. If however this is true there seems to be little need for the Gospel Peter is about to preach to Cornelius. If it means only that a good man like Cornelius has as much right as a Jew to have the Gospel preached to him it means that the ordinary man needs a moral conversion before he can have a Christian conversion; and indeed the conversion of Cornelius is not the change of life of one who has previously practised evil but the gift of the Spirit which issues in speaking with tongues (10.44–46). The conclusion reached after discussion (11.18), however, is that Gentiles as such may now be admitted to salvation, hitherto understood to be confined to Jews. From this conclusion not only those whose opinion is quoted in 15.1, 5 but the Council and the Decree appear to retreat. There are certain necessary conditions that Gentiles must fulfil. Later we learn that there is a report that Paul is teaching Diaspora Jews not to circumcise their children or to follow the (Jewish) customs – in a word, is teaching apostasy from Moses (21.21); Paul adopts James' suggestion as the means of clearing himself from this charge. Paul himself taught that circumcision must not be forced on Gentiles and that among Jews it was an adiaphoron: circumcision is nothing and uncircumcision is nothing (Gal. 6.15). According to Acts he observed Jewish feasts (20.16), though in Gal. 4.10 he speaks disparagingly of them. The Roman opinion is that the difference between Paul and other Jews is a matter of the interpretation of their Law (18.15), and though Luke, where the Romans trivialize the matter, sees its importance, he does not wholly disagree with Gallio. As with the OT as a whole, the Christians have understood the Law rightly, the Jews wrongly.

(j) *Gentiles and the Gentile Mission.* This matter has been almost sufficiently dealt with in the sections on the Law and the Jews; also in that on sources (pp. xxvi–xxxiv), for to a great extent Luke's sources may be regarded as those accounts of the origin and conduct of the mission to the Gentiles that he was able to collect. The chronological question of who first took the Gospel beyond Judaism to the Gentile world cannot be answered for Luke himself probably did not know. In his account of the Council (15.7) he allows priority to Peter, though he has described Philip's work before Peter's, probably because he had said (8.1) that when all other Christians were scattered from Jerusalem the apostles remained in the city. Mission was his theme, the mission to the Gentiles was the greatest of missions, and not its originator but its greatest leader was Paul. It is interesting that in Acts Paul does less than Peter and James to justify a mission to the Gentile world, invoking only (in ch. 15) the miracles that happened in the course of his missioning. He does not invoke the figure of Abraham as one who was justified by faith, without circumcision, and received a promise that included all the nations (Gen. 17.5; Gal. 4.17; Gen. 12.3; Gal. 3.9).

The earliest missions that included non-Jews were not (according to Acts) the result of planning by those who undertook them. Philip's mission to Samaria was the result of the persecution that scattered all the Christians (except the apostles) from Jerusalem. His encounter with the Ethiopian was the consequence of direct instructions given in the first instance (8.26) by an angel, subsequently (8.29) by the Spirit. Peter's visit to Cornelius was the result of co-ordinated directions given to the two men; it is made clear in his response to the vision (10.14) that Peter was not disposed to have dealings with Cornelius and that his resistance had to be broken down by divine pressure. When those who like Philip were driven from Jerusalem arrived in Antioch it is clear that their first intention was to preach only to Jews; at a second stage unnamed men from Cyprus and Cyrene included non-Jews in their scope. In view of this, and the resulting mixed church in Antioch, it may be (though it is not stated) that it was intended from the beginning that the mission to which Barnabas and Saul were committed (13.1–3) should include Gentiles. 13.5, however, refers only to preaching in the synagogues of Cyprus, and the meeting (13.6–12) with the proconsul Sergius Paulus seems to have been unpremeditated. It is a possible but quite uncertain conjecture that the success of this encounter (13.12) stimulated concern for the Gentiles. It is a further possible but quite uncertain guess that John Mark left his senior colleagues (13.13) because he disapproved of this unplanned step. From this point (according to Acts) Paul's own purpose was constant, and he usually adopted the method, on reaching any new town, of first visiting the synagogue, making use of hearers already collected to hear religious discourse, and leaving it when, as regularly happened, the Jews rejected his message, in order to concentrate on Gentiles. He never ceased to be concerned for his fellow Jews (e.g. 28.23; also Rom. 9.1–3; 10.1), but recognized in the Gentile mission a special vocation. This indeed is in Acts traced back to his conversion (9:15; 22.21; 26.17); rightly so, for this is confirmed in Gal. 1.16. The first journey (to use Luke's division of the material) includes a small circuit in Pamphylia and Pisidia; after this Paul moves more widely.

It is very probable that Jesus gave no explicit command to undertake a mission to the Gentiles. J. Jeremias[48] is probably right in the view that he foresaw after his death the eschatological pilgrimage of the nations to Jerusalem. Their joining with the Jews in one people of God would be one aspect of the end of history. After the resurrection the disciples found that there was to be an unexpected tract of history before the end. This extension of time made a mission to the Gentiles possible (see above, pp. lif.); but the mere extension of time was not sufficient to cause the Gentile mission. For causes we must look further. To some extent it may have been due to what might look like chance. A Gentile heard what the missionary was saying, accepted it, and manifested the spiritual and moral signs of a changed life. The preacher was faced with the question uttered by Peter at 10.47: How can I refuse to baptize one who shows the same marks of Christian existence as I do myself? He must be welcomed into the saved community. There were also hints in the story of Jesus. He undertook no mission outside Israel, but he did devote himself to and gave his life for those who though of Jewish race had wandered outside the religious framework of their people. If he could eat with tax collectors and sinners it is in fact surprising that Peter should hesitate to eat with Cornelius, and that, if Jesus declared all foods clean,[49] Peter should at first refuse to obey the order, 'Kill and eat' (10.14, 28; 11.3). No doubt sporadic conversions took place, but it was Pauline theological development that established work among the Gentiles, especially the recognition that the significant ancestor of Jesus was not David, the king of Israel, but Adam, the father of the race, and that God was not the God of the Jews only but of the Gentiles also (Rom. 3.29) – a God of half humanity would be only half a God.

[48] *Jesus' Promise to the Nations* (ET London, 1958), especially pp. 55–73.
[49] Mk 7.19 (not in Lk.).

This theological development is not found in Acts. Paul is called to go to the Gentiles, and he goes. There were other missions to the Gentiles. There were those of whom we learn most from the Pauline epistles but of whom we can see something in Acts: those who declared roundly that Gentiles might be accepted but only if they accepted circumcision and the Law (Acts 15.1, 5); perhaps there were also those whose existence is admitted though their authorization is denied at 15.24. Different groups insisted on various elements in Judaism; some upon all, the Galatian Judaizers on circumcision and the calendar, the Corinthian Judaizers on food laws, those who were responsible for the Decree on food laws, avoidance of idolatry, and chastity. The last may possibly be connected with the Seven of Acts 6.5. These or other Diaspora Jews may have been responsible for Stephen's speech (which opposes the Temple but accepts the Law) and the Areopagus speech attributed to Paul. Both of these speeches suggest an origin[50] in Hellenistic Judaism. It would be natural – and by no means improper – for a Hellenistic Jew who had become a Christian to edit and re-use a synagogue sermon in which he had combined Greek philosophy with OT religion, introducing a reference to Jesus at the end.

At this point should be mentioned also the so-called 'God-fearers'. For their existence, the nomenclature applied to them, and their possible role in Acts, see pp. 154f. Here it suffices to state without discussion that there were Gentiles who found Jewish ethics, theology and worship attractive, but not to the extent of becoming proselytes. Some of them probably had some contact with the local synagogue. Christian preachers offered to them, as they offered to all, a form of Judaism, stripped of its least attractive features, in particular of the rite of circumcision. If there were no evidence at all, it would seem probable that some of these should adopt the Christian way of admission to the people of God, and thus come to form the nucleus of a non-Jewish, uncircumcised element in the newly formed church.

(k) *Ethics.* Acts contains hardly any direct ethical instruction. The mission speeches include the call to repent, and this implies a change in moral behaviour; note especially 26.20, with the demand that hearers should show works, moral acts, that will demonstrate the sincerity of the repentance they profess. Even here however (cf. 2.38; 3.19; 17.30) there is no attempt to specify the works that might have

[50] See pp. 97, 265f.

this effect. The only example of specific ethical instruction is in 20.33–35, where Paul, addressing the Ephesian elders (it is of course Christians whom one would expect to receive ethical teaching), speaks of the example he has given and urges them not to depend on charity but to work as he has done so as to help the weak. He invokes a saying attributed (somewhat improbably – see the note) to Jesus: It is more blessed to give than to receive. Cf. 1.21, 22: the twelfth apostle who is to take the place of Judas Iscariot must have accompanied Jesus throughout his ministry; this implies familiarity with the teaching, including the ethical teaching, of Jesus.

It is consistent with this that the Acts narrative is written on a good ethical level. Clearly the healing of the sick is regarded as a proper activity in which Christians, if they have the appropriate gift, ought to engage (3.1–10; 4.9 – the healing is a good deed; 4.30; 5.12–16; 8.6–8; 9.33, 40f. – raising the dead is a particularly notable act; 14.10; 19.11f.; 20.10–12; 28.8, 9), though compassion for the sick is not the only motive – miracles have evidential value. Violent attacks on Christians are clearly not approved, but no special sympathy is shown for Sosthenes (18.17), and the story of the sons of Sceva (19.14–16) is told with a measure of *Schadenfreude*. Lying and deceit are wrong (5.1–11); so are disloyalty (15.38) and cruelty (in an OT story, e.g. 7.19). Herod Agrippa however is struck down not because he beheaded James and imprisoned Peter but for the theological offence of accepting glory due to God alone (12.23). Courage and determination, in facing death (e.g. 21.13) or in a storm at sea (ch. 27), are virtues. Fornication and the shedding of blood (if this is what is meant – see the note) are forbidden in the Decree (15.20, 29; 21.25). The practice of magic is condemned (8.9; 13.6; 19.13–19).

The teaching of the apostles (2.42), we may suppose, would include ethical teaching though, in a Jewish community, there would be little need for it: high ethical principles were already taught and on the whole practised. Paul's teaching to Felix (24.25) was perhaps not unnecessary. If the Western text is followed the Apostolic Decree included the negative form of the Golden Rule, which certainly was familiar in Judaism. The general requirement of kindness and care for those in need is expressed in a number of ways. For the selling of property and sharing of resources (2.44f.; 4.32, 34, 35, 36, 37; 5.1–11; cf. 6.1) see further below. The church of Antioch sent to the needs of their fellow Christians in Jerusalem (11.29, 30; 12.25). Paul, on his last visit to Jerusalem, had come with alms (24.17). Almsgiving was among the virtues of Cornelius (10.2, 4, 31) and Dorcas was full of good works and charities (9.36, 39). Hospitality is a notable good work (16.15, 34; 21.8, 16). Paul took thought for his fellow travellers who had spent too long without food (27.33–38). Stephen's prayer for the pardon of those who stoned him is modelled on that of Jesus (7.60).

It is interesting to observe that virtue and charity are not confined in Luke's narrative to Christians. Cornelius' practice of charity and righteousness has already been noticed (10.2, 4, 31, 35). Paul's friends among the Asiarchs are not said to be Christians but they took thought for him and tried to protect him (19.31). Julius the centurion took steps to save Paul (27.43 – as other Roman officials had done), and the barbarians of Malta 'showed us no common kindness' (28.2).

Paul twice claims to keep, or to have done his best to keep, a good conscience (23.1; 24.16). If Paul himself uttered these words he probably added – aloud or under his breath – the words he uses in 1 Cor. 4.4, it is not by that that I am justified. For Luke they mean quite simply that Paul regularly tries to do what he believes to be the right thing.

At 21.9 Philip is said to have four daughters who were virgins and prophesied. One can only wonder what, if anything, lies behind this. Did their virginity permit them to prophesy? Was it a qualification for mention in the book? Or was Luke simply stating a set of facts: there were four of them; they had remained unmarried; they uttered prophecies?

The special interest in poverty and wealth, in the danger of riches and the importance of the care of the poor, which are frequently noted as characteristic of the Third Gospel, are present but less emphasized in Acts. They most often take the form of the organizing of charity for those in need. Paul's collection (Rom. 15.25–28, and elsewhere), which may be alluded to at Acts 24.17, is not mentioned in Acts 15 (but cf. Gal. 2.10). It is possible that the Antiochene collection (see above) refers to the same gift. Most relevant here, but discussed on pp. 34f., 65–8, 69–72, 87, are the sale of properties mentioned in 2.44f.; 4.32–37; 5.1–11 and the ministration of charity of 6.1. We should note also the use of the word fellowship (sharing) and the statement that the Christians had all things in common (2.44; 4.32). The ministry of 6.1 is comparable with familiar Jewish charities; the common possession of all goods calls to mind Greek proverbs, which no doubt were sometimes expressed in concrete arrangements, but within Judaism it finds a parallel only in the practices of the Qumran sect; see pp. 34f. It is not surprising that arrangements of this kind, natural in minority groups, should be found both at Qumran and among the Christians; it does not prove any close relation between them.

VII. CONCLUSION

In the preface to his gospel (Lk. 1.1–4) Luke claims to have associated with persons who may or may not have been able to supply him with accurate historical information about the life and teaching of Jesus but must have been involved in some way in the life of the early church. They are described as eye-witnesses and ministers of the word. Such contacts formed the basis of his affirmation, which was evidently important to him, of the continuity between the pre-crucifixion Jesus and the post-resurrection church. They will have been sources for Acts as well as (in a different way) sources for the gospel. They must also have been sources for Luke's own theological and religious thinking. What is to be made of the author and his book? In the following pages, which will necessitate a small amount of repetition of matters already dealt with, this question will be considered.

It will not be wrong to begin with the observation that Luke was a man who liked telling stories and was good at telling them. He was less good at the connections between the episodes he narrated; perhaps he was less interested in them. He had before him a similarly episodic model, Mark. For this he had no little respect; otherwise he would not have used so much of it. But it was capable of improvement, and he set about improving it. He improved the Greek style, shortened passages that were unnecessarily long, and used his economics in space to add a good deal of fresh material. His revisions and additions had the effect of producing a story less starkly theological, more 'human' in interest and feeling. When he had absorbed Mark that work was finished with; it was superseded and could be dispensed with. Fortunately there were Christians who did not agree, and retained it.

One can hardly suppose that pleasure in telling stories would suffice to produce a written work of some size. Interest in story-telling leads to an interest in history; and there were additional reasons for such an interest. Christianity was a religion, an institution, a system of thought – none of these terms is satisfactory, but they may suffice – that could maintain its identity only by recalling its origin, for when it was truly itself it was determined by its origin. Luke wrote at a time when the old sense of an imminent consummation of history had waned. In the early days there had been no need to remember because the future was short and the end immediate. Memories however were now in danger of fading. Someone had to take steps to secure the church's memory not only of Jesus but of the way in which the transition from Jesus to the church had been effected. Mark, and any other gospel there may have been, had not recorded this; Paul, whose letters (which Luke seems not to have known) contained valuable pieces of history, had not recorded it. Luke may not have seen the need as clearly as it has been stated here, but he, and so far as we know no one else, did something to meet it. In addition to the danger of forgetting there was the danger that moral and doctrinal standards might slip. Most societies tend to think of their origins as heroic days, in which members of the society stood firm in faith and morals and stood by one another. A picture of the past, perhaps an idealized past, will inspire and instruct the present. Luke's picture of first generation Christians was intended to do this for his generation. He was, moreover, aware of the dangers that he puts on Paul's lips in 20.29, 30. What was future to Paul in Miletus was still in the main future to Luke, but it was a good deal nearer and no doubt had already appeared on the horizon. There were those who spoke perverse things and drew away disciples into their own schismatic coteries. Let the warning stand and an appropriate example be provided. Example, both in preaching and in morals, is there in Acts, but it has little positive content. There is little ethical teaching in Acts, though it is clear that the Christians are expected to be, and on the whole are, 'good' people. And Luke has no theological doctrines that he wishes to commend beyond basic Christian conviction. He believes in God, conceived on the lines of the OT, though he is aware of a convergence between the OT and the best Greek thought. Jesus Christ is central in his thought but there is no attempt to think through the problems of the incarnation. He is Son of God (9.20), as all Christians knew, but the term itself carries with it no implication of 'being of one substance with the Father'; he is Lord and Christ, but there is at least one hint that he became Lord and Christ only at his exaltation (2.36); his death was the result of sin and ignorance, speedily put right by God (3.13–18), but only at 20.28 is there a suggestion that it was by his death that he redeemed mankind. Luke undoubtedly believed in the Holy Spirit, and at 5.3f. there is a hint that he is divine, but it is the phenomenology rather than the personality of the Spirit that interests Luke. He accepted the OT as the word of God, and to this extent stood with the Jewish people, but he would have taken the

Christian line that the OT must be interpreted in terms of Christ, not Christ in terms of the OT.

Luke does not argue a special theological position but, it seems, takes the line of the majority of Christians in the 80s and 90s of the first century. This however is a proposition that will call for careful examination. It is by no means clear what group of Christians can be reckoned as constituting a majority in the 80s. In the view of J. Jervell Jewish Christians were numerically a minority but exercised an influence out of proportion to their numbers; it was for example their concern for the theological legitimacy of the Gentile mission that is reflected in Acts. This is in many respects an important observation, but it calls for some modification. That the earlier decades of the century were marked by conflict, often bitter and unrelenting, appears without question from the Pauline letters. The church had now emerged into a period of relative calm; this had happened earlier than Baur (see pp. xliiif.) thought, and not quite in the way that Goulder maintains. It was not Paul who won, though it may go too far to say that he lost. Paul and James, the extremists of right and left, were both defeated by the centre party, whom we may call if we wish the Hellenists. It is their compromise that appears in the Apostolic Decree.[51] This Decree is clearly accepted by Luke as the basis of the Gentile mission and the guideline on which the mission was to be conducted. It also provided its theology, which appears in a different form in the Areopagus speech (17.22–31) – the doctrine of God on which Jews and pagan theists could unite, with a reference to Jesus attached to it. This is the theology that prevailed in this period of the church's life, taking inevitably variant forms in different places. It originated with Hellenistic Jews and was accepted by very many Gentiles. The reference to Jesus is minimal in Acts 7.52 and 17.31, and Luke himself, as is clear from many passages, when writing on his own would greatly increase it; so did e.g. 1 and 2 Clement and Ignatius; hardly Hermas. The theological substructure lasted till it was attacked by Marcion, who failed in the end to establish his exaggerated reaction. Acts made a substantial contribution to his defeat, and when this was grasped the book emerged from the obscurity into which it had fallen, and served the purpose of showing

[51] See J. Jervell, *Luke and the People of God* (Minneapolis, 1972); *The Unknown Paul* (Minneapolis, 1984), M. D. Goulder, *A Tale of Two Missions* (London, 1994); C. K. Barrett, in *FS* Jervell, pp. 1–10.

that the Creator God and the Redeemer God were one and the same, and that Paul was in agreement with the Twelve. Irenaeus and Tertullian were not wrong in seeing that Luke made these points, though making them was not his main intention.

Historically, then, Luke is right when he celebrates a Hellenist victory; Hellenists (if we may use the word) were a centre party and their Decree guided the church through an obscure period and continued to direct it for much longer. Luke was wrong in representing Paul as one of the victorious Hellenists; he describes himself (2 Cor. 11.22; Phil. 3.5) as a Hebrew. This is the central (though by no means the only) point on which any judgement of Luke as a historian and a theologian must be based.

There are many features of Acts that must win a favourable verdict on the author as a historian. There are fairly frequent references to contemporary events and institutions and they are on the whole satisfactory. Many examples are given in the commentary; here it may be sufficient to mention the two kings, Agrippa I and Agrippa II (Luke describes the death of the former in substantial agreement with Josephus and knows that the latter's sister was Bernice); the two Roman governors, Felix and Festus (there is behind 24.27 a problem in the date of accession, but it is non-biblical evidence that lacks conclusiveness); the two proconsuls, Sergius Paulus and Gallio (the latter's governorship in Achaea can be dated with some precision and there is probable epigraphic evidence for the former); the Emperor Claudius (there is evidence for food shortages during his reign and Luke cannot be blamed for some uncertainty with regard to the date of his expulsion of the Jews from Rome). To persons may be added places and institutions associated with them: Luke knows Philippi was a *colonia* and the title by which its magistrates were known; he knows of the Areopagus court in Athens and of the world-famous goddess of Ephesus, Artemis; of the connection of Ephesus with magic, of its Asiarchs, and of its town clerk; he knows that one might find a centurion of the *Cohors Italica* in Caesarea; that Appii Forum and Tres Tabernae, not in themselves important towns, were stages on the road to Rome; that to lay hands on a Roman citizen was a dangerous thing to do, but that to resist or oppose decrees of Caesar was equally dangerous, though a citizen might escape at least immediate punishment by an appeal to Caesar. Luke is less successful in his references to Jews and to Jewish affairs. His reference to Annas may perhaps with some difficulty be defended; Gamaliel is rightly named but Luke puts on his lips a historical howler in the mention of Judas and Theudas; it is difficult to accommodate the details of the events that led to the riot in the Temple with the regulations for vows, though Luke is right in representing the introduction of Gentiles into forbidden areas of the Temple as a very serious and provocative offence.

Luke, then, was in general well informed about persons, events, and institutions in the Graeco-Roman world of the first century, probably better informed than most of his contemporaries, than most of his readers. And he was no fool. Where he agrees with other historical sources, his evidence is confirmed; where he disagrees, or where other evidence is lacking, he must at least be taken seriously. These matters however are incidental to his purpose, for he was not writing political, social, economic, military, or institutional history, but Christian history, and it is in this field that he must be judged.

Little can be said about the first twelve chapters of Acts except that in outline they must represent, with many omissions, the sort of thing that must have happened in the early years of Christianity. This is not the place to discuss the historicity of the resurrection; 1 Cor. 15.4–8 is sufficient to prove that the earliest (pre-Pauline) Christians believed that the crucified Jesus had appeared alive to a number of their leaders. This belief is represented in Acts. The rest of the first five chapters is made up of some traditional narratives and of Lucan constructions which are not without historical foundation. Twelve was a significant number for the inner group of disciples; the Christians did believe themselves to be inspired by the Spirit of God; they must have made speeches to communicate their beliefs; there was a traditional group of miracle stories; there was trouble between the Christians and the Jewish authorities. With ch. 6 a new stage of historiography begins. The sources used are discussed at pp. xxviii–xxxi. Into Antiochene traditions Luke incorporates more Petrine stories, Jerusalem traditions, stories going back to Philip, and the tradition about Paul's earliest contacts with Christianity. This is serious historical material; what it lacks is continuity and chronological coherence. Luke has set down different accounts of how the mission to the Gentiles began. Only one of these, it seems, has a future. This is given at first in the Antioch-based narrative of chs. 13 and 14. It continues in the Pauline missions, of which traditions, some drawn from members of the Pauline circle, some collected locally in Pauline cities, are set out first in a sequence of missionary journeys.

These journeys of Paul as a missionary free to travel wherever he was led by the Spirit end in Jerusalem; from ch. 22 onwards Paul is not a free man, and the story of his encounters with Jewish and Roman authorities is very difficult to evaluate historically. Paul was not held incommunicado. Information about the various legal – and illegal – proceedings could have been got out; but in the narrative itself there is no indication that this happened, no mention of a friend who kept in touch with him except at 24.23. Luke makes nothing of this, and in any case it does not cover the events of chs. 25 and 26. From 27.2 Paul is again accompanied by one or more companions and it is possible to guess with some plausibility at passages inserted in traditions derived from them.

So far nothing has been said about ch. 15, and it is here that questionings arise that cannot but affect our judgement of the rest of Acts. The composition of the chapter is discussed in some detail below (pp. 221f., 226–8). It is Luke's work, though it is not without historical foundation. It contains however difficulties in itself, and more appear when it is compared with the direct Pauline evidence, especially that of Galatians. Did Paul help to produce, assent to, and disseminate a Decree to which, even when he deals with its subject-matter, he makes no reference? A Decree which tells his Gentile Christians of Jewish conditions (not indeed including circumcision) which they must fulfil if they are to be members of the people of God? The only possible answer is No.

At this point the question about Luke the historian runs into the question about Luke the theologian. For that Luke deliberately intended to calumniate Paul, ascribing to him views Luke knew that he did not hold, is inconceivable; he admired him far too greatly for this. The only alternative is that he did not truly understand him. That 'a man is justified by faith and not by works of the Law' (Rom. 3.28) is a proposition not covered by the one reference to justification in Acts (13.38, 39). The explanation of the misunderstanding is latent in the sketch of the last few pages. As Luke himself shows, the mission to the Gentile world did not have a single official beginning. It started independently in different places, through different persons, and on different lines. Among those who began it, in their own way, were Hellenistic Jews who had become Christians. They were the founders of the mixed church in Antioch; their way of theological thinking and of preaching is seen in Acts 7 and 17. Their mission continued and prospered; it became the main official line. But the line of development that Luke knew, admired, and described was Paul's; and he confused the two. Paul was connected with Stephen and Antioch (7.58; 8.1; 11.25f.; 12.25; 13.1–3; 14.26–28; 15.2; 22.20); he must have been Stephen's successor and continuator – this was the volte-face of his conversion. He began as an Antioch envoy; he must have continued to be one. So the Hellenistic Jewish compromise Decree was Paul's decree; and Paul not only lost the battle for a radically law-free Gospel, he lost his integrity at the same time: a strange fate for Luke's hero to suffer at Luke's hands.

It was the only point of serious difference between them. Elsewhere it is enough to say that Luke lacks Paul's profundity. Luke believes in Christ, crucified and risen; but does not think about pre-existence or, in any profound sense, deity, and on the whole (except at 20.28) thinks of the cross as an unfortunate error put right by resurrection, which happily sets the cross aside. He believes in the Spirit, who causes ecstatic speech, rather than love, joy, and peace. He believes in the church, but scarcely sees it as the body of Christ. He knows baptism and a Christian meal, but they are not focused on crucifixion, on dying with Christ and proclaiming the Lord's death till he come. All this does not mean that Luke disagreed with Paul; only that he was not so good at theology. And this takes us back to history; how close to Paul and his ministry did Luke stand?

Theology however must have another word. Is Luke's theology true? Or have we disfranchised a book from the NT?

It must not be assumed that omission, especially in Christological matters, implies contradiction; and Luke either tolerates, or perhaps fails to observe, a measure of contradiction. A superficial reader of Acts 2.36 will infer that Luke supposed that Jesus became Messiah and Lord at his resurrection. Luke's source may have meant this, and Luke may have accepted it as he transcribed the source. But Lk. 2.11 states with equal clarity that Jesus was born as Messiah and Lord. The reformulation in Acts reflects the impression made by the resurrection on those who experienced it.[52] No Christology is complete without the notion of pre-existence, but Christology has often lacked it. Luke's Christology lacks it, but this does not mean that Luke would have denied it, or needed to deny it. The same observation can be made with reference to the doctrine of atonement through the death of Christ. That Luke does not assert it (except at 20.28) does not

[52] See *Romans* 20–22, on Rom. 1.3, 4.

mean that he would have denied it, still less that his readers need deny it.

Comparison of Acts 17.22–31 with Rom. 1.18–25 raises sharply the question of the place in Paul's thought, and thus in Christian thought generally, of natural theology.[53] The speech must be read in the context that Luke has provided for it and as determined less by Stoic speculation than by the OT prophetic denunciation of idolatry. This denunciation Paul shared (so one learns – credibly – from Luke's own story); he was provoked (17.16) by the sight of a city overgrown with idols. What the Athenians had made of nature was not natural theology (in a proper sense) but natural idolatry. This is not inconsistent with Romans 1, but it lacks the distinctive Pauline analysis and we cannot think that the speech was delivered by Paul; it comes rather from Hellenistic Judaism, adapted for Christian purposes (see pp. 265f.).

It is in regard to the Law that the greatest problem arises. Luke never says anything more positive about the Law than Paul's 'holy, righteous, good, spiritual' (Rom. 7.12, 14); only once does he condemn it as a burden that neither we nor our ancestors have been able to bear (Acts 15.10), and he never describes it as the origin of sinful passions (Rom. 7.5). The Pauline dialectic is missing, and so is the radical rejection of the Law (legalistically conceived) as an agent of salvation. If Gentiles are to be saved they must accept certain legal conditions – a sharply reduced list of conditions but conditions nonetheless. It is not surprising that Paul was obliged to reject the Decree of Acts 15.29, or at least to ignore it. Nor is it surprising that, as the textual phenomena show,[54] the Decree was given different interpretations; it may sometimes have amounted to little more than a request for consideration and courtesy on the part of Gentile Christians taking meals with Jewish Christians.

It is at this point, as have seen, that Luke's lack of penetrating and radical thinking reacts upon the historical worth of his book. Those whose thought was like his own he can represent successfully even when he lacks precise contemporary sources. The preaching of Peter in the early chapters has, as has often been remarked, a primitive appearance, but it is the kind of primitiveness that belongs to the 80s

[53] See my lecture 'Paul as Missionary and Theologian' in *Jesus and the Word* (Allison Park, 1995), pp. 149–62.

[54] See on 15.20, 29 (pp. 233f., 237).

as well as the 30s, and indeed to countless excellent but unreflecting Christians in every age. It manifests an absolute loyalty to Jesus Christ as a person but little attempt to evaluate him as very man and very God – or even in less orthodox but equally reflective terms. With Paul a new dimension entered Christian life; and it is probably no more than truth to say that Luke (like many others) was unable to see the difference between an approach to the Gentiles that rested upon the discovery that Gentiles might be as good as Jews, and an approach that sprang from the shattering discovery that Jews were sinners just as much as Gentiles, though perhaps in a different way. It is certain that the author of Acts regarded Paul as the outstanding missionary to Jews and Gentiles, and that to find fault with him was no part of his plan. To identify him with the kind of Hellenistic–Jewish–Christian message accepted in his own day was for Luke a natural error; but it was an error, which needs correction from Paul's own letters and must not be allowed to determine our picture of the first Christian century. Both parts of the quotation from F. C. Baur given on p. xliv are true. Acts is a most valuable historical source for the history of early Christianity; but it attains its full value only when used with the strictest – historical and theological – criticism.

ACTS: ANALYSIS

Acts falls into two approximately equal parts, neatly divided by the account in ch. 15 of the Apostolic Council. It is impossible to draw up a clear, formal analysis of chs. 1–14. It does not appear to have been Luke's intention to write a logically developing narrative of the earliest years of the church and its mission. What was important to him was, first, to show that the Christian mission was the true and necessary outcome of the life and work of Jesus: he must therefore begin in Jerusalem, the scene of the crucifixion and resurrection. His second important concern was to show how this originally Jewish movement spread with equal or even greater effect into the Gentile world. Of this he could give no connected, chronologically disposed account; he used what sources he could find, and set them out as is shown below and discussed above (pp. xxxf.).

In the second part of his book he manifests the same interest. He recounts the way in which the Gospel spread further into the Graeco-Roman world, eventually reaching Rome in a representative fulfilment of the charge given by Jesus himself (1.8). In this part of the book, however, the spread of the Gospel is bound up with the life and work of one man, Paul, who is indeed accompanied and assisted by others but occupies the centre of the stage. It is no more than a biographical sketch, with many gaps, but in addition to its account of Paul's work as a preacher and pastor it also indicates the relation in which he stood to both Jewish and Roman authorities, and binds the two parts of the book together, since the beginning of his Christian life is shown in ch. 9 and his first steps as an evangelist appear in chs. 11, 13 and 14.

I. **NECESSARY PRELIMINARY STEPS:** THE RESURRECTION RE-AFFIRMED AND THE APOSTOLIC GROUP BROUGHT UP TO STRENGTH.

1. Introduction and Recapitulation (1.1–14)
2. Judas and Matthias (1.15–26)

II. **THE CHURCH IN JERUSALEM** ESTABLISHED BY THE GIFT OF THE SPIRIT, BY PREACHING, BY MIRACLE, IN FELLOWSHIP, IN MUTUAL LOVE AND CARE; ITS RELATION WITH JEWISH AUTHORITY.

3. The Pentecost Event (2.1–13)
4. Peter's Pentecost Sermon (2.14–40)
5. The Pentecost Community (2.41–47)
6. Temple Miracle (3.1–10)
7. Peter's Miracle Speech (3.11–26)
8. Arrest and Examination of Peter and John (4.1–22)
9. Return of Peter and John (4.23–31)
10. Sharing and Witnessing Community (4.32–35)
11. An Example: Barnabas (4.36, 37)
12. A Negative Example: Ananias and Sapphira (5.1–11)
13. Miracle-working or Supernatural Community (5.12–16)
14. Arrest and Examination of Apostles (5.17–40)
15. Rejoicing and Witnessing Community: 'Final' Summary (5.41, 42)

III. **PROBLEMS AND PERSECUTION LEAD TO THE BEGINNING OF EXPANSION:** HEBREWS, HELLENISTS, AND WIDOWS; APPOINTMENT OF THE SEVEN; STEPHEN, CONTROVERSIALIST, PREACHER, AND MARTYR.

16. Appointment of the Seven and Further Prosperity (6.1–7)
17. Attack on Stephen (6.8–15)
18. Stephen's Speech (7.1–53)
19. Stephen's Martyrdom (7.54–8.1a)
20. Persecution (8.1b–3)

IV. **THE GOSPEL REACHES SAMARIA:** PHILIP IN SAMARIA AND BEYOND.

21. Evangelization of Samaria; Simon Magus (8.4–25)
22. Philip and the Ethiopian (8.26–40)

XI. **PAUL'S MISSION BREAKS NEW GROUND:** AFTER COVERING SOME OF THE GROUND OF THE FIRST MISSION PAUL, AND HIS COMPANIONS CROSS OVER INTO MACEDONIA, REACH ATHENS, WHERE THE THEOLOGICAL APPROACH TO GENTILES IS SET OUT, AND MOVE ON TO CORINTH.

41. Territory of the First Journey Revisited (15.36 – 16.5)
42. Guided by the Spirit to Troas (16.6–10)
43. Paul and Silas at Philippi (16.11–40)
44. From Philippi to Athens (17.1–15)
45. Paul at Athens (17.16–34)
46. Paul at Corinth, with Return to Palestine (18.1–23)

XII. **THE MISSION BASED ON EPHESUS:** THE POSITION OF DISCIPLES OF JOHN THE BAPTIST IS REGULARIZED, PAUL EVANGELIZES EPHESUS AND ITS REGION, IS OVERTAKEN BY A RIOT, RETURNS TO OTHER PARTS OF GREECE, AND GIVES A PASTORAL ADDRESS AT MILETUS.

47. Apollos and the Twelve Disciples (18.24 – 19.7)
48. Paul's Successful Ministry at Ephesus (19.8–20)
49. Riot at Ephesus (19.21–40)
50. Back to Palestine, through Macedonia, Greece, and Troas (20.1–16)
51. Paul's Speech at Miletus (20.17–38)

XIII. **PAUL RETURNS TO JERUSALEM:** PAUL MEETS JAMES, AND A PLAN FOR HARMONY BETWEEN JEWISH AND GENTILE CHRISTIANS MISFIRES.

52. Journey to Jerusalem (21.1–14)
53. Paul and the Church of Jerusalem (21.15–26)
54. Riot at Jerusalem (21.27–40)
55. Paul's Temple Speech and the Sequel (22.1–29)

XIV. **PAUL AND THE JEWS:** PAUL APPEARS BEFORE THE COUNCIL AND IS SAFELY MOVED TO CAESAREA.

56. Paul Before the Council (22.30 – 23.11)
57. The Plot: Paul Removed to Caesarea (23.12–35)

XV. **PAUL AND THE ROMANS:** NEITHER FELIX NOR FESTUS NOR AGRIPPA CAN FIND ANY FAULT IN PAUL AND HE APPEALS TO CAESAR.

58. Paul and Felix (24.1–27)
59. Paul Appeals to Caesar (25.1–12)
60. Festus and Agrippa (25.13–22)
61. Festus, Agrippa, and Paul (25.23 – 26.32)

XVI. **PAUL REACHES ROME** AFTER A LONG AND DANGEROUS VOYAGE AND HAS MEETINGS WITH THE LOCAL JEWS.

62. The Sea Voyage (27.1–44)
63. From Malta to Rome (28.1–16)
64. Paul and the Jews in Rome (28.17–28)

XVII. **CONCLUSION:** PAUL SPENDS TWO YEARS IN ROME.

65. Conclusion (28.(29)–31)

I

NECESSARY PRELIMINARY STEPS (1.1–26)

1. INTRODUCTION AND RECAPITULATION 1.1–14

**[1] I wrote my first book, Theophilus, about all the things that Jesus
began to do and to teach [2] up to the day when, having through
the Holy Spirit given a charge to the apostles whom he had
chosen, he was received up. [3] To them, after he had suffered, he
also showed himself alive by many certain proofs, appearing to
them from time to time during forty days and speaking of the
things concerning the kingdom of God. [4] And as he was eating
with them he commanded them not to leave Jerusalem but to
await that which the Father promised – 'that which,' he said,
'you heard from me. [5] For John baptized with water, but you
shall be baptized with Holy Spirit, not many days from now.'
[6] They then, when they had assembled, asked him, saying, 'Lord,
is it at this time that thou art restoring the kingdom to Israel?'
[7] He said to them, 'It is not yours to know times and seasons which
the Father has placed within his own authority; [8] but you shall
receive power when the Holy Spirit has come upon you, and you
shall be my witnesses in Jerusalem and in all Judaea and Samaria
and up to the end of the earth.'**

**[9] When he had said these things, while they were looking, he
was lifted up, and a cloud took him up from their sight. [10] While
they were gazing into heaven, as he was going, there came two
men in white clothes, who stood beside them. [11] They said, 'Men
of Galilee, why do you stand looking into heaven? This Jesus who
has been received up from you into heaven will come in the same
way that you have seen him going into heaven.'**

12 Then they returned to Jerusalem from the mountain called
Olive Grove, which is near Jerusalem – a Sabbath day's journey
off. 13 When they entered the city, they went up to the upstairs
room where they were staying, Peter, John, James, and Andrew,
Philip and Thomas, Bartholomew and Matthew, James (son of
Alphaeus) and Simon the Zealot, and Judas (son of James). 14 All
these, in union with one another, were continuing in prayer, with
their wives, and Mary the mother of Jesus, and his brothers.

Acts begins with an Introduction. Some see this as extending to v. 5, others to v. 8, but it is better to include the whole of vv. 1–14. Apart from the Ascension this paragraph contains no specific events but general statements which forecast without anticipating the main features of the book: the directing presence of the risen Jesus, the theme of the Kingdom of God, the activity of the Holy Spirit, and the work of the disciples as witnesses. The Ascension is the first independent narrative in the book, but it has a parallel in the former of Luke's two volumes (Lk. 24.51). Indeed the whole paragraph (vv. 1–14) is paralleled more or less closely in the Gospel and is best regarded as a résumé of what the reader may be supposed to have already read. In contrast with this the next paragraph (though it too constitutes part of the preparation for what follows) breaks fresh ground.

Not only does the substance of vv. 1–14 reproduce material in the Gospel, but to some extent the language is the same, or similar. It follows with great probability that Luke himself wrote the paragraph and (with a possible exception to be noted below) did not use special source material. He was after all writing only what must have been common knowledge and belief among Christians. Resurrection appearances, teaching about the Kingdom of God, the promise of the Spirit, and the call to bear witness would be familiar not only from the Third Gospel but from other sources too. The exception is the account of the Ascension, but here Luke seems to be writing up in his own way a conviction that was gradually acquiring narrative expression in the later NT period.

The Introduction is a carefully constructed piece which achieves the following aims. (a) It refers the reader to the following volume and indicates its continuity with the Gospel; the Jesus of the Gospel is now alive after crucifixion. (b) It draws attention to the work of the Holy Spirit as characteristic of the new volume, a feature which also, through the connection with John the Baptist, strengthens the link with Lk. (c) It underlines the function of the apostles as witnesses. (d) It points out that the church and its witnessing activity are to extend throughout the world. (e) It emphasizes that details of the eschatological future, though determined by God, are not made known even to the apostles. (f) It lays down the eschatological framework within which the Christian story is to unfold: Jesus has been exalted to heaven; he will return as he went, on a cloud. It is between these points that the church lives, and its life is determined by them. (g) The church is a fellowship at whose heart are the named eleven apostles, chosen by Jesus himself; into this new family the earthly, physical family of Jesus is integrated.

To these points should be added the Christological significance of the Ascension. Luke does little to bring this out (cf. 2.34f.; Ps. 110.1), but it is clear that for him Jesus reigns at the right hand of God. He does not come to terms with the question what happened to the physical body of Jesus. Salvation was initiated by him in his ministry and will be consummated by him at the End. In the meantime he will occasionally appear on earth, but will for the most part operate through the Spirit.

1. The introduction follows a pattern common in ancient literature in that it contains a dedication and a reference to an earlier work. Cf. Lk. 1.1–4.

Theophilus is doubtless the same person as the one addressed more formally as *Most excellent Theophilus* in Lk. 1.3 – that is, if the intention is to refer to a real person. This would certainly appear to be the intention if the name were not capable of theological interpretation. It means either *Loving God* or, more probably, *Dear to God*, and could well have been used to suggest an ideal or representative Christian (or Christian inquirer). The formality of Lk. 1.3 on the whole favours a real person.

My first book. The common use of *first* in English (as in Greek) is not such as to warrant belief that Luke must have written, or have intended to write, more than two books. *Book* may refer to any kind of treatise, or to a section of such a work; here undoubtedly the reference is to Lk., whose content may be summed up as **all the things that Jesus began both to do and to teach**. *Began* is probably not to be regarded as an Aramaism or a Latinism; it hints that the work of Jesus was continued through the Holy Spirit and his apostolic witnesses in the book that follows. The combination of action and teaching is characteristic of both Lk. and Acts.

Dedication to a person and a summarizing reference to an earlier work have many parallels.

2. The text of this verse is in some confusion. The Old Uncial and Western texts diverge, and it is not easy to reconstruct the original form of the Western text – if indeed there was a single original form of the Western text (see Introduction, p. xx). This may have been

> In the day in which he chose the apostles through the Holy Spirit and commanded them to preach the Gospel.

The reference in the Old Uncial text (**he was received up**) to the Ascension (see below, pp. 6f.) corresponds to the run of the narrative and the importance of the event; this favours the Old Uncial text and may be tentatively accepted, though with the observation that the words may have been added by an editor to a text that did not contain them.

3. This verse continues the recapitulation of the first book. **Showed** combines the senses of *manifested* and *proved.* **Suffered** includes the suffering of death – hence **alive. Certain proofs.** Luke's word is defined by Aristotle as *compulsive* proof, leading to a necessary conclusion.

Appearing to them from time to time during forty days. No other part of the NT specifies the period during which resurrection appearances took place. Barnabas 15.9 suggests an Ascension on Easter Day; various gnostics suggested 18 months, 545 days, 550 days. These longer periods make possible teaching by the risen Jesus of special (gnostic) doctrines different from those contained in the gospels. Luke's **speaking of the things concerning the kingdom of God** means that Jesus' teaching after the resurrection was the same as it had been before it. *Kingdom of God* is several times used in Acts (8.12; 19.8; 20.25; 28.23, 31) as a summary of the Christian message. *Kingdom* was a term open to misinterpretation (17.7); v. 6 shows that before the Ascension and the gift of the Spirit even the disciples did not understand it.

4. Eating with them. Luke's word is difficult and may mean *lodging with them.* But *eating* is probable, and recalls the Lucan resurrection stories: Lk. 24.30, 31, 35, 41–3. These passages are given (a) as proof of the bodily reality of the risen Jesus, and (b) as indicating a common meal as the context of his self-disclosure. There is no stress here on (a), there are later references (2.42, 46; 20.7; 27.35) to the breaking of bread which may suggest a special context of fellowship with Christ. Luke's word may contain a special reference to *salt* and there are passages that suggest a special use of salt in the church's holy meal. It is however doubtful whether these are relevant.

The Eleven are **not to leave Jerusalem but to await that which the Father promised**. In the Lucan writings there is a special stress on Jerusalem as the holy place, the scene of crucifixion, resurrection (and appearances), ascension, and the gift of the Holy Spirit; possibly also of the parousia (see v. 11). There may be a connection between this saying and the reluctance of some to leave Jerusalem for a mission to the Gentiles. *That which the Father promised* is the gift of the Spirit; cf. 2.4.

5. It is assumed that the reader of Acts has read Lk. and therefore does not need to be informed about John. The verb **baptized** shows immediately which John is meant. According to Lk. 3.16 John made the promise, I am baptizing you with water, but there is coming he who is mightier than I . . . he will baptize you with Holy Spirit and fire. The original meaning of the last four words is open to dispute but Luke when writing his gospel may already have seen in them a reference to the Pentecostal event as he described it. 1.8 and 2.4 throw immediate light upon the effect of the gift of the Spirit, but Luke's book has been described as the 'Acts of the Holy Spirit', and the whole book must be read in order to obtain an adequate view of the Spirit's work. See Introduction, pp. lii–liv. It is not possible to harmonize the Lucan and Johannine (Jn 20.22) accounts of the gift of the Spirit.

6. They then. It is probable, not quite certain, that Luke refers to the same group who have been previously mentioned.

Lord. The word may mean no more than a respectful 'Sir'. But the person addressed is assumed to have power to put into effect the intention of God for his people. He is the Messiah. See further on 2.36 and Introduction, pp. liv–lvii.

Is it at this time that thou art restoring . . . ? A futuristic present. Are you about to do this now? The question has been held to prove the existence of a Zealot element among the disciples of Jesus, but in fact Luke uses the question to underline the non-nationalist character of the Christian movement. The question arises naturally in a Jewish context; restoration of sovereignty to Israel is regularly prayed for in the Eighteen Benedictions and in the Qaddish. Jesus refuses to provide a timetable for the fulfilment of God's eschatological purpose; the rest of the book will show that it is (according to Luke) in the life of Christians that God's sovereignty is expressed.

7. It is not yours to know times and seasons. Cf. Mk 13.32. It is not denied that there will be a restoration, but it is not even for apostles to know when this will happen. Such matters **the Father has placed within his own authority**; that is, *he has reserved them for his own decision*, rather than *appointed them by his own authority*. It is possible that this withholding of information reflects a time of disappointment over the delay of the parousia; certainly Luke has himself come to terms with the fact that there was to be a perceptible interval between the resurrection and the end. But here the primary intention seems to be to lay stress on the gift of the Spirit and the role of the apostles as witnesses, both mentioned in the next verse.

8. The verse looks forward to ch. 2 and receives a measure of interpretation from that chapter, in which the apostles, represented by Peter, act as witnesses, having received power through the gift of **the Spirit**. It raises the question, fundamental for the understanding of Acts, of the relation between the gift of the Spirit and the End. The Spirit is not so much a substitute for the End as an anticipation of the End in the present. What is promised to the apostles is the **power** to fulfil their own mission, that is, to bear oral testimony, to perform miracles, and in general act with authority. This power is given through the Spirit, and conversely the Spirit in Acts may be defined as the divine agency that gives this power. The Spirit is not defined here as the third of a Trinity of divine Persons, though it is co-ordinated with the Father and the Son (see especially 2.33; 5.3, 4; 10.38).

What follows sums up the contents of Luke's second volume. The apostles are to be **witnesses**, primarily to the resurrection (1.22), but this includes witness to all the other propositions of the Christian proclamation; cf. 26.22 (the suffering and resurrection of Christ); 10.39 (the whole story of Jesus); 13.31; 26.16. Cf. Isa. 43.10. The work is to begin **in Jerusalem**; see chs. 2–7; it will continue **in all Judaea and Samaria**; see 8, 9; and it will go on **to the end of the earth**. This is a stock phrase, and means that the mission will be universal, but Luke may well have had Rome (19.21; 23.11; 28) in mind as an inclusive figure: if the Gospel can be preached and the church established in Rome there is no limit to their possible extension.

Luke does not mention Galilee, not, it seems, because he regards it as already Christian territory but because he lacks material.

9. While they were looking. These words show that, in Luke's view, the Ascension was a historical event like any other that men might watch. The witnesses attest it. Jesus' work on earth is now complete. The event however is described in terms that recall stories of magic. **He was lifted up** (the word is normally used in a literal, physical sense); **a cloud took him up** (the verb means to take up by getting underneath). Borne up by the cloud Jesus disappeared; the group of disciples saw him no more. This was the last of the resurrection appearances; Luke is aware of the fact and of its meaning. Paul did not see Jesus in the same way as the other witnesses.

For the theology of the Ascension see above (pp. 2f.) and Introduction, p. lii.

10. Gazing is stronger than *looking* (v. 9); they were straining their eyes to see their departing Lord.

Two men, two angels; cf. Lk. 24.4. The whole event was supernatural, and, as the exalted Lord, Jesus must be attended by supernatural figures. Their **white clothes** help to identify the *men* as angels; cf. 2 Macc. 11.8; Mk 9.3; 16.5; Jn 20.12; Hermas, *Vision* 2.1; 3.5; *Similitude* 8.2.3.

11. Galilee. Not mentioned in v. 8. **Why do you stand?** This is not an Aramaism; Luke is a descriptive writer, and he visualizes the apostles as they *stand* gazing into heaven. But this is no time for a nostalgic gazing after the departing figure of Jesus; the interval between Ascension and parousia will not be short, and the church must set to work.

Who has been received up corresponds to *took him up* in v. 9. Cf. 4 Kdms 2.11 (Elijah); 1 QH 3.20 (Thou hast taken me up to an eternal height). Luke's account is in no way parallel to the rabbinic story of the four who entered into Paradise (B. Hagigah 14b), but there may be some relevance in the figure of Metatron, who is in heaven with God, to the belief that the ascended Christ is at the right hand of God (see on 2.33).

Will come in the same way, that is, with the clouds (Dan. 7.13). Luke has in mind the familiar picture of the Son of man (though it is only at 7.56 that the term is used in Acts; cf. Lk. 17.24; 21.27). He predicts the coming of Jesus as Son of man as an event that will in due course bring church history (which is just beginning) – and world history – to a close. He does not say when this may be expected to happen.

12. From the mountain called Olive Grove. For the Mount of Olives see Dalman, *SSW* 261–8; Murphy-O'Connor, *Holy Land*

84–6. The location of the Mount of Olives is given in 'sacred measure'. Taking a Sabbath day's journey to be 2,000 cubits and a cubit 56 cm the distance given is 1,120 m. This according to Dalman is the distance from the city to the summit of the mountain. It follows from this that Luke (or his source) was not following the stricter Qumran rule which set the limit at 1,000 cubits. It is possible that the distance was recorded in this way because at some point the Ascension was believed to have happened on a Sabbath. Luke himself cannot have believed this if he took seriously the forty days of v. 3.

13. This verse and the next end Luke's Introduction and prepare for the first of the events which constitute his work. They are a summary statement which, like his other summaries, could have been, and probably was, generalized out of details supplied by narrative tradition.

The disciples, having returned to Jerusalem, **went up to the upstairs room where they were staying**. It is possible that Luke thinks of the upper room where the Last Supper was eaten (Lk. 22.12; cf. Mk 14.15) but the Greek word used is different. There is no means of locating the room, no great probability in the view that it was in the Temple.

It can hardly be intended that all the persons mentioned were *residing* in one room, only that they habitually met there. The list of names (apart from the dropping of Judas Iscariot) corresponds with that in Lk. 6.14–16. There are a few changes in order. **Simon the Zealot** was in Lk. Simon called the Zealot, which may suggest that he was not really a Zealot. This may be insignificant. The word was not uncommon, and could be used in a good sense (cf. 1 Cor. 14.1; Titus 2.14; 1 Peter 3.13). On the Zealot party see *NS* 2.598–606.

14. In union with one another. Luke's word usually refers to unity of spirit, but in its frequent use in Acts often implies being physically together.

Prayer. Cf. 2.42. The word may mean *place of prayer* (cf. 16.13), but this meaning does not seem to be included here.

With their wives. This is the most natural way of taking Luke's Greek. It is sometimes argued that this cannot be the meaning because the persons concerned were witnesses, so that the women must be those of Lk. 24.1. Luke's Greek word means sometimes *wife* sometimes *woman*. At least one Western editor seems to have taken the text to refer to the families of the apostles, adding the words *and children*.

Mary the mother of Jesus is referred to here only in Acts; see Lk. 1; 2 *passim*. Luke evidently has, or intends to give, no further information about Mary's life after the resurrection. He indicates here that the earthly family of Jesus was taken up into his spiritual family. This is the point of the reference to Mary and of that to **his brothers**. These are never again mentioned in Acts; even James (12.17; 15.13, 21, 28) is not described as the Lord's brother, though he is so described in Galatians (1.19; cf. 2.9, 12). The present passage can neither prove nor disprove any of the theories of the relationship of the *brothers* to Jesus, though it is fair to add that the most natural meaning of Luke's word is *blood-brother*, that *foster-brother* is not impossible, and that *cousin* is very improbable.

2. JUDAS AND MATTHIAS 1.15–26

**15 In these days Peter stood up in the midst of the brothers and
said (the number of persons amounted in all to about 120),
16 'Brothers, the Scripture had to be fulfilled which the Holy
Spirit spoke in advance through the mouth of David, concerning
Judas, who acted as guide to those who arrested Jesus; 17 for
he had been counted among us and obtained the lot of this
ministry. 18 With the reward of his unrighteous act he purchased
a property. He fell flat on his face, burst in the middle, and all his
intestines poured out. 19 This became known to all the residents
of Jerusalem, so that the property was called in their language
Aceldama, that is, Blood Field. 20 For it is written in the Book of
Psalms, Let his steading be desolate and let there be none who
lives in it; and, Let someone else take his office. 21 So then of those
men who accompanied us in all the time the Lord Jesus went in
and out among us, 22 beginning from the baptism of John until
the day he was received up from us, one must become with us a
witness to his resurrection.'**

**23 They nominated two, Joseph called Barsabbas, who was
surnamed Justus, and Matthias. 24 They prayed and said, 'Thou,
Lord, who knowest the hearts of all men, show which of these
two thou hast chosen 25 to receive the position of ministry and
apostleship from which Judas fell away to go to his own place.'
26 They cast lots for them, and the lot fell on Matthias, and he was
voted in along with the eleven apostles.**

There is a parallel but different account of the fate of Judas in Mt. 27.3–10; there is no NT parallel to the election of a replacement for him. In Mt. Judas repents of his treachery and seeks to return the money he has been paid. He is rebuffed, and commits suicide; the chief priests use the money to buy the Potter's Field, to be used as a burying-place for foreigners, thereby fulfilling Jer. 32.6–9 (and Zech. 11.12, 13?). Henceforth the field is known as Blood Field. This name is all that Luke has in common with Matthew, and he gives it a different derivation (v. 19). Attempts have been made to harmonize the two stories; they cannot be said to be successful. Both must have followed independently upon a connection made between Blood Field and Judas. Another divergent tradition was given by Papias. Probably nothing was known of the fate of Judas. Speculation was concerned to warn possible traitors, one by stressing the pangs of remorse, the other by the threat of divine judgement.

Luke is interested in the theme of judgement, also, alone among NT writers, in the gap in the ranks of the apostles caused by Judas' defection. Acting as leader for the first time in Acts Peter takes steps to fill the gap; this, he says, is required by Scripture. Another motivation may lie below the surface: the number twelve corresponds to the totality of Israel (cf. Lk. 22.30), and bringing the number of apostles back to twelve reaffirms the fundamental mission to and responsibility for Israel as a whole.

Apart from the awkward parenthesis in v. 15 (see the note) there seems to be no way of disentangling sources, oral or written, for this paragraph. There are marks of Lucan style, and it is probably correct to think that Luke received from tradition the bare facts of Judas' unhappy death and the accession to the Twelve of Matthias after the resurrection. He would supply the OT references and the neat ordering of the story, which, as he presents it, enshrines his understanding of the role of the apostles. An apostle was not only one who could bear personal testimony to the resurrection of Christ (v. 22); he must also be one who had been a companion of Jesus throughout his ministry (vv. 21, 22). The apostles, thus qualified, fulfilled a task that could not be handed on to others, and it can hardly have escaped Luke's notice that his definition of an apostle had the effect of excluding Paul; see on 14.4, 14, and Introduction, pp. lviii–lx.

In this paragraph only in the NT is the lot used to determine a matter. Luke may have thought that only in this way could it be made clear that the choice had been the choice of Jesus (cf. v. 24 with 1.2).

15. In these days must mean between the Ascension and Pentecost. The church was ready to receive the Spirit but until the Spirit was given its work could not begin.

For the first time in Acts Peter stands out as spokesman and leader. His prominence continues until the beginning of Paul's first journey (ch. 13), is resumed in ch. 15, and is then dropped. Peter is also prominent in the gospels and in the post-apostolic age (cf. 1 Clement 5.4; Ignatius, *Romans* 4.3; *Smyrnaeans* 3.2). That he played a leading part in the early church is hardly to be doubted. Peter **stood up** in the midst of, probably, the whole Christian group (though note *with us* in v. 22). **Brothers** is frequently used in Acts for members of God's reconstituted family.

Said should introduce Peter's speech but is followed surprisingly by a parenthetical clause, which suggests that at this point the author may have been following a written source.

The number **120** = 12 × 10 and there are Jewish parallels for a system of one leader for every ten members. It may be that Luke based the number 120 on the twelve apostles, but this is unconvincing. A more interesting, but equally unproductive, question is how the 120 are related to the 500 of 1 Cor. 15.6.

16. Brothers, literally, Men, brothers; LXX style. The next words express Luke's belief about the OT as a whole. It was spoken through notable persons by the Holy Spirit, and what it foretells must needs be fulfilled since it is God's word. Some think that the reference here is to the passages quoted in v. 20; perhaps more probable is Ps. 41.10.

17. Lot: here, that which is assigned by lot. Contrast v. 26. What is allotted here is a *ministry*, a *service*, not an office.

18. Luke writes a brief but vivid account of the end of Judas. Judas (not, as in Mt., the chief priests) **purchased** (not simply acquired) **a property**; the word suggests an estate or farm. It represents the Aramaic word transliterated in the first two syllables of Aceldama. He bought it with **the reward of his unrighteous act** (rather than *his unrighteous reward*). **He fell flat on his face**; literally, *he became prone*. Neither ancient nor modern attempts to harmonize this with Mt. (he hanged himself and fell; he jumped (in suicide) or fell (by accident) from a roof) are convincing. For his death; cf. 2 Kdms 20.10 and Josephus, *War* 7.453.

19. If the matter became known to all the inhabitants of Jerusalem it was not necessary for Peter to tell his hearers the story. Luke is of course telling it for his readers.

in their language. As the next word shows, this language was (not Hebrew but) Aramaic. Again we have Luke writing for the benefit of his Greek-speaking readers, not Peter speaking for his Aramaic-speaking hearers.

Aceldama, a transliteration of the Aramaic *ḥ^{a}qel dama*, Field of Blood. The suggestion that the last two syllables should be derived from *damka*, sleep, so that Aceldama means *Field of Sleep*, and of those who sleep (in death), i.e. cemetery (cf. Mt. 27.7) has been sometimes too easily dismissed. The verb *d-m-k* can mean *to lie in the grave*. This of course is not Luke's understanding of the name. It is more probable that the story of Judas in the forms in which we have it arose from the field which bore this unusual name.

20. Scripture (two passages, one referring to past events, the other to what is to be done in the future) was not merely aware of what was to take place but made provision for it. Ps. 69(68).26 is taken to refer to Judas' displacement from his office, or perhaps to his death. Ps. 109(108).8 refers to his replacement. In each case the quotation uses the LXX, with some modifications. **His office** (*episkopē*) is almost exclusively a biblical and Christian word. Here it contains in itself no indication of the content of the office in question, but it is clear that Matthias will do what Judas would have done had he not defected, that is, he will, as one who had accompanied Jesus throughout his ministry, bear witness to his resurrection and thus establish the continuity between Jesus and the post-resurrection church. For the meaning of *episkopos* as applied to Christian ministers see on 20.28.

21. The qualifications laid down for appointment to the apostolic group are such as to exclude Paul. For the role of the apostles in Acts, and for the status accorded to Paul, see Introduction, pp. lviii–lx.

22. Beginning. All the gospels regard John the Baptist as the necessary beginning of their accounts of Jesus. The Greek here is awkward but not sufficiently difficult to warrant the hypothesis of translation from Aramaic. **The baptism of John** probably refers generally to John's baptizing ministry, not specifically to his baptism of Jesus.

One must become. *Must* because it is foretold and commanded in Scripture.

A witness to his resurrection. This brings out clearly the meaning Luke attached to the word *witness*. Nothing could make Joseph or Matthias more truly eye-witnesses than they already were; one of them was to assume the specific task of *bearing witness* to that which he had seen.

23. They nominated. The community as a whole put forward Joseph and Matthias. There is some textual authority for *He nominated*, referring evidently to Peter. It is unlikely that this represents an attempt to magnify the authority of Peter.

Joseph called Barsabbas, who was surnamed Justus, and Matthias. Joseph and Matthias are common names. *Barsabbas* probably means 'Son of the Sabbath', that is, one born on the Sabbath; possibly 'Son of the old man', that is, one born in his father's old age; or simply 'Son of Saba'. *Justus* suggests a connection with the Roman world, possibly even that like Paul he was a Roman citizen.

We know no more about them than we know about most of the Eleven. The NT is more interested in the fact that the Twelve existed than in what they did.

Apparently James the Lord's brother was not put forward as a candidate. Cf. Jn 7.5; he did not qualify.

24. Thou, Lord. Jesus; he chose apostles in the past (Lk. 8.13; Acts 1.2) and is to choose now. He **knows the hearts of all men**; cf. 15.8. The word occurs nowhere else in the Greek Bible, but the notion that God is aware even of men's secret thoughts, intentions, and sins is biblical.

25. The chosen candidate will **receive the position** (literally, place) that Judas lost. The place is one of **ministry** (service) **and apostleship**. *Place* is a common word (cf. e.g. 1 QS 2.23) and has no necessary reference to ordination; cf. 1 Cor. 14.16. *Service and apostleship* is a hendiadys: service consisting in apostleship. He will serve Christ by being an apostle.

This place Judas left (crossing a boundary) **to go to his own place**. This may mean that he forsook his proper role of witness to Christ and adopted that of traitor. More probably it refers to the consequence of his act (cf. 8.20). His appropriate destination would presumably be hell. Cf. Targum to Eccles. 6.6: On the day of his death his soul goes down to Gehinnom, the one place where all the guilty go.

26. The new apostle is selected by lot. This method of choice, for both religious and social purposes, was widespread among both Greeks and Romans; it is mentioned frequently in the OT, and the religious use was continued and extended in post-biblical Judaism, though deprecated by Philo.

They cast lots for them. Luke does not use the customary verb, and it is possible that this, when taken with **he was voted in along with**, may refer not to the casting of lots but the casting of votes. This however is unlikely. The lot was used in order that the choice might have no human element in it but be wholly Christ's.

Matthias takes his place but equally with Joseph Justus is thereafter lost to sight.

II

THE CHURCH IN JERUSALEM

(2.1 – 5.42)

3. THE PENTECOST EVENT 2.1–13

**1 When the Day of Pentecost had at length come, they were all
together in the same place, 2 and suddenly there came from heaven
a sound as of a powerful rushing wind, and it filled the whole
room where they were sitting, 3 and there appeared to them
tongues as if of fire, dividing up among them, and it rested upon
each one of them, 4 and they were all filled with the Holy Spirit
and began to speak with different tongues, as the Spirit granted
them to give utterance.**

**5 There were residing in Jerusalem Jews, pious men coming
from every nation under heaven. 6 When this sound was heard the
crowd assembled and were confounded, because each one of them
heard them speaking in his own language. 7 They were astounded,
and marvelled, saying, 'Why, are not all these men who are
speaking Galileans? 8 So how is it that we, each one of us, hear
them speaking in our own native languages? 9 Parthians, Medans,
and Elamites, those who live in Mesopotamia, Judaea and
Cappadocia, Pontus and Asia, 10 Phrygia and Pamphylia, Egypt
and the parts of Libya adjacent to Cyrene, resident Romans, 11 Jews
and proselytes, Cretans and Arabs, – we hear them speaking in
our tongues the great deeds of God.' 12 They were all astounded
and perplexed, saying to one another, 'What can this be?' 13 But
others mocked and said, 'They are drunk on sweet wine.'**

Chapter 1 leads the reader to expect that the work of Jesus will not be complete, and that his followers will not be fully prepared for their work, until a notable activity of the Holy Spirit has taken place. This expectation is fulfilled on the Day of Pentecost. The presence of the Spirit – the gift of God in the eschatological age – is made known in visible and audible manifestations, particularly in the fact that when Peter and his colleagues speak they are understood by all the members of a large and diverse crowd assembled in Jerusalem from many regions, each of whom hears them speaking in his own language. Some are impressed, others think the apostles to be drunk.

Luke appears to have two purposes in mind in this narrative. The first is to demonstrate the fulfilment of Jesus' promise: his followers will receive supernatural power. The second is to show that the church is from the beginning a universal society in which universal communication is possible. This twofold interest invites two comments.

(a) Neither the Pauline epistles, nor any other part of the NT, refers in this way to a special, 'founding', gift of the Holy Spirit. The closest, but still remote, parallel is Jn 20.22.

(b) Luke appears to understand the gift of tongues to mean the ability to speak in a variety of foreign languages, intelligible to those with the appropriate linguistic background. This is a different view of glossolalia from Paul's, as is shown in 1 Cor. 12, 14, where speaking with tongues is unintelligible except through a special gift. Was Luke writing so long after the Pauline period that he no longer understood what speaking with tongues meant? Or were there two kinds of glossolalia?

It is in the light of these facts that we must consider the origin of Luke's story. He was not an eye-witness of the events described. There is no doubt that the crucifixion of Jesus was followed by events charged with profound religious and emotional power and conveying acute theological perception. It is doubtful whether those who shared them would be able to make a distinction and say, This was the presence of the risen Christ, and this the work of the Holy Spirit. There is something to be said for the view that what we read in Acts 2 is a varied version (edited by Luke in accordance with his own views, and perhaps on lines suggested by alternative traditions) of the appearance to more than 500 mentioned by Paul (1 Cor. 15.6). Luke asserts (2.16) the fulfilment of Joel 2.28; how could this, for Luke, be manifested, except by some kind of ecstasy? And how could potential universality be better adumbrated than by universal audition?

A distinction has often been made between vv. 1–4 and vv. 5–13, but it seems more likely that Luke wrote the whole on the basis of the convictions outlined above and various traditions of outstanding events recollected from the earliest days of the church. He incorporated a separate list of nations and countries.

1. When the Day of Pentecost had at length come. It is not easy to derive this or any other translation with any confidence from Luke's Greek. There is probably loose writing here. *The Day of Pentecost.* For the name of the feast cf. Tobit 2.1; Josephus, *War* 6.299; in rabbinic literature it is *Sh^{e}buoth* or *'^{a}ṣereth* (completion (of Passover)). In the OT see Exod. 23.16; 34.22; Num. 28.26; and especially Lev. 23.15–21; Deut. 9–12. It was originally, and in the NT period continued to be, a Harvest Festival. Later, but not till the second century AD, it was connected with the giving of the Law. It is tempting to use this connection in the interpretation of the Acts narrative. (a) The gift of Torah was a divine revelation in which the nature and will of God were made known on the basis of his gracious act of deliverance and with the result of a covenant between himself and his people; the Christian Pentecost is the new revelation through the Holy Spirit, based upon the new act of redemption and deliverance and issuing in the formation of a new, or renewed, people of God, based upon a new covenant. (b) According to B. Shabbath 88b, Every word that proceeded out of the mouth of the Almighty divided itself into seventy tongues (languages) – that is, though only Israel accepted the Torah and promised to be obedient, it was heard by all the nations in their own languages. This interpretation however is not to be accepted. (a) The Rabbinic material is too late, and other evidence sometimes adduced is for various reasons not valid. (b) Nothing in Acts hints at the giving of the Law on Mount Sinai. A more important OT reference is the account of Babel (Gen. 11.1–9), the effect of which is now reversed.

They were all together in the same place. *All* may mean *All the twelve apostles* or *All the 120* (1.15). The gift of the Spirit was not confined to a special group of spiritual persons.

2. Suddenly. Context and LXX background confirm in this word a hint of *wondrous, awesome.*

A sound as of a powerful rushing wind. Cf. Gen. 1.2, but Luke does not use the word for *wind* (which also means *spirit*) that is used in Genesis. Luke is accumulating features characteristic of theophanies; cf. 1 Kings 19.11; Isa. 66.15; 4 Ezra 13.10; and descriptive of the giving of the Law: Exod. 19.18f. and passages based on this, e.g. Philo, *de Decalogo* 33. The **sound** echoed through **the whole room where they were sitting**.

3. Tongues: the word as used here must mean (in surprising contrast to v. 4) *something shaped like the tongue*; Luke probably means that one tongue-like flame rested on each person. Fire is sometimes said to have rested on the heads of rabbis as they studied or disputed about the Torah, but neither the thought of a divine presence resting upon the pious nor the image of fire is distinctively Semitic or biblical. It is very probable that Luke saw in this event a fulfilment of the Baptist's prediction (Lk. 3.16), though that may have referred originally to judgement by wind and fire.

4. There can be no doubt that Luke saw the event described here as the fulfilment of the promise of 1.5 (cf. v. 8); it therefore appears that filling with the Holy Spirit and baptism with the Holy Spirit are synonymous. His language however lacks consistency. It is not easy to say whether for him the Spirit, once given, is a permanent possession, or spasmodic. Thus at 4.8 Peter, at 4.31 the whole group, are filled with the Holy Spirit. On the whole the dominant view in Acts is that, though the Spirit is always constitutive of the Christian life, the Spirit is specially given to Christians in special need (cf. Lk. 12.12; 21.15), as on the Day of Pentecost, or at any appearance in court.

It is consistent with this that Luke should recognize special gifts of the Holy Spirit in phenomena such as speaking with tongues (cf. 10.46; 19.6). See above, p. 16; a special problem arises when Luke's account of glossolalia (in vv. 5–8) is compared with Paul's. Verse 13 suggests something more like Pauline glossolalia (madness, drunkenness). Did Luke have in mind a clear picture of the Pentecostal events? A clear picture of glossolalia in the Pauline church? It is unlikely that anyone in contact with the Pauline mission would have been unfamiliar with it. The word **different** may point to the editing of two sources, or perhaps be Luke's means of transforming glossolalia into a token of the universality of the Christian mission. It would be a mistake to suppose that glossolalia was – or is – a uniform phenomenon. Those who are sufficiently out of control of their own functions to speak with tongues do not pause to consider whether they are doing so in the same way as others.

They were all filled with the Holy Spirit. For *all* see on v. 1. Only to Peter are specific words ascribed.

5. The text of this verse shows several variations which may be summed up in the observation that the words **Jews** and **pious** are uncertain. *Jews* may have come in as a marginal note, perhaps intended to show that the *pious men* were Jews by religion though by race or residence they were Parthians, Medans, etc. Alternatively, *Jews* may have been dropped as inconsistent with Parthians, Medes, etc. The evidence for the omission of *pious* is slight. The use of the word at Lk. 2.25; Acts 8.2; 22.12; and of cognates at Heb. 5.7; 11.7; 12.28 means that it can hardly be taken to denote a special class of 'God-fearers' (see p. 155). If taken with *Jews* it would suggest that Luke was thinking of a great assembly of the best, most devout, most favourably disposed Jews, gathered in Jerusalem for the feast or for permanent residence. This however leaves us with the problem of **coming from every nation under heaven** and the languages referred to in vv. 8, 11. Luke wishes to represent the church as from the beginning inspired and universal. But he may be combining sources. Were all in the crowd born Jews (cf. v. 11, *proselytes*)? How did Jews come to use from birth (v. 8) so many languages? What was the origin of the list of nations?

6. When this sound was heard – possibly the sound of the wind (v. 2), much more probably (in view of v. 8b) the sound of speech.

The crowd were confounded. This is the verb of Gen. 11.7 and has been taken to suggest the reversal of the confusion of Babel. But Luke does not say that confusion was ended; it found a new cause.

7. Why, are not . . . ? The expression has been thought to be a sign of an Aramaic original; more probably Luke is imitating the LXX, and imitating it not in a literal rendering of Hebrew but in an internal corruption.

Galileans. It has been suggested that a contrast with *pious men* (v. 5) is intended, but Luke is here interested in language, not piety, possibly in the degree of education that might be expected of Galileans.

8. Our own native languages, literally, our own languages in which we were born. This does not seem a natural way for Jews to speak.

9–11. The list of names, including both countries and races, presents severe problems and has never been satisfactorily explained. Surprisingly (when its difficulty is considered) it shows little sign of textual corruption. **Judaea** (v. 9) has often been suspected of corruption, and there are ill-attested variants: Jews, Armenia, Syria, India. Since the careful examination by B. M. Metzger it has become impossible to hold the view that the list is based on 'astrological geography'. The most probable source is the lists of the various countries inhabited by Jews; the best is that of Philo in *Legatio ad Gaium* 281f. Luke's and Philo's lists are by no means identical; there is no question of direct literary connection. For Jews resident in the areas mentioned the reader should consult the index of *NS*; also Hemer 222f. There is no point in giving details here; Luke's only interest is in the wide spread of representation in Jerusalem on this occasion.

Romans in v. 10 means not *visitors from Rome* but *Roman citizens* (now residing in Jerusalem). For **proselytes** see p. 19.

We hear in v. 11 picks up the same word in v. 8. Between stands the list in a sort of apposition: *We hear* – we Parthians, etc. – *we hear* . . . The new sentence emphasizes that the miracle was one of speech. It is not merely that We hear each one in his language, but We hear them speaking in our tongues. The speakers were telling forth **the great deeds of God**. The word points to God's mighty acts in delivering his people and is used in ascriptions of praise; cf. 1 QS 1.21. The preachers are declaring with praise the new redemption that God has wrought for his people.

12. The verse stresses bewilderment. The crowd wondered what was going on.

13. Others after *all* in v. 12 is simply careless writing. Luke regularly indicates that the Christian message did not meet with unanimous acceptance. For **mocked**; cf. 17.32. **They are drunk.** Cf. 1 Cor. 14.23 for the effect of glossolalia at Corinth.

Sweet wine was sometimes contrasted with better quality wine – it was alleged, perhaps, that the Christians were getting drunk as cheaply as possible. The question is sometimes raised how new, sweet wine, incompletely fermented, could be available at Pentecost, just before the vine harvest. But Luke is winding up his narrative; he is aware of the criticism that Christians speaking with tongues sounded, to the unsympathetic hearer, as it they were drunk, and sees that the charge can be neatly used to introduce Peter's speech.

4. PETER'S PENTECOST SERMON 2.14–40

**14 Peter stood up with the eleven, lifted up his voice, and addressed
them, 'Fellow Jews, and all you who are residing in Jerusalem,
let this be known to you; give ear to my words. 15 These men are
not, as you suppose, drunk, for it is the third hour of the day.
16 On the contrary, this is what was said through the prophet.
17 In the last days, says God, it shall be that I will pour out my
Spirit upon all flesh; your sons and your daughters shall prophesy,
and your young men shall see visions and your old men shall
dream dreams. 18 Yes, upon my men slaves and my women slaves
I will in those days pour out my Spirit, and they shall prophesy.
19 I will give portents in heaven above and signs upon the earth
beneath, blood and fire and smoky vapour. 20 The sun shall be
turned into darkness and the moon into blood before that great
and manifest day of the Lord comes. 21 And every one who calls
on the name of the Lord will be saved.**

**22 'Men of Israel, listen to these words. Jesus of Nazareth, a
man marked out for you by God with mighty works and portents
and signs, which God did through him in your midst, as you
yourselves know, 23 this Jesus, handed over by God's determinate
counsel and foreknowledge, you, making use of men outside the
law, nailed up and killed. 24 But God, when he had loosed the
pangs of death, raised him up, because it was not possible that he
should be held by it. 25 For David says of him, I set the Lord always
in my sight before me; for he stands at my right hand, so that I
may not be moved. 26 For this reason my heart rejoiced and my
tongue exulted, yes, my flesh shall dwell in hope. 27 For thou wilt
not leave my soul in Hades, nor wilt thou permit thy godly one to
see corruption. 28 Thou didst make known to me ways of life, thou
wilt fill me with gladness in thy presence. 29 Brothers, I may say
to you with all freedom of the patriarch David both that he died
and that he was buried; and his tomb is with us to this day. 30 So
he was a prophet, and knowing that God had sworn to him an
oath to set on his throne one of his descendants, 31 he foresaw
what would happen and spoke of the resurrection of Christ, saying
that neither was he left in Hades nor did his flesh see corruption.
32 This Jesus God raised up, and all of us are his witnesses. 33 So,
having been exalted by the right hand of God, and having received**

from the Father the promise of the Holy Spirit, he has poured out this that you both see and bear. 34 For it was not David who ascended into heaven; he himself says, The Lord said to my lord, Sit at my right hand, 35 until I set your enemies as a footstool for your feet. 36 So let all the house of Israel know for certain that God has made him both Lord and Christ, this Jesus whom you crucified.'

37 When they heard this they were pricked in their consciences, so that they said to Peter and the other apostles, 'What are we to do, brothers?' 38 Peter said to them, 'Repent, and let each one of you be baptized in the name of Jesus Christ for the forgiveness of your sins, and you will receive the gift of the Holy Spirit. 39 For the promise belongs to you and to your children and to all who are far away, all those whom the Lord our God calls to himself.' 40 With many other words he testified to them and exhorted them, saying, 'Accept your salvation from this crooked generation.'

The first public proclamation of the Gospel presented by Luke is directly attached to the Pentecost event. This, Peter argues, cannot be explained as due to drunkenness; rather it is the fulfilment of Joel 3.1–5, which, as quoted by Luke, makes it clear that the final stages of history have been reached; the gift of the Spirit belongs to the last days. Since this is so, salvation is now offered to all who call upon God's name. At v. 22 Peter turns to the Christological proclamation that appears elsewhere (notably in chs. 3, 10 and 13). He appeals to the historical record. Notwithstanding his mighty works, which proved that God was with him, his own people in collaboration with the Romans rejected and killed Jesus. But God had set right this great wrong by raising Jesus from the dead. This was supported not only by eye-witness testimony but by the OT. Jesus, vindicated by resurrection and ascension, was now at God's right hand, and the Spirit had been given. Hearers who repented and were baptized would receive forgiveness and the gift of the Spirit.

Other speeches follow a similar pattern, and though there is no question of a word-for-word report of what Peter actually said, the question is raised whether this pattern, and the Christology it represents, belongs to the 30s of the first century or to the 80s and 90s (when Luke wrote). This question may be approached in various ways.

(1) The speech has been held to bear marks of Aramaic origin; its contents would then be likely to go back to the early Aramaic-speaking

years of Palestinian Christianity. The evidence for this is examined in the notes; it is not convincing.

(2) It is a fair comment that the speech shows no developed theology, especially when compared with the Pauline epistles. This however does not prove that it is early. In every generation there have been Christians whose theology was simply undeveloped, unsophisticated. There can be no doubt that the theology of the speeches is *Lucan* theology, probably, that is, the theology of the church as this was known to Luke (in the 80s and 90s). The question remains unanswered whether it was also the theology of the 30s.

(3) (a) Apart from what appear to be Lucan notes of Lucan interests (inspiration; universality) in vv. 33, 39, the speech contains nothing (from v. 22 onwards) to connect it with the occasion. (b) The surface meaning of v. 36 (see the note) is inconsistent with Luke's own Christology (though the wording is such that Luke could have interpreted it in his own way). (c) There is a special interest in David. (d) The speech shares a common pattern with other speeches in the first half of Acts. We may conclude, somewhat tentatively, that Luke in composing this speech (and others) made use of some traditional material, but we have not thereby answered the question of the date and origin of the material on which he drew. Nothing is demonstrably post-Pauline (or Johannine), but Christians may still have been preaching in this way at the close of the century. If however it is correct (see Introduction, p. xxxviii) that it was one of Luke's aims to provide an apostolic handbook for preachers it is probable that he would seek out the oldest traditional material he could find. But it is at least equally probable that he would not use it as a critical historian.

14. Peter . . . lifted up his voice. The expression may be described as a Septuagintalism, but it occurs also in Greek with no Semitic background. **Give ear** is another Septuagintalism.

And all you who are residing in Jerusalem. This suggests an address to Jews and non-Jews, but at v. 22 only Israelites are in mind. In v. 14 Luke wishes to make the point of universality.

15. The mocking charge of 2.13 is rebutted by the simple observation that it was too early in the day for men to be drunk.

16. Most MSS have **the prophet Joel**, but the Western text omits the name, which many copyists would have seen fit to add. At 7.42f.; 13.40ff.; 15.16f., Mincr Prophets are quoted but not named. That the Pentecostal event was the fulfilment of prophecy was of first importance to Luke. **This is** in v. 16 corresponds to *it* *shall be* in v. 17. God has now begun but not completed the work of fulfilment. Christians are living in the last days, but the last day has not yet come.

17. In this verse and those that follow there are several variants, most of which are intended either to make the quotation conform more closely to the text of the LXX or to make it fit more neatly into the circumstances of the Day of Pentecost. Thus **in the last days** is by some MSS conformed to Joel's *after that*. These MSS miss an important point. *After that* simply points to an indeterminate future; *in the last days* asserts that the events referred to are part of God's final act of redemption.

They shall prophesy. Christian prophecy plays an important part in Acts, see 11.27; 13.1; 15.32; 19.6; 21.9, 10. Sometimes but not always the prophets make predictions; they speak in a distinctive way that can be recognized as inspired; they function as servants of the church, comparable with teachers.

The prophecy of Joel was taken up in Judaism and understood to refer to an outpouring of the Spirit in the age to come, when prophecy would no longer be confined to a few. Joel 3.1 was associated with Num. 11.29.

See visions . . . dream dreams. These are in synonymous rather than antithetical parallelism; young and old (the order in Joel reversed) alike will receive supernatural revelations.

18. As in v. 17 (sons and daughters) no distinction is made between men and women. Cf. Gal. 3.28.

And they shall prophesy; an addition to the words of Joel, indicating the importance to Luke of prophecy.

19. I will give portents in heaven above and signs upon the earth beneath. Luke has made out of Joel two parallel lines, but his motivation was probably not poetical; he wished to add to heavenly portents, signs, miracles, worked by the apostles (and by Jesus before them, v. 22) which provided further proof that the age to come was now dawning.

20. The great and manifest day of the Lord is the last day, of salvation for his people and destruction for his enemies, the day of judgement. This great day, which will be such that no one will fail to recognize it, marks the end of the eschatological process. It is the day on which the Lord Jesus Christ descends from heaven (cf. 1.11) to consummate the story of the people of God. Thus the verse does much to make clear Luke's understanding of the divine plan. His story lies within the period limited on the one hand by the resurrection and ascension and on the other by the return of Christ. From the outset it is marked by the gift of the Spirit which initiates Christian prophecy. There will also be signs on earth, and of these Luke will give examples. These will be followed by celestial portents which have not yet appeared but will form the immediate prelude to the coming of Christ. This is a simple outline, but it holds the Christian story firmly to its origin in the historical mission of Jesus and allowed Luke to find, and expound to the church, the significance of its history, which – perhaps unexpectedly – had taken the place of an immediate parousia.

21. Everyone who calls on the name of the Lord will be saved. Joel was thinking of salvation on the great climactic day, and this conception of salvation is retained in the NT (e.g. Rom. 13.11, and regularly in Paul). Luke would probably not wish to deny this sense of the word, but for him salvation is an event that happens to the believer in the present time; so for example 2.47, and elsewhere in the NT (including occasionally Paul).

The word *name* occurs frequently in the early chapters of Acts (see 3.6, 11; 4.7, 10, 12, 17, 18, 30; 5.28, 40) and in such a way as to have led to the view that it has a magical sense; the name itself is an active power which can be employed by those who know how to invoke it. The sense in which Luke uses the word is however best defined by the two occurrences in the present chapter (vv. 21, 38). In the present verse it is used in the context of calling on the name of the Lord, that is, of invoking him in faith (cf. Rom. 10.14: invoking rests on believing). For v. 38 see below; and see further on 3.16.

22. Peter calls for the attention of the audience described in v. 14: **Listen to these words.** *The name of the Lord* (v. 21) is **Jesus of Nazareth**. *Of Nazareth* represents an adjective, *Nazōraios*. Some think that this was derived from the Hebrew root *n-ṣ-r*, which means *to guard, to observe*. This, it is suggested, was applied to Jesus and his followers as *the observants*. Others, using the passive participle *naṣor*, think it means that Jesus was *the guarded one*, *the Servant of the Lord*. It is much more likely that the adjective means *of* (*the place called*) *Nazareth*.

The first proposition about Jesus is that he was **a man**. This (not the notion of the incarnation of a divine being) is the starting-point of Luke's Christology, but he immediately introduces qualifications. He was a man **marked out for you**. Luke's word often means *appointed* but it can scarcely mean this here, since no office is named (see v. 36). **Mighty works and portents and signs** showed that Jesus was one who stood in a special relation with God. The words as used here refer to the miracles of Jesus. Their effect is sometimes said to be to represent Jesus as a 'divine man' (*theios anēr*), but this says both more and less than is warranted by Acts (see further p. 38). On the one hand, Acts affirms that Jesus was a man, and that God worked through him. On the other hand, in due course God made him *Lord* and *Christ* (v. 36): he occupied the pre-eminent executive role in God's predetermined plan of salvation.

23. God marked him out for you, but **you . . . nailed** him **up and killed him**. Notwithstanding the crucifixions by Alexander Jannaeus crucifixion was not a Jewish punishment in the Roman period; the Jews acted through (**making use of** – there may be a Semitism here) **men outside the Law**. This does not mean that the Romans were specially wicked, only that they lacked the privilege of the Law.

You killed; but this was **by God's determinate counsel and foreknowledge**. What appeared to be a free concerted action by Jews and Gentiles was in fact done because God foreknew it, decided it, and planned it. Cf. 4.27, 28. This must be noted, along with 20.28, as providing a theological framework for the otherwise uninterpreted affirmation, 'You killed him, but God raised him from the dead' (e.g. 3.15). Luke does not develop the theology; he himself says little more than that it would be false to charge Jesus with failing to foresee the consequences of his actions. It was God's intention that was being worked out.

24. God . . . raised him up. As in the miracles (v. 22), so in the resurrection the prime actor was God. Jesus indeed rose, but he rose because he was raised. The point of this (developed by Paul rather than Luke) is that the resurrection of Jesus was not an isolated and individual event but an anticipated part of the resurrection at the last day, brought forward in such a way that the rest of men might share it by faith.

When he had loosed the pangs of death. Luke borrows from the LXX (Ps. 17.6 or 114.3) a mistranslation, or misunderstanding, of the Hebrew, which must refer to *cords* not *pangs*. The mistranslation is not Luke's. An alternative interpretation of Luke's words implies a picture of Death (personified) as in labour: God *put an end* to Death's *travail pains*. Death was to bring forth no more children, have no more effect. There is some support for this in 1 QH 3.28, but it is less probable than Luke's dependence on the LXX. There may be a reference to this verse in Polycarp, *Philippians* 1.2.

It was not possible . . . , because his resurrection had been foretold in Scripture.

25. David is assumed to be the author of Ps. 15(16).8–11, quoted in vv. 25–8. The interpretation is given in vv. 29–31, where it will be argued that David is not speaking of himself but of the Messiah, and protection from death becomes deliverance from death.

At my right hand makes a verbal link with Ps. 110.1, quoted in v. 34.

26. The verse agrees with Ps. 15.9. Instead of **my tongue** (LXX) the Hebrew has *my glory*, originally perhaps *my liver*, used in parallel with *heart* as the seat of the emotions. **My flesh**, if it means *my physical body*, is more suitable to Luke's purpose; after death my body will rest in hope (of resurrection). The Hebrew would be more suitable still, since it means objective security rather than subjective hope.

27. This verse agrees exactly with the LXX of Ps. 15.10, which is in sufficient agreement with the Hebrew. Cf. 13.35. Luke understands the Psalmist to be expressing, in the person of the Messiah, the confidence that God will not allow his destiny to be that of the inferior, unhappy existence which was all that men looked forward to after death.

28. This verse agrees exactly with the first two clauses of Ps. 15.11. The Hebrew singular *way of life* means the way that is pleasing to God and therefore leads to life; Luke thinks of the ways out of death back into life. Joy arises not simply out of not being dead but from the **presence** of God.

29. Brothers. Cf. 1.16; but here the brothers are fellow Jews, not fellow Christians. Superficially Psalm 15 appears to refer to David. If this is its only reference it is irrelevant to the story of Jesus. The words translated here **I may say to you with all freedom** have been taken as an apology for the suggestion that David's body might have experienced corruption; they mean rather that Peter (at least as represented by Luke) believes that he may say this without fear of contradiction. There had been attempts (under John Hyrcanus and Herod) to rifle the tomb but the coffin had not been disturbed. The body had decayed, and the Psalm therefore could not refer to David himself. Peter will continue in the next verse to give his interpretation. If this has to be regarded as a misinterpretation of a mistranslation some questions are raised regarding the understanding of Scripture, especially in the OT.

30. Since in the Psalm David was not referring to himself he must have been speaking of another, and of whom should he have spoken but of the one who God had sworn (see 2 Sam. 7.12f.) should be descended from him and inherit his throne?

Had sworn . . . an oath. This is sometimes classed as a Semitism, but it is no more than a slight one, with fairly numerous parallels in Classical Greek.

31. David as a prophet foresaw what was to happen and spoke of the resurrection of the Messiah. The two clauses (**neither . . . nor**) are essentially synonymous, though the former refers to the destiny of the soul after death, the latter to the fate of the physical body. The Greek **Hades** corresponds to the Hebrew Sheol as the place of the dead.

32. This Jesus God raised up. Cf. v. 24. **All of us are his witnesses.** It would be equally possible to translate, *are witnesses of this fact*. For the two possibilities cf. 1.8 (*my witnesses*) and 1.22 (*witnesses to* (*of*) *his resurrection*).

33. The right hand of God is in Greek ambiguous. It may be instrumental (*by the right hand of God*) or locative (*to the right hand of God*). The agency of God in v. 32 seems decisive for the instrumental sense here.

Having been exalted (in the ascension) recalls Ps. 68(67).19 (cf. Eph. 4.8). The Psalm continues, Thou didst receive gifts, and this recalls, **having received from the Father the promise of the Holy Spirit**, this special gift being naturally mentioned in the context of Acts 2. There may be further echoes of Ps. 68(67), but how far his readers, and how far Luke himself, would have been aware of them it is impossible to say. They may however determine one exegetical question. Jesus received the promise (consisting) of the Spirit: does this refer to his baptism (Lk. 3.22 – himself endowed with the Spirit he was able to confer the same gift on others), or to a receiving that was part of his exaltation? The allusions to the Psalm are decisive in favour of the latter alternative. The Spirit was in turn given by Jesus to his disciples, with results that had been seen and heard. The words **from the Father** imply that Jesus is God's Son, but it is clear that Luke understood sonship in a mildly subordinationist sense.

34, 35. It was not David who ascended into heaven, but another. Cf. the argument in vv. 29–31 that Ps. 16(15).8–11 referred not to

David but to the resurrection of Jesus. Here the clue is given by Ps. 110(109).1, a passage that played an important part in early Christian thought in which it was used (a) to associate Jesus with and distinguish him from David – he was the Messiah; (b) to support the view that his apparent defeat was his way to glory; (c) to set out the new two-stage eschatology that Christians were obliged to adopt – they lived between the exaltation of Jesus and the final submission of all things to him; (d) to show that the ascended Jesus was not merely greater than David (who calls him Lord) but was related to God at whose right hand he sits. For the Christology see v. 36 and Introduction, pp. liv–lvii.

36. So: this verse sums up and states the conclusion of the speech so far. **All the house of Israel** may **know for certain that God has made** Jesus **both Lord and Christ.** It is implied that there was a time when the crucified Jesus was not Lord and Christ. When was he appointed to these positions, and what did they mean? The context strongly suggests that the appointment took place when God raised up and thereby vindicated Jesus. Cf. Rom. 1.4. This was not Luke's own view; he must have been using a source, which he could have taken to mean that the resurrection and ascension prove that God had already, before his ministry, made Jesus Lord and Christ (cf. Lk. 2.11). The non-Lucan Christology that is hinted at here bears witness to the impact made by the resurrection. It seems clear that Jesus did not publicly claim Messiahship in the course of his ministry, almost equally clear that it was impossible to exclude messianic categories from the discussion of his work. For those who accepted it, his resurrection proved that nothing less could be the truth; at the same time, returning from death, he appeared as Messiah in the role of a supernatural Lord. This title was certainly in use in Aramaic at an early date (1 Cor. 16.22). The quotation in v. 34 used Lord in two senses, first as the name of God, then as the title of another person, greater than David but distinguished from the God of the OT, though invited to sit at God's right hand. This is an unreflecting Christology. He who shares the throne of God shares his deity; and he who is God is what he is from and to eternity – otherwise he is not God. This truth, evident as it is, was not immediately perceived. On the Christology of Acts see further Introduction, pp. liv–lvii.

37. The speech breaks off and the tension is heightened as the hearers interpose a question: **What are we to do, brothers?** – *brothers* in the sense of fellow Jews. It is presumably their responsibility for the crucifixion (whom you crucified, v. 36) that leads to the question. It is addressed to **Peter and the other apostles**; all had been speaking (2.4), presumably on the same lines. The force of Peter's words in vv. 38, 39 is increased by the fact that they are an answer to a question. The people of God have put themselves in an impossible situation by rejecting God's own messenger; what is to be done?

38. The answer to the question is in two parts: **Repent**, which is in the plural and is presumably addressed to *the whole house of Israel* (v. 36), and **let each one of you be baptized**, which is directed to the individual members of the crowd. Baptism may then be thought of as an individualizing of the response that Israel as a whole should make. Repent(ance) is a fairly common word in Acts (2.38; 3.19; 5.31; 8.22; 11.18; 13.24; 17.30; 19.4; 20.21; 26.20) and occurs mostly in the context of conversion. It means turning away from sin (here specifically the sin of the crucifixion is in mind) but includes also the positive aspect of a turn to God. Both these aspects are involved in baptism, which leads to **forgiveness**, and is **in the name of Jesus Christ**. For *the name* see further on 3.16. The varying relation of baptism to **the gift of the Spirit** (cf. 8.16; 10.44; 18.26; 19.5f.) shows that the name is anything but a magical formula. It means that the person baptized becomes the property of, one of the company of, Jesus. The baptized belong to the renewed people of God in the last days. The eschatological reference of baptism is affirmed by the treatment of the gift of the Spirit in vv. 17–21. It is what God has promised for the *last days*; it is those who are baptized who receive it; thus it is through baptism that they enter into the newly realized eschatological conditions.

39. The promise belongs to you, the promise of the Holy Spirit, but beyond that of the covenant into which God enters with his people, whom, notwithstanding the crucifixion, he has not cast off (cf. Rom. 11.1, 2). **and to your children**. This refers not to the baptism of infants but to the future generally. **and to all who are far away**: Luke sees a further opportunity of bringing out the potential universality of the church. There is no need (in the light of Acts as a whole) to restrict the reference to Diaspora Jews. Cf. Isa. 57.19 and Ps.Sol. 8.33.

40. Luke is aware of the improbability that Peter should have spoken for no more than about three minutes; he has used the material available. **testified . . . exhorted.** These are important words in Acts. They are not to be wholly distinguished, but the former stresses the objective statement of Christian fact and truth, the latter the persuasion added by the speaker.

Accept your salvation. The verb *to save* is expressed in the passive imperative. This is often taken to be equivalent to a reflexive, 'save yourselves' (and the verb can be so used). Here however there is no possibility that men will save themselves except in the sense that they call upon him who has already called them. Here, and at 2.47; 11.14; 13.26, 46f.; 16.31; 28.28, salvation is a present event, but Luke does not abandon a future element in salvation. Salvation is from **this crooked generation**, so that one no longer shares its ways or its destiny.

5. THE PENTECOST COMMUNITY 2.41–47

**41 So those who accepted Peter's word were baptized, and in that
day there were added about 3,000 souls. 42 They persisted steadily
in the teaching of the apostles and in the fellowship, in the
breaking of bread and in the prayers. 43 Fear lay upon every soul,
and many portents and signs were done by the apostles. 44 All the
members of the believing community held all their belongings in
common, 45 and they would sell their property and possessions
and distribute them to all, as anyone from time to time had need.
46 Daily they continued together in the Temple, and breaking
bread at home they took food with rejoicing and in simplicity of
heart, 47 praising God and enjoying favour with all the people.
And daily the Lord added the saved to the community.**

The new paragraph begins at v. 41, which describes the origin of the new believing community, rather than v. 42, which proceeds with the description of the community life. The speech which ends at v. 40 was probably drawn (and edited with supplements) from a source; the origin of the new paragraph will be discussed below.

The speech is represented as extremely effective. The number 3,000 may be tradition; it is large but not totally incredible, for we are not to think of 3,000 cases of an individual process of conviction, which led from irreligion, or false religion, to a new faith expressed in a radical change of moral life. In most cases it could probably be expressed in the words, Jesus was Messiah after all. It would also be a mistake to think of formal liturgically executed baptisms. The reference to baptism may arise out of Luke's familiarity with the practice of his own day. The new believers entered upon the common life of Christians, of which four staple constituents are mentioned: the teaching of the apostles, fellowship, common meals, and prayer. They shared their property; as Jews, they continued to frequent the Temple. These activities (apart from visits to the Temple) have been familiar to Christians of all periods. Luke may simply have read them back from his own time.

There are however similar summary descriptions elsewhere (e.g. 4.32–35; 5.12–16) and the question of their purpose and origin must be considered. It is part of the truth that they were intended less to inform than to edify – here were examples for Luke's readers to follow. They add an element of continuity to the episodes of which Luke's book is made up, and indicate the passage of time – the miracle of 3.1–10 did not happen on the day after Pentecost. And they confirm Luke's central theme of the triumph of the word of God. The Gospel is accepted by more and more people and the quality of Christian life is maintained and developed in depth and intensity. Some see the core of the paragraph in vv. 42f.; then in vv. 44f. Luke expands fellowship in the sharing of goods, in v. 46 the Christian meal, in v. 47 prayer. But the whole passage shows Lucan characteristics of style, and the whole could have been constructed out of general knowledge of Christian life and institutions, with hints drawn from concrete incidents in the story.

41. Who baptized the 3,000, and where, is not stated. There is no reason to doubt that considerable numbers were convinced that something out of the ordinary had taken place and were prepared to accept the latest messianic claimant. Some would identify the 3,000 with the 500 of 1 Cor. 15.6. Luke does not say that all the 3,000 received the Holy Spirit (2.38).

42. They persisted steadily. The verb is important in Acts; see 1.14; 2.46; 6.4; 8.13; 10.7. They devoted themselves to four things, arranged in two pairs, which constitute both the general life of the Christian community and the community gathering in which that life is focused.

the teaching of the apostles: they listened to the apostles when they taught, and practised what they heard. Luke's vocabulary does not distinguish between the apostles' public proclamation and the development of this for the instruction of believers, though no doubt there was a difference.

the fellowship. This word may be taken in various ways: fellowship with the apostles, and with other believers; the sharing of v. 44; the breaking of bread; almsgiving (cf. Rom. 15.26; 2 Cor. 8.4; 9.13). It recalls the cognate verb (*to hold in common*) in v. 44, and there is no doubt that fellowship may be practically expressed in sharing with a view to almsgiving (also of course in a shared meal). There is an important use at Qumran (1 QS 5.1; 6.7) of a Hebrew word (*yaḥad*) of similar meaning, when members of the community are said to form a fellowship in the sphere of Torah and property. If for Torah is substituted *the teaching of the apostles* we have something that closely resembles Luke's description. With the **breaking of bread** we may compare the use of the cognate verb in v. 46; 20.7, 11; 27.35. The phrase undoubtedly points to a meal, denoted by the action with which a Jewish meal began. Luke probably uses it because it was the old traditional term for the fellowship meal in which Christians shared, and thus gave a touch of antiquity to his story. In Luke's own time this meal had coalesced with the meal that derived from the tradition of the Last Supper; see Lk. 22.14–20. When the combination of the two took place we cannot say with certainty. It may well have been Paul who interpreted the fellowship meal in terms of the bread and wine of the Last Supper.

The believers were also assiduous in **the prayers**. Cf. 1.14, where the singular *prayer* is used. The plural, with the article, implies that they not merely prayed but used certain specific prayers. Were they Christian prayers? Is there an allusion to the Lord's Prayer? Luke nowhere hints at a Christian set of prayers, so that (unless the plural is an intensive) *the prayers* are probably the familiar Jewish prayers. Some have suggested the Psalter, the Eighteen Benedictions, the Lord's Prayer, new Christian psalms and hymns; all plausible guesses, no more.

If in Luke's picture of the first Christians there is idealizing (and there is – Luke wrote to edify) it is to be found in *they persisted steadily*. What they are described as doing is so obvious that if Luke had not written it one would have conjectured it. Faithful adherence to the Christian way was what Luke meant to describe and by implication to commend.

43. Fear lay upon every soul. *Fear* is more than reverence; dread of the supernatural, which was evidently at work. *Every soul* is a Septuagintalism, not wholly un-Greek. For **portents and signs** see on 2.22. Jesus had performed miracles; so did the apostles. The way is prepared for the miracle in ch. 3.

44. All the members of the believing community, literally, All those who believed together. *Together* recalls the Qumran *yaḥad* (see v. 42). One might say that those who believed believed themselves into a society. As such a society they **held all their belongings in common**. Cf. 1 QS 1.11f.; 5.2 (referred to above). The Essenes described by Josephus also practised a community of goods. 'Riches they despise, and their community of goods is truly admirable; . . . They have a law that new members on admission shall confiscate their property to the order, with the result that you will nowhere see abject poverty or inordinate wealth; the individual's possessions join the common stock and all, like brothers, enjoy a single patrimony' (*War*

2.122). In Acts there is no *law* and other differences distinguish the church from the Essenes and the Qumran sect. The ideal however was well known and often practised, and was expressed in a familiar Greek proverb. In addition, belief that the world was to end shortly may have encouraged those who held it to get rid of their property, and some Christians may have suffered from exclusion from Jewish charities.

45. This verse describes the process presupposed by v. 44. It was dictated by love, not law. There is no evidence that the sharing of property was ever widely practised in primitive Christianity. Tertullian, *Apology* 39 is interesting; after saying that Christians have all things in common he adds that each does as he wills, no one is compelled, each acts voluntarily.

46. Daily. So the meals referred to later in the verse were not weekly celebrations of the Lord's resurrection but, much more probably, the necessary daily meals which the Christians took in common. **they continued together in the Temple**, as faithful Jews. Cf. 3.1. **breaking bread at home**. Cf. v. 42; the meals were taken *at home*, not in the meeting-house (as opposed to the Temple). This would be an anachronism. **they took food**. What is in mind here is a real, not a merely symbolic, meal. The **rejoicing** was eschatological; salvation was at hand. Few inferences regarding the conduct of these early Christian gatherings are possible. Most suggestions are guesses resting on a minimum of fact. Luke is probably describing the Christian meals of his own day, idealizing them, and setting them back in his description of the early days of Christianity. **simplicity of heart**. There is evidence for the use of the cognate adjective *simple*, to describe simple meals, in contrast with elaborate and luxurious ones. Luke may mean that simple fare was matched by, and was prompted by, plainness and honesty of speech and life.

47. praising God gives an appropriate sense to *rejoicing* in v. 46. **enjoying favour with all the people** underlines the innocence and simple honesty of *simplicity of heart*. This clause could mean *giving* God *thanks before all the people*, but this is less probable.

daily the Lord added the saved to the community. The number 3,000 was constantly increasing. A mistranslation has been suspected here, in that behind *to the community* (more literally, *together*) there may lie an Aramaic word that in another dialect may mean *greatly*, and in the failure of Aramaic to distinguish direct and indirect object. This could lead to, Daily the Lord added greatly to the saved. But this suggestion has been very widely abandoned.

the saved are those whom God calls into the fellowship of the redeemed community of the last days. For Luke's understanding of salvation see on 4.12.

6. TEMPLE MIRACLE 3.1–10

1 Peter and John were going up to the Temple at the hour of prayer, the ninth hour. 2 And a certain man, who had been lame from his mother's womb, was carried and placed every day by the Temple gate called Beautiful, to ask alms of those who were going into the Temple. 3 He saw Peter and John as they were about to enter the Temple, and asked to receive alms. 4 Peter fixed his gaze upon him (John too), and said, 'Look at us.' 5 The man paid attention to them, expecting to receive something from them. 6 But Peter said, 'Silver and gold I do not possess, but what I have I give you. In the name of Jesus Christ of Nazareth, walk!' 7 He took him by the right hand and raised him up, and immediately his feet and ankles were made sound. 8 He leapt up and stood and began to walk, and he went into the Temple with them, walking and leaping and praising God. 9 And all the people saw him walking and praising God. 10 And they recognized that he was the man who used to sit for alms at the Beautiful Gate of the Temple; and they were filled with wonder and astonishment at what had happened to him.

The story begins abruptly; there is no evident connection with the preceding paragraphs. This miracle, with consequences leading to 4.31 (see especially 4.12), is given as an example of healings that happened frequently (4.30; 5.12, 15, 16). The paragraph shows few traces of characteristically Lucan style; it was probably drawn from a (perhaps written) source, edited here and there by Luke. There may have been a collection of miracles done by Peter; cf. 9.32–43. The speech that follows (3.12–26) though drawn from a different source has been co-ordinated with the miracle; see pp. 41–44.

As a miracle story the paragraph shows most of the features that are familiar in both biblical and non-biblical parallels. The stage is set; the severity of the disease is noted; healer and healed confront each other; there is a word of command, with physical contact; the suddenness and completeness of the cure and its effect on the onlookers are underlined. An unusual feature is the association of John (who does nothing and says nothing) with Peter. This is probably Luke's work, though it is not clear why he should have added John to the story. Probably Luke wished to make clear that from the beginning the church, represented by the Twelve, acted as a fellowship (ch. 5 expands the two into twelve). Only Peter and John were known outside Palestine.

Peter and John are represented as devout Jews on their way to the Temple. They have no money but have it in their power to give a better gift. Luke is sensitive (see also 3.12, 16 – Lucan additions to his source) to the fact that the exercise of this power could lead to the belief that the apostles were 'divine men', a belief that some Christians may have held. Luke rebuts it, partly in his narrative, partly by his use of the word *name*, which is to be understood not as itself a magical formula but in the manner explained on 2.21, 38. This word represents one way, but only one way (for miracles and speeches can be reported without its use), in which the supernatural power of Jesus is brought into operation; or rather, it is one way in which the believing and obedient invocation of the power of Jesus is described. This is brought out in the accompanying speech; see pp. 46f.

The story is traditional; it can therefore tell us nothing about Luke's knowledge of the topography of Jerusalem. In any case our own knowledge regarding the Beautiful Gate of the Temple is too uncertain to enable us to pass any judgement.

1. the Temple. Luke is concerned to show that the apostles have not ceased to be faithful and observant Jews. Christianity is the true, fulfilled form of Judaism. **at the hour of prayer**, **the ninth hour**. For the hours of prayer see (among other passages) T. Berakoth 3.6; B. Berakoth 26ab; for Christian borrowing of the three hours see *Didache* 8.3; Tertullian, *Prayer* 25. Prayer at the ninth hour took its name from the Tamid, or Minhah, sacrifice, offered at that time (see Josephus, *Ant.* 14.65; Dan. 9.21, Judith 9.1).

John. For his association with Peter see vv. 4, 11; 4.13, 19; 8.14; all have the appearance of editorial additions. See above, p. 37.

2. lame from his mother's womb. Cf. 14.8; the language is conventional but may be Luke's own addition. The lame man was placed daily, in order to beg, **by the Temple gate called Beautiful**. Of the Temple gates Josephus writes that 'nine were completely overlaid with gold and silver, as were also their door-posts; but one, that outside the sanctuary, was of Corinthian bronze, and far exceeded in value those plated with silver and set in gold' (*War* 5.201). This is usually identified with the Nicanor gate: see M. Middoth 2.3. For the location of the Nicanor gate see Josephus, *War* 5.204, 205, which unfortunately is not clear; it may have been between the Court of the

Gentiles and the Court of the Women, or between the Court of the Women and the Court of the Men. But is the Nicanor gate the Beautiful gate? There is a tradition (not ancient) that the Shushan gate is intended. But no ancient source mentions a gate called Beautiful, and we can only guess at the location Luke has in mind. See further on vv. 3, 8, 11.

The lame man may have been sitting at the gate because, as one who had to be carried, he would not be allowed in the Temple itself. More probably the place was chosen because it was favourable for begging. It is not correct that it was forbidden to carry money into the Temple; it was forbidden to carry it ostentatiously.

3. Peter and John **were about to enter the Temple**, that is, they were still outside. This should mean that the Beautiful gate was an outer gate; this the Shushan gate was, the Nicanor gate was not.

4. The role of the apostles is first emphasized (**Look at us**), then freed from possible misunderstanding (3.12, 16).

5. This verse prepares the way for the dramatic effectiveness of the next.

6. The lame man's hope – to receive money – is to be disappointed. Peter and John have none to give. **Silver and gold** will refer to minted money. Luke presents the apostles as poor men. Cf. 2.44f.; 4.32, 34; the Christians shared their goods and did not consider that money belonged to them personally. But they had it in their power to give a better gift. **In the name of Jesus Christ of Nazareth, Walk!** A word of command addressed by the healer to the sick person is found in many miracle stories; in miracles performed by Christians there is a natural invocation of the name of Jesus. This is the first of a number of occurrences of *name* in chs. 3 and 4 (3.6, 16; 4.10, 12, 17, 18, 30; cf. 4.7). These are not to be understood as invoking magic; see above, p. 38. To say this is not to say that no early Christians ever understood the name of Jesus to have magical significance; it is very probable that some did so understand it (cf. e.g. Justin, *Trypho* 85). Luke however did not share their view and indeed did his best, especially in chs. 3, 4 and 19, to combat it.

For **of Nazareth** see on 2.22.

The word of command is simply **Walk**. This is expanded in some MSS.

7. He took him by the right hand and raised him up. Physical contact of this kind is common in miracle stories. **his feet and ankles**. It is true that the Greek words are used by doctors but they are not confined to medical books and therefore prove nothing about Luke's professional background.

8. He leapt up . . . stood . . . began to walk . . . went . . . walking . . . leaping: The verse is clumsy and repetitious, but this is hardly adequate ground for ascribing it to Lucan editing. *Leaping* may owe something to Isa. 35.6. It is not surprising that there is a good deal of textual variation.

The verse conveys the fact that the man was fully cured, conveys it (partly) in OT language, and adds that he praised God for his newly found health and accepted the company of his benefactors. This hardly proves that he became a Christian, though in view of v. 6 (*in the name of Jesus Christ*; cf. 4.12) Luke would no doubt think it probable that he would do so. Cf. 4.14.

into the Temple. As in v. 3, it is suggested that the Beautiful gate was an outer gate of the Temple.

9. all the people. For Luke's word see on 4.25. But here it means the Jerusalem crowd, especially those who at the time happened to be visiting the Temple. These will of course be mainly Jews; at 3.12 Peter can address them as *Men of Israel*.

10. The crowd recognized the man as the beggar who had been in the habit of sitting at the Beautiful gate. This meant that they recognized him as having received an astonishing cure. **they were filled with wonder and astonishment** – the usual reaction to a miracle. Luke is here writing up his story in conventional style, and is almost ready to introduce the speech for which he is preparing.

7. PETER'S MIRACLE SPEECH 3.11–26

11 While he was holding on to Peter and John all the people ran together to them at the portico called Solomon's Portico, full of amazement. 12 When Peter saw what was happening he addressed the crowd, 'Men of Israel, why are you astonished at this, and why do you gaze at us, as if by our own power or piety we had made him walk? 13 The God of Abraham, of Isaac, and of Jacob, the God of our fathers, has glorified his Servant Jesus, whom you handed over and denied in the presence of Pilate, when he had given judgment to release him. 14 You – of all people – denied the holy and righteous one, and asked that a man who was a murderer should be granted you as a favour. 15 You killed the author of life, whom God raised from the dead; we are his witnesses. 16 By faith in his name, his name made strong this man whom you see and know; the faith that comes through Jesus gave him this perfect health in the presence of you all. 17 And now, brothers, I know that you did it in ignorance, as also did your rulers; 18 but God in this way fulfilled the things he had announced beforehand by the mouth of all the prophets, namely, that his Christ should suffer. 19 Repent therefore, and turn, that your sins may be blotted out, 20 that there may come times of refreshment from the presence of the Lord, and that he may send the Christ who has been appointed for you, namely Jesus, 21 whom heaven must receive and keep until the times when all things are restored – times of which God spoke through the mouth of his holy prophets from the beginning. 22 Moses said, "The Lord your God will raise up a prophet for you from among your brothers, as he raised up me; you shall listen to him in all the things he shall speak to you. 23 And anyone who does not listen to that prophet shall be cut off from among the people." 24 And all the prophets, from Samuel and those who followed him, all those who spoke, also announced these days. 25 You are the sons of the prophets, and of the covenant which God made with your fathers when he said to Abraham, "And in thy seed shall all the families of the earth be blessed". 26 God raised up his Servant and sent him to you first, to bless you in turning each one of you from his wicked ways.'

Verse 11 is Luke's own editorial link connecting the sermon that follows with the miracle that precedes. It reduplicates the close of the story (3.10), adding only a reference to Solomon's Portico, which Luke knew from tradition to have been a place frequented by Christians. Solomon's Portico was within the Temple (but see the note on v. 11) and forms a suitable setting as the people's astonishment provides an occasion for an address which Luke has linked to the miracle by a few small additions, which also serve the purpose of preventing misunderstanding of the miracle itself. Luke's editorial procedures are discussed in the notes; the results of these discussions may be outlined here.

At the beginning of the Pentecost speech (2.15) a misunderstanding is corrected. Similarly v. 12, which shows several marks of Lucan style, was intended to show that the miracle could not be ascribed to Peter and John as holy men who by their own piety were able to force miraculous action out of God. This is an important Lucan theme. In 14.15 it takes a different form: Paul and Barnabas are not 'divine men'. In a Jewish context no one would express himself as the Lycaonians do in 14.11.

The special emphasis on Pilate's wish to release Jesus (v. 13) recalls the Lucan Passion Narrative. Verse 16 in its confused wording shows signs either of rewriting or of Lucan creation. In v. 18, *that his Christ should suffer*, is probably Lucan. In the Synoptic Gospels the usual expression is that *the Son of man* must suffer; but cf. Lk. 24.26, 46; Acts 26.23.

The rest of the speech is not characteristically Lucan. It repeats the essential points of the Pentecost address: Jesus has been wrongfully killed by the collusion of Jewish and Gentile authorities; God has raised him from the dead, and thus offers forgiveness and blessing to those who repent of their sins; all this has happened as the fulfilment of OT Scripture; further acts of fulfilment will bring about the consummation of the process of salvation which has now been initiated. A number of special points however are added. Of these a brief preliminary list will be given here.

(1) Jesus is described as God's servant (Greek, *pais*). This designation occurs in Acts only at 3.13, 26; 4.27, 30; also at 4.25 of David, which shows that there is no necessary reference to the Servant of Isaiah's Servant Songs.

(2) Pilate had decided to release Jesus. See Lk. 23.14–16, 22.

(3) In v. 14 Jesus is described as *the holy and righteous one*. These may be messianic titles; the latter occurs at 7.32, 22.14, the former nowhere else in Acts.

(4) In v. 15 Jesus is *the author of life*. Cf. 5.31; Heb. 2.10; 12.2.

(5) Verse 17 emphasizes the ignorance of the Jews as at least a partial excuse for their rejection of Jesus. Contrast 2.22.

(6) The expressions *times of refreshment* (v. 20) and *times when all things are restored* (v. 21) are without parallel in Acts. They lead to an emphasis on the parousia (though not an immediate parousia) not found in ch. 2.

(7) *Appointed* (v. 20) is not used elsewhere of the appointment of Jesus as Christ.

(8) In v. 23 Deut. 18.15, 16 is quoted; elsewhere in Acts only at 7.37.

(9) The threat of extirpation for all who will not hear the promised prophet (Deut. 18.19; Lev. 23.29) occurs only at v. 23.

(10) The promise to be fulfilled through *the seed of Abraham* (v. 25) occurs nowhere else in Acts; cf. Gal. 3.16, where the argument is different.

(11) In addition note the possibly liturgical background of *servant*; hints of a Joseph typology (a figure rejected and vindicated), the possible occurrence of Baptist tradition (vv. 19–21); the absence of any reference to Christian baptism.

It has been maintained that the speech bears witness to a very early stage of Christian belief in which Jesus was not held to have been the Messiah during his ministry nor to have become Messiah at his resurrection (cf. 2.36). He had been the prophetic forerunner of the Messiah, a forerunner who would in the end turn out to be the Messiah himself. Arguments for this view are as follows.

(1) Jesus is said to be the Servant of God; this suggests a prophet rather than the Messiah.

(2) He is said to be the prophet like Moses (v. 22).

(3) The *times when all things are restored* suggest the work of Elijah, the prophetic forerunner (Mal. 3.23; cf. Sirach 48.10).

(4) *The Christ who has been appointed for you* means (it is said) that Jesus has been designated Messiah but has not yet taken office.

Over against these points it may be said:

(1) The speech assumes the fulfilment of the OT as a whole, the coming of the Messiah himself, therefore, not only of a forerunner.

(2) There is a radical treatment of sin and evil; forgiveness is offered now.

(3) Those addressed (vv. 25, 26) are heirs of the covenanted salvation.

(4) Jesus is the unique 'seed of Abraham' (v. 25).

These matters will be discussed in detail below. See also, on Christology and eschatology, Introduction, pp. liv–lvii, lif.

11. all the people (the word as at 3.9; see the note) **ran together . . . at the portico called Solomon's Portico**. Peter, John, and the formerly lame man had entered the Temple (3.9); It follows that Solomon's Portico was within the Beautiful gate. The word *Stoa* (the transliteration may be preferred to Portico) 'is applied to various types of building with a roof supported by columns, but principally to a long open colonnade . . . It was employed especially in shrines and in the agora . . . The stoa was the general purpose building of the Greeks. It offered shelter from sun, wind, and rain. It could be used as council-chamber or court-house, market-hall or class-room; and also for informal conversation as in several Socratic dialogues' (R. E. Wycherley, *OCD* 1016). The position of this stoa is not known. The Old Uncial text has been translated here, the Western text puts the stoa outside the Beautiful gate. According to Josephus (*War* 5.184f.; *Ant.* 15.396–401; 20.220f.) it was on the eastern side of the Temple. The topography, and with it the textual problem, must be left in uncertainty.

12. Peter . . . addressed the crowd. The verb often means *to answer*, but it is used, especially in translation of Hebrew, to mean simply *to intervene* in speech. Here we may think of Peter as answering the question implied by the crowd's amazement and their mistaken supposition that Peter and John were themselves the sole cause of the cure.

Men of Israel. As at 2.22. A Jewish crowd would not think that the apostles were divine, but they might think of them, as of the 'Jewish charismatics', that they were men of pre-eminent piety, whose virtue gave them power with God. Simeon b. Shetah said to Honi the Circle-Maker, 'What shall I do to you? You importune God and he performs your will, as a son that importunes his father and he does his will, and of you Scripture says,' Prov. 23.25 (M. Taanith 3.8). The verse thus contains Lucan themes and Lucan constructions and stylistic features. It is probable that Luke wrote it to connect the speech, which he had from another source, with the miracle.

13. The God of Abraham, of Isaac, and of Jacob, the God of our fathers. The words have an OT ring; cf. Exod. 3.6, 15; Acts 7.32; and the first of the Eighteen Benedictions. Peter insists that the new message he is about to proclaim concerns no new deity but the

God of the OT. The OT reference becomes more precise with the words **has glorified his Servant Jesus**, which recall Isa. 52.13. This passage, the fourth 'Servant Song', goes on to describe the humiliation and suffering, followed by the vindication and glorification, of one described in Isa. 53.11 as *my* (that is, God's) *servant*. The extent to which the figure of the Suffering Servant appears in the NT and contributed to its Christology is disputed, but there is no doubt that the figure is alluded to here and in the context of suffering and exaltation. It would be mistaken to take the song of Isa. 52.13 – 53.12 as the only factor determining Luke's use of the word *servant* (Greek, *pais*). This word (which in Acts occurs only in chs. 3 and 4, and not at all in Isaiah 53) is also used of David (4.25), so that it must be taken as a royal title. It is applied to many OT figures. The Christian use seems to be a late first-century development. It may have been derived from Jewish prayers; it certainly found an early place in Christian liturgy (*Didache* 9.2f.; 10.2f.; 1 Clement 59.2–4, *Martyrdom of Polycarp* 14.1; 20.2; Barnabas 6.1; 9.2).

The exaltation of Jesus the Servant followed upon his rejection by the Jews. **you** is emphatic. You, of all men, handed over your own king. **when [Pilate] had given judgement to release him**. More strongly than Matthew or Mark, Luke emphasizes Pilate's reluctance to condemn and execute Jesus; see Lk. 23.4, 14, 15, 20, 22. Pontius Pilate was Roman governor of Judaea, AD 26–36.

The glorification of Jesus may consist in his resurrection and ascension, or in the fact that through him God cured the lame man. The Servant is associated with suffering and death, and the resurrection is mentioned explicitly in v. 15. But v. 12 suggests that 'not we but the glorified Jesus' performed the cure. It may well be that the source used by Luke saw the glorification of Jesus in the resurrection but that Luke, in adapting his source, saw the miracle as a token of Jesus' glory. Cf. v. 16. It may be right to see in this verse signs of a 'Joseph typology', see on 7.9f.

14. You, again emphatic, **denied the holy and righteous one**. There is much to be said for the view that the adjectives are not messianic but descriptive. This is reinforced by the contrasting description. Barabbas was **a man who was a murderer**. In addition however the adjectives may have conveyed some hint of messianic status. For *holy*; cf. Mk 1.24; Lk. 4.34; Jn 6.69; 1 Jn 2.20; Rev. 3.7. For *righteous*; cf. 7.52; 22.14. It is perhaps safe to say that the adjectives were chosen as conveying some hint of messianic status but mainly because of their moral content in contrast with the murderer.

You . . . asked that . . . a murderer should be granted to you as a favour. A papyrus of AD 85 contains some of the same wording: 'You were worthy to be scourged but I am granting you to the crowds as a favour.'

15. This verse forms with v. 14 a rhetorical unit of contrasting clauses.

You denied the holy and righteous one
    You asked for a murderer to be granted to you
You asked for a murderer to be granted to you
    You killed the author of life
You killed . . .
    the author of life
You killed the author of life
    God raised him from the dead

These contrasts arise partly out of the content of the verses but they suggest careful and skilful composition – a sharp contrast with the clumsiness of v. 16.

Jesus is described as **the author of life**. Luke's word is used sometimes for a *hero, founder and protector of a city*, sometimes for *first cause*. In Acts 5.31 (see the note) the meaning *founder, protector* is probably best, and this also fits the contrasts of the present verse. If the word is taken to mean *leader* it will be in the sense of leading the way *to life*. On the Christology of this speech see above, pp. 43f.; also Introduction, p. lvf.

We are his witnesses. Also possible is *We are witnesses of this fact*. Cf. 2.32. Each proposition implies the other. The statement of God's over-ruling of human sin and error may be intended to recall the story of Joseph.

16. This verse appears to be an insertion (v. 15 connects with v. 17) designed to show that as the miracle was not the work of Peter and John as 'divine men' neither was it due to the magical operation of the 'name'. The Greek of the verse is intolerably clumsy. The clumsiness has been explained as due to misreading of an original Aramaic. **His name made strong** could be put back into Aramaic as *taqqeph sh*[e]*meh*. With different pointing this could be read as *taqqiph sameh*, and translated *he made strong*. A better but still unsatisfactory suggestion is to follow those MSS that omit the preposition *by* at the beginning of v. 16 and connect that verse with v. 15: Of whom (or which) we are witnesses, and to the faith in his name. Perhaps the best suggestion is that Luke had two explanations of the miracle – 'The name has healed him, faith has healed him' – and combined them awkwardly. The verse is linguistically overloaded because Luke is introducing corrective material into it. He has combined the miracle story and the speech. After Peter's words in 3.6 he could hardly object to the proposition, **His name made strong this man**; hence his first addition, **By faith in his name**. Even this however was not sufficient, and v. 16b was added to make it clear that it was not the name but the faith accompanying – evoked by and directed towards – the name that saved. The faith in question is that of the apostles; the sick man was expecting money, not exercising faith.

17. And now. The speaker takes up his main point. He is leading up to v. 19, Repent! Peter's hearers may be to some extent excused: they did not know that they were killing the holy and innocent originator of life. He had been represented in a quite different light. Not only the common people but their **rulers** also showed their **ignorance**. Cf. Lk. 23.34; also 1 Tim. 1.13. For ignorance as a partial excuse in Acts see 13.27; 17.30; in the OT, Lev. 22.14.

18. God not only reversed your ignorant wickedness in putting Jesus to death by raising him from the dead, he actually used your folly as the means of fulfilling his own purpose which he had previously declared through all the prophets. This was not difficult, for his purpose was **that his Christ should suffer**. *Suffer* is used to include the suffering of death. This is a Lucan form of expression; it is also Lucan to predicate the suffering of the Messiah (not of the Son of man). The whole context speaks of the fulfilment of prophecy, and this points in the direction of Messiahship. This verse does not support the opinion that in Luke's view (or that of his source) Jesus was to become Messiah only in the future.

Luke asserts that God foretold through **all the prophets** that the Christ should suffer. He gives no reference, notwithstanding v. 13, to Isaiah 53 and the Suffering Servant.

19. Repent and turn: if the words are not synonyms (and in the LXX both translate the same Hebrew verb) repentance means turning from evil, turning is turning to good, or to God. The use of the two words is a means of emphasis. Repentance has two purposes, one expressed in v. 19b, the other in v. 20. The former is the immediate personal consequence. The sins of each penitent will be **blotted out**;

cf. Col. 2.14. Repentance has both personal and corporate aspects and is called for in the present, the blotting out of sins similarly is both personal and corporate, and in its personal aspect belongs to the present, the coming of the Messiah means corporate redemption in the future. These observations are necessary for the correct understanding of vv. 20, 21.

20. This verse raises two questions of great importance for the understanding of Luke's eschatology: the meaning of **times of refreshment** and of the phrase **who has been appointed for you**. It is helpful to take the latter list.

It has been maintained that the Greek participle translated here *who has been appointed* bears witness to a very early Christology according to which Jesus had not yet become Messiah but was predestined, appointed in advance, to be Messiah at the time of the parousia and judgement. Examination of the etymological derivation and of the use of the word (see 22.14; 26.16) does not confirm this interpretation. The (perfect) participle means that Jesus is in the condition of having been appointed (2.36 might suggest, at his resurrection; Lk. 2.11 says, earlier) Messiah, in which position he will act at the appropriate time.

From this conclusion we may turn back to *times* (plural) *of refreshment*. The plural alone is sufficient to show that the phrase is not a synonym for the sending of the Messiah at the time of the End, and it is consistent with this that *refreshment* suggests temporary relief rather than finality (cf. Exod. 8.11; Philo, *De Abrahamo* 152). Luke does not see the period that must (v. 21) intervene between the resurrection and the parousia as one of unrelieved gloom. There are repeated conversions; there are moments of collective inspiration; there are marvellous works of healing. All these come **from the presence of the Lord** and confirm the promise of final salvation.

21. Whom heaven must receive and keep. The one verb used in Greek can on occasion convey the sense of remaining where one is received. In Acts Jesus is received into heaven at the ascension (1.11); there he remains until the End. This will mean the *restoration*, the *return to its appointed state*, of the whole of God's creation. This recalls Malachi 3.22f., where God promises that he will send Elijah to restore the heart of father to son and the heart of a man to his neighbour. It has been said that Luke's noun (cognate with Malachi's verb) cannot have this meaning here. It is impossible that **all things God spoke through the mouth of his holy prophets** should be *restored*. The word must mean *establishment* in the sense of *fulfilment*. This argument is not convincing. The antecedent of the relative clause *of which God spoke* is not *all things* but **times**. Another, less probable, suggestion is that the genders of *all* and *which* may be masculine. The prophets spoke of and Christ brought about the restoration of the human race to the state in and for which it was created (cf. Rom. 11.32).

Through the mouth of his holy prophets. An OT expression, but Luke is more probably imitating the LXX than translating Hebrew or Aramaic.

22. Moses said. Deut. 18.15 (cf. Acts 7.37). It goes too far to speak of a typological representation of the eschatological period as a repetition of the times of Moses. Luke sees simply the fulfilment of a prophecy. Deut. 18.18, 19 is quoted at 4 Q Test 5–8 and may lie behind 1 QS 9.11, but these are not predictions of the coming of the Messiah. The Samaritans seem to have taken the passage as such a prediction. But in general the use of it is Jewish Christian rather than Jewish; cf. *Clementine Recognitions* 1.43.

23. The verse appears to be a combination of Deut. 18.19 with Lev. 23.29. Luke may have been quoting from memory; he may have been using a collection of *testimonia* in which the OT passages had already been combined. There may have been Hebrew collections of passages before the time of Christ. The verse supports the command of v. 22 with a severe threat in which it is not clear to what the word **people** refers. If it refers to Israel as the people of God the threat should mean that Jews who do not accept the messianic authority of Jesus not merely fail to become Christians but also cease to be what they have hitherto been, members of the people of God. The Jew who does not accept the Messiah ceases to be a member of Israel. He cannot be cut off from the *new* people, to which he has never belonged; he is cut off from the *old* people, which still exists, though only in order that it may become the new people. Whether Luke meant so much is doubtful. He probably thought the verse a powerful means of expressing in negative form what is positively stated in 4.12: salvation is to be had only in the name of Jesus Christ.

shall be cut off. See M. Kerithoth 1.1. This was a punishment carried out by God himself and thus distinct from all punishments inflicted by the community. It might take the form of premature or sudden death (cf. 5.1–11); but Luke probably has in mind what might be called excommunication.

24. This verse takes up v. 21. **All the prophets** spoke of the time when the messianic restoration would take place. After Moses came **Samuel** not only chronologically but as the greatest of the prophets.

The sentence seems to be a mixture of two constructions – another mark of inadequate revision, perhaps – but the reference to the successors of Samuel is clear enough. **all those who spoke** is here taken as adjectival to *all the prophets*; this is the only way to save Luke from the charge of writing an incomplete sentence. **these days** are the times just spoken of, the last days, of which the events of resurrection, ascension, and the gift of the Spirit mark the first.

25. All the prophets announced the coming days of salvation (v. 24), and **You are the sons of the prophets**; literally, for the persons addressed are of the same Hebrew stock, and in the sense that they are the heirs of the prophets, potentially the recipients of what the prophets foretold. Cf. 2.39. It is implied that if Gentiles are to be admitted to these blessings it will be subsequently and secondarily, by special arrangement; perhaps by the ordinary process of proselytization to Judaism. The question of a Gentile mission is not yet raised. See however the latter part of the verse, and v. 26.

The hearers are also **sons of the covenant**. As Jews, they are invited to share in the new covenant. This invitation is an inalienable right (cf. Rom. 11.29); but this is not the same as a right to the covenant itself.

Verse 25b is a conflation of Gen. 12.3; 18.18; 22.18. There is a somewhat similar conflation in Gal. 3.8, and it is possible that the passages (perhaps already conflated) were already to be found in a collection of OT texts. The word **families** is peculiar to Acts. It is possible that Luke took the word **seed** to refer to Christ, but his main thought is that Israel occupies a special place in God's purpose and receives the word of salvation before other nations. The promise to Abraham, however, is certainly taken to contain a promise that the blessing offered in the first instance to him and his family would be extended to non-Jews. The future promise, **shall be blessed**, can hardly mean anything less. Whether this is a correct rendering of the Hebrew is another question; probably it is not.

26. to you first. This implies that the offer of messianic salvation made to the Jews will be followed by another – to the Gentiles. Luke does not mean that there will be a subsequent sending of the Servant to the Gentiles. The second sending of the Messiah will be at the End (v. 20). It is the first sending, initially to and for the benefit of Jews, that will turn out to be of benefit to the Gentiles also. The question of a Gentile mission will be raised more than once in Acts, but for Luke it is not in principle a difficult question. It is God's intention to have a newly constituted people of which both the original heirs of the covenant and Gentiles, newly called through the Gospel, may be members. For both there is only one way into the inheritance: Jesus the Messiah.

God raised up his Servant could refer to the resurrection (cf. 13.33), but here, as it precedes the first sending of the Servant, it must mean that God brought him on the stage of history; cf. Deut. 18.15, 18; Judges 2.16.

For the use of *Servant* in Acts 3 and 4, see on v. 13. The content of the blessing that he brings is defined as **turning each one of you from your wicked ways**. *Turning* could be intransitive: *in that each of you turns from . . . Wicked ways* is not intended to differ from *sins* in v. 19.

The speech ends abruptly; the offer of salvation is implicit. There is no reference to the Holy Spirit or to baptism. This is not to say (notwithstanding the present participle in 4.1) that the speech is unfinished.

8. ARREST AND EXAMINATION OF PETER AND JOHN 4.1–22

**1 While they were speaking to the people, the priests and the
Captain of the Temple and the Sadducees came upon them, 2 vexed
because they were teaching the people and proclaiming in Jesus
the resurrection from the dead. 3 They laid hands upon them and
put them under guard until the next day; for it was already
evening. 4 But many of those who heard the word believed, and
the number of the men rose to about 5000.**

**5 On the next day their rulers and the elders and the scribes
were gathered together in Jerusalem, 6 with Annas the High Priest
and Caiaphas and John and Alexander and those who belonged
to the highpriestly clan. 7 They set them in the midst and inquired,
'By what power, or in what name, have you done this?' 8 Then
Peter, filled with the Holy Spirit, said to them, 'Rulers of the people
and elders, 9 if today we are being cross-examined about a good
deed done to a sick man, if you want to find out by what means he
has been cured, 10 then let it be known to all of you, and to all the
people of Israel, that it is in the name of Jesus Christ of Nazareth,
whom you crucified, whom God raised from the dead, that it is in
this name that this man stands before you fit and well. 11 He is the
stone, despised by you builders, who has become head of the
corner. 12 And in no other is there salvation, for there is no other
name under heaven and given to men by which we are to be saved.'**

**13 As they observed the boldness of Peter and John, and took
note of the fact that they were unlettered laymen, they were
astonished, and they recognized them as former companions of
Jesus; 14 and as they looked at the man who had been cured
standing with them they could find no reply. 15 They commanded
them to go out of the Council and discussed the matter with one
another. 16 They said, 'What are we to do with these men? For
that a manifest sign has been done by them is evident to all who
live in Jerusalem, and we cannot deny it. 17 But that it may spread
no further among the people, let us threaten them not to speak in
this name to a single person.' 18 They summoned them and ordered
them not to speak at all or teach in the name of Jesus. 19 Peter and
John answered and said to them, 'Whether it is right in the sight
of God to listen to you rather than to God, make up your own**

minds; [20] for we, for our part, cannot but speak the things that we have seen and heard.' [21] They repeated their threats and dismissed them because they could find no way in which they might punish them because of the crowd, for they were all glorifying God at what had happened; [22] for the man on whom this sign of healing had been done was more than forty years old.

Chapter 3 began with a miracle story to which Luke attached a specimen of Christian preaching, making at the same time a few narrative connections and explanatory points (especially 3.12, 16). He now returns to his narrative source which continues up to 4.31 and possibly into ch. 5. The opening words of ch. 4 link the fresh narrative material with the speech directly (*while they were speaking*), by Peter's proclamation of the resurrection and by the statement that many hearers believed. It appears however from v. 7 that it was the act of Peter and John that provoked the authorities rather than the speech. Luke is still combining narrative and discourse. There are a few Lucan expressions but for the most part Luke seems to have continued with the narrative source. Editorial work appears in that Peter and John are arrested for preaching the resurrection whereas in court the healing is inquired into, and in the recognition in v. 13 that Peter and John had been disciples of Jesus, a fact that was already known in v. 2.

Peter's reply to the Council (vv. 8–12) contains a brief version of the proclamation of Jesus as this appears in chs. 2, 3, 10, and 13. It may have been contained in the narrative source. The speech makes the points common to the early sermons. It points to Jesus, 'whom you crucified, whom God raised from the dead'. The language of Scripture is used in v. 11, which thus asserts the fulfilment of prophecy. The offer of salvation is made in v. 12, with the warning that salvation is to be had nowhere else. The boldness of the apostles is noted (v. 13), but the climax of the paragraph is to be found in vv. 19 and 20, where it is asserted that official Judaism, so far from being the mouthpiece of God, stands over against him, so that men must choose which of the two they will obey. Luke makes it clear that Christianity is not Judaism; at least it is not the Judaism of those who officially represent Judaism. Luke uses this characteristic story of outstanding Christians to restate the content of the Gospel, and to make clear the distinction between the apostles and their supporters, the Jewish authorities, and the common people.

See further on 4.23–31, which continues the present story.

1. **While they were speaking.** No words are attributed to John, who seems to be a secondary addition to the story; cf. 3.1, 4. Characteristically Luke represents the speech as unfinished; cf. 7.54; 10.44; 17.32; 22.22; 26.24. The interest of the narrative is thereby increased, but the speech is in fact complete, and Luke takes up the narrative thread.

The speech was made in Solomon's Portico; hence the arrival of the priests and of the Captain of the Temple. The latter is probably the *s*[e]*gan hakkoh*[a]*nim*, possibly one of his inferiors, the Man of the Temple Hill or the Man of the Sanctuary. These regulated the cultus, the priests, and the Temple police. **the Sadducees**. See an up-to-date account, with bibliography, in *NS* 2.404–14. Their chief strength was in the lay nobility; many but not all priests shared their opinions.

2. **they were teaching . . . proclaiming**. No difference is intended between the two verbs. The authorities were **vexed because they were teaching . . . the people** and in their teaching **proclaiming . . .**

proclaiming in Jesus the resurrection from the dead. If the words *in Jesus* are omitted there is no difficulty. Peter and John were proclaiming, as any Pharisee would, that at the time of the End there would be a rising from the world of the dead of at least some of those who had died. It would be understood that Sadducees should object. But how is *in Jesus* to be understood? The preposition may be instrumental: They proclaimed *by means of* (the story of) *Jesus the resurrection*. Alternatively, the meaning may be *in the case of Jesus*; this might include the thought that in the case of Jesus the ultimate resurrection had (representatively) taken place. In fact Luke's language loses clarity because he tries to say several things in one sentence. These are

1. The Sadducees were annoyed because the apostles were affirming what they denied.
2. The apostles now associated belief in the resurrection with the story of Jesus.
3. The resurrection of Jesus set the seal on his unique relation with God.

3. **put them under guard**, took them into custody. An alternative possibility is, *put them in prison*.

evening. Peter and John were going into the Temple at about 3 p.m. (3.1). A miracle took place, they went into the Temple, a crowd assembled, a speech was delivered, report of this spread to the authorities. Luke might well deduce that evening had now come.

4. Postponement of the trial till the following day makes it easy for Luke to insert a comment on the further growth of the believing community. For **hearing the word**; cf. 2.37 (also 2.41). In the present verse *hearing* is not the *hearing of faith*, since **many** (not all) **of those who** (physically) **heard believed** that is, became believers. There is no reference to baptism; cf. 2.41. The theme of expansion runs through Acts; see 2.47; 5.14; 6.1, 7; 8.6, 12; 9.31, 35, 42; 11.21, 24; 12.24; 13.48, 49; 14.1, 21; 16.5(14f.); 17.4, 11f., 34; 18.8, 10; 19.10, 20; 21.20. **men**: The word is the normal Greek word for adult males. There is no passage in Acts where it can be shown to include women, and in some we have *men and women*. The number 5,000 may therefore have to be increased by a number of women. There could have been as many as 5,000 men who had had some sympathy with Jesus and were persuaded by spiritual phenomena and miracles; but we cannot suppose that the church at this time took much trouble over statistics.

5. The verse begins with a construction that reflects, probably by way of the LXX, a Hebrew idiom. It leads to grammatical confusion in v. 6.

their rulers and the elders and the scribes. *Their* should refer to the 5,000 new converts but clearly means *the Jews*. For the *rulers* see 3.17. The three groups represent correctly what appears to have been the constitution of the Sanhedrin in the Roman period. See *NS* 2.210–18. The Mishnah (M. Sanhedrin 4.4) reflects conditions after AD 70. At 4.23 we have *chief priests* instead of *rulers*, but referring probably to the same group. They were members of high-priestly families, or leading priests. *Elders* might be priests or laymen. *Scribes* were rabbinic scholars, mostly Pharisees, who at this period were finding their way into what had previously been a predominantly Sadducean assembly.

These **were gathered together** – in the *lishkath haggazith*, the Store Chamber of the Temple (Josephus, *War* 5.144). There is a tradition that forty years before the fall of Jerusalem (and thus about the time of the crucifixion) meetings were transferred to the *ḥanuth* or *ḥanuyyoth*, *shop* or *shops* (*bazaar*).

Jerusalem may be mentioned explicitly as the heart of the old religion now confronted by its fulfilment.

6. The construction changes (see on v. 5) as Luke lists some prominent members of the Sanhedrin.

Annas the High Priest and Caiaphas. Luke is right in thinking that before the fall of Jerusalem the president of the Sanhedrin was the High Priest, wrong in thinking that this was Annas. Annas was High Priest AD 6–15; Caiaphas was High Priest AD 18–36. According to Jn 18.13 he was Annas' son-in-law. Luke's mistake may be explained by the fact that Annas continued to be an influential person; in addition to his son-in-law Caiaphas five of his sons became in turn High Priest. Indeed, some Jews may have maintained that he was still the true High Priest; the Romans who deposed him had no right to act in such a matter.

John and Alexander cannot be identified. For *John* some Western authorities read Jonathan; this could be a son of Annas who became High Priest in AD 37.

those who belonged to the highpriestly clan. Cf. the *rulers* in v. 5; 'The Captain of the Temple . . . the leader of the weekly course of priests, whichever course was on duty, and the leaders of the four to nine daily courses of this week . . . the seven permanent Temple overseers, to which belonged the four chief Levites . . . . three permanent Temple treasurers and their colleagues. The chief priests permanently employed at the Temple formed a definite body who had jurisdiction over the priesthood and whose members had seats and votes on the council' (Jeremias, *Jerusalem* 180). Appointments in the Temple were marked by nepotism.

7. in the midst may be used quite generally; but the 'Sanhedrin was arranged like the half of a round threshing floor so that they all might see one another' (M. Sanhedrin 4.3). In this setting *in the midst* would have a precise sense. Interest moves from resurrection (v. 2) to the miracle (ch. 3).

For **power** see 1.8; 3.12; for **name**, 3.6, 16. *Power* is supernatural force, capable of curing disease, *name* links the force with a person. The answer to the question is given in v. 10.

You and **this** are juxtaposed in Greek, emphasizing both. 'have men like you done such a thing as this?'

8. Peter. John drops out of the story, returning at v. 13.

Filled with the Holy Spirit. Peter had already been filled with the Spirit at 2.4. It is unlikely that Luke would be aware of any clash, which (if such it is) could be explained by the use of a new source. Luke is no doubt thinking of the promise of Lk. 12.12, fulfilled afresh at every time of need.

Rulers of the people and elders. Cf. v. 5 and 3.17. See also 23.5, quoting Exod. 22.27. Peter addresses the Sanhedrin respectfully; he speaks as a Jew to the leaders of the Jewish community.

9. If we are being cross-examined – a legal term, calling for a stronger translation than *examined*. Cf. 1 Cor. 9.3. The word is used of magistrates preparing rather than trying a case; this is suitable to the present context.

By what means, literally, *In whom* or *In what. In* has probably an instrumental sense, and the relative is better taken as neuter.

He has been cured could be translated, *He has been saved.* The word is used by Luke in both religious and secular senses, though the two come close together, especially in the present paragraph (see on v. 12), and the secular sense helps to establish the meaning of the verb when used in religious contexts. Man, who is spiritually lame and unable to act in the way it was intended that he should, is so restored as to be able to move and act freely.

10. Peter wishes the whole people to know his answer to the question. Power has been released through invocation of the name of Jesus.

whom you crucified, whom God raised from the dead: a standard formula in Acts (2. 23f., 36; 3.13–15; 4.27f.; 10.39f.; 13.27–31). The formulation recalls Gen. 50.20 in the story of Joseph, which is taken up by Stephen (7.9–16). The importance of the parallel is less than some suppose. It is fair to observe (1) that neither Stephen nor Peter points out the analogy, and (2) that if the analogy is in mind we are presented with the story of Jesus in the form of a tale with a happy ending: Joseph suffered, but it all came right in the end; Jesus was crucified, but God overcame even this disaster. There is little or nothing to suggest that the crucifixion was itself a victory, or that the death of Jesus was for our sins. This is as far as it goes a correct observation of Luke's simple theology, but it does not go quite far enough. See Introduction, p. lvi.

in this name; literally, *in this*, possibly *in* (or *by*) *this person.*

11. Peter assumes that his hearers (Luke that his readers) will detect the allusion to Ps. 118(117).22. The sentence is adapted to the flow of Peter's argument. It was familiar in early Christian argument and debate (Mt. 21.42; Mk 1.10; Lk. 20.17; 1 Peter 2.7; Barnabas

6.4), but it is surprising that Peter does not explicitly claim the support of the OT.

Head of the corner. The probable meaning is *coping-stone*, but the precise sense is not important. The despised stone has come to occupy the position of greatest prominence and honour.

12. in no other, probably *person* rather than *name*, which come in the next clause. *in no other person*, because *there is no other name . . .*

salvation, a 'key concept in the theology of Luke' (Marshall). Cf. v. 9, where the word is used for deliverance from physical ill and 27.20 where it means deliverance from shipwreck in a storm at sea. The theological sense of the word is to be understood by asking from what theological distress or disability or danger, corresponding to lameness or drowning, man needs to be delivered. See 2.40; those who are saved are saved from belonging to this perverse generation and sharing its fate; they are no longer perverse, and they will not experience the punishment of perversity. For the positive side of this see 2.47; the saved are added to a common stock and share a common life. Thus the primary meaning of salvation is detachment from the world of the unbelieving and from disbelief and attachment to the people of God of the last days.

This salvation is **in** Jesus. *in* is not used as in the Pauline *in Christ*, but has essentially an instrumental sense.

Believing is often connected with baptism, but not here, and it is a mistake to add baptism as if it were necessarily presupposed. Too narrow a baptismal interpretation of this verse leads to the notion that the name itself, once invoked, is in some way automatically effective; and Luke is at pains to show that this is not so (3.16; 19.13–16; cf. 8.14–17; 18.24–28).

no other name offers salvation. **under heaven** is used like the English *under the sun*.

given to men, literally, *among men*, a surprising expression. Perhaps *name* is moving in the direction of *person* (as at 1.15). Jesus was not a useful commodity given to men but a person who lived among them as the agent of God's salvation.

13. As they observed the boldness of Peter and John. *Boldness*, and its cognate verb, *to speak or act with boldness*, are common and important in Acts (2.29; 4.13, 29, 31; 9.27, 28; 13.46; 14.3; 18.26; 19.8; 26.26; 28.31). The idea originated in Greek political life with the fundamental meaning of declaring the whole truth, without fear or favour. Such fearless freedom the apostles exercised, and the council, observing this, took note that **they were unlettered laymen**. *Layman* is in the first instance the *private man* who stands over against the state (the *res publica*); hence the *plebeian,* hence the *unskilled person* who stands over against the expert in any art, the *layman*. Peter and John were (from the legal point of view), *laymen*, conducting their own defence.

Justin, *1 Apology* 39, may show knowledge of this verse: the Twelve who went out from Jerusalem into the world were laymen, not able to speak. Cf. Origen, *Contra Celsum* 1.62; *Clementine Recognitions* 1.62.

14. they could find no reply. The word used occurs in the promise of Lk. 21.15.

15. discussed – a Lucan word; there may have been Lucan rewriting here, but the exclusion of the disciples form the Court's private discussion of their case is a natural part of the narrative.

16. What are we to do with these men? By their rejection of Jesus the authorities feel themselves committed to the rejection of his followers, but the miracle has put them in an impossible position. Action against those responsible for it would be very unpopular.

17. But that it may spread no further among the people. The past must be left alone; the future may be secured. It is the Christian movement, which must be brought to an end; possibly simply, publicity for the sign. Threats may achieve this goal.

18. not to speak at all or teach. The tense of the verbs in Greek implies that they are to stop what they have hitherto been doing. The two verbs may be regarded as mutually reinforcing synonyms. If they are to be distinguished they will mean that the Council in seeking to forbid both public proclamation, such as we have seen exemplified in chs. 2 and 3, and the private teaching of individuals and small groups. Both activities are practised in the name of Jesus, and there is nothing to suggest that they differ in content as well as in setting.

19. listen to you rather than to God. *Listen to* is perhaps the best way of conveying the sense of hear and obey which the verb *hear* often includes in Hebrew. A Semitism has been found in the exclusive use of *than* ('we must obey God, not man'), but it is hard to maintain this in view of the famous saying of Socrates (Plato, *Apology* 29d), 'I will obey God rather than you' (the *rather than* construction is the same in Plato as here, and in 5.29). The words of Socrates had become proverbial, and were adopted in Hellenistic Judaism; cf. also 1 Sam. 15.22f.; Jer. 7.22f.; 2 Macc. 7.2; 4 Macc. 15.16–21.

It was open to the Council to reply, How should God issue commands to a Jew if not through the highest authority in Israel? Surely the Jewish layman will obey God by obeying the Council, as it interprets Torah. This in turn would invite reply.

20. we for our part (the pronoun *we* is emphatic), **cannot but speak the things that we have seen and heard**. Speak: present infinitive, as in v. 18; We cannot stop speaking. Cf. Amos 3.8. By the things that they had seen and heard Peter and John refer not to the miracle but to the crucifixion and resurrection (of which they were appointed witnesses) and the teaching of Jesus. To them, these constituted the word and command of God.

21. There is nothing the Council can do but renew the threats of vv. 17, 18. Punishment was impossible **because of the crowd**. The crowd **were all glorifying God at what had happened**, and would not have tolerated punishment for those who were responsible for it. It is also possible that the Council may have abstained from punishment on the ground that Peter and John were unlettered laymen (v. 13), who therefore could not be expected to know in advance the consequences of their actions; they could be punished only if, after the legal position had been explained, they repeated their offence. This legal point has been used in the discussion of Luke's sources (see Introduction, p. xxxi), but Luke himself shows no awareness of it. According to Luke, it is fear of the crowd's reaction that motivates the Council.

22. the man . . . was more than forty years old. It has been suggested that this verse was originally the close of the narrative of 3.1–10. The man's mature age makes the cure particularly striking, but Luke cannot have intended the logical consequence (note **for**) of his words – that the crowd would not have been glorifying God had the man been only twenty. This must be regarded as an example of inadequately revised language.

9. RETURN OF PETER AND JOHN 4.23–31

**23 When they had been released they came to their own people
and reported what the chief priests and elders had said to them.
24 They, when they heard it, together lifted up their voice to God
and said, 'Master, thou who didst make heaven and earth and
sea, and all the things that are in them, 25 who, by the mouth of
our father David, thy servant, through the Holy Spirit, didst say,
Why did the Gentiles behave insolently and the peoples make
vain plans? 26 The kings of the earth stood there and the rulers
were gathered together against the Lord and against his Christ.
27 For of a truth in this city Herod and Pontius Pilate, with the
Gentiles and peoples of Israel, were gathered together against
thy holy Servant Jesus, whom thou didst anoint, 28 to do the things
which thy hand and thy counsel foreordained should happen.
29 And now, Lord, look upon their threats, and grant thy servants
to speak thy word with all boldness, 30 as thou stretchest out thy
hand for healing and signs and portents happen through the name
of thy holy Servant Jesus.' 31 And when they had made their
prayer, the place in which they were assembled was shaken, and
they were all filled with the Holy Spirit and continued to speak
the word of God with boldness.**

Peter and John may have seemed (3.1 – 4.22) to have been acting on their own, but in truth they were acting in relation to and on behalf of their own people, to whom they now return. After reporting, they join the rest in a prayer which restates their (Luke's) view of the matter. Their God is the God of the OT and of Judaism, the Creator (v. 24), and the Lord of history (v. 25b; v. 26, quoting Ps. 2.1, 2; v. 27, recalling the gospel story). The crucified Jesus is now alive and at work (vv. 28–30); the gift of the Spirit is renewed (v. 31).

The use of the word Servant (v. 27) links this paragraph with those that precede it, and it is made clear that the word does not in itself mean Messiah (the Servant is anointed to become Messiah), and is not exclusively connected with Isaiah 53, since it is used (v. 25) of David. It is disputed whether Luke himself composed the prayer or derived it from the liturgical practice of the church. The answer probably lies between these alternatives. The appeal to God as Creator and the use of Scripture recall the prayer of 1 Clement 59–61; the

Christological use of the term Servant belongs to the late first century. Luke probably composed the prayer, based on current use but adapted to the circumstances. It forms a fitting climax to the story that begins at 3.1. It is affirmed that Peter and John did well to cure a sick man; that their proclamation of God's word was as valid as it was effective; and that the work of the church will go forward with God's blessing. An interest in Christian origins was combined with a desire, by the example of the past, to comfort, encourage, and advise the church of Luke's own day.

23. When they had been released. See 4.21. **they came to their own people**. Luke's phrase often refers to members of one's own family, expanding to fellow countrymen, fellow soldiers in an army; here of course to fellow Christians. Cf. 12.12; 24.23. It is not made explicit whether we are to think of the other ten apostles, of the 120 (1.15), or of the 5,000 (4.4). Irenaeus, *Adversus Haereses* 3.12.5, already interprets 'to the church'. Luke probably means the community as a whole, but not the whole of it; probably of a church gathering such as he himself knew, able to meet in a private house.

the chief priests and elders. Cf. 4.5, 6. Peter and John reported what they had said, but evidently with no intention of obeying it.

24. together: see on 1.14. **lifted up their voice**: see on 2.14. It is not quite correct to say that vv. 24b–28 have nothing to do with the situation: the church in any distressful situation does well to recall God as Creator and Lord of history. It may however be true that in these opening verses Luke is recalling familiar expressions.

Master. A relatively uncommon word for God; see Lk. 2.29; 2 Tim. 2.21; 2 Peter 2.1; Jude 4; Rev. 6.10. It is seldom used in the LXX, never in the Psalms. Not used by Paul, it seems to have been introduced into Christian liturgical use towards the end of the first century (e.g. *Didache* 10.3, 1 Clement 59.4; 60.3; 61.1, 2). The prayer that follows belongs to that setting; Luke composed it, using words and phrases that were familiar. **thou who didst make heaven and earth and sea.** Cf. Ps. 146(145).6. For the theme of creation in early Christian prayer see *Didache* 10.3, 1 Clement 59.4, Justin, *Trypho* 41, 1 *Apology* 65.

25. In the opening part of the verse there is much textual confusion, which is probably due to the fact that what appears to be the oldest Greek text is practically incapable of analysis or translation. This has been explained as due to Luke's error in reading the original Aramaic; he mistook *hi'* for *hu'*. This explanation has now been almost universally, and rightly, abandoned. Some think of a primitive textual corruption, or of a combination of different ways of introducing the quotation. Fortunately the sense of the clause is not in doubt. Three things are affirmed. (1) God said (what follows); (2) He said it through the Holy Spirit; (3) He said it by the agency of David (as the author of the Psalter).

our father David, thy servant. *Servant* is not exclusively Christological, or necessarily drawn from Isaiah 53.

The prayer recalls the prayer of Hezekiah (Isa. 37.16–20), and opens with the quotation of Ps. 2, 2.1 in v. 25b, 2.2 in v. 26. Each verse agrees exactly with the LXX. The same two verses are quoted at the end of the first column of 4 QFlor; unfortunately only fragments of the beginning of column 2 are preserved, but the use of the Psalm seems to be similar to Luke's. The true members of Israel are attacked by Gentiles. Probably there is Palestinian material in the background of Acts, but the use of the LXX and the reference in v. 27 to Luke's gospel must be borne in mind.

Peoples (plural) is strange here as it is in v. 27 (with Israel). It is due to exact following of the LXX text. **behave insolently** renders Luke's Greek; it is not a good rendering of the Hebrew. **vain plans**: vain because inevitably it is the Lord's will that will be done.

26. The kings of the earth. The Psalm generalizes. For Luke they are Herod and Pontius Pilate. In this verse **the Lord** is clearly distinguished from **his Christ**. It is mistaken to suppose that whenever *Lord* is used of *Christ* he is being identified with the God of the OT.

27. gathered together introduces Luke's interpretation of the Psalm. Neither Herod nor Pontius Pilate was a king, though both were rulers. Luke presumably thought of Herod as, like Pilate, a Gentile. For Herod see Lk. 3.1; and *NS* 1.340–53. For Jesus as *servant* see on 3.13; the word is not equivalent to Messiah, for God **anointed** him and thus made him Messiah (the Anointed One). Cf. 2.36 and especially 10.38. It is Luke only (Lk. 23.12) who reports the reconciliation of Herod and Pilate at the time of the crucifixion. Did he know of the reconciliation and invoke Psalm 2 to show that God himself had determined it? Did he know the Psalm as a messianic prophecy and invent a fulfilment? In the Gospel there is no reference to the Psalm; Luke would hardly invent a fulfilment and fail to mention what was being fulfilled. But there is no other evidence for a quarrel and reconciliation. Lk. 8.3 and Acts 13.1 hint that Luke may have had access to the Herod family, and it may be that he heard a story about Herod and Pilate which reflection finally led him to connect with Psalm 2.

28. Herod and Pilate came together in order to do what they thought fit, but they were in fact tools in the hand of God who used them to carry out his own purposes. **thy hand** – as at 4.30; 11.21; 13.11, but the image is not peculiar to Luke or indeed to the Bible. **thy counsel** is a Lucan characteristic.

29. And now. The prayer passes from the past to the future. This break was hardly to be avoided and does not mean that Luke is turning from liturgical quotation to his own composition. He has used in the main traditional Christology to construct his own prayer throughout.

For **look upon** cf. Lk. 1.25; for **threats**, 4.17, 21; for **boldness**, see on 2.29. The **word** of God (or, of the Lord) is in Acts a very common term for the Gospel proclaimed by Christian preachers: 4.29, 31; 6.2, 7; 8.14, 25; 11.1; 12.24; 13.5, 7, 44, 46, 48, 49; 15.35, 36; 16.32; 17.13, 18.11; 19.10, 20; in other passages *word* is used without pronoun or divine name.

30. Preaching and miracle-working are both to be continued. God's work in **healing** has the effect of **signs and portents**, done through the **name** of Jesus. The occurrence of *name* in a prayer implies that the church has no (magical) control over it and its effectiveness.

31. This verse brings to an end the first part of a major section, beginning at 2.1, that Luke composed with care. It narrows Luke's intention to say that its purpose was to comfort persecuted Christians; this intention, if present, was subordinate to that of painting an impressive picture of Christian beginnings. The section ends as it began, with the gift of the Spirit, whose presence is shown by physical portents, here **the place was shaken**; cf. Ps. 114.7; Isa. 2.19, 21 – but there are extra-biblical parallels too. **they were filled with the Holy Spirit** – all who were present; see on v. 23. There is no ground for thinking that only apostles are intended. **with boldness**: see on v. 29. Gifts such as speaking with tongues may be included here, but not to the exclusion of normal speech.

10. SHARING AND WITNESSING COMMUNITY 4.32–35

32 The whole company of those who had become believers had one heart and one soul, and not even one of them would say that any of the things that belonged to him was his own, but they held all things in common. 33 And with great power the apostles bore testimony to the resurrection of the Lord Jesus, and great grace was upon them all. 34 Nor was anyone in want among them, for those who were owners of lands or houses would sell them and bring the price of the things that had been sold 35 and they would lay them at the apostles' feet, and distribution was made to each one, as anyone from time to time had need.

Luke marks a second stage in the development of his story by a second summary passage. Cf. 2.41–47; the same points are made, with emphasis on the sharing of goods and the care of the poor, but reference to common Christian meals is omitted. Apostolic testimony to the resurrection of Jesus is included. The picture of the church is an idealized generalization; a serious exception will appear in 5.1–11. Luke had in the stories of Barnabas and of Ananias and Sapphira ground for thinking that members of the community disposed of their possessions in the common interest and used this information as part of his picture of the church when the church was at its best. He provides his readers with a good example, but does not suggest or hint that church members ought at all times to dispose of their capital assets, and it is clear from the rest of the book that they did not do so. In this respect Luke's account differs widely from the rule of Qumran.

That Luke's account is idealized does not mean that it has no foundation in fact. The teaching and example of Jesus, the problems of Galileans living in Jerusalem, the example of the Pharisees and of Qumran, eschatological expectation, together with precedents outside Judaism – these may all have contributed to spontaneous sharing.

32. There are several features of Lucan style, and a close parallel with 2.44, 45. This suggests that Luke is using familiar material to construct a summary passage, which he considered desirable at this point. Some see the Shemaʿ as supplying the language and thought here, others a mixture of OT language (*one heart and soul*) with the Greek proverb, 'Friends have all things in common'. It is worth noting that the combination is to be found in Aristotle: 'the proverbs . . .

"one soul" and "property of friends is common"' (*Nicomachean Ethics* 98 (1168b)).

33. The apostles had been promised **power** (1.8) for their work; this could be manifested in miracles (2.22; 3.12; 4.7), but here is expressed in powerful, convincing speech – or possibly in both.

great grace was upon them all. It is not clear whether *grace* is used here in the sense that it has at 2.47 (*favour* with all the people) or denotes the active favour of God, who approves of what the apostles are doing and encourages and helps their work. The parallel in Lk. 2.40 and the absolute use of *grace* lend greater probability to the latter view. *Upon them all*: all the apostles or all the Christians? In view of vv. 32, 34, probably the latter, though if v. 33 is drawn from a source the source may have had the apostles only in mind.

34. Nor was anyone in want among them; *in want* suggests the fulfilment of Deut. 15.4. 6.1 suggests some breakdown in the arrangements; 5.1–11 another kind of breakdown. Clearly Luke is presenting an ideal picture. This persists in the second half of the verse: **those who were owners of lands or houses would sell them**. The word *them* is not expressed in Greek. It would be possible to suppose that Luke's meaning was that property-owners sold *some of* their possessions, but it is probable that Luke, correctly or incorrectly, wishes to describe a great movement of generosity which could be spoilt only by the meanness and deceitfulness of 5.1–11.

35. Imperfect tenses are used in **bring** (v. 34) and in **lay** and **distribution was made** in order to describe a regular practice of which the apostles continued to be the administrators until the new appointments of 6.2–6. To *lay things at a person's feet* seems to be a Lucanism, mainly in this context (4.37; 5.2; 7.58).

as anyone from time to time had need, the same words as in 2.45. It is possible that Luke is using a source that repeated itself or that he is using the same source twice; it is more probable that the phrase is his own (or taken by him from current use) and that he is punctuating his narrative from time to time with summaries that he himself constructed. See pp. 32f.

11. AN EXAMPLE: BARNABAS 4.36, 37

**36 Joseph, who was named by the apostles Barnabas (which is translated 'Son of Exhortation'), a Levite, a Cypriote by birth,
37 since he owned a piece of land, sold it, and brought the money and laid it at the apostles' feet.**

The practice of selling one's property and devoting the proceeds to the common good is illustrated by the story of Barnabas, a person who is mentioned elsewhere as, for a time, a companion of Paul's (9.27; 11.22, 30; 12.25; 13; 14; 15.2, 12, 22, 30, 35). The relation between them comes to an end in 15.36–41. If therefore Luke (or the author of a source used by him) belonged to the Pauline group he may have had sufficient contact with Barnabas to have learned what is here described. The contact may have come by way of Antiochene tradition.

In Acts as it stands the story of Barnabas illustrates the general statements of 4.32–35 (cf. 2.44, 45); in fact Luke probably constructed his summaries on the basis of traditions such as this one about Barnabas.

This paragraph, taken with 5.1–11, shows that the sale of property and sharing of the proceeds was in fact not a universal practice; if it had been there would have been no point in singling out Barnabas for special mention. Wholesale community of goods must be regarded as Luke's idealizing generalization of what was done by some.

Some take Barnabas to have been a Diaspora, Hellenistic Jew. In fact he was, according to Acts, a Hebrew (6.1). He was an early member of the Jerusalem church; though not one of the Twelve he was trusted by them so that they accepted Paul on his recommendation (9.27), and used him as an accredited inspector in Antioch (11.22).

36. Joseph ... **Barnabas** is always in the NT referred to as Barnabas. For double names see on 1.23. The name Barnabas is Semitic (*Bar* is Aramaic *son of*). **Exhortation** is a probable, not a certain, rendering. The word can be used for encouragement, exhortation – a sermon – given in a synagogue service (13.45). At 15.31 it could mean *comfort*. The cognate verb can mean *to exhort* (e.g. 2.40; 11.23; 14.22); it may mean *to comfort* (16.40; 20.12). It is probable that the noun here means *exhortation*, and that *son of exhortation* means *preacher*. The story in Acts is in accord with this.

How this was derived from the Aramaic that must have accompanied *Bar* is not clear. There is no better suggestion than *n[e]biyya* (*prophet*) or *n[e]bi'utha* (*prophecy*). If the name means *Son of comfort* it has the same meaning as Manaen (13.1), and there is the possibility of confusion at Antioch.

Barnabas was **a Levite**. On Levites see *NS* 2.250–6, 284–7. According to Num. 18.20; Deut. 10.9 a Levite should not have owned an estate. For **Cyprus** see on 13.4; it is possible that the island was chosen as a field for evangelism because it was familiar to Barnabas.

37. The language of this verse is similar to that of 4.34f.

12. A NEGATIVE EXAMPLE: ANANIAS AND SAPPHIRA 5.1–11

[1] A man, Ananias by name, together with his wife Sapphira, sold a property [2] and kept back part of the price. His wife was privy to this. He brought part of the price and laid it at the apostles' feet. [3] Peter said, 'Ananias, why has Satan put it into your heart to deceive the Holy Spirit and keep back some of the price of the land? [4] While it remained did it not remain yours? And when it had been sold was it not under your authority? Why did you plan this act? You lied not to men but to God.' [5] When Ananias heard these words he fell down and expired, and great fear came upon all those who heard of it. [6] The young men rose up, prepared his body for burial, carried him out, and buried him. [7] There was an interval of about three hours; then his wife came in, not knowing what had happened. [8] Peter said to her, 'Tell me, did you sell the land for so much?' 'Yes,' she said, 'for so much.' [9] Peter said to her, 'Why did you agree to tempt the Spirit of the Lord? Behold, the feet of those who buried your husband are at the door, and they will carry you out.' [10] Immediately she fell at his feet and expired. The young men came in and found her dead. They carried her out and buried her beside her husband. [11] Great fear came upon the whole church and upon all those who heard these things.

At first sight, this paragraph forms a pair with the preceding one (4.36, 37). Barnabas provides a good example of generous care for the poor, Ananias and Sapphira provide a bad one. Luke probably intended the story to be taken in this way, but analysis of the narrative shows that the matter is not so simple. Ananias and Sapphira did make provision for the poor. True, they could have given more generously, but they are blamed not for avarice but for deceit. If the story were abstracted from its context we should probably say that it was intended to teach (1) the wickedness and danger of attempting to deceive God, and (2) the supernatural power, insight, and authority of Peter. Luke took a primitive story and adapted it for his own purpose. It is to be noted that Luke does not say that Peter killed Ananias and Sapphira and does not use the opportunity of representing Peter as a 'divine man' Peter does not say, 'You have lied to *me*'.

This shows that though Luke thinks of Peter as at this stage the leading member of the one Christian community he does not think of him as embodying that community in himself.

What was the origin of the story? There are OT parallels; see especially Leviticus 10; Joshua 7; 1 Kings 14. It has been suggested that it originated in the early deaths of two church members. Through death (it was believed) they would miss the parousia and the kingdom; they must therefore have done something exceptionally wicked. There may be an analogy with Qumran: only entry to the inner circle called for renunciation of all property. Ananias and Sapphira had tried to get the best seats at the cheaper price. It is probably enough to say that Luke used a traditional story to show that deceit does not pay.

1. Ananias (the Hebrew name of Shadrach, Dan. 1.6; 3.13) is introduced in a way that has parallels in the OT (e.g. Job 1.1). The Hebrew name, borne by several Tannaim and Amoraim, means *The Lord is gracious*, alternatively, with a different spelling (Neh. 3.23), *The Lord hears*. A more correct spelling would be Hananias, but there is little point in abandoning the familiar form. Another Ananias appears in the narrative of Paul's conversion (9.10–17; 22.12), and a third as High Priest (23.2; 24.1). The present Ananias cannot be identified, though the earliest among the Tannaim was Captain of the Temple (see on 4.1), and thus lived before AD 70. The name **Sapphira** is the feminine of a Hebrew adjective meaning *beautiful*. Inscriptions demonstrate the use of the name in Jerusalem at about the relevant time.

sold takes up the verb of 4.34, 37. **property** looks back to 2.45; in older Greek it suggested personal rather than landed property; later it came into use for an estate, farm, or field. The ordering of the material here is Luke's, so that we cannot say that Ananias and Sapphira were motivated by the desire to share the good impression made by Barnabas.

2. Ananias **kept back part of the price**. Luke's word suggests the secret misapplication of part of a larger sum which belongs to a group. Cf. especially Josh. 7.1. He thus **laid at the apostles' feet** (4.35, 37) only a **part of the price**. Had there been no deceit Ananias' act would not have been without merit.

his wife was privy to this – a note that prepares for the second part of the story.

3. why has Satan put it into your heart . . . ? Cf. Lk. 22.3. For Luke, Satan is the supernatural power opposed to God; cf. 26.18. The meaning probably is that Satan has himself entered into Ananias, rather than that he has put into Ananias' mind the evil intention of deceit. The result of Satan's act is expressed by two infinitives: **to deceive the Holy Spirit** and **to keep back some of the price**. These seem to refer not (as is sometimes said) to one offence but to two: deceiving (or attempting to deceive) the Holy Spirit; defrauding the church's charity. The second infinitive supplies the content or method of the first (to deceive . . . by withholding), but each act is independently significant.

4. While it remained did it not remain yours? And when it had been sold was it not under your authority? Thus the sale of property and distribution of the proceeds was voluntary. It is implied that when Ananias brought part of the price he either directly or implicitly claimed that he was bringing the whole. Whether this gives a historically true picture is another question. See 4.34.

You lied (the verb is the same as *deceived* in v. 3 but takes a different case) **not to men but to God**. Ananias' crime is twofold: he has withheld money; he has attempted to deceive. Taken with v. 3, *to God* may hint at but hardly asserts the divinity of the Holy Spirit.

5. Ananias . . . fell down and expired. *Expired* is used by physicians but is not exclusively medical, nor (notwithstanding v. 10 and 12.23) does it in itself imply a sudden or unpleasant death. It is not stated that Peter killed Ananias or wished him dead, but **great fear** implies the impression that supernatural and dangerous powers were at work.

6. The young men (a different but related word is used in v. 10) are not an official group but active members of the community, quick to relieve their elders of a necessary but unpleasant duty. One is reminded of the *young men* who formed the subordinate troops of the kings of Israel (e.g. 1 Sam. 14.1; 21.5). **rose up**, an OT pleonasm. **prepared the body for burial** (the verb could mean *to lay out* or *to cover with a shroud*; both are included in a simple preparation for burial).

7. For the simple method of detecting falsehood; cf. Susannah 44–62.

8. Peter's question may be said to provoke Sapphira's lie; he does nothing to help her to confess and repent. It is possible, but not probable, that Peter's question is indirect: *Tell me whether . . .*

9. to tempt the Spirit of the Lord. Cf. v. 3. For tempt; cf. 15.10; the word and the notion belong to the OT; cf. Exod. 17.2. They mean *to provoke*, 'seeing how far you can go'. Whether *the Lord* refers to God or Christ remains uncertain. **the feet,** an OT expression; cf. Isa. 52.7; 59.7; Nahum 1.15). Peter predicts (**they will carry you out**) Sapphira's death; whether he causes it is not stated. Cf. pp. 69f. The narrative does not warrant rationalizing explanations of death caused by grief or shock.

10. Immediately heightens the effect and the sense of the supernatural. Cf. v. 5. For **expired** cf. 5 and for **young men** cf. v. 6.

11. For **great fear** cf. v. 5. At this point more than reverence is intended. Fear falls first upon the church, then upon all those, presumably on the edge of the Christian group, who heard what had happened.

the whole church, the first occurrence in Acts of the word church; see Introduction, pp. lviiif. The phrase suggests the total number of Christians, but at the time this was identical with the local church of Jerusalem.

13. MIRACLE-WORKING OR SUPERNATURAL COMMUNITY 5.12–16

[12] Many signs and portents among the people were done at the hands of the apostles, and they were all together in Solomon's Portico, [13] and of the rest no one dared join them, but the people praised them. [14] Believers were added to the Lord in increasing numbers, crowds both of men and of women, [15] so that people carried out the sick even into the streets and laid them on mattresses and stretchers, in order that as Peter passed by at least his shadow might fall on one of them. [16] The crowd from the cities round about Jerusalem came together, bringing the sick and those who were afflicted by unclean spirits; all of them were healed.

This summary passage connects the narrative in the rest of ch. 5 with the stories of chs. 3 and 4; the thread was in danger of being lost in the story of Ananias and Sapphira. The material in the summary (miracle; the use of Solomon's Portico; the awed reaction of the crowds to recent events, presumably including the deaths of Ananias and Sapphira; Peter's outstanding activity as healer and exorcist) could easily have been derived from the surrounding traditional narratives.

The paragraph is however surprisingly ordered – or disordered. There are bad joins between vv. 12a and 12b; 13a and 13b, 14; 14 and 15, 16. Put differently, miracle-working is the theme of vv. 12a, 15, 16; the relation of the Christians to the population of Jerusalem that of 13; the success of the apostles' preaching that of 14; and 12b stands on its own. Because of this, editors have made suggestions for improvement; for example, it has been proposed that vv. 15, 16 should be placed between 12a and 12b; or that v. 14 should be regarded as Luke's insertion, dividing the original paragraph. These suggestions however are unnecessary. The connections are not good, but there is usually (see the notes) something to be said in favour of them, with the exception of v. 12b – and Luke was interested in places and local colour. Probably he wrote the paragraph himself to introduce – or reintroduce – the traditional material written up in 5.17–42.

12. Many signs and portents. See 2.43. **among the people**, the (Jewish) population of Jerusalem; see 4.25. **at the hands of the apostles**: not necessarily *by the laying on of hands* – Luke uses a

Septuagintal expression. Miracle-working is now dropped till v. 15. Did vv. 12b, 13 open a traditional summary? Perhaps Luke added v. 12a to connect, representatively, with 3.1–10.

all together; see 1.14. **Solomon's Portico**, see 3.11. Apparently, in Luke's view, this was a regular meeting place for Christians, who probably had no meeting-house of their own.

13. of the rest. One view is that *of the rest* means Christians other than the apostles; more probably it refers to non-Christians. The verse suggests that the assembled Christians formed a distinct group on their own, and that to **join** the group was understood to be virtually equivalent to becoming a Christian, for in view of v. 14 Luke cannot mean that no one dared to become a Christian; many did so. There is a superficial contradiction between v. 13 and v. 14 and it has been argued that *join* represents a Greek word that mistranslates Aramaic that in fact means *contend with*. This is linguistically possible, but unnecessary. No one joined the Christian group unless he was prepared to become a Christian. The Christians were however (according to this verse) popular and left in peace.

14. Believers were added to the Lord. For *added*; cf. 2.41, 47. *The Lord* is Jesus, thought of as the head of the new community, who gains more and more adherents; less probably, *Believers in the Lord were added* (*to the church*). **Crowds both of men and of women.** The concern for the role of women often noted in the gospel continues in Acts.

15. It is often observed that this verse would connect better with v. 13 than with v. 14; it is however probably correct to say that the **so that** with which the verse begins looks back to the whole paragraph, especially perhaps v. 12a. Luke combines statements about conversions with statements about cures.

It is hardly possible to distinguish between **mattresses** and **stretchers**. No more astounding piece of miracle-working is described in the NT; Peter does not need to speak, to touch, or, it seems, to give any attention to the sick person. Parallels of a sort can be cited, but it is probably correct to say that in ancient thought it mattered little whether a miracle was worked by the shadow, the hands, or the words of the miracle-worker. In any case the agent here is God.

16. Not surprisingly, news of what was happening in Jerusalem spread beyond the city. **afflicted** is a word used, but not exclusively, by medical writers. It proves nothing about the author of the book. **all of them were healed**. The summary could not end more impressively.

14. ARREST AND EXAMINATION OF APOSTLES 5.17–40

17 The High Priest, and those who were with him, the local party
of the Sadducees, rose up. They were filled with envy, 18 and laid
their hands on the apostles and put them in prison publicly. 19 But
an angel of the Lord opened the doors of the prison by night, led
them out, and said, 20 'Go, stand and speak in the Temple to the
people all the words of this Life.' 21 When they heard this they
entered the Temple at dawn and began to teach. When the High
Priest and those who were with him arrived they summoned the
Sanhedrin and all the Senate of the children of Israel and sent to
the gaol that they might be brought. 22 But the agents when they
arrived did not find them in the prison. They returned and
brought their report, 23 saying, 'We found the gaol closed in all
security and the guards standing at the doors, but when we opened
them we found no one inside.' 24 When the Captain of the Temple
and the chief priests heard these words they were at a loss
concerning them to know what this might mean. 25 Then some
one came and reported to them, 'See, the men whom you put in
prison are standing in the Temple and teaching the people.'
26 Then the Captain of the Temple went off with the agents and
brought them, not however with violence, for they feared the
people, lest they should be stoned.

27 When they had brought them they set them in the Sanhedrin,
and the High Priest asked them, 28 saying, 'We strictly ordered
you not to teach in this name. And now you have filled Jerusalem
with your teaching, and you wish to bring this man's blood upon
us.' 29 Peter and the apostles answered and said, 'We must obey
God rather than men. 30 The God of our fathers raised up Jesus,
whom you killed by hanging him on a tree. 31 This man did God
exalt by his right hand to be a ruler and saviour, to give
repentance to Israel, and the forgiveness of sins. 32 And we are
witnesses of these things, and so is the Holy Spirit, whom God
has given to those who obey him.'

33 When they heard this they were incensed, and wished to kill
them. 34 But there rose up one of the Sanhedrin, a Pharisee called
Gamaliel, a teacher of the Law held in honour by all the people;
he urged that the men be put outside for a little while, 35 and said
to the members of the Sanhedrin, 'Men of Israel, take heed to

yourselves with regard to these men and consider what you are about to do. [36] For some time ago Theudas rose up saying that he was somebody, and a number of men, about 400, adhered to him; he was killed, and all those who followed his lead were dispersed and came to nothing. [37] After him, Judas the Galilean rose up in the days of the census and drew a company after himself. He too perished, and all those who followed his lead were scattered. [38] And now, I tell you, steer clear of these men and let them alone, for if this plan or this deed comes from men it will be destroyed; [39] but if it is of God you will not be able to destroy them, and you may find yourselves fighting against God.' They took his advice, [40] summoned the apostles, beat them, commanded them not to go on speaking in the name of Jesus, and dismissed them.

At first sight this paragraph seems almost a doublet of 4.1–22 (see Introduction, pp. xxxf.). There are however significant differences. (1) The apostles have been warned and are now liable to punishment (4.18–21; 5.28). (2) The miracle of ch. 3 is now left behind; the apostles are attacked on the ground of their teaching. (3) The word *servant*, characteristic of chs. 3 and 4, is not used. (4) The new chapter includes a miraculous rescue by an angel. (5) It also contains punishment – a beating. (6) It also contains the intervention of Gamaliel. (7) Not two apostles only but the whole group suffer.

These all represent points that Luke will have wished to make, and the paragraph as a whole may be regarded as his own composition, designed, with 5.41, 42, to conclude the first main section of his book. Most could have been written on the basis of general knowledge – Paul himself (1 Cor. 15.9; Gal. 1.13, 23) confirms early persecution and therefore trials. Gamaliel's speech is no doubt Luke's own composition and contains unfortunate errors (see the notes on vv. 36, 37), but Gamaliel's attitude is intelligible and credible within Judaism.

17. The High Priest, according to 4.6, Annas. **the Sadducees** (see on 4.1) form a **party**; so do the Pharisees (15.5; 26.5) and, in the opinion of others, the Christians (24.5, 14; 28.22). **rose up**: a Septuagintal pleonasm; cf. 5.6. In Acts it often introduces fresh action. The success of Christian preaching (5.14) filled the Sadducees with **envy**, though it is possible to give the word a better sense – *a holy zeal* for the truth as they believed it to be.

18. They laid their hands (4.3) **upon the apostles**, on this occasion on all the apostles, not on Peter and John only. They **put them in prison publicly**; *publicly* could be taken as an adjective, *put them in the public prison.* This would recall a Latin expression.

19. In the course of the night the apostles were delivered from prison by an angel. Cf. 12.4–10, and 16.25–34 where Paul and Silas are released by an earthquake. **an angel of the Lord** (often with the definite article) is an OT expression (e.g. Gen. 16.7). The effect of the angel's intervention is to increase the confidence of the apostles and the wrath of their opponents.

20. The apostles have been released in order to continue their work. They are to **stand** (cf. 2.14) **in the Temple** and **speak to the people**. The Temple is the centre of the old religion and the place where they are sure to find a large concourse of people. Their message is described as **all** (omitting nothing out of fear or tact) **the words of this life**. *This life* may mean *this way of life*, more probably the new life (cf. 11.18; 13.46, 48) offered by Jesus as *the author of life* (3.15).

21. The apostles did as they were told and **entered the Temple at dawn**. The gates were closed at night but must have been opened in time for the sacrifice at daybreak. They **began to teach**; this is not distinguished from proclamation.

Luke's somewhat careless expression cannot mean that the High Priest and his entourage arrived at the place where the apostles were teaching but at the place where the Sanhedrin should meet. The distinction between **Sanhedrin** and **Senate** is not clear. The general sense of the verse however is clear; the apostles are to be brought from prison to appear before the court.

22. The reader of course does not share the surprise of the High Priest's agents.

23. we found no one inside. It would be wrong to press this to mean that only the apostles had been in prison. *No one* means *no one of those whom they sought.*

24. The perplexity of the **Captain of the Temple** (see 4.1) and of **the chief priests** (also 4.1) is understandable.

25. More information arrives. They **are standing in the Temple and teaching the people**; that is, They are doing precisely what they were told to do.

26. The Captain of the Temple and **the agents** were officers of the Council and undertook practical tasks, such as arresting criminals. The apostles were popular figures (5.13) so that the authorities had to tread carefully. They feared lest they should be stoned. Such a stoning could not be a formal legal penalty, since the only authority that could inflict such a penalty was the Council itself. Luke is evidently thinking of a popular move by which a crowd threw stones at unpopular people. At 7.58, 59 Luke uses a different verb; whether he there means the same kind of stoning is a difficult question; see the note.

27. Judicial proceedings begin. For the arrangement of the Sanhedrin see on 4.7. It is interesting that the High Priest makes no reference to the surprising disappearance of the apostles from prison; this incident may have been an addition to a story which did not originally contain it.

28. After v. 27, a question is to be expected, but (except in some MSS) no question follows but a statement. **We strictly ordered you**: the Greek is either a translation or more probably an imitation of a Hebrew construction. The High Priest is referring to 4.17, 18. So far from obeying this order the apostles have **filled Jerusalem with** the forbidden **teaching**. Coupled with objection to what is evidently regarded as erroneous and undesirable teaching goes sensitivity to what was taken as a personal accusation. The Sanhedrin feels that it is being accused of responsibility for the death of Jesus. See 2.23; 3.13, 17; 4.11, 27; 10.39; 13.27, with on the whole increasing emphasis on the role of the rulers.

29. Once more, Peter takes the lead, using words so similar to those of 4.19 that they suggest that the two 'trial scenes' are duplicates. For the Socratic parallel see on 4.19. The principle – of the supreme authority of God – is one highly characteristic of Judaism itself, in which it had been established at a high cost in suffering. Peter's application of it, in its context, is new and shocking because it sets over against each other God and those men who were best qualified to expound God's command as expressed in his Law.

30. The God of our fathers. As at 3.13 Peter begins by emphasizing that he is introducing no new God but is speaking of the God of the (Jewish) fathers. The Christian faith is the fulfilment, not the contradiction, of Judaism. **raised up**. This may refer to the resurrection, or to God's act in bringing Jesus on the human scene. The occurrence of *exalt* in v. 31 suggests the former alternative. **hanging him on a tree** (cf. 10.39) recalls Deut. 21.22, 23 (and Gal. 3.13), but, unlike Paul, Peter makes no theological use of the OT reference. He may not have been aware of it but have simply used familiar Christian language.

31. This man did God exalt . . . to be a ruler and saviour. As the object of divine action Jesus becomes its subject. It is possible that *exalted* covers both resurrection and ascension, more likely that resurrection is covered in v. 30 (see the note) and that exaltation refers to the further events. For *ruler* see on 3.15; here it does not differ widely from *lord* (cf. 2.36). For *ruler and saviour* cf. 2 Clement 20.5. *Saviour* is characteristic of later NT writings; its pagan associations may have discouraged its early use. Here however the work of the Saviour issues in **repentance . . . and the forgiveness of sins**. God offers not vengeance but pardon. **His right hand** is ambiguous, as at 2.33. Here also the instrumental sense may be preferred to the local.

32. we are witnesses of these things. Cf. 1.8 and many other passages. **and so is the Holy Spirit**. Cf. Jn 15.26f.; but Luke, unlike John, is probably thinking of such phenomena as speaking with tongues, which serve as a sign of God's presence and activity. **whom God has given**, at but not only at Pentecost. Luke will recount frequent bestowals of the Spirit to believers – **those who obey him**.

33. they were incensed. The same word is used (*cut to the quick*) at 7.54. They **wished**; many MSS have a similar word, *they planned*. It might be said that each implies the other.

34. one of the Sanhedrin (not, as has been asserted, its president), **a Pharisee called Gamaliel**. For the Pharisees see *NS* 2.381–403. Luke represents them as more favourable to the Christians than the Sadducees were, probably because of their belief in resurrection. For Gamaliel see *NS* 2.367–8; Rabban Gamaliel I, a Tanna of the first generation, is intended, according to 22.3 the teacher of Paul. He was **a teacher of the Law held in honour by all the people**. This is a correct account of Gamaliel; cf. Josephus, *War* 5.527; M. Sotah 9.15. He prefers to put his point of view in the absence of the apostles; the Sanhedrin can speak more freely and they will avoid giving the apostles the impression that they may perhaps be right. Cf. 4.15.

35. and consider: these words, not in the Greek, are inserted in order to make clear that the sentence is in the form of an indirect question. The matter is open, and there are precedents which it will be useful to consider.

36. Theudas. See Josephus, *Ant.* 20.97, 98. An impostor, Theudas, persuaded the people to follow him to the Jordan which, he said, would at his command be parted so that they could cross. But the procurator, Fadus, sent a squadron of cavalry, who slew many and took many prisoners, including Theudas, who was beheaded. This story corresponds well enough with the words attributed to Gamaliel, but Fadus was procurator in AD 44 – years after Gamaliel is said to have spoken.

37. After him. This can mean only, After the time of Theudas. **Judas the Galilean rose up in the days of the census.** His resistance to the *registration* or *census* conducted in AD 6 by Quirinius (Lk. 2.2) is described by Josephus (*Ant.* 18.4–10, 23; *War* 2.(56).118) in an account which agrees substantially with the words attributed to Gamaliel. Josephus does not describe the end of Judas, but he certainly did not prevent the census, and Luke's **He too perished** may well be correct. His followers, according to Josephus (*War* 2.118; *Ant.* 18.9), became the foundation of the Zealot movement.

If the identifications of Judas and Theudas given here are correct, Judas did not rise up *after* Theudas, but nearly forty years before him; indeed Theudas did not initiate his revolt until at least ten years after Gamaliel was speaking. The simplest explanation of Luke's text, and the only one that does not involve him in some error, is that there was another Theudas, otherwise unknown, who took up arms some time before Judas. This is possible; it does not seem probable. Another explanation is that Luke had misread Josephus, *Ant.* 20.102, in which Judas (though correctly dated) is mentioned after the reference to Theudas. It is worth noting that this hypothesis would mean that Luke was writing Acts after AD 93, when the *Antiquities* was published. This is a possible source of error, but many other mistakes are possible, and though Luke seems to have made one of them we do not know which.

The MS D uses an expression that seems to mean that Theudas committed suicide. This is inconsistent with Josephus' account of Theudas, and might possibly point to another Theudas, whose dates, if we knew them, might be more accommodating. But this is most improbable.

38. Gamaliel draws the inference from his examples. Wrongdoing brings its own reward. So, **let them alone**. If their activity is of merely human origin it will come to nothing.

39. but if it is of God you will not be able to destroy them. It is hardly possible to believe that the words of vv. 36, 37 were spoken by Gamaliel, but the conclusion is one that he might have reached. See M. Aboth 4.11: Any assembling together that is for the sake of

Heaven shall in the end be established, but any that is not for the sake of Heaven shall not in the end be established.

Perhaps **you may find yourselves** . . . ; or, **lest you find yourselves** . . . You may find yourselves inadvertently sinners. Gamaliel's advice and warning prevail.

40. They **beat them**. The apostles could be punished because they have disobeyed the explicit command of 4.18, but in fact the Council do little more than reinforce their earlier warning.

This verse continues in v. 41, here treated as the beginning of a very short summary paragraph.

15. REJOICING AND WITNESSING COMMUNITY: 'FINAL' SUMMARY 5.41, 42

[41] So they went from the presence of the Council, rejoicing that they had been counted worthy to be treated with ignominy for the sake of the Name, [42] and all day in the Temple and at home they did not stop teaching and telling the good news that the Christ was Jesus.

With these two verses Luke brings to an end the first stage of his work. He has demonstrated the truth of the resurrection (1.3); his story will fill the interval between Jesus' departure and return (1.11); inspired by the Holy Spirit the disciples will bear witness to Jesus, eventually through the whole world (1.15–26). Jesus' promise of the Holy Spirit has been fulfilled (2.1–4), and Luke gives four accounts of the apostolic testimony (2.24–40; 3.12–26; 4.8–12; 5.30–32). The community increases in number, prays, practises charity, performs miracles. Its leaders are exposed to attack but enjoy divine protection and rejoice not least that they have the privilege of suffering for Christ. They continue the work of teaching and evangelizing. On this foundation the story can develop. It has two bases: the apostles continue to use the Temple, that is, they think of themselves as Jews; and they bear witness to Jesus as Christ, that is, as the fulfilment of Judaism. The next step will lead us outside Jerusalem.

There can be little doubt that Luke composed this short summary, which is in his style, is based on the stories he has already told, and serves a literary purpose.

41. This verse completes the narrative of 5.17–40 but looks at it from a new point of view. Luke sums up the past with a view to the future.

from the presence, literally, *from the face*. Luke imitates the LXX. **worthy to be treated with ignominy** – an intentional oxymoron. The thought is not exclusively Christian. **For the sake of the Name** – a new use of *name* (cf. 3.16). It represents the person who bears it.

42. at home, *in* their own private *houses*; the words could mean, *in their* specifically Christian *meeting-house*. Cf. 2.46 for the phrase, and 2.2 for a house (or *room*) where Christians met.

the Christ was Jesus. It would be possible to translate, *the anointed Jesus*. Much more probably, *the Christ* is the subject of the implied assertion: the Christ is Jesus – that is, the promises are fulfilled; God is already active in saving his people. The apostles and their followers thus embark on a course of deliberate disobedience.

III

PROBLEMS AND PERSECUTION LEAD TO THE BEGINNING OF EXPANSION

(6.1 – 8.3)

16. APPOINTMENT OF THE SEVEN AND FURTHER PROSPERITY 6.1–7

1 In these days, as the number of the disciples was increasing, there arose a complaint on the part of the Hellenists against the Hebrews, to the effect that their widows were being overlooked in the daily ministration of charity. 2 The Twelve summoned the whole company of the disciples and said, 'It is not acceptable that we should forsake the word of God and serve at table. 3 But, brothers, look out from among you seven men of good repute, full of the Spirit and wisdom, whom we will appoint over this business. 4 For our part, we will continue in prayer and in the ministry of the word. 5 This proposal pleased the whole company, and they chose Stephen, a man full of faith and of the Holy Spirit, Philip, Prochorus, Nicanor, Timon, Parmenas, and Nicolas, a proselyte from Antioch. 6 They set these men before the apostles, and when they had prayed laid their hands on them.

7 And the word of God grew and the number of disciples in Jerusalem increased greatly. A large number of the priests gave their obedience to the faith.

It is important to take this paragraph on its own. It is separated by 6.7 (a Lucan summary) from the stories of Stephen and Philip and from the Antiochene tradition (see Introduction, p. xxxi), which nevertheless have some connection with it. The summary brings out Luke's intention of showing how a minor deficiency in administration was speedily set right and led to the emergence of a new group of leaders and the expansion of the church. Luke is not giving an account of the origin of the order of deacons, though his narrative reflects what had probably become in his own time the accepted manner of appointing ministers. For the meaning of the terms *Hellenists* and *Hebrews* see on v. 1. The Seven who, according to v. 5, were appointed to care for the poor, were probably evangelists (see 21.8) as much as social workers.

Luke's use of his material is guided by three convictions. He believed that the early years of the church were exemplary, evil (Ananias and Sapphira) and inefficiency being immediately dealt with; that the unity or the church and its link with Jesus were based on the Twelve; the developments in the church led to its extension. He was aware of the fact that in Jerusalem in the early years there were Greek-speaking Jews who had at their head a group of seven men, about whom he knew as much – or as little – as he knew about the Twelve. The difference between the two groups he did not know, except that the Twelve held priority in time and in authority. The two groups had the same functions: both were at once evangelists and carers for the poor (for the apostles, see 4.35, 37; 5.2). Luke (see on v. 1) suggests the traditional term *Hebrews* for the apostles, and *Hellenists* for the Seven, or at least for the widows who were their responsibility. His contribution in this paragraph was to isolate the theme of charity and to link it specifically with widows, which was natural enough, and to represent the difficulty as immediately overcome by the intervention of the Twelve, with whose approval the Seven were appointed to an official position.

The few points explicitly affirmed in this edifying story, especially the existence of the two groups, may well be correct, but many questions remain not only unanswered but lying beneath rather than on the surface. These include: What were the distinctive views of the Seven? Of the Twelve? How were they related to each other and to official Judaism? Were the Seven related, in doctrine, in practice, in person, with the Samaritans? With the Jews of Qumran? How was Saul related to them? In the beginning? Subsequently? What role did they play in the period covered by Acts? In later years? On these questions see the notes below.

1. In these days. There is no attempt at precise chronology, but clearly Luke is thinking of the time when the church was still confined to Jerusalem. **there arose a complaint**, like the complaining of the Israelites in the wilderness (e.g. Num. 11.1), **on the part of the**

Hellenists against the Hebrews. It is difficult to define these terms, especially *Hellenist*, which until much later is used only in Acts (9.29; 11.20) and dependent passages. *Hellenist* has been taken to mean *Greek*, that is, *Gentile*; this however is improbable. It is to be noted that Luke uses it in three different senses, and therefore did not have in mind a clearly defined party; here it probably refers to Jews who habitually spoke Greek; what remains quite uncertain is the extent to which they had acquired, with the language, Greek ways of life and thought. *Hebrew* means Jewish, and, in the NT, not only capable of using the Jewish language (Semitic – Hebrew or Aramaic) but valuing the beliefs, traditions, history of their people, though not all will have valued these in the same sense as Paul (2 Cor. 11.22; Phil. 3.5).

The *complaint* was that **their widows were being overlooked in the daily ministration of charity**. Widows were always a vulnerable group; there may be a special reference to widows of Diaspora Jews who came to spend their last years, and to die and be buried in or near Jerusalem. Their widows would often be left with no nearby family members or friends to care for them. Charitable distribution recalls, but not precisely, the Jewish custom of providing a *tamḥui* to the casual poor (but the widows would be resident) and a *quppah* given to members of the community.

2. Here only in Acts is the term **The Twelve** used as a designation of a special group of disciples. They are apparently the same as *the apostles* (v. 6), but the term may be a mark of Luke's use of a fresh source. There was a group of twelve at Qumran (1 QS 8.1), but the common number is not enough to suggest any connection. **It is not acceptable** – probably to God: it is not his will . . . ; possibly *to us, the Twelve*. **the word of God**, probably *preaching*; cf. 2.41; 4.4, 29, 31; and frequently. See however on v. 4, *the ministry of the word*. **serve at table**, that is, to serve food to (e.g.) the widows. *Table* is sometimes used for a banker's counter (e.g. Lk. 19.23); it is possible though unlikely that the word here refers to financial arrangements.

3. Seven men of good repute are to be found; cf. 16.2; 22.12. They must also be **full of the Spirit**, showing all the marks of the work of the Holy Spirit, **and of wisdom**, for Luke not a theological term. The seven must have spiritual and natural gifts. **We will appoint**: the Twelve appear to be ready to accept the congregation's choice.

4. In the division of labour between the Seven and the Twelve, **the ministry of the word** has been taken to refer to *doctrinal* *discussion*, but it is usually and rightly understood of the work of proclamation. Cf. the use of *the word* in v. 2.

5. The list of seven names has been held to imply the use of a written source; this is probably but not certainly correct. All the seven bear Greek names; this suggests but by no means proves that they were of Diaspora origin.

Stephen, a fairly common Greek name. See 6.8 – 8.2; 11.19; 22.20.

Philip, a name borne by several kings of Macedon, including the father of Alexander the Great. See ch. 8; 21.8 (where he is called the Evangelist).

Prochorus, not a common name.

Nicanor. It is surprising that this name should be given to a Jew; see 1 Macc. 7.26.

Timon, a not uncommon name.

Nicolas, a common Greek name. **a proselyte from Antioch**: this probably implies that the rest were born Jews, and may imply that they were Palestinian in origin. Luke's use of the word Hellenist (see on v. 1) must not be taken to mean that they were necessarily of the Diaspora; in any case the word is not applied to the Seven. Nicolas was a proselyte, a full convert to Judaism who had as such, in all probability, cut himself off from family and friends and was prepared to endure scorn and dislike. He would not be prepared to sit loose to the laws and customs of his adopted people; it is probable that his six colleagues shared his devotion to the Law.

The name Nicolas occurs nowhere else in the NT, but cf. Rev. 2.6, 15, which refer with disapproval to the teaching of the Nicolaitans. As early as Irenaeus and Eusebius this sect was said to have been founded by the Nicolas of Acts 6. There is nothing to support this view, though it may be that a gnostic sect claimed descent from this (semi-)apostolic figure in order to add to its authority.

6. They must refer to *the whole company* (v. 5); these will also form the subject of **when they had prayed laid their hands on them**. There is no question that this is the grammatical meaning of Luke's words. The Western text rewrites the sentence and makes the apostles lay their hands on the Seven. In v. 3 the apostles say *we will appoint* but this is already covered when the apostles accept those who are set before them. The laying on of hands (cf. 13.1–3) signifies the blessing which accompanies the committing and the undertaking of a new kind of service.

7. The word of God as the apostles continued to preach it (vv. 2, 4) had continually increasing influence and effect. The church is created and sustained by the word. The increasing **number of the disciples** now included a **large number of the priests**. These **gave their obedience to the faith**. *Faith* must here stand for the content of Christian belief and life. Cf. Rom. 1.5; 10.16.

17. ATTACK ON STEPHEN 6.8–15

[8] Stephen, full of grace and power, began to work great portents and signs among the people, [9] but there rose up some of those who belonged to the synagogue called the Synagogue of the Libertines, both Cyrenians and Alexandrians, and of those who came from Cilicia and from Asia, disputing with Stephen, [10] and they were unable to withstand the wisdom and the Spirit with which he spoke. [11] Then they suborned men who said, 'We have heard him speak blasphemous words against Moses and God.' [12] And they stirred up the people and the elders and the scribes, and they came suddenly upon Stephen, seized him and carried him away, and brought him to the Sanhedrin. [13] They set up false witnesses, who said, 'This man never stops speaking words against the Holy Place and the Law; [14] for we have heard him say that this Jesus of Nazareth will destroy this place and change the customary rules which Moses handed down to us.' [15] And all who were sitting in the Sanhedrin fixed their eyes on him and saw his face as if it had been the face of an angel.

It is important at this point to have in mind the whole narrative sequence of 6.1 – 8.3, which contains (a) the reference to Hebrew and Hellenist widows; (b) the names of seven appointed to special service; (c) the disputes and arrest of Stephen; (d) Stephen's speech; (e) Stephen's martyrdom and the general persecution. (a) and (b) are based on a traditional list of names of men who had some connection with charitable work in Jerusalem but became leaders distinct from the Twelve and were connected by tradition with the founding of a mixed Jewish and Gentile church in Antioch. (c) has its sequel in (e); both paragraphs show signs of compilation. In 6.8–15 the charge against Stephen is given twice. In 7.54 – 8.1 it is hard to decide whether Stephen's death was the execution of a sentence passed in a court of law or a lynching. These duplications suggest the combination of sources. An alternative explanation is that the story of Stephen was written up by Luke in the light of the account of the trial and death of Jesus. Some such combination of sources and editing might account for the narratives as we have them.

There is probably truth in both views – that Luke was freely writing up tradition and that he made use of sources that had already achieved a definite form. Luke has written with too great freedom to permit the complete disentangling of sources, but his freedom has been to some extent inhibited by the existence of formulated material which he did not feel free to jettison altogether even when use of it resulted in some repetition and inconsistency. Verses 10 and 11 may be taken to lead on to the lynching story contained in 7.54 – 8.1, vv. 12 and 13 (with their references to elders, scribes, and the Sanhedrin) to the trial and judicial execution narrative, and v. 15 to the heavenly vision of 7.55. To this v. 14 is probably Luke's own addition, adding fresh substance to the charge and, more important, linking the story of Stephen with that of Jesus. Verses 8 and 9 are Luke's means of linking his account of the appointment of the Seven (which he had constructed) to the Stephen (Antiochene) tradition on which he now embarks.

8. Stephen, full of grace and power. Cf. 6.3, 5; it is unlikely that Luke intended these different descriptions of Christian leaders, of Stephen himself, to mean different things. *Grace* is here a general term, the favour of God expressed in an abundance of gifts; *power* is the result of the work of the Holy Spirit (cf. 1.8) – here its effect is that Stephen **began to work great portents and signs**, as the Twelve had done (2.43; 4.30; 5.12). In this respect at least Stephen is not inferior to them.

It is not said that Stephen gave any attention to the proper distribution of alms and the care of the Hellenist widows. The connection between him and the charitable arrangements is secondary, except to the extent that the Seven may have first come to prominence as agents of charity.

9. the Synagogue of the Libertines, both Cyrenians and Alexandrians, and of those who came from Cilicia and from Asia. On the synagogue see *NS* 2.423–54; also *Background*, 53–5, 204–6. Its primary use was for the reading and exposition of Scripture, for prayer, and for instruction, but it served also as a meeting-place for Jews and might have residential accommodation attached to it (see below). It is not clear, and is not agreed, how many synagogues are referred to here. Some think that five were intended, one for each of the groups mentioned, others that there were two, others, with perhaps greatest probability, that the one occurrence of the word means that Luke had in mind only one synagogue, and that all the groups shared in it.

Libertines, freedmen. Many Jews, In various parts of the Roman world, enjoyed this status, that of the freed slave who had not become a citizen. We may think of Jewish freedmen drawn from various parts of the Diaspora. For *Cyrenians*; cf. 11.20; 13.1; also Lk. 23.26 and Acts 2.10. For Jews in Cyrenaica see *NS* 3.60–62. For *Alexandrians* cf. 18.24. There was a numerous and varied Jewish population in Alexandria; see *NS* 3.42–4. For *Cilicia*; cf. 15.23, 41; Gal. 1.21; but the most famous of Cilicians was Saul (21.39; 22.3; 23.34). For Jews in Cilicia see *NS* 3.33f. For *Asia*; cf. 2.9; 16.6; 19.10; 21.27, and see *NS* 3.17–36. It is understandable that Hellenistic Jews who remained Jews and did not become Christians should be incensed with those of their number who, in their view, betrayed the ancestral faith. Cf. 9.29.

It is not impossible that the synagogue here referred to should be that known to have existed in Jerusalem, founded by Theodotus, son of Vettenus, and provided with residential accommodation for Jews coming from abroad. The name Vettenus recalls the Roman *Gens Vettena*, and it could be that the father, or an earlier ancestor, of Theodotus had been a slave of one of the Vetteni and given his freedom.

10. The members of the synagogue argued with Stephen in vain. Cf. 4.14, and note the fulfilment of the promise of Lk. 21.15. **the wisdom and the Spirit**. The wisdom with which the Spirit supplied him.

11. Then they suborned men. There is a close parallel in the *Martyrdom of Polycarp* 17.2. Stephen is accused of speaking **blasphemous words against Moses and God**. It is evident that Luke regards the accusation as slanderous, that is, Stephen did not so speak. For the question whether Stephen did speak against Moses see pp. 96–8; in the speech attributed to him in ch. 7 he speaks very highly of Moses (e.g. 7.20, 35). He blasphemed God only if Jesus, whom Stephen accepted as Messiah, could be held to have done so. The accusation recalls that against James (Josephus, *Ant.* 20.200); in Luke's time it had probably become customary.

12. the people are persuaded to change the good opinion of Christians that they had held, according to 5.26. For the **elders and the scribes** see on 4.5. The mob seize Stephen and carry him to the authorities; from this point in Luke's narrative the proceedings become more formal.

13. They set up false witnesses. The story of Jesus is recalled; see e.g. Mt. 26.59, 60; Mk 14.56, 57. The theme of false witness brought against the righteous and godly is an OT one: Ps. 27.12; 35.11; Prov. 14.5; 24.28.

This man never stops speaking words against the Holy Place and the Law. The charge is similar to that of v. 11. To speak against Moses is to speak against the Law; in ch. 7 Stephen speaks highly of the Law (7.58). *Place* could in itself denote synagogue (e.g. that of the Libertines), but v. 14 shows decisively that the Temple is meant.

14. this Jesus is contemptuous. **of Nazareth**: see on 2.22.

The witnesses have been said in v. 13 to be *false*, but there is material in the sayings of Jesus (as recorded by Luke) that comes close to justifying what they asserted. See Lk. 21.6, 24, and cf. Mt. 24.2; 26.61; 27.40; Mk 13.2; 14.58; 15.29; Jn 2.19; also Gospel of Thomas 71 (Jesus said: I shall de[stroy this] house and no one will be able to build it [again]).

the customary rules which Moses handed down (both written and oral traditions are covered) **to us**. These are laws, not mere customs of no authority. Again, the accusers could cite evidence from the teaching of Jesus: Mk 7.15, 19; Mt. 15.15–20. These are not in Lk., but see Lk. 6.1–11; 13.6–17; 14.1–6. Whether or not Stephen said so, it seems that a strong case can be made for the belief that Jesus did foretell the destruction of the Temple (perhaps not by himself), and that he did change Mosaic regulations, even if he regarded his changes as fulfilment rather than destruction.

This passage gives an interesting and important insight into Luke's understanding of Christianity. He recognizes that the new faith may seem to disrupt the old, but to maintain this is a falsehood, misrepresenting both Jesus and those who preach his Gospel. This is not the way in which Paul expresses the dialectic of Law and grace; it is a historian's way rather than a theologian's. We can hardly assert that Stephen and his colleagues preached a law-free Gospel.

15. They **saw his face as if it had been the face of an angel**. Cf. Gen. 33.10; 1 Sam. 29.9; 2 Sam. 14.17; Esther 5.2; and especially Exod. 34.29–35; also Joseph and Aseneth 14.9. The description prepares the way for Stephen's (inspired) speech, and perhaps for the vision of 7.55. Cf. *Martyrdom of Polycarp* 12.1.

18. STEPHEN'S SPEECH 7.1–53

**1 The High Priest said, 'Are these things so?' 2 He said, 'Brothers
and Fathers, listen. The God of glory appeared to our father
Abraham while he was in Mesopotamia, before he came to live in
Haran, 3 and said to him, Leave your land and your family, and
go into the land that I will show you. 4 Then he left the land of
Chaldea and settled in Haran. And there, after the death of his
father, God transferred him into this land in which you now live,
5 and he gave him no inheritance in it, not even space to plant his
foot, and he promised to give it in possession to him and to his
seed after him, although he then had no child. 6 God spoke thus,
that his seed should be sojourners in a foreign land and that the
native inhabitants would enslave them and ill-use them 400 years.
7 And the nation they serve as slaves I will judge, said God, and
afterwards they will come out and worship me in this place. 8 And
he gave him the covenant of circumcision; so he begot Isaac and
circumcised him on the eighth day, and Isaac begot and
circumcised Jacob, and Jacob begot and circumcised the twelve
patriarchs.**

**9 'The patriarchs were jealous of Joseph and sold him into
Egypt, but God was with him 10 and rescued him out of all his
afflictions and gave him grace and wisdom in the eyes of Pharaoh
king of Egypt, and he appointed him ruler over Egypt and over
all his household. 11 But famine came upon the whole of Egypt
and upon Canaan, and great affliction, and our fathers found no
food. 12 When Jacob heard that there was corn in Egypt he sent
our fathers, on the first occasion. 13 And on the second Joseph
was made known to his brothers and Joseph's race became known
to Pharaoh. 14 Joseph sent and summoned Jacob his father, and
all the family, in all seventy-five souls. 15 And Jacob went down
into Egypt, and died, he himself and our fathers too, 16 and their
bodies were transferred to Sychem and laid in the tomb that
Abraham bought for a sum of money from the sons of Emmor in
Sychem.**

**17 'Now as the time for the fulfilment of the promise that God
made to Abraham drew near the people grew and multiplied in
Egypt, 18 until there arose a different king over Egypt, who did
not know Joseph. 19 He tricked our race and ill-treated our fathers,**

causing them to expose their infants, that they might not be
preserved alive, [20] At this time Moses was born, and was a splendid
child. For three months he was cared for in his father's house,
[21] and when he was exposed Pharaoh's daughter took him up and
cared for him as a son. [22] Moses was trained in all the wisdom of
the Egyptians, and was powerful in his words and deeds. [23] But
when he had completed the span of forty years it came into his
mind that he should visit his brothers, the sons of Israel, [24] and
when he saw one of them being unjustly treated he defended him,
and avenged him who was being wronged by smiting the
Egyptian. [25] He supposed that his brothers understood that God
was giving them deliverance by his hand, but they did not
understand. [26] On the next day he appeared to them as they were
fighting and tried to reconcile them and make peace. He said,
Men, you are brothers; why are you wronging one another? [27] He
who was injuring his neighbour thrust him aside, saying, Who
appointed you a ruler and judge over us? [28] Do you wish to kill
me, as yesterday you killed the Egyptian? [29] At this word Moses
fled and became a sojourner in the land of Midian, where he
begot two sons.

[30] 'When forty years were up an angel appeared to him in the
wilderness of Mount Sinai in a fiery flame in a bush. [31] When
Moses saw it he marvelled at the sight. As he approached so as to
look closely the voice of the Lord was heard: [32] I am the God of
your fathers, the God of Abraham, Isaac, and Jacob. Moses
trembled with fright and did not dare to look closely. [33] The Lord
said to him, Take off the shoes you are wearing, for the place on
which you are standing is holy ground. [34] I have indeed seen the
ill-treatment of my people who are in Egypt and I have heard
their groaning, and I have come down to rescue them. And now
come, let me send you to Egypt. [35] This Moses, whom they
disowned when they said, Who appointed you a ruler and judge?
– this man God sent as ruler and redeemer, with the aid of the
angel who appeared to him in the bush. [36] This man brought them
out: for forty years he did portents and signs in the land of Egypt,
at the Red Sea, and in the wilderness. [37] It is this Moses who said
to the children of Israel, God will raise up a prophet for you,
from the midst of your brothers, as he raised up me. [38] This is he
who was in the assembly of God's people in the wilderness, with
the angel who spoke to him on Mount Sinai and with our fathers,

**who received living oracles to give to us. 39 Our fathers would not
be obedient to him but thrust him aside and, in their hearts,
returned to Egypt, 40 and said to Aaron, Make us gods to go before
us; for this Moses, who brought us out of the land of Egypt, we
do not know what has happened to him. 41 And in those days they
made a calf, offered sacrifice to the idol, and made merry over
the works of their hands. 42 God turned and handed them over to
worship the host of heaven, as it is written in the Book of the
Prophets: Did you bring me sacrifices and offerings forty years
in the wilderness, O house of Israel? 43 You took up the tent of
Moloch, and the star of your god Raiphan, the images which you
made for worship, and I will transport you beyond Babylon. 44 Our
fathers had the tent of testimony in the wilderness, as he who
spoke to Moses charged them to make it, according to the pattern
that he had seen. 45 Our fathers, with Joshua, entered into the
succession and brought in the tent when they dispossessed the
Gentiles, whom God drove out before the face of our fathers, up
to the time of David. 46 He found favour with God and asked that
he might provide a sacred dwelling-place for the house of Jacob.
47 But Solomon built God's house. 48 Yet the Most High does not
dwell in things made by human hands, as the prophet says,
49 Heaven is my throne, earth is the footstool of my feet. What
sort of house will you build me, says the Lord, or what is the
place where I will rest? 50 Did not my hand make all these things?**

**51 'Stiff-necked and uncircumcised of heart and ears that you
are! You are always contradicting the Holy Spirit; as your fathers
did, so also do you. 52 Which of the prophets did not your fathers
persecute? They killed those who announced beforehand the
coming of the Righteous One, of whom you have now become
betrayers and murderers, 53 you who received the Law at the
ordinance of angels, yet did not keep it.'**

This long speech was evidently important to Luke. Stephen, outstanding member of the Seven (6.5), has been arrested on the charge of blaspheming God and attacking Moses (as giver of the Law) and the Temple. The High Priest asks (7.1) whether the charge is true, a question that cannot be answered with a simple Yes or No. Certainly the speech is not a straightforward courtroom 'Defence', but that does not mean that it is irrelevant to the situation. Whence did Luke derive it? It is unlikely that he composed the whole himself; if he had done so the specifically Christian material would probably have appeared much earlier than v. 52. It has been argued that polemical insertions (vv. 35, 37, 39, 42, 48–53; perhaps 25, 27) have been introduced into an edifying account of OT history that has OT and Jewish parallels (e.g. Deuteronomy, Joshua 24, Ezekiel 20, Nehemiah 9, Psalm 105(104), Josephus, *War* 5.376–419), but these parallels themselves contain critical features. Moreover, if polemics had been Luke's aim, why should he have embedded his polemics in so much non-polemical material? We may ask also why Luke, if himself composing the speech, missed so many opportunities of making Christian points. The power of god to bring salvation out of evil and suffering is illustrated in the stories of Joseph and Moses; the parallel with Jesus is never mentioned.

This is not to say that the speech as a whole is irrelevant, even if it fails to get to grips with the immediate situation. Stephen still holds fast to the God of the Fathers; the new faith is the fulfilment of all that the old, represented by Abraham and Moses, rightly stood for, but it is a fulfilment so radical that it finally disintegrates the institutionalism that had for so long been the people's temptation. It is however only at the end that Luke makes the point that the whole record is crystallized in the crucifixion of Jesus.

Though the speech attacks the Temple (and so far proves rather than disproves the charge brought against Stephen) it does not oppose the Law. The treatment of this theme is not Pauline. The covenant God made with Abraham was a covenant of circumcision (v. 8), Moses gave deliverance (salvation) to his people (v. 25); God made Moses a ruler and redeemer (v. 35); Moses received living oracles to give to *us*.

We have thus a speech in which (a) the history of Israel is reviewed; (b) the patriarchs are honoured; but (c) Moses is accorded a more than human dignity; (d) correspondingly the Law is spoken of with great respect; but (e) the Temple is treated with no respect at all. The most probable explanation of this is that Luke gives us, in outline, the sort of sermon that might be preached in a Diaspora synagogue and could easily be taken over when Hellenist Jews became Hellenist Jewish Christians. It may be that similar sermons can be traced in Acts 14 and 17.

The speech, which can hardly have been spoken by Stephen in the circumstances described, recovers great historical value as a document of that sector of Judaism with which Stephen and his colleagues are said to have been associated. It is a valuable source for our knowledge of first-century Judaism and in addition gives us a glimpse of a non-Pauline line along which Christianity moved into the Gentile world. It does not stand close to Qumran, where criticism of the Temple is based on other grounds. It demonstrates Luke's view of the relation between Judaism and Christianity. They share a common origin in God's call of Abraham, in God's promise to him, and in the fulfilment of this promise in the living oracles given to Moses, but Christianity belongs to that critical prophetic strand of Judaism which refuses to substitute institutions for the word of God, and claims that the final conflict between the two came to a head in the story of Jesus.

1. Are these things so? The question means in effect, Are the facts stated in the accusation true? Do you admit the charge? not simply, Did Jesus in fact say this?

2. Brothers: cf.1.16; **and Fathers**: only here and at 22.1.

The God of glory (cf. Ps. 28(29).3) **appeared to our father Abraham.** It is emphasized that Stephen speaks as a Jew concerned for the honour of the national religion.

while he was in Mesopotamia, before he came to live in Haran. According to Gen. 12.1 God addressed the words that follow to Abraham after the move to Haran (Gen. 11.31, He came to Haran and lived there). The difference from the OT seems to serve no purpose and is presumably an error.

3. Here Stephen (Luke) follows closely the LXX text of Gen. 12.1.

4. Stephen resumes his narrative. It is now, not at the earlier point given by 11.31, that Abraham settles in Haran. Here Terah (Abraham's father, not named in Acts) dies; cf. Gen. 11.32, according to which Terah dies in Haran, but before Abraham's call. This discrepancy has been used to demonstrate dependence on the Samaritan Pentateuch, and thus a connection between Stephen (and his colleagues) and the Samaritans. According to Gen. 11.26 Terah was 70 when Abraham was born, and according to Gen. 12.4 Abraham was 75 when he left Haran for Canaan. Terah was thus 145. His age at death was 205 (Gen. 11.32), so that he thus had 60 years to live after Abraham entered the promised land. The Samaritan Pentateuch gives not 205 but 145 years as Tarah's age at death and so represents him as dying at the time when Abraham left for Canaan. Luke (Stephen) may have used this Samaritan text, but this is not a necessary conclusion. The mistake is easily made in using the Hebrew (or Greek) text; Philo too made it.

God transferred him. There is great stress on God's action. Abraham did not choose his (and his descendants') place of residence.

in which you now live. A Diaspora Jew speaks to Palestinian Jews.

5. God gave Abraham not the land in actual possession but the promise that he would give him the land as a possession. Cf. Gen. 12.7; 13.15; 17.8; 48.4.

6, 7. More OT passages are seen to be in mind. See Gen. 15.13f.; also Exod. 2.22; 12.40; 3.12.

the native inhabitants would enslave them and ill-use them. No subject is expressed in Greek, but there is no doubt what is meant.

400 years. In Gal. 3.17 the interval between the promise to Abraham and the giving of the Law is 430 years (Cf. Exod. 12.40). Calvin observes that redemption came before the Temple and the giving of the Law.

they will come out and worship me in this place. Cf. Exod. 3.14, *on this mountain*. Stephen seems to change the goal of the Exodus form Sinai to Sion. For *place* as referring to the Temple see 6.14; though whether (in view of what follows) Stephen would regard Temple worship as the goal of the Exodus is questionable.

8. In addition to the promise Abraham was given a covenant, an agreement that assured the promise. This consisted of circumcision. Cf. Gen. 17.10–13; 21.4. The covenant meant, on man's side, that every father must in every generation circumcise his male children. This requirement the Fathers carried out. Stephen does not suggest that in the Christian dispensation circumcision has lost its place. Critical of the Temple, he is not critical of the Law.

9. The story continues; see Gen. 37.11, 28; 39.2. It may be that Luke had in mind that Jesus was sold into the hand of his enemies, and that by his 'brothers'; even so, **God was with him**.

10. The OT story continues; see Gen. 39.21; 41.38–45; also Ps. 104(105).21.

he appointed him ruler. It would be natural to take this to mean, He, Pharaoh, appointed over all his, Pharaoh's, household, But cf. Gen. 45.8; it is God who controls the events of history. Cf. 4.28.

11. Once more, Luke sums up a long narrative in a few words, some of which recall the OT though there is no quotation.

food. Luke's Greek word means almost invariably *fodder*, *forage* – food for cattle. This may be intended – the patriarchs were graziers; or the word may be used exceptionally to mean human food.

12. The first clause gives the sense of Gen. 42.2, but in wording differs almost completely from the LXX.

on the first occasion is a somewhat unclear way of saying that Jacob's sons were sent twice – which is itself a simplification of the story in Genesis. On *first* (rather than *former*) see on 1.1. There is no necessary implication of a third visit.

13. on the second. See on v. 12. Cf. Gen. 45.2, 16. **Joseph's race became known to Pharaoh**, i.e. it became known that he was a Hebrew. Alternatively the words could mean that his *family* became (personally) known to Pharaoh.

14. This verse sums up the narrative of Gen. 45.9–11; 46.

seventy-five souls. In addition to the material in Genesis see Deut. 10.22 (where the number is 70) and Exod. 1.5 (where the LXX has 75, the MT 70; 4 Q Exod. has 75). Philo, *On the Migration of Abraham* 199–201 notes that Exod. 1.5 (LXX) has 75 and that Deut. 10.22 has 70; he offers no historical explanation but allegorizes. Jubilees 44.33 offers the explanation that five died, childless, in Egypt.

15, 16. Again Stephen summarizes, using language for the most part different from that of the LXX. There are also matters of substance to note.

(a) At the end of v. 16 Abraham is mentioned instead of Jacob. See Gen. 33.19. This passage has been confused with Gen. 23.3–20.

(b) Jacob was buried not (as these verses might suggest) at Sychem (= Shechem) but at Hebron. According to Josh. 13.32 Joseph was buried at Hebron; the OT does not tell us where the other sons of Jacob were buried. The original name of Hebron was Kirjath Arba, the city of Four, from which Jewish tradition deduced that four were buried there – Abraham, Isaac, Jacob, and (a majority view) Adam.

(c) It has been concluded that Stephen (Luke) was either expanding Josh. 24.32 to cover Joseph's brothers or was dependent on local Shechemite tradition. If the latter alternative is adopted we may have a further (see v. 4) link between Stephen and the Samaritans. This must be judged not impossible, but not probable.

17. the time for the fulfilment of the promise of vv. 6, 7: the promise made by God to Abraham was thus to be fulfilled at the Exodus – a Jewish not a Christian view. Contrast Gal. 3.16, 19.

For the growth of the people see Exod. 1.7. Luke abbreviates.

18. Exod. 1.8.

19. The first part of the verse summarizes Exod. 1.9–14; the attack on the children is in 1.15–22.

20. Moses . . . was a splendid child. In Exod. 2.2 Moses is describes by the adjective that ordinarily means simply *good*; the LXX appear to have taken it in terms of physical appearance. Targum Yerushalmi I takes the adjective to mean that Moses was born at six months; his mother saw that the premature infant was capable of living, and kept him for the next three months.

21. Cf. Exod. 2.5. **Pharaoh's daughter took him up**: literally perhaps, but the verb is used in Koine Greek for acknowledging one's child or adopting a child.

22. Philo, *Moses* 1.21–24, gives a full account of the education of Moses – an account which no doubt reflects his own Graeco-Egyptian education. According to Jubilees 47.9 Moses' education was Jewish. Luke's source, whatever it may have been, was concerned simply to glorify Moses, as was the whole Jewish tradition. This intention appears in the words, He **was powerful in his words and deeds.** Here Luke has slipped, for Moses was not powerful in speech (Exod. 4.10–16). The Lucanism (Lk. 24.19) slips in inadvertently.

23. when he had completed the span of forty years. See Deut. 34.7; According to Siphre § 357, 150a, Moses was in Egypt forty years, in Midian forty years, and for forty years he led Israel.

visit. The word includes more than the conventional sense; Moses intends to come out of his royal environment not only to see but to assist his fellow Israelites. Cf. Lk. 1.68; 7.16.

24. The sentence is not clearly expressed though it is not hard to fill in the gaps that Luke has left. The person **being unjustly treated** (or *injured*) must be an Israelite, though this is not stated. The person causing the injury must be an Egyptian, though this is not stated till the end of the verse. See Exod. 2.12.

25. Stephen (Luke) introduces the theme of the divinely chosen ruler whose role is misunderstood by those who should gratefully look to him as their leader; cf. the story of Abraham (vv. 4, 5). The case of Moses is developed at greater length and is treated is such detail as to suggest that the speaker thinks of him as a type of Jesus; this point however is never made in the speech. See on v. 35. **deliverance** could be translated *salvation*.

26. On the use of Exod. 2.13f. in vv. 26–28 see Hatch, *Essays*, 169: 'the narrative portion of the text differs from that of Exodus, but the dialogue nearly agrees and is probably a quotation'.

Reconciliation, it is said, is a work of the 'divine man'; but not of him exclusively.

27. With the words of the man (**Who appointed you a ruler and judge over us?**) the text of the LXX (Exod. 2.13) is taken up and followed precisely. The question is rhetorical, but Luke would of course answer – God.

28. The words are those of Exod. 2.14 (LXX). Moses is dismissed as a mere bully.

29. Such complete failure to understand his intention (cf. v. 25) was too much for Moses, who **fled**. He **became a sojourner**, not a permanent resident, **in the land of Midian**, on the east coast of the Gulf of Aqaba. **two sons**: Gershom (Exod. 2.22; 18.3) and Eliezer (Exod. 18.4).

30. Another period of **forty years** elapses (cf. v. 23). For the burning bush; cf. Exod. 3.1, 2 (where both MT and LXX have not Sinai but Horeb). Sinai was not in Midianite territory but on the other side of the Gulf of Aqaba.

Angels appear in God's service and for the benefit of his people but it is God who speaks.

31. Again a somewhat more circumstantial narrative is abbreviated. See Exod. 3.3–5.

32. I am the God of your fathers, the God of Abraham, Isaac, and Jacob. In Exod. 3.6 the word *am* is expressed, as it is not here, *father* is used in the singular, and *God* is repeated before *Isaac* and *Jacob*. This would be insignificant were it not that the Samaritan Pentateuch, against the Hebrew, LXX, Vulgate, and Peshitto, has the plural *fathers*; some have seen here evidence for a link between Stephen and the Samaritans (cf. v. 4). The evidence is worthless: in Exod. 3.15f. the plural *fathers* appears in the Hebrew and all versions and assimilation would be inevitable.

33. Stephen (Luke) alters the order of the OT, where similar words occur in Exod. 3.5. The removal of shoes (probably as bearing uncleanness which it would be difficult to remove) on approaching a holy place was (and is) a common religious rite. See M. Berakoth 9.5.

34. The verse is based on Exod. 3.7, 8, 10. **groaning** may come from Exod. 2.24; 6.5.

35. At this point there begins what has been described as a Moses hymn, analogous to the Christ hymn of Col. 1.15–20. (1) The man rejected by the people becomes ruler and lord; (2) he becomes deliverer through signs and wonders given by God; (3) he is both prophet and prototype of the Coming One; (4) he is mediator between God and people; (5) he is the receiver and giver of words of life; (6) the people reject him. There is no doubt that this verse and those that follow give high honour to Moses; whether they constitute a *hymn* is another question. If it is a hymn, where did it originate? Among Jews or Christians? If among Christians, cf. 1 Cor. 10.2. If among Jews we have an example of the post-biblical development in Jewish thought which saw Moses as the founder of a religion.

Moses had been rejected by his fellow countrymen, but God overruled their reaction for their own good. Cf. the story of Joseph (vv. 9–16). **Who appointed you a ruler and judge? – this man God sent as ruler and redeemer.** The word *ruler* is retained; *judge* is dropped, but Moses is said to be *redeemer* of his people. The word here refers to *deliverance*, *liberation*; it is not implied that a price has to be paid to effect this. Moses was not sent without supernatural authority and assistance; these were given by **the angel**.

36. The verse rearranges the Exodus story. Cf. *Assumption of Moses* 3.11.

37. Stephen quotes Deut. 18.15, as Peter does in 3.22. Neither in this verse nor in the speech as a whole is it claimed or implied that the prophecy is fulfilled in Jesus.

38. Moses **was in the assembly of God's people.** The Greek word is *ekklēsia*, often translated *church*; see on 5.11, and Introduction, pp. lviif. Here as in v. 37 Stephen (Luke) does not hint at the Christian development of the term.

the angel who now accompanies Moses is not the angel of v. 35. This angel spoke on Mount Sinai, presumably giving the Law (cf. v. 53). Reverence now puts God at a further remove from human affairs.

Moses **received living oracles to give to us**. Cf. Ps. 118(119). 50. The phrase is not to be restricted to the Ten Commandments; the whole of Torah was life-giving; see Deut. 30.15–20; 32.47; Mt. 19.17; M. Aboth 2.7 (The more study of the Law the more life . . . if he has gained for himself words of the Law he has gained for himself life in the world to come). In Stephen's speech there is no disparagement of the Law (except in its relation to the Temple).

to us. Stephen associates himself with his Jewish hearers. There is a well-supported variant *you*, but there would be on the part of Christian copyists a desire to distinguish Stephen from the Jews.

39. thrust him aside. *him* is not expressed in Greek, and it is possible though not probable that the unexpressed object of the verb should be *them – the living oracles* of v. 38.

in their hearts they **returned to Egypt**, not a very clear way of speaking of their desire to return. Slavery in Egypt was better than freedom coupled with the service of God and the rigour of life in the desert.

40. The people's request is expressed in the words of Exod. 32.1, 23, with a few slight changes. **this Moses** is contemptuous.

41. The complete apostasy of the people is described in the OT story, though here for the most part Stephen (Luke) uses his own words.

the works of their hands refers to the calf as a man-made and thus idolatrous object. Never had a people been so privileged or so completely negated their vocation.

42a. God turned. This rendering takes the Greek verb as intransitive: God changed his attitude to the Israelites. The verb could however be transitive with *them* as its unexpressed object: *God turned them over, gave them up*. **to worship**. The word means *to serve* and sometimes, but by no means always, has the specific sense of the service of divine beings. **the host of heaven**, the heavenly bodies, regarded as gods.

42b, 43. Stephen supports his charge of idolatry by quoting, from the Book of the (Twelve Minor) Prophets, Amos 5.25–27. Amos 5.26 is quoted in CD 7.14f., where it is combined with Amos 9.11 (quoted in Acts 15.16) and Num. 24.17. The first line is cited in exact agreement with the LXX (which agrees almost completely with the MT). **Did you bring me sacrifices and offerings forty years in the wilderness?** The interpretation of this clause depends on where the stress is laid. We may say, *Did* you bring me . . . ? with the implied answer, No, at that time we did not (cf. Jer. 7.22). Alternatively: Was it *to me* that you brought . . . ? with the implied answer, No, it was to false gods. A further possibility is: Did you offer sacrifices in the desert, I should like to know? No; and you were quite right not to do so; your sacrificial cult now is nothing but sacrifice to pagan gods. There is fairly general agreement that Stephen's understanding of his quotation is that in the desert the Israelites were idolaters.

forty years in the wilderness. Stephen agrees with the LXX except in order.

You took up the tent of Moloch. This again agrees with the LXX, but MT has *You have taken up Sikkuth your king*. CD 7.14 agrees with MT except in the verb: it has, And I will banish. What must be noted here is (a) Stephen quotes the LXX rather than the Hebrew (or Targum, though he is nearer to this than to MT); and (b) in Hebrew, Greek, and Aramaic, and for Stephen and Qumran, Israel is accused of idolatry.

In the next lines (**and the star . . . made for worship**) Stephen's changes from the LXX are slight; the MT differs in many ways. (In the MSS of Acts the name *Raiphan* appears in many forms.) As far as meaning is concerned, the differences between Stephen and the OT (whether Greek or Hebrew) are not important. What does it matter whether a false god is called Sikkuth or Moloch, Kiyyun or Raiphan? They are all false gods, to worship them is idolatry, and it will be punished.

beyond Babylon. Amos has, *Beyond Damascus*. Stephen's only concern is that idolatry is to be punished by exile. He may have thought that deportation to Assyria was more accurately expressed by *beyond Babylon*; he may have thought of the deportation (later than Amos) to Babylon; he (Stephen or Luke) may have been guilty of a lapse of memory.

44. the tent of testimony, a regular LXX term for the Tabernacle. It is clear that Stephen (Luke) thinks the Tabernacle preferable to the Temple; see below and cf. Heb. 8.1–5. **Our Fathers**: those of the Exodus. **charged**: the verb cognate with the noun *ordinance* in v. 53. Cf. Exod. 25.1, 9, 40. **he who spoke to Moses** is of course God. There is a positive command to make a tent; a house (vv. 47, 49) is different.

45. Our fathers are now the next generation of Israelite ancestors. **entered into the succession**, took their turn after Moses. **up to the time of David.** This must relate to the use of the Tabernacle. The construction of this verse is not clear.

46. David **found favour with God**; cf. 2 Kdms 15.25. He **asked that he might provide**: asked for himself that he might provide, that is, have the privilege of providing. Cf. 2 Sam. 7.2, 5. **a sacred dwelling-place for the house of Jacob**. Cf. Ps. 131(132).5. In agreement with the Psalm, many MSS of Acts read *for the God of Jacob*; this however is the easier reading and *house* is read by old and important MSS and should be accepted. In fact the two readings have substantially the same meaning. A dwelling for the God of Jacob is a temple for him to dwell in; a dwelling for the house of Jacob is (in this context) a place that the house of Jacob may use as a temple, that is, as a dwelling for their God. The prophet Nathan at first approved David's desire, later forbade it, with the promise that David's son should build a house for God's name.

47. But Solomon built God (Greek, him) **a house.** A statement of fact. Early Christians however would take David's son (in Nathan's prophecy) to be (not Solomon but) the Messiah – Jesus. Solomon wrongfully anticipated the work of Christ.

48. the Most High. In the OT this is a common name or description of God. It is also used of Zeus and was sometimes thought by the heathen to be a suitable term for the solitary Jewish deity; it may also have been used in syncretistic Jewish cults. He does not dwell **in things made by human hands**. In Greek, this is the word *in* with one compound word, which is used in the LXX in a uniformly bad sense and connected with idolatry. Used of the Temple it must have been highly offensive in Jewish ears.

But at the beginning of the verse is probably strongly adversative (Solomon built a house but should have done no such thing), not slightly so (Solomon built a house, but we must not think that God is confined to it). The verse states only what the OT already knows (1 Kings 8.27); but it is to be noted that Stephen picks out not the many OT passages that glorify the Temple but some of the few that criticize it. There is here sharp criticism, probably rejection, of the Temple. It must be remembered that in Acts 1–5 Christians continue to use the Temple, and that (according to Acts – see 21.26) Paul was prepared to do so. A twofold attitude to the Temple matches Luke's attitude to Judaism in general. See Introduction, pp. lxv–lxvii.

49, 50. Isa. 66.1, 2, quoted in close agreement with the LXX. Most though not all OT scholars are agreed that the prophecy did not originally constitute an attack on the Temple, but this seems to be how Stephen (Luke) understood it. Cf. 17.24f. Many, perhaps most, Jews of the Diaspora had to practise their religion without use of the Temple. Stephen appears to have denied, as Jeremiah (7.21–6) had done before him, that God required the sacrificial worship that was the Temple's *raison d'être*; he (or Luke) may have thought it inconsistent with the majesty of God.

51. Stephen's apostrophe of Israel is expressed in OT language, but it is not a quotation of any OT passage. Cf. Exod. 33.3; Lev.

26.41; Jer. 6.10; Deut. 10.16; Jer. 4.4; Jubilees 1.7, 23; 1 QS 5.5; 1 QpHab 11.13.

You are always contradicting the Holy Spirit. Cf. Isa. 63.10. **as your fathers did**: the evidence in the speech is repeated and amplified in v. 52ab. **so also do you**: this is implied in the persecution of Stephen but the chief point is in v. 52c. According to Stephen, the history of Israel consists of messages addressed by God to his people, and of his people's disobedience and recalcitrance.

52. Stephen's words are an exaggeration, pardonable no doubt in the circumstances. The OT does not provide evidence for the persecution and killing of all the prophets, though the verse itself provoked the development of apocryphal legends designed to support it.

the Righteous One. Cf. 3.14, with the note. In the present passage it is hard to avoid the conclusion that it is a title. **betrayers and murderers**, by handing Jesus over to Pilate and thus securing his death.

53. The *betrayers and murderers* were the more culpable because they had received the highest privileges. They had **received the Law at the ordinance of angels**. Cf. v. 38, Gal. 3.19; Heb. 2.2. In Galatians only is the participation of angels seen as a relative disparagement. For the presence of angels see Deut. 33.2, taken up in many Jewish texts. At Qumran CD 5.18 is not a close parallel.

keep is to observe obediently. The killing of Jesus is the climax of disobedience. It seems probable (see p. 97) that the reference to Jesus was added as a new climax for a Hellenistic Jewish sermon, originally intended to expose the errors of the people and summon them to repentance and true obedience.

19. STEPHEN'S MARTYRDOM 7.54 – 8.1a

54 As they listened to these things they were cut to the quick and gnashed their teeth against him. 55 But he, full of the Holy Spirit, gazed into heaven and saw the glory of God, and Jesus standing at God's right hand. 56 He said, 'Look, I see the heavens opened, and the Son of man standing at God's right hand.' 57 They shouted with a loud voice, stopped their ears, and together rushed at him.
58 They threw him out of the city and stoned him; and the witnesses laid down their clothes at the feet of a young man called Saul.
59 And they stoned Stephen, as he called upon the Lord, and said, 'Lord Jesus, receive my spirit.' 60 He knelt down and cried with a loud voice, 'Lord, do not let this sin stand against them.' And when he had said this he fell asleep.

1 Saul was in full agreement with his killing.

There is some reason to think that in 6.8–15 two sources were combined; a similar phenomenon is to be found in the new paragraph. The simplest forms of this hypothesis is that 6.9–11; 7.54–58a constitute a 'lynching' source (in which Stephen is the victim of a popular move) and 6.12–14; 7.58b–60 a 'trial' source (in which Stephen is condemned by a court). Just as in ch. 6 *we have heard* is repeated (vv. 11, 14; cf. also vv. 11, 13, *suborned*, *set up*), so stoned is repeated in 7.58a, 59. This separation of two sources is fundamentally sound, but it cannot be held in its simplest form. There are many different theories. Luke's editorial hand has been at work; he has introduced Saul and thereby shown ignorance of Jewish legal procedure (see the note on v. 58). He had the story of the death of Jesus in his mind.

That there should have been two accounts of the death of Stephen bears witness to the impression made by the event in the church's memory. This is the more readily understandable if it did indeed make a deep impression on Saul. See Acts 22.20; yet Paul never in the extant epistles mentions Stephen.

Luke in this paragraph wishes to show that the evangelistic move to the Gentiles was rooted in Jerusalem Christianity. But just as Stephen's speech shows an at least partially negative attitude to Judaism, so his martyrdom represents the No of Judaism to the Gospel. Perhaps this was a No that had to be spoken before the

Gospel could be taken outside the limits within which it was born (cf. not only 13.46; 18.6; 28.28 but also Romans 9–11), and was (after the resurrection of Jesus, and indeed as part of this) the supreme example of the power of God to bring good out of evil (cf. p. 97).

The historicity of the event and, assuming its historicity, its date must be considered in the light of Jn 18.31. The correctness of John's statement is disputed. If it is incorrect there is no problem. If it is correct the problem may be answered by the suggestion that the event took place during the interregnum between the recall of Pilate and the arrival of his successor. But this interval was short and late, thus making Paul's conversion impossibly late. It may be best to infer that Stephen died at the hands of a mob – this would solve the problem.

54. Listening to Stephen's speech provoked the hearers to greater rage. For their expression of it cf. Ps. 34(35).16.

55. Luke knows that Christians are given special help by the Holy Spirit at times of special need (cf. 4.8; for Stephen and the Spirit cf. 6.3, 5, 10). The Spirit enables Stephen to see a vision of heaven and face death. The vision shows that God is taking Stephen's part. Cf. Targum Pseudo-Jonathan Gen. 27.1: Isaac's defective sight is explained. 'When his father bound him he saw the throne of glory, and from that moment his eyes began to become dim.' The present verse and the next recall the question, which gave rise to much dispute within Judaism, and between Jews and Christians, whether there is anyone, any other power, who may share the throne of God. Here it is said that Jesus was standing at God's right hand. Cf. 3 Enoch 16.3–5 (Aḥer [Elisha b. Abuya] saw Metatron sitting on a great throne and said, There are indeed two powers in heaven. Then, at the command of the Holy One, the Prince struck Metatron with sixty lashes of fire and *made him stand to his feet*). Jesus is already standing. See further on v. 56.

56. Here only outside the gospels does *the Son of man* (with the article) occur in the NT. Here only, and in v. 55, is Jesus (the Son of man) said to stand, rather than sit, at the right hand of God. Most NT passages are affected by Ps. 110.1. There have been many attempts to explain why the Son of man should here be described as standing. Most see him as in some sense rising for the assistance or support of Stephen, or to welcome him to heaven; he rises to minister as priest in the heavenly Temple or to plead in the heavenly court. Perhaps the best suggestion is that the Son of man is standing because he is about to come – to the martyr at the time of his death as at the end he will come to all men.

57. The council had been angered by the speech; now (whether or not they saw in the vision Stephen reported a threat to the unity of God) they would hear no more. But can the subjects of the verbs in this sentence be the members of the council? Does Luke move from a 'trial' source to a 'lynching' source? **They . . . stopped their ears** could follow immediately upon 7.53, but it would be wrong to suppose that it must have done so.

58. They threw him out of the city and stoned him. The legal process of stoning is described in M. Sanhedrin 6.1–5. The place of stoning was far from the court. The person to be stoned was stripped and thrown down from a height at least twice that of a man. This might suffice. If he still lived a witness took a stone and dropped it on his heart. If he still lived he was stoned by all Israel. Only Luke's *they threw him out of the city* corresponds to this. It is possibly a lynching that is in mind here, but the word for *they stoned* is the same as that used in v. 59.

The introduction in the last words of the verse of **a young man called Saul** is a fine touch of Luke's dramatic instinct. His word tells us little about Saul's age. Acts 26.10 seems to claim that not long after the stoning of Stephen he had a vote in courts that passed sentence on Christians. In a legal stoning the witnesses did not throw stones and had no need to take off their clothes.

59. they stoned, the same word as in v. 58; there is no means here of distinguishing between sources.

he called upon. It is surprising that in Greek no object is expressed. It is of course easy to take one out of the words attributed to Stephen. For the use of **Lord** with **Jesus**; cf. 2.36. For the prayer; cf. Lk. 23.46, though there the verb is different. It is presupposed that the speaker has a **spirit** which survives the death of the body and may be entrusted to the divine protector.

60. He knelt down. Luke's wording is a Latinism (cf. 17.9; 19.38). Stephen continues his prayer. **Lord** presumably refers to Jesus, as in v. 59. **do not let this sin stand against them**. *Stand* is sometimes used in financial contexts and this may be the image here: *stand in their (moral) account*. The word may also mean *establish*, the opposite of *forgive*. There is no difference in meaning. Cf. Lk. 23.34 (but note the omission by important authorities).

As Calvin points out, Stephen's prayer shows in its two parts faith and love: a good example of a Christian death.

he fell asleep. This word for death is used elsewhere in the NT, in the OT, and in post-biblical Judaism. But it is not exclusively biblical.

1a. Saul: see v. 58. **killing** – so, rather than *death*. Like the reference in v. 58 this is probably Luke's own editorial work.

20. PERSECUTION 8.1b–3

[1] At that time there arose a severe persecution against the church in Jerusalem, and all were dispersed through the districts of Judaea and Samaria, except the apostles. [2] Devout men buried Stephen, and made loud lamentation over him. [3] Saul violently attacked the church, and going into house after house and dragging off men and women handed them over to prison.

This short paragraph is probably Luke's own work, an introduction to the combined stories, in chs. 8–12, of Paul, Peter, Philip, and the unnamed disciples who took the Gospel to Antioch. Chronological sequence throughout these chapters is obscure, and the present paragraph lacks clarity. Verse 2 concludes the story of Stephen. It may be the end of the 'lynching' story (see p. 91), but *devout men* suggests Luke's work, and Luke was probably responsible also for vv. 1 and 3. One of his sources spoke (8.4; 11.19) of *those who had been dispersed* (*scattered*) and he prepared for this by saying that *all were dispersed* (v. 1); *except the apostles* prepared for 9.27, but overlooks 9.26. It is a reasonable inference that it was the remaining Six (cf. 6.5) and their adherents who were obliged to leave Jerusalem. Saul's persecuting activity in v. 3 prepared for ch. 9, and for 22.4, 19; 26.9–11.

That this paragraph is due to Lucan editing does not rob it of historical value. Persecution scatters; and we have Paul's own word for his work as a persecutor (1 Cor. 15.9; Gal. 1.13, 23; Phil. 3.6; cf. 1 Tim. 1.13).

1b. At that time, literally, *On that day.* Luke means that the persecution followed without delay. For **the church** see on 5.11 and Introduction, pp. lviif. So far as Luke has told us, there was at this time no church except in Jerusalem. Like the Jewish, the Christian Diaspora (limited at this time to Judaea and Samaria) was in part due to persecution. **all were dispersed**; Luke excepts **the apostles** in view of 9.26f. Luke presumably meant what he wrote, but there may well have been other exceptions.

2. This verse interrupts the connection between vv. 1 and 3.

The general sense of the word translated **buried** is clear, but not its precise meaning. The Mishnah (M. Sanhedrin 6.5, 6) prescribes funeral rites and limits the degree of mourning for executed criminals.

loud lamentation is either an indication that Stephen's death was due to lynching, not to a court decision, or that his friends defied the court, or that the Mishnaic regulations were not yet in force. But the verse is probably Luke's insertion of what seemed to him a suitable close for his account of Stephen.

Devout men. Again the meaning is not precise. The word seems to be one that Luke uses (2.5; 8.2; 22.12; Lk. 2.25) for 'good' Jews who if not already Christians are ready to be persuaded.

3. Saul is the chief agent in the persecution of v. 1. **House after house.** It is sometimes asked whether these were private residences or meeting-houses. The answer is that there is no difference. The Christians met in the (larger) houses of (wealthier) Christians.

IV

THE GOSPEL REACHES SAMARIA

(8.4–40)

21. EVANGELIZATION OF SAMARIA: SIMON MAGUS 8.4–25

**[4] So then those who had been dispersed went on their way,
preaching the word as good news. [5] Philip went down to the city
of Samaria and proclaimed Christ to them. [6] With one accord
the crowds paid attention to the things said by Philip as they
listened and saw the signs that he performed. [7] For unclean spirits,
crying with a loud voice, came out of many, and many paralysed
and lame people were cured; [8] and there was great joy in that
city.**

**[9] A certain man, Simon by name, had for some time past been
in the city practising as a magus and astounding the Samaritan
nation, saying that he was someone great. [10] All of them, from the
least to the greatest, paid attention to him, saying, 'This is the
power of God called great.' [11] They paid attention to him because
for a long time he had been astonishing them by his magical
practices, [12] but when they believed Philip as he preached the good
news about the kingdom of God and the name of Jesus Christ
they were baptized, both men and women. [13] Simon himself also
became a believer, and when he had been baptized he continued
in Philip's company, and as he beheld the signs and mighty works
that were done he was astonished.**

**[14] When the apostles in Jerusalem heard that Samaria had
received the word of God they sent to them Peter and John, [15] who
went down and prayed for them that they might receive the Holy
Spirit, [16] for it had not yet fallen on any of them; they had only**

been baptized in the name of the Lord Jesus. [17] Then they laid
their hands upon them and they received the Holy Spirit. [18] When
Simon saw that the Spirit was given through the imposition of
the apostles' hands he brought them money, [19] and said, 'Give me
too this power, that anyone on whom I lay my hands may receive
the Holy Spirit'. [20] So Peter said to him, 'May your money perish
with you, because you thought to acquire God's gift by money.
[21] You have no part or lot in this matter, for your heart is not
straight in the sight of God. [22] Repent of this wickedness of yours,
and beseech the Lord, if perhaps your intention may be forgiven,
[23] for I see that you are full of bitter poison, bound by un-
righteousness.' [24] Simon answered, 'Do you pray to the Lord on
my behalf that none of the things you have spoken may happen
to me.'

[25] So they bore their testimony and spoke the word of the Lord
and returned to Jerusalem; and they evangelized many villages
of the Samaritans.

This passage combines a number of themes that are important in Acts. Luke has brought them together into a single connected story, though it seems clear that vv. 5–13, in which Philip is the central Christian character, and vv. 14–24, in which he disappears and is replaced by Peter and John, were originally distinct.

Verse 4 is Luke's own introduction (perhaps based on a reference to Antioch – see the note); in v. 5 begins the account of Philip's (see 6.5) preaching in Samaria. Many are converted and baptized, including Simon the Magus, who is introduced in vv. 9–12. At this point Philip disappears till 8.26. Peter and John arrive on the scene (v. 14) and by prayer and the laying on of hands supply what previously had been wanting: the Holy Spirit falls on the new converts. Simon then offers money for the right thus to bestow the Holy Spirit and is rebuked by Peter, who, with John, makes a missionary tour back to Jerusalem. Luke does not describe the relation between the Seven (Philip) and the Twelve (Peter and John). He notes a new stage in the expansion of Christianity, shows the unity of the church, and offers implications regarding Simon, baptism, and the Holy Spirit.

Christian writers in the second century saw in Simon the founder of a gnostic sect. This is not how Luke describes him; Luke's magi (here and in ch. 13) are magicians, not proto-gnostics. Simon's fault is – simony. Luke is sensitive to money matters in general, and attempts to make profit out of the supernatural arouse his indignation.

That the Spirit is conferred through the ministry of Peter and John, not through that of Philip, points not to a difference in status but to the fact that God gives the Spirit (Luke is thinking of inspiration with manifestations such as speaking with tongues) not in consequence of payment or of liturgical correctness but as and when he sees fit. The church has the Spirit as guide and defender, but it has this privilege as a gift which it may depend on but cannot control and never possesses in its own right.

Attempts to divide the passage into neat segments drawn from a variety of sources are not convincing, though there are occasional repetitions of words that may suggest the use of sources: *pay attention* in vv. 6, 10, 11; *astound*, *astonish* in vv. 9, 11, 13; *great* in vv. 9, 10; *believed*, *baptized* in vv. 12, 13. The most probable explanation is that Luke possessed various pieces of information about Simon which he combined in one narrative. It must not be forgotten that 21.8 suggests some measure of contact between the author of Acts and Philip. He is putting together, perhaps not without historical justification, information that connected Philip with Simon and thus with Samaria and the tradition of evangelization by the Seven; Peter and John are introduced in order to show that the Seven were allies, not rivals, of the Twelve. If this is so the hypothesis that Samaria was evangelized by Hellenists and that the apostles took over their work, and that this is reflected in Jn 4.38, will not stand. A more interesting gospel passage is Mt. 10.5. If there were Christians who were doubtful whether Samaritans should be evangelized the exploratory mission of Peter and John would be intelligible.

Traditionally this passage (with Acts 19.6) has been used as the basis for the practice of confirmation as a post-baptismal rite. It cannot be said that Luke takes it in this way.

4. those who had been dispersed resumes 8.1 and points forward to 11.19, which some think to be the original continuation of the present verse, since **went on their way** (literally, *passed through*) requires a destination. This verb often suggests a missionary journey; this suits the context here. It could have been part of an Antiochene source, into which Luke interposed a group of illustrative stories about Philip and also about Peter (9.32 – 11.18); it was necessary to add also Saul's conversion to prepare for 11.25.

5. Philip cannot be (for Luke) the apostle, since the apostles remained in Jerusalem (8.1). On the Samaritans see *NS* 2.15–20. The NT regularly takes them as occupying a middle position, neither full Jews nor mere Gentiles. Philip has reached this middle point (cf. 1.8). The geographical location is not clear because though some MSS have **the city of Samaria** others have *a city of Samaria*. This variant treats *Samaria* as a region in which there are several cities; Luke does not know, or at least does not name, the city in question. The reading with *the* will either refer to the capital city (though in Luke's time this was called Sebaste) or assume that in the province there was only one city – this is not as unlikely as it might seem, if *city* means a place of some size. It is against *the city* that Samaria (Sebaste) was a highly hellenized community, not so much Samaritan as Gentile; this however may have led copyists to change *the city* into *a city*. If the latter reading is accepted one may consider the suggestion that the unnamed city was Gitta, according to Justin (*1 Apology* 26) the home of Simon Magus.

7. The meaning of the verse is clear though the language is a little confused. The cures are described conventionally; Luke is writing up a tradition that may have told him little more than that Philip visited Samaria.

8. This verse could have been followed by v. 12. Verses 9–11 interrupt the sequence and were probably drawn from a different source.

9. The new source (see v. 8) introduces **Simon**, who is not mentioned elsewhere in the NT, but was regarded by later Christians as the founder of the gnostic sect of the Simonians. According to Justin Martyr (*1 Apology* 26; cf. 56; *Dialogue with Trypho* 120.6) he was a Samaritan who came from Gitta, and was honoured by an inscription in Rome which spoke of him as a god: *Simoni Deo Sancto* (cf. Tertullian, *Apology* 13). This statement is now very widely taken to be an erroneous reference to an inscription discovered in 1574, which runs, *Semoni Sanco Dio Fidio*, a dedication to a (probably) Sabine god, Semo Sancus. In Acts Simon is described not as a gnostic but as one **practising as a magus**. He is one of a class that Luke strongly dislikes; he has illicit dealings with the supernatural, and makes money out of them (see below, pp. 121f.; and cf. 13.6–11; 16.16–24; 19.11–20, 23–40). There is no reason to think that Simon was in fact a gnostic and that Luke has downgraded him into a magus for polemical reasons. His claim is to be **someone great**. This is quite unexplicit, but see v. 10.

10. See v. 6; Simon had occupied the position that Philip had now taken. **from the least to the greatest**: not a Greek idiom, possibly taken from Hebrew by way of the LXX.

This is the power of God called great. This looks like a popular expression of the words ascribed to Simon in v. 9, but *This is* may be based on an *I am*, used in aretalogical statements (e.g. the 'divine man' in Origen, *c. Celsum* 7.8f., says, I am God, or God's child, or divine spirit). It may be that *power* itself means god, *of god* being Luke's explanatory supplement (cf. Lk. 22.69 with Mk 14.62), but there is precedent for the notion that the supreme God is accompanied by powers. This distinction is found in Philo, though he can also refer to God himself as the 'highest and greatest power'. Heretical Judaism countenanced the belief that there were two (or more) ruling powers in heaven; see M. Sanhedrin 4.5; B. Hagigah 15a; 3 Enoch 16.3; also the notes on 7.55f. Simon may have held the belief that of many Powers of God he was the great one. Or it may be that Simon was not a speculative gnostic theologian downgraded by Luke but a very ordinary magician upgraded so as to appear a 'divine man'. By doing this Luke would find himself able to kill two objectionable birds with one stone.

11. A curiously repetitive verse. Luke seems to be gathering up material about Simon so as to make the transition back to Philip; hence at the end of the verse a comma, not a full stop.

12. They believed. Faith is the correct reaction to the preached word, but it is unusual that it should be directed to the preacher; the first step however to faith in a full theological sense is to recognize, What this preacher says is true. The content of **the good news** that Philip preached is **the kingdom of God and the name of Jesus Christ**. In Acts *the kingdom of God* often serves as a general summary for the content of preaching (e.g. 28.23). For *the name* see on 1.3; 3.6, 16. Philip's Gospel is a statement of Christian truth in which at least the terminology of eschatology is retained.

The believers were **baptized**; Luke no doubt thought that no further reference to the name was necessary (see v. 16). **both men and women**: both were equally exposed to persecution (8.3), both equally are offered the benefits of the Gospel.

13. Simon . . . became a believer . . . baptized. There is nothing in this verse to suggest that Simon was less sincere or in any way a less satisfactory convert than the other Samaritans. The verse shows stylistic signs of Luke's editorial hand.

14. Luke made it clear at 8.1 that the apostles remained in Jerusalem; news reached them that **Samaria had received the word of God** (that is, had believed, come to faith). No reason is given for the mission of Peter and John (as in chs. 3, 4 and 5, only Peter speaks). Verses 15f. suggest that they may have been sent to convey a gift that Philip had been unable to provide, v. 17 to carry out a rite (the laying on of hands) that only apostles were entitled to perform. The parallel with 11.22 (Barnabas sent to Antioch) may suggest inspection, or the taking over by the Twelve of a mission initiated by others (cf. Jn 4.38, and see p. 117). All that can be said with confidence is that here, as in ch. 6, Luke wished to show that the Seven and the Twelve acted in harmony, but that new Christian developments needed to be integrated, and to be seen to be integrated, with the movement that flowed authentically from the work of Jesus (cf. 1.21f.). The mission to Samaria is part of the movement whose links with Jesus are affirmed by the apostles whom he chose. It is a part of a wider mission inspired by the Spirit, who is Lord over the process, not to be coerced whether by payment or by ritual actions.

15. went down. The word is regularly used for journeys from the capital, irrespective of the elevation of the destination.

16. So their baptism did not have the effect of conferring the Spirit. For Luke's view of the relation between baptism and the gift of the Spirit see Introduction, pp. lx–lxii; also for the meaning of **in the name**. Some (including Calvin) think that what was lacking was not the general grace of the Spirit, without which there is no Christian life, but the special endowment that results in spiritual gifts, such as prophecy.

17. For the laying on of hands in Acts see on 6.6. For its use in the context of baptism see 19.6 (and perhaps 9.12, 17). The narrative element in the verse is clear; less clear is Luke's purpose in including it. He does not mean that baptism carried out by Philip was defective; see 8.38. He does not mean that the gift of the Spirit is contingent upon the laying on of hands; see 10.44, where the Spirit is given before baptism and there is no reference to the laying on of hands. He does not mean that baptism is complete and effective only in the presence of an apostle; see once more 8.38 and 9.17f. This is a special case. Luke is concerned (see above) to show how the new mission was integrated into one apostolic mission and that the Seven and the

Twelve collaborated. He is about to tell of Simon's wish to buy the power to communicate the Spirit: there must have been some ecstatic manifestation to evoke this desire. Luke wishes further to show that the Spirit is not controlled by human agencies, whether liturgical or financial.

18. When Simon saw . . . See on v. 17: in this gift of the Spirit there was something to *see*.

19. Give me too – that I may have it as well as you – **this power**. Luke (see e.g. 19.13–20) greatly dislikes the use of the supenatural for money.

20. May your money perish with you. Peter shares Luke's dislike. This attitude is widespread in Greek literature.

21. You have no part or lot in this matter. His request shows that Simon has no place in the Christian movement. *Matter* could be translated *word*, and it may be that there is a specific reference to Christian proclamation. **your heart is not straight in the sight of God**. Simon is attempting to cheat God, to infringe the divine prerogative of bestowing the Spirit in accordance with his own will.

22. The only thing for Simon to do is to **repent**. The theme of repentance occurs frequently in Acts, here only with reference to a particular sin (other than the rejection of Jesus) and here only is the sin introduced by the word literally rendered *from* (Greek, *apo*). This goes naturally with the Hebrew for *turn*, which has the frequent transferred meaning *repent*, and Luke's use of *from* has been thought to be a Semitism and to justify the conclusion that we have here the very words of Peter and a proof of the historicity of the incident. This is an unconvincing argument. The OT connection between *turn* and *repent* inevitably brought with it the use of *from*; cf. Heb. 6.1; Justin, *Dialogue with Trypho*, 109.1. Peter does not regard penitence as impossible.

23. I see that you are full of bitter poison, bound by unrighteousness. The translation is uncertain. The first part of the assertion, if it stood alone, could well mean, 'You are destined for bitter anger, that is, to experience the wrath of God (unless you repent).' The difficulty lies in finding a way of taking the next words in a corresponding sense. 'You are destined for the bondage (in hell) deserved by unrighteousness' might be possible but is not convincing. Much better would be, 'In your present state of mind you are in bondage to unrighteousness.' But then, what does the first phrase mean? One could say, 'You are in a state of bitter anger,' but bitter anger was not Simon's sin. It seems better to take this in the sense *bitter poison*, a possible meaning of Luke's word (literally, *gall, bile*).

24. Do you pray. Simon's *you* is emphatic. 'You have urged me to pray; pray for me (or, on my behalf).' It is probably unfair to Simon to suggest that he is still moving in the sphere of magic, in that he believes that a prayer offered by Peter will have automatic effect. That he may be truly penitent is suggested more strongly by the Western text. **the things you have spoken** suggests that the words of v. 23 refer to punishments, but this is not necessarily so. Peter has spoken of perdition in v. 20. The issue of Simon's penitence is not clear because Luke was not greatly interested in it; the personal fate of Simon was not his major concern. The second-century identification of Simon with Simonianism should be viewed with scepticism.

25. they probably refers to Peter and John. Philip is dealt with in the next verse. Peter now disappears until 9.32, John (apart from being his brother's brother, 12.2) completely. If their visit was an inspection it has cleared the way to evangelism in Samaria. For the contrast, or contradiction, with Mt. 10.5 see above, p. 117.

22. PHILIP AND THE ETHIOPIAN 8.26–40

[26] An angel of the Lord spoke to Philip, and said, 'Get up and travel at midday on the road that goes down from Jerusalem to Gaza; this is deserted'. [27] He got up, and went. And there was an Ethiopian man, a eunuch and minister of Candace, Queen of the Ethiopians, who was in charge of all her wealth. He had gone to worship in Jerusalem, [28] and was returning, sitting in his chariot and reading the prophet Isaiah. [29] The Spirit said to Philip, 'Go up to this chariot and join it.' [30] Philip ran up, heard him reading the prophet Isaiah, and said, 'Do you, I wonder, understand what you are reading?' [31] He said, 'How should I be able to, unless someone guides me?' And he asked Philip to get up and sit with him. [32] The passage of Scripture that he was reading was this: As a sheep he was led to slaughter, as a lamb before the one who shears it is dumb, so he does not open his mouth. [33] In his humiliation his judgment was taken away. Who shall recount his generation? For his life is taken away from the earth. [34] The eunuch took up the conversation and said to Philip, 'Pray, about whom does the prophet say this? About himself or about someone else?' [35] Philip opened his mouth, and, taking this Scripture as his starting-point, proclaimed to him the good news of Jesus. [36] As they travelled along the road they came upon some water, and the eunuch said, 'Look, here is some water; what prevents me from being baptized?' [38] He gave orders for the chariot to come to a halt and the two of them went down into the water, Philip and the eunuch, and Philip baptized him. [39] When they came up out of the water the Spirit of the Lord caught away Philip and the eunuch saw him no more, for he simply continued on his way, rejoicing. [40] Philip arrived at Azotus; he continued on his way, evangelizing all the cities till he came to Caesarea.

The story is told in a straightforward style, though with appeal to supernatural influence. Supernatural powers direct Philip and cause him to fall in with an Ethiopian eunuch who is a high official in his country. The traveller is reading the OT; Philip interprets it to him in Christological terms; the eunuch seeks and is given baptism; Philip is removed to Azotus by extraordinary means; and the eunuch proceeds on his way. It is the story of a conversion, and Luke uses it to illustrate the power of the Gospel and the oversight by God of the Christian mission.

But Luke is pursuing the pattern of expansion adumbrated in 1.8 and it is natural to ask how the story fits into the pattern. The traveller was an Ethiopian, not a Jew by birth, and as a eunuch could not be a proselyte. He was thus a stage more remote from the people of God than Cornelius, whose story follows in ch. 10.

It is well to remember the reappearance of Philip in Caesarea at 21.8. Directly or indirectly Luke must have obtained information about Philip's activities. He had given one such story in 8.5–13 and combined it with stories about Simon Magus and Peter. It was natural to proceed with the second Philip story as soon as the Magus was out of the way and Peter and John had returned to Jerusalem, and to do so with little regard to chronology. It will be noted that both the work of Philip (8.40; 21.8) and that of Peter (9.32 – 10.1) converge on Caesarea, where there was at an early stage a mixed Jewish and Gentile church. This however points to the difference between the story of the Ethiopian and that of Cornelius, both of whom are described as neither born Jews nor proselytes, but sympathetically interested in Judaism and its religion. The difference is that after his baptism the eunuch saw Philip no more (v. 39) but returned to Ethiopia, whereas Cornelius was baptized as one of a group who formed the kernel of a church.

There is no means of checking the historicity of the narrative unless it can be assumed that angels do not exist or that they do not order missionaries about or provide transport for them. Even if these assumptions are true it might be possible to retell the story in outline without angelic intervention.

There is no evidence of a first-century church in Ethiopia.

26. The story is resumed from 8.13, the new development being ascribed to divine initiative by the reference to **An angel of the Lord**. Later instructions will be given by the Holy Spirit; here, as in ch. 10, there is little difference in this respect between the two agencies (8.26, 29; 10.3, 19). The conversion of the Ethiopian was planned not by Philip but by God.

travel at midday; or; toward the south. Luke's word means *midday* but was also used of the position of the sun at midday, the south. *South* fits the geography approximately, whether Philip is starting from Samaria or Jerusalem. *Midday* may be preferred precisely because noon was no time to travel under a hot sun. It was by going at a time he would not choose that Philip would meet a man ready for conversion.

the road that goes down from the hills to the sea, but the word is also used for returning from pilgrimage. **this is deserted**. The road, or Gaza? Grammatically *this* could apply to either. But the road from Jerusalem to Gaza is said not to be desert, and the old town of Gaza, sacked by Alexander Jannaeus in 96 BC, long remained desolate, even when a new town was built. **Gaza** was one of the five cities of the Philistines (1 Sam. 6.17). It was rebuilt in 56 BC by Gabinius, again destroyed in AD 66.

27. an Ethopian, It was God's plan that Philip should meet him. The Ethiopian kingdom was not the modern Ethiopia but the Sudan; its capital was Meroe. The Ethiopians, 'last of men' (Homer, *Odyssey* 1.23), were remote enough to enjoy a reputation for piety, but for Luke and his contemporaries OT references would be more important: Ps. 68(67).32(31), Let Ethiopia hasten to stretch out her hands to God; Zeph. 3.10. The man was **a eunuch**. Such men were excluded from the Lord's people (Deut. 23.1(2)), though later a distinction was made between one impotent from birth and one subsequently mutilated (M. Yebamoth 8; cf. M. Niddah 5.9). The matter is further complicated by the fact that the Hebrew word *saris* had originally nothing to do with sexual impotence but referred to persons of state. The religious disqualification of the eunuch is both recognized and removed in Isa. 56.3–5. This clearly refers to physical disability ('I am a dry tree') but promises to the pious eunuch 'in my house and within my walls a monument and a name better than sons and daughters'. The Ethiopian traveller was *a eunuch* **and minister of Candace**, **Queen of the Ethiopians**, an officer of some importance. Luke seems to have taken *Candace* as a personal name; in fact it appears to transliterate the title that appears in Ethiopic inscriptions as *k(e)ut(e)ky*. His function is defined: he was **in charge of all her wealth. He had gone to worship in Jerusalem**. In what sense? He was not a Jew; he could not become a proselyte. If it is right to speak of a special class of 'God-fearers' or 'half-proselytes' (see on 10.2) he may have been one of such men. One must ask whether a man could be found of whom all these predicates were true: he was an Ethiopian; he was a eunuch; he belonged to the ruling class of his people; he read the Bible; he went on pilgrimage to Jerusalem. Does he in the expansion of the church represent an earlier stage than Cornelius? Perhaps because of the favourable prophecy in

Isaiah 56? But Luke does not quote this passage. Probably we must be content to take the story as a piece of tradition about Philip which Luke placed here not because it fitted into his scheme of Christian expansion but because this was the point at which he was dealing with Philip.

28. The Ethiopian **was returning in** – or, *on* – **his chariot**; not a luxurious vehicle. The most we can say of it is that Luke thought it capable of holding two passengers. It cannot have moved very rapidly (it was probably ox-drawn) since Philip was able to run and join it (v. 30). The Eunuch was fortunate to possess for himself a copy of a biblical book; he must have been enthusiastic in the pursuit of such features of the Jewish religion as were open to him. He was **reading** aloud, as was customary in antiquity.

29. Previously an angel had directed Philip (v. 26); now **the Spirit** does so.

30. Philip ran up, quickening his pace. He **heard him reading** (aloud) **the prophet Isaiah**. The brief exchange which follows has been described as a 'gem of Greek conversation' (W. L. Knox). It was right to use a journey for study (e.g. B. Erubin 54a; cf. M. Aboth 3.8).

31. The OT is not self-explanatory; for Luke, it needs Christological interpretation. The OT bears witness (so Luke, like other NT writers, believed) to Jesus Christ, but the witness is intelligible only if one is able to begin with Jesus. This is the advantage that Philip has over the Ethiopian (cf. v. 35).

32, 33. The passage the eunuch was reading was Isa. 53.7, 8. Since he was reading as he made a long journey it is reasonable to infer that he could have in his mind more than the few lines given in these verses; and it may be reasonable to infer that Luke regarded them as conveying the sense of the whole. They do not contain the word *Servant* or the notion of vicarious sacrifice. Luke may have thought the passage adequately summarized without them.

Isaiah is quoted in agreement with the LXX, with only a few small variations. In two places the Hebrew differs from the Greek:

LXX: In his humiliation his judgement was taken away

Hebrew: From (as a result of) oppression and judgement he was taken off

LXX: For his life is taken away from the earth

Hebrew: For he was cut off from the land of the living

The meaning of v. 32 is reasonably clear; the Ethiopian may well be excused for failing to understand v. 33. Whom is the prophet portraying?

34. The Ethiopian's problem is the identification of the Servant referred to – not by that designation in the verses quoted but in the passage as a whole. The prophet himself, or some other? Judaism had no agreed answer to this question. There is a good summary of opinions by J. Jeremias in *TDNT* 5.678–700, except that doubt must be cast on the belief that any Jews identified the Servant with the Messiah. It does not seem that the Servant was taken to be the Messiah at Qumran.

35. Philip opened his mouth. Another of Luke's OT phrases; cf. 10.34; 18.14. In Rabbinic use it came to mean 'to open' even 'to give a lecture on Scripture'. He **proclaimed to him the good news of Jesus**, presumably identifying Jesus with the person described in **this Scripture**. Exactly how this identification with the contents of vv. 32, 33 is effected is not clear. Verse 32 presumably implies that Jesus dies a sacrificial death (though the sheep is not killed but shorn). Verse 33a may be taken in two ways: *either* he was humiliated and his right to fair trial was taken away; *or* even in his humiliation the judgement against him was taken away, that is, cancelled. Verse 33b can hardly be understood unless *his generation* is taken to mean *his disciples*, who will become innumerable. Verse 33c is ambiguous like v. 33a: *either* his life is taken away, *or* he has been taken up into heaven.

36. Philip and the eunuch, **as they travelled along the road . . . came upon some water**. This is not surprising; there is good winter rainfall along the coastal strip.

What prevents me . . . ? This has been thought to represent the liturgical inquiry used at a baptism, but *What prevents?* is a fairly common idiom for *Why not?*

37. In what seems to be the original text the question is left unanswered. A number of MSS supply the continuation: *If you believe with all your heart it is permitted. He answered, I believe that Jesus Christ is the Son of God* (or similar words). It will be observed that the word *believe* is used in different ways. Philip uses it of confident trust in God (or Christ), the eunuch of the acceptance of a dogmatic proposition.

38. He (that is, the eunuch) **gave orders**. Both men **went down into the water**, and Philip (in Greek, *he*, but there is no question who is meant) baptized the eunuch. No words are quoted, but a form could easily be constructed from passages such as 2.38; 8.16. There is nothing (apart from the long text of v. 39) to say what was the consequence of baptism. Nothing suggests that Stephen was not competent to baptize. This is not why Luke introduces Peter and John at 8.14.

39. the Spirit of the Lord caught away Philip. For the verb; cf. 2 Cor. 12.2, 4; 1 Thess. 4.17; Rev. 12.5; also Jn 6.15.

for he simply continued on his way, rejoicing. *For* means that the eunuch saw Philip no more, for he, unlike Philip, simply continued his journey. There is a secondary variation, comparable with v. 37: *The Holy Spirit fell upon the eunuch* (the expected consequence of baptism), *and an angel of the Lord caught away Philip*.

40. The Spirit brought Philip to **Azotus**, the OT Ashdod, modern Esdud, just over twenty miles up the coast from Gaza. Philip continues his evangelistic journey.

Caesarea is a further fifty-five miles or so up the coast as the crow flies. Important cities on the way were Jamnia and Antipatris (23.31). Lydda (9.32–35) and Joppa (9.36–43; 10.5–23) lay east and west of the road respectively, but not far from it. At Caesarea the Roman authorities had their seat. The town was Greek, with a Jewish element. According to Josephus, *War* 2.457, the whole Jewish population (20,000) was massacred in AD 66.

Philip reappears at Caesarea at 21.8, in a 'We-passage' (see Introduction, pp. xxxi–xxxiii. It is not unreasonable to consider the possibility that Philip provided a link between the finished work and some of the stores of the first eight chapters.

V

SAUL THE GREAT EVANGELIST PREPARED FOR MISSION (9.1–31)

23. SAUL'S CONVERSION 9.1–19a

**[1] Saul, still breathing threatening and murder against the disciples
of the Lord, approached the High Priest [2] and asked from him
letters to Damascus, to the synagogues, so that if he found any,
men or women, who belonged to the Way, he might bring them
as prisoners to Jerusalem. [3] As he was on his way, he was drawing
near to Damascus; suddenly a light from heaven shone round
him. [4] He fell to the ground and heard a voice saying to him, 'Saul,
Saul, why are you persecuting me?' [5] He said, 'Who art thou,
Lord?' The other answered, 'I am Jesus, whom you are persecuting. [6] But get up and go into the city, and it will be told you
what you must do.' [7] The men who were travelling with him stood
still, struck dumb; they heard the voice but saw no one. [8] Saul got
up from the ground, and when he opened his eyes he saw nothing;
but they led him by the hand and brought him into Damascus.
[9] For three days he saw nothing, and neither ate nor drank.**

**[10] In Damascus there was a disciple called Ananias. In a vision
the Lord said to him, 'Ananias.' He said, 'Here I am, Lord.' [11] The
Lord said to him, 'Get up and go to the street called Straight
Street, and in the house of Judas seek for one called Saul, a
Tarsiote, for behold he is praying, [12] and in a vision has seen a
man, Ananias by name, come in and lay his hands on him, so that
he may recover his sight.' [13] Ananias answered, 'Lord, I have
heard about this man from many people – heard how much harm
he has done to thy saints in Jerusalem; [14] and here he has authority
from the chief priests to arrest all who call upon thy name.' [15] The**

**Lord said to him, 'Go, for this man is a chosen vessel to me, to
bear my name before nations and kings and the sons of Israel;
[16] for I will show him what he must suffer for my name's sake.'
[17] Ananias went off, entered the house, laid his hands upon him,
and said to him, 'Brother Saul, the Lord has sent me, Jesus, that
is, who appeared to you on the road by which you came, that you
may recover your sight and be filled with the Holy Spirit.' [18] And
immediately something like scales fell from his eyes. He recovered
his sight, got up, and was baptized. [19] And when he had taken
food he grew stronger.**

That Luke narrates this event twice more (22.6–16; 26.12–18) measures the importance that it had for him. The existence of the parallels justifies us in taking vv. 1–19a as a unit; otherwise there would be much to be said for including vv. 19b–22, which set the seal on the story of conversion by showing the new convert as engaged in Christian work in Damascus. The three accounts have much in common but are by no means identical. They may be set out as follows.

	Acts 9		*Acts 22*		*Acts 26*	
1.	Paul is travelling to Damascus	v. 3	Paul is travelling to Damascus	v. 6	Paul is travelling to Damascus	v. 12
2.	A light shines about him	v. 3	A light shines about him	v. 6	A light shines about him	v. 13
3.	He falls to the ground	v. 4	He falls to the ground	v. 7	All fall to the ground	v. 14
4.	A voice addresses him	v. 4	A voice addresses him	v. 7	A voice addresses him in Hebrew	v. 14
5.	Saul, Saul, why are you persecuting me?	v. 4	Saul, Saul, why are you persecuting me?	v. 7	Saul, Saul, why are you persecuting me?	
6.					It is hard for you to kick against the goad	v. 14
7.	Who art thou, Lord?	v. 5	Who art thou, Lord?	v. 8	Who art thou, Lord?	v. 15
8.	I am Jesus, whom you are persecuting	v. 5	I am Jesus the Nazarene, whom you are persecuting	v. 8	I am Jesus, whom you are persecuting	v. 15
9.					Paul is commissioned as missionary to Jews and Gentiles	vv. 16–18

	Acts 9		Acts 22		Acts 26	
10.			Companions see light but do not hear	v. 9		
11.			What shall I do?	v. 10		
12.	Paul is sent into Damascus for instructions	v. 6	Paul is sent into Damascus for instructions	v. 10		
13.	Companions hear the voice but do not see	v.7				
14.	Paul gets up, blind	v. 8	Paul is blind	v. 11		
15.	Paul is led into Damascus	v. 8	Paul is led into Damascus	v. 11		
16.	Paul, blind, eats and drinks nothing for three days	v. 9				
17.	Ananias is introduced and told of Paul's calling	vv. 10–16	Ananias is introduced	v. 12		
18.	Ananias heals Paul	vv. 17, 18	Ananias heals Paul	v. 13		
19.	Paul is baptized	v. 18	Paul is baptized	v. 16		
20.	Paul eats	v. 19				
21.			Vision in the Temple; Paul is commissioned as missionary to Jews and Gentiles	vv. 17–21		

The agreements are much more important than the disagreements. These can for the most part be accounted for by the contexts in which the story is placed. The agreements are due in part to the appearance in all three accounts of common features of theophanies: the light, the prostration of the recipient of the vision, the supernatural voice, the authoritative commands, the commissioning. See e.g. the story of Heliodorus in 2 Maccabees 3 and the conversion of Aseneth in *Joseph and Aseneth*. These resemblances, however, though clear, are relatively superficial. More important as parallels are the OT stories of the call of prophets, notably Isa. 6.1–13; Jer. 1.4–10; cf. Gal. 1.15. These have led to the view that the event should be described not as a conversion but as a call, or commission. Saul worshipped the same God afterwards as before. This is true; but it is now Jesus who determines his thought of God, and he knows that what is required of him is to put his trust not in his own legal, moral, and religious achievements but solely in Jesus Christ. This was a radical change of religious direction, and it was accompanied by as radical a change of action: the active persecutor became an even more active preacher and evangelist. If such radical changes do not amount to conversion it is hard to know what would do so. The element of vocation however is also present and must not be underestimated; see 9.6, 15; 22.15, 21; 26.17, 18, 20, confirmed by Gal. 1.16.

A number of questions are left over by the three conversion narratives in Acts.

(1) How and when was the substance of the Gospel conveyed to Paul? He claims that it came to him by revelation (Gal. 1.12) and that he was not taught it. The fact that he vehemently persecuted the church implies knowledge of Christian belief. He knew what he was trying to stamp out. What he now discovered was that it was true.

(2) In Acts 9 a large part is played by Ananias. Did Paul (in the epistles and in Acts 26) omit him in order to show his independence? Did Luke include him in order to establish agreement between Paul and Jerusalem? Neither extreme position is correct. The appearance of Christ was, to Paul, so commanding that other figures faded into insignificance. And Ananias acts (according to Luke) not as a representative of the church but of God.

(3) In the epistles Paul claims that Christ appeared to him as to the other apostles. This makes him an apostle (1 Cor. 9.1; 15.5–8). In Acts the appearance to Paul is separated from the other appearances by the ascension, and Paul is apparently not an apostle (see on 14.4, 14). What was Paul's position in the church and what was his relation to those who were apostles before him (Gal. 1.17)? See Introduction, pp. lixf. No one (if we may trust Acts) made a greater contribution to the fulfilment of the commission given in 1.8; and that this contribution should be made outside the narrow boundaries of officialdom is not insignificant.

Luke probably received not three different accounts of Paul's conversion but only one, which he adapted to the circumstances in which he used it. He probably thought that in ch. 9 he was supplying the basic facts in as striking a manner as possible. The account in ch. 22 is adapted to the Jewish audience to which it is addressed. The version in ch. 26 is abbreviated and suited to Festus and Agrippa. The basic facts come more or less directly from Paul and are paralleled in the epistles. How far such details as the light, the fall, the blindness, the conversation, the role of Paul's companions and of Ananias can be traced back in the tradition we have no means of knowing.

1. still. Saul's fierce opposition to the new movement did not abate with time. **threatening and murder** may be a hendiadys: *threats of murder*, but Luke probably means that death was not only threatened but inflicted; cf. 26.10. **the High Priest**. Cf. 4.6, where the High Priest is named as Annas; Caiaphas, mentioned with him, was the High Priest recognized by the Romans.

2. Saul **asked from** the High Priest **letters to Damascus**. To issue such letters would presuppose authority, on the part of the High Priest, to require, or at least to request, action by local Jewish communities outside Palestine and under a different civil government. Whether such authority existed and, if it did, how it was exercised cannot be determined with certainty. It is however unnecessary to suppose that Paul's actions carried, or needed, any authority beyond the confines of Judaism. Given the goodwill of the synagogues in Damascus it would be quite possible for Jews known to be Christians to 'disappear' and subsequently to find themselves in unwelcome circumstances in Jerusalem. The important historical question is that of the relation between the High Priest and Sanhedrin and provincial synagogues. It is unfortunately a question to which no precise answer can be given. Known compliance with Sanhedrin policies may have been a reason contributing to the choice of Damascus as a place in which to pursue anti-Christian action.

Damascus was about 135 miles NNW of Jerusalem, a large and prosperous commercial city, a member of the Decapolis League, with a large Jewish population. How there came to be Christians in Damascus we do not know; a useful reminder of the fact that Luke gives us not a full account but a few glimpses of the early spread of Christianity. There is no ground for connecting the Christians at Damascus with the Qumran sect. For Saul's indiscriminate readiness to arrest Christians of both sexes cf. 8.3.

The Christians are described as **those who belonged to the Way**. This use of *Way* recurs at 19.9, 23; 22.4; 24.14, 22; cf. 16.17; 18.25, 26. Its background is disputed. The closest parallels are to be found in the Qumran literature, where however the Way was understood as strict observance of the Mosaic Law. This is not how even the most conservative Jewish Christian groups understood their 'Way', though

Qumran and Christian groups have in common the exact performance of what is understood to be the revealed will of God.

3. light is a common feature of theophanies, e.g. Ps. 27.1; 78.14; Isa. 9.2; 42.16; 60.1, 20; Micah 7.8; also in non-biblical use. Paul himself understood the event as revelation (Gal. 1.12, 15); for Luke light is a physical representation of the divine glory of Christ.

4. Saul fell to the ground; another feature of theophanies. Cf. Ezek. 1.28; Dan. 8.17; Rev. 1. 17. For 2 Maccabees and *Joseph and Aseneth* see above, p. 131. Paul is addressed by his Hebrew name, *Sha'ul*; cf. 26.14. His companions fail to perceive the significance of what is taking place.

why are you persecuting me? Saul was persecuting Christians. Traditional interpretation has laid great stress upon the implied unity of Head and members. This is not wrong, but Luke's thought is not profoundly theological; any leader is injured if his followers are attacked.

5. Who art thou, Lord? The question corresponds to the **I am** that follows. Though Saul has not yet identified his interlocutor, *Lord* is not simply a polite address (*Sir*). The reply identifies the speaker as Jesus, once dead, now alive and unquestionably more than man. The discovery that the crucified Jesus was in fact alive agrees with Paul's own accounts of the origin of his Christian life (Gal. 1.15, 16; 1 Cor. 9.1; 15.8; cf. Phil. 3.7–11) and was the root of the new understanding of the OT and interpretation of Judaism that were the foundation of his theology.

6. But get up and go into the city. Further instruction is not to be given by the roadside. But it is not correct to say that Paul is now referred to the church to learn Christian doctrine. Saul is brought into contact with one disciple who is told in a vision not to instruct Saul in Christian doctrine but to cure his blindness. It is probable but not certain that Ananias baptized Saul but there is no mention of instruction then or before Paul begins to preach (9.20). Luke is indeed concerned to represent Saul as integrated into the life of the church as a whole but he does not represent him as a derivative person acting under direction from 'the church'.

7. The men who were travelling with him. Luke does not say who they were; he is interested in them only in that their reaction brings out more forcibly the effect of the event on Saul and at the same time establishes its objectivity. In the interests of security travellers went in groups rather than singly.

they heard the voice but saw no one. Contrast 22.9. It may be possible to explain the difference between the two statements by the different ways of using the Greek verb *to hear*, but it is probably best to suppose that Luke, without regard to consistency, wished in each narrative to express the thought that all recognized a supernatural event but only one understood its meaning. Supernatural beings become visible when and to whom they choose; cf. Deut. 4.12; also Homer, *Odyssey* 16.154–63.

8. when he opened his eyes he saw nothing. Saul's blindness is the result of his supernatural encounter; physically, one might say, he is blinded by the light of v. 3 (cf. 22.11). Blindness is not a punishment but a mark of the powerlessness of the hitherto powerful persecutor. Led by the hand, and not at all as he intended, Saul enters Damascus.

9. The blindness lasted **for three days**, during which Saul **neither ate nor drank**. It is a reaction that hardly calls for explanation and is not to be understood as an anticipation of the pre-baptismal fast (*Didache* 7.4; Justin, *1 Apology* 61; Tertullian, *On Baptism* 20).

10. Luke takes up the second character in his story, **Ananias**, here described as **a disciple**, that is, *a Christian*, presumably a local Christian not a refugee, since he has heard of, not experienced, Paul's activities in Jerusalem. In 22.12 he is devout according to the Law; in ch. 26 he does not appear. **The Lord** (Jesus; see v. 17) calls him by name. He replies, **Here I am**, **Lord**, using a LXX rendering of a Hebrew idiom.

11. The Lord gives specific directions, which appear to have the effect of diminishing Ananias' readiness to obey. Saul is lodging in **Straight Street** (*Straight* is a name, not simply a description), **in the house of Judas**, a person otherwise unknown but presumably a Jew. Saul is a **Tarsiote** – the first reference in Acts to Tarsus, an important Hellenistic city; see 21.19. Its prosperity was based on the linen industry; in the first century BC it became important in philosophy. For Jews in Tarsus see *NS* 3.33f. Saul is **praying**; he needs the help Ananias can bring.

12. Saul's second **vision** is indirectly reported. He has seen Ananias doing what in fact he later did. Ananias will **come in and lay his hands on him**. This has nothing to do with baptism. The purpose is explicit: **that he may recover his sight**. To Luke the laying on of hands was a gesture of blessing whose precise meaning was determined by its context.

13. Ananias fears that Saul is still out to persecute; prayer and vision must be a hoax. He has **heard about this man from many people**; he has not himself known persecution. It is the Lord's **saints in Jerusalem** who have been attacked, his *holy ones*; that is, persons specially devoted to and belonging to God. The word is often used of Christians by Paul, not frequently (9.32, 41; 26.10), and not theologically developed (but see 20.32; 26.18) in Acts.

14. Ananias is well informed; see vv. 1, 2, with slight differences in wording. His continuing hesitation emphasizes the wonder of the conversion.

15. Ananias' objection is overruled. The Lord gives reasons for his instructions, speaking in the biblical style that Luke considers suitable for such purposes. **this man is a chosen vessel to me**. The use of *vessel* (or *instrument*) reflects OT usage; *chosen* could refer to Paul as one of the *elect* (that is, a Christian) but must here be understood in the light of the following words: Saul is one whom the Lord has singled out for special service. He is **to bear my name**, an unusual expression, but cf. 8.12. *The name* (of Christ) sums up the Christian message, which Paul will take throughout the world.

nations rather than Gentiles, because the Greek word has no article (the article is added by some MSS so as to make the sentence conform to the familiar designation of Paul as 'apostle of the Gentiles').

16. for I (emphatic) **will show**. The emphatic *I* explains the unexpected *for*. You, Ananias, need not hesitate to perform the task I am giving you, for I myself will be personally engaged in it. Paul's sufferings are described in the rest of Acts; the epistles, especially 2 Cor. 11.23–33, present a grimmer picture. Luke wishes to show at the same time how much Paul suffered and how the power of God delivered him from suffering.

17. Ananias was convinced and carried out his instructions. He addresses Saul as **Brother**, that is, as fellow Christian, though he is not yet baptized. The laying on of hands is certainly not a rite subsequent to baptism; as usual in Acts, it is a sign of blessing, here an act of healing. **that you may recover your sight** takes up v. 12. By the gift of **the Holy Spirit** Paul is made to stand on the same level as the original apostles (2.4), though this means no more than that he is a Christian (2.33, 38, etc.). No visible or audible phenomena mark the gift of the Spirit.

18. something like scales fell from his eyes. Cf. Tobit 3.17; 11.12. The word *scales* is occasionally used by medical writers, but it is widely used in many senses and does nothing to prove that Luke was a physician. In fact the description of the cure is looser than one would expect from a professional.

Saul **was baptized**; presumably by Ananias. Cf. 22.16 (with the note).

19a. Saul is now a Christian and needs no further instruction or authorization. **when he had taken food he grew stronger**. There is nothing here to suggest a reference to the eucharist. Paul had eaten nothing for three days (v. 9); it is not surprising that he felt better after taking food.

24. SAUL FROM DAMASCUS TO JERUSALEM 9.19b–30

**19 Saul was some days with the disciples in Damascus 20 and
immediately in the synagogues he proclaimed Jesus, affirming
that he was the Son of God. 21 Those who heard him were
astonished, and said, 'Is not this he who in Jerusalem made havoc
of those who invoke this name, and had come here for this very
purpose, to bring them bound before the chief priests?' 22 But
Saul grew stronger and stronger and confounded the Jews who
lived in Damascus, teaching that this man was the Christ.**

**23 When many days were completed the Jews plotted to kill
him, 24 but their plot became known to Saul. They were watching
the gates day and night in order to kill him, 25 but his disciples
took him by night and let him down by the wall, lowering him in
a basket.**

**26 When he reached Jerusalem he tried to join the disciples,
and they were all afraid of him because they did not believe that
he was a disciple. 27 But Barnabas took him in hand, brought him
to the apostles, and told them how on the road he had seen the
Lord and that the Lord had spoken to him, and how in Damascus
he had spoken boldly in the name of Jesus. 28 And he was with
them, going in and going out, at Jerusalem, speaking boldly in
the name of the Lord. 29 He spoke and debated with the Hellenists,
but they tried to kill him. 30 When the brothers learned this they
brought him down to Caesarea and sent him off to Tarsus.**

When this passage is compared with the epistles difficulties arise. According to Gal. 1.17 Paul after his conversion went away to Arabia. Acts knows nothing of this journey; Paul preaches in Damascus till he goes to Jerusalem. According to 2 Cor. 11.32f. Paul escaped from Damascus in a basket when threatened by the Ethnarch of King Aretas. In Acts he is threatened by Jews, and the escape is not, as in 2 Corinthians, a humiliation but almost a triumph. According to Gal. 1.17 Paul delayed his visit to Jerusalem three years. In Acts, after escaping from Damascus Paul makes straight for Jerusalem. The difficulty here is not only chronological. In Acts Paul meets the apostolic body who after initial scepticism, accept him as a fellow preacher, he preaches in Jerusalem until driven out by the Hellenists. In Galatians he stays in Jerusalem only a fortnight and sees only

Peter and James. Again, if we accept Paul's own 'three years', why were the apostles suspicious of him? After so long a time it must have been recognized that he had genuinely become a Christian and a missionary and was not an *agent provocateur*, and mediation by Barnabas would not be necessary. It may be that what lay behind any hesitation the Jerusalem group may have had was not doubt of Paul's sincerity but disagreement with his theological understanding of the Christian faith. If that was so a role may still be found for Barnabas.

Luke's interests can be clearly seen. (1) He wishes to show Paul in close association with the church and as a preacher of orthodox doctrine; he preaches that Jesus is the Son of God (v. 20) and the Christ (v. 22). Through the mediation of Barnabas he is accepted by the apostles, not as a fellow apostle but as an acceptable evangelist. Luke's position here must not be overstated. He does not say that the apostles gave any sort of validation to Paul's ministry or imparted to him the content of the Gospel. But they did not say, He is an impostor, or, He is a heretic. How far this is a historically correct and complete account of relations between Paul and the Jerusalem church is another question.

(2) Luke characteristically depicts the victory of the word of God in the lives of those who speak it. In Damascus and in Jerusalem his enemies attack Paul in vain. Stephen may perish but he has a successor – another proposition that invites historical questions.

(3) Attacks on the church not only fail; they aid the spread of the Gospel. Paul, threatened in Jerusalem, is sent to Caesarea and Tarsus.

Paul was a great preacher; he must (Luke is sure) have preached in Damascus. His escape from Damascus was probably widely known and often told. Of course Paul had contacts with Jerusalem and must have preached there. It is not difficult to see how the paragraph was built up on the basis of traditionally known events, helped out with inferences, some not wholly correct. Luke is correct in maintaining the two points, though there is tension between them: Paul was a great independent evangelist, Paul was not out of harmony with the apostles who guaranteed the connection between Jesus and the church. But Luke is wrong in some details, and also in that he misses the stormy atmosphere that often disturbed the relations he describes.

Luke has brought Paul on the stage and introduced him; he may now be left at Tarsus (v. 30) till he is summoned to Antioch (11.25f.).

19b. A new paragraph seems to begin here, though it is closely connected with what precedes. **the disciples in Damascus** suggests a gathered group – which is in any case likely. **some days**: *many days* suggests a longer period, though Luke seems to use both expressions when he has no precise length of time in mind.

20. immediately, without waiting for further instruction or commission. In Gal. 1.16 Paul *immediately* goes off to Arabia. Paul's proclamation is summed up in the affirmation that Jesus **was the Son of God**. Elsewhere in Acts Jesus is said to be the Son of God only at 13.33, in the quotation of Ps. 2.7. The term is somewhat more frequent in Lk., but in special Lucan material it is used only at 1.32, 35. It can hardly be claimed that it is one of special significance to Luke or that he was making a special point of the claim that Paul was the first to use it. It was traditional and filled out the use of **proclaimed**. There is no indication in Acts of a belief in the essential identity of the Father and the Son. Luke is simply reporting that Saul now came out clearly and positively on the Christian side.

21. The astonishment of those who heard Saul's preaching is hardly surprising. **made havoc** is the word used for the same action in Gal. 1.13, 23.

22. For his part, **Saul** simply grew **stronger and stronger**. That Saul, after a specific call to act as missionary to the Gentiles, should begin by arguing with **the Jews who lived in Damascus** may seem strange but according to Luke Paul's regular pattern of ministry was to begin with the Jews and then turn to the Gentiles. Paul taught that **this man**, Jesus, **was the Christ**. Luke probably takes this to be identical in meaning with v. 20; that is, in v. 20 *Son of God* does not have a metaphysical meaning but is a correlate of Messiahship.

23. The language of the verse is characteristically Lucan; Luke is writing up a story he knew in outline from tradition.

24. At this point the narrative becomes strikingly parallel to but not identical with that of 2 Cor. 11.32, 33, where it is the Ethnarch of King Aretas who was plotting to seize Paul. It is surely correct to identify the two occasions, and to suppose that Paul knew whom he had to fear. Luke probably did not know the source of the threat and supposed on general principles that it must be the Jews. Aretas died in AD 39; we do not know what sort of official his Ethnarch was. It may be that from AD 37 to 39 Aretas was ruler of the city; no coins of the Emperor Gaius (Caligula) have been found there.

25. his disciples is probably the correct reading; the alternative is *the disciples*, a much easier reading, which would refer simply to the local Christians. Who were *his disciples*? Possibly *his converts*, Christians who owed their faith to Paul and stood particularly close to him; but no answer to this question is entirely satisfactory.

26. Read superficially the verse presents no problems. It was natural that Saul, now himself a Christian, should seek to join the disciples in Jerusalem. It was equally natural for the disciples not to trust him; would he not prove to be a surreptitious infiltrator, perhaps an *agent provocateur*? Read in the light of Galatians the verse is full of problems. Paul had been called to go to the Gentiles; why go to Jerusalem? In fact he went not to Jerusalem but to Arabia, to Jerusalem only three years later. Then he saw not 'the apostles' but Cephas and James only. After three years how could anyone doubt his sincerity? Did Paul seek, and does Luke represent him as seeking, authorization and legitimation from the original apostles? This has been maintained, but there is no word in either Acts or Galatians to justify the opinion. The historical Paul in fact did his best to live in unity with the Twelve; in this he succeeded less well than appears in Acts. See Introduction, pp. xliiif., lixf., lxxxiif.

27. Barnabas. See on 4.36. Later he will appear as Paul's colleague in Antioch (11.25, 26), his travelling companion on the mission of help to Jerusalem (11.27–30; 12.25), his fellow missionary (13; 14) delegate with him from Antioch to the Jerusalem Council (15.2). Later still he will separate from Paul (15.37–40; Gal. 2.13), perhaps not permanently. One wonders why Barnabas accompanied Paul, and whether the apostles would have received Paul if Barnabas had not vouched for him.

to the apostles suggests, to the whole company of the apostles. Contrast Gal. 1.18f.: Peter only, with James (who may or may not be an apostle). Paul's account must be accepted. Probably Luke knew that there was a visit to Jerusalem and inferred, wrongly, that it included a meeting with all the Twelve.

and that the Lord had spoken to him. *The Lord* is not expressed in Greek, and *he had spoken to him* might mean *Paul had spoken to Jesus*. A further possibility is to translate not *that* but *what*: *how he had seen . . . what he had said . . . and how in Damascus . . .*

he had spoken boldly. The verb is used at 9.28; 13.46; 14.3; 18.26; 19.8; 26.26. It does not suggest ecstatic speech but points to a blunt statement of the truth regardless of the consequences. To speak **in the name of Jesus** is more than to speak about him; it is to speak on his behalf, almost in his person.

28. going in and going out. Saul was not only with the apostles but shared their activities; there is nothing to suggest that he did not do so on equal terms.

29. the Hellenists (some MSS have *Greeks*); see on 6.1. Those with whom Stephen disputed (6.9: Cyrenians, Alexandrians, Cilicians, Asians) were presumably Hellenists in the sense of Jews with roots in the Greek-speaking world, but Luke does not use this word to describe them, though he probably wishes to suggest that Saul entered into the same conflict as Stephen. In himself as in his opponents Paul was for Luke the new Stephen, a great Hellenist Christian leader.

30. the brothers: see on 1.15. **sent him off**: the words suggest a journey by sea, but this is not certain. We hear no more of Saul until Barnabas goes to Tarsus to bring him to Antioch (11.25f.). How he occupied the intervening period Acts does not tell us. Paul records (Gal. 1.18, 21) that after his short visit to Jerusalem he went into Syria (where Antioch was situated) and Cilicia (where Tarsus lay). Between this time and his next visit to Jerusalem (Gal. 2.1) he remained personally unknown to the churches of Judaea – a fact which is more easily harmonized with Gal. 1.18f. than with Acts 9.26–29.

25. THE CHURCH IN JUDAEA, GALILEE, AND SAMARIA: A SUMMARY 9.31

[31] So the church throughout Judaea, Galilee, and Samaria had peace; it was being built up and walked in the fear of the Lord under the influence of the Holy Spirit, and it increased in numbers.

This verse, standing on its own, can hardly be anything other than a summary editorial note, inserted by Luke; cf. 2.42–27; 4.32–35; 5.12–16; 6.7. It looks forward, introducing the journey that takes Peter eventually to the founding of a mixed church, including Gentiles, at Caesarea (11.18). The formula itself is backward-looking, and here means that the new development will rest on a sound foundation. Galilee, of which nothing has so far been heard, is mentioned to show that the church is now settled and established in all Jewish areas, including half-Jewish Samaria. It is at peace and flourishing, and ready for further expansion.

31. For **the church** see on 5.11. Luke uses the word, normally in a local sense, to denote the community of Christians, said here to be functioning as it should, without further theological definition. For its presence in Judaea see 1.8; 2.9; 8.1; for Samaria, 8.4–25. Galilee has not been mentioned, and will be mentioned, but not as a mission field, only at 10.37; 13.31. Probably there were few Christians there.

The church **had peace**, that is, it now lived an undisturbed life. **it was being built up** numerically, and as its members made progress in piety. **the fear of the Lord** is a common OT expression. **under the influence of** is an attempt to give a comprehensive sense to a word translated sometimes *exhortation*, sometimes *comfort*, sometimes *encouragement*. Luke means that the church grows as it should only through the operation of the Holy Spirit.

The sentence as a whole is changed into the plural number (*the churches*, with corresponding verbs) by the Western text. The Western editor was not influenced by a different view of the church but wished to show how extensive the Christian body had become. Except at 20.28 Acts uses the word *ekklēsia* to denote a local church, and probably does so here. The area described is not so large that the Christians in it could not be regarded as constituting a unit.

VI

THE FIRST PREACHER TO GENTILES AND THE FIRST GENTILE CHURCH

(9.32 – 11.18)

26. PETER'S MIRACLES ON THE WAY TO CAESAREA 9.32–43

**32 It happened that Peter passed through all these areas and came
down also to the saints who lived at Lydda. 33 There he found a
man called Aeneas who for eight years had lain on his bed; he
was paralysed. 34 Peter said to him, 'Aeneas, Jesus Christ has
healed you; get up and make your own bed.' And immediately he
got up. 35 And all those who lived in Lydda and in the Plain of
Sharon saw him and turned to the Lord.**

**36 In Joppa there was a woman disciple called Tabitha (which,
translated, is Dorcas). She was constantly practising good works
and giving alms. 37 In those days it happened that she fell sick and
died. They washed her body and laid it in an upper room. 38 Since
Lydda was near to Joppa the disciples, when they heard that Peter
was there, sent two men to him, with the request, 'Please do not
hesitate to come to us.' 39 Peter got up and went with them. When
he arrived they took him up to the upper room, and all the widows
were present with him, weeping and displaying the tunics and
cloaks that Dorcas made while she was with them. 40 Peter put
everyone out, knelt down, and prayed. He turned to the body and
said, 'Tabitha, get up.' She opened her eyes, and when she saw
Peter she sat up. 41 He gave her his hand and raised her up. He
called the saints and the widows and presented her to them alive.
42 This became known through the whole of Joppa, and many
believed in the Lord. 43 Peter stayed on a number of days in Joppa,
with a man called Simon, a tanner.**

Peter, apparently engaged on a missionary tour or on an inspection of Christian centres (cf. 8.14), or possibly simultaneously on both, came to Lydda and to Joppa, where there were already groups of Christians (see on vv. 32 and 36). Luke tells us nothing of the foundation of churches in Lydda and Joppa; we may guess, but with little confidence, that they were the work of Philip on the way from Azotus to Caesarea (8.40). In Lydda there was a sick man, Aeneas, probably a Jewish Christian, whom Peter healed. News of this led to many conversions in the area, and to a request to Peter to visit Joppa, where a woman, Tabitha (Dorcas), noted for charitable work, had died. She was raised from death by Peter, and there were more conversions. The two stories are similar in form and may have been combined before Luke used them (part of an early *Acts of Peter*?). Both serve as a further demonstration of the power of Jesus working through Peter (cf. 5.15, 16), and bring Peter on the way to Caesarea. The Christian group in Joppa includes a clientele of widows (cf. 6.1; 1 Tim. 5.9–16); they are not an order; they are not said to perform any service for the church (but see on v. 39); they are rather its beneficiaries.

We have no means of dating Peter's journey through Lydda and Joppa; the group of widows suggests a fairly advanced development. It is attractive to suggest that 12.17 (when Peter went to *another place*) marks the point at which Peter left Jerusalem for a wider mission field; but see on that verse.

The story of Cornelius (ch. 10) was of great importance to Luke (see 15.7). Here he is preparing for it. It seems probable (see pp. 153f.) that it was Caesarea's own traditional account of the foundation there of a mixed Jewish and Gentile church. The two miracles may always have been attached to the Caesarea story, to explain how Peter came to be within reach of Caesarea. Alternatively, Luke found them as a piece of loose tradition which he decided to use as an introduction.

32. Peter passed through. The verb may (cf. 8.4, 40) suggest a missionary, preaching, journey, but here its meaning is bound up with the phrase **through all these areas**, which is a guess at the meaning of the words *through all* . . . , no noun being supplied with *all*. We may possibly anticipate **saints**: Peter visited all the Christians. Some have seen here an Aramaism, meaning *all the land*. It is a good suggestion that, if Luke begins here to use a new source, this source, before Luke edited it, would explain the reference of *all*. To Luke *the* *saints* will be Christians; it is conceivable that the postulated source gave the word a different meaning (Essenes?), but there is nothing to support this conjecture. **Lydda** is the OT Lod, later Diospolis. See *NS* 2.190–8. It was a day's journey from Jerusalem on the road to Joppa.

33. Aeneas. The name neither suggests nor excludes Jewish origin; it occurs in Palestinian inscriptions. He was probably a Christian; if he had been converted by his cure Luke would have remarked on this. **for eight years**: *possibly from the age of eight.*

34. The name of Jesus is not invoked (contrast 3.6), but Peter's words here explain what the name of Jesus means when the phrase is used; it is none other than Jesus (certainly not Peter) who effects the cure. **Jesus Christ has healed you.** The verb is either perfect or present, according to the accentuation; many prefer, *Jesus Christ heals you.*

The command to the sick man to **get up** is familiar in healing stories; so is carrying away the bed on which the sick person has lain. Here, **make your own bed** (with a view to packing it up and taking it away) might be translated, *Lay a table for yourself*, with a view to having a meal. This seems less probable. **immediately** – another characteristic feature of miracle stories; cf. 3.7.

35. A note of the reaction of onlookers is another characteristic of miracle stories. **the Plain of Sharon**, the coastal plain, at that time thickly populated and famous for its fruitfulness. They **turned to the Lord**; for *turning* as a conversion word; cf. 3.15; 11.21; 14.15; 15.19; 26.18, 20; (28.27).

36. Joppa. On this town see *NS* 2.110–14. It was essentially a Greek city, so that when Peter reached it he was on the way to a Gentile environment (ch. 10). In Joppa there were *disciples* (v. 38); undoubtedly for Luke, Christian disciples, conceivably but improbably, in a source, others. Among them was **a woman disciple called Tabitha** (in Greek, **Dorcas**). It is probable that in the mixed society of Joppa both names, Aramaic and Greek (for *roe*, *gazelle*) were in use. **She was constantly practising** (literally, **full of**) **good works**; these are specified in v. 39.

37. Tabitha **fell sick and died**. The body was prepared for burial; washing was customary among Greeks, Romans and Jews (e.g. M. Shabbath 23.5). So was anointing, not mentioned here. She was laid **in an upper room**; cf. 1.13; 20.8. Luke may be thinking of a regular place of Christian assembly.

38. Joppa was about ten miles from **Lydda**. **two men**: cf. 10.7. **Please do not hesitate to come to us.** Luke's Greek is often taken as a polite form of imperative, or rather request: Please come, be so good as to come. It is however difficult to avoid the sense of hesitation or delay which is found in classical use, where the word is used (without Luke's negative) of reluctance, caused by shame, fear, pity, cowardice, or indolence. Here it hints that Peter might for some reason be unwilling to come. Why? Hardly because the distance was too great. Because Joppa was a Greek city (v. 36)? Because the Christians in Joppa were not Jews? The latter possibility would throw Luke's chronological scheme into confusion.

39. Peter got up, a biblical pleonasm. **the upper room** (v. 37). **all the widows**, not as an order (cf. 1 Tim. 5.9–16) but as poor. This may mean that Acts is earlier than the Pastoral Epistles and casts some doubt on the view that they were written by the same author. The picture of the weeping widows has the effect of representing Peter as not only powerful but as compassionate. **tunics and cloaks**, inner and outer garments. **while she was with them**; this has been taken to mean that Tabitha had had a workshop with the widows; more probably it means only *while she was alive*.

40. Peter put everyone out. *Everyone* is in Greek masculine; it could include the widows, but must include also some men. The same words occur at Mk 5.40 (where they are omitted by Luke). Peter **prayed**. Cf. 4 Kdms 4.33. Peter did not effect cures in his own right but by appealing to divine power (cf. 3.12). **Tabitha, get up.** The name suggests that Peter was speaking Aramaic. His words recall the words of Jesus to the daughter of Jairus as these are given at Lk. 8.54, but even more as they stand in Mk 5.41 (*Talitha koum*). But though there is confusion in some MSS of Mk, *talitha* is not a name, and the resemblance is a matter of coincidence. **She opened her eyes**, cf. 4 Kdms 4.35. **she sat up**, cf. Lk. 7.15. The story is told in conventional miracle form.

41. He . . . raised her up does not refer to raising her to life; she is already alive. Peter helps her to her feet. **the saints** are the local Christian community; it would be wrong to infer that the widows were not also Christians.

42. The news of so marvellous an event spread rapidly and encouraged faith – the appropriate response to the Christian message.

43. Peter stayed on . . . with a man called Simon, a tanner. The name must be traditional; pure invention would never have invited confusion by making Simon Peter stay with another Simon. Tanners were despised in Judaism; so for example M. Ketuboth 7.10. They were suspected of immorality, and their work involved a bad smell. It may be significant that Peter was willing – or perhaps obliged – to stay in a low-class house, and with one of very doubtful repute in Jewish eyes.

a number of days is a characteristic expression. Luke himself would not know how many.

27. PETER AND CORNELIUS: CAESAREA 10.1–48

**[1] A certain man in Caesarea, Cornelius by name, a centurion
belonging to the Cohort called Italica, [2] pious and God-fearing
with all his household, making many charitable gifts to the People
and constantly at prayer to God, [3] saw plainly in a vision, at about
the ninth hour of the day, an angel of God, who came in to him
and said, 'Cornelius.' [4] He stared at him, and struck with fear
said, 'What is it, Sir?' The angel said to him, 'Your prayers and
your charitable gifts have come up before God for his remem-
brance. [5] So now you must send men to Joppa, and send for one
Simon who is surnamed Peter. [6] He is lodging with one Simon a
tanner, who has a house by the sea.' [7] When the angel who spoke
to him went away, Cornelius called two of his servants and a
pious soldier from among those who attended him, [8] and when he
had explained the whole matter to them he sent them to Joppa.**

**[9] On the next day, while they were on their way and drawing
near to the city, Peter about the sixth hour went up on the roof to
pray. [10] He felt hungry, and was wanting to eat. While they were
preparing a meal a trance fell upon him [11] and he saw heaven
standing open and a sort of vessel descending, like a great sheet
let down on the earth by the four corners. [12] In it were all the
quadrupeds and reptiles of the earth and birds of heaven. [13] There
came a voice to him, 'Get up, Peter, slaughter and eat.' [14] But
Peter said, 'Certainly not, Lord, for I have never eaten anything
profane or unclean.' [15] Again, a second time, a voice came to him,
'Things that God has cleansed, do not you treat as profane.' [16] This
happened three times, and immediately the vessel was taken up
into heaven. [17] While Peter doubted in himself what the vision he
had seen might mean, Behold, the men who had been sent by
Cornelius, having asked after Simon's house, came and stood at
the gate. [18] They called and asked, 'Does Simon who is surnamed
Peter lodge here?' [19] While Peter was reflecting on the vision, the
Spirit said to him, 'Here are some men looking for you. [20] Get up
and go down and go with them, with no hesitation, for I have sent
them.' [21] Peter went down to the men and said, 'I am the man you
are looking for; what is the reason on account of which you have
come?' [22] They said, 'Centurion Cornelius, a righteous man and
one who fears God, of good reputation with the whole nation of**

the Jews, was instructed by a holy angel to send for you to come
to his house and to hear words from you.' 23 So he asked them in
and put them up.

On the next day he arose and went with them, and some of the
brothers from Joppa accompanied him. 24 On the next day he
entered Caesarea. Cornelius was awaiting them, and had gathered
his relatives and closest friends. 25 As Peter entered, Cornelius
met him, fell at his feet, and did him reverence. 26 But Peter raised
him up, saying, 'Get up; I too am myself a man.' 27 Conversing
with him, he went in, and found many assembled. 28 He said to
them, 'You know that it is unlawful for a man of Jewish race to
attach himself to or approach a man of another race; but God
has shown me that I should not call any human being profane or
unclean. 29 For this reason, when I was sent for I came without
gainsaying. So I ask you for what reason you have sent for me.'
30 Cornelius said, 'Four days ago, at this very hour,' I was saying
the ninth hour of prayer in my house when behold, a man stood
before me in bright clothing, 31 and said, Cornelius, your prayer
has been heard and your charitable gifts have been remembered
before God. 32 So send to Joppa and summon one Simon who is
surnamed Peter. He is lodging in the house of Simon a tanner, by
the sea. 33 So I sent for you at once, and you were so kind as to
come. Now therefore we are all in the presence of God to hear all
that has been laid upon you by the Lord.'

34 Peter opened his mouth and said, 'Of a truth I perceive that
God has no favourites, 35 but that in every nation he who fears
him and works righteousness is accepted by him. 36 The word
which God sent to the children of Israel, bringing the good news
of peace through Jesus Christ (he is Lord of all) . . . 37 You know
the event that happened throughout the whole of Judaea,
beginning from Galilee after the baptism that John proclaimed,
38 Jesus of Nazareth, how God anointed him with the Holy Spirit
and power, who went about doing good and healing all who were
overpowered by the devil, for God was with him. 39 And we are
witnesses of all that he did in the land of the Jews and in
Jerusalem. They killed him by hanging him on a tree; 40 God
raised him up on the third day and granted to him that he should
be revealed, 41 not to all the People but to witnesses who had been
appointed beforehand by God, namely to us, who ate and drank
with him after he had risen from the dead. 42 And he charged us

to proclaim to the People and to testify that he is the one who has been marked out by God as judge of the living and the dead.
43 All the prophets bear witness to this, that everyone who believes in him receives through his name the forgiveness of sins.'
44 While Peter was still speaking these things the Holy Spirit fell upon all who were listening to his speech. 45 And the circumcised believers who had accompanied Peter were astonished that the gift of the Spirit had been poured out upon the Gentiles too –
46 for they heard them speaking with tongues and magnifying God. Then Peter spoke up: 47 'Can anyone forbid the water so as to prevent from being baptized these men who have received the Holy Spirit, just as we did?' 48 And he gave orders for them to be baptized in the name of Jesus Christ. Then they asked him to stay on for some days.

The story told in this chapter is repeated, more briefly, in ch. 11, and alluded to in 15.7–9. Clearly it was important to Luke. It was important as marking the climax of the extension of the Gospel – to Jews, to Samaritans, to the Ethiopian who was all but a proselyte, and now to a Gentile, with the conclusion of the matter expressed in 11.18. The story however is not as simple as may appear on the surface, and there is a long history of critical discussion – too long for a full account here.

Questions arise in regard to the chronological placing of the story. Had not Philip's baptism of the eunuch settled the question of the admission of Gentiles? And after 11.18 why was it necessary to send Barnabas (11.22) to inspect the work at Antioch? And after the 'First Council of Jerusalem' (11.1–18) why was it necessary to raise the questions of 15.1, 5 and to have a Second Council? Further significant questions are raised when the details of the story are considered.

(1) The story is set out as a notable step in the progress of the Gospel into the non-Jewish world. Yet the story also emphasizes how close Cornelius is to Judaism. One would have expected to meet a less God-fearing Gentile.

(2) Peter's vision gives rise to a group of problems. Does Peter think that the Lord is tempting him to do what is wrong? Does he think that Jesus is interested in the distinction between clean and unclean foods? What of Mk 7.15–19? (The matter is further complicated by the fact that this Marcan passage has no parallel in Lk.) After the vision, how can the Council of Acts 15 persist in the

distinction between foods that do and foods that do not cause uncleanness? Does the meaning of the vision switch from clean and unclean foods to clean and unclean persons?

(3) If 11.1–18 be taken as it stands, ch. 15 is superfluous, unless we take it to be dealing not with the admission of Gentiles but with the conditions of (table-)fellowship between Jewish and Gentile Christians – and there is something to be said for this view. The first question was, May they come in? The second question was, Now that they are in, how are they and we (Jewish Christians) related to each other? What Jewish rules must they keep? That this was the purpose of the Council of Acts 15 does not accord with 15.1, 5, but may be inferred from some of the evidence.

This proliferation and complication of problems means that neither the origin nor the interpretation of Acts 10 is likely to be simple. It is clear that Luke intended to represent a decisive step, perhaps the decisive step, in the expansion of Christianity into the non-Jewish world. This expansion rests upon the fact that there is no respect of persons with God (10.34). Non-Jews are welcomed, and the only sign of their initiation is baptism. Peter not only baptized but ate with them (11.3; cf. 10.48). That he ate with uncircumcised Gentile Christians is confirmed by Gal. 2.12 (though he withdrew under threat from James). But the history was more complex than this. Luke can hardly have invented the story; if he did so he produced for himself a number of unnecessary difficulties.

The best suggestion is that in, or behind, the story of Acts 10 and 11 we have its own account of the foundation in Caesarea of a church that included Gentiles, and of the final recognition in Jerusalem that this had been a proper step. This step was so unprecedented, and so full of (at the time only partially perceived) theological meaning, that it was probably recorded in more churches than one, even if only in their folk memory. Antioch had a similar recollection, which was not attached (except in the second degree – see 11.22, 25) to any of the great names but only to certain men of Cyprus and Cyrene (11.20), acting as a result of, or in association with, the expulsion of Hellenist Christians from Jerusalem.

Luke has not simply taken over the Caesarean story. (1) The difficulties in the story of Peter's vision have already been described (pp. 152f.). Can this have been an original part of the Caesarean narrative? (2) At 8.40 Philip came to Caesarea; at 21.8 he is still there. Did he make no contribution to the founding of a church in

Caesarea? This however builds too much on 8.40 and assumes the chronological priority of the stories about Philip.

It is better to conclude that there was current in the church at Caesarea a story of its founding by Peter, which included the assertion that it was from the beginning a church that included Gentiles, and that this was accepted by the Christians in Jerusalem. Luke also received by tradition an account of Peter's vision, explaining 'How Peter changed his mind' – perhaps not on the question, What may you eat? but, With whom may you eat? Even so, the vision needed reinterpretation.

It is right here to note the theological question, often missed but seen and wrestled with by Calvin. If (v. 34) in every nation he who fears God and works righteousness is acceptable to God, and if Cornelius is therefore already accepted, why preach to him? Why baptize him? Calvin concludes that Cornelius already knew Christ, though in the manner of the fathers of old who hoped for salvation by a Redeemer not yet revealed. But Calvin mistakenly attributed to Luke his own depth and acuteness of theological thought. Luke means that God judges men fairly in accordance with their opportunities. God looks with favour on those who, as far as they know him, fear him and, as far as they know what righteousness is, practise it, and he will make it possible for those who have advanced so far to go further. He prefers to speak about one thing at a time, and is not speaking here about God's love for the sinful.

1. For the introduction of a new character and a new story cf. 8.9. For **Caesarea** see on 8.40. There were many Jews in the city but the principal language was Greek. Luke has run out of information about Philip, and turns to his story about the founding of the church in Caesarea. The name **Cornelius** was borne by many Romans. **A centurion** commanded a century (100 men), two centuries made a maniple, three maniples a **cohort**, ten cohorts a legion. These were paper figures, not always adhered to. As they rose in seniority through the legion, centurions became persons of consequence and when they retired were normally given equestrian rank. We know that Cohors II Militaria Italica Civium Romanorum Voluntariorum was in Syria some time before AD 69. Cornelius seems to be surrounded by family and friends and had perhaps retired and settled in Caesarea; in this case the soldier of v. 7 would also have retired.

2. Cornelius was **pious and God-fearing**. These words may be simply descriptive of Cornelius as an individual, or they may categorize him as one of a special class of persons, not Jews, not proselytes, but attracted to the synagogue by their acceptance of Jewish religious and ethical principles and general sympathy with the Jewish way of life. Such persons are often described as 'God-fearers'. The term 'half-proselyte' has been used, meaning one who is half-way to being a proselyte. That there were such persons is clear; that they constituted a recognized division of the synagogue community and bore the title 'God-fearer' is not. This question (of great importance for our knowledge of Judaism and the surrounding society in the Graeco-Roman world) is not important in the present passage. What is important is (a) that some Gentiles were attracted to Jewish ethics, theology and worship, but did not become proselytes; (b) that in some places (one is known) they formed a recognized and valued element in the synagogue community, though the degree of their religious attachment to it is not specified and remains unknown; (c) that such Gentiles presented a great opportunity to Christian evangelists; (d) that Luke was aware of this. See further on 13.16.

In his piety Cornelius carried *his household* with him. It was expressed in almsgiving and prayer, both characteristic features of Jewish religion, and connected with each other.

3. Cornelius saw **plainly** – so that there was no possibility of mistake – **in a vision**: in Acts this word is always used of some kind of supernatural appearance. **at about the ninth hour of the day**, so that the vision was not a nocturnal dream. For the *ninth hour* as a time of prayer see on 3.1.

an angel of God. Angels play a considerable part in Acts in prompting action in accordance with God's will; see 5.19; 8.26; 12.7; 27.23. In this story supernatural interventions fit neatly together to show that the conversion of Cornelius was due to God's initiative. Cornelius is addressed by name; cf. 9.10.

4. Several words in this verse are characteristic of Luke, who is probably writing up a story he has been told. Cornelius' good works are remembered to his advantage, by God; cf. Ps. 141.2; Sirach 35.16f.; Tobit 12.12; Phil. 4.18; Heb. 13.15f. God will act for Cornelius' advantage by bringing him within reach of the Gospel. He will do this because Cornelius has shown by his devotion and charity that he deserves it. This theme runs throughout the narrative; it is reasonable to ask whether it is consistent with, for example, Paul's theology.

5. Specific directions are given which Cornelius must fulfil if he is to take advantage of God's favourable offer. He must send for **Simon who is surnamed Peter**. For **Joppa** see on 9.36.

6. He is lodging, another Lucan word. **a house by the sea**. This will help the messengers. The tanner's unclean occupation called for supplies of water.

7. Cornelius sent two of his servants. The Greek has *he* but there is no doubt who is meant. *Servants* translates a word that means *household slave*; evidently (v. 8) these were men with whom their master could share confidential matters. The **soldier** was **pious**, like his master (v. 2). If (see above) Cornelius had retired he might well have retained on a private basis the services of a soldier who was retiring at the same time.

8. Cornelius **explained**, recounted (another Lucan word), **the whole matter to them**. They were in his confidence. **he sent them to Joppa**, a distance of about thirty miles. For the time taken on the journey see v. 9 and the note.

9. Luke takes up Peter's strand of the story. People and events fit together in a way that shows God's hand at work. After the vision at 3 p.m. the messengers cannot have left before 5 p.m.; they will have done well to arrive at noon (**the sixth hour**) **on the next day**. Were they mounted? Did they travel through the night? Did they leave on the day after the vision, so that *the next day* is one day later still? Luke makes no attempt to work out details that do not affect the substance of the story, and did not ask how Cornelius could forecast the time of Peter's arrival so as to have a considerable company assembled to meet him (v. 24).

There are parallels to the use of **the roof** for prayer. Midday was not a usual time for prayer (as the ninth hour was); it was a fairly regular time for *prandium*. It is probably pointless to attempt to fit the narrative into Jewish, Greek, or Roman habits of eating and prayer. Probably for Luke apostles were men who prayed more frequently than most.

10. He felt hungry: apparently only after he had gone up to the roof to pray. *Hungry* is a rare word, found elsewhere only in a medical author. **to eat** must here mean *to have a meal*, though usually it means *to taste*. There is no point in the reference to Peter's desire for food and the preparation of a meal if it is not intended to prepare for the form in which Peter is instructed in the vision. He desires food; let him slaughter for himself. **While they were preparing**: hardly the tanner alone. The tanner and his servants? Local Christians (9.38, 42)? – many would be glad to serve the apostle.

11. heaven standing open: cf. 7.56. This is a standard feature of apocalyptic and other visions. **a sort of vessel**. The Greek word (*skeuos*) has so wide a use as to be almost equivalent to the English *thing*, but it is often used for (any sort of) *container*. The vessel is **like a great sheet**. The word means *fine linen, a piece of fine linen, a piece of any cloth*, such a piece of cloth used for a specific purpose, *a woman's dress*, the *sail of a ship*. It has been suggested that it was the ships' sails, seen from the roof of a seaside house, that determined Peter's mental picture. If the event is to be thought of as historical and psychologizable this is not impossible.

12. It is clear from the context that Luke is thinking of a collection of every kind of living creature; cf. Gen. 1.20 (for birds), 24 (for the rest). The OT (e.g. Lev. 20.25) distinguishes clearly between clean creatures, which might be eaten, and unclean, which might not.

13. There came a voice to him. The vision is accompanied by a word of command. **slaughter**. The word retains from its primary meaning at least the overtones of *sacrifice*. Peter is called upon to perform a religious act, which will be completed by eating.

14. Certainly not, Lord. Peter recognizes that the command comes from God (*Lord*), but refuses to obey. Why? The only rational explanation is that he supposes that the Lord is testing him, to see whether he will obey the Law regarding food or not; cf. 1 Kings 13.18. This does not seem probable; it may be better to say that Luke (Peter) failed to see the logical implication of what was said. **I have never eaten anything profane or unclean.** Peter, a Galilean (not notorious for strict observance of the Law), who had found the Law an intolerable burden (15.10)? Peter was not only a Galilean; he had been a disciple of Jesus. Was he aware of Mk 7.14–23, or anything like it in the tradition of Jesus? And why does Peter assume that, out of all the animals there are, he was expected to pick out an unclean one? A further problem will arise at v. 28. **profane**, or *common*. The word means that which is not one's own but is *common* to a group or society. The *sacred* means that which is proper to God alone; that which is common to human society thus becomes un-sacred, profane. For the adjective with animals and food cf. 1 Macc. 1.47, 62; 4 Macc. 7.6.

15. The supernatural voice is heard again, in balanced form, with **you** over against **God**. The verb with *you*, cognate with the adjective *profane*, at 4 Macc. 7.6 means *to make profane*. Here however its sense is determined by v. 28, though it is true that calling, or treating, a thing (or person) *profane* amounts to making it *profane*, since it is rejected and not used (cf. Rom. 14.14). This Peter must not do with **things that God has cleansed**. It makes no difference whether we understand this as *has cleansed* or *has counted clean*. The distinction between clean and unclean exists in the mind of God, so that what God *counts as* clean, objectively *is* clean. Does this mean that the OT was wrong in making its distinction between clean and unclean animals? Or has God changed his mind? If the latter, should we associate the change with Mk 7.19? But there is no parallel to Mk 7.19 in Lk. It must be remembered that in v. 28 the vision is interpreted not in terms of food but of men. This must again be related to vv. 34, 35, and to the cleansing of 15.9. On the whole, the context seems to require that what is being given in the vision is a revelation of what eternally is in the mind of God, though it is arguable that God in the past willed to keep Jews and Gentiles separate in order later to unite them in the way that seemed to him good.

16. This must refer to the conversation. The vessel is removed after the repetition.

17. While Peter was wondering what the vision meant the next stage in the story was reached. **Behold** gives a 'biblical' flavour to the narrative but does not prove the use of a Semitic source. **the men who had been sent by Cornelius**, having made the natural inquiries **came and stood at the gate**. *Gate* might imply a large building, but the word could be used of an ordinary house door. Cf. 12.13.

18. See vv. 5, 6.

19. An angel spoke to Cornelius (v. 3); a voice spoke to Peter (vv. 13, 15); now the Spirit speaks. Luke's theology is not so developed as to suggest that he is making any distinction. **Some men.** Many MSS have *three men*, Codex Vaticanus has *two*, a few have no numeral. The last may well be original; many MSS filled in *three*; B, thinking the soldier a guard rather than a messenger, put *two*. Or possibly *two* was original; some copyists 'corrected' to *three*, some omitted.

20. with no hesitation. This could be rendered, *making no distinction.* For Luke's verb see 11. 12; 15.9; Rom. 14.23; James 1.6. **I have sent them.** *I* is presumably the Spirit. It was an angel who gave the command to Cornelius. See on v. 19. For Luke, all these instructions came from God.

21. Peter obeys the Spirit's command.

22. The description of Cornelius is taken up from v. 2.

to his house is not merely circumstantial; to enter Cornelius' house is what a Jew might be expected to be unwilling to do; hence the stress that Cornelius is **righteous** (observing the Law) and a synagogue adherent (if this is what **one who fears God** means).

23. Peter gives proof of his readiness to have dealings with Gentiles and to enter a Gentile house by inviting Gentiles into the house where he is staying.

On the next day, the day after Peter's vision. This (unless we add a day between vv. 8 and 9) is the day after Cornelius' vision, so that we are now on the third day of the narrative. Peter was accompanied by some (six, according to 11.12) of the Joppa Christians.

24. On the next day. Cf. v. 23. We reach the fourth day of the event.

Cornelius . . . had gathered his relatives and closest friends. Cornelius evidently believed that the message was not for him alone. No doubt he would make sure that his guests were all relatively 'unobjectionable' Gentiles. If Cornelius was a soldier still in the service *relatives* would mean (wife and) children. *Closest friends* are probably friends so close as to be almost like relatives.

25. Peter now enters Cornelius' house, a more significant step than entering Caesarea (v. 24). Cornelius met him and, recalling his vision and the voice that he had heard, assumed that he must be more than man, and greeted him accordingly. His action could have been simply an expression of the respect naturally accorded to a notable religious teacher, but Peter's reply (v. 26) shows that more was intended. If Cornelius had in any degree accepted Judaism he could not have thought Peter divine; he may have taken him to be an angel. Cf. Rev. 19.10; 22.9.

The grammar of the opening words is not clear; this probably accounts for a number of variant readings.

26. But Peter raised him up, saying, 'Get up, I too am myself a man.' This is not the way to treat an apostle; cf. Rev. 19.10 and Wisdom 7.1. Important as the apostles may be, Luke does not think of them as 'divine men'. See p. 38 and elsewhere.

28. You (the visitors from Joppa may well be included) **know that it is unlawful for a man of Jewish race** . . . See Jubilees 22.16: Keep yourself separate from the nations, and do not eat with them; and do not imitate their rites, nor associate yourself with them. A Gentle would recognize that to a Jew many things were contrary to what was laid down in the Law and must therefore be avoided. 'They sit apart at meals, they sleep apart' (Tacitus, *Histories* V 5). **to attach himself to**: the verb is that of 5.13. Luke exaggerates the legal requirement, which is accurately given in *NS* 2.83: 'The statement in Acts that a Jew may not associate with Gentiles . . . does not mean that such an association was forbidden, but that each such association was a cause of defilement.' **But God has shown me** . . . The language is so closely parallel to that of v. 14 that it is impossible to suppose that *has shown* does not refer to the vision. In v. 14 however the words *profane*, *unclean*, refer to animals and their use for food. In the present verse they refer to human beings. Do this conclusion and the vision truly belong together? It is true that the two propositions are closely related; unclean food was a major cause of Gentile uncleanness. But though related they are by no means identical, and the difference is important in any consideration of the sources and composition of this chapter. See p. 154.

29. This is repetitive of vv. 21f., but gives Cornelius the opportunity to inform the assembled company, and also allows Luke a form of emphasis.

30. Four days ago, at this very hour. The Greek is confused and confusing; this is its probable meaning. For the chronology see vv. 23, 24. **I was saying the ninth hour of prayer.** This seems to be the meaning. If Cornelius (Luke) means simply *I was praying at the ninth hour* the construction of the last four words is abnormal. **a man stood before me in bright clothing** – clearly the angel of v. 3. For the use of *man*; cf. 1.10. For the clothing; cf. Mt. 27.3; Mk 16.5; Lk. 23.11; 24.4; Jn 20.12.

31. Paraphrases v. 4.

32. Paraphrases vv. 5, 6.

33. Cornelius had immediately done as he was commanded; see vv. 7, 8. **I sent for you at once, and you were so kind as to come.** *I* and *you* are in emphatic contrast: *I sent* and *you came*. *You were so kind as to come*, an idiom, more often with the meaning *Please* . . .

The contrast continues in the second part of the verse: *we* are present to listen to what *you* say. It is a solemn occasion (**in the presence of God**), Peter has a message given him by the Lord – **all that has been laid upon you by the Lord**.

34. For **Peter opened his mouth** cf. 8.35; it adds a solemn (and biblical; e.g. Job 3.1) touch to the proceedings. **Of a truth** is also biblical.

God has no favourites, literally, *God is no accepter of persons*, a biblical expression based on Hebrew that means to raise up the face (of one who has prostrated himself?), hence *to show favour*. It is not clear whether it is Peter's vision (v. 28) or the evident fact that God, through his angel, has had dealings with Cornelius, that leads Peter to this conclusion; perhaps both. Cf. Rom. 2.11, where the emphasis is different. Peter recognizes that a Gentile may be as good as an Israelite, and be treated by God with equal favour; Paul is compelled against his natural wish to recognize that Jews, like Gentiles, are sinners in God's eyes.

35. God does not practise favouritism. **in every nation** appropriately qualified persons are acceptable to God whether they are Jews or belong to some other race. Two requirements are laid down: **he who fears** God **and works righteousness**. Fearing God is not here a matter of the technicality of v. 3, but of holding God in due reverence. Working righteousness cannot mean observing all the precepts of the Law, as a born Jew or proselyte would, for Cornelius, being uncircumcised (11.3), was not a proselyte. It may be that observance of the commandments of the sons of Noah (regarding judgements, blasphemy, idolatry, incest and adultery, murder, theft, and eating meat containing blood; see *NS* 3.1.171, 172) was in mind. Almsgiving (v. 2) was important – for the Gentile an equivalent to what Israel had in the sin-offering (B. Baba Bathra 10b; not a unanimous opinion). For the theological problem perceived here by Calvin see above.

36. The language of this verse, of v. 37, and to some extent also of v. 38 is so difficult as to be untranslatable. Fortunately the general sense is clear. The historic mission of Jesus to Israel is summed up as in 2.22; it leads to crucifixion and resurrection. The awkward construction is further complicated by textual problems, of which the most important is the omission by many MSS of the word *which*. If this word is omitted the verse will stand on its own: *He* (God) *sent the word to the sons of Israel, proclaiming the good news of peace through Jesus Christ* (*he is Lord of all*). *Word* is not used personally; it is the message proclaimed by Jesus, and it is good news because it brings peace between men and God (cf. Lk. 2.14) but also, since Jesus is Lord of all (not of Jews only), between Jews and Gentiles. But what if *which* is included? *Which* becomes the object of the verb *sent*, and *the word* (in the accusative case and therefore an object) is left in suspension. It seems that we must either accept the short text without *which* (this leaves us with the unanswerable question why anyone should have put it in), or conclude that Luke, after writing his parenthesis (he is Lord of all) forgot how the sentence was intended to run. This is better than taking *you know* out of v. 37 and better than an explanation based on a hypothetical Aramaic original.

37. The opening words are relatively clear. **You know the event that happened** (if *you know* is taken with v. 36 – see the note – *the event* will be in apposition with *the word*) **throughout the whole of Judaea**. Peter appeals to his hearers' knowledge as he does at 2.22, but what is natural enough in Jerusalem is strange in Caesarea. Luke is using traditional preaching material. It is not clear why *Judaea* should be singled out for an event located mainly (in Luke's gospel) in Galilee.

Beginning is a participle which does not agree with *the word* or with anything else in the sentence. There are textual variants and conjectures, but we must conclude either that there was a primitive corruption of the text or that Luke wrote a sentence which (grammatically) he ought not to have written and probably did not intend to write, and never reread and corrected his first draft.

The work of Jesus is dated **after the baptism that John proclaimed**, as in Mk. For John the Baptist in Acts see 1.5, 22; 13.24. There may be an allusion to Isa. 52.7 or Neh. 2.1 (or both).

38. Jesus of Nazareth. Here only the place name, elsewhere in Acts the adjective *Nazoraean* is used. **God anointed him with the Holy Spirit and power.** There may be a reference here to the baptism of Jesus; see v. 37. *God anointed him*; that is, made him Messiah, the Anointed One. This seems probable, but see 2.36; 3.20, with the notes. He **went about doing good and healing** . . . The tenses of the Greek verbs suggest that his ministry regarded as a whole was made up of a continuous series of acts of beneficence. **the devil** was responsible not only for possession but for illness in general; God was making through Jesus a decisive attack on him. Cf. Mk 3.23–27. **God was with him.** This could be said of many in the OT. Luke's Christology is undeveloped.

39. And we are witnesses. For this theme see 1.8, 22; 2.32; 3.15; 5.32; 13.31; 22.15; 26.16. At this point witnessing seems to be restricted to the events of the ministry of Jesus; witness to the resurrection will be mentioned in v. 41. The ministry was confined to **the land of the Jews and** . . . **Jerusalem**. This raises sharply the question what, if anything, may be expected to happen in Caesarea.

They killed him. No subject is expressed; one is implied by *the land of the Jews* and *Jerusalem*; Peter regards the Jews as morally responsible. **by hanging him on a tree**. See 5.30 (and cf. Gal. 3.13; Deut. 21.23).

40. Upon crucifixion follows resurrection. Cf. 3.15; 4.10; 5.30. In none of these passages is there reference to **the third day** (1 Cor. 15.4; Lk. (13.22); 18.33; 24.7, (21), 46; and in Mt.). Mk has *after three days*, meaning probably *after a short time*, *soon*. The fact but not the date is significant here.

God **granted to him**; cf. 2.27 (= Ps. 16.10); 14.3; a Septuagintalism. **that he should be revealed** represents an adjective sometimes used for presenting a person or thing in open court – here the witnesses (vv. 39, 41) are available for identification.

41. The **witnesses** whom God had **appointed beforehand** were **us**; The following words show that Luke was thinking of the Twelve, who a**te and drank with him after he had risen from the dead**. See 1.3, 4; also Lk. 24.36–43; eating and drinking prove the physical reality of the risen body of Jesus (contrast Tobit 12.19).

It may be that Ignatius, *Smyrnaeans* 3.3, shows knowledge of this verse.

42. The witnesses are charged to proclaim the truth to the (Jewish) people. This is that he has been appointed Judge. That he will preside at the last judgement does not in itself claim that he is divine, though it does mean that he has been entrusted with a divine function.

43. All the prophets bear witness to this, that everyone . . . It would be possible to translate, *To him all the prophets bear witness that* . . . , but elsewhere in Acts prophets are not said to bear witness to Christ but rather to certain facts about him (2.16, 30; 3.18, 21, 24; 13.27, 40; 15.15; 24.14; 26.22, 27; 28.23, 25). The prophets' testimony is **that everyone who believes in him receives through his name the forgiveness of sins**. For *forgiveness* see 2.38 (and the note); for *name* see 3.16 (and the note). Isa. 33.24; 55.7 are possibly relevant prophetic passages, but Jer. 31.34 is probably more important. *Everyone who believes in him* is important; the only requirement is faith. Without saying so (and, according to Luke's narrative, without knowing that he had done so) Peter has prepared for what follows.

44. While Peter was still speaking. According to 11.15, Peter was beginning to speak. In fact he has finished the common outline of preaching in Acts. Luke is concerned to emphasize the spontaneity of the Spirit's action, and its unexpectedness. For the gift of the Holy

Spirit see on 2.4. The gift was experienced by **all who were listening**, but Luke is thinking primarily of the Gentiles present, who, on the basis of nothing but the proclamation of Jesus, had manifestly been brought within the scope of salvation.

45. And the circumcised believers: cf. 11.2. They are simply circumcised, not a circumcising party, and are not to be blamed (and Luke does not blame them) for the astonishment they feel at the pouring out of the Spirit **upon the Gentiles too**. For *pouring out*; cf. 2.17, 18, 33 (Joel 3.1, 2). The parallel between these Gentiles and the original disciples is emphasized at v. 47; 11.15; 15.8.

46. That the Spirit has been given is proved (as usual for Luke) by audible phenomena. The Gentiles speak with tongues, as the apostles did at Pentecost (2.4; see on this verse for glossolalia). They were **magnifying God**; the word is common in the LXX (e.g. Ps. 33(34).3). Peter is obliged to respond to the situation.

47. Peter's conclusion is that there is no reason why Cornelius and his friends should not be baptized. The conclusion is understandable but makes some assumptions. It assumes that Cornelius and his friends wish to become Christians. This is perhaps justifiable. It assumes that to become a Christian one must be baptized. This agrees with 2.38, but the requirement is not universal in Acts (see Introduction, pp. lxif.). It assumes that there is, or might be, unwillingness to permit Gentiles to receive baptism. This would be understandable, at least in the sense that circumcision might be required to accompany baptism. This is countered by the rhetorical question which expects the answer No.

In this story baptism follows upon the gift of the Spirit. In 2.38 the gift of the Spirit is the consequence of baptism. In 8.16 the gift is not given till after the laying on of hands. It is doubtful whether Luke maintained, or indeed had heard of, hard and fast rules in this matter. See Introduction, pp. lxif.

48. And he gave orders for them to be baptized in the name of Jesus Christ. Peter apparently did not carry out the baptism himself.

Then they asked him to stay on for some days. *They* must be Cornelius and his friends. 11.3 implies that Peter accepted the invitation though it meant staying with an uncircumcised Gentle. He recognized them as Christians, and as 'clean'. Peter's staying with Cornelius allowed time for the story to reach Jerusalem; see 11.1.

28. PETER AND CORNELIUS DEBATED 11.1–18

**[1]The apostles and the brothers who were in Judaea heard that
the Gentiles also had received the word of God. [2]When Peter
went up to Jerusalem those who represented circumcision debated
with him, [3]saying, 'You went into the house of uncircumcised
men and ate with them.' [4]Peter began to set things out for them
in order, saying, [5]'I was in the city of Joppa praying, and in a
trance I saw a vision, a sort of vessel coming down like a great
sheet let down from heaven by the four corners, and it came right
up to me. [6]I peered in and considered it, and saw the quadrupeds
of the earth, and wild beasts, and reptiles, and the birds of heaven.
[7]And I heard a voice saying to me, Get up, Peter, slaughter and
eat. [8]But I said, No indeed, Lord, for nothing profane or unclean
has ever entered my mouth. [9]The voice answered a second time
from heaven, Things that God has cleansed, do not you treat as
profane. [10]This happened three times, and the whole was drawn
up again into heaven. [11]And immediately there were three men
standing by the house in which we were, sent to me from Caesarea.
[12]The Spirit told me to go with them, making no distinction; there
went with me also these six brothers and we went into the man's
house. [13]And he reported to us how he had seen the angel in his
house, who stood and said, Send to Joppa and summon Simon
who is surnamed Peter. [14]He will speak to you words by which
you will be saved, you and all your household. [15]As I began to
speak the Holy Spirit fell upon them, as he had done upon us at
the beginning, [16]and I remembered the word of the Lord, how he
said, John baptized with water, but you shall be baptized in the
Holy Spirit. [17]If then God gave to them when they believed in the
Lord Jesus Christ the same gift as he gave to us, who was I to be
able to stand in God's way?' [18]When they heard these things they
fell silent and glorified God, saying, 'Why then, to the Gentiles
also God has given that repentance that leads to life.'**

The greater part of this paragraph is devoted to an abbreviated repetition of the story told in 10.1–48. This is called for by the report of the Cornelius episode that came to the ears of the Jerusalem church (v. 1) and evoked objection on the part of those who valued their Jewish as well as their Christian status (vv. 2, 3). Peter's reply was his own account of what had happened; the objectors then recognized that God had made it possible for the Gentiles to repent and thereby receive life.

It is important to distinguish two questions that are raised by the Cornelius story. May a Jew, even if a Christian and going about Christian duties, have domestic and table-fellowship with a Gentile? And, May those who are not Jews become Christians, and, if they wish to do so, is it necessary that they should first be circumcised as Jews before being baptized as Christians? The questions, though distinct, are of course closely related. Peter's narrative argument is accepted in the proposition (v. 18) which generalizes what was manifestly true about Cornelius and his company: God has granted to Gentiles, uncircumcised, salvation (life).

This conclusion constitutes a problem. Does it not already answer the requirements maintained in 15.1, 5 and discussed at the Council of ch. 15? This problem cannot be fully discussed till ch. 15 is reached, but it may be noticed here that the discussion in the present chapter moves from the propriety of entering a Gentile dwelling (v. 3) to the wider question of the conditions of salvation (v. 18), but that in ch. 15 moves in the reverse direction, from the conditions of salvation (15.1, 5) to what appears to be a food law regulating relations between Jewish and Gentile Christians (15.29). There are various possibilities: the Lucan chronology is mistaken; Jewish attitudes hardened between ch. 11 and ch. 15; the questions were too complicated for Luke to set out in the space at his disposal, perhaps too complicated for him (writing at a later period) to understand. These suggestions may all prove to be true.

This leads to the question of the literary source of the paragraph. See what is said above (pp. 152–4) on ch. 10. The Caesarean church's story of its own origin probably concluded with the recognition by Jerusalem of its legitimacy. It may be that behind v. 18 there was a much more restricted approval of what had happened in Caesarea.

A further historical question may be raised, that of the role and position of Peter in the story. It is clear that in the end he carries the church with him, but its members; evidently feel free to call his actions into question. There was no automatic approval of what he had done. It is worth noting that there is no reference to James.

1. The apostles and the brothers together make up the whole church: its leaders with the rank and file. For *apostles* see 1.2; for *brothers* see 1.15. **The Gentiles also had received the word of God**, had accepted it so as to become believers; cf. 8.14; 17.11.

2. Peter went up to Jerusalem, evidently still his base. **Those who represented the circumcision**, literally, *those of the circumcision*. The same words are used at 10.45 with the addition of *believers*; this must be understood here also.

3. You went into . . . ; a question is possible, *Did you go into* . . .? It is also possible though unlikely that the question should be, *Why did you go into* . . . ? These variant translations make little difference to the general sense.

You went into: *the house* is not in the Greek but is implied. **and ate with them**. This is not stated in 10.25, but may reasonably be taken to be implied. The house would certainly be unclean and the food might be, though Cornelius, it seems, was not the sort of man (10.2) to insult a Jew by offering forbidden food. The accusation is that Peter entered into an association that can hardly have failed to produce some measure of uncleanness. This could be removed; and the objectors do not raise the question of the admission of Gentiles into the Christian church (though this is what is accepted in v. 18). They speak as Jews to a Jew who has entered into social relations with a Gentile.

4. Peter's answer is simply to relate what had happened; as the Lucan narrative unfolds it is this relation that takes the event out of the area of Judaism (Why did Peter eat with Gentiles on Gentile premises?) and into that of developing Christianity (May Gentiles become Christians and if so on what terms?).

Peter began to set things out for them in order. *began* is pleonastic, but Hellenistic rather than Semitic idiom; it may have been suggested by *in order*. He set about giving a logical development. The narrative that follows is closely related to and often verbally repeats that of ch. 10. The existence of the two accounts shows how important Luke considered the event to be.

5. See 9.43; 10.9, 10, 11.

6. I peered in, literally, *into which having peered*. Construction and verb are both Lucan. There is substantial agreement with 10.12.

7. The construction as in 10.13.

8. has ever entered my mouth. Like 10.14 but with a Hebrew idiom.

9. In agreement with 10.15.

10. As in 10.16.

11, 12a. These verses sum up 10.17–23a, from Peter's point of view. **in which we were**. *we* might be Peter, the tanner, and the members of his household; more probably Peter and those who were to accompany him.

12b. Cf. 10.23b. **these six brothers**. The number is added. **we went into the man's house**. Peter thus admits the first part of the charge made in v. 3. *the man*: Cornelius of course is meant, but in the retelling of the story he has not been mentioned. Apparently Luke, abbreviating somewhat carelessly, did not see anything important in the description of Cornelius as *God-fearing* (10.2).

13, 14. The unnamed *man* proceeds to tell his story. These verses abbreviate 10.30–33. Not only Cornelius himself but his **household** will be **saved**.

15. As I began to speak does not agree precisely with 10.44, even if *begin* is used in Semitic fashion (see on 1.1). **at the beginning** makes the parallel with the event of Pentecost more emphatic. The divine initiative has placed Cornelius and his colleagues in the same position as the Christian leaders in ch. 2.

16. I remembered the word of the Lord. The saying appears to go back to John the Baptist; but see 1.5. The use of this saying leaves the reader in doubt whether Christian baptism called for the use of water (though 8.36; 10.47 make it clear that Luke was familiar with a Christian rite in which water was used as it was in John's). On baptism in Acts see Introduction, pp. lx–lxii.

17. Repeats the argument of 10.47 in rather different terms. **If then God gave to them when they believed . . . the same gift as he gave to us.** *Belief* is not mentioned in ch. 10, but one may reasonably suppose that the reaction to Peter's address was belief in Jesus; Peter and his fellow apostles had believed in Jesus long before the day of Pentecost. It was when Cornelius and his friends believed that they received the gift of the Holy Spirit.

The rest of the sentence is not well expressed. Peter could have forbidden the use of water (10.47); he could not prevent God from doing what he intended, still less could he prevent God from doing what he had already done. The question is really a double one: (1) Who was I that I should . . . ? and (2) Was I able to . . . ?

18. When they heard these things they fell silent and glorified God. *They* must be *those who represented circumcision* (v. 2). Their objection was silenced by the spontaneous action of God. They do not say, You were after all justified in going into a Gentile house and eating there, but **to the Gentiles also God has given that repentance that leads to life** (salvation; cf. 5.20; 13.46, 48). There is no hint that the men should now be circumcised. This raises problems in regard to ch. 15; these are to some extent mitigated if we read the sentence as a question: *Has God actually given to Gentiles . . .* ? For the connection between repentance and salvation; cf. 2.38; 3.19; 5.31; 20.21; 26.20.

There is no immediate connection with what follows, in which a new beginning of the Gentile mission is described.

VII

THE CHURCH FOUNDED AT ANTIOCH AND APPROVED BY JERUSALEM

(11.19–30)

29. FOUNDATION OF THE CHURCH AT ANTIOCH (11.19–26)

[19] Those who had been scattered by the persecution that arose on account of Stephen went on their way as far as Phoenicia, Cyprus, and Antioch, speaking the word to none but Jews only. [20] But there were some of them, men from Cyprus and Cyrene, who when they came to Antioch spoke also to the Hellenists, as they told the good news of the Lord Jesus. [21] The hand of the Lord was with them, and a large number who believed turned to the Lord. [22] The report about them came to the ears of the church that was in Jerusalem, and they sent out Barnabas to make his way to Antioch. [23] When he arrived and saw that the grace of God was at work he rejoiced, and exhorted them all to continue with the Lord in the purpose of their hearts, [24] for he was a good man, and full of the Holy Spirit and of faith. And a considerable number was added to the church. [25] Barnabas went off to Tarsus to seek out Saul, [26] and when he had found him brought him to Antioch. It now happened that they met in the church for as much as a whole year and taught a considerable company, and that in Antioch for the first time the disciples came to bear the name of Christians.

In 10.1 – 11.18 we have heard what appears to be the story of the beginning of the mission to the Gentiles. This is located in Caesarea. In the new paragraph we have a second account of what may equally be taken to be the beginning of the mission to Gentiles. It is located in Antioch. It is not surprising that there should be two such stories.

At some time a church arose in Caesarea, some of whose members were not Jews and did not become Jews. At some time a similar mixed Christian group came into being at Antioch (as is confirmed by Galatians). There is no doubt that both these churches came into being, but we cannot be certain which came into being first; there is no need to suppose that either church knew how or when – or even that – the other was founded.

The foundation at Antioch is ascribed to *those who had been scattered by the persecution* connected with Stephen (8.1, 4). They were Jews, and did not at first extend their mission to Gentiles. When eventually they did so, with remarkable results, it was important to Luke, perhaps also to the Jewish evangelists, that this step should be, and should be seen to be, a valid expression, result, and continuation of the work of Jesus. This was achieved by the sending of Barnabas (4.36f.; 9.27), who was more than satisfied. He took part in the work and went off to Tarsus to look for Saul (9.30). The two took up residence in Antioch and became leading members of an established and flourishing church.

There are signs of Luke's work in the paragraph (see e.g. vv. 19, 21, 24), but there is also material that probably was not his own; Luke would not have invented a mission in Cyprus before Paul's (v. 19 before 13.4–12) or Gentile converts in Antioch (vv. 20, 25f.); he would probably have had Barnabas sent by the apostles in Jerusalem. Luke has traditional material at his disposal and probably collected it in Antioch or through Antiochene contacts. The passage opens immediately, with no attempt to date the events it describes; this probably means that Luke did not intend to assert that they happened after the events at Caesarea (10.1 – 11.18). He was collecting information about the extension of the Gospel to the Gentile world, and wished to show that this new development, like that at Caesarea, was not an independent innovation but was based on the original Jerusalem Gospel. This was confirmed in two ways. The evangelists were those who, originating in Jerusalem and having the stamp of the Twelve's approval (6.1–6), had been driven out by persecution; and once the innovation had been made it was examined and approved by Barnabas.

The theory (see Introduction, p. xxxi) that a continuous Antiochene source connects 8.1, 4 with the reference to *those who had been scattered* is now widely abandoned, but this paragraph may well be Luke's edited version of the story of its origin current in the church of Antioch, which was certainly an early foundation and had links with Jerusalem (Gal. 2.11–14). The visit of Barnabas may be Luke's own invention, but visitations from Jerusalem to Antioch are confirmed by Acts 15.1, 5 and Gal. 2.11, 12. There is little to be said for the view that Antioch was evangelized from Galilee. If Luke is correct in saying that it was at Antioch that believers were first called Christians some light is thrown on the make-up of the church, for the new designation was probably needed when it became clear that believers who had left their old Gentile way of life were no more Jews than they were heathen; they were in fact a third race, Christians.

19. For **Those who had been scattered by the persecution that arose on account of Stephen** see 8.1, 4. As 8.4 indicates, they preached as they travelled, **speaking the word to none but Jews only**. **Phoenicia** was not an 'official' provincial name. It included Sidon, Tyre, and Byblos. The Phoenicians were widely known as traders, and as founders of Carthage. **Cyprus** was visited by Paul and Barnabas (13.4 – where nothing suggests an earlier mission). The island was a minor senatorial province. Julius Caesar gave it to Cleopatra, Augustus took it back. **Antioch**, though founded as late as 300 BC by Seleucus I, was one of the greatest cites of antiquity. There were many Jews in Antioch, and they received many privileges from its founder.

20. The missionaries must have been normally resident in Jerusalem (8.1) but some were not of Palestinian origin. Some were **men from Cyprus** (see on v. 19), others were from **Cyrene**. Cyrene is mentioned at 2.10; cf. 6.9; 11.20; 13.1. The name will probably include not only the city but also the region (Cyrenaica), long settled by Greeks, and Greek-speaking, but with a large population of Jews. These men spoke not only to Jews but also to others who in some MSS are called Hellenists (*hellēnistai*), in others Greeks (*hellēnes*). *Hellenists* is probably correct; cf. 6.1; 9.29. The word now has a third meaning. At 6.1 the Hellenists were Greek-speaking Jewish Christians; at 9.29 they were Greek-speaking Jews who were not Christians; here the context requires that they should be Greek-speaking Gentiles, not necessarily, not probably, natives of Greece. In dealing with early Christian history it is well to use the word Hellenist with great care.

21. That the new step was successful is expressed by Luke in one of his 'biblical' phrases, **The hand of the Lord was with them**; cf. 4.28, 30; 13.11; also Lk. 1.26. Luke is imitating rather than translating.

22. News of the conversion of the Hellenists reached Jerusalem. Cf. 11.1. The word **church** (*ekklēsia*) is used again at v. 26 and at 13.1; 14.23, 27). It was perhaps characteristic of the Christians (v. 26) at Antioch. Luke evidently understood **Barnabas** (a fellow Cypriote) to have been appointed to represent Jerusalem as inspector, charged to find out what was happening at Antioch, and presumably – if necessary – to put an end to it. Some, pointing out that at 11.30; 12.25 Barnabas is a delegate from Antioch to Jerusalem, and that at 13.1 he is a leading member of the church at Antioch, think that he was one of the Hellenists who were driven from Jerusalem and founded the church at Antioch (8.1; 11.19). There are no good grounds for this view. In 4.36, 37 Barnabas appears as a very early and generous member of the church at Jerusalem; he is not mentioned in ch. 6; in 9.26 he is able to introduce Paul to the apostles; in Gal. 2.13 he sides with James and Peter against Paul, though he seems to be back as a Pauline colleague at 1 Cor. 9.6.

23. Barnabas saw what was going on, but it is described not in human terms but as the grace of God. It was this that caused the conversion of the Hellenists. The construction is somewhat unusual and suggests a certain predicative sense in the adjectival phrase (**of God**): he saw the gracious work that was going on and was obliged to recognize that it was of God. Barnabas **exhorted them all to continue** in their relation (of faith, v. 21) to the Lord. This indicates the objective direction of their continuance; its subjective character is given by **the purpose of their hearts** – *heartfelt purpose*. Barnabas is here acting as an *apostle* of the Jerusalem church. The verb that describes his sending in v. 22 is *exapesteilen*.

24. Barnabas judged as he did because **he was a good man, and full of the Holy Spirit and of faith**. To Luke it was so evident that the Gentiles must be included in the Christian mission that he was convinced that any good and honest Christian must approve of the step taken in Antioch; those mentioned in 15.1, 5 had small chance of a favourable comment. *Full of the Holy Spirit and of faith* is a Lucan expression; cf. 6.5 (of Stephen). Cf. also 6.3, 8. The result of the whole process – the approach to the Gentiles and the visit of Barnabas – was (as is usual in Acts) an increase in the number of believers.

25. Barnabas went off to Tarsus. At 9.30 Saul, whom the Hellenists were seeking to kill, was sent, presumably for his safety, to Tarsus, according to 22.3 his native place. Barnabas, who knew

Saul well enough to commend him to the apostles (9.27), now knew him as an ardent evangelist, experienced in dealing with Hellenists (though we must remember that now, in ch. 11, the word is differently used). That there was a close relation between Barnabas and Saul is not only confirmed in the later chapters of Acts; it is evident in the epistles: 1 Cor. 9.6; Gal. 2.1, 9, 13 (*even* Barnabas). Cf. Col. 4.10. Gal. 2.13 connects both men with Antioch. That a connection between Saul, Barnabas and Antioch existed is certain; if it did not come about in the way described by Acts we do not know how it originated.

26. The text at the beginning of this verse is confused and the original wording must remain uncertain.

they met in the church. It is disputed whether Luke's verb means *to join in the services of the church* or *to be entertained, accommodated.* It could mean both, as in F. J. A. Hort's paraphrase, 'were hospitably received in the Ecclesia' (*The Christian Ecclesia*, 1914, 61).

Christians. The ending *-ianus* is Latin, and, with a name, was used to describe partisans; thus *Caesariani*, *Galbiani*, *Pompeiani*, *Augustiani*. *Christ* had probably become virtually a proper name, and Christians were the partisans of Christ, his adherents. It is doubtful whether the name originated during the time when Saul and Barnabas worked together in Antioch – Luke does not quite say that it did. It was probably used in Pompeii between the earthquake of AD 62 and the destruction of the town in AD 79. It is probably contained in *CIL* 4.679 (see E. Dinkler in *Signum Crucis*, 138–41). It is a not unreasonable suggestion that it reflects a situation in which Christians were becoming numerous and were clearly distinguished from Jews. The word is used at 26.28 and at 1 Peter 4.16, later by Ignatius, *Ephesians* 11.2; *Romans* 3.2; *Magnesians* 10.3; *Polycarp* 7.3. See also Tacitus, *Annals* 15.44; Suetonius, *Nero* 16.2; Pliny, *Epistles* 10.96; Lucian, *Alexander* 25, 38; *Peregrinus* 11; 12; 13; 16.

30. THE CHURCH AT ANTIOCH INDEPENDENT 11.27–30

[27] **In these days prophets came down from Jerusalem to Antioch.**
[28] **One of them, Agabus by name, stood up and declared through the Spirit that there was to be a great famine over the whole inhabited earth; this happened in the time of Claudius.** [29] **Each of the disciples, as he prospered, determined on service, to send to the brothers who lived in Judaea.** [30] **This in fact they did, in that they sent to the elders by the hand of Barnabas and Saul.**

The church at Antioch proved both its independence and a continuing relationship by sending aid to the church in Jerusalem to which it owed its origin, in its founders (those who had been scattered – 8.1, 3) and in Barnabas (11.22). The core of the paragraph was probably drawn from Antiochene tradition; it was the sort of thing the church would be glad to remember. The tradition may well have included reference to Paul and Barnabas, whose connection with Antioch is confirmed by Gal. 2.13. The narrative builds up to the commissioning in 13.1–3. Luke's editorial hand can probably be seen at a number of points. He may have developed a prophecy of famine in Judaea into a world-wide famine. He knew Agabus (21.20) and may have introduced his name as that of a representative prophet. The reference to Claudius comes from one who could look back to the 'time of Claudius' (fourteen years in fact) as a relatively short period. Christian charity is no longer a wholesale disposal of capital but what it is with Paul, a giving out of earnings (1 Cor. 16.2; 2 Cor. 9.7).

The present visit of Paul to Jerusalem is, in Acts, his second, that in Acts 15 his third. But ch. 15 corresponds most closely with Gal. 2.1–10, and this suggests that the two 'visits' are in fact duplicate accounts of one visit. This however is perhaps too simple an account of a very complex matter. See further the notes on ch. 15 and Introduction, pp. lxxxiif.

What must be noted in this paragraph, in addition to such important points as a tradition that an early prophet had foretold a great famine and Luke's knowledge that Paul had on some occasion brought to Jerusalem the proceeds of a collection, is the Antiochian interest that runs through 11.17–30. The story originates in Jerusalem and returns to Jerusalem. The extension of the Gospel to the Gentiles, the problems this causes, and the resolution of these problems, are major Lucan interests, which Luke pursued wherever he could find them. He may have regretted that the story of Antioch was less eventful than that of Caesarea.

27. In these days is a vague note of time. It could refer to the year of 11.26, or to a later time. **prophets**: the first reference in Acts to Christian prophets; see 13.1; 15.33; 21.10; cf. 2.17, 18; 19.6; 21.9. For wandering prophets at more or less the time at which Acts was written see *Didache* 11.7–9. In the present passage and at 21.10 prophets foretell the future. This role is not mentioned at 15.32. In the Pauline epistles the prophets speak the word of God to the congregation (though this need not exclude prediction). The prophets **came down from Jerusalem to Antioch**. There is no need to explain the movements of wandering charismatics, but it may be that in v. 28 (see the note) Luke introduced the words *over the whole inhabited earth*. If the famine was in fact universal no church would have been able to help any other; the forecast may have referred only to Jerusalem (and Judaea – see 21.10 for Agabus). It was to Jerusalem that help was sent.

28. One of them, Agabus by name. Agabus is presumably a Semitic name. Ezra 2.45 refers to Hagabah, 2.46 to Hagab. The Hebrew *ḥagab* means *locust*. Another possibility is suggested by an inscription which contains the female name *ʿagabah*. Agabus (it seems pedantic to write Hagabus) comes from Jerusalem and appears at Antioch and Caesarea – an itinerant prophet (cf. *Didache* 11). **He declared . . . that there was to be a great famine over the whole inhabited earth.** Luke's word means *the inhabited land*, and *land* may mean a particular country, the Greek world, the Roman world, the whole world. The last seems to be Luke's meaning, though he may have exaggerated an original reference to a more local famine, perhaps in Judaea (see on v. 27).

this happened in the time of Claudius. Claudius was Emperor from AD 41 to 54. There are several references to famine in his time; see especially Josephus, *Ant.* 20.101, which refers to a *great famine* in the time of Tiberius Alexander, who was procurator of Judaea AD 46–48. This must have been aggravated by the Sabbatical year of AD 47–48 (see M. Sotah 7.8). This was after the death of Herod Agrippa (12.23), but the present verse dates (if it dates anything) the prophecy, not the event, and Luke puts the visit after Agrippa's death (12.24).

The Western text of this verse begins: There was great rejoicing, and when *we* met there spoke . . . If this reading is accepted we have here a use of the first person plural that anticipates 16.10, normally taken as the beginning of the 'We-source'. On this see on 16.10, and Introduction, pp. xxiiif. The reading is perhaps sufficiently accounted for as a characteristic Western attempt to make the history both livelier and more authoritative.

29. Each of the disciples (Luke does not continue to use the word Christians – 11.26), **as he prospered, determined** . . . The charitable organization was different from that described in the earlier chapters. Christians were engaging in business, and some at least were prospering. Each, it seems, was free to decide what he should do with his profits. This was the way Paul conducted his collection (2 Cor. 9.7). The aim was **service**, the word Paul uses (Rom. 15.31; 1 Cor. 16.15; 2 Cor. 8.4; 9.1, 12, 13). It is also a Lucan word (1.17, 25; 6.1, 4; 12.25; 20.24; 21.29).

30. It must not be assumed that **they sent** immediately after the visit of the prophets. **to the elders**. Christian elders are here mentioned for the first time. See later 14.23; 15.2, 4, 6, 22, 23; 16.4; 20.17; 21.18. Jewish elders are mentioned at 2.17; 4.5, 8, 23; 6.12; 23.14; 24.1; 25.15. There were *elders* also at Qumran, but there is no ground for supposing that there was any connection except a common dependence on the OT tradition. The Christian institution is more likely to be modelled on the elders of the local synagogue. **Barnabas and Saul** resemble the pairs in which Jewish envoys entrusted with the carrying of money were sent.

VIII
RETURN TO JERUSALEM
(12.1–25)

31. JAMES, PETER, AND HEROD 12.1–23

[1] At that time King Herod laid his hands on some of those who
belonged to the church so as to harm them. [2] He killed James, the
brother of John, with the sword. [3] When he saw that this was
pleasing to the Jews he went on to arrest Peter also. These were
the days of Unleavened Bread. [4] He seized Peter and put him in
prison, handing him over to four squads of four soldiers each to
guard him, with the intention of bringing him up to the people
after Passover. [5] So then Peter was being kept in the prison, and
prayer was being earnestly offered to God by the church on his
behalf.

[6] When Herod was about to bring him forward, that night
Peter was asleep between two soldiers, bound with two chains,
and guards posted before the doors were keeping the prison. [7] And
behold, an angel of the Lord came and stood over Peter and light
shone in the prison cell. He struck Peter's side and awakened
him, saying, 'Get up quickly.' His chains fell from his hands, [8] and
the angel said to him, 'Fasten your belt and put on your sandals.'
He did so. The angel said to him, 'Put on your cloak, and come
with me.' [9] He went out and followed, and did not know that what
was being done by the angel was true, but supposed that he was
seeing a vision. [10] When they had passed through the first watch
and the second they came to the iron gate that led to the city; this
opened to them of its own accord. They went out and traversed
one street, and immediately the angel left him. [11] Then Peter came
to his right mind, and said, 'Now indeed I know that the Lord

has sent his angel and rescued me out of the hand of Herod and from all that the people of the Jews were expecting.' [12] When he had considered this he went to the house of Mary, the mother of John called Mark, where many were assembled and praying. [13] He knocked at the door in the gateway and a girl called Rhoda came forward to answer the knock. [15] When she recognized Peter's voice she did not open the door for joy, but ran in to report that Peter was standing at the gateway. [15] But they said to her, 'You are mad.' She however persisted that it was so. They said, 'It is his angel.' [16] Peter went on knocking; when they opened the gate they saw him and were astonished. [17] Peter motioned to them to be quiet, and recounted to them how the Lord had brought him out of the prison, and said, 'Report these things to James and the brothers.' Then he went out, and went to another place.

[18] When day broke there was no small confusion among the soldiers as they wondered what had become of Peter, [19] When Herod looked for him and did not find him he examined the guards and ordered them to be led off for punishment. He went down from Judaea to Caesarea and stayed there.

[20] He was angry with the Tyrians and Sidonians. Together they presented themselves before him, and having got Blastus, the king's chamberlain, on their side, they asked for peace, because their country was supplied by that of the king, [21] On an appointed day, Herod put on royal robes, sat on the tribune, and addressed them. [22] The assembly called out, 'The voice of a god, not of a man!' [23] Immediately the angel of the Lord struck him down, because he did not give God the glory. He was eaten by worms and expired.

This paragraph is not distinctively Lucan in style and is easily detachable from the thread of narrative; v. 25 could follow immediately upon 11.27–30. It is the more important to ask what purpose the paragraph seemed to Luke to serve. It is in three parts: (a) the death of James, part of an attack on the church (vv. 1, 2); (b) the arrest ,and escape of Peter (vv. 3–19); (c) the fate of Herod (vv. 20–23).

There is no way in which the main thread of narrative is affected by (a). It may have been Luke's intention to balance the 'success stories' of chs. 10 and 11, and the miraculous escape of Peter, with a piece that recognizes the fact of opposition and the vocation of

Christians to suffer for their faith. But it is probably best to conclude that (a) stands where it does because it was attached in tradition to (b).

(b) also is a persecution story. It shows interest in Herod as well as Peter; for this cf. 13.1 and Lk. 8.3. Luke's main concern however is twofold. In the first place it gives a striking example of the power of God to watch over his word and protect those who proclaim it. Secondly, it may contain a hint of how leadership in the Jerusalem church was transferred from Peter (who went to *another place*, v. 17) to James (also v. 17). This point, if it is valid, is best thought of as Luke's addition to a story of divine deliverance, in which the emphasis lies upon God's spontaneous intervention – Peter does not even understand what is happening to him. After the departure of the angel (v. 10) a number of names are introduced (Mary, John Mark, Rhoda). Cf. 9.32–43 (Aeneas, Dorcas, Simon). Elsewhere in early Christian tradition Mark is connected with Peter (1 Peter 5.13; Eusebius, *HE* 3.39.15; 5.8.3). In the rest of Acts he appears with Paul (12.25; 13.5, 13; 15.37; cf. Col. 4.10; Philemon 24; 2 Tim. 4.11). It is doubtful whether Luke included this story of Peter's supernatural release to balance that of Paul (16.25–34); doubtful also whether his intention was to clear Peter of the suspicion of having run away.

(c) calls for little comment here. A parallel account of Herod's death is given by Josephus; we have two popular, Jewish and Christian, reports; both saw the hand of God in the punishment of the man who claimed to be God, or allowed the claim to be made on his behalf.

The paragraph as a whole – (a), (b), and (c) – is a carefully constructed unity. Luke winds up one part of his book and prepares the way for another. The story of the Twelve (who now, apart from Peter's brief appearance in ch. 15, disappear) ends gloriously, with martyrdom and miracle, and only the sophisticated will note the logical and theological gaps in the story.

1. At that time. A vague note; for the date of Herod's death see on v. 20; for the relation between this and the 'famine visit' of Barnabas and Paul see on 12.25.

King Herod is Herod Agrippa I, or rather Julius Agrippa I; he bears the family name Herod only in Acts. The Agrippa of 25.13 – 26.32 was his son, Agrippa II. Drusilla (24.24) and Bernice (25.13) were his daughters. Agrippa I was the son of Aristobulus and grandson of Herod the Great. He was born in 10 BC and had a varied career. See

NS 1.442–54; also Schwarz, *Agrippa I*. Eventually, in part through his friendship with the Emperors Gaius and Claudius, he governed as wide an area as his grandfather. Notwithstanding his Roman and Greek contacts he seems to have been recognized as, especially when in Judaea, a good Jew (M. Sotah 7.8; Josephus, *Ant.* 19.292–4, 331). It would be in this character that he acted against James and Peter.

some, not all; this probably means an attack on the church through its leaders. **the church**: see on 5.11, and Introduction, pp. lviiif.

2. For **James, the brother of John**, see 1.13; Mk 3.17. **with the sword**. This has been taken to mean that the charge against James was political rather than religious. Herod may have seen Christianity as a political threat to his government. This is possibly but not quite certainly true. It is supported by v. 3 if that means that Herod first acted on his own, subsequently discovering that what he had done pleased the Jews. According to an epitome of Philip of Side (*c.* AD 430), 'Papias in his second book says that John the Divine and James his brother were killed by Jews.' There is nothing in Acts to support the belief that John also suffered an early martyrdom. See *St John* 103f.

3. Herod is here distinguished from **the Jews**, to whom his action was pleasing. **he went on to arrest Peter also**. Luke's Greek is a Hebraism, probably due not to translation but to imitation of the style of the LXX. **These were the days of Unleavened Bread.** An awkwardly inserted parenthesis. See Lk. 22.1; Luke evidently did not distinguish between Passover and Unleavened Bread.

4. four squads of four soldiers each. Details of the guard are given in order to heighten the miracle. We do not know where Peter was imprisoned; some think of the Antonia (see p. 336). It was Herod's intention to bring Peter **up to the people** (not for trial but for execution) after **Passover** (see v. 3) – recalling sacrifice (the crucifixion), or deliverance (resurrection)? Passover night was expected to be a night of messianic deliverance, and this belief was continued and reinterpreted in the Christian Pasch (Easter) and the eucharist. There is a curious echo of this story in the *Epistula Apostolorum* 15. Luke does nothing to bring out the Paschal significance of his story.

5. the church naturally prays for the imprisoned Peter. It is rightly pointed out that in chs. 22–28 there is no such reference to prayer for Paul.

6. Passover is presumably now past (v. 4). **that night**. Cf. Exod. 12.12. But Luke is telling a vivid story, not working out a typological scheme. The **two chains**, like the guard, bring out the magnitude of the miracle.

7. And behold – an imitation of OT idiom – **an angel of the Lord** recalls the OT, but see 5.19, and for the whole narrative 5.19–25. The appearance of the angel is naturally accompanied by **light**; cf. 9.3; 22.6; 26.13. The parallel to the release of Peter provided by the release of Dionysus in Euripides' *Bacchae* was already noticed by Origen (*Contra Celsum* 2.34); this was applied to the figure of the 'divine man' (see p. 42); Apollonius of Tyana takes his leg out of his fetters and puts it back again. But Peter has no power in himself to release himself, but acts under instructions.

8. Fasten your belt and put on your sandals. Cf. Exod. 12.11. But Luke is probably thinking of common-sense instructions, which show that God is at work.

9. Peter obeys, but without understanding what is happening. The thing seemed not to be **true**, in the sense of *real*.

10. the first watch and the second. It is easy to guess that, of the four guards (v. 4), two were chained to Peter, one stood before an inner and one before an outer door. **the iron gate** unfortunately gives no clue to the identity of the prison. After **They went out** the Western text adds, *they went down the seven steps*. Nothing is known of these steps. The variant may rest on (though it does not prove) local knowledge on the part of the Western editor. **The iron gate opened to them of its own accord.** There are many parallels; miraculous escapes made a popular theme in ancient imagination. There is a good example in the Jewish historian Artapanus (quoted in Eusebius, *Praep. Ev.* 9.27.23, tr. J. J. Collins): When the king learned this, he confined him [Moses] in prison. But when night came, all the doors of the prison opened of themselves, and some of the guards died, while others were relaxed by sleep and their weapons were broken. Moses came out . . .

They **traversed one street**. Perhaps, *went along the main street until its intersection by a lane*.

For Peter's eventual recognition of the truth; cf. that of Nebuchadnezzar in Dan. 3.95: God has sent his angel and delivered his servants. **out of the hand**, a LXX idiom. **the people of the Jews** – the last three words emphasize the now apparent distinction between Jews and Christians.

12. John called Mark. See above, p. 181. Of **Mary**, his mother, nothing else is known. It is striking that no man is mentioned as her husband, Mark's father; somewhere behind Luke's narrative lies a tradition of a Christian family in Jerusalem where the father either was already dead or had not become a Christian.

many were assembled and praying. Cf. v. 5. If we accept Luke's numbers (2.41; 4.4) the Christians could not all have met in any private house, however large (v. 13). In view of their incredulity at the report of Peter's presence (vv. 15, 16) they can hardly have believed that their prayer was likely to secure his release; possibly his constancy even in death. But Peter knows where to go. The connection may be personal (note the traditional relation between Peter and Mark) or the house may have been Christian headquarters. There is no mention of other apostles, or of any official leadership.

13. The door in the gateway. This suggests a large house with a large *gateway* or *gatehouse* in which was set a *wicket-door* that would be used for ordinary purposes. See however v. 14. **a girl** (cf. Jn 18.17) **called Rhoda**. Either a young woman member of the family (or of the church) or a slave; mention of her name suggests the former alternative. The name was used for slaves (it means Rosebush), but was also the name of, for example, the lady who owned the slave Hermas (Hermas, *Vision* 1.1.1).

14. Rhoda **recognized Peter's voice** (so that she was probably a Christian) and was so delighted that **she did not open the door** (the word translated *gateway* in v. 13).

15, 16. Rhoda's report was not believed: she must be out of her wits. Initial disbelief emphasizes the wonder of the deliverance. Her mistake could perhaps have been caused by the appearance of an **angel**. Judaism believed in protecting and guiding angels, and these were sometimes thought to resemble the human beings whom they protected. See Gen. 48.16; Tobit 5.4–6, 21; Mt. 18.10; Hermas, *Vision* 5.7. Final astonishment underlines further the fact that the prayer meeting had not expected Peter's release.

17. Peter motioned to them, a word not infrequently used of an orator's gesture. See 12.17; 13.16; 19.33; 21.40. **He recounted to them**: the relation is given in the briefest terms; contrast the repetition of the story of Cornelius in ch. 11 and the repetition of Paul's conversion in chs. 22 and 26. The report is to be passed on **to James and the brothers**. Luke assumes that his readers will know who *James* is. He must be a person of considerable importance; this is confirmed by Galatians 2 (especially 2.12, where, it seems, Peter accepts the authority of James). From Gal. 1.19 we infer that he was one of the brothers of Jesus (but **brothers** in this verse is used differently – of fellow Christians). James will reappear in chs. 15 and 21. He seems to have become leader of the church in Jerusalem, with some sort of claim to wider, perhaps universal, authority.

Peter **went out** of the house, **and went** (the word may, but need not, mean *travelled*, implying a journey beyond the city) **to another place**. That Peter did engage in missionary activity is attested in the NT (Acts 9.32 – 10.48; 1 Cor. 9.5; Gal. 2.11–15). But Luke was deeply interested in the Gentile mission, and if this had been in his mind he would probably have mentioned it. Probably by *another place* he meant simply that Peter got clean away, to a place where Herod was unlikely to lay hands on him – another town, or a house not known as a Christian meeting-place. There is nothing to suggest a journey to Rome, or that he was handing over leadership to James, though in ch. 21 James seems to be in charge. It is probably anachronistic to think of regional delimitations of authority, or indeed of the kind of authority that could be so delimited.

18. no small confusion was a natural result of Peter's disappearance.

19. led off for punishment. The Western text makes explicit that the punishment was death. The verb *led off* is often used for *to arrest, to take to court, to take to prison*, but the stronger sense is called for in the light of a principle widely accepted in antiquity.

Herod left Jerusalem; Luke says **from Judaea**, but he is not using the word in its official sense, for **Caesarea** was in Judaea. Caesarea on Sea is meant; see on 10.1. This note of place leads to the next part of the story and may give its date. Josephus, *Ant.* 19.343 says that Herod went to Caesarea in order to celebrate spectacles in honour of Caesar; see on v. 23.

20. He was angry, not *at war with*, because Sidon was in the province of Syria.

The Tyrians and Sidonians appeared **Together** (for the word see on 1.14). They needed good relations with Herod because they drew their food supplies from his kingdom. This seems surprising after 11.27–30, but the famine there referred to came some years after Herod's death.

they asked for peace. This sounds like a cessation of hostilities, but see above. It seems that we must think of economic sanctions applied by Herod against the two cities. Of **Blastus** we know only what Luke tells us. This means that Luke is independent, and has a source other than Josephus, who tells the story of Herod's death in *Ant.* 19.343–53 (cf. *War* 2.219; Eusebius, *HE* 2.10.3–9).

21. Herod put on royal robes, no doubt splendid ones. Josephus says that he wore a silver robe which was caught by the rays of the morning sun. From a **tribune**, or raised platform, he **addressed** the Tyrians and Sidonians, and presumably others also (see v. 22). The verb means *to make a public speech*, but is sometimes used pejoratively of a demagogue's speech aimed at flattery and winning popularity. Neither Luke nor Josephus says that Herod himself claimed to be divine.

22. The Western text adds that Herod was reconciled with the Tyrians (but not with the Sidonians?), and they no doubt joined the assembly (the people of Caesarea?) in their acclamation, which presumably Herod was happy to accept. This was intolerable sin (cf. Ezek. 38.2, 6, 9) and was immediately punished.

23. the angel of the Lord. Cf. Peter's angel in v. 7. Failure to glorify God – rather than themselves – is noted as fundamental sinfulness in Rom. 1.21. In consequence Herod was **eaten by worms**, a single word in Greek, used elsewhere of vegetable matter, not used by physicians. He **expired**, the word used elsewhere in the NT only of the deaths of Ananias and Sapphira (5.5, 10). Biblical and early Christian writers (and many others) often relate the deaths of persecutors and other bad characters. Among very many examples we may note Judith 16.17; *Apocalypse of Peter* 27; 2 Macc. 9.5–12 (Antiochus Epiphanes, ending in v. 12 with, It is right to be subject to God, and no mortal should think that he is equal to God).

In a long and detailed discussion K. Lake argues (*Begs.* 5.46–52) that Herod died in AD 44; *NS* 1.452 agrees. D. R. Schwarz, however, concludes that he died 'between September/October 43 and January/February 44, and most probably at the very beginning of this period' (111).

32. A CONNECTING LINK 12.24, 25

24 The word of God grew and multiplied. 25 Barnabas and Saul returned, having fulfilled their service in Jerusalem, and having picked up as companion John who was called Mark.

It would be possible, and some think better, to treat these two verses as part of the preceding paragraph, 12.1–23. But as 11.27–30 stands apart from (though it also introduces) 12.1–23, so also does 12.24f. The two verses are transitional and were undoubtedly provided by Luke himself. Verse 24 is a very characteristic Lucan piece. God so orders events that, though James the apostle and Herod the persecutor die, though Peter gives place to James, his word grows and multiplies. In v. 25, whatever be the solution of the textual puzzle (see below), the mission of Saul and Barnabas on behalf of the church of Antioch is brought to a successful conclusion, and Luke is able to take up his Antioch material in ch. 13. Thus 12.24f. has links with 11.27–30, gives the conclusion of 12.1–23, and prepares for 13.1–3. It is right to let it stand as a very short unit.

A consecutive reading of Luke's text may suggest that the 'famine visit' and Herod's death took place at approximately the same time. In fact the famine is to be dated about three years later; the relief visit must be later still; after the journey of chs. 13 and 14? At the same time as the 'Council visit' (15.1–5)? At this point there is no material for the discussion of these questions. See p. 222.

24. The attack by Herod, supported by the Jews, had an effect opposite to that intended. **grew** and **multiplied** go somewhat awkwardly with **The word of God**, one of Luke's favourite terms for the Christian message. He means, of course, that preaching of the Gospel increased in effectiveness and in effect, so that the number of believers multiplied. This sums up chs. 1–12.

25. The mission of 11.30 was duly completed, but the words in which its completion is described raise a notorious textual problem. The text of Greek MSS and early versions takes three forms:

(a) to Jerusalem
(b) to Antioch
(c) from Jerusalem [two different Greek words are used for *from*; in many MSS *to Antioch* is added].

Of these readings it may be said that (b) and (c) are manifestly 'corrections' of the very difficult (a), and that (a), as given above, is so difficult as to be impossible. Some have dealt with this impasse by conjecturing a primitive corruption of the text and reordering the words of (a) so as to yield *having fulfilled their ministry to* (or, *in*) *Jerusalem*. Conjecture however is unnecessary; the words as written may be taken in the way suggested. It is not the most natural, but is a quite possible, way of taking them.

For **John who was called Mark** see on 12.12. Luke may have deduced his statement from 12.12 and 13.5.

IX

ANTIOCH INITIATES THE WIDER MISSION (13.1 – 14.28)

33. BARNABAS AND SAUL COMMISSIONED FROM ANTIOCH 13.1–3

1 In Antioch, in the local church, there were prophets and teachers, Barnabas and Symeon (called Niger) and Lucius (of Cyrene), Manaen (an intimate friend of Herod the Tetrarch), and Saul.
2 While they were waiting upon the Lord and fasting, the Holy Spirit said, 'Set apart for me Barnabas and Saul for the work to
which I have called them.' 3 Then they fasted and prayed and laid
their hands on them, and sent them on their way.

This paragraph marks a major departure in Luke's story. Up to this point, missionary work, especially in relation to Gentiles, has been unplanned, almost fortuitous. Here, though the initiative is still ascribed to the Holy Spirit (v. 2), two associates of the local church are sent on an evangelistic journey through country in no sense properly Jewish.

The paragraph, which recounts a meeting of church leaders in the course of which Barnabas and Saul are commissioned as missionaries, is probably based on Antiochene tradition, with Lucan editing. Prophets and teachers (see on v. 1) are not Lucan words for church leaders; Luke's own preferred *presbyters* (*elders*) is not used. Luke himself associates church gatherings with eating rather than with fasting, and *waiting upon the Lord* is used elsewhere in Luke–Acts only at Lk. 1.23. On the other hand, 'the Holy Spirit said' is a Lucan expression (see 10.19 and note), and the imposition of hands recalls 6.6. It is impossible to assert that the story of Antioch was told as a continuous whole, but 13.1–3 stands in the midst of a considerable sequence in which the church of Antioch looks back to its origins (11.19–26), establishes its independence (11.27–30), and also relates its own contribution to Christian missionary expansion (13.4 – 14.28). The whole is written from an Antiochene point of view on the basis of information probably supplied at least in part by Antioch. The most probable view is that Luke found in Antioch some account of churches having some connection with Antioch as centre and collected stories that referred to them, perhaps were current in them. The speeches, notably the synagogue sermon at Pisidian Antioch, are probably his own composition. There is no specific connection between the speeches and the places at which they are said to have been given, but this does not mean that Paul did not visit the cities in question. It would be natural and proper (14.26f.; 15.36) for Antioch to keep in touch with churches founded by their envoys, and Luke if he visited Antioch would be in ready contact with a valuable supply of information. It is true that there was trouble between Paul and one element in the church at Antioch (Gal. 2.13), but (according to Acts) Paul returned and spent some time there (18.22f.).

Thus we have (as might be expected) in this paragraph a combination of Antiochene tradition, which may run back to a fairly early date, with Lucan editing, which belongs to the date of composition of Acts. The resulting picture of the early church and its ministry is accordingly complex. It is to Luke's historical credit that he does not introduce the word *presbyter* (see v. 1), or any of the words that were coming into use at the time when he and the author of the Pastorals were writing. We should note however the action of the Spirit in prophecy (cf. 1 Tim. 1.18; 4.14) and the laying on of hands (1 Tim. 4.14; 2 Tim. 1.6). It would be not only anachronistic but mistaken to describe the event as ordination: both Barnabas and Saul had already acted as ministers, and afterwards Saul was (according to both Acts 18.3; 20.34 and the Epistles) no more than a part-time church worker. What is described is a matter of function, not office; two of the brothers are sent to carry out a particular task. There is no attempt to draw legitimacy for this from Jerusalem; the Holy Spirit is the sole and adequate source of legitimacy.

1. In Antioch, in the local church; cf. 5.17 (the local party of the Sadducees). However 12.25 is interpreted the scene has now changed from Jerusalem to Antioch, where **there were prophets and**

teachers. For prophets; cf. 2.17f.; 11.27. Teachers are mentioned here only in Acts, but cognate words are frequent (1.1; 2.42; 4.2, 18; 5.21, 25, 28, 42; 11.26; 13.12; 15.1, 35; 17.19; 18.11, 25; 20.20; 21.21, 28; 28.3). Luke's own preferred word for ministers is *presbyters* (*elders*; 11.30; 14.23; 15.2, 4, 6, 22, 23; 16.4; 20.17, at 20.28 called also *episkopoi*, *bishops*). The words used in the present passage probably represent the organization of the church at Antioch; Luke is probably editing Antiochene tradition. For the association of prophets and teachers; cf. 1 Cor. 12.28; *Didache* 15.1. At 14.4, 14 Paul and Barnabas are apostles; but see the notes.

The two general terms are followed by the names of five men who were presumably prophets or teachers, or possibly both. For Barnabas see 4.36; 11.22, 25f. He accompanied Saul in the journey of chs. 13 and 14, but separates from him at 15.39f. (cf. Gal. 2.13). **Symeon** is distinguished from Simon Peter (Symeon at 15.14; 2 Peter 1.1) by the addition of **called Niger**; this tells us nothing of Symeon's race (cf. Josephus, *War* 2.520). **Lucius** is distinguished by **of Cyrene**; cf. 11.20. For **Manaen** cf. 4 Kdms 15.14; it is a free transliteration of *Menaḥem, Comforter*. **Herod the Tetrarch** (cf. Lk. 3.1) is thus distinguished from Herod (Agrippa I) in ch. 12. **Intimate friend** was a court title. For Luke's interest in the Herods cf. Lk. 8.1. Last in the list, **Saul**.

2. There is little probability in the suggestion that we should read here **While** *we* **were waiting on the Lord** (cf. 11.28). Luke's 'We-source' (see Introduction, pp. xxxi–xxxiii) did not begin here. In itself, *waiting upon* has no specific religious connotation; this however develops in the LXX and in later Christian literature, and gives rise to the English word *liturgy*. There is nothing in this context to suggest the eucharistic liturgy; prophesying, teaching, and prayers are more probable. Nor is there anything to suggest that the community as a whole was present.

Fasting is not frequently enjoined in the OT, nor was it frequently practised in Judaism (but always on the Day of Atonement, e.g. Lev. 16.29; cf. Acts 27.9). It is naturally associated with prayer.

In the course of the meeting, **the Holy Spirit said**, presumably through one of the prophets (but cf. 8.29; 10.19; 11.2), **Set apart for me Barnabas and Saul**. Cf. Num. 16.9; 1 Chron. 23.13. *Set apart* is the word used by Paul of his divine call (Rom. 1.1; Gal. 1.15). The work to which the two men have been called is not described here; it will be given in the content of the rest of the book.

3. Three steps are taken before the missionaries are sent on their way: fasting, prayer and the imposition of hands. Fasting (see v. 2) accompanies the appointment of presbyters at 14.23; it is not mentioned at 1.21–6 or 6.6. The church (leaders) could hardly fail to pray for those whom the Holy Spirit had designated as his agents. The laying on of hands was an additional circumstance of prayer. There is some resemblance here to rabbinic ordination, but this could hardly apply to Paul who was already a teacher. The two men became apostles of the church of Antioch (14.4, 14; see the notes), but we do not know how Jewish apostles (*sh*[e]*liḥin*) were commissioned. The church (14.26f. shows that all were involved) committed their brothers to the grace of God for the task ahead, to which they had been called. Luke does not discuss the relation between this commissioning and the apostleship Paul had received in and with his conversion, partly no doubt because even in his time terminology had not sufficiently hardened.

34. BARNABAS AND SAUL IN CYPRUS 13.4–12

4 So they, having been sent out by the Holy Spirit, came down to
Seleucia, and thence they sailed away to Cyprus. 5 Having arrived
in Salamis they proclaimed the word of God in the synagogues of
the Jews. They had John, too, as assistant. 6 When they had passed
through the whole island as far as Paphos they found a man who
was a magus, a Jewish false prophet whose name was Bar-Jesus.
7 He was with the Proconsul, Sergius Paulus, an intelligent man.
He summoned Barnabas and Saul, and sought to bear the word
of God. 8 But Elymas the Magus (for that is how his name is
translated) resisted them, seeking to turn away the Proconsul
from the faith. 9 But Saul, who bore also the name Paul, filled
with the Holy Spirit, fixed his gaze upon him, 10 and said, 'You
son of the devil, full of every kind of deceit and every kind of
fraud, enemy of all uprightness, will you not stop perverting the
ways, the right ways, of the Lord? 11 See now, the Lord's hand is
upon you, and for a time you will be blind and will not look upon
the sun.' And suddenly mist and darkness fell upon him, and he
went about seeking someone to lead him by the hand. 12 Then,
when the Proconsul saw what had happened, he became a
believer, surprised by the teaching about the Lord.

Information gathered by Luke in Antioch (see above, pp. 189f.) may have been little more than a list of names: Antioch, Seleucia, Salamis, Paphos. Luke did not find much on Cyprus to fill them out, but wrote out in his own style what was available. He probably knew the Pauline theological principle, 'To the Jew first, and also to the Greek' and gave it narrative application, beginning in Salamis. He knew a tradition that associated John Mark with Barnabas, and associated him with and later dissociated him from Saul. In Paphos he may have combined two stories: Barnabas and Saul *found* the magus, the proconsul *summoned* them.

The combination of tradition and Lucan editing may help to solve one of the outstanding minor puzzles of Acts. Up to 13.8 the name Saul has always been used; from 13.9 the missionary theologian is always Paul. This, as the epistles show, was the name commonly in use in Christian circles. *Saul* brought out the bearer's roots in Judaism and was probably also the name used in the old Antiochene tradition.

If Luke drew on both Antiochene and other local traditions he would use them to make the points he wished to make to his contemporaries. The following interests have been suggested. (1) Apologetic – Paul was on friendly terms with a proconsul; other Roman authorities might learn from this precedent; (2) Paul took precedence over his colleagues, such as Barnabas; (3) magic was an evil to be fought; (4) Paul was the equal of Peter. The last does not in fact seem to be a Lucan interest – that Peter and Paul, for example, both oppose magic does not make them rivals but allies.

4. Paul and Barnabas were **sent out** not so much by the church of Antioch as **by the Holy Spirit**. They went first to **Seleucia**, a port near the mouth of the Orontes, founded about 300 BC by Seleucus I. It was a station of the Roman fleet.

There had been an earlier mission in Cyprus (11.19), where there was a large Jewish population. The epistles do nothing to confirm a Pauline visit to Cyprus, but there is no reason to doubt it.

5. Salamis had been the capital of Cyprus, but its harbour silted up and about 200 BC it was superseded by Paphos. They preached **in the synagogues** (6.9), for Paul a regular practice (13.14; 14.1; 17.1, 10, 17; 18.4, 19; 19.8). There is no reason why Paul should not have made a practical application of his theological principle.

John is presumably the man of 12.12, 25. Luke's word **assistant** is used at Lk. 1.2 (*ministers of the word*) and at Acts 26.16 of Paul. It is used of any subordinate assistant, also of a variety of special servants and helpers in social, political, and military contexts which do not seem relevant here. Chapter 12 suggests that Mark's family was of some importance in the church of Jerusalem; it seems probable that his functions in the missionary party were not confined to care of their material needs but included a share in the work of preaching and healing. His participation in this ends at 13.13.

6. When they had passed through the whole island. *Passed through* may refer to a preaching tour (8.4). No account of such a tour has survived; Antiochene records may have retained only the names of Salamis (at the east end of the island) and Paphos (at the other end). A road along the south coast, which Paul and Barnabas may have traversed, connected the two. The two large towns could well be taken as representative of **the whole island**.

Paphos had supplanted Salamis (v. 5). There was an Old Paphos, which went back to Mycenean times, but long before the first century it has been supplanted by a new town, ten miles further north, closer to the sea, and with a better harbour.

they found (it is not implied that they had looked for him) **a man** who was all that Luke disliked – **a magus** (cf. ch. 8), **a false prophet** (perverting a good institution), and a Jew (and Jews were always making trouble for Christians). His name is given in this verse as Bar-Jesus. This must be Aramaic and mean Son of (= *Bar*) Jesus (Joshua). It is not clear how this comes to be *Elymas* in v. 8, but cf. v. 10, where *Son of the devil* plays on *Son of Jesus*.

7. Bar-Jesus **was with**, that is, was at the court of *the Proconsul* (as a senatorial province Cyprus was governed by a proconsul), **Sergius Paulus, an intelligent man.** A Latin inscription, dated in the reign of Claudius (AD 41–54), refers to five men as Curators of the River Tiber. One is L. Sergius Paulus, who could quite possibly have gone from his curatorship to Cyprus. Another inscription which gives us only the (Greek) letters *s e r g* is less helpful. There is some evidence connecting the Sergii Pauli with Pisidian Antioch (13.14). Could this have affected Paul's travel plans?

This *intelligent man* sought out Paul and Barnabas. Luke does not say that they sought out him, or any other Gentile.

8. No answer has yet been given to the question how the name **Elymas** can be regarded as a translation of the Aramaic Bar-Jesus. *Elymas* is not a Greek word. One must be content to conclude either that there has been a primitive corruption of the text or that Luke, possessing two divergent strands of tradition, one giving the name as Bar-Jesus, the other as Elymas, concluded that the one form must be a translation of the other. He might have remembered that the Latin *Paul* is not a *translation* of the Semitic *Saul* (v. 9).

The Proconsul evidently looked with favour on the Christian message, a reaction which the magus wished to discourage, no doubt seeing in it a threat to his livelihood.

9. Saul, who bore also the name Paul. This is the first use of the name *Paul*; after this *Saul* is never used except in the repetitions of the conversion story (22.7, 13; 26.14). Paul is an alternative name, not a newly given one. For a possible reason for the change made by Luke see p. 193.

filled with the Holy Spirit, specially equipped for a special purpose. Cf. 2.4; 4.8.

10. You son of the devil. Luke has no love for those who have illicit, and probably profitable, dealings with the supernatural. The magus is soundly cursed, use being made of his name Bar-Jesus. Cf. 8.20–23. **fraud**. Luke's word may be only a synonym for **deceit** but probably adds the sense of making money by deception and trading on credulity. **Uprightness**, or righteousness; but the word has here an ethical, rather than Paul's theological sense. In Acts it is used only here and at 10.35; 17.1; 24.25.

the ways, the right ways, of the Lord. Cf. Hos. 14.10; also Prov. 10.9.

11. Paul's words to Elymas are given in biblical, that is, Septuagintal, idiom. See e.g. Judges 2.15 (*the hand of the Lord*); Job 19.21 (*not seeing the sun*). But there are parallels elsewhere.

for a time. The punishment of Bar-Jesus is to be limited in time. Presumably Paul hoped that a limited period of blindness would lead the magus to repentance. Luke does not say whether it had this effect. Cf. 8.24.

12. Luke has left the sentence in such a form that the relation between verbs and objects has to be sorted out by the reader. The translation offered here follows the order of the words as well as possible and takes Luke's *of* the Lord as an objective genitive.

It has been maintained that Sergius Paulus was not truly converted (courtesy being perhaps mistaken for conviction) because he was not baptized. This argument would mean that there were no conversions on this missionary journey; there is no reference to baptism.

35. THROUGH PAMPHYLIA TO PISIDIAN ANTIOCH
13.13–52

**13 Paul and his party put out from Paphos and came to Perge in
Pamphylia, but John separated from them and returned to
Jerusalem. 14 But they went on from Perge and arrived at Pisidian
Antioch. On the Sabbath day they went into the synagogue and
sat down. 15 After the reading of the Law and the prophets the
presidents of the synagogue sent to them, saying, 'Brothers, if you
have any word of exhortation for the people, say it.' 16 Paul rose
up, and having gestured with his hand said, 'My fellow Israelites,
and you who fear God, listen. 17 The God of this people Israel chose
our fathers and exalted the people during their sojourn in the
land of Egypt. With uplifted arm he brought them out of it, 18 and
for about forty years he nourished them in the wilderness, 19 and
he overthrew seven nations in the land of Canaan, and gave them
(the Israelites) their land as an inheritance, 20 for about 450 years.
After this he gave them judges up to the time of Samuel the
prophet. 21 After that they asked for a king, and God gave them
Saul, the son of Kish, a man of the tribe of Benjamin, for forty
years. 22 He removed him, and to be king raised up for them David,
of whom he said by way of testimony, 'I have found David, the
son of Jesse, a man after my heart; he will do all my will.' 23 Of
this man's seed, God, in fulfilment of his promise, has brought to
Israel a saviour, Jesus, 24 after John, before his coming, had
proclaimed to all the people of Israel a baptism of repentance.
25 As John was completing his course, he said, 'What do you
suppose me to be? I am not what you think; but see! there is
coming after me one of whom I am not worthy to loose the shoes
of his feet.' 26 Brothers, you who belong to the family of Abraham,
and those among you who fear God, to us has the message of this
salvation been sent. 27 For the inhabitants of Jerusalem and their
rulers, though they did not recognize him or the words of the
prophets, which are read every Sabbath, sat in judgment upon
him and so fulfilled the prophetic message. 28 Though they found
no valid capital charge against him they asked Pilate that he
should be killed. 29 When they had completed all the things that
had been written about him, they took him down from the tree
and laid him in a tomb. 30 But God raised him from the dead. 31 In**

the course of many days he appeared to those who had come up with him from Galilee to Jerusalem; these are now his witnesses to the People. 32 And we are bringing you the good news of the promise made to the fathers – 33 the good news that God has fulfilled it for us their children, by raising up Jesus. This is as it stands written in the second Psalm: Thou art my son; today have I begotten thee. 34 But that he raised him from the dead, no more to return to corruption, he has affirmed in this way: I will give you the holy and sure promises of David. 35 Therefore he says also in another Psalm: Thou wilt not allow thy Holy One to see corruption. 36 For David, having served his own generation by the will of God, fell asleep and was added to his fathers and saw corruption. 37 But he whom God raised up did not see corruption. 38 So let it be known to you, brothers, that through this man forgiveness of sins is proclaimed to you, and from all those things from which you could not be justified by the Law of Moses, 39 in this man everyone who believes is justified. 40 Beware therefore lest there come upon you that which was spoken in the prophets: 41 See, you despisers, and marvel and fade away; for I am working a work in your days, a work which you will not believe, even though someone explain it to you.'

42 As Paul and Barnabas were going out people begged them that these things might be spoken to them on the next Sabbath. 43 When the synagogue broke up, many of the Jews and devout proselytes followed Paul and Barnabas, who conversed with them and urged them to continue in the grace of God. 44 On the next Sabbath almost the whole city was gathered together to hear the word of the Lord. 45 When the Jews saw the crowds they were filled with envy and contradicted the things that Paul was saying, blaspheming. 46 But Paul and Barnabas grew bold and said, 'It was necessary that the word of God should be spoken first of all to you, but since you thrust it aside and judge yourselves unworthy of eternal life, see! we are turning to the Gentiles. 47 For thus has the Lord given us charge: I have appointed thee as a light for the Gentiles, to be a means of salvation up to the end of the earth.'

48 When the Gentiles heard this they rejoiced and glorified the word of the Lord, and those who were appointed to eternal life became believers. 49 And the word of the Lord was spread abroad through the whole region. 50 But the Jews incited the devout

women of high standing and the leading men of the city; they raised a persecution against Paul and Barnabas and drove them out of their borders. [51] But they shook off the dust of their feet against them and came to Iconium. [52] And the disciples were filled with joy and with the Holy Spirit.

The missionary journey continues by sea from Paphos to Perge; the party then strikes inland to a different Antioch (on the borders of Pisidia). If the framework of chs. 13 and 14 is supplied by Antiochene tradition (*Syrian* Antioch) we must conclude that Luke uses a different source for the synagogue sermon delivered by Paul, which resembles those given by Peter in chs. 2, 3, and 10. Speeches in Acts differ in relation to audiences rather than speakers; those delivered by Paul in chs. 17 and 20, where the audiences are different, are different from this one.

The speech resembles that of Stephen in ch. 7 in that it contains a sketch of OT history. In this it probably reflects the exegetical debate that must have gone on as soon as Jewish Christians began to make their views heard in the synagogue. There is a creditable attempt to look beyond isolated proof-texts at the history of Israel as a whole and to see in it a pattern of God's action. We may go further if a suggestion is adopted which sees in the sermon points of contact with the proem form of synagogue homily. In this form a proem text is used of which at least one word must be shared with the Haftarah (prophetic lection) of the day. It is suggested that the proem text was 1 Sam. 13.14, which was linked with the seder (Torah lection), Deut. 4.25–46, by Acts 13.17–21. The haftarah was 2 Sam. 7.6–16, and Acts 13.22–41 is a typical proem homily. The suggestion, made by J. W. Bowker, is to be found in *NTS* 14 (1967), 96–111.

Paul's sermon is in two parts; this and other matters of detail will be considered below. In the final offer of salvation occurs the only reference in Acts to justification by faith. It occurs appropriately on Paul's lips, but the wording is not characteristically Pauline. This, like the paragraph as a whole, must be regarded as Luke's own work as he takes up a traditional speech and adapts it to the circumstances. At the end (v. 46) Paul announces his intention of leaving the Jews in their unbelief and turning to the Gentiles. This is to be taken not as a once-for-all irrevocable decision but rather as a recurring pattern in his ministry. It corresponds with the Pauline proposition, 'to the Jew first and also to the Greek', which to Paul himself was primarily a theological statement, though it may well be that he sometimes gave it a practical application. The synagogue provided a ready-made audience.

13. Paul and his party. Paul is included (as in classical use of Luke's idiom) and is now thought of as its head.

Perge (near modern Murtana) is near but not on the coast of Asia Minor. It could be reached by ship on the River Kestros, where there was a port about two miles from the town. Perge was an important centre for the worship of Artemis; there is no evidence for the presence of Jews, though there were not a few in **Pamphylia**, which in AD 43 Claudius had united with Lycia to make a senatorial province.

John separated from them. This was, according to 15.38, a blameworthy desertion. There have been many guesses why John Mark left them and went to Jerusalem; none is anything other than a guess. Col. 4.10; Philemon 24; 2 Tim. 4.11, even if not written by Paul, give a good hint of later reconciliation.

14. They **arrived at Pisidian Antioch**. There were many towns called Antioch, related to, in many cases founded by, members of the family of Antiochus (one of the successors of Alexander the Great). This Antioch was properly in Phrygia, but on the borders of Pisidia (there was a Phrygian Antioch, on the Maeander). There was a substantial Jewish population; the evidence of Acts is confirmed by Josephus. Paul and Barnabas attended the Sabbath service in the synagogue (for this institution see 6.9). They **sat down**. Early synagogues often had stone benches along two or three of the walls. There may in addition have been wooden benches which of course have not survived. It seems that Essenes and members of the Qumran sect sat.

15. For the order of worship in the synagogue see *NS* 2.447–54. 'As principal parts of the service, the Mishnah mentions the recitation of the *Shema*ʿ, the Prayer, the reading of the Torah, the reading of the prophets, the priestly blessing. To this was added the translation of the portion of Scripture read aloud, . . . and its exposition by means of an elevating discourse' (p. 448). **the presidents of the synagogue**; normally there was only one, who was responsible for arranging the service, including the sermon (if there was one). More than one president implies a large community. **Brothers.** Paul and Barnabas are fellow Jews. **word of exhortation**, hortatory discourse, sermon. **if you have any word**. It has been suggested that this should be taken as an indirect question: *Tell us if you have* . . . On this view, vv. 16–41 are not Paul's *word* but a preliminary announcement of it.

Then (v. 44) next Sabbath the whole city is gathered together to hear the word of the Lord. This is grammatically possible, but cannot be accepted. Verses 16–41 *are* a sermon on the Acts pattern; v. 43 (*continue*) implies that some have already been converted; v. 46 that the *word of God* has already been spoken. One supposes that the president recognized that Paul was a trained and qualified rabbi.

16. Paul rose up. He would not be sitting on the dais and must stand in order to be seen and heard. **gestured with his hand**; cf. 12.17; 19.33; 21.40. This, like the standing position, suggests the Greek rhetor rather than the synagogue preacher.

My fellow Israelites. This address would take in all Jews in the synagogue. **and you who fear God**. This (*and you*) might be supposed to refer to a different group, either to *proselytes* or to those often referred to as *God-fearers*, persons who were attracted to the beliefs and life of the Jews, attended the synagogue, and followed some but not all Jewish ordinances, without taking the radical step of becoming proselytes. The existence of such a group is hardly in question (see on 10.2); proselytization was often a matter of more than one generation – the father was a sympathizer and the son became a proselyte. What is in question is the degree of formality with which such a group was related to the synagogue and the technical use of the word God-fearer (*theosebēs*; in the NT only at Jn 9.31, which is irrelevant) to describe it. There is inscriptional evidence that bears on these questions, but it is two centuries later than Paul's visit to Pisidian Antioch, and belongs to a distant place (Aphrodisias). It is more probable that in this verse Paul is addressing Jews (this is certain) and proselytes. Why should he leave out proselytes and address a group of, doubtless well disposed, outsiders? In v. 26 he speaks to proselytes; in v. 43 proselytes are described by the participle *God-fearing* (here, *devout*). In the present verse, Paul (as represented by Luke) is probably addressing Jews and proselytes; or, just possibly, he is defining Jews: 'My fellow Jews, yes, you who fear God as no other nation does.' At v. 46 he turns to Gentiles; and of course God-fearers were Gentiles.

17. Paul embarks on a sketch of the history of Israel. He is speaking of **The God of this people Israel**. He has not invented a new God but proclaims the fulfilment of the intention of the one God. He leaps over 500 years or so of history, not naming the patriarchs (contrast Stephen in ch. 7). God is the God of Israel not in the sense that Israel selected him out of a number of possibilities. He chose them and brought them out of Egypt **With uplifted arm** – a Septuagintal expression. Cf. Exod. 6.1, 6; 32.11.

18. for about forty years. See Deut. 16.35; Num. 14.33, 34.

he nourished them. This translates the Greek verb *etrophophorēsen*, which, with the primary meaning *supplied with food*, becomes more generally *cared for*, as a nurse. There is a variant reading consisting of the almost identical verb *etropophorēsen, he put up with their ways, endured them, bore with them.* There is little to choose between the evidence for each. Many prefer *put up with*; the alternative, *nourished* may be chosen (though not with complete confidence) because, in the context, Paul is dealing not with Israel's wayward conduct (in this his speech may be contrasted with Stephen's) but with the benefits bestowed on them by God.

19. There are more textual variants here, caused no doubt by the fact that though the drift of the argument is reasonably clear the wording is occasionally obscure.

seven nations. See Deut. 7.1; cf. Josh. 3.10; 24.1; at Deut. 20.17 there are six. **gave . . . as an inheritance**: a mainly Septuagintal word, which is sometimes *give* (so evidently here) and sometimes *receive as an inheritance.* At 1 QM 11.8f. they become the eschatological foes of Israel.

20. about 450 years. This must (as *about* indicates) be an approximation. It is hard to see how the available data can make 450 years. **judges**. Luke takes the Greek word from the LXX. It is not a good rendering of the Hebrew; the 'judges' were national leaders rather than judicial functionaries. **Samuel** was both a judge and a prophet; here he is given his place as a prophet.

21. they asked for a king. See 1 Kdms 8.5, 10; 10.21–6. **Saul . . . a man of the tribe of Benjamin.** So was Saul of Tarsus. The suggestion that the preacher mentioned this as a matter of pride overlooks the next verse. **for forty years**. This is not given in the OT; 1 Sam. 13.1 is corrupt. Forty years can be found in Josephus, *Ant.* 6.378, contradicted by *Ant.* 10.143.

22. Saul reigned for a time, but God **removed him**, and **raised up . . . David** in the sense of bringing him forward to be **king**. God's **testimony** to David conflates Ps. 88(89).21a and 1 Kdms 13.14, which are combined also in 1 Clement 18.1. The quotation in Acts bears resemblance not only to both MT and LXX but also to the Targum of 1 Samuel 13.

23. From David, Paul leaps over the centuries to Jesus. The reference to David is emphatic. It was **Of this man's seed** that God brought **to Israel a saviour, Jesus**. There is no attempt at this point to define saviour, or salvation. See vv. 38f.

24. This verse is added in the form of an afterthought: we must not forget to mention the forerunner, John the Baptist. His importance in the early Christian understanding of the eschatological significance of the work of Jesus is deeply attested in Acts; see 1.5.

John . . . proclaimed to all the people of Israel a baptism of repentance. Its distinguishing feature was that it was accompanied by, and was an outward sign of, repentance. *All the people* is emphatic. The whole of Israel must repent.

25. As John was completing his course. The imperfect tense implies an overlap between the ministries of John the Baptist and of Jesus (cf. Jn 3.23, 24; 4.1).

What do you suppose me to be? I am not what you think. The Greek sentence begins with the interrogative pronoun *What?* (some MSS, less probably, have the masculine *Whom?*). The question is straightforward; the response follows, *I am not*, and this must receive the supplement given above. The whole however constitutes an awkward and unusually ordered sentence, and some have argued that the interrogative pronoun is used as if it were the relative pronoun, so that the sentence would run continuously, What you think me to be I am not. The awkwardness of the construction adopted here is not adequate justification for turning the interrogative into a relative; alleged parallels to this are unconvincing. Fortunately the sense of the verse is not affected: John denies that he is the Messiah; nothing else can be intended.

26. Paul addresses the whole company as **Brothers**. They are divided into two groups. There are those **who belong to the family of Abraham**; these will be Jews by race. There are also **those among you who fear God**; these are proselytes rather than 'God-fearers' (see v. 16). They are *brothers*, they are *among you*, not simply physically present but belonging to the same company. There is some evidence for omitting **and** before *those among you*. If this reading is accepted the phrase is restrictive: Descendants of Abraham – those at least in this company who truly fear God, to you . . .

This salvation looks back to v. 23. For *salvation* see on 4.12.

27–29. These verses contain a somewhat confused version of the traditional account of the death and burial of Jesus. It is probably this confusion that led to a variety of Western variants which cannot be dealt with here; they do not affect the essential meaning of the passage.

the inhabitants of Jerusalem and their rulers (here both are blamed) unwittingly fulfilled the prophetic Scriptures, which, though they read them regularly, they failed to understand. **they found no valid capital charge against him**. *Valid* represents Luke's meaning – that Jesus died an innocent man – rather than his text. The Jews brought a capital charge against Jesus; what was lacking was the evidence to prove it. Notwithstanding this, **they asked Pilate that he should be killed**. Verse 29a repeats v. 27: those who killed Jesus **completed all things that had been written about him**. It must however be an oversight when Luke continues **they** (there is no indication of a change of subject) **took him down from the tree and laid him in a tomb**. It was Joseph of Arimathea who took down the body of Jesus (Lk. 23.53). The body was taken down *from the tree*. Cf. 5.30; 10.39; and see Deut. 21.22; Gal. 3.13. Luke makes no theological use of the reference.

30. Cf. 3.15; 4.10; 10.40; also v. 37.

31. Jesus, raised by God from death, **appeared to those who had come up with him from Galilee to Jerusalem**, that is, to those defined in 1.2, 22 as possible replacements for Judas. The word *appeared* is that used by Paul in 1 Cor. 15.8, and in 1 Cor. 9.1 he insists upon his having seen Jesus. It seems unlikely that he would have expressed himself as he does here and in v. 32; the speech (as seems in any case probable) is Luke's composition rather than his. To Luke, Paul was an outstanding evangelist but not an apostle in the same sense as the Twelve. See on 14.4, 14, and Introduction, p. lix.

32. we, emphatic, and presumably in contrast with the witnesses of v. 31. It goes however too far to say that Luke is here dealing with the authority of the next, post-apostolic, generation; for Luke, Paul is a unique figure.

the promise, now fulfilled, was made **to the fathers**. This will include more than the patriarchs in view of the references to David that follow. The Gospel, it is implied, fulfils the forward-looking meaning of the OT as a whole.

33. for us their children. This is the best of several variants. It is possible to take *for us* with **by raising up Jesus**. These words probably do not refer to the resurrection but to God's action in sending his Son – *raising up* Jesus as in the past he had raised up judges and prophets. **written in the second Psalm**. The reference is to what we know as Ps. 2.7, but a well-attested variant has *the first Psalm*. There is patristic evidence that the first two Psalms (as we reckon them) were combined as one; Luke may have written *first*.

The Psalm speaks of God's Son, and if in the first part of the verse *raised up* refers to the resurrection, this becomes the time of Jesus' adoption into the divine family (cf. Rom. 1.4). More probably the reference is to the baptism (Lk. 3.22 – note the Western text here). In any case the understanding of sonship is messianic rather than metaphysical.

34. The resurrection is affirmed here, with reference to Isa. 55.3 (and, in v. 35, Ps. 16.10), which is given in the form, **I will give you the holy and sure promises of David**. This agrees with both the MT and the LXX, except that these have not *I will give* but *I will make an eternal covenant*. The word *promises* is an insertion in the translation; the text itself has (with the LXX) *the holy things* (noun not specified); the MT has *mercies*. It should be added that the Hebrew for *mercy* is *ḥesed*, the Hebrew for *holy* (in this verse) is *ḥasid*. Presumably Paul (Luke, or his traditional source) thought the notion of *covenant* irrelevant at this point. The conjectured supplement *promises* must be related to the use of the word *ḥasid* in Ps. 16.10, quoted in the next verse, where it must mean *the Holy One* – Jesus, who did not experience corruption. The scriptural argument of the two verses may be paraphrased: I will fulfil for you (Christians) the holy and sure (promises made to) David by raising up, by not allowing to see corruption (not David himself but) his greater descendant, who was himself holy. It would be possible, instead of *promises made to David* to have *promises spoken by David*, or God's *holy and faithful dealings with David*, now reproduced in his dealings with the people of David's messianic descendant.

35. For the quotation of Ps. 16.10, see on v. 34. It is used as in 2.27. The quotation is introduced here by the words **in another Psalm**. The word *Psalm* is not in the text of Acts, which reads simply *in another*. It is natural to look back past the Isaiah quotation in v. 34 to the reference in v. 33 to Psalm 2, though it might be better to play for safety and say *in another place*.

36. As in 2.29, the death, burial, and corruption of David's body shows that the Psalm cannot refer to him. Not that David did not do all that might be expected of mortal man. The words used however are not clearly arranged. There are two verbs and two dative cases, and the following arrangements are all possible.

(a) David, having served the will of God, fell asleep in his own generation.

(b[1]) David, having in his own generation served the will of God, fell asleep.

(b[2]) David, having in his own generation served by the will of God, fell asleep.

(c) David, having served his own generation, by the will of God fell asleep.

(d) David's own, human, generation, is contrasted with the Messiah, who is of divine generation.

The last is very improbable; none of the others can be discounted as impossible – and it makes little difference which is chosen.

fell asleep: see on 7.60. **was added to his fathers**: Luke chooses to use a biblical expression for death; see e.g. Judges 2.10; cf. 3 Kdms 2.10. And David **saw corruption**.

37. Not so Jesus. For Luke, the resurrection is the reanimation of a dead body and its emergence from the grave. At this point the OT argument is concluded and the last part of the discourse begins.

38. Let it be known to you: a Lucan expression (2.14; 4.10; 28.28).

The consequence of God's action in Christ is **forgiveness of sins**. See on 2.38; here forgiveness is developed in terms of *justification*. Neither here nor in v. 39 does Luke attempt to explain what is meant by *justify*, *justification*. His use of **from** suggests that **justified** does not have its usual Pauline forensic sense, but means something more like *release from*: Forgiven, the believer is set free from sin, sins no more. This meaning may perhaps be found in Rom. 6.7, not elsewhere in Paul. Luke hardly means, in this verse, though he appears to say, that the Law of Moses suffices to justify from some sins but not from all; he means that the Law is inadequate; for justification something more is needed. But he rightly sees that though forgiveness and justification are not identical they are closely related. He writes as one who wishes to do full justice to Paul but has less than full understanding of his theology.

39. in this man can be taken either with **everyone who believes** or with **is justified**. 'Believing in him' is a simpler concept than 'being justified in him', and more in harmony with Luke's style.

40. Forgiveness, justification, are freely available on the basis of faith alone. But the consequence of refusal is disaster, and this has already been made known by the OT prophets. Quotation of Hab. 1.5 follows.

41. The quotation is given in substantial but not complete agreement with the LXX. **I am working a work in your days.** Paul (Luke) refers to the work that God has done in Christ; and the unbelief of Israel, their rejection of God's work, has been foretold. This theme will be worked out further, in narrative terms, in the remainder of this paragraph. See v. 46; also 18.6; 28.28. An alternative interpretation sees the Gentile mission as the work God is now performing. 1 QpHab 2.1–10 sees the passage in Habakkuk as referring to the renegades of the last days, but does not refer to Gentiles.

42. The remainder of the narrative is probably Luke's own work. **As Paul and Barnabas** . . . Luke does not supply the names; they are added in the translation because it is clear that they are intended. **people begged**. The text has simply *they begged*. This will refer to the Jews, who wish to hear so striking a message again, but many MSS have *the Gentiles*. It is assumed that there will be no further opportunity of hearing a sermon till next Sabbath. There were synagogue meetings on Monday and Thursday, but most Jews, being at work, would not be able to attend them.

43. When the synagogue broke up. *Synagogue* is now of course not the building but the gathering. **devout proselytes**. The noun had by this time acquired a precise meaning; these are full converts to Judaism. The participle translated *devout* (or *worshipping*) is that which may sometimes denote 'God-fearers' (see on 10.2) but here can only be descriptive. **Jews** are Jews by birth; *proselytes* are Jews by conversion. These two groups **followed Paul and Barnabas**. In Acts this verb always (12.8, 9; 21.36) refers to literal following, and does so here. Paul and Barnabas continued the work of persuasion and evidently some of the hearers accepted the message, for they were urged **to continue in the grace of God**. On *grace* see on 11.23.

44. On the next Sabbath, that referred to in v. 42. **was gathered** – no doubt in and around the synagogue.

45. the Jews, that is, some of them. Some had been favourably impressed (v. 43). They would have been glad to make an equal impression on their pagan neighbours. **they** . . . **contradicted**. They contradicted what Paul was saying and this meant that they were **blaspheming** (rather than *reviling* Paul), since what Paul was saying was the word of God.

46. Paul and Barnabas grew bold and said. They did not hesitate to give a theological evaluation of the rejection of their message. They do not explain why **It was necessary that the word of God should be spoken first of all to you**. The reason is apparent in the first lines of Paul's sermon: the Christian message was the fulfilment of Israelite history and especially of Israelite prophecy. No other people had so clear a right to hear what God had now to say. Yet **you thrust it aside and judge yourselves unworthy of eternal life**. It is seldom that Luke writes in this ironical vein. **we are turning to the Gentiles**. This means neither that Paul had not preached to Gentiles in the past nor that he would not preach to Jews in the future. Cf. 18.6; 28.28; also Rom. 11.26.

47. Turning to the Gentiles is justified by Isa. 49.6, quoted (apart from two small omissions) in agreement with the LXX. The support of Scripture was of course of great importance to the Christian preacher. At Lk. 2.32 very similar language is used of Christ himself: he is a light for revelation to the Gentiles. Paul is a light of the Gentiles only in virtue of the Christ whom he preaches. Christ is a light of the Gentiles as he is preached by his servants.

48. When the Gentiles heard this they rejoiced; a way of salvation had been opened to them, and it was not fenced with the unwelcome rite of circumcision. They **became believers**, and thus **glorified the word of the Lord** which they had heard. Believers were **those who were appointed to eternal life**. This is as unqualified a statement of absolute predestination as is found anywhere in the NT. Those believed who were appointed (the passive implies, by God) to do so. The rest, one infers, did not believe, did not receive eternal life, and were thus appointed to death. It is arguable that rejection was the result of willed human action; they *thrust aside* the word of God. But Luke does not make this explicit; nor does he say anything about the work of the Holy Spirit. Luke, who was a narrator rather than a theologian, was apt to put down on its own the aspect of any question that concerned him at the time of writing, and did not, as Paul did, insist upon a rounded view obtained by viewing theological issues from all sides.

For the language, cf. B. Berakoth 61b: Blessed art thou, Akiba, for thou hast been appointed to the life of the age to come.

49. And the word of the Lord was spread abroad, one might translate, *was carried through*. This implies the work of others, assisting Paul and Barnabas. **region** is not a political term (though

Ramsay takes it to refer to Phrygia Galatica; see on 16.6). It means the whole neighbourhood of Antioch.

50. The Jews went beyond verbal opposition (v. 45). They **incited the devout women**, presumably not Jews. They were not only devout but **of high standing**. **and the leading men of the city**. Some of the leading families are known to have been associated with the cult of the god Men. They may have attacked Paul and Barnabas because they were a threat to the cult.

51. The reference to Iconium, taken up in 14.1, probably indicates Luke's resumption of the list of places evangelized by the missionaries from (Syrian) Antioch, into which he had inserted a sermon. The symbolic act of shaking the dust off their feet (Mt. 10.14; Lk. 10.11) implies on the part of Paul and Barnabas a paradoxically new evaluation of the people of God – no longer the recalcitrant Jews of (Pisidian) Antioch but the group of Christian believers, whose existence is attested by 14.21, 22 as well as by v. 52.

they . . . came to Iconium. This was within the area added in 25 BC to the old Kingdom of Galatia and thus formed part of what is sometimes known as 'South Galatia' (see on 16.6). It was a notable city, under Claudius allowed the name of Claudiconium. It possessed a synagogue (14.1).

52. Luke, as usual, makes it clear that persecution cannot halt the Gospel or deprive Christians of joy. They are filled with the Holy Spirit (cf. 2.4).

36. IN AND AROUND LYSTRA 14.1–23

[1] In Iconium they followed their custom and entered the synagogue of the Jews, and so spoke that a great company of both Jews and Greeks became believers. [2] But the unbelieving Jews incited the Gentiles and poisoned their minds against the brothers. [3] So they stayed a considerable time, speaking boldly in the Lord, who bore witness to the word of his grace by causing signs and portents to be done at their hands. [4] The population of the city was divided, and some were on the side of the Jews, others on the side of the apostles. [5] But when there was a move on the part of both Gentiles and Jews, along with their rulers, to outrage and to stone them, [6] they perceived this and fled for refuge to the cities of Lycaonia, Lystra and Derbe, and the surrounding region, [7] and there they were occupied in evangelism.

[8] In Lystra there used to sit a man, powerless in his feet, lame from his mother's womb, who had never walked. [9] This man heard Paul speaking. Paul fixed his eyes on him, and when he saw that he had the faith for healing, [10] he said with a loud voice, 'Get up, and stand erect on your feet.' He jumped up and began to walk. [11] The crowds, when they saw what Paul had done, lifted up their voice in Lycaonian and said, 'The gods have come down to us, made like men.' [12] They called Barnabas Zeus and Paul Hermes, because he took the lead in speaking. [13] The priest of the Zeus whose holy place was outside the city, with the crowds, brought out to the gates bulls and garlands, and wished to offer sacrifice. [14] But when the apostles Barnabas and Paul heard this, they tore their clothes and sprang into the crowd, shouting, [15] 'Men, why are you doing these things? We too are men, of like passions with yourselves, who bring you the good news that you should turn away from these vain things to the living God, who made heaven and earth and sea and all the things that are in them. [16] In generations gone by he permitted all the Gentiles to go their own ways; [17] yet he never left himself without witness in that he did good and sent you from heaven rain and fruitful seasons, filling your hearts with food and gladness.' [18] It was with difficulty that, by saying these things, they prevented the crowds from sacrificing to them.

[19] But there came Jews from Antioch and Iconium; they got the crowds on their side, stoned Paul, and dragged him outside

the city, supposing that he was dead; [20] but when the disciples surrounded him he got up and went into the city. On the next day he left with Barnabas for Derbe. [21] When they had evangelized that city and made a considerable number of disciples they returned to Lystra, Iconium, and Antioch, [22] strengthening the souls of the disciples, exhorting them to abide in the faith, and explaining to them that it is through many afflictions that we must enter the kingdom of God. [23] When they had appointed for them elders in each church they prayed, held fasts, and committed them to the Lord in whom they had put their faith.

It is probable that the Christians at (Syrian) Antioch preserved the memory of, and perhaps links with, the churches of Cyprus, Perge, (Pisidian) Antioch, Lystra, and Derbe. To what may have been little more than a list of names Luke has been able to attach both narrative and preaching material. Traces of Luke's style and interest are spread through the whole section, which as it stands must be regarded as his own composition. This is not to say that it is fictitious; he had information of various kinds.

Luke probably had least information about Iconium; vv. 1–6 are an application of the familiar theme of Jewish opposition. In v. 6 he seems to return to the itinerary, into which he inserts a long piece on events at Lystra (vv. 8–18), which has the effect of leaving the initial reference to Derbe (v. 6) in the air, not resumed till v. 20. The story of Lystra could be lifted out of the text without leaving a noticeable gap. The essential matter is the cure of a lame man, followed by a short speech in which Paul and Barnabas refuse to be treated as gods. The discourse (vv. 15–17) anticipates some of the themes of the Areopagus speech (17.22–31). These will be discussed in relation to the fuller treatment at that point. It is very doubtful whether the Paul we know from the epistles made even to Gentiles a speech that owed so much to natural theology; it is much more like the approach to the Gentile world of Hellenistic Judaism. It is very unlikely that this impromptu speech was preserved in traditions kept at (Syrian) Antioch. To a possible Antiochene reference to Lystra Luke has added a conventional miracle and a Hellenistic Jewish speech.

After the acclamation in vv. 11–18 reaction follows in vv. 19, 20. Behind these verses there may lie some information from Antioch, but as they stand they are very questionable. It is 100 miles from

Antioch to Lystra, another sixty from Lystra to Derbe. Luke has not fully investigated the tradition.

Verses 22 and 23 are Luke's conclusion. They contain his own *theologia crucis*: the way into the kingdom of God leads through suffering. The churches are provided with elders (*presbyters*), a word Paul never uses in his letters. It is Luke's word; this does not mean that Paul would take no thought for the care of churches he had founded.

Only in this chapter is Paul described as an *apostle*, as also is Barnabas. Elsewhere this term is reserved for the Twelve (excluding Judas Iscariot and including Matthias), who are apostles as defined in 1.21, 22. See the notes on vv. 4, 14, where the word is used. From the literary point of view it may be best to conclude that the word *apostle* occurred in the Antiochene material on which Luke drew, but it was used not in the sense of 'one belonging to the Twelve, appointed by Jesus himself but to mean 'one sent out as a missionary by the church (of Antioch)'.

1. Iconium. See on 13.51. It lay on the Via Sebaste, connected westwards with Pisidian Antioch, eastwards with Lystra and Derbe.

they followed their custom and entered. Many translate *entered together* or *entered with the Jews*. There was little point in saying these things. The reference to *their custom* is better; notwithstanding the troubles in Antioch there was no change of policy or tactics. The result was the same as that at Antioch (13.42f.). How the **Greeks** heard what Paul and Barnabas had to say is not clear. Luke does not describe them as either proselytes or 'God-fearers' (10.2). Many Jews and Greeks **became believers**, but v. 5 suggests that more did not.

2. The **unbelieving Jews** caused the **Gentiles** (not as in v. 1 *Greeks*) to be disaffected towards **the brothers**. If Luke intends a difference between *Greeks* and *Gentiles* (but he is not writing with great precision) the former may be, the latter may not be, synagogue adherents; but this is quite uncertain. *The brothers* could be the numerous believers of v. 1 (but had they had time to become a recognizable group?) or the two preachers. Again, we look in vain for precision.

3. There is a difficult connection between vv. 2 and 3. The Jews incited the Gentiles against the brothers **so** Paul and Barnabas stayed a considerable time . . . This is not impossible. Paul and Barnabas stayed because the brothers needed their support; the greater the opposition the bolder they became. This could be so, but it has been suggested that vv. 2 and 3 should be reversed in order. This however is improbable; a number of Western variants show that the text was already causing difficulty at a very early date. Luke's characteristic vocabulary appears in this verse; he was probably making the most of little information: there must have been Jewish opposition, the preachers must have been fearless and persistent, and so on. The Lord encouraged them **by causing signs and portents to be done at their hands**. The signs and portents are not an end in themselves but bear witness to **the word of** God's **grace**

4. Some of the population were **on the side of the Jews**, believing Paul and Barnabas to be deluded, or determined in their own interests to delude the people. **others** were **on the side of the apostles**. *The apostles* suggests here most naturally Paul and Barnabas; but except at v. 14 (see the note) nowhere else in Acts is either of the two described as an apostle; this term is restricted to the eleven named in 1.13 together with Matthias (1.26). In terms of the definition given in 1.21f. Paul certainly, Barnabas probably, could not have been in this sense an apostle. Yet Paul describes himself as an apostle (e.g. Rom. 1.1), and insists on his apostolic status (1 Cor. 9.1). He probably thought of Barnabas as an apostle (1 Cor. 9.6; Gal. 2.1, 9), and of others too (Rom. 16.7). The following explanations have been suggested. (1) Luke was careless and in this verse contradicted his own definition. This does not explain the fact that in the conversion story, and from 14.15 to 28.31, Paul is never called an apostle. (2) Luke knew that he must not call Paul an apostle (apart from the definition, to do so would provoke controversy) but admired him so greatly that the word slipped in accidentally. (3) *The apostles* here does refer to the Twelve; it was their message that Paul and Barnabas preached (13.31, 32) so that to agree with Paul and Barnabas was to be on the side of Peter, John and the rest. If he meant this Luke should have expressed himself more clearly. (4) Paul and Barnabas were *apostles* in a different sense. They had been sent by the church of Antioch (13.1–3) to which they reported after their mission (14.26, 27). They were apostles of churches (2 Cor. 8.23). After this point Paul was no longer an apostle of Antioch, or of any other church; he worked on the lines described in Gal. 1.1.

If (4) is accepted, as it probably should be, we are dealing here with an old Antiochene source.

5. Those who were on the side of the Jews (v. 4) prevailed, and there was violent action against the missionaries.

6. the cities of Lycaonia, Lystra and Derbe. These were not the only cities in Lycaonia, though this was not a thickly populated or developed area. Cilicia lay to the south, Cappadocia to the east, Phrygia to the north, Pisidia (see on 13.14) and Isauria to the west. In 25 BC part of Lycaonia, with other regions (see on 16.6), had been joined to the old kingdom of Galatia to form a province. *Lystra* lay SSW of Iconium, six hours distant on the 'Imperial Road'. It is the modern Khatyn Serai. Derbe was about sixty-five miles distant from Iconium.

7. and there, in the cities and surrounding country. Luke lacks precise information about the contents of the next verses. He uses an imperfect tense to express a continuous operation.

8. Luke leaves generalities for a particular event, which may have been reported in Syrian Antioch or have been picked up by Luke locally or from a travelling companion. The language recalls 3.2; in both places Luke is using his Septuagintalizing style.

9. The lame man had heard Paul speaking; where, we do not know. There is no reference to a synagogue in Lystra. **Paul fixed his eyes on him**; a Lucan expression. **faith for healing**: the verb could be translated *to be saved*, and though *healing* is here the primary sense the other will not have been absent from Luke's mind; see on 4.12.

10. Healing is effected by a word of command (in **a loud voice**). It is instant and complete: **He jumped up and began to walk.**

11. The crowds, not unnaturally, were deeply impressed. They expressed themselves in their own language, **Lycaonian**. This language is not known, but its persistence is inferred from the use of Latin in official inscriptions. This shows that Greek was not current. How far the Lystrans had understood Paul and Barnabas we do not know; had they understood better they might not have thought the speakers gods. **The gods**: it would be mistaken to infer that the Lystrans believed in no more than two; they may have thought of the two gods mentioned in the legend referred to in v. 12.

Barnabas was taken to be **Zeus, Paul Hermes**, though the Lycaonians, speaking their own language, no doubt used different names (Pappas and Men, perhaps). Chrysostom thought that Barnabas was identified with Zeus because of his impressive appearance. Paul was Hermes **because he took the lead in speaking**. This is not how Paul describes himself in 1 Cor. 2.1–5, or how his opponent describes him in 2 Cor. 10.10; cf. 11.6. Did Luke know him personally? The identifications may have a different explanation. Ovid tells the story

(*Metamorphoses* 8.618–724) of the aged couple Philemon and Baucis who unknowingly entertained Zeus and Hermes in a location not inconsistent with the area of Lystra. The story may have been popularly known and led to the belief that Zeus and Hermes had returned.

13. The priest of the Zeus whose holy place was outside the city. There is a Western variant preferred by many: *The priests of the local Zeus outside the city.* The only serious difference lies in the number of the priests involved. He or they brought **bulls and garlands** with a view to sacrifice to the two gods. These objects were brought **to the gates**; whether of the city or of the temple it is impossible to say.

14. the apostles Barnabas and Paul. See on v. 4. Here there is a Western reading which drops the word *apostles*; it also introduces a false concord, using a singular participle with **Barnabas and Paul**. This makes it grammatically the more difficult reading, possibly therefore to be preferred. If it is accepted, the designation of the two men as apostles loses its only unambiguous support in Acts.

Some think that Barnabas and Paul reacted slowly to the blasphemous identification of them with gods because they did not understand what was being said in the Lycaonian language. It is very doubtful whether Luke intended to describe a slow reaction. The two men took immediate steps to disclaim divinity. Tearing one's clothes is a reaction to blasphemy (see M. Sanhedrin 7.5).

15. Men, not on this occasion *Brothers*. **We too are men, of like passions with yourselves.** Cf. James 5.17; Wisdom 7.3; 4 Macc. 12.13. Not gods, but men, and bringers of **good news**. Idols, from which the Lystrans must turn, are **vain things**. This word is used in the LXX for **false gods**; this use does not occur in non-biblical Greek, but its meaning *empty talk*, *vain* or *foolish persons*, would make it intelligible to a Gentile audience. The true God is **the living God**, defined as Creator in language based on the OT; see Exod. 20.11; Ps. 145(146).6; cf. Acts 4.24. As in the Areopagus speech Paul does not appeal to the OT but uses the OT to express thoughts which some at least of the audience would recognize and approve. There is no reference or allusion to Jesus; contrast 17.31 and still more 1 Thess. 1.9, 10. No doubt some Christian preachers would adopt the step-by-step method: Monotheism first, Christology only when this has been established. Whether Paul did so must be considered doubtful.

16. God had created the universe yet the Gentile inhabitants of Lystra now had to be told about him and drawn away from misleading substitutes. How was it that they had not known him? Because, with the exception of his own people, Israel, who are not mentioned here, he had himself withdrawn from human affairs to the extent of leaving all the Gentiles to manage on their own. In view of this they may be excused; cf. 17.30, and contrast Rom. 1.20.

17. God did not intervene in the affairs of the Gentiles, as he did in the affairs of Israel; but this did not mean that his hand could not be discerned by anyone who was minded to look for it, nor did it mean that the Gentiles were uncared for. The goodness of God in the natural order is a widespread theme. So e.g. M. Berakoth 9.2 (For rain and good tidings one should say, Blessed is he, the good and the doer of good). It was used as an argument by some early Christian writers, e.g. 1 Clement 19, 20; Justin, *2 Apology* 5.2.

18. Some MSS add, after **they prevented the crowds from sacrificing to them**, that *they told them to go home*. As the sequel shows, they had lost public support.

19. there came Jews from Antioch and Iconium. A long journey; hardly less than 100 miles. But Colonia Lystra had put up a statue in (Pisidian) Antioch and there may have been some contact otherwise unknown between the two towns.

Paul, but apparently not Barnabas, was stoned. Paul was the better known figure; he had worked a notable miracle and made a public speech. If Luke was embroidering scanty Antiochene tradition he may have drawn in a traditional stoning (2 Cor. 11.25). It is certainly correct to say that Luke's purpose was to show that there was increasing opposition from Jews, and that God overcomes opposition. **supposing that he was dead**. Luke is careful not to say that Paul was dead.

20. We do not know whether Luke believed that Paul had been seriously injured and was miraculously cured, or that he had – miraculously – escaped serious injury. In one way or another God protects his servants; his word will always triumph. Paul, one would suppose, was in reasonably good health, since, after showing his determination by entering the city, **On the next day he left with Barnabas** on the sixty-mile journey to Derbe (see on v. 6).

21. The work in Derbe was successful and no opposition was recorded. To Luke Derbe was probably no more than a name on an Antiochene list. There had been difficulties and opposition in Lystra,

Iconium and Pisidian Antioch. This did not prevent the missionaries from returning; rather, it made return desirable. The disciples needed support and advice.

22. The support was given: **strengthening the souls of the disciples**. With **to abide in the faith** cf. 13.43, *to continue in the grace of God*. Luke would have agreed that these were complementary elements in the Christian life. In further guidance to disciples Luke introduces his own understanding of the theology of the cross: **it is through many afflictions that we must enter the kingdom of God**. Elsewhere in Acts (see on 1.3) *the kingdom of God* serves as a summary of Christian truth. Some think that here it belongs to the present, others that it is entered at death, and thus represents an individualizing of eschatology (cf. 7.55, 56). But here the meaning is probably broader. The kingdom is the final state of blessedness that believers will enter if they continue in faith and grace. The tribulations are related to the Jewish apocalyptic notion of messianic travail pains, the affliction that must precede the good time to come. It is a mark of Christian existence.

23. Paul and Barnabas provided **elders** for the disciples, helping them to withstand the troubles they were sure to encounter (v. 22). This meant ordination in that it gave to some Christians a special kind of responsibility and service; cf. 6.6; 13.1–3; 20.17, 28. On the development of the ministry in Acts, see Introduction, pp. lixf.

The word *elder* (*presbyter*) seems not have been used at Antioch; Luke introduced it from the practice of his own time. He evidently thought it proper that the appointment should be accompanied by prayer and fasting; there is no reference to the laying on of hands. It is not clear whom Paul and Barnabas **committed** . . . **to the Lord**, the disciples or the elders. It is unthinkable that they omitted to pray for any of the disciples, but Luke may have had the elders specially in mind.

37. BACK TO ANTIOCH 14.24–28

24 They passed through Pisidia and came to Pamphylia. 25 Having spoken the word in Perge they went down to Attalia, 26 and thence they sailed away to Antioch, whence they had been committed to the grace of God for the work that they had now completed. 27 When they arrived and had assembled the church they reported the things that God had done with them, and that he had opened a door of faith for the Gentiles. 28 They stayed no short time with the disciples.

The importance of this paragraph, probably based on the Antiochene record but rounded out by Luke with traces of his own style throughout, is that it matches 13.1–3. The whole narrative of chs. 13 and 14 is set in an Antiochene framework, though with insertions from other sources. Luke emphasizes in v. 27, and indeed throughout, that the mission had opened a door of faith to the Gentiles. This will have been welcomed in (Syrian) Antioch (cf. 11.20), but it met with a different attitude in Judaea (15.1). This attitude and its overcoming laid the foundations for the rest of the book.

24. They passed through. Cf. 8.4; they may well have preached on the way, as for example in Perge (v. 25). For **Pisidia** see 13.14, for **Pamphylia**, 13.13.

25. Having spoken the word: one of Luke's ways of describing the work of Christian preachers, though he usually adds a defining genitive to *the word*. **they went down to Attalia**. Perge was some miles upstream, Attalia (modern Antalya) was on the coast, a seaport of relatively recent (*c*. 150 BC, by Attalus II Philadelphus) foundation. Attalia adds nothing to the story of the mission. It was presumably in the Antiochene itinerary.

26. whence they had been committed to the grace of God, at 13.1–3, with fasting, prayer, and the laying on of hands. It was natural that they should return. *Grace* nowhere in Acts receives a precise theological definition. It refers to the active love of God which enables men to do his will (4.33; 6.8) and several times has particular reference to the protective care of God (15.40; 20.32). **for the work**: the words used by the Holy Spirit at 13.2. **that they had now completed**. It is not implied that the church at Antioch would no longer be concerned about Paul and Barnabas.

27. When they had assembled the church. *The church* is the local community of Christians (*the disciples* of v. 28), perhaps particularly as assembled. Paul and Barnabas were commissioned by it, and now exercise leadership by calling the members together. **they reported the things that God had done with them**: not what they had done; as e.g. at 3.12, apostles and others do not act on the basis of their own power or piety. Conversions and healings were alike the work of God. Cf. 15.4, 12. God **had opened a door of faith for the Gentiles**. For Luke (who has written chs. 8, 10, and 11) this cannot mean that this journey was the beginning of the conversion of Gentiles, but, in his story, it has the effect of leading to Acts 15, and thus establishing the mission to Gentiles on a firm footing; cf. Gal. 2.9. *A door of faith*: some take the genitive *of faith* to be objective (*leading to faith*), others subjective (*a door by which faith enters*). Possibly better than either alternative is to take the genitive as appositional: a door (*into salvation*) *consisting of faith*. Luke would probably have been willing to accept all three interpretations.

28. They stayed no short time. The words are repeated at 15.35; the account of the Council may have been inserted at this point.

the disciples are *the church* (v. 27) resolved into its individual components. The equivalence must be borne in mind when other occurrences of *disciples* (e.g. 18.23; 21.4) are considered.

X

THE COUNCIL IN JERUSALEM

(15.1–35)

38. DISPUTE IN ANTIOCH 15.1–5

**1 Certain people came down from Judaea and began to teach the
brothers, 'Unless you are circumcised in accordance with the
Mosaic practice you cannot be saved.' 2 Between them and Paul
and Barnabas no small measure of contention and discussion
arose, and they appointed Paul and Barnabas, and certain others
of their number, to go up to the apostles and elders in Jerusalem
about this subject of dispute. 3 So, having been sent on their way
by the church, they travelled through both Phoenicia and
Samaria, recounting the conversion of the Gentiles, and they gave
great joy to all the brothers. 4 When they reached Jerusalem they
were welcomed by the church and the apostles and the elders
and reported the things that God had done by means of them.
5 But there stood up some believers who belonged to the party of
the Pharisees, saying, 'It is necessary to circumcise them and
command them to observe the Law of Moses.'**

At the end of ch. 14 Paul and Barnabas report to the church that had sent them out on their mission. In the course of the mission Gentiles had been converted to Christianity. This had already happened in Antioch itself (11.20f.); it seems to have evoked no comment and Barnabas had approved (11.22–24). Now however travellers from Judaea assert that such converts may become members of God's people only if they are circumcised and keep the Law. This question must be settled in Jerusalem, whither Paul, Barnabas, and some others must travel. The debate that follows is rightly described as the centre of Acts (see below, p. 226). The present small paragraph is important because it sets out clearly the question at issue. This concerns not the terms on which Jewish Christians and Gentile Christians may have fellowship, especially at the common Christian meal (though this question undoubtedly lurks in the background and was important), but whether circumcision and observance of the Law are necessary for salvation.

There are literary signs of Luke's editing throughout the paragraph, but this does not mean that Luke has simply invented his material. We have the evidence of Galatians that there was a meeting in Jerusalem attended on the one side by James, Peter, and John, and on the other by Paul, Barnabas, and at least one other – Titus (Gal. 2.1–10). We know that envoys from James went to Antioch and caused a division between Jewish and Gentile Christians (Gal. 2.11–14). The correspondence is not exact, for in Acts the Jerusalem travellers to Antioch appear first and the Council follows; in Galatians the order is reversed. We may say that Luke knew that there was a meeting in Jerusalem; that Jerusalem made trouble in Antioch; that there was a compromise Decree; that when he wrote (in the 80s or 90s) the church was at peace. He did not know precisely how these data were to be fitted together, but had no intention of painting a picture of a disorderly and inharmonious church.

See further on § 39 and Introduction, pp. lxixf., lxxxiif.

1. Certain people came down from Judaea – to Antioch (14.25–8). Cf. Gal. 2.12, *from James*; this must mean, *from Jerusalem*. The visitation in Acts precedes the Acts Council, the visitation in Galatians follows the Galatian Council. If the two Councils are to be identified one writer is presumably in error. This must be borne in mind.

These visitors **began to teach the brothers**; the use of *brothers* is Luke's and shows, as is in any case clear, that Luke regards uncircumcised believers as Christian brothers. The visitors evidently did not; in their belief, without circumcision there could be no salvation. They do not say: Gentiles cannot be saved at all. They say: You cannot be saved unless you are circumcised. This almost all Jews would have allowed. A Gentile might enter the Jewish fold if he complied with the regulations; and all male Jews, by birth or by proselytization, were circumcised. Exceptions to this requirement are very hard to find.

you cannot be saved. For the meaning of *saved* see on 4.12. In the present context we may paraphrase it as 'to receive in full the benefits provided by God for his people', without specific reference to particular benefits. Luke makes it clear that not table-fellowship but salvation is the theme that is under discussion. It might have seemed that this question had been settled at 11. 18. Cf. Gal. 2.3.

2. no small measure of contention and discussion. The wording (as elsewhere in this paragraph) suggests Luke's work; sharp dispute is intended. **Paul and Barnabas** are leaders in the church of Antioch (11.26) and its trusted delegates (13.1–3), but in **they appointed** the pronoun cannot be certainly identified. Probably *they* are the Christians of Antioch, but *appoint* sometimes comes near to *order*; did the Judaean visitors summon the ringleaders to Jerusalem? For the Western text see below. **certain others**; cf. Gal. 2.1, Titus.

Paul, Barnabas, and the others are to go to Jerusalem to enter into discussion with, or (if we follow an important variant in the Western text) be judged by, **the apostles and elders**. For *apostles* see on 1.21–26; for *elders* on 11.30; 14.23; and for both, Introduction, pp. lviii–lx. A large part in the account of the Council is played by James. He is not an apostle; he is never called an elder. It is probably true that he owed his influence to a special relation with Jesus (Gal. 1.19) and to the strength of his character and convictions rather than to any definable office.

3. The representatives were **sent on their way by the church**; this suggests (see v. 2) that it was the church rather than the Judaeans who were responsible for their journey. On their way they recounted **the conversion of the Gentiles**. In Acts as it stands this will refer primarily to chs. 13 and 14; it is worth noting that 11.21 would suffice as a reference if the mission of these chapters is thought to be misplaced; see p. 222. This account **gave great joy to all the brothers**. Public opinion was on their side, and the battle was over before it was fought. We know however from the Pauline epistles that there was some very sharp fighting – a fact that must be borne in mind when the historicity of Luke's narrative is considered.

Phoenicia (see 11.19; 21.2) is not a precise geographical term. It describes the coastal area of Palestine stretching northward from Carmel and bordering in the south on **Samaria**.

4. This verse reproduces the themes of vv. 2, 3. Luke represents the journey to Jerusalem as something like a triumphal progress. The Gentile mission has begun and it is clear that nothing will stop it. This intended emphasis provides a better explanation of the repetition than a theory of parallel sources. They **reported the things that God**

had done by means of them. Paul and Barnabas had been his agents but the work was his doing. This proved that it was right; it needed no further defence.

the church here probably refers to those Christians who did not hold office, as **apostles** or **elders**. Some think that this verse describes a preliminary open meeting; in 15.6 there is a meeting of apostles and elders alone.

5. But there stood up some believers who belonged to the party of the Pharisees. For *party* see on 5.17; for *Pharisees* on 5.34. These Pharisees had presumably come to believe that Jesus was the Messiah without changing their view of the Law. The question before the Council is still, 'On what terms may Gentiles be saved, that is, become Christians?' and not 'On what terms may Jewish Christians and Gentile Christians have fellowship, including table-fellowship, in one body?'

39. COUNCIL IN JERUSALEM 15.6–29

**6 The apostles and elders gathered together to look into this
matter. 7 When much discussion had taken place, Peter stood up
and said to them 'Brothers, you know that in days of old God
made his choice among you that through my voice the Gentiles
should hear the word of the Gospel and believe; 8 and God, who
knows the human heart, bore testimony to them when he gave
them the Holy Spirit, as he had done to us, 9 and he made no
distinction between us and them when he cleansed their hearts
by faith. 10 So now why do you put God to the test by laying on the
neck of these disciples a yoke which neither our fathers nor we
were able to bear? 11 On the contrary, we believe that it is through
the grace of the Lord Jesus that we shall be saved, in the same
way as they.' 12 The whole company fell silent, and they listened
to Barnabas and Paul as they narrated the signs and portents
that God had done among the Gentiles through them. 13 When
they had ceased speaking, James joined in, saying, 'Brothers,
listen to me. 14 Symeon has reported how God at the first took
action so as to take out of the Gentiles a people for his name; (15)
and with this the words of the prophets agree – as it is written:
16 "Afterwards I will return, and I will build up again the tent of
David that has fallen down, and I will build up again its ruins,
and I will raise it up, 17 in order that the rest of mankind may
seek the Lord, even all the Gentiles upon whom my name has
been named." So says the Lord, making these things 18 known
from of old. 19 Therefore for my part I give my judgement that we
should not make trouble for those who from the Gentiles turn to
God, 20 but write to them that they should abstain from the
defilements caused by idols, from fornication, from that which
has been strangled, and from blood. 21 For Moses from generations
of old has in every city those who proclaim him, since he is read
out every Sabbath in the synagogues.'**

**22 Then the apostles and the elders, along with the whole
church, decided to choose men from among themselves to send to
Antioch with Paul and Barnabas; [they chose] Judas called
Barsabbas and Silas, leading men among the brothers, 23 and
wrote for them to deliver [as follows:] 'The apostles and the elders,
your brothers, to the brothers in Antioch, Syria, and Cilicia, who**

**come from among the Gentiles: Greeting. [24] Since we had heard that some of us had disturbed you by what they said, unsettling your souls, – men to whom we had given no such instructions –
[25] we, when we met together, decided to choose and send men to you along with our beloved Barnabas and Paul, [26] men who have devoted their lives to the name of our Lord Jesus Christ. [27] So we have sent Judas and Silas, who will report the same things to you by word of mouth. [28] For the Holy Spirit and ourselves have reached the decision that we should lay upon you no other burden except these necessary things: [29] that you should abstain from things sacrificed to idols, from blood, from things that have been strangled, and from fornication. If you keep yourselves from these things you will be doing right. Farewell.'**

The meeting planned in the preceding paragraph takes place. It does not take the form of a trial (see 15.2) but rather of a general discussion of Christian practice. At the outset there is much debate, which Luke does not report. He assigns speeches to Peter, who is in favour of a liberal attitude; to Barnabas and Paul, who show that God, by granting miracles, has blessed the Gentile mission; and to James, whose attitude is less clear. He agrees with Peter, but indicates that some concessions must be made to Jewish convictions. The whole company agree with their leader, and a letter is written in the name of all, disowning those who have caused trouble at Antioch and stating the Decree proposed by James.

The paragraph is rightly described as the centre of Acts. It is the best example of a pattern that occurs several times. A difficulty is encountered; steps are taken to deal with it; as a result not only is the problem solved, a notable advance takes place. There are notable examples of this pattern in chs. 6 and 19. In ch. 15 the extension of the Gospel to the Gentiles (which runs through chs. 1–14) is threatened; the Council deals with the problem; not only is the problem solved, its solution leads to further advance (15.35, and the rest of the book). Chapter 15 may thus be said to determine the shape of Acts as a whole.

Different views have been taken of the origin of the paragraph. It has been described as an 'imaginative reconstruction by Luke', though from this description the letter and the Decree (vv. 23–29) are often excepted. Many see here the use by Luke of a variety of traditions; some think of oral, others of written traditions. It is wise not to be over-confident, and to bear in mind the possibility that there were traditions of both kinds. Some think it possible to distinguish between Antiochene and Jerusalem traditions, traditions of trouble in Antioch and of the Decree. The best course is to begin with an open mind, recognizing that Luke would probably here (as elsewhere) collect whatever material he could find and use it uncritically but in line with his purpose of showing how the Christian message was taken to the world and resulted in a world-wide community.

Luke's story invites comparison with Galatians 2, in which also a Jerusalem meeting is described. The same persons are involved; the main field of discussion is in each case the questions raised by the extension of the Christian mission to the Gentile world. In Galatians the conclusion reached is that Paul and Barnabas may continue their work among the Gentiles, with, it seems, no demand for circumcision, while the Jerusalem apostles continue their mission to Jews. The Acts story begins on these lines but ends with a Decree most readily understood as regulating the conditions on which Jewish and Gentile Christians may have fellowship, especially table-fellowship, with one another. In Galatians there is no reference to the Decree, nor does Paul mention it elsewhere. To this we should add that both Acts and Galatians mention the visit to Antioch of a delegation from Jerusalem. In Acts this happens before the Council, in Acts 15.1–5. Judaeans tell the Gentile Christians of Antioch that they must be circumcised and keep the Law. In Galatians it happens after the Jerusalem meeting. Certain people come to Antioch from James and put an end to the practice of shared Jewish–Gentile meals, dividing the church and even separating Barnabas and Paul. Paul rebukes Peter for his change of attitude. This seems to mean that at this point there was no agreed Decree on common meals. Paul maintained his position and stood by the Gentiles.

Assuming Paul to have been neither stupid nor dishonest, though doubtless like all men fallible in memory, his account, which is first-hand, must be accepted where it differs from Luke's. The course of events may be reconstructed as follows (see further, Introduction, pp. lxxxiif.).

Paul, finding his work threatened by Jewish Christian demands that Gentle converts should be circumcised, went up to Jerusalem, that he might not run in vain (Gal. 2.2). Apart from an encounter with false brothers (who are distinguished from the apostles) the meeting was not inharmonious. There was agreement that Paul should go to the Gentiles (to evangelize them), the Jerusalem apostles to the Jews. This was well, so far as it went, but it did not take into account what should be done in churches with a mixed Jewish and Gentile membership. In Antioch it was at first assumed that since all were Christians all might eat together. The messengers from James (Gal. 2.12) must have said something like, We agreed that Gentiles might be accepted as Christians without circumcision but we did not say that Jews might so far cease to be Jews as to have unrestricted dealings with Gentiles. The two leaders, James and Paul, dug in their heels, and it was (see the discussion below) the Hellenistic Jewish Christians who found a way out by proposing the Decree – which Paul did not accept.

In Luke's report, however, the Decree (proposed here by James) fits into the framework Luke has provided: it sets forth conditions of salvation. And Galatians shows that the demand for circumcision had not been abandoned but still threatened to destroy Paul's work. Luke's simplification of a complicated sequence of events makes dating virtually impossible; probably a year or two after the famine (11.28).

6. *The church* of 15.4 now disappears (but see v. 22 and perhaps v. 12); the matter is left to **The apostles and elders**. Of the apostles (cf. ch. 1) only Peter speaks; Barnabas and Paul make a contribution but their words are not quoted; James proposes a solution which is accepted. *Elders* (presbyters) probably represent the church order with which Luke himself was familiar. At 13.1 the church at Antioch has prophets and teachers; there, probably, Luke follows, here he edits, an Antiochene source. There is no record of any contribution from the elders; the apostles (in Luke's view) were the decision-makers.

7. When much discussion had taken place – Luke does not report it, no doubt because it was not in his source – **Peter stood up**. He appeals to common knowledge: **you know**. His first sentence contains several obscurities. One would expect the opening words to mean *from* days of old, but **God made his choice among you** shows that we must translate **in days of old**. But when were *the days of old*? Probably the early days of the Christian movement; it is not till v. 15 that it is pointed out that God showed his intention in the time of the OT prophets.

The next words also are ambiguous, but it seems best to take the object of **God made his choice** to be the accusative and infinitive clause (in Greek) **the Gentiles should hear . . . and believe**. Peter refers no doubt to the story of Cornelius; what was required from him was not that he should be circumcised but that he **should hear the word of the Gospel and believe**. The verse affirms the priority of Peter in the Gentle mission, though in the rest of the book Paul is beyond question its leader, whereas Peter disappears. It would be in accord with Luke's eirenic interest (displayed not least in this chapter) that he should present the two as of equal standing – one the first, the other the greatest. The same interest might account for Luke's silence regarding the rest of Peter's career, of which some features from a Pauline point of view were scarcely creditable (especially Gal. 2.11–18).

Peter speaks first; it is not so clear as some think that James was now the head of the Jerusalem church. The Gentle mission originated within the apostolic tradition.

8. who knows the human heart; see on 1.24. God truly knew the sort of men that Cornelius and his friends were, and **bore testimony to them**, that is their fitness for hearing and accepting the Gospel. He gave this testimony **when he gave them the Holy Spirit** (10.44; cf. 10.35). This gift was the visible, or audible, sign of his approval (10.46), and it placed Cornelius and his friends in the same position as the first disciples. God had done for them **as he had done to us**.

9. By giving to Gentiles the same gift of the Holy Spirit that he had given to the apostles God made it clear that **he made no distinction between us and them**. Peter's inference is clear: since God did not require circumcision before giving his gifts it was not for men to demand it. Corresponding to this gift is an act: **he cleansed their hearts by faith**. *Cleansing*, an image not frequently used in Acts, occurs in the Cornelius story (10.15; 11.9) but in a different sense. There, Peter must not hesitate to approach those whom God has cleansed; here, cleansing results from the faith with which Cornelius and others respond to the word. *Faith* must be understood in the same sense as *believe* in v. 7. The cleansing of the heart probably means for Luke the forgiveness of sins (cf. 13.38f.) and inward renewal with a view to future obedience.

10. Peter begins to bring his brief speech to a conclusion with a rhetorical question. **why do you** . . . ? means, *you ought not to* . . . It is absurd to expect Gentiles to put up with what we Jews cannot endure. **why do you put God to the test** . . . ? God has already by his action (at Caesarea) made clear that it is his intention to incorporate the Gentiles as they are – without circumcision or any other legal observance – in his people, so that to hinder their reception by legal stipulation is wantonly to provoke him. For *putting God to the test* see e.g. Exod. 17.2. Men are seeing 'how far they can go' with God, insisting on that which is plainly contrary to his will. This use of *test*, *tempt*, is almost exclusively biblical. For **yoke** in a bad sense; cf. 1 Tim. 6.1; Gal. 5.1; Barnabas 2.6. In Rabbinic use (e.g. M. Aboth 3.5), the yoke of the Law, the obligation to obey it, is a blessing and a privilege. With this attitude Peter's words do not agree. It may be correct, as is often maintained, that these are the views not of Peter's time but of Luke's. They do not agree with Peter's attitude to food laws as expressed in 10.14; 11.8. But Peter, unlike Paul, was not a Pharisee, and showed variability of character (not only in the gospels but at Gal. 2.12–15). But if no Jews (**our fathers**) had been able to **bear** (*endure*, *put up with*) the Law it is hard to know why it was so diligently preserved, studied, and obeyed – not to say loved.

11. The language of this verse is superficially Pauline, but lacks Paul's precision. **the grace of the Lord Jesus** recalls 2 Cor. 8.9, but there is no attempt to say what grace means. It is however clear that grace does not mean works of the Law, so that the general sense is clear. It is as **we believe** that **we shall be saved**. The word *saved* is in Greek an infinitive, and it could be put into English as *we shall be saved*, *we are saved*, or *we have been saved*. In Greek idiom the future reference seems most likely, but this is not certain. Peter (Luke) would probably be content to say, Salvation is by faith, and leave it at that.

We believe that we shall be saved **in the same way as they**. *They* is most naturally taken to refer to the Gentile believers, but *our fathers* is the nearest antecedent and cannot be excluded as a possibility, though a less likely one. The saints of the OT were saved by faith; so shall we be.

12. The whole company fell silent – the general body of believers, not *all the apostles and elders*.

Barnabas and Paul now play their part in the discussion. They tell of the **signs and portents** (a Lucan phrase) that accompanied their work among the Gentiles. It was God who had performed these signs; he would not have done them had he disapproved of the mission on which the two were engaged.

There is much to be said for the view that the reference to Paul and Barnabas here, and other references in 15.1–35, were insertions by Luke. There is no difficulty in conjecturing a source that ran: The whole company fell silent, and James joined in . . . If Luke did make the insertion he could have done so (a) because he knew that the two had been present at a Jerusalem conference (Gal. 2.1–10), (b) because he believed that the two were of Stephen's Hellenist group, and that that group must have been represented.

13. James is presumably the James of 12.17 and 21.18, a person so well known that Luke does not think it necessary to identify him. A James is mentioned among the brothers of Jesus (Mk 6.3) and as a witness of the resurrection (1 Cor. 15.7). It is probably the same James who appears in Galatians (1.19; 2.9, 12). See in addition the two accounts of his martyrdom: Josephus, *Ant.* 20.200 and Eusebius, *HE* 2.23.4–18. In these he has a great reputation for Jewish piety. In Acts 15 he appears to be in harmony with Peter, Barnabas, and Paul. Whether the other evidence confirms or contradicts this is a question that cannot be avoided.

Brothers – Fellow Jews or Fellow Christians; or in this case both.

14. Symeon imitates the Hebrew form of the name *Simon*.

at the first. Cf. *in days of old* (v. 7). The event belongs to the beginning of the Christian story and was the first of its kind. **God . . . took action.** Luke's verb is often translated *to visit* and could be so translated here if it were not followed by an infinitive. For the language cf. Deut. 14.2. In a different context James could simply be referring to the distant past when God chose Israel to be his special people. He is however taking up Peter's reference to the Cornelius story, but does so in language based on the LXX. James speaks throughout (not only in vv. 16f.) as a Hellenistic Jew dependent on the LXX.

15. What God did in drawing Cornelius though uncircumcised into his people fulfilled what he had through the prophets promised to do. **prophets**, plural, but only Amos 9.11f. is quoted. *Prophets* may be a reference to the book of the Twelve (minor) Prophets; but it is better to take **as it is written** as introducing a specimen quotation (cf. 7.42).

16. I will build up again the tent of David that has fallen down. In Amos 9.11 the fallen tent of David is presumably the Davidic royal house which came to an end with the fall of Jerusalem in 587/6 BC. The last chapter of the book (its authorship need not be considered here) promises its restoration. James (Luke) may have understood this to refer to the coming of the Messiah, with the inference, Now that Christ has been raised from death the way is open for Gentiles to enter into the people of God; or to the restoration of Israel to sovereignty, implying that the conversion of Gentiles must wait upon the conversion of the Jewish people. That there were some who held the latter position is supported by the fact of Paul's argument against it in Romans 9–11; the text of Amos 9.11 could have been used to support their position. That text was also used at Qumran; see CD 7.15, 16 and 4Q Flor 1.11–13. These passages emphasize not only the coming of the Messiah but the importance of the Law. James however continues the quotation, and it is here that the entry of the Gentiles into the people of God becomes explicit.

17, 18. Here James quotes Amos 9.12 in agreement with the LXX (there are a few small variations that need not be noted here). The Hebrew text differs. It runs as follows (in the RSV translation):

> That they may possess the remnant of Edom and all the nations who are called by my name, says the Lord who does this.

When this is compared with the LXX, it appears that the remnant of Edom becomes *the rest of mankind*; this becomes the subject of a new verb, no longer they may possess but *may seek* (with *the Lord* as object). The Hebrew promises the victory of Israel over what is left of Edom; the LXX predicts that the rest of mankind (= the Gentiles) will seek the Lord.

The question that arises here is whether James would have been likely, in a Hebrew- (or Aramaic-) speaking environment to hang his argument on a Greek text. It is a question on which different views have been held. It is not impossible; it does not seem likely.

Amos 9.12 ends with the words *who does this*. James continues (we must now say *make* rather than *do*), **making these things known from of old** (there are several variants). Some have seen this as a quotation of Isa. 45.21; it is probably simply an added gloss.

19. Therefore looks back to the quotation and to v. 14. **for my part I**. The pronoun is emphatic. This is what *I* say. And not only *say*. **I give my judgement.** Luke's verb could mean no more than *I give my opinion*, but it is the word of a judge. 'I decree' is too strong, but James is at least acting as chairman and expressing what he takes to be (and wishes to be) the sense of the meeting. The impression of James' prominence gains some support from the absence of an accusative subject for the verb *make trouble*. It is not wrong to supply the first person plural (as in **that we should not make trouble for those** . . .), but James does not express this, and the singular could be understood: *I am deciding not to trouble . . .* , with the implication that the speaker decides what shall or shall not be done. **those who from the Gentiles turn to God**, turn from whatever pagan gods they had previously worshipped to the God of the Jews, as now believed in by Christians. It was this that led to the conviction that they should now behave as Jews.

20. Gentile converts are not to be *troubled*; but that is not the end of the matter. **write to them that they should** is to be understood somewhere on the scale between *We are writing with the suggestion that you might consider . . .* and *These are our written instructions*: *You shall abstain . . .* In this proposal James moves gently; vv. 23–29 are stronger. Four abstentions are called for.

(1) **from the defilements caused by idols**. The word *defilements* does not in itself refer specifically to food but would certainly include defilement contracted through eating idolatrous sacrifices (cf. v. 29; 21.25). It may be that there was an original prohibition of idolatry in general terms which in practice (cf. 1 Corinthians 8; 10) came to be focused on the eating of sacrificial food.

(2) **from fornication**. Luke's Greek word means *prostitution, fornication, uncleanness*. It is used however at 1 Cor. 5.1 of one who has taken his father's wife. This is expressly forbidden at Lev. 18.8, which occurs in a passage that deals with forbidden degrees in marriage. These are made to apply not only to the native Israelite but also to 'the stranger who sojourns among you', and some think that such laws were now applied to Gentile Christians. But the word fornication (Greek, *porneia*) does not occur in this OT passage, nor is there reason to think that it was ever used of marriage within the forbidden degrees.

(3) **from that which has been strangled**. This probably means meat which, not having been killed in accordance with Jewish rules, still contains blood. This interpretation is difficult because it seems to be duplicated by the fourth abstention (see below). The Greek word was perhaps used of the flesh of an animal that died of itself, or of a beast which, alive or dead, had some blemish. But we do not know that Luke's word was used in this way.

(4) **from blood**. The prohibition of the consumption of blood is frequent in the OT: Gen. 9.4; Lev. 7.26, 27; 17.10–14; Deut. 12.16, 23. But, since loss of blood means loss of life, the same word came to be used also of *bloodshed*, in particular of *murder*. The possibility that this is the meaning of James' abstention must not be excluded; if

accepted it would mean that there would be no redundancy in the third and fourth abstentions.

What are the background and origin of these abstentions? Several suggestions have been made.

(a) They are practical rules bearing on the convert's life. The fundamental requirement was that he should abandon his old idolatrous religion. In v. 20 this is stated in absolute terms; in v. 29 and 21.25 it is recognized that eating food offered to idols would be for many Gentiles the easiest way to relapse into idolatry. Jews had long known that the temptation to idolatry came most often through the butcher's shop and the brothel: avoid idolatry and fornication. Thus understood the rules would concern salvation, not table-fellowship only.

(b) The requirements may have been based on the commands given to Noah and believed to be applicable to all races. These appear in their earliest form in Jubilees 7.20; as later developed they forbid idolatry, blasphemy, murder, incest, stealing, perverting justice, and eating flesh containing blood. The parallel is not close, and nothing in Acts recalls Noah.

(c) A widely accepted parallel is to be found in the regulations given in Leviticus 17 and 18 for Gentiles living among Jews. These require that sacrifices must be brought to the door of the tent of meeting (17.8f.); that blood must not be eaten (17.10–14); that what dies of itself or is torn by beasts must not be eaten (17.15f.); that the forbidden degrees must be observed (18.6–30). These commands may be said to cover the prohibition of fornication (if interpreted of marriage rules), what is strangled (if interpreted as suggested above) and blood (if this means eating rather than shedding blood). The connection is not close.

(d) A better background, which can be readily combined with (a), is provided by a group of rabbinic passages in which it is urged that, though in persecution a Jew is not expected to give his life on any minor issue, there were three matters on which no compromise was possible: idolatry, the shedding of blood and incest. These cover Luke's idolatry, blood and fornication (which would include incest). They do not cover *what is strangled*; this could have been added to facilitate common meals. It is worth noting that there is some correspondence also with the legal observance possible for Diaspora Jews; much of the Law could be observed only in Israel.

The interpretation of this verse is complicated by a number of variant readings.

(a) *and fornication* is omitted by one very old papyrus, which unfortunately is not extant at v. 29 and 21.25. This is probably no more than a slip on the part of the copyist.

(b) *that which has been strangled* is omitted by a group of Western authorities. The omission makes it possible to understand the Decree as a purely moral (and not ritual) order.

(c) After *from blood* the Western text adds the Golden Rule in its negative form: *the things they do not wish to happen to themselves not to do to others*. This, underlines the Western, ethical, form of the Decree. The Golden Rule in positive form appears in Mt. 7.12; Lk. 6.31. It was already in use in Judaism; see e.g. Tobit 4.15; B. Shabbath 31a (Hillel: What is hateful to yourself, do not to your neighbour).

21. For Moses from generations of old has in every city those who proclaim him. For the wide dissemination of Jews in and beyond the Graeco-Roman world see *NS* 3.3–86. *Every city* is scarcely an exaggeration. James explains what he means by the proclamation of Moses: **he is read out every Sabbath in the synagogues**. Every synagogue service (see p. 200) included the reading of the Torah of Moses.

For means that this verse contains the reason for an earlier statement, but it is not clear which earlier statement is in mind. (1) It may look back to v. 19: It is not for us to trouble the Gentiles since Moses already has enough preachers to take his part and Gentiles who want the Law can get it in the synagogue. (2) It may look back to v. 20: It is necessary to lay some obligation on the Gentiles since Moses has everywhere so many adherents. (3) It is possible but unlikely that it looks back to the quotation in vv. 15–18: We can see the fulfilment of Amos's prophecy in the large number of those who proclaim the Law. The whole passage is obscure, and it is possible that Luke intended both (1) and (2): It is not necessary to trouble the Gentiles seriously (by demanding circumcision), but it is necessary to trouble them a little (by the Decree). Alternatively, Luke may be placing traditional material in a new setting and thereby giving it a new meaning.

22. The apostles and elders, now **with the whole church, reach a decision**. *The whole church* is clearly the church of Jerusalem, with a handful of delegates from Antioch. It does not claim authority for itself, the authority is that of the Holy Spirit (v. 28), but it is not shown how the mind of the Holy Spirit is made known. Luke is not interested in such questions of legal validity and authority.

The company **decided** (the word is common in 'official' Greek) to write to the church at Antioch, sending the letter by **Paul and Barnabas**, together with **Judas called Barsabbas and Silas**. The name *Judas* occurs several times in Acts; this Judas (for his surname see on 1.23) appears only in the present context; nothing else is known of him. *Silas* became an important partner for Paul in succession to Barnabas. He is quite possibly the Silvanus of 2 Cor. 1.19; 1 Thess. 1.1, 2; 2 Thess. 1.1; possibly the Silvanus of 1 Peter 5.12.

23. The letter follows. Some think that the whole was derived by Luke from a written source; it is perhaps more probable that he composed the letter, deriving the Decree itself (v. 29) from widely known tradition. **The apostles and elders** now act on their own, without *the whole church*. The place-names may well be original. The Decree was not intended to apply only to Antioch; see 16.4 for its distribution by Paul and Silas. **Syria and Cilicia** suggest more than the hinterland of Antioch. For Antioch see on 11.19; 13.1; 14.28. For Cilicia see on 6.9. Syria, a Roman province, was the large tract of land in northern Palestine.

24. The sentence that begins at this point is written in finished style; whether it was composed by Luke or received by him from tradition is difficult to determine. Luke certainly regarded the Decree as a most important part of the tradition he received about the vital issue of the expansion of the Christian faith, and it is not unreasonable to suppose that he created a fitting setting (including, it may well be, not only the letter but the whole account of the Council) for it.

The present verse looks back to 15.1; the trouble-makers are emphatically disowned – **men to whom we had given no such instructions**. This seems clear, but the reader is bound to ask questions which Luke does not answer. If the circumcisers of 15.1, 5 had had no backing would they have caused so much trouble and precipitated a high-level conference? If they had no backing at the time, had they later, in Galatia and Corinth? Who wrote the commendatory letters of 2 Cor. 3.1? And we must distinguish between, We gave no charge at all, and We gave no charge concerning circumcision.

Another question arises at the beginning of the verse. A reading followed by many commentators speaks of *some who have gone out from us*, who may have exceeded their commission but carried weight because they could appeal to *us*, who sent them. A variant reading, however, omits *who had gone out*, so that the trouble-makers become *some of us* – presumably some of the apostles and elders. This is an old reading and should probably be accepted (as it is in the translation).

25. decided, as at vv. 22 and 28. The word suggests a *decree*, not an *opinion*. The sending of the **beloved Barnabas and Paul** implies that there was no difference of opinion between the Jerusalem apostles and the Antiochene missionaries.

26. Further description of Barnabas and Paul follows. They **have devoted their lives to the name of our Lord Jesus Christ**. The words used suggest at first *have given their lives*, but this was manifestly not so. Devoting their lives (= themselves) *to the name* will mean *to preaching the name*.

27. So connects with v. 25. We have decided to send others with Barnabas and Paul *so* **we have sent Judas and Silas**. For these two see v. 22. **who will report the same things**. The construction here (surprisingly after some very good Greek) recalls the construction of a Hebrew circumstantial clause. Could it reflect the Hebrew in which this letter was originally composed?

28. On what ground the Council felt able to affirm that the Holy Spirit had concurred in their conclusion is not stated. There is no suggestion that any of the speakers spoke under inspiration. It is well to reflect that Paul, it seems, did not accept the validity of the Decree. See Introduction, p. xxxii.

we should lay upon you no other burden. Very similar words occur at Rev. 2.24. The same passage (2.20; cf. 2.14) condemns fornication and the eating of things sacrificed to idols. It seems probable that there is a reference here (the earliest) to the Decree, or at least a version of it. **no other burden except these necessary things**. The Greek expression here is unusual, but there is no doubt about its meaning; it refers to certain *necessary requirements*. Necessity, compulsion, are plainly set down. It is not said, You Gentiles are completely free of legal requirements, but as a matter of courtesy to your Jewish brethren you might be so kind as to abstain from . . . This is important for the understanding of the Decree; Luke at any rate understood it as a matter not of courtesy but of compulsion, and therefore presumably as a condition of salvation (15.1, 5).

29. This verse repeats what is given in v. 20 as James' judgement. There are some variations in order; an exhortation and greeting are added; and instead of *the defilements caused by idols* we have **things sacrificed to idols**, which has the effect of specifying the most likely cause of defilement. There are textual variants similar to those of v. 20.

40. PAUL AND BARNABAS RETURN TO ANTIOCH 15.30–35

30 So they, when they had been dismissed, went down to Antioch, and when they had gathered the company together they delivered the letter. 31 When they had read it they rejoiced at the comfort that it brought. 32 Judas and Silas, who also were prophets, speaking at length, encouraged and strengthened the brothers. 33 After spending some time [in Antioch] they were released by the brothers in peace [to return] to those who had sent them. [34 But is seemed good to Silas to remain there.] 35 But Paul and Barnabas stayed on in Antioch, teaching and preaching the word of the Lord along with many others.

This paragraph is the necessary complement to the preceding one, and could have been, probably was, constructed by Luke by means of it. The only substantial addition to what could be inferred from the letter of 15.23–29 is that Judas and Silas were prophets.

30. So they – the group mentioned at 15.23 – **when they had gathered the company together**; this clearly refers to the whole church of Antioch (cf. 15.12). As in 13.1–3 there is no reference to elders at Antioch; v. 32 may imply that there were prophets.

31. they . . . rejoiced, that is, the Antiochenes. They rejoiced because they felt that they had got what they wanted. **comfort**: the word means sometimes *exhortation* or *encouragement*. Here however it is *comfort*: they were relieved that the leading Jewish Christians in Jerusalem had not insisted that they should be circumcised.

Had they got what they wanted? Had their objection been simply to the offensive and painful rite of circumcision? Or had they objected to the principle of legal requirements (however slight) as a condition of their salvation? Or are 15.1, 5 misleading, the real point at issue being not, On what terms may Gentiles be saved? but, On what terms may Gentile Christians eat with Jewish Christians? The only question that can be answered here with any confidence is, How did Luke view the matter?

32. Judas and Silas (see 15.22) joined in the operation. They **also were prophets**. *Also* – in addition to Paul and Barnabas? Or in addition to native Antiochene prophets? **the brothers**: as in v. 30 there is nothing to suggest a hierarchy of ruling members in the church at Antioch.

33. the brothers. Cf. v. 32. **in peace**: not only on good terms but in a general situation of Christian wellbeing.

If this verse is read on its own it suggests that both Judas and Silas, perhaps Paul and Barnabas too, returned at this point to Jerusalem. Luke does not mean this. At v. 35 he says that Paul and Barnabas stayed on in Antioch; 15.40 suggests without quite proving that Silas stayed on too.

34. This verse is probably a Western addition to the original text, designed to show that Silas did stay in Antioch. MSS differ in detail but the general sense is: But Silas decided to stay there; only Judas went away.

35. Paul and Barnabas stayed on in Antioch, as much at home there as in Jerusalem. They worked **with many others**, see 11.19; 13.1. For **teaching the word of the Lord** see 18.11; for **preaching the word of the Lord** see 8.4; for **the word of the Lord** see e.g. 8.25; 15.36.

XI

PAUL'S MISSION BREAKS NEW GROUND (15.36 – 18.23)

41. TERRITORY OF THE FIRST JOURNEY REVISITED 15.36 – 16.5

[36]After some days, Paul said to Barnabas, 'Let us return and visit the brothers from city to city, every one of them, in which we proclaimed the word of the Lord, to see how they are faring.' [37]Barnabas wished to take with them also John, called Mark; [38]Paul however took the view that they should not take with them this man who had parted from them in Pamphylia and failed to accompany them to the work. [39]There arose a sharp disagreement so that they separated from each other, and Barnabas took Mark and sailed away to Cyprus, [40]while Paul chose Silas and went off, committed by the brothers to the Lord's grace. [41]He passed through Syria and Cilicia, strengthening the churches.

[1]He now reached Derbe and Lystra; and there was a certain disciple there whose name was Timothy, the son of a Jewish woman who was a believer and of a father who was a Greek. [2]This disciple had a good reputation with the brothers in Lystra and Iconium. [3]Paul wished him to go with him, and took and circumcised him on account of the Jews who were in those parts, for they all knew that his father had been a Greek. [4]As they passed through the cities they delivered to the believers for their observance the decrees that had been decided by the apostles and elders who were in Jerusalem. [5]So the churches were confirmed in faith and increased in number daily.

The motivation and plan of the movements detailed in this paragraph make on the surface good sense. To check the welfare of the Christian societies established on the first journey was an elementary Christian duty. Paul however would not have the untrustworthy Mark (13.13), Barnabas' relative and protégé, as a travelling companion. Disagreement led to separation and Paul found a new travelling companion in Silas (15.22). Paul, with Silas, began to retrace his steps in reverse order and in Lystra he encountered Timothy, whom he circumcised and added to the party.

The outline of the passage is thus straightforward, but it raises a number of problems, discussed in the notes. The plan of revisiting 'First Journey' churches is speedily given up (16.6). Disagreement about Mark is understandable, but in Gal. 2.13 a different cause of dispute is given. Acts tells us nothing of the intervention in Antioch by James and of Paul's reproof of Peter and separation from Barnabas over the issue of common meals. Were the two grounds of contention connected? Had Mark left Paul because the mission was more and more turning to Gentiles? And had he persuaded Barnabas?

Another problem has Timothy as its focus. Paul, who had (Gal. 2.3) vigorously resisted the attempt to have Titus circumcised and had carried his point at the Council, circumcised Timothy. It is just credible that Paul did this, but only just. He might have reasoned: As he is, Timothy is neither Jew nor Gentle; we cannot undo the Jewishness of his mother; we can give him the circumcision his Gentile father would not permit. Thus all ambiguity is resolved. This is possible; not probable. No other suggestion is better. If this one is rejected, if Luke has given us at best a partial account of Paul's break with Barnabas and an incorrect account of Timothy, the authorship of Acts by one of the Pauline circle is called in question. The best we can say of this paragraph is that Luke was dependent on popular stories, which he did not, perhaps could not, check with Paul, with Barnabas, with Timothy, or with the church in Antioch.

36. It was a prudent and responsible suggestion that converts made and churches established on the journey of chs. 13 and 14 should be revisited. The task would be done thoroughly, **from city to city, every one of them**. The usage of the English verb *visit* requires an addition to *visit* . . . **to see how**. The plan in this form was not carried out. After Derbe and Lystra Paul and Silas entered on new ground.

37. Barnabas wished to take with them John, called Mark. Cf. 13.5. See also 13.13; 15.38; also Col. 4.10; 2 Tim. 4.11; Philemon 24. According to Col. 4.10 Mark and Barnabas were related.

38. Paul rejects Barnabas' suggestion. Mark **had parted from them in Pamphylia** and was not a proper person to trust as a travelling companion. Acts 13.13 does not necessarily suggest a blameworthy separation; in the present context a different verb is used, and **failed to accompany them to the work** suggests dereliction of duty. There have been attempts, based on the tenses of the Greek verbs used in v. 37 and here, to lessen the difference between Paul and Barnabas, but they are unconvincing. 2 Tim. 4.11, however, whether written by Paul himself or not, indicates that Mark was eventually accepted back into the Pauline circle.

39. The disagreement between Paul and Barnabas was in fact sharp; the partnership of chs. 13 and 14 was broken. **Barnabas took Mark and sailed away to Cyprus** – his native place (4.36).

A different ground of controversy between Paul and Barnabas is given in Gal. 2.13. The rebuke Paul delivered to Peter in Gal. 2.14–18 would have applied equally to Barnabas, who was carried away by Peter's hypocrisy. Nothing is said in Galatians about Mark. It may be that there were two distinct quarrels; it may be that there was one quarrel with two elements; it may be that Paul gives the true ground of separation and Luke prefers to find a personal rather than a theological reason for the split. There is no reason to think the story about Mark a pure invention.

40. Paul, now in need of a travelling companion for the journeys that lay ahead of him, **chose Silas**; see on 15.22. It is pure conjecture, but it may be correct, that Paul set out on a new mission with a new companion because he had lost his battle at Antioch (Gal. 2.11–14). Luke says however that he was commended **by the brothers to the Lord's grace**. On the new journey he begins in what might be described as the Antiochene mission field, but soon leaves it.

41. He (accompanied by Silas) **passed through Syria and Cilicia.** In Antioch he was in Syria. Cilicia, at times administratively joined with Syria, lay to the north at the northeastern angle of the Mediterranean, and stretched west perhaps as far as Pamphylia, which Paul had visited on the first journey. Cf. 9.30; on the way to Tarsus Paul must have passed through Syria and Cilicia, but we do not know if at that time he was preaching and founding churches. There were churches there for he strengthened them, and the Decree had been sent there (15.23).

1. The new paragraph makes a new beginning, probably the beginning of a new source of information. *Syria and Cilicia* (v. 41) could be inferred from the letter (15.23). **Derbe and Lystra** not only recall the earlier journey (see p. 214); they introduce an important new fact. The narrative is now probably based on local information.

and there was, literally, And, behold . . . Luke writes in his 'biblical' style. **Timothy** was to play an important part in Acts (16.1; 17.14, 15; 18.5; 19.22; 20.4) and in the Pauline letters. He was a **disciple** – a Christian. He is not mentioned in the account of Paul's earlier visit, and one guesses that he was not converted at that time, though at 1 Cor. 4.17 Paul speaks of him as his child. His mother also was a Christian (according to 2 Tim. 1.5 called Eunice). His father was not. She was a Jewess, his father was a Greek – that is, a Gentile. The marriage was thus in Jewish law illegal. Jewish law also required that in a mixed marriage the child should follow the nationality of the mother. Timothy ought thus to have been circumcised on the eighth day after birth, though of course a Gentile father might have forbidden this. It has however been shown that this law of matrilineal descent was not in operation in the first century. See further on v. 3.

Silas now disappears from the story till 16.19; Timothy (after v. 3) till 17.14.

2. Lystra and Iconium: with *Derbe*, towns of the first journey. The towns were not, in the days of foot travel, very close together, but no doubt the Christians in each found it useful to keep in touch.

3. Paul wished him to go with him. 1 Thess. 1.1; 3.2, 6 are sufficient to show that a man called Timothy accompanied Paul on the 'second missionary journey'. The existence of the two Epistles to Timothy, though Paul did not write them, shows that Timothy survived Paul. For Luke Timothy would have been a useful and probably available source of information.

With this desire, Paul **took and circumcised him on account of the Jews who were in those parts**, that is, in the Derbe–Lystra area. This statement creates one of the most difficult problems in Acts. Paul (according to Acts) had just been contending successfully for Gentile freedom from the Law, specifically from circumcision. The controversy was sharp: Gal. 2.3–5; 5.2; 1 Cor. 7.18. Why should Paul have circumcised Timothy? Perhaps (it is said) because in the course of the mission Paul would wish to take him into synagogues and Jewish places of prayer. But (in Acts) Paul never does this; in any case, uncircumcised Gentiles favourable to Judaism were admitted to at least some synagogues (see on 10.2). If (see on v. 1) it was held that Timothy's maternal ancestry, if it did not legally make him a Jew, connected him so closely with Judaism as to make it desirable for him to live as a Jew (**all knew that his father had been** – this suggests that he was now dead – **a Greek**), there would perhaps have been a case for circumcising him – 'to make an honest Jew of him' – but it is doubtful whether Paul would have accepted it. It is just possible, though it seems unlikely, that Paul would have circumcised Timothy so as not to raise problems in dealing with Jews. It is more probable that Luke was mistaken. It is a question on which students of Acts are divided.

4. they delivered to the believers; literally, *to them*, but the pronoun cannot refer to *the cities* and there is no other possibility. **the decrees** corresponds to the verb used in 15.28 (cf. 15.22, 25). The word does not suggest a request for considerate and courteous behaviour aimed at making possible harmonious common meals, rather it means ordinances that must be observed by those who wish to be members of the group that ordains them. It was **the apostles and elders** who decided the decrees; nothing is said now of the main body of the church (15.12, 22). And Paul is made to act as an agent of the Jerusalem apostles in a way hard to reconcile with Galatians.

5. This verse is a summary, reminiscent of the summaries that punctuate the earlier part of Acts (2.42–47; 4.32–35; 5.12–16; 6.7; 9.31). It is Luke's conclusion of the paragraph that began at 15.1. As on other occasions, we see the emergence of a problem, its speedy and effective solution, and its outcome in greater progress and expansion for the churches.

42. GUIDED BY THE SPIRIT TO TROAS 16.6–10

**[6]They passed through Phrygia and Galatian territory, having been forbidden by the Holy Spirit to speak the word in Asia;
[7]they came opposite Mysia and tried to go into Bithynia, but the Spirit of Jesus did not permit them to do so. [8]They arrived at
Mysia and came down to Troas. [9]A vision appeared to Paul in the night: a man of Macedonia was standing, begging him with the words, 'Come across into Macedonia and help us.' [10]When
Paul had seen the vision, immediately we sought to leave for Macedonia, concluding that God had called us to evangelize them.**

The journey begun in 15.41 reaches Troas by the end of v. 8. The course of it as described in vv. 6–8 raises several notoriously difficult questions, but Luke emphasizes that at every stage the travellers receive supernatural guidance. This continues in vv. 9, 10 where Paul is directed by a vision to cross over to Macedonia. What must be noted here is the introduction into the narrative of the first person plural, *we sought* (v. 10). The first impression given by this is that the person who wrote it was present at the events he describes. This first impression may be but is not necessarily correct, and many different views are held about the 'We-passages', which begin at this point (but see on 11.28; 13.2). See Introduction, pp. xxxi–xxxiii. Nothing in the present passage points to the identity of the fellow traveller implied by the first person plural.

6–8. The Greek of these verses bristles with grammatical and geographical obscurities and ambiguities. It seems best, at the risk of creating an appearance of dogmatism, to base the comment on the translation provided, pointing out alternatives and giving reasons for the choices made.

They passed through Phrygia and Galatian territory. The subject, no longer that of 16.5, must now be Paul, Silas, and Timothy. The question that arises here is whether *Phrygia* is to be regarded as a noun or is an adjective, in which case it would share with *Galatian* the government of *territory*. The political geography that lies behind this question is the incorporation in 25 BC of part of Phrygia (and some other districts) in the newly formed province of Galatia, which was based upon the old kingdom of Galatia. Did the travellers go through (what remained of) Phrygia and Galatian territory, or through territory that was (or had been) Phrygian but was (now) also Galatian, through what has been called (though the expression is not known to have been used in antiquity) 'Phrygo-Galatic territory'? The translation offered here takes *Phrygia* as a noun, partly because of the route involved (see below) and partly because of the similar but not identical expression at 18.23 (*the Galatian territory and Phyrgia*), where Phrygia can hardly not be a noun.

They took this route because they had **been forbidden by the Holy Spirit to speak the word in Asia**. This means that the route they took was a consequence of the Spirit's prohibition. Phrygia and Galatia constituted a route alternative to a route through Asia, which presumably had been contemplated. This new route will bring them to a point **opposite Mysia**, where again they are diverted by the Spirit, who turns them back from **Bithynia**. The alternative view, which takes the travellers through 'Phrygo-Galatic territory', brings them up to the frontier of Asia, where the Spirit turns them back. This means translating not **having been forbidden**, but *they were now*, after passing through 'Phrygo-Galatic territory', *forbidden*. Is this possible? The answer is that it is very unlikely. **Having been forbidden** translates a Greek aorist participle. Such participles regularly refer to action before that of the main verb (here, *they passed through*); occasionally they refer to action contemporaneous with the main verb; extremely seldom do they refer to subsequent action. When these considerations are taken together it seems (though some take a different view) that Luke's meaning is that Paul thought of preaching in Asia but was forbidden to do this. Instead he went through Phrygia and Galatia and came to Mysia, which was part of Asia and therefore had to be avoided. He thought of going to Bithynia to the north but again was prevented. So **they arrived at Mysia** (for this meaning of the verb see Acts 24.7), and must have passed through some part of it since **Troas is** in Mysia.

It remains to look at a few details in these verses. On **Phrygia** and **Galatia** see above – and see a map. The data given here bear on the question of the destination, and thus on the date, of the Epistle to the Galatians; but this is not a matter to be considered in a study of Acts. **The Holy Spirit – the Spirit of Jesus**. No difference is intended. One can only think that Luke liked variety in theological terminology. **Mysia** was a northern part of the province of **Asia**, a wealthy and highly civilized part of Asia Minor, based upon a number of city-states, still at least partially independent. It was bordered on the north by Bithynia, on the south by Lycia, on the east by Galatia, on the west by the sea. See further on ch. 19. Bithynia lay to the east of Mysian Asia and stretched eastward along the south coast of the Black Sea. Pompey the Great organized Bithynia as a province in union with Pontus (further east). During the first century it was a senatorial province though its position on the route to the east led to an unusual measure of imperial interference. Troas, in full Alexandria Troas, was founded by Antigonus (323–301 BC). It was a free city; under Augustus it became a colony. In addition to 16.11; 20.5, 6 see also 2 Cor. 2.12; 2 Tim. 4.13.

9. Supernatural guidance is now given in a new form. **A vision appeared to Paul in the night.** The word *vision* is frequent in Acts; That it appeared *in the night* probably means that we should think of it as a dream. The man who appears is a *Macedonian*, recognizable as such by his request, . . . **Macedonia** . . . **help us**. He is vividly described, **standing**, **begging**, saying. **Come across** implies coming from one side of a barrier (here the Thracian Sea, the northern part of the Aegean) to the other. **Help us** is a surprisingly vague expression, possibly intended to convey the thought that the Macedonians were aware of their need of help but not of the particular help that Paul could offer.

Much is sometimes made of the move from Asia to Europe. This is an error. The whole journey was within the Roman Empire of which both Mysia (Asia) and Macedonia were provinces. In Philippi Paul would speak the same Greek that he had spoken all the way from Antioch.

10. immediately expresses unhesitating obedience to a divine command. **we sought**: the immediate but not necessarily correct impression is that the writer was one of the party concerned. It is often supposed that he had just joined, and might be 'Luke', the author of the book as a whole. It could be Silas or Timothy who here begins to speak. There is no point in making or recording conjectural identifications. This may be done when every 'We-passage' has been considered; see Introduction, pp. xxxi–xxxiii. All agreed that **God had called us to evangelize** the Macedonians. The next part of the book is determined.

43. PAUL AND SILAS AT PHILIPPI 16.11–40

**11 We set sail from Troas and made a straight run to Samothrace,
and on the next day to Neapolis, 12 and thence to Philippi, a leading
city of the province of Macedonia, a colony. We stayed in the city
several days. 13 On the Sabbath day we went outside the [city]
gate by a river, where we supposed that there was a place of
prayer. We sat down and spoke with the women who had
gathered. 14 A woman, Lydia by name, a dealer in purple from
the city of Thyatira, who worshipped God, listened; the Lord
opened her heart to give attention to the things spoken by Paul.
15 When she and her household were baptized she asked us, 'If
you have judged me to be faithful to the Lord, come into my
house and stay;' and she constrained us to do so.**

**16 It happened that as we were on our way to the place of
prayer, a slave girl who had an oracular spirit met us; she made
much profit for her owners by giving oracles. 17 She followed Paul
and us, crying out, 'These men are slaves of the Most High God;
they are proclaiming to you a way of salvation.' 18 She did this for
many days. Paul could endure it no longer, turned, and said to
the spirit, 'I command you in the name of Jesus Christ to come
out of her.' It came out at once. 19 When her owners saw that the
hope of their profit had departed, they seized Paul and Silas and
dragged them into the Agora before the rulers. 20 Having brought
them to the magistrates they said, 'These men, who are Jews, are
greatly disturbing our city, 21 and are proclaiming customs which
it is not lawful for us, who are Romans, to receive or practise.'
22 The crowd joined in the attack upon them and the magistrates
tore off their clothes and commanded [their officers] to beat them.
23 When they had laid many stripes upon them they cast them
into prison, ordering the gaoler to guard them securely. 24 He,
having received such a command, put them in the inner prison
and secured their feet in the stocks. 25 At midnight Paul and Silas
in their prayers were singing psalms to God, and the prisoners
were listening to them. 26 Suddenly there was a great earthquake
so that the foundations of the prison were shaken. Immediately
all the doors were opened and the bonds of all [the prisoners]
were loosed. 27 The gaoler woke up, and when he saw the doors of
the prison standing open he drew his sword and was about to kill**

himself because he supposed that the prisoners had escaped. 28 But Paul called out with a loud cry, 'Do yourself no harm, for we are all here.' 29 [The gaoler] asked for lights and sprang in. He was trembling, and fell down before Paul and Silas. 30 He brought them outside and said, 'Gentlemen, what must I do to be saved?' 31 They said, 'Believe in the Lord Jesus and you will be saved – you and your household.' 32 And they spoke to him the word of the Lord, together with all who were in his house. 33 He took them in that hour of the night and washed them clean from the effect of the blows they had received, and he was baptized, he and all his family, immediately. 34 He brought them up into his house, prepared a meal, and rejoiced with all his household, because he had come to faith in God. 35 When day broke, the magistrates sent the lictors, saying, 'Release those men.' 36 The gaoler reported these words to Paul, saying, 'The magistrates have sent that you should be released; so now depart and travel on in peace.' 37 Paul said to them, 'They have beaten us publicly, uncondemned, men who are Romans; they have put us in prison; and will they now put us out secretly? No, indeed; rather let them come themselves and lead us out.' 38 The lictors reported these things to the magistrates. When they heard that they were Romans they were afraid, 39 came and placated them, and having brought them out asked them to leave the city. 40 When they had come out of the prison they went into Lydia's house, and when they had seen the brothers they encouraged them, and left.

The use of the first person plural which begins at 16.10 continues through the earlier part of the new section. Verbs or pronouns in the first person plural occur in vv. 11, 12, 13, 15, 16 and 17; that is, the narrator expressly represents himself as present on the journey from Troas to Philippi, as visiting the place of prayer and entertained by Lydia, and as addressed by the prophesying girl. From this point 'We' disappears; this however means, or need mean, no more than that it was only Paul and Silas who were arrested and imprisoned – the narrator no longer played an active part in the story. If we are to think of the author (real or supposed) of a source (or of the book itself) it is reasonable to think that he joined Paul's party at Troas, accompanied him to Philippi and remained there after Paul had left, rejoining the party at Philippi in 20.5, 6. There are features of the narrative that suggest local knowledge (see e.g. the notes on vv. 13, 20). Against such realistic features must be placed the earthquake – not the earthquake itself but the fact that it was strong enough to release all the prisoners but gentle enough to do them no harm, and sufficiently localized to have escaped the notice of the town officials. It may be that the implied eye-witness was no longer present after v. 17; he, or the author using the eye-witness as source, added such local traditions as he could find. In this chapter we may have to distinguish eye-witness recollection, local tradition, the elaboration of local tradition, and the editorial work of the final author. See Introduction, pp. xxxi–xxxiii.

11. Troas. See 16.8. **made a straight run**: cf. 21.1; a word used especially of ships. **Samothrace**: an island at the northern extremity of the Aegean; many came here to be initiated into the mysteries practised at the temple of the 'Great Gods'. Paul and his companions presumably spent the night here and came **on the next day to Neapolis**, the port of Philippi, the base of Brutus and Cassius at the battle of Philippi (42 BC).

12. thence to Philippi, about ten miles inland, made a colony by M. Antonius after the victory of 42 BC and subsequently augmented by Octavian (Augustus). As a *colonia* it was treated, in justice and administration, virtually as if it were on Italian soil. It was **a leading city of the province of Macedonia**: the text here is uncertain; this gives the probable sense.

13. Again there is a textual problem. **On the Sabbath day** (for the expression cf. 13.14) **we went outside the [city] gate by a river** (the Gangites, or Cangites), **where we supposed that there was a place of prayer** (or, where a place of prayer was accustomed to be – there are other variants). The various forms of the text hint without actually asserting a probability that a synagogue (*place of prayer* is often simply *prayer*, but the word was used for a place, not necessarily a building, where Jews met for prayer and instruction) would be found by a river, or other water. There is good but perhaps not quite conclusive evidence that such places were chosen if available. See *NS* 2.440–42.

We sat down and spoke with does not suggest a formal synagogue service; contrast 13.5, 14f. For Luke's interest in and concern for women, and in the conversion of women to Christianity, see 1.14; 8.3, 12; 9.2; 16.1; 17.4, 12, 34; 18.2, 26; 21.5; 22.4.

14. Lydia, a fairly common name, was **a dealer in purple from the city of Thyatira**. There was a large dyeing industry. The colour *purple* was derived from the purple-fish (*porphyra*), though madder-root was also used to produce the colour. It is not clear whether Lydia was a commercial traveller in purple cloth who visited Philippi frequently enough to know her way to the place of prayer, or had opened a retail establishment there. A fragmentary Latin inscription from Philippi (*CIL* 3.664.1) appears to refer to dealers in purple. For Thyatira; cf. Rev. 2.18, 29. Several local inscriptions refer to guilds of dyers.

For another business woman in the NT cf. Chloe (1 Cor. 1.11). Lydia was **one who worshipped God**. This is the expression used at 10.2, on which see the note. It may be that she was a Gentile adherent of the synagogue, a Jewish sympathizer, but the words do not necessarily mean more than that she was a devout woman. As the informal meeting proceeded she listened. She heard, but it was **the Lord** who **opened her heart,** leading her to faith. For the theological issue raised here see 13.48.

15. On baptism in Acts see Introduction, pp. lx–lxii. There is no reference here to the *name*, to water, or to the Holy Spirit. No instruction is mentioned. Lydia's household are baptized with her. There is nothing to tell us whether it included young children or not. There are occasional but few instances of women as heads of households. **come into my house and stay**. The word house/household has now changed its meaning.

16. the place of prayer. See on v. 13. **a slave girl**. Luke's word has various meanings. At Jn 18.17 it must mean *maidservant* or possibly *female slave*. Here it must mean *slave* since the girl has **owners**. *Prostitute* is not impossible but would be unsuitable for Rhoda, of whom the same word is used at 12.13. The girl had **an oracular spirit**. The word here translated *oracular* was drawn originally from the name of the snake or dragon which was killed by Apollo; it was the priestess of Apollo who delivered the oracles at Delphi. It is clear that Luke understood the girl to be the victim of possession. It is possible that there is an allusion to the Witch of Endor (1 Sam. 28.7). It appears that the being eventually driven out had supernatural knowledge of what Paul and his colleagues were doing (v. 17). **she made much profit for her owners by giving oracles**, a matter evoking Luke's disapproval; he regularly objects to profits made by the abuse of spiritual agencies. *Giving oracles* is a word never used of OT or Christian prophets.

17. She followed . . . crying out. The tenses of the Greek verbs reinforce the repeated action explicitly stated in v. 18. **Paul and us**:

Paul is the most important person; *we* are his entourage. The girl is, Luke believes, genuinely possessed by a demon who has supernatural knowledge of Paul and his message.

the Most High God. *Most High* is a designation of God common in the LXX of the Psalms and of Daniel; it is common also in Sirach. It occurs in Philo and Josephus and is also used of Zeus. The word, attested in some inscriptions, seems to have been used sporadically in Hellenistic Judaism. A resident in Philippi, with no first-hand knowledge of Judaism, might well identify the one Jewish God with the highest god in his own pantheon. For **slaves** of God see 2.18; 4.29. The word is Pauline (e.g. Rom. 1.1) and goes well with the description of God as exalted in majesty and power.

The servants of God proclaim **a way of salvation**. For *way* cf. 9.2 (but in the present passage the meaning is *way to*), and for *salvation* cf. 4.12. The *way* will be briefly stated in v. 31.

18. The incident is clearly regarded by Luke as an exorcism. Cf. Lk. 4.35.

19. Loss of profit is treated by Luke as the real cause of the action taken by the girl's owners; the charge they bring in v. 21 is therefore a falsehood, and Luke intends that it should be seen as such. Cf. 19.25. They **dragged them into the Agora**. The earliest meaning of *agora* was *assembly*, then *place of assembly*, but especially *market-place*. A Greek market-place however was used for many, including judicial, purposes. **rulers** is a general term. For the question whether these *rulers* are the same as *the magistrates* see on v. 20.

20. having brought them to the magistrates, a different word from *rulers* in v. 19. The Greek (*stratēgos*) is a standard equivalent for the Latin *praetor*, though the original meaning of the Greek word was military, of the Latin judicial. At an earlier time the magistrates of colonies (such as Philippi) were called *praetors*. Later they became *duoviri*, but this is difficult to put into Greek and it is understandable that *stratēgos* should be retained. But were these the same as the *rulers* (v. 19)? *Either* the rulers sent the complainants to the law officers, *or* they went to the rulers who assumed their legal function as magistrates. The former alternative is better; the latter seems a pointless repetition. Instead of *rulers* we might say *leading people*.

The first charge is that of causing a disturbance; cf. 17.6; 24.5.

21. The ancient principle was that Roman citizens must practise the state cult and might in addition practise only those cults that had been sanctioned by the Senate. This principle was relaxed in the early

Empire provided that a new cult was compatible with citizenship. Here the principle is revived, (a) perhaps because an isolated colony in a Greek environment might feel it necessary to stress Roman 'otherness', and (b) Paul and Silas were Jews, and though Rome was tolerant towards Jews there was some feeling against proselytization. The juxtaposition of *who are Jews* (v. 20) and **who are Romans** suggests this. Did Paul present his message as a version, the only true version, of Judaism? Cf. 18.2.

22. the magistrates tore off their clothes. Whose clothes? The pronouns throughout the sentence seem to refer to Paul and Silas, and for judges to tear off their own clothes in horror is a Jewish rather than a Roman or Greek custom, whereas to tear off an offender's clothes before beating him has many parallels. **their officers** is not expressed in Greek. In English some such supplement is necessary with the active infinitive. Such a beating should not have been inflicted on Roman citizens; see on v. 37.

23. The thought is not well expressed. It is unlikely that the magistrates themselves tore the clothing off the backs of Paul and Silas (v. 22), and in the present verse though the sense is clear enough it is not always grammatically clear which are the subjects of the verbs, the magistrates or their attendants. It has been observed that it would be possible to pass directly from this point to v. 35, leaving the possibility that Luke might have inserted the supernatural story of the earthquake into a much more matter-of-fact event.

24. The gaoler picks up *securely* from v. 23, puts his prisoners **in the inner prison**, and secures **their feet in the stocks**. It is not certain whether *the stocks* are to be regarded as a means of security or an instrument of torture. Classical passages suggest security, Eusebius speaks of the stocks as an instrument of torture applied to Christian martyrs. Probably the same appliance was used for both purposes.

25. Paul and Silas in their prayers . . . A natural recourse for Christians in distress. Cf. 12.5; James 5.13. Paul and Silas were singing OT Psalms or new compositions on similar lines (cf. the hymns in the Lucan infancy stories and the Qumran Hodayoth). Singing in prison may be a literary convention, intended to show the coolness, courage, and faith of the prisoners. Luke, with the earthquake and release to come, is building up a dramatic story, but it is not necessarily at this point unhistorical. Men in prison for their faith have praised God.

26. there was a great earthquake. In the eastern Mediterranean earthquakes were as familiar in antiquity as they are today. Luke does not ascribe this one to divine providence, though he will certainly not have thought it fortuitous. Origen (*contra Celsum* 2.34; cf. 8.41f.) takes up Celsus' allusion to the story of Dionysus in Euripides, *Bacchae* (see especially 447f.: Spontaneous fell the chains from off their feet;/ The bolts drew back untouched by mortal hand). For other possible connections between Acts and Euripides see 21.39; 26.14.

The place of the supernatural in Luke's day calls for notice if not discussion. The observation that earthquakes do happen, and that prisoners have sometimes escaped without knowing the circumstances of their escape, is fair enough. To be added to it is Luke's conviction that a special providence protected Paul as God's agent in the evangelization of the Gentiles. Paul does not himself ascribe his escapes from the perils of 2 Cor. 11.24–27 to miracles.

27. Because he supposed ... Presumably the gaoler would think that the punishment for allowing the prisoners to escape would be an alternative worse than suicide. Cf. 12.19. Dramatic effect is heightened and the question of v. 30 prepared for, but the point has been questioned. The earthquake might well be accepted as an excuse.

28. How in the middle of the night and in the course of an earthquake Paul knew that all the prisoners were present is the sort of question Luke does not think of asking. Paul knows that God is ordering all things for good. But he is not acting as a 'divine man'. He does not free himself.

29. The subject changes, without notice in the Greek. The gaoler naturally **asked for lights and sprang in** – into the *inner prison*, unless Paul and Silas had already emerged. He **fell down before** them, no doubt taking them to be 'divine men'. On this error see v. 28. Luke is moving swiftly on to the climax of the story in vv. 30, 31.

30. He brought them outside and said ... The conversation proceeds without interruption by the earthquake. **Gentlemen**: the word need be no more than a polite address, though the context suggests a man moved by supernatural events and probably taking his prisoners to be divine. **what must I do to be saved?** *saved* may have a purely secular connotation. The gaoler has contemplated suicide; how can he escape the trouble he is in? There is however a supernatural aura in the events that have taken place and *saved* (cf. 4.12) has already something of its religious sense.

31. The religious sense of *saved* is immediately taken up. **Believe in the Lord Jesus** (many MSS add *Christ*) **and you will be saved.** Paul and Silas reply in terms that rest upon an accepted formula; cf. Rom. 10.9; Phil. 2.11. Jesus is presented as a divine figure, the origin of *the way of salvation* (v. 17). A divine being who would be insulted when his servants were publicly ill-used and was powerful enough to send an earthquake to release them was one to command allegiance. This is a form of Christian belief neither profound nor exalted, but the historian must remember that this is what Christianity must have looked like to many in the first century, whether believers or unbelievers. **you and your household**. Cf. v. 15. It cannot be maintained that *household* here includes infants, since not only were all baptized (v. 33), all heard the word of the Lord and rejoiced (v. 32). For the relation of the salvation of the household to the faith of one member see 1 Cor. 7.14–16 (on which see *1 Corinthians* 164–7).

32. the word of the Lord, one of Luke's standard terms for the Gospel. **all who were in his house**, all his *household* – all who were capable of hearing and understanding.

33. The gaoler acted immediately – **in that hour of the night** – in care of his prisoners, and **was baptized**, **he and all his family**. Cf. v. 31. Whatever be the historical value of his account of events in Philippi, it may probably be inferred that Luke and his readers would find nothing incredible, or improper, in a baptism following immediately, without instruction, upon conversion and profession of faith.

34. The gaoler **brought them up into his house** and **prepared a meal**, literally, *prepared a table* for a meal. He and his **household rejoiced**. There is nothing to support the view that this meal, prepared as an act of gratitude and compensation, was a eucharist. If he had meant this Luke would have made his meaning clear, perhaps using the phrase, *the breaking of bread.* But every Christian fellowship meal was at least potentially a eucharist, and the gaoler **rejoiced** . . . **because he had come to faith in God**.

35. When day broke the magistrates were again at work and, having presumably heard of the earthquake (though they do not refer to it), send to **Release those men**. Their messengers are **the lictors**. So they would be called in Rome itself; in Greek literally *rod-carriers*, men bearing a rod or staff of office, carrying out official duties, making arrests, and so forth.

36. The lictors brought their message to the gaoler, who passed it on to Paul.

37. Paul did not find this somewhat casual treatment satisfactory. It was illegal to beat a Roman citizen, and Paul stresses the enormity of the offence by adding **publicly**. They had been publicly insulted and disgraced by the punishment they had received. Honour and shame were important themes in Graeco-Roman society; it is possible that they seemed more important to Luke than to Paul, who was not in the habit of laying claim to things to which he was entitled (1 Cor. 9.12). Luke may have thought it worth while to make the point in order to discourage magistrates elsewhere from precipitate violence. For Paul's claim to be a Roman citizen see 22.25, 28, and the note. Paul never in the epistles makes any reference to his citizenship; and he received three Roman beatings (2 Cor. 11.23, 25). Why does he stand on his dignity in Philippi? Possibly because this was the first occasion; subsequently he would act differently.

38. The lictors report back to the magistrates; for their reaction see on v. 37, and cf. 22.29

39. It might be said that the text translated here suffers from undue brevity (*placated* is an unusual rendering of Luke's word but its usual sense is duplicated by *asked*); brevity is amply made up in a long Western expansion. It runs (in Codex Bezae):

> They arrived at the prison with many friends and asked them to leave, saying, In reference to your affair we did not understand that you were innocent men. And they brought them out and begged them with the words, Go out of this city, lest there be another riot with the people crying out to us against you.

This adds picturesque detail, and emphasizes the innocence and dignity of Paul and Silas and the obsequiousness of the magistrates.

40. Lydia and the gaoler are the only converts so far mentioned, so that we do not know who **the brothers** are. Luke writes a little absent-mindedly. The first person plural is dropped, the narrator disappears; either he has already left Philippi or the first person is a literary device, or interest is naturally focused on the two witness-bearers who have suffered in the cause.

44. FROM PHILIPPI TO ATHENS 17.1–15

**1 They followed the road through Amphipolis and Apollonia and
came to Thessalonica, where there was a synagogue of the Jews.
2 Paul, in accordance with his custom, went in to them on three
Sabbaths and argued with them on the basis of the Scriptures,
3 expounding them and submitting that it was necessary that the
Christ should suffer and rise from the dead, and, 'This man is
the Christ, Jesus, whom I am proclaiming to you.' 4 Some of them
believed and accepted their lot with Paul and Silas, also a large
company of the God-fearing Greeks, and not a few of the leading
women. 5 The Jews became jealous, took to themselves evil men
from among the market-place louts, gathered a crowd, and set
the city in an uproar. They gathered at the house of Jason and
sought to bring them out to the people. 6 When they did not find
them they dragged Jason and some brothers before the politarchs,
shouting, 'These men who have led the whole world into revolt
have come here too. 7 Jason has taken them in; and they are all
acting contrary to the decrees of Caesar saying that there is
another king, Jesus.' 8 They disturbed the crowd and the
politarchs, as they listened to these [charges], 9 and from Jason
and the others they took security and dismissed them.**

**10 Immediately, in the course of the night, the brothers sent off
Paul and Silas to Beroca. When they arrived they went into the
synagogue of the Jews. 11 These [Jews] were more liberal than
those in Thessalonica; they received the word with all eagerness,
searching the Scriptures daily [to see] if these things were so.
12 So many of them became believers; also not a few of the Greek
women of good standing, and men. 13 But when the Jews from
Thessalonica knew that the word of God had been preached by
Paul in Beroea also they came there too stirring up and disturbing
the crowds. 14 Immediately, at that very time, the brothers sent
Paul away to travel to the sea. But Silas and Timothy remained
there [in Beroea]. 15 Those who were accompanying Paul brought
him as far as Athens; they left with instructions for Silas and
Timothy that they should come to him as quickly as possible.**

The next significant stop made by Paul and Silas in Macedonia is at Thessalonica. The mission there begins with considerable success

(vv. 1–4). Opposition on the part of the Jews leads the politarchs (v. 6) to take relatively mild action (vv. 5–9); Paul and Silas are sent off to Beroea, where they receive a more favourable welcome (vv. 10–12). Jews from Thessalonica pursue the missionaries to Beroea. The Beroean Christians send Paul away to the sea and bring him to Athens. Silas and Timothy remain in Beroea, with instructions to join Paul as soon as possible.

All this makes a logically connected narrative. It was probably a continuous composition by Luke himself, showing signs of his customary vocabulary and style. The place-names were probably derived from an itinerary; this is supported by the fact that no incidents are recorded for Amphipolis and Apollonia. The names (one may suggest) were on a list in Antioch; Luke collected material at, or about, Thessalonica and Beroea, but could find nothing to report, beyond their presence on a list, about Amphipolis and Apollonia. The name Jason suggests contact with local tradition, the use of the correct word *politarch* (see v. 6) either contact or a good knowledge of Roman provincial administration.

Paul is correctly represented as preaching Christ crucified and risen. The (possibly deliberate) misunderstanding of Christ's kingship (v. 7) probably often created a problem for Christian preachers.

1. They followed the road. Luke's Greek verb embodies the word for *road* and may possibly intend an allusion to the Via Egnatia, which the travellers would be using. This was the main land route from Rome to the East.

Amphipolis, the capital of the first district of Macedonia, was so called because it was surrounded on two sides by the River Strymon, and was visible from both sea and land. **Apollonia** was further inland. It is possible that the two towns formed stages on the way to Thessalonica. There is no record of preaching in them, possibly because the preachers found no synagogue to serve as a point of entry. **There was a synagogue** at **Thessalonica**, a large and populous city. It may have been the existence of the synagogue that persuaded Paul and his colleagues to stay. There is no other evidence for the presence of Jews in Thessalonica before the second century.

2. Paul, in accordance with his custom (13.5, 14; 14.1; cf. 16.13), **went in to them**, those who might be expected to be found in the synagogue – Jews, with perhaps a few interested Gentiles. **on three Sabbaths** could be *for three weeks* but cf. 13.27, 42, 44; 15.21; 18.4. Phil. 4.16 (cf. 4.9) and 1 Thessalonians suggest that Paul stayed in Thessalonica a good deal longer than three weeks. Paul **argued** in the synagogue, the argument evidently turning on the interpretation of the OT.

3. He argued on the basis of the Scriptures (v. 2). The argument consisted of **expounding** and **submitting**, affirming. *Expounding* is literally *opening*, a Greek word to which there is in this sense no parallel (except Lk. 24.32) of relevant date. The corresponding Hebrew *to open* is used with a related but not identical meaning: 'to open a lecture or sermon with a Bible passage'. There is no doubt of Luke's general meaning here – a biblically based argument – but it would be hazardous to assert that his language was based on a Jewish model. At Qumran, CD 5.3 and 1 QH 18.20 are scarcely relevant. No attempt is made to show which passages in the OT are held to prove that the Messiah must suffer and die and be raised from the dead.

4. Some of them (Jews and proselytes in the synagogue – others are mentioned separately) **believed and accepted their lot with Paul and Silas**. One is inclined to translate *threw in their lot with* but the verb is passive and means *were assigned to*. Luke held a predestinarian view of conversion (13.14; 16.14) and may have thought that those who attached themselves to Paul and Silas did so because God had appointed them to this end.

The believing Jews and proselytes were joined by **a large company of the God-fearing Greeks**. See 10.2; 13.43, 50; 16.14; 18.7. On the relation of these persons to the synagogue see pp. 154f. The present verse distinguishes them from proselytes and shows that notwithstanding their piety they were classed as *Greeks* (Gentiles). There was also a group of **leading women**. An alternative translation (required by the Western reading) is *wives of leading men*. For Luke's interest in women and their share in the church see 1.14; 5.1; 8.3, 12; 9.2; 13.50; 16.1, 13, 14; 17.1, 2, 34; 18.2; 21.5; 22.4; 24.24.

5. The Jews became jealous, fearing that they were losing control of the synagogue and their appeal to religious non-Jews.

the market-place louts. This certainly gives the meaning that Luke attached to his word, though it has several meanings, of which the others are neutral or favourable. The grammatical subject of **gathered a crowd** must be *the Jews*, though one suspects that *the louts* may have been intended. It would be easy to **set the city in an uproar** and blame the Christians. **They gathered at**, perhaps *set upon*. **Jason** is certainly known only through this passage. The name occurs at Rom. 16.21 as that of a Jewish helper of Paul; the name Jason might be a Greek substitute for Joshua. It is not impossible that Jason of Thessalonica travelled to join Paul at Cenchreae (Rom. 16.1), but quite uncertain.

The trouble-makers sought to bring **them** (Paul and Silas) **out to the people**. It is disputed whether *the people*, who should be an orderly official assembly, are or are not to be distinguished from the riotous *crowd* mentioned earlier.

6. Paul and Silas were not to be found, either because they were well hidden or because they were not in Jason's house. Other victims, however, **Jason and some brothers**, would serve. It is probably, though not certainly, implied that Jason too was a (Christian) brother. The men were dragged **before the politarchs**. This was the correct title in Macedonia for the non-Roman magistrates of a city. The more important the city the greater the number of politarchs. In the time of Augustus Thessalonica had five, later six. Use of the correct title does not establish the historicity of the whole story, but it demonstrates contact at some stage with Macedonia.

The charge was that **these men who have led the whole world into revolt have come here too**. The sense of Luke's verb is given by 21.38 (the Egyptian rebel led an armed revolt against Rome) and by v. 7: they are acting contrary to imperial decrees and attempting to set up a rival emperor.

7. Jason has taken them in. It is implied that if Jason is not a Christian he is at least a sympathizer. **They . . . all**: Jason, the brothers, Paul and Silas; any other Christians available. **the decrees of Caesar**. What decrees? It would be understandable that a mob should not show much legal precision. Thessalonica was a free city and *decrees* would not be binding on the magistrates. Some suggest that they were the enactments that banished the Jews from Rome (see pp. 276f.). Others think of edicts against predictions (especially political predictions). These were enforced through the local administration of oaths of loyalty, carried out by the politarchs. *Kingdom of God* is an expression that runs deep into the gospel tradition and could easily give colour to the accusation that Christians were supporters of a rival emperor.

8. They disturbed the crowd. Cf. v. 5. Was this the first step towards persuading the duly constituted *people* to take action against the Christians?

9. they took security. Linguistically a Latinism, and legally a practice borrowed by the Greeks from Rome. **Jason** is made to give security for the good behaviour of his guests (who are promptly sent away); but since security is taken from **the others** also they are evidently all charged to maintain good conduct.

10. the brothers, not the *brothers* of v. 6, but the community as a whole. 1 Thessalonians (e.g. 1.4, for *brothers*) is sufficient proof that after a short ministry Paul left a church in Thessalonica; so also is 20.4. **sent off Paul and Silas to Beroea**. This city was well chosen for flight; it was large and populous; forty-five miles WSW of Thessalonica, it lay off the Egnatian Way which Paul had followed so far. The presence of Jews is confirmed by inscriptions (*NS* 3.67, 68). Notwithstanding the troubles in Thessalonica (v. 5) Paul and Silas went without delay to the synagogue.

11. Their reception here was more favourable than it had been in Thessalonica. **These [Jews] were more liberal**. Luke's adjective referred originally to noble birth but came to be applied to noble behaviour. Luke means that the Beroean Jews allowed no prejudice to prevent them from giving Paul a fair hearing. They **search[ed] the Scriptures** to see whether Paul's assertions were correct. His fundamental message was evidently understood by Luke to be (a) that the OT affirms the coming of a Messiah who will suffer and rise from the dead, and (b) that Jesus was this Messiah. The NT nowhere else uses the word *search* for the study of the Bible; it is more often used in legal contexts for the examination of witnesses. This is in fact the sense in which it is used here. Paul has set up the Scriptures as witnesses; does their testimony, when tested, prove his case?

12. After their examination of Paul's biblical argument **many of them [the Jews] became believers**. Also **not a few of the Greek**, that is, not Jewish, **women of good standing**. For Luke's adjective descriptive of the women cf. 13.50. They (and the **men**) are not said to be *God-fearing*. For Luke's frequent references to women converts see v. 4.

13. The successful preaching in Beroea was naturally unpleasing to the Jews of Thessalonica, who came to Beroea stirring up trouble. If the Christians could be found responsible for disturbances in the city they would no doubt be expelled without examination of their teaching.

14. It was important to get **Paul** (no doubt the main target of attack) away quickly, and **the brothers**, the Christian community, acted without delay. They sent him away **to travel to the sea**. Some question this rendering of the Greek, and there are variant readings.

The most interesting alternative has the brothers sending Paul *as if* to the sea; this was a feint, and he would in fact travel by land. This could be correct, but the simple *to the sea* seems better, though it is fairly pointed out that it would accord with Luke's custom to name the port of departure.

Silas and Timothy were to stay in Beroea. Timothy has not been mentioned since 16.1–3, and some think that 1 Thess. 3.2 means that up to that point he was not known in Thessalonica. It is not however necessary to infer that he had not been with the party. 1 Thess. 3.2 might be intended to assure the Thessalonians that one who had hitherto been slightly regarded as a junior assistant was in fact a trusted lieutenant.

15. Macedonian companions saw Paul on his way **as far as Athens**. They returned with instructions that Silas and Timothy were to join him **as quickly as possible**. According to Acts (18.5) they caught up with him at Corinth. 1 Thess. 3.2 suggests that Silas and Timothy, or at least Timothy, had joined him in Athens.

There is some free rewriting in the Western text at this point. Codex Bezae includes the words: He passed by Thessaly, for he was forbidden to proclaim the word to them.

45. PAUL AT ATHENS 17.16–34

**16 While Paul in Athens was waiting for Silas and Timothy his
spirit was vexed within him as he saw that the city was overgrown
with idols. 17 So in the synagogue he disputed with the Jews and
the devout persons and in the Agora every day with those he
chanced to meet. 18 Some of the Epicurean and Stoic philosophers
argued with him, and some said, 'What does this third-rate
journalist want to tell us?' Others said, 'He seems to be a preacher
of foreign gods.' For he was preaching the message of Jesus and
the resurrection. 19 They got hold of him and brought him to the
Areopagus, saying, 'May we know what this new teaching, spoken
by you, is? 20 For you are bringing strange things to our ears. We
should like to know therefore what these things mean.' 21 For all
the Athenians and the resident foreigners had leisure for nothing
but to say or hear some novelty.**

**22 Paul stood up in the midst of the Areopagus, and said,
'Gentlemen of Athens, I see that you make a great display of
piety. 23 For as I passed by and looked at your objects and
instruments of worship I saw among other things an altar on
which was inscribed, To an unknown god. What therefore you
worship in ignorance, that I proclaim to you. 24 The God who
made the world and all the things that are in it, since he is Lord
of heaven and earth does not live in shrines made by human
hands, 25 nor is he served by human hands as though he were in
need of anything, since he himself gives to all life and breath and
all things. 26 He made of one origin every race of men to dwell
upon the whole face of the earth, having appointed foreordained
seasons and the boundaries of their habitation, 27 with a view to
their seeking God, and, perhaps, by groping after him, find him,
though indeed his being is not far from each one of us. 28 For in
him we live and move and are; as indeed some of your own poets
have said: "We too are his family." 29 Since then we have our
being as God's family, we ought not to suppose that the divine
being is like gold or silver or stone, an object carved by man's art
or imagination. 30 So the times of ignorance God has overlooked,
but now he is commanding men that they should all everywhere
repent, 31 inasmuch as he has set a day on which he will judge the
whole world in righteousness by a man whom he has appointed.**

Of this appointment he has provided proof in that he raised him from the dead.'

[32] When they heard of the resurrection of the dead some mocked, but others said, 'We will hear you on this topic again.' [33] So Paul went out of their midst. [34] But some men adhered to him and believed, among whom were Dionysius the Areopagite, and a woman, Damaris by name, and others with them.

Paul reached Athens alone, where he awaited Silas and Timothy. Shocked by the idolatry of the city, he discoursed in the synagogue and the Agora. His reception was mixed: and when he addressed the Areopagus court the response was again divided. A few disciples however were made. This outline of events is to some extent confirmed by 1 Thessalonians. There is however in the narrative no use of the first person plural. There are a few features that suggest acquaintance with Athens, but these can for the most part be accounted for as based on general knowledge and literary allusion, and if the author had himself been in Athens he need not have been there in Paul's company. Of course, in any city Paul would take advantage of every opportunity, in synagogue and market-place, to commend the Gospel, but the summary of his message in v. 18 (Jesus and the resurrection) recalls that in Rom. 10.9.

The speech attributed to Paul (vv. 22–31) is a different matter. Athens, with a few local notes, may have been found by Luke in an itinerary, but the speech is his own work, a summary of the kind of address to Gentiles that Hellenistic Christians had inherited from Hellenistic Jews. It is a different approach from that found in Rom. 1.18–31. Paul's approach to the Gentile world is essentially Christocentric (see especially 1 Cor. 2.2), and his criticism of Gentile society, though Jewish in its line of argument, develops the attack on idolatry found in the Wisdom of Solomon in a way that is ultimately Christologically determined. The Areopagus speech lacks this determining Christological factor. That Paul sought to turn his hearers from their idols to the living and true God is proved by 1 Thess. 1.9, 10, but he could do this by his preaching of Christ crucified. That he sometimes engaged in polemical speech against materialism, idolatry, and polytheism may well be true; these ways of thinking are open to philosophical attack, but, if we may judge from the epistles, such negative themes did not constitute the basis and prime content of Paul's message.

To say this is not to disparage Luke's work or the preaching of his contemporaries. It had in Luke's time become clear (as it had not in Paul's) that Christianity was to spend some time in a world that had an important intellectual element and that it was necessary that Christians should be able and willing to converse with those who represented this element (just as it had long been necessary for Jews to do so). It was however Luke, not Paul, who perceived this, and Paul would have insisted on what Luke does in fact with some success achieve: the restriction of the use of philosophy to those themes which it shares with the OT. And he would not have relegated Christ to a concluding footnote.

16. Paul in Athens was waiting for Silas and Timothy. See 17.15. Athens was not what it had been in the days of Pericles, but it was well treated by Rome and respected in its role of notable university city. As far as Acts is concerned, Paul waited for his colleagues in vain: they joined him in Corinth (18.5). But 1 Thess. 3.1f. shows that Timothy at least had been with Paul in Athens.

Paul's **spirit** (his inward life) **was vexed within him**. *Vexed* is the verb cognate with the noun *sharp disagreement* in 15.39. **the city was overgrown with idols**. Luke's word *overgrown* may suggest the luxuriant vegetation of a forest; there were idols everywhere, and Paul had not abandoned his Jewish belief that there was only one God and that he was to be worshipped without the use of images. The artistic excellence of the images was of no concern to him.

17. in the synagogue he disputed with the Jews and the devout persons. *In the synagogue* (see on 6.8), as at Thessalonica and Beroea, but here the synagogue is dealt with in one sentence. There were many synagogues but only one Athens, and in Athens the most important place was **the Agora**. The *devout persons* are presumably Gentile sympathizers with Judaism; see on 10.2.

Disputed and *Agora* both recall the figure and habit of Socrates. So does **those he chanced to meet**. This recalls Socrates' readiness to converse with anyone willing to converse with him. For the Socratic dialectical method, which grew out of market-place arguments, see e.g. Plato, *Republic* V. 454. Luke, as a man with at least a popular education, can hardly have failed to think of Socrates as he described Paul's work in Athens. For the archaeology and topography of this part of Athens see the Princeton publication, *The Athenian Agora*. 1953 onwards.

18. Among those with whom Paul conducted conversations were **Epicurean and Stoic philosophers**. These may be mentioned because their opinions are reflected in the speech that follows. If we are to conceive a god who created the universe it is ridiculous to bring him a pig or a sheep as if he were a hungry beggar, or to suppose that he could be localized in a building. This was Epicurean criticism of popular religion. The Stoics believed that the human race was one, proceeding from a single point of origin, that there was a divine being, and that it was man's duty to live in accordance with this indwelling god. From one point of view the speech can be looked on as an attempt to see how far a Christian preacher can go in company with Greek philosophy.

Paul's critics use to describe him a word that means 'one who picks up and retails scraps of knowledge, an idle babbler, gossip' (LS 1627). If one borrows the English word **journalist** it must be understood to refer not to distinguished journalists of high ability, but to the less able representatives of the profession.

The hints at the figure of Socrates noted in v. 17 now become more definite in what is almost an explicit quotation. According to Xenophon the charge brought against Socrates was (in addition to the corruption of the youth) that he was guilty of not believing in the gods believed in by the city and of bringing in new deities. It was alleged that Paul **seems to be a preacher of foreign gods** – an action to which the Athenians were notoriously sensitive. Paul was **preaching the message of Jesus and the resurrection**. It is possible but not likely that this was taken to refer to two gods – Jesus and Anastasis (Greek for *Resurrection*).

19. They got hold of him. Luke's word may imply an arrest, with or without violence, or a friendly approach – Come and let us talk this over. The intention was probably to bring Paul to the Areios Pagos court (not necessarily for a formal trial); less probably to bring him to the Areios Pagos hill for an open-air discussion. The history of the Areopagus court in the first century is obscure, but it remained the supreme authority in Athens, with the right to interfere in any aspect of corporate life and to try cases of any kind. It met often but perhaps not always on the Areopagus hill. The court, or some members of it, make a polite inquiry: **May we know**... ?

20. This verse is little more than a duplicate of vv. 18, 19. It seems like a simple request for information, but it is worth while to recall the words of Josephus with reference to Athens: The punishment of those who bring in a strange god has been determined as death (*Against Apion*, 2.267).

21. The Athenians' search for novelty had become proverbial. This fact makes it difficult to know whether Luke was writing of what he had himself observed in Athens or was quoting common opinion.

the resident foreigners. Many visitors came to Athens, some as serious students, others as tourists.

22. Paul stood up. This would be expected in Athens, not in a synagogue. **in the midst of the Areopagus**. This is consistent with the view that sees in the Areopagus a court rather than a hill.

Gentlemen of Athens. Cf. *Men of Galilee* (1.11), and many other examples in Acts. Here however the familiar words of Socrates are recalled. **I see that you make a great display of piety.** 'I perceive that in all things ye are too superstitious' (AV). Was Paul placating, flattering, or attacking the Athenians? The question is disputed, and turns on the meaning of Luke's adjective. This however cannot in itself answer the question. The word means *religious*. To the sceptic, this means *superstitious*; to the religious, judgement depends on whether the religion is one that he shares, or at least approves, or is one that he rejects. We shall see that Paul's attitude (as represented in this speech) is not simple: he has however noted with vexed disapproval, that the city is full of idols. The adjective as used by Luke is in the comparative form and is introduced by a word normally translated *as*. These facts complicate the question further. The comparative may hint at a superlative, *as* hints at *as if*. Athens presents a show of (idolatrous) piety, but it is an unreal, uninformed piety directed towards a deity who remains unknown (v. 23). Paul was not the only person to comment on Athenian religiosity.

23. I saw . . . an altar on which was inscribed, To an unknown god. *An altar*, or possibly *the base of a statue*; certainly, a religious object. No object in Athens bearing this inscription is known to archaeologists; Jerome already rejected the accuracy of Luke's account. 'The inscription on the altar was not, as Paul asserts, "To an unknown god", but "To the gods of Asia. Europe, and Africa, gods unknown and foreign"' (*To Titus*, 1.12). Jerome may be right; but not everything that existed 2,000 years ago is still to be seen, or was to be seen in Jerome's time. In any case, the use made of the (supposed) inscription is the important matter.

An unknown god: the noun is masculine, but it is, surprisingly, taken up in neuter pronouns. **What . . . you worship in ignorance, that I proclaim to you.** *In ignorance* picks up *unknown* (in Greek the two words are cognate). *Ignorance* was characteristic of their worship. They were religious, but their religion was uninstructed. Paul was now proclaiming what they must know if their religion was to be real, even though much of the speech that follows contains material that would not have sounded strange to religious Athenians, and Paul, in this speech, never reaches what in his Gospel was (to the heathen world) totally unknown.

It is important not to give too heavy a theological treatment to Paul's (Luke's) sentence. The speaker is not dealing with the question of the knowability, or unknowability, of God. He is introducing a speech in which he hopes to build on what is already in his hearers' minds, and to add material that would give their natural religion a new direction and content.

24. Paul proceeds with a proposition familiar to Jews, and scarcely less familiar to Greeks. That God created the world is stated not only in Gen. 1.1, but, in varying degrees of explicitness, in many other passages, e.g. Exod. 20.11; Isa. 42.5; Wisd. 9.1, 9. This is taken up by Philo and Josephus. Plato's *Timaeus* is an account of creation very different from that of Genesis except in the notion of divine causation, and there are other references to creation in Greek literature. Cf. also 1 QH 1.13–15. In Acts 4.24 the language is even closer than the present passage to the language of the OT. As a universal Creator and Lord, God is not to be confined within a space circumscribed by human invention and manufacture. Cf. 7.48–50. Judaism used such polemic against heathen temples, but it is rightly observed that Luke does not present the Hellenistic Jewish argument that God can be known from creation; he is known only by the word, or Gospel; God's creatorship is known by faith.

25. It is ridiculous to suppose that God needs service by human hands. He made everything; how can he need anything? In addition to the original work of creation he continues to give **to all life and breath and all things**. *Life* and *breath* are hardly to be distinguished – they reinforce each other; *all things* is deliberately vague. There are many parallels to the verse, biblical, Jewish, non-Jewish. Isa. 42.5 is close, but Isaiah's *Spirit* is omitted because the Spirit is given not to all but to believers; *the people* (which suggests Israel) becomes *all*, and *all things* is added. Cf. Ps. 50.12f.; 2 Macc. 14.35; Tobit

7.17; 3 Macc. 2.9; Mt. 11.25 = Lk. 10.21. *Corpus Hermeticum* 5.10 is interesting: All things are in thee, all things come from thee; thou givest all things and receivest nothing.

26. He made of one origin every race of men. The word *origin* is an explanatory addition, interpreting Luke's *of one* with reference to the biblical account of one primal man and rejecting the reading of those MSS that add the word *blood*: *of one blood*, an alternative way of expressing the unity of the human race. The word *made* also calls for interpretation. It is probable that it is equivalent to *created* and not a modal verb to be taken with **to dwell** and *to seek* (v. 27). There is a further ambiguity in *every race of men*, which could be rendered *the whole race of men*. On this see below.

Men were thus made **to dwell upon the whole face of the earth**, and God **appointed fore-ordained seasons and the boundaries of their habitation**. The meaning of *seasons* and *boundaries* is disputed. The main possibilities are:

1. (a) God has ordained the various areas in which the races live, and the periods in history of their dominance.

   (b) As (a) but the periods are those not of history but of apocalyptic; that is, they belong to the future.
2. The areas are the different zones of the earth and the seasons are the seasons of the year.

This question is connected with that noted above: *every race of men* goes with 1 (a – less probably b); *the whole race of men* goes with 2. The parallel with 14.17 points to the meaning *seasons* (of the year). Passages from Qumran have been quoted on either side: in favour of 1(a), 1 QH 1.16f., in favour of 2, 1 QM 10.12–16. See also 1 QM 2.6–15; 1 QS, 1.14, 15. A clear-cut decision is scarcely possible; in any case, the point made is that all the affairs of men and nations are in God's hands.

27. The human race was disposed in areas of the earth's surface, and under climatic conditions, calculated to make human life possible, but physical existence was not the final purpose for which men were made. They were made (not in the sense of *compelled* – see v. 26) **with a view to their seeking God**. Seeking God is a theme of the OT (e.g. Isa. 51.1; 55.6.), where though it is to a great extent a matter of the will there is also an intellectual element, which was developed in Hellenistic Judaism (e.g. Philo, *On the Special Laws*, 1.36). The search for God is not an impossible one, though success is not certain. The next clause, **and perhaps by groping after him find him**, expresses confidence in the final *find*, but some uncertainty and doubt in the Greek construction, represented here by *perhaps*. God intends men to seek, and this implies an intention that they should find. The word *grope* is well illustrated by Homer, *Odyssey* 9.416, where the blinded Cyclops is described as 'groping with his hands' in search of Odysseus and his men. The transferred sense of the word does not imply a hopeless quest, and this is reinforced by the affirmation that God **is not far from each one of us**. That God *exists* in nearness refers here not to his presence with those who acknowledge him but to his nearness to all. This was a Stoic belief.

Commentators point out, correctly, the difference in emphasis between seeking and knowing God in the OT and in the Greek philosophers, the former stressing the moral and religious, the latter the intellectual element. It is however well to ask whether Luke had seen as clearly as modern students the difference between the biblical and the philosophical search. All used (more or less) the same words; must they not mean the same? To analyse the distinction too sharply may mean missing Luke's point.

28. For in him we live and move and are. *For* shows that this verse is intended to supply the basis for the statement in v. 27 that God is not far from each one of us. It is in him that we exist. The threefold assertion has a Stoic ring, for the Stoics connected life with movement and movement with being, but the formulation has no precedent and it may be due directly to Paul (Luke). It is true that the reference to *the poets* may refer backward as well as forward and some earlier poet may have coined the phrase, but there is no evidence to support this. In Luke's mind, *in him* must be understood, as v. 27c shows, in a personal, not a pantheistic sense; this modification of the Stoic view was probably already made in Hellenistic Judaism.

some of your own poets. The plural may conceal ignorance of the actual author, suggest that the words were written by more than one, or (this seems unlikely) be a conventional way of introducing a quotation. The words quoted – **We too are his family** – are found in Aratus, *Phaenomena* 5, as was already observed by Clement of Alexandria (*Stromateis* 1.19). There is a similar half-line in the Hymn to Zeus by Cleanthes. For Aratus, the words are pantheistic, and must be distinguished from superficially parallel Christian statements. There is no reference to regeneration but to a relationship which all human beings share as God's creatures. This is used in the attack on idolatry which continues in v. 29.

29. The argument runs back from human beings to **the divine being** (Luke uses a neuter word). Since we are the thinking and feeling persons that we are, we ought not to suppose that the divine being is made of metal or wood. We deny our own proper being if we identify our progenitor with material objects.

Idolatry was condemned by Jews and Christians, also by some pagan philosophers, though it seems that the general view was that actual identification of the image with the deity was too absurd to warrant discussion. For the prophetic attack on idolatry see Isa. 40.18–20 and many other passages, especially in Deutero-Isaiah and Jeremiah. Wisdom (especially 13.10–19) takes up the attack in Greek, as does Philo (e.g. *On the Decalogue*, 66). Among Gentile writers see e.g. Seneca *Epistle* 31.11; Lucretius, 1.63–80; Plutarch, *On Superstition* 6.

30. The necessity of repentance (v. 29) is clear. The divine, Paul has argued, must not be identified with material objects, but (according to Luke, v. 16) the Athenians were making this identification all over their city. This was due to ignorance, which perverts the piety that accompanies it into superstition. The story of Athens was the story of **the times of ignorance**. From nature the Greeks had evolved not natural theology but natural idolatry. God did not will or approve this ignorant idolatrous worship, but he did not suppress it; he **overlooked** it. It was not however his intention that men should continue in this ignorant idolatry; he has now issued his command **that they should all everywhere repent**.

The summons to repentance may be regarded as parallel to the manifestation of God's righteousness in Rom. 3.26. In each case there is an implicit charge that God's righteousness has been impugned; does he not care what his creatures do? There is no reference in this speech to the manifestation of God's saving righteousness in Christ. It is however important that the defect of Greek religion is seen to be not merely intellectual; man is guilty of having withdrawn from fellowship with his Creator. Repentance is called for as well as education.

31. The requirement of repentance is supported by the sanction of judgement. God has appointed **a day on which he will judge the whole world in righteousness**. He has also appointed the judge, **a man**. The Western text adds his name, *Jesus*, but this would never have been omitted had it stood in the original text. Both the use of the word *man* and the omission of the name are worth noting. Luke of course was aware that his readers would know to whom he was referring; he must have known that members of the Areopagus would not. Both the absence of the name (Paul does not tell the Areopagus that the world will be judged by an insignificant Jewish provincial) and the use of *man* have the effect of universalizing the thought of judgement, for though it goes too far to see in *man* a translation of the Aramaic *bar nasha'* (Son of man) it means that there is a representative man to whom God gave special status when **he raised him from the dead**. This act provides **proof** (elsewhere in the NT this word is translated *faith* but *proof* is a valid though unusual meaning) that the appointment has been made.

32. The speech is ended. The proclamation of the resurrection is in all senses the crucial point. Athenians, like the rest of mankind, will believe or mock. This is how Luke represents the matter. **When they heard of the resurrection of the dead some mocked**. 'There is no resurrection' is a proposition that can be quoted from many places in Greek literature. So some of Paul's hearers. Another group react differently: **We will hear you on this topic again**. Some take this to be the same reaction as that of the former group, but Luke is not setting out to describe the visit to Athens as total failure, great though the difficulties were. The Greek construction (*On the one hand . . . on the other*) is decisive. The two groups cannot be saying the same thing – not even the same thing in different words.

33. Paul went out of their midst. This (cf. v. 22) confirms that by *Areopagus* is meant a company of people, not a locality.

34. This verse agrees with v. 32: the work in Athens was difficult but not without fruit. There is no mention here of baptism, though there are believers. Dionysius the Areopagite is otherwise unknown. According to Dionysius, bishop of Corinth in the second century, the Areopagite was the first bishop of Athens (Eusebius, *HE* 3.4.10; 4.23.3). He was sometimes confused with Dionysius of Paris (*c.* AD 250) and with the author (Pseudo-Dionysius, *c.* AD 500) of a number of mystical writings.

46. PAUL AT CORINTH, WITH RETURN TO PALESTINE 18.1–23

[1] After these things Paul left Athens and came to Corinth, [2] and found a Jew, Aquila by name, of Pontus in origin, who had recently come from Italy, with Priscilla his wife, because Claudius had issued an edict that all the Jews should leave Rome. Paul approached them, [3] and because they were of the same trade he stayed with them and worked; for by trade they were tentmakers. [4] Every Sabbath he argued in the synagogue and sought to persuade Jews and Greeks; [5] but when Silas and Timothy came down from Macedonia Paul was constrained by the word, testifying to the Jews that the Christ was Jesus. [6] When they opposed him and blasphemed Paul shook out his clothes and said to them, 'Your blood be upon your own heads; I am clean. Henceforth I shall go to the Gentiles.' [7] He moved away from there and entered the house of Titius Justus, one who reverenced God, whose house was adjacent to the synagogue. [8] But Crispus, the Archisynagogue, became a believer in the Lord, with all his household, and many of the Corinthians when they heard this believed and were baptized. [9] In the night the Lord said to Paul in a vision, 'Do not be afraid but continue to speak and do not fall silent; [10] for I am with you and no one will set upon you so as to harm you, for I have a people, a large people, in this city.' [11] He stayed a year and six months teaching the word of God among them.

[12] When Gallio was proconsul of Achaea the Jews with one accord set upon Paul and brought him to the place of judgement, [13] saying, 'This man is persuading people to worship God in a manner contrary to the law.' [14] As Paul was about to open his mouth, Gallio said to the Jews, 'If there had been some matter of injury or wicked deceit, you Jews, I should of course have been forbearing with you; [15] but if they are disputes about talk and words and the law that you observe, you will have to see to it yourselves; I have no wish to be a judge of these things.' [16] And he drove them from the place of judgement. [17] They all took hold of Sosthenes the Archisynagogue and beat him before the place of judgement; and none of these things troubled Gallio.

[18] Paul stayed on a number of days, took his leave, and sailed away to Syria. With him were Priscilla and Aquila. He had shaved

**his head in Cenchreae, for he had a vow. [19] They reached Ephesus
and there he left them; he himself went into the synagogue and
argued with the Jews. [20] When they asked him to stay a longer
time he did not consent, [21] but took his leave with the words, 'I
will come back to you, God willing.' Then he set sail from Ephesus
[22] and landed at Caesarea. He went up and greeted the church
and came down to Antioch.**

**[23] Having spent some time there he left, passing through, in
order, the Galatian territory and Phrygia, strengthening all the
disciples.**

This paragraph unites a number of Lucan themes. Paul continues his travels and visits two notable cities: Corinth and Ephesus, which are to become important Christian centres. He is assisted by colleagues, including new ones. There are contacts with secular history which make it possible to establish dates. There is opposition from Jews, and fair dealing from Roman authorities. Notwithstanding Jewish opposition, Paul himself behaves as a Jew, taking a vow.

All this Luke will have enjoyed writing. Every piece contributes to the picture of Paul that he wished to convey. There is no first person plural in this section (see on 16.10), but it does not follow that the section contains nothing but Luke's invention. Of some matters there is confirmation in the epistles, and the expulsion of the Jews from Rome and the proconsulship of Gallio are confirmed in secular history. It is probable that Luke wrote the whole in the form in which we read it, but many concrete details, showing no special Lucan interest, make it probable that he is drawing on some kind of Paul-source. The name, for example, of Titius Justus (v. 7) serves no special purpose, and Luke would have gained nothing by inventing it. But the whole section shows Lucan editorial management; Luke wrote up in his best style pieces of information, some derived from the Pauline circle and some, perhaps, collected in Corinth.

Two important historical questions arise, the first out of the reference to the expulsion of the Jews from Rome. See on v. 2; if the view of the date rejected there is accepted, Pauline chronology as a whole is affected.

The second question arises at the end of the paragraph. Paul's vow (if it was not Aquila's – see the note on v. 18) fits into Luke's picture of Paul as a good Jew; but is it credible? It is hardly covered by 1 Cor. 9.20. And why did Paul make this journey to the East, on which nothing happens east of Ephesus, and Jerusalem is not mentioned? It is possible that Luke felt it necessary both for Paul to secure a foothold in Ephesus (vv. 19–21) and to leave clear a period when Priscilla and Aquila were in charge. Or it may be that Paul, having heard of the threatened destruction of his work in Galatia by men who, rightly or wrongly, assumed the support of Jerusalem, hurried back to find out what was going on, and then returned through Galatian territory and Phrygia (v. 23) to put things right.

1. After these things, that is, at the end of the Athenian episode. **Paul . . . came to Corinth.** For some account of Corinth see *1 Corinthians* 1–3. *2 Corinthians* 1, 2; but especially Murphy-O'Connor, *St Paul's Corinth*. Old Corinth had been wealthy and influential but came to an end in 146 BC, when the Consul Lucius Mummius, after the battle of Leucopetra, killed the citizens or sold them into slavery, and levelled the city with the ground. After 100 years of desolation, Julius Caesar refounded the city as a colony (*Colonia Laus Julia Corinthiensis*). Its natural advantages enabled it to regain its prosperity; it probably did little to shake off the reputation for immorality that the old city had acquired.

2. Paul **found a Jew**, **Aquila by name**, probably already a Christian since it is not said that he was converted by Paul. It was surprisingly good fortune to find (a search is not implied) one who was a Jew, a fellow-tradesman, and a Christian. For Jews in Corinth see *NS* 3.64–66. For Aquila see Acts 18.18, 26; Rom. 16.3; 1 Cor. 16.19; 2 Tim. 4.19. He **had recently come from Italy**, but came originally from **Pontus** (see 2.9). He had come with his wife, **Priscilla** (in the epistles Prisca). Aquila is never mentioned without her, and it is clear that she was an outstanding person in her own right. The two had come to Corinth **because Claudius had issued an edict that all the Jews should leave Rome**. Aquila cannot have been a Roman citizen; the edict would not apply to citizens. The edict of expulsion is confirmed by Suetonius, *Claudius* 25: He expelled from Rome the Jews who were constantly rioting at the instigation of Chrestus. (One plausible guess is that *Chrestus* is a corruption of *Christus* and that the Jewish community in Rome had become intolerably agitated through Christian preaching.) Suetonius does not date this event. Orosius (fifth century) says that a passage in Josephus dates it in AD 49. The passage cannot be found in the extant works of Josephus but the date is probably correct, though there is evidence (in Cassius Dio) that Claudius took action (but not expulsion) against the Jews in

AD 41. **Paul approached them** – because they were Jews, because they were Christians, in the hope of earning a living at his trade? We do not know; possibly for all three reasons.

3. they were, Paul and Aquila, though Aquila and Priscilla have been suggested. **tentmakers**. This is the etymological rendering of Luke's word, and there is no reason why it should not be accepted, though some prefer *leather-worker*. An inscription bears witness to the existence in Rome of a corporation of tentmakers. **he stayed with them**; perhaps *lodged with them*. According to Rom. 16.3–5; 1 Cor. 16.19 there was a church at their house and all Gentile Christians had reason to be grateful to them. It is probable that they were wealthy and entertained not only Paul but other Christians also. Paul's readiness to work to support himself was a theme important to Luke, both in itself and as an example to future ministers (20.34, 35).

4. he argued in the synagogue. Cf. 17.17. A fragmentary inscription bears witness to a *synagogue of the Hebrews* in Corinth (see *Background* 53). **Every Sabbath**. The weekly service provided a ready-made congregation; if Paul was not invited to preach he could at least converse with those present. **Jews and Greeks**. The latter were presumably Gentiles who attended the synagogue. Paul turns decisively to the Gentiles at v. 6.

5. when Silas and Timothy came down from Macedonia. They had been left in Beroea with instructions to join Paul as soon as possible (17.14, 15). It was now according to Acts that they did so. But 1 Thessalonians (see 1.1; 3.2, 6) suggests that at least one of them had been with Paul in Athens. This can be fitted in only by telling a much more complicated story than Luke's. He may not have known the full story, or have deliberately simplified it.

Paul **was constrained by the word**, which is treated almost as a personal agent. A variant, *by the Spirit*, is probably a simplification. Another possible translation is *confined himself to the word*; Silas and Timothy could earn enough for three so that there was no need for Paul to spend time in tentmaking. **that the Christ** – the Jews knew that there would be a Messiah – **was Jesus**. Cf. 2.36.

6. When they ... blasphemed. The word could mean *reviled* (Paul), but the context suggests that they were rejecting the claim made by Paul (v. 5).

Paul shook out his clothes. The same word (*shook*) is used at 13.51, but of shaking the dust from one's feet. It is clear at least that Paul is breaking off relations with the Jews against whom he performs this symbolic act. **Your blood be upon your own heads**: You, not I, will be responsible for the loss you suffer in rejecting the Gospel. **I am clean. Henceforth I shall go to the Gentiles.** This could be translated, *Clean, I shall go to the Gentiles.* The alternative, though possible, would not be Lucan in style. Cf. 13.46; 28.28. Luke evidently thinks of this as a frequently repeated pattern, not as a once-for-all event.

7. He moved away from there, that is, from the synagogue, though the Western text takes it to mean from Aquila (no longer lodged with him). Some think that Luke was concealing, at least not publishing the fact, that Paul was expelled from the synagogue. The new host of Paul's preaching and teaching is **Titius Justis** (other forms of the name appear in various MSS). The Latin use of *nomen* and *cognomen* is correct but there is no *praenomen*. He was **one who reverenced God**; see 10.2. His **house was adjacent to the synagogue**. This may have been convenient but would be unlikely to promote good relations.

8. Crispus; cf. 1 Cor. 1.14. As **Archisynagogue** (see 13.15) he was a notable convert but was evidently unable to take all his people with him. He was, however, accompanied by **all his household**; for the expression, and the question whether Luke intended the reader to understand that little children and infants were included, see on 16.15, 31–3. It is not said here that *all the household* (or *Crispus* himself) were baptized, but that they believed. Many others followed (Stephanas and his household had preceded – 1 Cor. 16.15). Luke says, **Many of the Corinthians believed . . . and were baptized**, presumably both Jews and Gentiles.

9. In the night the Lord said to Paul in a vision. The message of encouragement stands at this point to mark the transition from work in the synagogue to unrestricted mission to Gentiles (v. 6) and to prepare for the attack of v. 12. The Jews may be unbelieving, but there will be others. **Do not be afraid**. Cf. Deut. 31.6; Josh. 1.6, 9; Isa. 41.10; Jer. 1.8. **continue to speak and do not fall silent**. The translation represents the forms of the Greek verbs used.

10. Paul is to continue to speak fearlessly **for I am with you**. There are similar promises in the OT; cf. e.g. Exod. 3.12; Isa. 43.5. A second ground for courage is that, as will appear, there are in Corinth many who are, potentially and by predestination (cf. 13.48), God's people.

11. a year and six months. For the dating of Paul's work in Corinth see on vv. 2 and 12. It seems to be implied that at least the greater part of the eighteen months fell before the attempt to bring Paul before Gallio. The *days* of v. 18 are probably additional. **teaching the word of God** must as v. 13 shows include mission preaching. *The word of God* is one of Luke's usual terms for the content of the Christian message.

12. When Gallio was proconsul of Achaea. Achaea had been a senatorial province since 27 BC and was therefore governed by a proconsul. *Gallio* was originally L. Annaeus Novatus, brother of the writer and philosopher Seneca, but he was adopted by Junius Gallio, and became L. Junius Gallio Annaeanus. The date of his proconsulship in Achaea is given by an inscription (see *Background* 51f.) which is dated by a reference to the 26th acclamation of Claudius. This fell probably between 25 January and 1 August AD 52 (possibly at the end of the previous year). This means that Gallio became proconsul in 51 (summer) or possibly in 50 if, as was less usual, he held office for two years. Paul had probably, not certainly, already spent nearly 18 months in Corinth (see on v. 11). It is a reasonable guess (little more) that Paul's opponents would take an early opportunity of winning the new proconsul to their side. It is consequently reasonable to suggest that Paul appeared before Gallio in the Autumn – say, September – of AD 51. This would mean, if we may trust Acts, that he arrived in the Spring – say, March – of the year 50; see *Romans* 4f. These dates are consistent with v. 2, if we may accept (see the note) 49 as the date of Claudius' expulsion of the Jews.

the Jews . . . brought him to the place of judgement. The *place of judgement* is determined by the presence of the judge, not topographically. This means that we cannot identify the place in Corinth to which Paul was brought.

The crime of which Paul was accused was not one (as we might say) on the statute book. The case was *extra ordinem*, a (technically) extraordinary one.

13. to worship God in a manner contrary to the law. What law? Roman or Jewish? Gallio (v. 15) takes it to be Jewish law, which as proconsul he has no intention of enforcing within a Roman colony, in which only Roman law would be recognized. This may have been a misinterpretation, possibly a deliberate misinterpretation. The Jews may have thought that the best way of attacking Paul was to accuse him of commending a religion that Romans could not legally adopt (cf. 16.21; 17.7). This might have been a dangerous though not a legally sound charge, for at this period proselytism and circumcision (though the latter was frowned upon) were not strictly contrary to law and did not become so till the time of Domitian (emperor AD 81–96). This was probably (see Introduction, p. xxv) the time at which Luke was writing, and later conditions may have coloured his story.

14. Paul is prepared to offer a defence but Gallio cuts him short and dismisses the case. He decides that no **injury** has been inflicted or **wicked deceit** practised. **I should . . . have been forbearing with you**, presumably, that is, I should have listened to your accusation. **If there had been** . . . This, in the Greek construction, is an unfulfilled condition. Contrast v. 15.

15. if they are disputes about talk and words . . . This is an open condition, and Gallio implies that it represents the truth. **the law that you**, not Romans, **observe**. See on v. 13. The Jews must see to such things. They had of course courts of their own for this purpose.

16. Gallio had no patience with the Jews. If Luke's account is correct he judged that they were wasting the time of his court; either the charge was irrelevant (a matter of Jewish theology) or there was not even *prima facie* evidence that Paul constituted a danger to the Empire. Either way, the precedent was a useful one for Christian apologists.

17. They all took hold of Sosthenes. Who **beat** Sosthenes? According to the Western text, *all the Greeks*. This is probably correct interpretation. Jews were often unpopular; they were for the moment out of favour and it would be safe to attack one of them. But it may be that *they all* is to be interpreted by *them* in v. 16: the Jews beat Sosthenes for mismanaging the case against Paul. Or *all* may be *all*: the Jews beat him for inefficiency, the Greeks on general principles. There is a Sosthenes at 1 Cor. 1.1, but the name was a common one. Sosthenes may have succeeded Crispus, or the synagogue may have had more than one archisynagogue.

none of these things troubled Gallio or, *Gallio cared for none of these things*. He evidently thought that public order was not threatened and that it would do no harm if some angry people vented their wrath on a Jew.

18. Paul stayed on a number of days. This suggests a relatively short addition to the 18 months of v. 11. He **sailed away to Syria**. This is often thought of as the end of Paul's Second Journey. So little happens between this point and his return to Ephesus from the East that some prefer to speak not of Second and Third Journeys but of only one journey. It is a matter of words.

Paul was accompanied by **Priscilla and Aquila**. The couple travelled widely.

He had shaved his head in Cenchreae, for he had a vow. Paul or Aquila? Aquila is the grammatical antecedent, but Paul is the main character in the story, and is the subject of the next verb (in v. 19). Other questions arise. Why should either man take a vow? What sort of vow was it? The Nazirite vow meant cutting the hair at the end of the period of the vow; the suggestion that it was customary to cut it at the beginning and then let it grow till the end is unsupported by evidence. Vows were sometimes taken before a difficult and dangerous undertaking; this might be connected with the vision of v. 9 or the appearance before Gallio; but Luke does not say so. It has been suggested that it is part of Luke's (unhistorical) presentation of Paul as a good Jew; but Luke makes nothing of it, and Paul had no particular occasion to make himself a Jew to the Jews (1 Cor. 9.20) in this way. Accordingly some suggest that the vow was not a Jewish vow but a natural Greek reaction to a message received in a dream or vision; but that Paul should be willing to be a heathen to the heathen seems even less likely than that he was becoming a Jew to the Jews. If we ascribe the vow to Aquila we avoid some difficulties for the simple reason that we know less about Aquila. One can only guess that Luke found something about a vow in the itinerary he was following and reproduced it.

For **Cenchreae** see Rom. 16.1. It was the eastern port of Corinth (the western was Lechaeum), situated on the Saronic Gulf and the natural port of embarkation for eastward voyages.

19. Ephesus, mentioned now for the first time, was missed, with the whole of Asia (16.6), on the outward journey. It was the chief city of Asia, the residence of the governor. It lay at the mouth of the Cayster, a city of great size and importance, commercially and culturally. The temple of Artemis was the greatest of the seven wonders of the word. See further on 19.1.

Paul **went into the synagogue and argued with the Jews**. No synagogue has been excavated in Ephesus, but it is unthinkable that so large and important a city did not have a community of Jews. *Argued*, not *preached*; perhaps no opportunity was given. Cf. 17.2.

20. Paul was welcomed, but did not agree to stay. He had other plans; see vv. 21–23.

21. Paul promised to return and was soon back in Ephesus; 19.1.

God willing is a pious formula, with pagan as well as Jewish parallels. The thought is Pauline: 1 Cor. 4.19; 16.7; cf. Heb. 6.3; James 4.15; also e.g. Plato, Epictetus.

This verse contains a major Western addition. Paul explains his early departure with the words, *I must at all costs keep the coming feast day in Jerusalem.* Cf. 20.16. If the words are original, and if Paul left Corinth not long after September (v. 12), he may have been thinking of the Day of Atonement (though this was a fast, not a feast) or of Tabernacles. More probably the Western editor thought it necessary to give a reason for Paul's hurried departure – it did not occur to him to add explicitly that Paul did visit Jerusalem. Did Paul feel strongly about the Jewish calendar? See on 20.16, and cf. Gal. 4.10.

22. Paul **landed at Caesarea**, which is not in Syria (v. 18), but in Judaea. Luke may not have been clear about the geography; the ship may have been compelled by northerly winds to pass by Antioch (where Paul spent some time on the return journey). He may have intended to visit Jerusalem, if not for a feast (v. 21) for some other reason (see below). For Caesarea see on 8.40. **He went up and greeted the church.** It is natural to think of the church in Caesarea. But *to go up* was often used of a visit to a capital, and *the church* was sometimes used for the (mother) church of Jerusalem. It may be that a visit to Jerusalem took place. That the name *Jerusalem* is not mentioned is of course most easily explained if Paul did not go there. But it is not unreasonable to suggest that Paul paid a flying visit to find out what support the trouble-makers in Galatia and Corinth had, and if possible to stop the trouble at its source. The same interest would determine his route in v. 23. This would explain his haste, and might also explain Luke's silence.

For **Antioch** see on 11.19. Here too there may have been trouble to deal with; see Gal. 2.11–14.

23. passing through, in order, the Galatian territory and Phrygia. Cf. 16.6, where the order of places is reversed. Here the phrase *in order* makes it almost necessary to take *Galatian territory* and *Phrygia* as two distinct areas. See 19.1 for Paul's route to Ephesus. Paul's aim, as he passed on his way, was to strengthen **the disciples** in their faith. The suggestion that in these parts there were *disciples* but no churches (the word is not used) makes nonsense of Luke's understanding of discipleship.

XII

THE MISSION BASED ON EPHESUS (18.24 – 20.38)

47. APOLLOS AND THE TWELVE DISCIPLES 18.24 – 19.7

[24] A certain Jew, Apollos by name, an Alexandrian in origin, an eloquent man, arrived in Ephesus. He was powerful in the Scriptures. [25] He had been instructed in the way of the Lord and was fervent in the Spirit as he spoke and taught accurately the things concerning Jesus, though he knew only John's baptism. [26] He began to speak boldly in the synagogue. When Priscilla and Aquila heard him they took him in, and expounded the way of God to him more accurately. [27] When he wished to pass on to Achaea the brothers encouraged him and wrote to the disciples that they should welcome him. When he arrived he supported those who through grace had become believers, [28] for he vigorously debated with the Jews, showing publicly through the Scriptures that the Christ was Jesus.

[1] It was while Apollos was in Corinth that Paul passed through the hill country of the hinterland and came down to Ephesus, where he found certain disciples. [2] He said to them, 'Did you receive the Holy Spirit when you became believers?' They said to him, 'We did not hear if there is a Holy Spirit.' [3] He said, 'Into what then were you baptized?' They said, 'Into John's baptism.' [4] Paul said, 'John baptized with a baptism of repentance, telling the people that they should believe in the one who was coming after him, that is, in Jesus.' [5] When they heard this they were baptized into the name of the Lord Jesus, [6] and when Paul laid his hands upon them the Holy Spirit came upon them, and they spoke with tongues and prophesied. [7] The total number of the men was about twelve.

It would be easy to make out of what is here treated as a single paragraph two distinct paragraphs, one about Apollos (18.24–28) and one about a group of disciples (19.1–7); easy, but misleading, for the most difficult problems and the most important observations would be missed. Each, taken on its own, seems to make reasonable sense, but it is impossible to read either 'on its own', and it may be assumed that Luke intended each to be read in the light of the other. When they are so read a parallel and a difference immediately stand out. In the first we meet a man who has received John's baptism and no other; he is given some instruction and then is not merely received into the church but continues a preaching activity he has already begun. In the second, there are (about) twelve who are in the same position; they must receive a new baptism and the imposition of hands before they take part in Christian activities. Why was Apollos treated differently? Because he was already *fervent in the Spirit*? What instruction did Priscilla and Aquila give him? The twelve were *disciples*, a word which in Acts almost if not quite always means Christian disciples. Were they only disciples of John? How could it be that they had never heard of the Holy Spirit?

The two paragraphs are united by two themes, the work of John the Baptist, and the Holy Spirit, inadequate and adequate marks respectively of the Christian faith. There is evidence for the continued existence of groups of disciples of John after their master's death. They must, if they wished to become Christians, have presented a problem to the church. What was to be done with them? It is probable that different answers to the problem were given and that the two fundamental ones are reflected in our paragraph. Some would hold: All that they need is to be instructed more fully in what Christians believe about Christ. Others would take the view that they were essentially like other unbaptized unbelievers and must enter the church through the only door universally recognized. Luke can hardly be supposed to have put the two stories together in order that his readers might be informed about diverse attitudes to the disciples of John in the first century. He probably collected both in Ephesus and used them to show Paul in a new role, as one who brings together Christians of different origins.

Some discussions of this paragraph are vitiated by the assumption that Luke rigidly assumed the necessity of ecclesiastical regulations, including the requirement of baptism. This was not so. See Introduction, pp. lx–lxii.

24. The new paragraph assumes the existence of a church in **Ephesus**. It can hardly have been founded by Paul in the few days that he had spent there; possibly by Priscilla and Aquila (18.19f.). **Apollos** (some MSS have other forms of the name) came there. He is almost certainly the Apollos of 1 Cor. 1.12; in this epistle he is a colleague of Paul's. He was a **Jew, Alexandrian in origin** (for the expression; cf. 18.2). The name Apollos is scarcely known elsewhere. He was moreover **eloquent** (Luke's word could be translated *learned*, but at this time education was to a great extent education in rhetoric) and **powerful in the Scriptures**, in his understanding of them and in his application of them in preaching and debate.

25. Apollos **had been instructed in the way of the Lord**. The most natural way of understanding these words is that Apollos was an instructed Christian. For Christianity as *the Way* see on 9.2. It is most improbable that the Essene way is intended. He was also **fervent in the Spirit** (it is possible that the meaning is *fervent in spirit*, that is, enthusiastic), and **taught accurately the things concerning Jesus**. Cf. 28.31. So far it appears that Apollos was an inspired and accurate Christian teacher. Yet he had not received Christian baptism; only that of John. This might mean that he had been baptized by John himself in Jordan, or that he belonged to one of the groups of followers of John who seem to have persisted long after John's death.

The questions that arise out of the text are clear. Was Apollos a Christian? If he was, how had he escaped baptism? If he was not, why was he not baptized now? The questions are not answered here, or in v. 26.

26. to speak boldly is the mark of one who is *fervent in the Spirit*. Apollos was already a teacher (v. 25); v. 26 means that **he began** to practise his teaching in the Ephesus synagogue, not that he began to do what he had done nowhere before. Could this mean, could it in an earlier form of the story have meant, that he was a Jewish, not a Christian preacher?

Priscilla and Aquila heard him and were favourably impressed, but concluded that though he already *taught accurately the things concerning Jesus* (v. 25) he needed further instruction in **the way of God**. If v. 25 had referred to *the way of God* and v. 26 to the way of the Lord it would have been natural to think that Apollos had been at first a Jewish preacher turned into a Christian preacher by Priscilla and Aquila. But this (though it might be true) is not what Luke says.

Perhaps the point is that Apollos is (nearly) sound doctrinally and may therefore be accepted forthwith, whereas the disciples (19.2) were ignorant of a fundamental element of Christian theology and therefore needed to begin from the beginning, with baptism.

27. Apollos **wished to pass on to Achaea**. For *Achaea* see on 18.12. We know (1 Cor. 3.5, etc.) that Apollos worked in Corinth. We do not know why he wished to go to Achaea, nor do we know whether he intended to travel by sea, sailing across the Aegean, or to make the long land journey through Macedonia. **the brothers** (for this designation of Christians see 1.15 and many other passages) **encouraged him and wrote to the disciples**. This was a commendatory letter; cf. 2 Cor. 3.1; Rom. 16.1; Col. 4.10. Luke's words could mean that the Ephesian Christians encouraged their Achaean brothers to welcome Apollos, but this is less probable.

Having arrived in Achaea (one may guess at Corinth, but other Achaean towns cannot be excluded) Apollos gave support to **those who through grace had become believers**. Cf. 15.11; that they became believers was due only to the grace of God. Luke does not develop the theme of grace as Paul does, but makes it clear that faith comes through divine not human initiative. It would be possible to take *through grace* with *gave support* (*he supported them through grace*) but it seems better to take the adverbial phrase with the nearer verb.

At this point the Western text differs sharply from the text translated here. Codex Bezae runs as follows.

> When some Corinthians who were residing in Ephesus heard him speak they asked him to cross over with them to their country. When he agreed to do so the Ephesians wrote to the disciples in Corinth [asking] that they would welcome the man. When he took up residence in Achaea he gave much help in the churches through grace, for he vigorously debated with the Jews . . .

This may be pure fancy, but it is not impossible that the Western editor knew traditions still in his time current in Corinth.

28. Apollos **debated with the Jews vigorously** and **publicly**. The debate naturally took the form of a scriptural demonstration **that the Christ was Jesus**. Jews and Christians agreed that there was, or was to be, a Christ. Christians asserted that this Christ was to be found in Jesus. Luke finds it unnecessary to specify the Scriptures used.

There are further Western variants, probably bearing witness to a time when it was felt that the wording of Acts could be handled with some freedom.

1. Apollos had gone to Achaea (18.27); it is not surprising (especially with 1 Corinthians in mind) that he should find himself in the largest city of Achaea, **Corinth**. At this time, **Paul passed through** (possibly preaching as he went; cf. 13.6) **the hill country of the hinterland and came down to Ephesus**. Literally, *Paul passed through the upper regions*. The precise meaning of this phrase is not clear. The adjective is rare, and is not used elsewhere as a geographical term. It may refer literally to *hill country* or to the *hinterland* (here, of Ephesus). Paul was said at 18.23 to be passing through *the Galatian territory and Phrygia*; the present verse takes up the same journey and presumably refers either to the same territory or, more probably, to the country between Phrygia and Ephesus. Paul was personally unknown to the churches of Colossae and Laodicea (Col. 2.1) and therefore probably did not use the route that follows (more or less) the line of the Maeander but a more northerly one. The route through the valley of the Cayster was shorter and would also make possible the use of *upper regions* in both available senses: the hinterland was elevated.

So **Paul . . . came down to Ephesus**. When Rome took over the kingdom of Attalus III in 133 BC Ephesus was already a large and notable city. It continued to expand in wealth and architectural splendour and was the residence of the proconsular rulers of Asia. Further points will be noted below (pp. 291, 296). In Ephesus Paul **found certain disciples**. One would expect *disciples* in Luke's narrative to be Christians, but the ensuing narrative raises difficulties about this. See below.

2. Paul asks the disciples, **'Did you receive the Holy Spirit when you became believers?'** It is not clear why Paul should immediately ask this question, and the disciples' reply is surprising. **'We did not hear if there is a Holy Spirit.'** Is it conceivable that Christian disciples should have said this? Is it conceivable that disciples of John the Baptist should have said it? Jesus had promised that the disciples would be baptized with the Holy Spirit (1.5; 11.16), and John had foretold this (Lk. 3.16). Readers of the OT must have been aware of the existence of the Spirit. A variant (. . . *that any receive the Holy Spirit*) is clearly a secondary 'improvement' of the text. One suggestion is that the words mean, 'We did not *at our baptism*

(John's) hear whether there is a Holy Spirit – it spoke of nothing but repentance and forgiveness.' In any case, these disciples could not have been teaching accurately the things concerning Jesus, as Apollos did. Their *doctrine* was defective; this was where they differed from him. See 18.26, above.

3. The disciples' strange reply leads to a further question. **'Into what then were you baptized?'** This (with the answer) is not Luke's usual use of *into*. The meaning however of both question and answer is clear. But if they were Christian disciples why had they not received Christian baptism? One suggestion is that they were disciples whom Apollos (see 18.24–28) had taught; he knew the facts about Jesus but only John's baptism.

4. One might have expected Paul to reply to the disciples, John's baptism was a baptism with water; the new baptism, foretold by John and now given in the name of Jesus, is a baptism with the Holy Spirit. Instead he takes up another part of John's prediction. John foretold **one who was coming after him . . . Jesus**.

The last words of the verse may be read in different ways: either, the Coming one, that is, as you, being Christians though unbaptized, know, Jesus; or, the Coming One, who, I now inform you disciples of John, is to be identified with Jesus, in whom you should now believe.

5. They were baptized into the name of the Lord Jesus. We now have the usual *into the name*; on this see pp. 38f. and Introduction, pp. lx–lxii. Some think that passive verb (*they were baptized*) implies that Paul, though he laid hands upon them, did not himself baptize the disciples: a possible but not a necessary inference. Barth (*CD* 4.4.62, 75) thought that *when they heard* and *they were baptized* applied to the crowds that heard John; *they* were baptized in that baptism into the name of Jesus, and therefore, like Apollos, received no further baptism. It seems very improbable that Luke intended this.

6. the Holy Spirit came upon them when Paul laid hands upon them. For the relation between baptism, the laying on of hands, and the gift of the Spirit see on 8.17, also Introduction, pp. lx–lxii. The story of Apollos is sufficient to show that Luke required no rigid sequence of events. **they spoke with tongues and prophesied**. See on 2.4. For Luke this was the clearest indication that the Spirit was at work. Cf. 10.46. Whether the Paul who wrote 1 Corinthians would have been satisfied with this outcome of his work is another matter.

7. Luke is interested in numbers, and likes to give them. He is also aware that he can as a rule give only approximations, and indicates this by the use of **about**. This also shows the improbability of the view that Luke was thinking of an Ephesian 'Twelve' in any way parallel to the Twelve (apostles) of Jerusalem.

48. PAUL'S SUCCESSFUL MINISTRY AT EPHESUS 19.8–20

[8] Paul went into the synagogue and spoke boldly, for three months arguing and persuading about the kingdom of God. [9] But when some grew hard and disbelieved, and spoke evil of the Way, in the hearing of the populace, he separated from them and withdrew the disciples, arguing daily in the school of Tyrannus. [10] This lasted for two years, with the result that all who lived in the province of Asia heard the word of the Lord, both Jews and Greeks. [11] God performed no common works of power by Paul's hands, [12] so that sweatbands and sweatcloths were carried from contact with his skin to the sick, and their diseases left them and the evil spirits went out.

[13] Some of the itinerant Jewish exorcists set about naming the name of the Lord Jesus over those who had evil spirits, saying, 'I adjure you by Jesus whom Paul preaches.' [14] There were seven sons of a certain Sceva, a Jew, a chief priest, doing this. [15] But the evil spirit answered them, 'I know Jesus and I am acquainted with Paul, but who are you?' [16] and the man in whom the evil spirit was leapt upon them, overpowered them all, and mastered them, so that they fled from the house naked and wounded. [17] This became known to all, both Jews and Greeks, who lived in Ephesus; fear fell upon them all, and the name of the Lord Jesus was magnified. [18] Many of those who had believed would come, confessing [their sins] and disclosing their magical practices. [19] A good many of those who practised magic gathered their books together and burned them in the presence of all. They counted up the prices [of the books] and found that they came to 50,000 silver [drachmae] [20] Thus the word of the Lord grew mightily and prevailed.

The first part of this paragraph (vv. 8–10) describes in summary form Paul's two-year ministry in Ephesus. It follows the usual pattern. Paul begins in the synagogue and is able to continue there for three months before he is obliged to move to a non-Jewish site. The result of his unusually long period of teaching in the city is the dissemination of his message through the whole of Asia. All this could be the entry under 'Ephesus' in a Pauline itinerary. Verse 8 reproduces words used in 18.19; it is possible that all the intervening material was introduced by Luke into the itinerary from other sources. The outline of vv. 8–10 raises no serious historical problems. The rest of this section (together with 19.21–40) is best understood as consisting of local traditions picked up by Luke in Ephesus. Their historical value is uneven. Ephesus was a great centre of magical practices and it is not surprising that Paul should leave the impression of an opponent of magic. This is expressed in various ways – by his appearance as a more striking wonder-worker than his rivals (vv. 11, 12), as one who discomfited the professional exorcists (vv. 13–17), and as one who banished magic from the city (vv. 18, 19). The paragraph is wound up with a Lucan summary (v. 20).

8. Paul went into the synagogue. Cf. 18.19. There is no reference here to a previous visit to the synagogue, to Apollos, or to the disciples of 19.1–7. The present verse could be describing the beginning of Paul's work in Ephesus. For Jews in Ephesus see *NS* 3.22, 23, 28, 122, 123. For the surprising lack of evidence of a synagogue community see on 18.19. **for three months**. After this Paul remained in Ephesus for a further two years (v. 10), and the whole period is summed up at 20.31 as three years (counting inclusively). Three months was a long time for Paul to be tolerated in a synagogue. **arguing and persuading** suggest reasoned debate; **spoke boldly** may, but need not, mean inspired speech. **the kingdom of God** is a term Luke uses in Acts as a summary of the Gospel preached by the apostles and others; see for example 20.25.

9. some grew hard, hardened their hearts against Paul and his message. Cf. Exod. 7.3; Rom. 9.18; also Acts 13.48, but Luke will have been more inclined to blame the recalcitrant synagogue members than the divine decree. For **the Way** as a term for Christianity see on 9.2. To whom did the opponents speak **evil**? Luke's word may be taken to mean (a) the Christians in the synagogue, with a view to making them give up their faith; (b) the synagogue community as a whole, so as to bring about the expulsion or punishment of the Christians; (c) the general public, persuading them not to become Christians and perhaps to persecute those who were. **the populace** is perhaps the best choice.

Paul in response **separated from them and withdrew the disciples. the school of Tyrannus.** The name is not uncommon in inscriptions at Ephesus. The Greek word *scholē* most often refers to people, but must here mean a *building*, in which instruction was given. *Tyrannus* may have been a philosopher, otherwise unknown, or the owner of the building. Paul taught here **daily** – perhaps more frequently than the synagogue would have been available. At the end of the verse Codex Bezae adds *from the fifth hour to the tenth* – possibly the siesta hours when the room would normally not be in use.

10. This lasted for two years. See v. 8; 20.31. The dates are probably between Autumn 52 and Spring 55.

In this period **all who lived in the province of Asia** (see 16.6) **heard the word of the Lord**, spreading outward from the chief city. It is not said that Paul himself proclaimed the word everywhere. For example, he had not himself evangelized Colossae (Col. 1.7; 2.1). Revelation 2 and 3 are good evidence for the existence of churches in a number of the main cities. No doubt Luke knew that Asia was one of the earliest and most successful mission fields, and that the churches included **both Jews and Greeks**.

11. The preaching of the word of the Lord was accompanied, as often in Acts, by **works of power** (the words *sign* and *portent* are not used after 15.10). It was God who performed them **by** (or through) **Paul's hands**.

12. sweatbands and sweatcloths. Precise definitions are not easy to find. Probably both were sweatrags, the former worn on the head to prevent sweat from running into the eyes, the latter carried in the hand for general mopping up. It seems important that they should have been in contact with Paul's skin. Physical contact between the healer and the sick person is a common feature of miracle stories; the wonder is heightened here in that the contact is indirect. It is customary to point out the parallel with the effect of Peter's shadow (5.15f.). The parallel is valid, but it is doubtful whether Luke went out of his way to draw up a precise but varied balance between Peter and Paul. He was probably more concerned to show that Paul could beat the Ephesian magicians at their own game. This theme continues in the following verses.

13. Paul's success as healer and exorcist prompted imitation. For Jewish exorcists see *NS* 3.342–79. Solomon's legendary powers as exorcist were believed to have been transmitted, through incantations and formulas, to first-century exorcists. For the use outside orthodox Christian circles of the name of Jesus see Mk 9.38–41. That it continued is shown by Rabbinic disapproval of the practice. The story that follows, in which *the name* has anything but the desired effect, Luke could take as confirming his own understanding of it (see on 3.6).

I adjure you by Jesus whom Paul preaches. In the NT Christians do not use the word *adjure*. *Whom Paul preaches* seems to be used here simply as a definition.

14. There were seven sons of a certain Sceva, a Jew, a chief priest. *Chief priest* could be *high priest*. But there is no Sceva in the list of Jewish High Priests otherwise known. The word is used in the plural in the gospels and in Acts (e.g. 4.1) to denote members of the Jewish priestly aristocracy or of a Jewish court. It could be so used here; a migrant Jew took his title with him. It has been suggested that Sceva was a renegade Jew who had become a high priest in the imperial cult. Or – perhaps likeliest – Sceva adopted the title as an advertisement. The text however does not say that Sceva himself practised as an exorcist.

15. the evil spirit has been implied (v. 14) but not expressly mentioned. **Jesus . . . Paul . . . but who are you?** Each of the two names is introduced in Greek by the definite article. It is hard to explain this in terms of Greek usage; the point may be, *The great Jesus . . . the great Paul, who in comparison are you?* This would at least make sense. Cf. Mk 1.34; also Acts 16.17.

16. the man in whom the evil spirit was. It seems that the spirit can speak (v. 15) but can act only through its host. The would-be exorcists are discomfited. The man **leapt upon them and overpowered them all**. *All* translates a Greek word that normally means not *all* but *both*. This does not agree with *seven* in v. 14. There are a few later papyri in which the word means *all*, and it is perhaps best to suppose that Luke gives us the earliest known example of this use. No other explanation is convincing. The seven **fled from the house**. No house has been mentioned. The story as a whole is untidy (it is rewritten in Codex Bezae); it may be that Luke incorporated into the story of Paul an incident that did not belong to it. Paul does not drive the spirit out; it is, in some sense, on Paul's side.

17. Not surprisingly, such events became **known to all, both Jews and Greeks, who lived in Ephesus**. Abuse of *the name* was ineffective. It was a means of access to the person whose name it was. Hence (in a Septuagintal expression) **the name of the Lord Jesus was magnified**.

18. confessing is a verb that usually has an object; in the translation **their sins** is supplied, but it would be possible to take **their magical practices** as the object of both *confessing* and **disclosing**. *Magical practices* translates a word that could mean *practices* in general, but it is used in relation to magic and the connotation is appropriate in the present context.

19. A good many (Luke uses one of his characteristic imprecise words of quantity) **of those who practised magic**. Ephesus was noted for the practice of magic, and *Ephesian writings* was a term used for the sort of **books**, containing incantations and spells, that were burned. For an example of a magical papyrus see *Background* 34–7. **They counted up the price of the books.** The meaning of *they* is not specified; if it does not refer to the owners of the books a subject may be taken out of **all**. People in general estimated the value of the books. No unit of currency is mentioned; *drachmae* must be supplied. To estimate the value rather than the number of the books is a Lucan touch. Luke does not like magic but he specially dislikes the use of it for making money. In the Roman world magic was officially discouraged but almost universally believed in. Only sceptics such as Lucian (not Christians, who disapproved but did not disbelieve) denied its power.

20. A characteristic concluding summary. Cf. 6.7; 12.24. Luke here brings one incident to a close and is about to embark on a fresh piece of tradition which is not connected with the last, except so far as 19.26 refers to the success of the mission described in vv. 11–20.

49. RIOT AT EPHESUS 19.21–40

**[21] When these events were done, Paul formed the intention to pass
through Macedonia and Achaea and travel to Jerusalem. He said,
'After I have been there I must see Rome too.' [22] He sent into
Macedonia two of his assistants, Timothy and Erastus, and
himself extended his stay in Asia.**

**[23] At that time there arose no small disturbance concerning
the Way. [24] One Demetrius by name, a silver-smith, by making
silver shrines of Artemis provided the craftsmen with no small
amount of business. [25] He gathered them and the workmen
engaged in this business together, and said, 'Men, you know that
our prosperity arises out of this business; [26] and you see and hear
that not only in Ephesus but in almost all Asia this fellow Paul
has persuaded and led astray a large crowd of people, saying that
these that are made with hands are not gods. [27] Not only does this
mean for us a risk that this line of business may come into
disrepute but also that the temple of the great goddess Artemis
may be reckoned as nothing, and she whom all Asia and the
inhabited world worship will be cast down from her greatness.'**

**[28] They listened to this and were filled with rage, and shouted,
'Great is Artemis of the Ephesians.' [29] The city was filled with
confusion; they seized Gaius and Aristarchus, Macedonians and
travelling companions of Paul's, and rushed with one accord into
the theatre. [30] Paul wished to go [into the theatre] to the people,
but the disciples would not permit him to do so. [31] And some of
the Asiarchs, who were well disposed to him, sent and begged
him not to go into the theatre. [32] Some shouted one thing, others
another; for the assembly was confused, and the majority did not
know why they had come together. [33] Some of the crowd instructed
Alexander, and the Jews put him forward. Alexander made a
gesture with his hand and wished to make a defence to the people,
[34] but when they recognized that he was a Jew there arose one cry
from all, who for about two hours shouted, 'Great is Artemis of
the Ephesians.'**

**[35] The town clerk stilled the crowd and said. 'Men of Ephesus,
what man is there who does not know that the city of the
Ephesians is temple warden of the great Artemis and of the Stone
that fell from heaven? [36] Since these matters are not open to**

contradiction you must remain quiet and do nothing rash. [37] For you have brought these men [here] who are neither guilty of temple profanation nor blasphemers of our goddess. [38] So if Demetrius and the craftsmen associated with him have a suit against anyone, courts are held and there are proconsuls: let them accuse one another. [39] And if you seek anything more than that it will be dealt with in the lawful assembly. [40] For as for this day, we run the risk of being accused of riot, there being no cause for it. We shall not be able to give a reason for this meeting.' With these words he dismissed the assembly.

This paragraph falls into two parts. The second, vv. 23–40, must be based on information, oral or written, derived by Luke from Ephesus. The great temple of Artemis is known – but all the world had heard of this; Artemis herself is referred to, with the popular adjective *great*; so are the Asiarchs and the town clerk. Paul's fellow travellers, Gaius and Aristarchus, are involved, and could have provided information. Some of the objections that have been made to the historicity of the account are superficial and unconvincing. The story makes good sense.

The first, and much shorter, part of the paragraph (vv. 21, 22) is of a different kind. Paul determines to make a roundabout journey to Jerusalem, travelling by way of Macedonia and Achaea. After visiting Jerusalem he will go to Rome. Two of his assistants, Timothy and Erastus, are sent ahead into Macedonia; Paul will follow them and continue into Greece. The two assistants were probably engaged in Paul's collection for the relief of poverty in Jerusalem, which surprisingly is not mentioned. The journey ends at 21.15 and bears clear marks of being based on an itinerary, with very few narrative insertions.

21. Paul formed the intention. The Greek word for *spirit* occurs here but there is no reference to the Holy Spirit; the word *spirit*, in the sense of human spirit, is needed with the verb to express the thought of intention. Paul's intention is **to pass through** (the verb may suggest a preaching mission; cf. 13.6) **Macedonia** (see 16.9) and **Achaea** (see 18.12) **and travel to Jerusalem**. The journey itself begins at 20.1, the riot (v. 23) intervening. The final visit to Greece (20.2, 3) seems to follow on the Corinthian troubles that form the background of 2 Corinthians (see 2 *Corinthians* 5–21). All this Luke omits, though it is difficult to think that he was totally unaware of it.

It was not a story that he wished to tell. Jerusalem must be visited first, but after that **I must see Rome too**. This more remote objective was beginning to fill Paul's mind, according to Acts, and according to Paul himself (Rom. 15.22–29). For Paul, Rome was to be a staging-post on the way to Spain. This Luke does not mention, possibly because he knows that Paul did not get so far; in any case, for him Rome was more important.

22. Timothy was sent to Corinth (and could have been sent through **Macedonia**) at 1 Cor. 16.10 (cf. 4.17). A visit by **Timothy** to **Macedonia** (Philippi) is contemplated in Phil. 2.19–23; this could have been from Ephesus, more probably from Rome. An **Erastus** is mentioned at Rom. 16.23; probably not the same person. See also 2 Tim. 4.20. In what way they assisted Paul is not specified, but Timothy at least exercised pastoral responsibility.

Paul **extended his stay in Asia**. Cf. possibly 1 Cor. 16.8.

23. A new narrative, complete in itself and free (except in v. 26) from any reference to Paul's work in general, begins here. Luke may have heard it told in Ephesus, or by Ephesian Christians elsewhere.

24. Demetrius was a common name; it is unlikely that there is any connection with 3 John 12. Instead of **by making** it would be possible to translate, *who made . . . and* **provided** . . . The translation given here is chosen because it binds the narrative together. It was by making the silver shrines that prosperity was provided. An Ephesian inscription mentions one M. Antonius Hermeias, a **silversmith**, and a guild of silversmiths. **silver shrines**: a shrine is a temple, or the most sacred inner part of a temple. It is probable that the silver shrines were small portable shrines carried in religious processions. As a Greek goddess, **Artemis** was the daughter of Zeus and Leto, worshipped already in Mycenaean times. She was a virgin, who helped women in childbirth, a huntress armed with a bow, the goddess of death. The establishment of an Ionian colony at Ephesus led to assimilation of the Greek Artemis to oriental deities. Worship of a goddess seems to have been practised in Ephesus before the arrival of the Greeks, and images have often been interpreted as many-breasted, suggesting that she was a fertility goddess. Reinterpretation of the breasts as bull's testicles reinforces the notion of fertility but recently this has been contested. See further on v. 27.

It has been suggested that the Greek *naous poiōn* (*making shrines*) was a corruption of *neopoios* (there are variant spellings), the term used in the Roman period for the officials elected by the city tribes to supervise the fabric of the temple of Artemis. But the only ground for this suggestion is our ignorance of the custom of making silver shrines.

Demetrius **provided the craftsmen** who actually made the shrines **with no small amount of business** (v. 23).

25. Demetrius **gathered** the craftsmen (v. 24) **and the** relatively unskilled **workmen . . . together**. He appealed to their common knowledge and self-interest: **You know . . .**

26. in almost all Asia. It must be remembered that Paul had assistants (19.22; cf. Col. 1.7; 2.1). But no doubt Demetrius was prepared to exaggerate. **has persuaded and led astray**, persuaded them to move from one side, from one religion, to the other. **This fellow Paul** (deliberately disrespectful) says **that these that are made with hands are not gods.** Did anyone in Ephesus believe that the wooden and stone images were gods? See above, p. 272. Probably not many; but probably many did think that there was something more than a symbolic relation between image and deity, and it soon became clear that Christianity was mounting a major attack on such religions as that of Artemis. Both could not prevail, and the business of Demetrius and his colleagues was in real danger.

27. Demetrius puts business considerations first but adds a religious point. There is **a risk that this line of business may come into disrepute**. If people no longer buy silver shrines silversmiths will suffer. Lack of respect for **the temple of the great goddess Artemis** will also have economic consequences. And the universally worshipped deity **will be cast down from her greatness**. Demetrius hardly exaggerates the wide respect in which Artemis was held; the adjective *great* was regularly applied to her.

The effect of Christianity on pagan religion is shown in Pliny's account (*c.* AD 110–112, in Bithynia–Pontus) of the restoration of paganism when Christianity was repressed: 'It is agreed beyond question that the temples which have been almost deserted are beginning to be thronged, and the sacred rites, long neglected, are seen to be resumed.'

28. Demetrius' speech had its intended effect in rousing his colleagues in opposition to the Christian movement. For the adjective **great** see on v. 27. The crowd use the popular local cry.

29. The effect of Demetrius' speech spread: **the city was filled with confusion**. The rioters **seized Gaius and Aristarchus, Macedonians and travelling companions of Paul's**. The name *Gaius* recurs at 20.4; on the possibility of identification see on that verse. In

20.4 there is also an Aristarchus, who is a Macedonian. At 27.2 there is an Aristarchus who is a Macedonian from Thessalonica; no doubt the same man. *Travelling companions* is used in 2 Cor. 8.19, and may have come to be used as a semi-technical term for an assistant in Paul's work. Such men were presumably publicly known and thus natural targets for the mob's violence.

the theatre at Ephesus was an imposing building. Estimates of its capacity vary; the lowest seems to be 24,000. It was used for the town's meetings.

30. It was not Paul's intention to avoid dangers to which his subordinates were exposed; he wished **to go to the people**, that is, **into the theatre**. This however **the disciples would not permit**. Paul's life was too valuable to be risked in this way. For the question whether these events are reflected in 1 Cor. 15.32; 16.9; 2 Cor. 1.8 see *1 Corinthians* 365f.; *2 Corinthians* 63f. The answer seems to be, 'Possibly in 1 Cor. 15.32.'

31. It was not only Christian disciples who were concerned for Paul's safety. There were also officials who were ready if not to take his part at least to advise caution. **some of the Asiarchs who were well disposed to him**. The Asiarchs were undoubtedly leading figures in the province, but details of their function are obscure. There is evidence that suggests that it was from among the Asiarchs that the provincial high priest of the emperor was chosen, but the relation between these offices probably changed from time to time. *Martyrdom of Polycarp* 12.2 refers to the Asiarch Philip. It is only some of the Asiarchs who were friendly to Paul, and their attitude was informal and at most advisory. There is no ground for questioning the veracity of Luke's statements.

32. the assembly. The Greek word is *ekklēsia*. For the Christian use of this word see on 5.11 and Introduction, pp. lviif. In its non-biblical sense it is correctly used at v. 39 (see the note) of the duly constituted assembly of citizens (held in the theatre, see v. 29); the use in vv. 32 and 40 is doubtful since the assembly seems to be informal, unofficial, and riotous. More suitable words are used at vv. 30, 33, 36, 40. The use of *ekklēsia* however is understandable; the persons concerned were those who would be summoned to a lawful assembly, even though they were not at the time engaged on lawful business.

the majority. Codex Bezae uses a different word. This also could mean *the majority* but might mean *the best people* – even they did not understand what was going on.

33. Some of the crowd. Alternatively, *Some put forward from the crowd* . . . Why should the Jews put forward one of their own number (v. 34)? Perhaps because they were not always differentiated from the Christians, who had provoked the mob, or because they were known to be opposed to idolatry and were generally unpopular.

34. See v. 33 for the anti-Judaism of the crowd.

Great is Artemis of the Ephesians. See v. 28, especially for the popular use of *great*.

Verses 33 and 34 contain, in Greek, a number of unusual expressions. Verse 32 would join well with v. 35. It seems reasonable at least to raise the question whether vv. 33, 34 were added to a narrative that did not originally contain them. Possibly Luke supplemented by local inquiry a narrative that he found in a travel record. He may have had a special reason for making the addition; perhaps Alexander was at the time of the riot, or subsequently became, a Christian. Cf. Mk 15.21; Rom. 16.13.

35. See on v. 34; v. 35 could be linked with v. 32.

The town clerk. The Greek word was the title of an official at Ephesus (and at other Greek cities). It seems that some of the wealth of Artemis got into the city treasury and that the town clerk might not have welcomed inquiry. He appeals to public knowledge. **the city of the Ephesians is temple warden of the great Artemis**. A *temple warden* was originally a person; transference to the city is easy to understand. **and of the stone that fell from heaven**. This object was probably some form of meteorite, perhaps having human form.

36. No one – that is, no one who matters – disputes these facts, so that there is no reason for riot. The Christians, of course, did dispute them, but it was obviously possible to discount the opinion of a few misguided people.

37. Misguided and (in the town clerk's argument) misjudged. **these men . . . are neither guilty of temple profanation nor blasphemers of our goddess**. The wisdom and inaccuracy of the town clerk's statement are both apparent. On another occasion he might well have said that Paul and his colleagues were guilty of both offences; on this occasion however his intention was to quiet the mob, and no doubt it could be said with some plausibility that Paul's primary aim was to proclaim Christ rather than to discredit a rival to him, and the Christians were not profaning or robbing the temple or blaspheming in a vulgar way. The town clerk's speech cannot be judged unhistorical because it was tactful.

38. The town clerk points out to Demetrius that there are **courts** in which private suits may be presented in due form of law and that there is therefore no occasion for riotous assembly. **and there are proconsuls**. There was of course only one proconsul of the province of Asia; the plural is a plural of category. Luke is not to be accused of ignorance of an elementary and universally known fact.

39. Anything beyond a private civil action will be dealt with **in the lawful assembly**. Demetrius would not have had to wait long for a hearing. According to Chrysostom (*Homily* 42.2) there were three meetings a month; according to an inscription, one; perhaps the need had increased by Chrysostom's time. For *assembly* (in Greek, *ekklēsia*) see on v. 32.

40. The syntax of this verse is very confused; some think that there has been a primitive corruption of the text.

In the first clause it seems that the town clerk is saying that the real risk is not in loss of business but in trouble with the police for disturbing the peace; **riot** is a strong word. **there being no cause for it** could be *there being no man guilty*. It is almost impossible to make sense of the next clause as it stands. Literally it runs, Concerning which (that is, the *cause* of the previous clause?), we shall not be able to render account. This becomes much easier if with some MSS we omit the negative: There being no reason concerning which we shall be able to give an account of this concourse. But the easier reading is seldom to be preferred. There is much to be said for the suggestion that the author wrote the sentence in several forms and omitted to delete rejected words. Even this however does not deal with the fact that the verse seems to permit two different impressions (not translations). The town clerk wishes to send everyone home in peace and quiet, but he may be arguing: (1) We are running the risk of being accused of riot and insurrection, and there will be no defence, for there is no rational ground or excuse for what has happened; that is, we shall get what we deserve; *or* (2) We are running the risk of being accused of riot and insurrection, even though we have not done anything for which we cannot plead that there was just cause; punishment inflicted by the proconsul will be undeserved, but nonetheless unpleasant. It may be that Luke was not clear in his own mind how the situation should be viewed, or that the town clerk wanted to 'have it both ways' and used ambiguous arguments designed to appeal to different sections of the crowd.

An important parallel has been drawn with the civic speeches of Dio Chrysostom, in which the old city state defends its reputation and autonomy against centralizing authority. This confirms (if confirmation is needed) a date for Acts before the Antonine emperors.

A further important observation is that an element of Acts apologetic is brought out by the story and by the town clerk's comment. It is not Christianity but its opponents who constitute a threat to established order.

50. BACK TO PALESTINE, THROUGH MACEDONIA, GREECE, AND TROAS 20.1–16

**[1] After the uproar had ceased Paul sent for the disciples, gave them
an exhortation, said farewell, and set out to travel to Macedonia.
[2] When he had passed through those parts and exhorted them in
much preaching he came into Greece; [3] when he had spent three
months [there] and a plot was made against him by the Jews as he
was about to leave for Syria, he made up his mind to return through
Macedonia. [4] There were associated with him Sopater the son of
Pyrrhus, a Beroean, of the Thessalonians Aristarchus and
Secundus, Gaius of Derbe and Timothy, and the Asians Tychicus
and Trophimus. [5] These went on ahead and waited for us in Troas.
[6] We sailed from Philippi after the Days of Unleavened Loaves and
came to them at Troas after five days; there we stayed seven days.**

**[7] On the first day of the week, when we had gathered to break
bread, Paul, since he was about to leave on the morrow, discoursed with them and prolonged his speech till midnight. [8] There
were many lamps in the upper room in which we had met, [9] and a
young man, Eutychus by name, sitting by the window, was being
gradually overcome by deep sleep as Paul discoursed longer and
longer, until having been finally overcome by sleep he fell from
the second floor, and was picked up dead. [10] Paul went down, fell
on him, embraced him, and said, 'Stop making a disturbance, his
life is in him.' [11] He went up, broke bread, and ate; he conversed
further until dawn, and so left. [12] They took up the boy alive, and
were no little comforted.**

**[13] We went on ahead to the ship and set sail for Assos, where
we were to take up Paul, for so he had given orders, since he
himself intended to go by land. [14] When he met us at Assos we
took him up and came to Mitylene. [15] Thence we sailed, and on
the following day came opposite Chios; on the next day we reached
Samos, and the day after that we came to Miletus. [16] For Paul had
chosen to sail past Ephesus in order that he might not have to
spend time in Asia, for he was making haste so as to be, if possible,
in Jerusalem on the Day of Pentecost.**

The structure of this section is clear. The first six verses describe the opening stages of Paul's roundabout return from Ephesus to Palestine.

When the uproar in Ephesus is over he leaves for Macedonia, addresses the Christians in those parts, and makes his way to Greece. After spending three months there he determines to sail for Syria; his plan is changed by a Jewish plot, and he decides to return by the way he came, through Macedonia. In v. 4 we learn the names of the men accompanying Paul, but no sooner are they named than they (or some of them) separate from him, go ahead, and wait for *us* – for now the first person plural is reintroduced – in Troas. Here there are Christians and the party join them at the common meal, which becomes the occasion of a miracle. The journey is resumed in v. 13 and the following verses contain little but geography until at the end comes the note that Paul omitted Ephesus from his route because he wished to be in Jerusalem for the Day of Pentecost.

For the most part what we have here is a list of names which was almost certainly taken from a Pauline itinerary. Three points may however be noted. (1) It was at this time that the complicated and stormy relationships that can be seen in the letters to Corinth were settled – settled at least to the extent that Achaea in the end contributed to Paul's collection (Rom. 15.26; see 2 *Corinthians*, 21, 25–28). Unless Luke was completely – and surprisingly – ignorant of the Corinthian episode, he decided that it was better omitted. (2) The miracle of Eutychus is not in itself connected with Troas (or any other location) and could be lifted out without damage to the context. It may have been heard by Luke in Troas and inserted into the itinerary. (3) Paul's reason for not taking in Ephesus is surprising; one would not have thought that he would be so eager to attend a Jewish feast.

Some think that the *we* referred to in this paragraph comes from a different writer from the other *We* passages. There is no good ground for this view. It is worth noting that *we* ceased in Philippi (16.17) and is resumed at Philippi (20.5f.).

1. If, as some think, Paul left Ephesus because he was driven out, Luke does not say so; indeed, that Paul stayed till **the uproar had ceased** suggests the opposite. According to 19.21 he had already intended to leave. That he exhorted **the disciples**, and **said farewell**, does not suggest undue haste. For **Macedonia** see on 16.9.

2. those parts – presumably of Macedonia on the route to Greece.

3. when he had spent about three months in Greece. This seems to be the occasion when Paul paid his third visit to Corinth (2 Cor. 12.14; 13.1) and won at least some support for his collection. He was now on the way to Jerusalem, bearing the fruits of his appeal. It was at this time that Romans was written (Rom. 15.23–28).

Paul's plans for his return to **Syria** were changed by a **plot . . . made against him by the Jews**, in consequence of which **he made up his mind to return through Macedonia** – by land; it is probable that his original intention was to go by ship, and it is a good suggestion (though incapable of proof) that the Jews, probably on pilgrimage to Jerusalem for Passover, were travelling on the ship that Paul was intending to use, causing him to change his plan and travel overland. The Western text, however, attributes the change of plan to direct intervention by the Holy Spirit.

4. It is certain that the journey undertaken here had as one purpose, perhaps its primary purpose, the conveying to Jerusalem of the proceeds of Paul's collection. That Luke does not mention this (except in the hint of 24.17) is a surprising fact. Reasons for his silence can only be conjectural. According to 1 Cor. 16.3f. it was Paul's intention that local representatives should take the money to Jerusalem, perhaps in his company. It is reasonable to infer that those mentioned in this verse, except perhaps Timothy, were such local representatives rather than assistant missionaries.

Sopater the son of Pyrrhus, a Beroean. The name *Pyrrhus* is omitted by some MSS. Sopater is not mentioned elsewhere in the NT, but some identify him with Sosipater (Rom. 16.21).

of the Thessalonians Aristarchus and Secundus. *Secundus*, a Latin name, does not occur elsewhere in the NT. For *Aristarchus* see 19.29; he reappears at 27.2; cf. Col. 4.10; Philemon 24.

Gaius of Derbe and Timothy. Derbe and Lystra (probably Timothy's home – see 16.1) were both Lycaonian towns. *Of Derbe* translates the adjective *Derbaios*; a variant reading has *Doub(e)rios*, which means *of Doberos*, a town in Paeonia, at that time part of Macedonia. This would give us a Gaius who was a Macedonian; cf. 19.29. This reading however is probably not to be accepted.

the Asians Tychicus and Trophimus. Tychicus is mentioned at Eph. 6.21; Col. 4.7; 2 Tim. 4.12; Titus 3.12. For Trophimus see 2 Tim. 4.20. The references are sufficient to show that both men were companions of Paul's.

5. These (the men just mentioned; some think only Tychicus and Trophimus) **went on ahead and waited for us in Troas** (see 16.8). They waited for *us*; it is implied that whoever was responsible, in whatever way, for the We source joined Paul at Philippi (v. 6). *We* has not occurred since ch. 16 and it is possible that the writer had remained in Philippi throughout the intervening period.

6. We sailed from Philippi. *We*: see on v. 5, and for the We passages in general see Introduction, pp. xxiiif.

the Days of Unleavened Loaves. Luke still uses the Jewish calendar as a means of dating events; there is no Christian 'Easter' that he can refer to. Luke seems not to have distinguished Unleavened Loaves from Passover; see Lk. 22.1 (The Feast of Unleavened Loaves which is called Passover). **We . . . came to them at Troas after five days.** The note of time is unusually expressed but it can hardly mean anything other than that the voyage lasted five days. The journey in the opposite direction lasted only two (16.11). Experts seem to agree that an easterly wind could make so great a difference.

there we stayed seven days. It is often said that this, with the next verse, implies that Paul arrived and left on a Monday. It would be better to say that if he did leave on a Monday he must have arrived on the preceding Tuesday. Tuesday to Monday is seven days, counting inclusively.

7. On the first day of the week. See on 17.2. This probably refers to Sunday evening, but could refer to Saturday evening, when the first day of the Jewish week began. **when we had gathered to break bread**. The first person plural continues; but if the Troas incident was originally a separate piece the *we* could have been incorporated into it from the itinerary. For breaking bread see 2.42, 46; 27.35, with the notes. There is nothing to suggest that this was anything other than a church fellowship meal, accompanied by religious discourse and conversation. For a general consideration of such meals and their possible relation with the eucharist see Introduction, pp. lxiif. The meal took place in a private house, as at this time most, perhaps all, church meetings must have done.

Paul . . . discoursed with them. The meaning of the word varies between *dialogue* and *discourse*. Paul had spent seven days in Troas, was about to leave, and could hardly hope to see these Christians again; so he spoke **till midnight**. Even if the meeting began with supper he must have spoken at considerable length. It was the first day of the week (even if it was Saturday evening). Observance of the Jewish Sabbath is already abandoned in the NT (Col. 2.16); early in the second century the two observances were taken to be typical of the Jewish and Christian religions respectively (Ignatius, *Magnesians* 9.1). Pliny in his letter to Trajan (*Epistles* 10.96.7) says that on a set day the Christians met early in the morning and again in the evening. There is nothing in his words to suggest (though this is often assumed) that one of these meetings was, the other was not, sacramental.

The reference here to the first day of the week has been made the basis of an attempt to find a precise date in Pauline chronology. The argument is that Paul left Troas on Monday (vv. 7, 11); he therefore began his seven-day stay in Troas on Tuesday. He arrived after a five-day journey from Philippi (v. 6). He must have left Philippi on Friday. This was after the Days of Unleavened Loaves (v. 6), therefore Passover in that year fell on a Thursday. The Passover of AD 57, calculated by the full moon, fell on a Thursday. This was true of no other of the neighbouring years. It follows that Paul's journey took place in AD 57. Superficially attractive, the argument falls to pieces as soon as it is examined. (1) Lk. 22.1, 7 show Luke's ignorance or carelessly imprecise statement of the relation between Unleavened Loaves and Passover. (2) Passover in fact coincided with the first of the days of Unleavened Loaves, so that if Unleavened Loaves ended on a Thursday Passover must have been on a Friday. (3) 'After the days of Unleavened Loaves' does not necessarily mean, 'on the day after the last day of Unleavened Loaves'. (4) The time of full moon in the first century can be calculated now with greater accuracy than it could be observed at the time. (5) Even if the 5 and 7 of v. 6 came from the itinerary we cannot be confident of their precise accuracy, nor do we know whether the last day of the 5 coincided with the first day of the 7.

8. There were many lamps. Some think that the lamps account for the drowsiness of Eutychus, others that they were used to promote wakefulness. In a meeting that lasted all night (v. 11) lamps would in any case be needed. **upper room**, an upper storey of the house (see v. 9).

9. a young man, Eutychus by name. Eutychus means *fortunate*, and might well have been selected for one who in a story was raised from death. But the name was a common one, and the historicity of the story cannot be dismissed on account of it.

being gradually overcome by deep sleep . . . finally overcome by sleep. The tenses of the Greek participles bring out vividly the gradually increasing drowsiness and its climax. In the Qumran community falling asleep in the assembly was punishable by exclusion for thirty days (1 QS 7.10). There is no hint of disciplinary procedure here. Eutychus' accident provides the occasion for a miracle and serves no other purpose.

from the second floor. So in English usage. The Greek contains the word *third* but denotes a building on three levels, of which the highest (ground floor, first floor, second floor) might be called the *third*. The better houses of antiquity seem for the most part to have been one-storey buildings. The dwellings of the poor were apartment houses of several storeys.

was picked up dead. Luke says and means *dead*, not *as if he were dead*. Luke was capable, if he wished, of saying that a person appeared to be but was not dead; see 14.19.

10. The miracle (it can hardly be doubted that Luke intended the story to be taken in this way) is described in conventional miracle language, perhaps with special allusion to the Elijah and Elisha stories of the OT; see 3 Kdms (1 Kings) 17.17–24; 4 Kdms (2 Kings) 4.18–37.

11. He went up, from the street to the second floor, **broke bread**: the purpose of the gathering, v. 7; see the note there; **and ate**. Luke's word normally means *to taste*, but in Luke's use it is *to eat*, *to take a meal* (see Lk. 14.24; Acts 10.10; 23.14; the only exception, Lk. 9.27, is taken directly from Mk and is in any case metaphorical). It would therefore be mistaken to infer that the reference was to a sacramental meal in which only a fragment of bread was tasted. The subject is Paul, the centre of interest, not Eutychus. **he conversed further until dawn**. Luke's verb (cf. Lk. 24.14, 15; Acts 24.26) does not mean *to address a public meeting* but *to engage in conversation*. No doubt on such occasions Paul did the lion's share of the talking, but it was not an entirely one-sided engagement. **and so**: *so* picks up the preceding (Greek) participles – *went up*, *broke*, *ate*, *conversed*; a classical use.

12. All that remains is to make explicit the happy ending of the story.

13. We went on ahead to the ship. The 'We' passage continues, but *we* now means, as the next words show, the Pauline party without Paul. We **set sail for Assos**, a town on the mainland, founded from Lesbos in the eighth century BC. From 133 BC it was under Roman rule. Paul meanwhile proceeded from Troas to Assos by land – why, we do not know. There is nothing to suggest that he made an evangelistic tour. The suggestion that he was liable to seasickness is exegetical despair.

The sailing party was to **take up Paul** at Assos, **for so he had given orders**; Luke's word is often somewhat stronger than *made arrangements*.

14. The plan was duly put into effect. **we took him up**; the word can be used generally but here clearly means *into the ship*. **And** we **came to Mitylene**, the largest town on the island of Lesbos, an important centre of Greek life, commerce, and art. The cult of Augustus (or Augustus and Rome) had been established here as early as 27 BC.

15. The journey continues. **on the following day** we **came opposite Chios**, too long a stretch to be covered in one day. Apparently they sailed between the island of Chios and the mainland. Chios may mean the island or its main town, situated on its east coast. It had been made a free city by Sulla (86 BC).

Samos, another of the Ionian islands, separated from the mainland by a narrow channel. In 21/20 BC Augustus made Samos a free city, a privilege withdrawn by Vespasian. The first person plural returns with **we reached** (the word could mean *we passed by*, a meaning which may lie behind Codex Bezae's reference to a call at Trogyllium).

It was between Chios and Samos that the ship sailed past Ephesus (see v. 16) and came to **Miletus**, an ancient, prosperous, and influential city. There is evidence of a Jewish element in the population.

16. For Paul had chosen to sail past Ephesus. This presumably means that he had chosen a ship whose calling places did not include Ephesus. He would hardly be able to direct the ship's course. He made this choice **in order that he might not have to spend time in Asia**. It would have been difficult not to spend time on local contacts and responsibilities in and around Ephesus. And he was in a hurry to reach **Jerusalem** for **the Day of Pentecost**.

Whether Paul reached Jerusalem in time for the feast we do not know. It might have been possible given favourable conditions, but the feast is not mentioned in the account of his stay in Jerusalem. Would Paul have been so keen to attend a Jewish feast? Gal. 4.10 suggests disparagement of calendrical observances; cf. Rom. 14.5f. Would he have saved much time by stopping at Miletus instead of Ephesus? Estimates of the time needed for sending a message across and bringing the Ephesian elders (20.17) over vary from two days to six. Other motives are possible. Some think that Paul had made Ephesus too hot to hold him, a fact that Luke chose to suppress. Paul was conveying a large sum of money to Jerusalem, and might have felt safer in Miletus than in Ephesus. If Luke had been simply inventing a setting for a speech he would probably have put it in Ephesus. If there was a tradition of a great farewell speech in Miletus he might have thought fit to ferry the elders across in order to provide a partly Ephesian audience.

51. PAUL'S SPEECH AT MILETUS 20.17–38

**17 From Miletus Paul sent to Ephesus and summoned the elders
of the church. 18 When they reached him he said to them, 'You
[elders] know how, from the first day I set foot in Asia, I conducted
myself towards you for the whole time I was with you, 19 serving
the Lord with all humble-mindedness and tears and afflictions
that befell me through the plots of the Jews. 20 [You know] that I
kept back none of the things that were profitable for you, so as
not to declare them to you and teach you in public and in private,
21 testifying to both Jews and Greeks repentance towards God
and faith in our Lord Jesus. 22 And now behold I am going to
Jerusalem, bound in the Spirit, not knowing the things that will
befall me there, 23 only that the Holy Spirit in city after city testifies
to me that bonds and afflictions await me. 24 But I take my life to
be of no account as valuable to myself so that I may finish my
course and the ministry that I received from the Lord Jesus – the
ministry that consists in testifying the Gospel of the grace of God.
25 And see now, I know that all of you, among whom I went about
proclaiming the kingdom, will see my face no more. 26 Therefore
I affirm to you this day that I am clear from the blood of all men,
27 for I kept nothing back so as not to proclaim to you the whole
counsel of God. 28 Take thought for yourselves and all the flock in
which the Holy Spirit has appointed you bishops, to shepherd the
church of God, which he saved and acquired through his own
blood. 29 I know that after my departure fearsome wolves will
come into your company, not sparing the flock, 30 and from among
yourselves men will rise up speaking perverse things so as to draw
away disciples as their followers. 31 Watch therefore, remembering
that night and day for three years I did not cease admonishing
each one with tears. 32 And now I commit you to God and to the
word of his grace, to him who is able to build you up and to give
you the inheritance among all those who have been sanctified. 33 I
desired no one's silver or gold or clothing. 34 You yourselves know
that these hands ministered to my own needs and to those who
were with me. 35 In all ways I showed you that it is necessary to
work like this and to help the weak, and to remember the words
of the Lord Jesus, [to remember] that he himself said, 'It is more
blessed to give than to receive.'**

[36] When he had said these things he knelt down with them all and prayed, [37] A good deal of lamentation arose on the part of all, and they fell on Paul's neck and kissed him, [38] grieving most of all at the prediction he had uttered, that they should see his face no more. They saw him off to the ship.

A brief introduction (vv. 17, 18a) and a concluding note (vv. 36–38) provide a framework for a long address by Paul. The framework may certainly be considered Luke's own writing. Verse 17 provides a suitable audience for the speech, which forms an important part of Luke's presentation of the figure of Paul. That Paul (for whatever reason) did not on this journey visit Ephesus was a datum of tradition; that he made a speech in Miletus may have been. Miletus was in his journey the nearest point to the great centre of population, and since Paul could not, or did not, go to Ephesus, Ephesus was brought to him, represented by the elders of the church, who could on behalf of the church as a whole hear Paul's farewell and learn what he had to teach about pastoral responsibility. The speech completed, there must be leave-taking, the more serious a matter because Luke makes it clear that this is a final farewell.

The speech defies analysis. It proceeds from point to point, with many repetitions. Its form is that of the farewell, of which there are many examples in the Bible and elsewhere. Its themes are those of the farewell address in Luke 21 (take heed; watch) but the eschatological basis of the Gospel discourse has disappeared. There is a warning of coming problems in the church, but none of coming judgement. The church order presupposed belongs to Luke's period rather than Paul's, and Paul's own ministry, at least in the East, has reached its end (v. 25).

A stronger case for Luke's knowledge of (some of) the Pauline letters can be made here than anywhere else in Acts, but even so there is no convincing literary allusion, nor even any recognition of the fact that Paul ever wrote a letter. How could a writer such as Luke be unaware of the fact, or, knowing it, fail to mention it?

The literary problem is at its sharpest in relation to the Pastoral Epistles. That the author of Acts wrote the Pastorals has been argued with great force. The parallels are real and substantial, and there can be little doubt that Acts and the Pastorals were produced in similar circumstances and at times not very remote from each other. There are differences, however, for example in the development of Christian institutions. And, though both Acts and the Pastorals have the highest respect for Paul, whereas the Pastorals represent him as the pre-eminent apostle, Acts will scarcely use the word apostle in describing him.

17. From **Miletus** (20.15) **Paul sent to Ephesus** (20.16) **and summoned the elders of the church**. For *elders* see 14.23, for *church* see 5.11; on both words see Introduction, pp. lvii–lx. At v. 28 the *elders* are called *bishops*; see on that verse. It is probable that we see here the constitution of the church as it was known to Luke: a community led by a group known indifferently as elders and bishops. Paul in the epistles never uses the word *elder*: *bishop* occurs once, in Phil. 1.1. Both words occur in the Pastoral Epistles – one of many contacts between this speech and those epistles. It is unlikely that there is any connection between the Christian elders and the elders who had a place in the constitution of Ephesus.

18. You is emphatic (cf. 10.28; 15.7): You elders know, if no one else does. It is likely that many of the elders would have been chosen from among the earliest converts, who had had the opportunity of observing Paul's ministry, which he describes in the following verses, at first hand and from an early time. The speech begins in the manner of a farewell, with a defence of the speaker's conduct; cf. e.g. 1 Sam. 12.2f.

19. This verse contains a striking number of parallels with the Pauline epistles. They are not quotations; they do not prove that Luke had read the epistles; but they do show contact with the Pauline tradition, so that this verse may be said to depict a speaker who could have written the letters.

serving the Lord. See especially Rom. 12.11 (unless *serving the time* is read); also Rom. 16.18; 1 Thess. 1.9, and Paul's frequent description of himself as a *servant of Jesus Christ* (e.g. Rom. 1.1; 1 Cor. 7.22; Gal. 1.10; Phil. 1.1).

He serves **with all humble-mindedness**. Cf. Rom. 12.16; 2 Cor. 7.6; 10.1; 11.7; 12.21; Phil. 2.3; 4.12. The use of *all* is Pauline.

tears. Cf. 2 Cor. 2.4. **afflictions that befell me through the plots of the Jews**. Cf. 1 Thess. 2.15.

20. You know is taken from v. 18, but repetition is called for in English. Here and at v. 27 Paul emphasizes that he has withheld nothing; the elders and indeed the whole church at Ephesus have received from him the whole of Christian truth. Luke's motive here does not seem to be the desire to point out Paul's courage in speaking unwelcome truths but rather to emphasize the completeness of his Gospel. He probably has in mind the secret teaching of the Gnostics and their claim to possess a secret tradition from Paul which he had withheld from the church at large. Paul had made his proclamation **in public** and taught **in private**. It is implied that anything beyond the known and publicly recognized teaching of Paul was not **profitable**.

21. testifying to both Jews and Greeks: cf. Rom. 1.16; 10.12; 1 Cor. 1.24; 10.32; 12.13; Gal. 3.28; Col. 3.11. The content of Paul's testimony is described as **repentance towards God and faith in our Lord Jesus**. Paul very seldom, in the epistles, refers to penitence, and for faith in Christ prefers a different form of words, literally 'faith of (not in) Jesus Christ'. The words used here in Acts do however recall Rom. 10.9. Here it may be said that repentance is called for because men have not treated Jesus as Lord; faith is summed up in the acceptance of the resurrection. Paul himself prefers the more objective statement. Luke, like the Pastorals, is apt to give a subjectivized version of Paulinism.

22. From this point (to which he will return, v. 25) Paul turns to the future and the lot that awaits him. **I am going to Jerusalem, bound in the Spirit.** We know that Paul is on his way to Jerusalem. *Bound in the Spirit* is not clear either in construction or in meaning. In a literal sense Paul was not yet bound, but he was under divine constraint to continue on a course that must sooner or later lead to his arrest. Moreover, as the next verse states explicitly, the Holy Spirit was constantly witnessing to him that this would be the result of his actions. Paul knows that he must go to Jerusalem, but does not know **the things that will befall** him **there**; that is, he does not know what form *bonds and afflictions* (v. 23) will take.

23. Paul knows no details of what will happen to him in Jerusalem, only that the visit will be a painful one; he must face imprisonment.

It is correctly observed that the 'divine man' of antiquity knows his approaching end. What must be observed here is that Paul professes ignorance of exactly what will happen, that he does not know anything in himself but is given limited information by the Holy Spirit, and that the Holy Spirit gives the same information to all who happen to be present at the time. On apostles as 'divine men' see e.g. 3.12.

24. The text and the construction of the opening clause are alike obscure. The text translated here is the most difficult of three. Though difficult grammatically the general sense is clear. Life itself is worth less to Paul than the fulfilment of his calling. There are further variants but the opening clause will continue: My purpose in discounting the value of my life is that I may . . .

so that I may finish my course. Paul frequently uses images drawn from the games, but never the noun used here.

After using his athletic image Paul speaks directly of the task assigned to him. The word **ministry** is sometimes (Rom. 15.3; 2 Cor. 8.4; 9.1, 12, 13) in the epistles used for Paul's ministry to the poor saints, that is, to his collection. It is very unlikely that this is referred to here; Luke never mentions this collection (except possibly at 24.17). The ministry is **testifying the Gospel of the grace of God** (cf. 9.15; Gal. 1.16). Other allusive references to Paul's message occur in vv. 25, 27, 28, and 32. For the theme of grace cf. 14.3; 20.32.

25. This is a farewell speech, and Paul turns to the future. **you . . . will see my face no more**. Personal contact is at an end. Luke could hardly have written this verse (and v. 38) if he had known that Paul returned to Asia.

For **I went about**; cf. 9.32; if the whole of Asia is in mind (cf. 19.10) there may be a reference to missionary tours, but probably the writer is thinking of Paul's long residence in Ephesus during which he went about **proclaiming the kingdom**. This is the original text though various MSS in different ways amplified this minimum summary. But *kingdom* means in effect the recognized content of Christian preaching, and is so expressed in order to bring out the continuity between the teaching of Jesus and the preaching of the post-resurrection church.

26. Therefore I affirm to you this day. Paul affirms in the strongest terms the testimony of his conscience to his blameless behaviour in Ephesus (or Asia), and in particular to his complete openness in declaring the truth about God and his purpose. **I am clear**, cf. 18.6; also, for the sense, Ezek. 3.18–21; 1 Thess. 2.10. The formulation is Lucan rather than Pauline. Paul is responsible for no man's (eternal) death through neglecting to preach the Gospel to all and to deliver it in all its fullness.

27. I kept nothing back. Cf. v. 20. **the whole counsel of God**. *Counsel* is a Lucan, and especially an Acts (2.23; 4.28; 5.38; 13.36; 19.1 (if the Western text is followed); 20.27; 27.12, 42), rather than a Pauline, word. Here it must refer to God's plan for the redemption of all mankind.

28. This verse is both the practical and theological centre of the speech, the practical centre because the speech's aim is to urge the Ephesian elders (and, through them, the Christian leaders of Luke's day) to do their duty conscientiously and effectively, and the theological centre because it states the significance of the death of Christ and at the same time brings out the ground of the church's ministry in the work of the Holy Spirit.

The elders are bidden **to take thought for** themselves, that is, to maintain the quality and integrity of their own Christian life, and to take thought for the church, in which they hold a responsible position. The church is described as a **flock**, which the elders must **shepherd**. The language of shepherding is not Pauline, but after Paul's time the image became common; see Jn 21.15–17 (and cf. 10.11, etc.); 1 Peter 2.25; 5.2–4; Eph. 4.11; Heb. 13.20; Jude 12. It rests upon familiar OT passages, e.g. the story of David; Ps. 23; Jer. 3.15; 23.1–4; Ezek. 34.1–24; but it is also used of rulers and leaders in the non-biblical world. The Christian shepherd is one who is able to guide and also to protect against the agencies that mislead and endanger Christians.

It was the Holy Spirit who appointed the elders. This does not differ essentially from 14.23; it is those whom the Spirit has chosen and prepared by his gifts whom the church may appoint to act as shepherds.

It is clear that the same persons, who act as shepherds, are described both as elders (v. 17) and as bishops (*episkopoi*, v. 28). The same equivalence appears in Titus 1.7 and very probably in 1 Tim. 3.2. It is implied in Philippians, where *episkopoi* and deacons are mentioned but not elders. The word *episkopos* is used of officials in many social groups. The background of the word has been found at Qumran in the word *m*[e]*baqqer*; see especially CD 13.7–9. A direct connection is however unlikely. More important is the LXX use of the cognate verb, which suggests the saving act in which God visited and redeemed his people. This defines a ministry in which God's redeeming visitation is applied to and brought before the minds of church members.

The elders or bishops are to act as shepherds of **the church of God**. For *church* see on 5.11 and Introduction, pp. lviiif.

The church is the people whom God **saved and acquired** (one word in Greek). He did this **through his own blood**. This expression was found theologically difficult by copyists who made various changes. Some, accepting what is almost certainly the correct (and difficult) reading, translate it, *through the blood of his Own*, *his Own* being taken as a title of Christ. It is very unlikely that a trained theologian would write, of God, 'his own blood'. But Luke was not such a theologian, and the natural way of reading the Greek should probably be adopted (as in the present translation). It was enough for Luke that when Jesus Christ shed his blood on the cross he was acting as the representative of God; he was God's way of giving life, blood, for the world. How the blood shed on the cross saved a people for God is a question which it would be wrong to pursue at great depth because it probably did not occur to Luke to inquire deeply into it. Luke nowhere else asserts so plainly that it was the death of Jesus that brought into being the redeemed people, but the form – and indeed the existence – of his two-volume work, hinging on crucifixion and resurrection, implies so much. And with that Luke seems to be content.

29. Paul's **departure** (on his travels? in death? or both, a generalization? – 'as soon as I am out of the way') will lead to the entry of **fearsome wolves**, an image suggested by the description of the church as a flock (v. 28). The adjective is literally *heavy*; *oppressive*, *savage*, is probably the sense intended, though the emphasis may perhaps be on *strong*, *formidable*, rather than *ferocious*. The wolves **will come into your company**, that is, they come in from without. They may be Jewish or Gentile teachers who make their way into the church and propagate false doctrine within it. For the fulfilment of this verse, and of v. 30, see the Pastorals and Revelation. The observation bears on the relative dates of the books.

30. and from among yourselves men will rise up, in contrast with those who come in from without (v. 29). Heresy and schism will arise within. *Yourselves* should apply to the Ephesian elders, but Luke is probably thinking of the church at large.

There is nothing in the present passage to suggest in which ways the truth would be perverted or who would attempt to set up rival communities over against what Luke regarded as the true church. It is clear that a time is contemplated when orthodoxy and heresy would be clearly differentiated, and when the church would be an institution with clearly defined frontiers. It did not always appear so simple. Gnostic teachers, for example, emerging within the church would often regard themselves as its most faithful, or at least as its most intelligent and advanced members.

31. The speaker now turns from the future to the past. The two are deliberately mingled, and united by the word **Watch**. This recalls apocalyptic passages (e.g. Mk 13.34, 35, 37; 1 Thess. 5.6) but here it refers not to watchful preparedness for the coming of the Son of man but to vigilance in caring for the continuing life of the church. **night and day** must be read in the light of v. 34: when Paul was not working for his living he was constantly employed as a pastor. **for three years**; see 19.8, 10. This was work over which he shed **tears**; cf. 2 Cor. 2.4. It could be summed up in **admonishing** (a Pauline word: Rom. 15.14; 1 Cor. 4.14; 1 Thess. 5.12,14; Col. 1.28; 3.16; 2 Thess. 3.15; the cognate noun in 1 Cor. 10.11; Eph. 6.4; Titus 3.10). He admonished **each one**, not the 'spirituals' only – an anti-gnostic point?

32. Paul exhorts his hearers; he also commits them **to God and to the word of his grace**. The two elements in this commendation form in fact one: *to God, who is active in the word of grace*, which you proclaim and by which you live. Since these elements belong together the grammatical question of the antecedent of **who/which is able to build you up** . . . becomes less important. It is the word of God, but that means God in his word, who is able to build up the elders and the church they serve. The building up of the church belongs to the present age; **the inheritance** will be received in the age to come. It is not clear why Paul (Luke) should say **among all those who have been sanctified** instead of *all the saints* (*holy ones*). It is important, however, that the Ephesian elders take their place in a larger company. The *inheritance* has an important OT background. See e.g. Deut. 33.3, 4; Ps. 15(16).5; Wisd. 5.5. Cf. also 1 QS 11.7, 8; 1 QH 11.11, 12.

Polycarp may show knowledge of this verse: *Epistle* 12.2 (May God . . . build you up . . . and give you part and lot among his saints).

33. Paul, again looking into the past, justifies his conduct in Ephesus (and, no doubt, Luke means to imply, elsewhere) using language similar to that of Samuel in 1 Sam. 12.3. What he had done he had not done for money (had he been accused of this? Cf. 2 Cor. 12.16–18), or other material advantage.

34. Not only did Paul show no desire for others' property (v. 33); not only does he work for his own living; he works also for the benefit of others.

You yourselves know, but Luke wishes to inform his readers, **that these hands** – the speaker shows them to his hearers – **ministered to my own needs and to those who were with me**. Cf. 18.3; 1 Cor. 4.12. In 1 Corinthians 9 Paul (using a saying of Jesus different from that quoted in v. 35) argues that it is right that preachers of the

Gospel should be maintained by those to whom they minister, though he himself chooses to make no use of the principle in relation to the church of Corinth. He did accept gifts from other churches (1 Cor. 9.6–18; 2 Cor. 11.7–11; Phil. 4.10–18).

35. it is necessary to work like this and to help the weak, and to remember . . . You must do all these things. Luke takes the view that church elders should work for their living and be in a position to help those who cannot do so; they must like Paul be ministers in their spare time.

Just as in 1 Cor. 9.14 Paul clinches his argument that preachers ought to be supported by the congregation by quoting a saying of Jesus, so here he confirms in the same way his advice to elders to support themselves. **It is more blessed to give than to receive.** The saying has many parallels in ancient literature, from which it was probably taken. It should not be taken in an absolute sense ('giving is blessed, not receiving'), or pressed to the implication that the poor, who have nothing to give, get no blessing. It addresses one who has a choice between giving and receiving; for him, giving is the better course.

36. For the farewell prayers; cf. 21.5. This and the next two verses are probably Luke's construction, a framework for the speech.

37. A good deal, a common Lucan expression. See 18.18. **They fell on Paul's neck**. Cf. Lk. 15.20; in the OT cf. Gen. 33.4; 45.14; it describes an emotional embrace, here accompanied by a kiss.

38. that they should see his face no more. See v. 25. This was a final parting. This could have been a mistake; Paul might have returned to the East. But it seems very unlikely.

They saw him off to the ship. Cf. 20.13. The Greek article does more than the English (**the**) to hint that it was the ship in which he arrived, but falls short of proving it.

XIII

PAUL RETURNS TO JERUSALEM

(21.1 – 22.29)

52. JOURNEY TO JERUSALEM 21.1–14

**1 When we had separated from them and set sail we made a
straight course and came to Cos, and on the next day to Rhodes,
and thence to Patara. 2 We found a ship crossing to Phoenicia,
embarked, and set sail. 3 Having raised Cyprus and left it on our
left we sailed to Syria and landed at Tyre, for there the ship was
discharging its cargo. 4 We sought out the disciples and stayed
there seven days. They told Paul through the Spirit that he should
not go to Jerusalem. 5 But it happened that, when we had completed the [seven] days, we left and set out on our journey while
they all, with their wives and children, saw us off as far as outside
the city. We knelt on the beach, prayed, 6 and said farewell to one
another. We embarked on the ship, while they returned home.**

**7 We continued the voyage from Tyre; we arrived at Ptolemais,
greeted the brothers, and stayed with them one day. 8 On the next
day we left and came to Caesarea. We entered the house of Philip
the evangelist, who was one of the Seven, and stayed with him.
9 He had four daughters, virgins, who prophesied. 10 We stayed
on for many days, and there came down from Judaea a prophet,
Agabus by name. 11 He came to us, took Paul's belt, bound his
own feet and hands, and said, 'Thus speaks the Holy Spirit: So
shall the Jews in Jerusalem bind the man whose belt this is, and
deliver him into the hands of the Gentiles.' 12 When we heard
this, we and the local residents begged [Paul] not to go up to
Jerusalem. 13 Then answered Paul, 'What are you doing, as you
weep and break my heart? for I am ready not only to be bound**

but even to die in Jerusalem for the name of the Lord Jesus.' [14] Since he would not be persuaded we fell silent, with the words, 'The Lord's will prevail.'

The journey continues; similar voyages, requiring similar lists of place-names, occur in other ancient sources. A different kind of parallel has been found in 2 Kings 2.1–12, where Elisha accompanies Elijah from place to place, Elijah repeatedly predicting his imminent departure, to the subdued lamentation of the prophets, but there is nothing in Luke's narrative that suggests that he had the OT in mind.

The source of the narrative is disputed. The first person plural recurs in vv. 1, 2, 3, 4, 5, 6, 7, 8, 11, 12, and 14, and it is natural to think that Luke is here using the first person plural itinerary that occurs elsewhere in the book. Not all agree, and it is true that signs of Lucan style suggest his redactional hand. An important question is whether vv. 8b, 9 belong to the source or to the redaction; if to the source it means that there is at least a second-hand, conceivably a first-hand, connection between the author of Acts and one of the Seven, whose story runs back to ch. 6. It is interesting to note that Agabus, previously mentioned at 11.28, is now (v. 10) described as if he were an unfamiliar character. Information about him may have reached Luke along two different channels. It seems probable that the person responsible for the *We* and for the itinerary met Agabus here.

We have in this paragraph a clear example of what Luke appears to have done throughout the journey narrative. There is an itinerary, which gives in simple terms a list of places touched at, probably noting a few additional matters that bear on the journey and its route, notably the plot of 20.3, the halt in Miletus (20.15f.), and the encounter with disciples at Tyre (21.3f.). To this travel source Luke added incidents which (in all probability) he learned by local inquiry: the miracle at Troas (20.7–12), the farewell at Tyre (21.5f.), perhaps the meeting with Philip (21.8f.) and the prophecy of Agabus (21.10–14). The third component consists of theological comment on the meaning of the journey. The most important such comment is the speech at Miletus (20.18–35), which shows Paul's pastoral care for the whole church and foretells both his approaching suffering and the perils of heresy and schism which lie ahead. In addition to the speech there are repeated references to Paul's suffering and his determination to face and accept it.

1. we had separated from them. Luke's word suggests a parting made with difficulty; they were loath to part.

we made a straight course (see 16.11) . . . **to Cos**. This implies a north-east wind, which was usual. After Samos, going south, Cos was the next sizeable island; it was the home of Hippocrates and the site of the medical school founded by him. For Jews on Cos see *NS* 3.69; Trebilco 13, 134f.

to Rhodes. The ship was following the chain of inshore Aegean islands. There is little evidence of Jews at Rhodes but see 1 Macc. 15.23. **Patara** was on the mainland, in Lycia. The Western text here adds a call at Myra.

2. A change of ship was necessary. Some have guessed that **We found** a fresh ship in order to make greater speed or to avoid a plot (cf. 20.3). It is simpler to think that the first ship was going no further, a larger ship was needed to cross **to Phoenicia** – no longer a coastal voyage. In Greek as in English the present participle **crossing** is used with future reference.

3. Cyprus: see 11.19. They left it on their left, passing to the right, that is, to the south of it following a direct line from Patara (Myra).

Syria: see 15.23. The word is used here in the sense of Phoenicia.

Tyre was the most notable city on the Phoenician coast. It had been destroyed by Alexander the Great in 332 BC but speedily regained prosperity. There were Jews here (*NS* 3.14f.). For the earlier story of Tyre see 2 Sam. 5.11; 1 Kings 5; Isa. 23; Ezek. 26–28. Estimates of the time required for this voyage vary from three to five days.

was discharging its cargo. Tyre was a great trading centre. On this journey Antioch is not included. This may have been simply through failure to catch a convenient boat; it may have been that the church of Antioch, after the troubles of Gal. 2.11–21, was no longer open to Paul. The question is worth asking, though there is no means of finding an answer.

4. the disciples: one of Luke's common terms for a local Christian community. **We . . . stayed there seven days.** Cf. 20.6. Paul was (according to Acts) in a hurry to reach Jerusalem, but was obliged to wait for the unloading and reloading of his ship. *The ship* in v. 6 implies in Greek, with some probability, that it was the ship previously mentioned.

They told Paul through the Spirit that he should not go to Jerusalem. *Through the Spirit*: presumably, showing the phenomena of inspiration. Luke does not express himself clearly. His words taken strictly would mean either that Paul was deliberately disobedient to the will of God or that the Spirit was mistaken in the guidance given. Luke cannot have intended either of these. It is probable that what he meant but failed adequately to express was something like what is written in vv. 10–14. The Spirit acting through prophets foretold that the journey to Jerusalem would bring Paul suffering, and his friends, acting under the influence not of the Spirit but of human concern, sought to dissuade him from going there.

5, 6. The language of these verses is Lucan and gives a correct description of the smooth beach at Tyre. **We knelt on the beach, prayed, and said farewell to one another**, a Christian leave-taking. The travelling party **embarked on the ship**; the article is anaphoric – the ship already mentioned (v. 4). **they returned home**, literally, *to their own* (*places*); cf. Jn 16.32; 19.27.

7. We continued the voyage. The word could be rendered, *Having completed the voyage*, and some think Luke's meaning to be that the journey from Ptolemais to Caesarea was made by land.

Ptolemais was an important port. It was an ancient town, formerly Acco (Judges 1.13; 4 Q pls[a] 2.23), renamed after himself by Ptolemy V (285–246 BC). There was a Jewish population, also Christians, **the brothers**. That **we . . . stayed with them** no more than **one day** (contrast seven days each at Troas and Tyre) probably means that Paul's group was proceeding by ship and that the ship stayed only one night.

8. On the next day corresponds to *one day* in v. 7. **Caesarea**: see 10.1 and the note. **We entered the house of Philip**, last heard of at Caesarea (8.40). If the 'we' material is to be thought of as a source it can hardly be insignificant that its author lodged with a Christian whose memories extended as far back as Acts 6, and probably earlier. See pp. 88, 128 and Introduction, p. xxviii.

Philip is described as **the evangelist, who was one of the Seven**. In the NT the word evangelist occurs only here and at Eph. 4.11; 2 Tim. 4.5, but cf. 8.12, 35, 40, where Philip *evangelizes*. The word seems to have dropped out of use and to have had no precise significance. Eusebius (especially *HE* 3.37.2) seems to have regarded it as applicable to those who followed the apostles in mission preaching and founding churches. An *evangelist*, not an apostle; one of the *Seven*, not one of the Twelve. But the *Seven* remained in technical use even less than evangelist.

9. He had four daughters, virgins, who prophesied. Cf. the three daughters of Job in Testament of Job 48–50. Eusebius (*HE* 3.39.9) recalls information which Papias claimed to have derived from the daughters of Philip.

That women should prophesy in gatherings of Christians is confirmed by 1 Cor. 11.5 and by Acts 2.17; it appears to be denied by 1 Cor. 14.34; 1 Tim. 2.11f. No doubt the practice varied from part to part of the church. Attitudes tended to harden against participation by women, but Luke, towards the end of the first century, must have held that it was legitimate and edifying for women to prophesy. The story of Agabus that follows (cf. 11.27–30) shows that for Luke prediction was an important part of prophecy; for Paul the emphasis lies elsewhere.

The four prophesying daughters were *virgins*. It is hard to tell whether Luke relates this as a simple fact or as a condition relevant to prophecy. If they had not been virgins would they have prophesied? If they had not been virgins would they have been allowed to prophesy? The women bidden in 1 Cor. 14.35 to be silent are married. For Luke's own view it is relevant that Priscilla, who taught Apollos, was married and that the prophetess Anna (Lk. 2.36) was a widow.

10. Agabus: see 11.28. There is no indication how Agabus has been occupied in the meantime, or whether his prophesying constituted an office or was an occasional act, occurring only when prompted by the Spirit. He is introduced here as if he were a fresh character in Luke's story. This suggests that the present reference was contained in the We source (or some other source) in which Agabus had not previously been mentioned. Agabus is said to come **from Judae**a: but Caesarea was in Judaea – that is, from the Roman administrative point of view. This *from Judaea* may reflect Jewish use.

11. Agabus **bound his own feet and hands** – an acted parable, a prophetic sign comparable with those of the OT prophets. His prophecy is predictive, and its fulfilment will appear in the following chapters, though not precisely, for, the Jews do not themselves bind Paul, nor do they hand him over to the Gentiles. Luke however is not a writer who notices or is concerned about neat correspondences; he may moreover in **deliver him into the hands of the Gentiles** be thinking of the arrest and trial of Jesus, which will provide a pattern for Paul's. The story as a whole, however, requires that the Jews should have laid before the Romans some accusation against Paul.

12. we, Paul's travelling companions, are joined by **the local** Christian **residents** in begging Paul **not to go up to Jerusalem** at the cost Agabus has described.

13. break my heart. *break* is a rare and strong word; it is not clear whether *breaking Paul's heart* here means *with sorrow* or by *weakening his resolve*. The latter suits the present context better. But Paul was **ready . . . even to die . . . for the name of the Lord Jesus**. Cf. 5.41; 9.16. For the use of *name* in Acts see pp. 38, 39.

14. Paul is not to be persuaded. It is clear to him that his duty calls him to Jerusalem (Why? Not apparently to preach; to convey the proceeds of his collection? To secure the unity of the church? To act as well as speak his testimony to the Crucified?) and nothing will deflect him from it. This is part of Luke's picture of the heroic missionary – and is not inconsistent with the epistles.

The Lord's will prevail. The Lucan version of the Lord's Prayer does not contain the words, Thy will be done; it follows that there is here (cf. v. 11) a probable allusion to the Passion story (Lk. 22.42). The hearers recognize in Paul's words the will of God, and, unwelcome as this is, they pray that it may be done.

53. PAUL AND THE CHURCH OF JERUSALEM 21.15–26

**[15] After these days we packed up and set out on the journey up to
Jerusalem. [16] Some of the disciples went with us from Caesarea,
bringing us to the man we were to lodge with, Mnason, a Cypriote
and an early disciple. [17] When we reached Jerusalem the brothers
welcomed us gladly.**

**[18] On the next day Paul went in with us to James, and all the
elders were present. [19] When he had greeted them he related in
detail the things that God had done among the Gentiles through
his ministry. [20] When they heard it they glorified God and said to
him, 'You see, brother, how many tens of thousands there are of
those who have believed among the Jews, and they are all zealous
for the Law. [21] They have been informed about you that you teach
defection from Moses, telling all the Jews who live among the
Gentiles that they should not circumcise their children or walk
in accordance with the customs. [22] What then? They will certainly
hear that you have come. [23] So do this that we tell you. We
have four men who have a vow on them. [24] Take these men with
you, be purified with them, and pay their expenses that they
may shave their heads, and then all will know that there is
nothing in the things they have been told about you, but that
you yourself also conform, observing the Law. [25] But concerning
those Gentiles who have believed we ourselves wrote an injunction with the decision that they should be on their guard against
food sacrificed to idols, blood, strangled meat, and fornication.'
[26] Then Paul on the next day took the men with him, was purified
with them, and entered the Temple, notifying the fulfilment of
the days of purification until the offering was offered for each of
them.**

This is a passage of equally great importance and difficulty. The opening verses retain the first person plural of the travel narrative, and may well have brought it, or one section of it, to a close. The warm welcome given to Paul would form a suitable conclusion, and from this point the story is focused on Paul and not on *us*. The action taken by Paul at the request of James and his colleagues is represented as the origin of all the following events, up to Paul's arrival in Rome. Yet after v. 27a the four vow-makers disappear from the scene, and a new charge – of bringing Greeks into the Temple – is brought against Paul. Combined with such plainly historical questions (see on vv. 21, 24, 25) are theological questions which at the same time bear upon the historicity of the narrative. Would the Paul whom we know from his letters have acted in the way described in this paragraph? It is very doubtful, though the possibility cannot be excluded that in the interests of peace he allowed himself to be persuaded, perhaps against his better judgement, to take part in the legal requirements laid upon those who had taken vows. If so, the outcome must have speedily shown him the error of his decision.

Another factor calls for consideration here, though in Luke's story it is noticeable by reason of its surprising absence. Paul had brought to Jerusalem the product of his collection for the benefit of the poor in Jerusalem. What became of it? When was it handed over? There are obvious possibilities at v. 17 or at vv. 18, 19. But Luke is silent (see however 24.17). It has been suggested that James, perhaps with excellent intention, perhaps to Paul's dismay, announced, 'We shall use part of this gift to pay the expenses of our four poor Nazirite brothers, and will do so in your name, so as to still the rumours that you no longer care for the ancestral religion, and to show that you observe the Law.'

Had James ulterior motives? Did he hope to discredit Paul in the estimation of Gentile Christians? Did he even hope to ensnare him into the Temple and provoke the riot that ensued – in which, as in the whole legal process that followed, there is no indication that the Christians of Jerusalem made any move to aid the apostle of the Gentiles? We have no means of answering these questions, though we cannot avoid asking them, and v. 25 remains ambiguous; see the note. James and his colleagues may have honestly feared for the success of their mission to Jews if Paul should be allowed too much freedom. His hope to secure the unity of the church by means of his collection failed. It may be that this is why Luke omitted the collection from his story.

15. After these days, presumably the days of 21.10, though the expression means sometimes simply *After this*. **we** (the first person plural continues) **packed up**. The word is used in this sense in relation to a journey; possibly of equipping horses – could it be that Paul was travelling on horseback? Even on horseback the distance (sixty-seven miles) from Caesarea to Jerusalem could hardly be covered in one day; see the variant reading in v. 16.

16. The general sense of this verse is clear, though it contains a number of grammatical uncertainties, which cannot be discussed here.

Some of the disciples accompanied Paul and his party from Caesarea, bringing them to **Mnason**, with whom they were **to lodge**. But where? Somewhere in the long stretch between Caesarea and Jerusalem? Or, ignoring intermediate stops, in Jerusalem? The text translated here does not help (though v. 17 strongly suggests that Jerusalem was reached only as a subsequent stop after that with Mnason). The Western text is very difficult to reconstruct here, since Codex Bezae is badly damaged, but it appears to have run: they brought us to those with whom we were to lodge, and when we reached a certain village we were with Mnason . . . In this text it is clear that Mnason did not live in Jerusalem but in a village (doubtless between Caesarea and Jerusalem). In substance this may well be correct, but the Western text is probably a common-sense interpretation of a less clear original.

The name Mnason occurs nowhere else in the NT, but was not uncommon. It is Greek, but may have been chosen as an equivalent of Menahem or Manasseh, or some other Semitic name. Mnason was probably a **Cypriote** Jew. See on 4.36. He was also **an early disciple**. For the adjective cf. 15.7. Here it means that Mnasons's discipleship went back to the earliest days, that is, either the earliest days of Christianity in Jerusalem or to the beginnings of Paul's mission in Cyprus (13.4–12) – possibly to neither of these, since Barnabas the Cypriote had been a Christian before Paul's mission. The reference to Mnason is probably traditional; it is hard to see what Luke would have gained by inventing him.

17. Whether traditional material continues in this verse is more doubtful. **we reached** suggests that the We source continued. **the brothers welcomed us gladly**; this was not what Paul had expected; see Rom. 15.30, 31. Some explain the welcome by the suggestion that the *brothers* whom Paul first encountered were Hellenistic Jewish Christians. But Luke goes on to represent James also as friendly and convinced that the charge against Paul (v. 21) was not true and could be readily disproved. The narrative must be examined verse by verse.

18. On the next day (one of Luke's regular expressions) **Paul went in with us** (now clearly distinguished from Paul) **to James**. The verb and preposition convey a hint of entering the presence of a great person, and James (who must be the Lord's brother, 15.13) is now undoubtedly the leading Christian in Jerusalem. The impression is strengthened by the presence of **all the elders** (see 11.30; 14.23; 20.17, 28; and see Introduction, pp. lviii–lx. But the most striking feature of the verse is the absence – here and in v. 19 – of any reference to Paul's collection.

19. When he (Paul) **had greeted them he related in detail the things that God had done among the Gentiles through his ministry.** There is no doubt that Luke does regard the mighty works done in the course of the mission as at least part of its justification (see 15.12), but there is no clear reference to miracles at all. The events described must consist primarily in the conversion of Gentiles. As frequently, Luke makes it clear that the great works were not done by the missionaries but by God through the missionaries. They were done *through Paul's ministry*; the Greek noun is *diakonia*, a word Paul sometimes uses of his collection; but this is not even hinted at here. It is what has happened *among the Gentiles* that is of interest to James.

20. they glorified God: the Christian authorities in Jerusalem are (according to Luke) delighted to hear of the success of the Gentile mission; and they address Paul as **brother**. But they draw attention to the **tens of thousands there are of those who have believed among the Jews**. The last words do not refer to Gentiles living among Jews, but to believers who are Jews, and clearly do not cease to be Jews, for **they are all zealous for the Law**. There are some who wish to omit the words *who have believed* – those who complained were Jews but not Christians. There is no authority, and no justification, for the omission. Luke is describing Christian believers who were devotees of the Law. He may exaggerate their numbers, but probably gives a not inaccurate picture of the Jerusalem church.

Were James and the elders quoting a complaint or sharing in it? They do not condemn the attitude of those who bring charges against Paul, and apparently feel that he must do something to clear his reputation; but they believe, or at least hope, that he will do this.

21. They have been informed. By whom? Luke does not tell us; he may be thinking of those whom he mentions in 15.1, 5, but since he evidently believed the charge to be false he must be thinking of trouble-makers who spread false reports. Since however they do not appear, the general picture of a harmonious apostolic age is maintained, though it is only the surface that is smooth. There is an influential anti-Pauline movement.

The report is that Paul teaches **defection from Moses**, that is, from the Law of Moses. The allegation is illustrated by, and may even be alluded to, in a saying attributed to R. Eleazar of Modiim (*c.* AD 120–140) (M. Aboth 3.12): If a man profanes the Hallowed Things and despises the set feasts . . . and makes void the covenant of Abraham our father [i.e. undoes the effect of circumcision], and discloses meanings in the Law which are not according to the *Halakah*, even though a knowledge of the Law and good works are his, he has no share in the world to come.

Those concerned are **the Jews who live among the Gentiles**, Diaspora Jews. The question is no longer (as in 15.1, 5) the circumcision of Gentile converts to Christianity but whether Jews who become Christians should circumcise their children and obey other legal regulations, in other words, retain their Jewishness.

Did Paul in fact teach Jews to abandon circumcision and other provisions of the Law? Opposite answers have been given to this question. It is hard to believe that he *forbade* Jewish parents to circumcise their children but he probably classed those who insisted on and made much of the rite as 'weak' (Rom. 14; 15; 1 Cor. 8; 10). He certainly taught his fellow Jews to sit loose to legal regulations (see e.g. Gal. 2.12–14; 1 Cor. 10.25, 27) and regarded circumcision as an irrelevancy (1 Cor. 7.19).

22. They will certainly hear that you have come. There is a variant reading, with sufficient support to mean that it must be taken seriously, which contains a Greek word that may mean 'the (local) church as a whole' (as at 15.30) or 'a (possibly disorderly) crowd' (as at 21.36). If the variant is accepted, James says either 'We shall have to have a church meeting' or 'There is sure to be a riot'. If however the words were originally in the text it is hard to see why they should have been omitted. The riot undoubtedly happened.

23. We have four men who have a vow on them. The *vow* is more like a Nazirite vow (see on 18.18) than any other, but difficulties arise as the story proceeds; see below.

In Luke's narrative James and his colleagues take the view that only public action on Paul's part will clear his name. To consider whether this was so would require more knowledge than we possess of the structure of the Jerusalem church, the authority of its leaders, and the extent to which their writ ran in the Diaspora. The incident of the vows and the attendant sacrifices disappears from the story as soon as it happens.

24. The plan is now outlined in detail; some of the details are however obscure. **Take these men with you**, not only, Accompany them, but, Undertake responsibility for the procedure they must follow. **be purified with them**. This is not clear. It cannot mean, *Enter into the vow with them*, for the Nazirite vow lasted thirty days. It seems that the men had during the period of the vow incurred some uncleanness and that Luke supposed (wrongly) that Paul would be obliged to share in the act of purification. Alternatively, Paul himself needed purification before entering the Temple, or entering into the vow procedure, because of his residence outside the land of Israel. Luke, it seems, was imperfectly informed (but we cannot suppose that James was) about the regulations for vows and uncleanness.

pay their expenses. There is no problem here. Purification required sacrifice, and sacrifices cost money. Would this come from Paul's collection? We do not know, but the question cannot be avoided. **that they may shave their heads**. This expression probably covered the whole process of release from the vow – offering the he-lamb, ewe-lamb and ram, and the associated meal offering; cutting off and burning the hair. By doing all these things, or sharing in them, Paul would show that **there is nothing in the things they have been told about** him. They would prove that he did **conform, observing the Law**. Would they, and did he? The question is not whether Paul would on occasion do things that Jews did; 1 Cor. 9.20 proves that he would. The question is whether Paul was prepared to use a special occasion to suggest something that was not true, namely, that he too (**you yourself**), just like the ardent Jews who suspected his loyalty, was regularly observant of the Law as understood within Judaism. Readiness to do this is not covered by 1 Corinthians 9, and if Paul's motives in performing this single act were seen to be false his Jewish critics would have been - rightly - more enraged than by simple apostasy. It is not surprising that the plan broke down.

25. But concerning those Gentiles who have believed. The present concern of the Jewish believers (v. 20) is not with Gentile believers; their behaviour has already been regulated. It is presupposed that the Decree of 15.29 applied not to a limited area only but to all Gentile Christians. Jewish Christians are not asking that Gentiles should be made Jews, only that Jews should not be made Gentiles through the abandonment of circumcision and other legal requirements. It is easy to see how this concern would arise. If Paul expected Jews to eat with Gentiles, unless the Decree was observed he was expecting them to give up some of their Jewishness. This may account sufficiently for the reference here to the Decree, though perhaps not for the citation of all the details. On the surface, it seems that Paul is being informed of the Decree as if he knew nothing about it, although, according to Acts, he was present when it was formulated, approved of it, and was one of its sponsors. The repetition may be introduced in order to inform Paul's companions, or to remind the reader; it may be that this is how the Decree was introduced in the 'We source'; it may be that we have here a trace of a divergent tradition which did not represent Paul as having previously been concerned with the Decree. The last of these possibilities (not incapable of being combined with others) may well be true, but, as suggested above, Luke's presentation of the matter is not impossible. 'Here is a new point; the old one (conditions for the admission of Gentiles) was settled long ago.'

we ourselves wrote an injunction. *We* is emphatic. A reader unfamiliar with ch. 15 would suppose that it referred to James and the elders (v. 15). Taking Acts as a whole it must mean, You Paul and I James. But was it necessary to give Paul that information?

they should be on their guard against. At 15.20, 29 the word used is *abstain from*. It is doubtful whether Luke intended, or noticed, any difference in meaning. For the content of the Decree see on 15.20, 29.

Historical questions of great importance focus on this verse. See below; also Introduction, pp. lxvii–lxx.

26. Paul assents to the proposal and begins to put it into effect.

was purified with them. Cf. v. 24; and see the note on that verse for the question whether Paul would need to be purified, possibly on his return from residence abroad in Gentile territory. Cf. Num. 6.9; this suggests that the men have not reached the normal completion of their vow but are renewing it after incurring defilement.

notifying the fulfilment of the days of purification. Again; cf. Num. 6.9f.

until the offering was offered for each of them. This would mark final discharge from the vows.

54. RIOT AT JERUSALEM 21.27–40

**27 When the seven days were almost completed, the Jews from
Asia, having seen Paul in the Temple, stirred up the whole crowd
and laid their hands upon him, 28 shouting, 'Men of Israel, help!
this is the man who teaches all men everywhere against the People
and the Law and this place. Moreover, he has also brought Greeks
into the Temple and has profaned this holy place.' 29 For they had
previously seen Trophimus the Ephesian in the city with him and
supposed that Paul had brought him into the Temple. 30 The whole
city was excited and there was a tumultuous concourse of the
people. They laid hands on Paul and dragged him outside the
Temple; and immediately the gates were shut. 31 While they were
seeking to kill him word went up to the tribune of the cohort that
all Jerusalem was in an uproar. 32 He immediately took soldiers
and centurions and ran down upon them. When they saw the
tribune and the soldiers they stopped beating Paul. 33 Then the
tribune came up, got hold of him, and commanded him to be
bound with two chains. He inquired who he might be and what
he had done. 34 Some in the crowd called out one thing, others
another. Since he was not able to get trustworthy information
because of the tumult he ordered him to be brought into the
barracks. 35 When he got on the steps he was actually carried by
the soldiers because of the violence of the crowd, 36 for the whole
multitude of the people were following, shouting, 'Away with
him!'**

**37 As he was about to enter the barracks Paul said to the
tribune, 'May I say something to you?' He said, 'Do you know
how to speak Greek? 38 So are you not the Egyptian, who in the
past raised and led out into the desert four thousand men of the
sicarii?' 39 Paul said, 'Truly I am a Jew, of Tarsus in Cilicia, a
citizen of no mean city. I pray you, permit me to speak to the
people.' 40 He gave permission; Paul stood on the steps and
gestured to the people with his hand. There was dead silence, and
Paul called out to them in the Hebrew language.**

Quickly read, this paragraph gives the impression of a straightforward account of violent events in the Temple, happening at a point determined in relation to the process of purification in which, according to

21.23–26, Paul had agreed to take part. Paul however was accused not of anything amiss in the rite of purification but of bringing into the part of the Temple from which Gentiles were excluded Trophimus the Ephesian. This charge, Luke clearly implies, was not true. Paul was beaten, the city was in an uproar; the Roman tribune intervened at the head of his troops, brought Paul into the barracks, and began to interrogate him, believing him to be an Egyptian trouble-maker. Paul sought and obtained permission to speak to the crowd.

This appears to be, and is, a plain tale, and whatever its origin every part of it is possibly historical. There are however points of difficulty, some real, some imaginary. These will be noted in the commentary.

Paul was not without companions in Jerusalem, and it is presumably to them that Luke (who could himself have been one of them, though probably he was not) owes this story and some of those that follow. There is no use of the first person plural, nor could this be expected. The conversation between Paul and the tribune must be based on conjecture. There is little or nothing improbable in it. See the note.

27. When the seven days were almost completed. This is most naturally understood in terms of Num. 6.9 to mean that the four men who had undertaken (Nazirite) vows had incurred some uncleanness, for removing which a seven-day period was necessary. Alternatively, Paul might have needed to remove uncleanness due to his residence abroad. This too would require seven days in view of Num. 19.11–13, since outside the land of Israel one might unwittingly come into contact with graves.

the Jews from Asia. These had already caused trouble for Paul (20.19). It is to be noted that (according to Acts) it is Jews, not Jewish Christians (21.20f.) who make trouble for Paul.

28. Men of Israel. See 2.22 and the note. **this is the man who teaches all men everywhere** (this must mean *all Gentiles*) **against the People and the Law and this place**. This is a different charge from that of 21.21, where Paul is alleged to teach *Jews* not to observe the Law. In the epistles Paul does not teach against the People (Romans 9–11; but note 1 Thess. 2.14–16); his teaching about the Law is complex, with positive and negative elements; and he does not refer to the Temple. Luke of course regards the accusation as false.

he has also brought Greeks into the Temple. The next verse names only Trophimus. A notice on the Temple wall forbade non-Jews, on pain of death, to enter beyond the Court of the Gentiles. See *NS* 2.285f.; *Background*, 53. In 1 QpHab 12.6–9 the Wicked Priest defiles the Temple; it is mistaken to see in this a reference to Paul.

29. Trophimus, from Asia: 20.4. Had the others mentioned in that verse not reached Jerusalem? Or was it that only Trophimus had been seen and recognized? **they . . . supposed**, quite illogically, but naturally enough if they believed Paul to be capable of any offence against Judaism.

30. immediately the gates were shut: possibly not the outer gates, but the gates of the inner courts. The authorities would shut the gates to prevent further profanation – perhaps by the murder of Paul.

31. While they were seeking to kill him. One would have thought that they could have succeeded in their desire long before a report could reach army headquarters. **word** is not a formal report; it is nearer to *rumour*. **went up**, literally, to the Antonia tower, which overlooked the Temple. See *NS* 1.361, 362, 366. Troops were kept here during festivals. For **cohort** see on 10.1; a **tribune** was the commander of a cohort. **all Jerusalem was in an uproar**. It was the sort of event that could easily get out of hand, and it was the purpose of the Roman garrison to nip such disturbances in the bud.

32. soldiers and centurions. For *centurions* see on 10.1. The plural means at least two, so that – at least on paper – 200 men or more might be involved. This intervention had the intended effect; the crowd stopped beating Paul.

33. Then the tribune came up. That the tribune himself led his forces and began the interrogation suggests that the disturbance was taken very seriously. **two chains**: perhaps attached to two soldiers, one on each side.

who he might be and what he had done. The two dependent questions are differently expressed in Greek. The first is quite open – he might be anyone; the second assumes that he has done something to cause the trouble.

34. The tribune could get no trustworthy information from the crowd. **the barracks** will be the Antonia (see v. 31).

35. the steps, which linked the Temple to the Antonia. See Josephus, *War* 5.243. **he was actually carried by the soldiers**, not because he was too weak to walk (and so would be unable to make the speech of ch. 22) but, as Luke says, **because of the violence of the crowd**.

36. the whole multitude of the people were following. Hence *because of the violence* in v. 35. **Away with him!** Cf. Lk. 23.18; Acts 22.22; Jn 19.15; *Martyrdom of Polycarp* 3.2; 9.2. Cf. also Isa. 53.8; with Acts 8.33. Luke probably intends to recall the story of Jesus.

37. about to enter the barracks. See v. 35. The tribune is surprised (for a reason that will appear in the next verse) that Paul can speak Greek.

38. So are you not the Egyptian . . . ? This sentence may be taken as a question, expecting the answer Yes, or as a negative statement: Since you speak Greek you cannot be the Egyptian. Egyptians however could for the most part speak Greek, so that the negative statement is unlikely. Since Paul does not speak to him in Aramaic the tribune reaches the tentative conclusion: You could be the Egyptian; are you not he? The Egyptian had **raised and led into the desert four thousand men of the sicarii**. For the Egyptian see Josephus, *War* 2.261–3; *Ant*. 20.169–72. The Egyptian's forces were put down by Felix but he himself escaped, so that the tribune's question was quite reasonable. The population of Jerusalem had assisted the Romans in repulsing him; they might be doing so again. According to Josephus, he had led his army *out of* the desert to the Mount of Olives. Luke says *four thousand men*, Josephus thirty thousand. The difference has been explained by confusion of two Greek numerals: the letter *delta* (Δ = four) and the letter *lambda* (Λ = thirty). The *sicarii*, according to Josephus, carried concealed daggers, in form resembling Roman *sicae*, with which they committed many murders in the time of troubles leading up to the Roman war. If the tribune took Paul to be the leader of such a group he could hardly be expected to treat him gently.

39. Paul is **a Jew**, not an Egyptian, a Jew **of Tarsus in Cilicia**. For Tarsus and its significance see on 9.11. The civic status of Jews in Hellenistic cities was not uniform, and **a citizen of no mean city** may not have any very precise meaning. For Roman citizenship see on 22.25. We have little evidence concerning Jews in Tarsus, and cannot be certain that Paul meant much more than *resident in*, especially as he goes on to use what is almost a quotation from Euripides (*Ion* 8; cf. *Hercules Furens* 849). 'no mean city of the Greeks'. Paul refers again to his Tarsiote citizenship in 22.3, this time depreciating it in comparison with his residence in Jerusalem.

40. He gave permission. It seems improbable. The outcome was renewed violence (22.22f.), which might well have been expected. Would it not have been prudent to hustle Paul into the Antonia – in the interests of security, supposing Paul to be guilty, in his own interests, supposing him to be innocent? Perhaps the fact is that *Luke* needs a speech to clarify his story. **Paul stood on the steps**; see v. 35. He **gestured to the people with his hand**. Cf. 13.16, and other passages, for the orator's gesture.

in the Hebrew language. It is probable that Aramaic is intended. See *NS* 2.20–28.

55. PAUL'S TEMPLE SPEECH AND THE SEQUEL 22.1–29

**[1] 'Brothers! Fathers! Listen to the defence that I now bring to
you.' [2] When they heard that he was addressing them in the
Hebrew language they gave even greater silence. He went on: [3] 'I
am a man, a Jew, born in Tarsus in Cilicia, brought up in this
city, educated strictly in the ancestral Law at the feet of Gamaliel,
being zealous for God, as are all of you today. [4] And I persecuted
this Way to the death, binding and delivering to prison both men
and women, [5] as the high priest and all the company of elders
bear me witness. From them also I received letters to our [Jewish]
brothers and journeyed to Damascus, in order that I might bring
those [Jewish Christians] who were there bound to Jerusalem,
for punishment. [6] It happened to me as I travelled and was
drawing near to Damascus, about midday, that suddenly there
shone round about me from heaven a great light. [7] I fell to the
ground and heard a voice saying to me, "Saul, Saul, why are you
persecuting me?" [8] I answered, "Who art thou, Lord?" And he
said to me, "I am Jesus the Nazoraean, whom you are
persecuting." [9] Those who were with me saw the light, but did not
hear the voice of him who was speaking to me. [10] I said. "What
am I to do, Lord?" The Lord said to me, "Get up and go into
Damascus; there you will be told about all the things which it has
been appointed for you to do." [11] When I was unable to see because
of the glory of that light I was led by the hand by those who were
with me and came into Damascus. [12] One Ananias, a pious man
according to the Law, who had a good reputation with all the
resident Jews, [13] came to me, stood by me and said, "Brother Saul,
regain your sight." In that very hour I looked upon him. [14] He
said, "The God of our fathers has appointed you to know his will
and to see the Righteous One and to hear a voice from his mouth,
[15] for you shall be a witness for him to all men of the things you
have seen and heard. [16] And now what are you going to do? Get
up, get yourself baptized and wash away your sins by calling on
his name." [17] And it happened to me when I had returned to
Jerusalem and was praying in the Temple, that I fell into an
ecstasy [18] and saw him saying to me, "Make haste and depart
quickly from Jerusalem because they will not receive your
testimony about me." [19] And I said, "Lord, they themselves know**

that I was engaged in imprisoning and beating from synagogue to synagogue those who believe in thee, [20] and when the blood of Stephen thy witness was shed I was myself standing by and approving and keeping the clothes of those who were killing him." [21] He said to me, "Go, for I shall send you far from here to the Gentiles."'

[22] They listened to him up to this word and [then] they lifted up their voices saying, 'Away with such a man from the earth, for it is not fit that he should live.' [23] As they were shouting and flinging off their clothes and throwing dust in the air, [24] the tribune ordered that he should be brought into the barracks, saying that he should be examined with the scourge in order that he [the tribune] might know why they were so shouting him down. [25] But when they stretched him out for the lash Paul said to the centurion who was standing there. "Is it lawful for you to scourge a Roman – and one not even tried at that?" [26] When the centurion heard this he approached the tribune and reported the matter, saying, "What are you going to do? This man is a Roman." [27] The tribune approached him and said. "Tell me, are you a Roman?" "Yes" he said. [28] The tribune answered, "I acquired this citizenship at a high price." Paul said, "But I was born a citizen." [29] Immediately those who were about to examine him stood back, and the tribune was afraid when he recognized that [Paul] was a Roman, and that he had bound him.

The staple content of the speech which Paul, with the consent of the tribune, makes to the riotous crowd is an account of his conversion. This event is described three times in Acts: in ch. 9, here, and in ch. 26. For the event itself see Section 23. Here the account is adapted to the Jewish audience to which it is addressed. The High Priest himself is invoked to testify to Paul's Jewish zeal (v. 5), Ananias is described not as a disciple but as a devout observant of the Law (v. 12), who speaks in the name of the God of our fathers (v. 14), it is in the Temple that Paul receives his instructions (v. 17), and it is only when he claims to have been sent by God to the Gentiles that he provokes dissent (vv. 22, 23). It is not so clear that the speech was suited to the particular Jewish audience who heard it. Paul was accused of teaching against the People, the Law, and the Holy Place, and of having profaned the Temple by bringing Gentiles into it. In the background lurks the charge that he teaches Diaspora Jews apostasy from Moses.

None of these accusations is touched upon except indirectly, in the assertion that Paul is a good Jew trained by Gamaliel, a persecutor of Christians, and an authorized representative of the High Priest. These are however matters of fundamental importance. His conversion was within, not from, Judaism. He was and remained a Jew, and had lived in the Gentile world only as the result of a direct command from God, which he had done his best to avoid (vv. 18–21). These are all relevant considerations; and they set the stage for the rest of Acts.

The dramatic structure of the rest of the book is completed when the mob violence that interrupts the speech brings the Romans fully into the action. It was the tribune's duty to preserve order, hence to remove one who was evidently provoking disorder. It was conventional to 'examine' such a person by the use of the lash. It was natural that a Roman citizen should wish to save himself from a possibly fatal flogging by drawing attention to his status and rights. Whether Paul was a Roman citizen, and how in the circumstances he could prove that he was one, are questions to consider below.

Most of the arguments that have been brought against the historicity of the speech are unconvincing, though without question there are redactional elements in it and the whole is the result of Luke's editing of a traditional conversion story. Equally it is impossible to demonstrate its historicity; who, in the circumstances described, took notes of it? That Paul did make, or attempt to make, a speech, and that the outcome was the triangular Paul–Jews–Romans relationship which dominates the rest of Acts, is probable enough; certainly something brought the triangle into being.

1. Paul shows respect for his audience by adding **Fathers** to his customary **Brothers**. It has been rightly pointed out that **defence** is the theme of the remaining chapters of Acts. Paul claims to be committing no offence against either Judaism or Rome.

2. in the Hebrew language. See 21.40. **they gave even greater silence**, a conventional phrase. In the OT see Job 34.29. Silence implies attention.

3. I am a man a Jew. The point will be emphasized throughout the speech as Paul argues that Christianity is not opposed to Judaism but fulfils it.

born in Tarsus in Cilicia: another way of putting what is said in 21.39.

brought up in this city. Is *this city* Tarsus or Jerusalem? The answer often given has been Tarsus, but Jerusalem probably has the better claim, so that Paul is asserting that not only his higher education but his earlier training also had been located in Jerusalem, whither presumably the family had moved. For **Gamaliel** see on 5.34; a highly respected teacher and authority. Under such a teacher it is not surprising that Paul should be **zealous for God**. As a wise speaker he associates himself with his hearers: **as are all of you today**.

4. Proof of Paul's zeal follows. **I persecuted this Way to the death**. So ardent a persecutor of Christians could not fail to be a zealous Jew. Almost the whole of this verse appears in 9.2, 3. Cf. 26.10. Some think that *to the death* exaggerates Paul's persecution.

5. Cf. 9.1, 2. Here **the company of elders** is associated with the High Priest – as in fact they would be.

6. The construction differs from that of 9.3 but most of the significant words are found in both accounts. The present verse adds **about midday**, making the story more circumstantial and perhaps showing that the event was no dream but an objective occurrence.

7. Again, the construction differs but the significant words are found in 9.5.

8. This verse substantially reproduces 9.5. Here the name of Jesus is followed by **the Nazoraean**. For this word see on 2.22.

9. The parallel is found in 9.7. The most interesting difference is that in 9.7 we have *they heard the voice* (Greek, genitive case) *but saw no one*, but here **Those who were with me saw the light, but did not hear the voice** (Greek, accusative case). It is true that in Greek the verb *to hear* takes sometimes the accusative and sometimes the genitive, and attempts have often been made to explain the difference by means of this fact. But such attempts have often overlooked the further facts that in 9.4 we have *He . . . heard a voice* (accusative) and in 22.7 *I . . . heard a voice* (genitive). It is doubtful whether Luke was very interested in the question which case should follow the verb.

10. What am I to do, Lord? These words do not occur in ch. 9. They express admirably Paul's readiness to accept any charge laid upon him. The Lord's words however are closely parallel in the two accounts.

it has been appointed for you to do. The perfect tense suggests that Paul's mission is part of the eternal purpose of God.

11. There are close parallels with 9.8. *Saul got up from the ground* (in 9.8) was hardly necessary in view of the command in v. 10 and his subsequent activity.

12. The second part of the story introduces Ananias though without his long introductory vision and conversation with Christ. In ch. 9 Ananias is *a disciple*; here he is **a pious man according to the Law, who had a good reputation** (for this expression; cf. 6.3; 16.2) **with all the resident Jews**. If, as is probably intended, both descriptions are true we have an example of what Luke displays as an ideal – the good Jew is a good Christian.

13. The opening words give the sense of 9.17a, but that verse adds that Ananias laid his hands on Saul, and the simple command **regain your sight** replaces a much longer sentence. In both passages Ananias begins with the words **Brother Saul**, accepting Paul as already a Christian brother.

14. Ananias here gives the substance of what is said to him by the Lord in 9.15; the wording is in the main different.

The God of our fathers: *our* shows that Ananias is a Jew and not merely a Jewish sympathizer. He and Saul are servants of the God of the OT; it is implied that Christianity is the true version of Judaism and Christians are heirs of the OT. Saul has been **appointed** (cf. 9.15, *chosen vessel*) **to know** God's **will, to see the Righteous One, to hear a voice from his mouth**. *God's will* as far as Paul himself is concerned is dealt with in vv. 15, 16. Luke may mean that Paul will understand better than others God's purpose in and plan for saving mankind, more probably perhaps that he will live on exceptionally intimate terms with God. *The Righteous One* here must be a title of Christ rather than a simple estimate of his character. See on 3.14.

15. This verse corresponds to 9.15b. **to all men** clearly must include Gentiles, but (if we are to follow Luke's presentation of the matter) the crowd do not see the implication of the Gentle mission till it is made explicit in v. 21. **you shall be a witness for him**: neither here nor in ch. 9 or ch. 26 is Paul told that he is to be an apostle; see on 14.4, 14, and Introduction, pp. lviii–lx. He has seen the Lord, as he himself claims (1 Cor. 9.1; 15.8), but not in his earthly ministry.

16. This verse is paralleled in narrative form in 9.18b.

get yourself baptized. The verb *baptize* is expressed in Greek in the middle voice. This is not reflexive (*baptize yourself*) but probably does emphasize the fact that baptism takes place as the result of a decision made by the baptized person. **wash away** reinforces the interpretation of the middle voice given here. Baptism is for the washing away, that is, the forgiveness, of sins. There may be a special reference to Paul's work as a persecutor, but the words attributed to Ananias are probably formulaic rather than specific. **calling on his name** helps to interpret the use of *in(to) the name* in other baptismal sayings. See on 3.6, pp. 38, 39. The name is not a magical instrument effecting supernatural results; the name is invoked, that is, it signifies faith and obedience directed towards Christ. There is no reference here to the Holy Spirit.

17. The construction of the Greek in this verse is extremely confused; the meaning however is clear. Paul, omitting what is contained in 9.19b–25, tells part of the story of his conversion and commissioning which appears neither in ch. 9 nor in ch. 26. After the events near and in Damascus he returns to Jerusalem and enters the Temple (in which in the epistles he shows no interest) for prayer. This seems to contradict Gal. 1.15. Prayer turned to **ecstasy**; cf. 10.10; 11.5, also 2 Cor. 12.1–5.

18. Why Paul returned to Jerusalem we are not told; possibly with the intention of fulfilling his call by bearing witness to his own people of what had happened. This however (he was told) would fulfil no useful purpose. **depart quickly from Jerusalem because they will not receive your testimony about me**. Luke's intention may be to emphasize that Paul's own intention was to be a missionary to Jews; it was only at the Lord's own direction that he turned to the Gentiles.

19. And in this verse and the next Paul appears to argue with the Lord. He would be an effective witness to Jews. They know his past and would be obliged to recognize that only a supernatural event could change the course of his life.

20. See 7.52; 8.1. **Stephen thy witness**. *Witness* is in Greek *martys*, whence the English *martyr*. Stephen has been a witness; so will Paul be. It seems probable that Luke understood Paul to have taken Stephen's place, especially as the leader of a world-wide mission. This was probably only superficially true. See Introduction, pp. lxxxiif.

21. He said to me, Go . . . The Lord overrules Paul's objection and renews his command, making it more specific. **I shall send you far from here to the Gentiles**. The surprising tense of *shall send* is probably due to the thought that the fulfilment of the mission belongs to the future. The thought that the God of Israel, should will a mission to the Gentiles is too much for the crowd.

22. They listened, imperfect (continuous) tense in Greek, **and then** . . . *Then* is implied by the Greek aorist tense, which is contrasted with the continuous *listened.* **Away with such a man** recalls 21.36, also Lk. 23.18; Jn 19.15; and Isa. 53.8, quoted at Acts 8.33. It is possible that Luke wished to draw a parallel between the suffering of Jesus and that of Paul. **from the earth**: this could be, *from the land* (of Israel); he should be driven out. But the next words, **it is not fit that he should live**, show that the crowd were asking for death, not deportation.

Is this an interruption, or has Paul said what he wants to say?

23. In addition to shouting the crowd find other ways of expressing their feelings. **flinging off their clothes**. Some translate *waving*. It is unnecessary to distinguish too nicely. **throwing dust in the air**. The motive is the same. The dust is not a threat that stones will follow, but a token of frenzy which will in due course throw anything that comes to hand.

24. The tribune (see 21.31) decided that it was time to put a stop to the riot by removing and dealing with the man who had provoked it. **The tribune ordered that he should be brought into the barracks** (the Antonia; see 21.34). Safe now from the mob, Paul is exposed to new danger, he is **to be examined with the scourge**, the recognized way of 'interviewing' a slave or other lower class and possibly reluctant witness. It is the tribune's intention to find out why they were so shouting him down; it is possible that he had not fully understood the (Hebrew or Aramaic) speech.

25. The prisoner about to be given a lashing would be tied to some sort of frame. The word translated **lash** refers to *leather thongs*, which could be understood as cords used for tying or, more probably, the thongs of which the lash was composed. There is a centurion in charge, and Paul addresses him. Cf. 16.37; the Lex Porcia and the Lex Julia forbade (with certain exceptions) the lashing of a Roman citizen. Paul was not only uncondemned, he had not even been tried. His claim to citizenship would be ineffective (and might lead to death) if it could not be proved true. It is possible that Paul was carrying his *diploma*, a small wooden diptych which would attest his registration (and birth) as a Roman citizen. Why did he not disclose his citizenship earlier? We do not know the answer to this question. Verses 25–29 may be Luke's addition to the narrative, appended rather than more appropriately worked in.

26. There are several unimportant textual variants in this verse, but the sense is clear. That the centurion's question is a warning is shown by the context and by the **for** that follows. 'You had better be careful. This man is a Roman.'

27. The centurion had approached the tribune; the tribune now approaches Paul, wishing to verify the claim that Paul has made. **Tell me, are you a Roman?** There is some stress on *you*: You, whom at first I took to be the Egyptian rebel (21.38), whom I have heard speaking to the Jews in their own Aramaic and claiming to be one of their race, you who have just escaped with your life from a violent mob – are *you* a Roman?

28. The tribune had grounds for viewing Paul's claim with scepticism. He himself had not been born a citizen but had acquired the citizenship, and it had cost him a large sum: **I acquired this citizenship at a high price**. There may be a special point in mind here. The tribune's name was Claudius Lysias (23.26); this means almost certainly that he became a citizen under the emperor Claudius (AD 41–54). There was much selling of the citizenship under Claudius; at first the price was high, later it dropped. The tribune may be saying, I acquired the citizenship when it cost a large sum, and implying, You no doubt got it cheap. He is deflated by the reply, **But I was born a citizen** – and therefore did not purchase the citizenship at any price.

29. those who were about to examine him stood back, and the tribune was afraid. They had already offended against the law by binding Paul – assuming that he was as he asserted a citizen. No one in Luke's narrative questions the assertion. It was not illegal for the tribune to arrest a citizen if he believed him to be a threat to public order.

At this point the Greek text of Codex Bezae as now extant comes to an end. The Latin part of this MS ended at v. 20.

XIV

PAUL AND THE JEWS

(22.30 – 23.35)

56. PAUL BEFORE THE COUNCIL 22.30 – 23.11

**30 The next day, wishing to know the truth, that is, what accusation
was being brought by the Jews, [the tribune] took off his bonds
and ordered the chief priests and all the Sanhedrin to assemble.
He brought Paul down and caused him to stand before them.**

**1 Paul fixed his eyes on the Sanhedrin and said, 'Brothers, up
to this day I have conducted myself before God with an entirely
good conscience.' 2 The high priest Ananias ordered those who
were standing beside him to strike him on the mouth. 3 Then Paul
said to him, 'God will strike you, you whitewashed wall. You – do
you sit there to judge me according to the Law, and do you
contrary to the Law command me to be struck?' 4 Those who
were standing there said, 'Do you insult God's high priest?' 5 Paul
said, 'I did not know, brothers, that it was the high priest, for it is
written, You shall not speak evil of a ruler of your people.' 6 Paul
noticed that one part of them was made up of Sadducees, the
other of Pharisees, and cried out in the Sanhedrin, 'Brothers, I
am a Pharisee, the son of Pharisees; it is for the hope of the
resurrection of the dead that I am on trial.' 7 When he had said
this there arose a conflict of Pharisees and Sadducees, and the
company was divided. 8 For Sadducees say that there is no
resurrection, nor angel nor spirit, while the Pharisees confess
belief in both. 9 There arose a loud outcry, and some of the scribes
on the side of the Pharisees rose up and contended, saying, 'We
find no evil in this man; and what if an angel spoke to him, or a
spirit?' 10 There was a great conflict, and the tribune became**

afraid lest Paul should be torn in pieces by them. He ordered the detachment to come down, seize him out of their midst, and take him into the barracks. [11] In the following night the Lord stood by [Paul] and said, 'Be of good courage, for as you have testified in Jerusalem to the things concerning me so must you bear witness in Rome too.'

This is an important paragraph, not least because it adumbrates a number of themes that will continue through the rest of the book. It has also evoked a number of criticisms which it is useful to discuss because they help to make clear the sort of historian Luke was.

Thus in v. 30 it is said that the tribune 'took off Paul's bonds'. This evokes the comment, If already on the previous day the possibility that Paul was a Roman citizen had arisen, why did the tribune wait twenty-four hours before correcting his error? But Luke is writing his own story, not composing (or copying) a police report, and wishes Paul to appear in this context as a free man.

In the same verse the tribune orders the Sanhedrin to meet. The word is probably ill-chosen. It might have been better to say that he persuaded the Sanhedrin that it would be a good thing for them to meet; it would give them a chance to put their case, and they could serve him as a fact-finding (and fact-interpreting) body. It is true that this leaves us with an unclear legal position, but it means that we see what Luke wishes us to see: Paul, Jerusalem and Rome standing face to face. And in fact they did so stand; Luke's history is so far justified.

Again, it is incorrect that the prisoner should open the proceedings (v. 1) and that the High Priest should initiate a physical attack (v. 2) on one who had not been tried, still less found guilty. True, but Luke does not claim to report every speech, and wishes his readers to see the courage with which Paul will face every kind of attack (v. 3). Some might cringe but not he. And in the next verse he will show how good a Jew, how obedient to Torah, he is.

Paul's *divide et impera* tactics in v. 6 have also evoked criticism; arguments *ad homines* are always open to such attacks, and it probably did not take the Pharisees long to see that when they and Paul spoke about resurrection they did not have precisely the same thing in mind. Again Luke has made the points he wished to make. (a) Paul was a faithful Jew. (b) He as a Jew of the Pharisaic kind, so that Pharisees are nearer than Sadducees to Christians and should be encouraged.

(c) The central issue for Christians is the resurrection – the resurrection of Jesus. (d) The Jews are too divided to take effective action. It is most improbable that Luke, or any other Christian, was present at the meeting of the Council; Luke has written up the story. But these points are historical – that is, they represent positions held by historical persons, whether the modem historian shares them or not.

30. The opening words suggest that the tribune wished to use the Sanhedrin in an advisory capacity. He wished **to know the truth**, namely, **what accusation was being brought by the Jews** against the Roman citizen (as the man himself claimed) who was in his custody. It was a natural, and indeed inevitable, inquiry. **ordered** is perhaps not the word Luke should have used; the Sanhedrin did not take orders from a tribune. They were however probably pleased to have an opportunity of putting their case against Paul. Did the tribune intend to be present, and was he present, at the meeting? Luke does not answer this question. It is doubtful whether a Roman tribune would run the risk of leaving a Roman citizen unguarded among his enemies; a non-Jew could not have attended a *formal* meeting of the Sanhedrin. It is perhaps the word *formal* that should be queried.

chief priests: see on 4.5. **Sanhedrin**: see on 4.6. **brought Paul down**, from the Antonia (see on 21.31) to the Sanhedrin's place of meeting; see on 4.5, and cf. *NS* 2.223–5.

1. Brothers. If this address is not purely formal it may mean that Paul regards the members of the Sanhedrin as equals, not as judges or superiors. **I have conducted myself before God with an entirely good conscience.** This could include his work as a persecutor. 'I have always done what (at the time) I thought was right.' Luke's verb (*politeuesthai*) meant originally to live as a free citizen of a city (*polis*), or to take part in the government of such a city; mainly in Jewish and Christian use it came to have a more general meaning. *Before God* is particularly relevant because the Jewish state existed under the sole supreme rule of God himself. Paul asserts, In the sight of God, the Ruler and Lawgiver of the Jewish nation, I have acted as a good citizen. It reads too much into the text to find here a 'theology of the good conscience'.

2. Paul, of course, should not have opened the proceedings. That he does so emphasizes the informality of the meeting, or perhaps simply means that Luke, who was not setting out or claiming to supply a full shorthand account of the proceedings, saw no point in wasting space with, 'Now, what have you to say for yourself?' The

High Priest could hardly claim informality as an excuse for his contribution to the inquiry. **Ananias**: cf. 24.1. He was appointed by Herod of Chalcis, and was in office AD 47–59. He has a mixed reputation in contemporary references but not of personal violence. Why did he order **those who were standing beside him to strike Paul on to mouth**? The context suggests that he was indignant at Paul's claim to be a conscientious Jew: and so he might well be, for Paul's conscientiousness would have destroyed Judaism as currently understood. An alternative explanation is that he disapproved of Paul's speaking before he was questioned. For the blow and the response; cf. Jn 18.22f.

3. God will smite you; this is most naturally understood in terms of divine judgement. At some future time God will punish you; unrighteous action will meet with its reward. Luke may have had in mind the actual fate of Ananias, murdered by revolutionaries at the beginning of the war (so Josephus, *War* 2.441). The intention however may be to express an imprecation (= May God smite you). The two interpretations may be combined; a curse may be uttered with the conviction that it coincides with God's judgement and is therefore sure to take effect.

you whitewashed wall. The image may recall the white-washed or plastered wall in Ezekiel 13, especially 13.14f.: an insecure wall, though outwardly it appears secure. Cf. CD 8.12. Or the whitewashing may suggest hypocrisy, as at Mt. 23.27 (but this saying appears in a different form in Lk. 11.44).

according to the Law. The court may have been convened by the Roman tribune but (at least in Luke's mind) it considered itself to be applying the Law to an Israelite accused of apostasy. **contrary to the Law**. See Lev. 19.15, which may be regarded as requiring fair play for the person accused. In the Mishnah the tractates Sanhedrin and Makkoth go out of their way to emphasize this requirement.

4. Do you insult God's high priest? The words can be punctuated with either a question mark or a full stop: *You are insulting . . .*

The Greek term *high priest* occurs only seldom in the canonical books of the OT. It was in the main a post-canonical development; and to prefix *God's* was no doubt intended to emphasize the offence; it is no common man you insult but the high priest who has been appointed by and thus represents God himself. Cf. the reaction to Jesus' reply to the High Priest in Jn 18.22 (Is that how you answer the high priest?).

5. I did not know . . . that it was the high priest. This is one of the most puzzling sentences in Acts. Apparently Paul withdraws his disrespectful remark on the ground that he did not know that the person who ordered him to be struck was the High Priest. Is failure to recognize the High Priest conceivable on the part of one who in the past had been a trusted agent of the highpriestly party? It is true that there had been a change of high priest and it may be that Paul's previous visit to Jerusalem had been at the time when Ananias had been sent to Rome. But who should have presided over the Sanhedrin but the High Priest (if present)? Some think that Paul meant that he did not know that it was the High Priest who had given the order. Many have suggested that Paul spoke ironically, but the address, **brothers**, and the quotation of Exod. 22.27 are against this. Others suggest that Paul withdrew because the time had not yet come for final conflict; or one might translate, I did not know that there was (that there could be) a high priest (under Roman occupation). Or, Paul's sight was defective; or he remembered his own words, When we are abused, we bless; when we are persecuted, we are forbearing (1 Cor. 4.12). It may be that Luke was concerned to represent Paul as a better Jew than his opponents. This was probably Paul's own belief, but he would hardly have expressed it in so crude and unbalanced a way. There is historical material behind this paragraph, but it is deep and remote and it is well to recognize limits to our ability to interpret it.

In Exod. 22.27 the Hebrew has the singular *ruler*; most MSS of the LXX have the plural, *rulers*.

6. Paul noticed. A lapse either of thought or of expression on Luke's part; the historical Paul would not notice because he would have been well aware of the mixed composition of the Sanhedrin. On Sadducees see p. 54, on Pharisees, p. 79. Paul claims to **be a Pharisee, the son of Pharisees**. Presumably his father was a Pharisee; but *son of Pharisees* may point to a line of Pharisees in the family or may represent the Semitic 'son of' construction which describes essential characteristics.

Paul claims that it is as a Pharisee, in the interests of Pharisaic doctrine, that he is **on trial**. Strictly speaking, the Sanhedrin were not trying a case but ascertaining facts (22.30); but it may well have seemed like a trial, and it suited Luke's purpose to make it appear so. As a translation, **hope of the resurrection** treats *hope and resurrection* as a hendiadys; it makes little difference if the two nouns are taken separately. Paul's belief in the resurrection of Jesus would be impossible if the Sadducees' belief that resurrections do not happen were accepted, but the Pharisees' willingness to believe in general terms in resurrection does not make them believers in the resurrection of Jesus. Paul's argument here has been described as not far from lying. It was not the Pharisaic doctrine of resurrection that he represented. The argument may possibly be not his but Luke's; when Paul in Phil. 3.5f. refers to his Pharisaic background it is in a different way. If the resurrection of Jesus is thought of as a partial and preliminary anticipation of the general resurrection the argument may to some extent be justified; but it is doubtful whether Luke had enough theological subtlety to think of this.

7. *Divide et impera*. Paul's intervention had the effect desired (at least, by Luke). The word **conflict** is a strong one; see v. 10, where the repetition of the word has suggested to some that vv. (6)7–9 are a Lucan insertion, or redaction.

8. For Pharisees and Sadducees see above on v. 6.

That **Sadducees say that there is no resurrection** is not a problem; see Mt. 12.18 (and parallels), and e.g. Josephus, *War* 2.165. But that they say that there is no **angel or spirit** is a different matter. The Sadducees accepted the authority of the written Torah, and this contains many references to angels and spiritual beings. The suggestion that Luke thought (wrongly) that those who denied the resurrection must be rationalists and deny angels and spirits too is not convincing. Better is the view that the Sadducees denied the existence of an intermediate state in which those who had died lived as angels or spirits until the general resurrection. It is possible to take *angel or spirit* in apposition with resurrection: the Sadducees did not believe in resurrection, whether as angel or as spirit.

These possibilities may explain a second difficulty. **the Pharisees confess belief in both**. This appears to refer to resurrection, angels, and spirits – not two but three. It may be that *both* has been wrongly used for *all*; cf. 19.16. It may be that *angel or spirit* is to be understood as a unit. Or, perhaps best, the Pharisees accept both angels and spirits as possible resurrection, or pre-resurrection, forms of being.

9. a loud outcry. Cf. 22.23 for the cognate verb. The court behaves like a rioting mob. For defence of Christians by Pharisaic scribes; cf. 5.34, 39 (Gamaliel). **We find no evil in this man**. Cf. 23.29; 25.25; also Mt. 27.23, and especially Lk. 23.4, 14, 22. It seems that Luke wished to draw attention to the similarity between the innocent suffering of Paul and that of Jesus.

what if an angel spoke to him, or a spirit? *What* is added to a conditional sentence that lacks an apodosis. The wording should perhaps be explained in terms of v. 8. The appearance of the risen Jesus might be thought of as his existence as angel or spirit between death and resurrection.

10. It is clear that if the tribune was not actually present at the council meeting (v. 30) he was not far away. His fear **lest Paul should be torn in pieces by them** is to be understood literally (see v. 9). The size of **the detachment** is not stated and cannot be determined. The tribune would order out of the men available to him the force he thought suitable.

11. Paul is comforted by a vision and a heavenly voice. Cf. 18.9f.; 27.23f. The encouragement constitutes implicit commendation of the past (Paul's bearing witness in Jerusalem is evidently approved) and prediction of the future (he need not fear that he will die in Jerusalem since he will survive to bear witness in Rome).

Luke's comment on the present incident is not that Paul has used a clever trick to get out of trouble but that he has borne the witness he was intended to bear and that the Lord has protected him and will continue to do so.

57. THE PLOT: PAUL REMOVED TO CAESAREA 23.12–35

**[12] When day broke the Jews made a plot and bound themselves
by oath, saying that they would neither eat nor drink till they
had killed Paul. [13] Those who made this conspiracy were more
than forty in number. [14] They approached the chief priests and
elders and said, 'We have bound ourselves with an oath to eat
nothing until we have killed Paul. [15] So do you make a representation to the tribune, with the Sanhedrin, that he may bring
him down to you, as though you wanted to make a further inquiry
into his case with a view to reaching a decision; but we, before he
comes near, will be ready to kill him.' [16] But the son of Paul's
sister heard of the ambush, came and entered the barracks, and
reported the matter to Paul. [17] Paul called one of the centurions
and said, 'Take this young man to the tribune, for he has
something to tell him.' [18] So he took him, brought him to the
tribune, and said, 'The prisoner Paul called me and asked me to
bring this young man to you since he has something to say to
you.' [19] The tribune took him by the hand, withdrew privately,
and asked, 'What is it that you have to tell me?' [20] He said, 'The
Jews have planned to ask you to bring Paul down to the Sanhedrin
tomorrow, on the pretext of making some more accurate inquiry
about him. [21] Now do not you be persuaded by them; for above
forty men of them are lying in wait for him, men who have bound
themselves with an oath not to eat or drink until they have killed
him, and they are ready now, awaiting your promise.' [22] So the
tribune dismissed the young man, with the command not to tell
anyone 'that you have given me this information'.**

**[23] He summoned two of the centurions and said, 'Get ready
two hundred soldiers to go to Caesarea, with seventy cavalry and
two hundred lancers. [They are to be ready] from the third hour
of the night, [24] and to provide beasts in order to mount Paul and
bring him safely to Felix the governor.' [25] He wrote a letter, as
follows: [26] Claudius Lysias to His Excellency the governor Felix:
greeting. [27] I came up with the troops and rescued this man, who
had been taken by the Jews and was about to be killed by them,
when I learned that he was a Roman. [28] Wishing to discover the
ground on which they accused him, I brought him down to their
Council. [29] I found that he was accused over disputes arising out**

**of their Law but under no charge calling for death or imprison-
ment. 30 When it was made known to me that there was to be a
plot against the man I immediately sent him to you, commanding
his accusers also to state the case against him before you.**

**31 So the soldiers, in accordance with their instructions, took
Paul and brought him by night to Antipatris. 32 On the next day,
having let the cavalry go on with Paul the infantry returned to
the barracks. 33 The cavalry entered Caesarea, delivered the letter
to the governor, and also presented Paul to him. 34 He read the
letter, inquired of what province Paul was, and having found out
that he was from Cilicia 35 said, 'I will hear you when your
accusers also are present.' And he ordered him to be guarded in
Herod's praetorium.**

In chs. 24, 25 and 26 Paul's story is based on Caesarea, where he is in Roman custody, custody designed not only to prevent him from stirring up trouble but also to protect him from the Jews, whose motives, and the loyalty of whose actions, were under suspicion. The present paragraph effects the transfer of Paul from Jerusalem to Caesarea, and the reader asks whether Luke made it up for the purpose or drew it from tradition. Stylistically there is little doubt that the composition is Luke's work. It was however a piece which he was under no obligation to write. Paul had to be taken to Caesarea, but Luke could have written, The tribune, hearing of a plot against Paul's life, sent him by night and under guard to Caesarea. That he did not write in this simple way leads to a probable inference that he found in the tradition the story of the nephew and of the surprisingly powerful force that escorted Paul to Caesarea. Paul had friends in Jerusalem, even if only those whom he brought with him. Again, if it is correct that Paul spent his youth in Jerusalem (22.3) it is not impossible that a married sister lived there. On the other hand it may be argued that in this paragraph the Sanhedrin is united in opposition to Paul, whereas in the preceding one it is divided. Such discontinuities did not trouble Luke, whose interest and ability lay rather in the narrating of vivid scenes than in drawing out logical connections and progressions. It is probable both that the story has some foundation and that Luke gave it its present form.

The letter (vv. 26–30) is another matter. It is most improbable that Luke could have obtained access to Roman archives whether in Jerusalem or in Caesarea. The letter includes, with a little variation on events described in chs. 22, 23, the points Luke wishes to make: the trouble was caused not by Paul but by Jews; the only matter at issue was the interpretation of Jewish Law; Paul had committed no offence against the state. The tribune must have written a letter; was he not bound to have made these points? So Luke would think.

12 the Jews can hardly mean more than *some Jews* but Luke takes them to be representative of general Jewish opposition to Christianity, at least in its Pauline form. **a plot:** at 19.40 the word was translated *meeting*, but it can be used, as here, for a secret meeting held for a special purpose. **bound themselves by oath**. They undertook to accept the ban of the synagogue if they failed in their purpose. Abstinence from eating and drinking is thus augmented by a religious sanction. If those who took this vow were not released from it they should have died. See, in the Mishnah, Nedarim 3.1–3: Four kinds of vows the Sages have declared to be not binding: vows of incitement, vows of exaggeration, vows made in error, and vows [that cannot be fulfilled by reason] of constraint . . .

These Jews are determined on Paul's death; and the story of a plot going to such lengths is not necessarily to be dismissed as unhistorical because it accords with the picture of the Jews that Luke wishes to paint. Paul sometimes went in danger of his life (2 Cor. 11.24–26).

13. more than forty. Too many for a successful conspiracy; but they may have thought they would have to fight a well-armed Roman guard.

14. the chief priests and elders. See pp. 55f. Official Jewish collaboration was necessary if Paul was to be placed in a situation in which he could not be defended by Roman swords.

15. The conspirators having disclosed their plot indicate the part that must be played by the authorities. **make a representation**. The word is not easy to translate. It is used in legal contexts at 24.1; 25.2, 15. Here it means little more than *ask*, but its legal associations may be suggested by a phrase sometimes found in legal use: *make a representation.*

with the Sanhedrin. There are two difficulties here. *The chief priests and elders* (v. 14) virtually are the Sanhedrin; and are the Sanhedrin *with* the plotters or the tribune? Luke is writing somewhat carelessly, but probably wishes to suggest as much Jewish involvement in the planned assassination as possible. **to make a further inquiry . . . making a decision**. The long phrase is needed to translate one word which was a technical term in legal use: *to decide or determine a suit*. Both process and result must be expressed in the rendering.

do you make . . . but we . . . The authorities must play their part, the assassins will play theirs. **will be ready** is in Greek a present tense, expressing vividness: *There we are, all ready . . .*

bring him down to you, presumably from the Antonia. Luke probably had no more details to communicate. The plan was clear enough.

16. the son of Paul's sister. We know nothing else about members of Paul's family, but 22.3 suggests the possibility that some may have been living in Jerusalem. **the ambush**. The word can be used for *trickery* or *treachery* of any kind, but in v. 15 it seems that some kind of *ambush*, the primary sense of the word, is in mind.

came and entered translates the Greek text as usually punctuated, but it is clumsy and the first word could equally well or better be translated *was present*. It could then be connected with what precedes: Paul's nephew was present when the plot was made. He now has access to Paul. This is by no means impossible, especially if Paul was in the Antonia for protection rather than punishment.

17. Paul can summon a centurion and send a message to the tribune. He is not in the ordinary sense imprisoned.

18. The prisoner Paul. He is nevertheless a prisoner. He is not free to leave. It might be dangerous to let him go.

19. withdrew privately, making it easier for the young man to speak freely.

20. on the pretext of making. There is much variety in the text here, but it is probably the Sanhedrin, not the tribune, who wish to make further inquiry.

21. Most of this verse relates with only small variations in wording matters that we already know.

your promise. This is the usual meaning of Luke's word and should be accepted here, though some prefer *consent* or *assent*. There is no substantial difference. If the tribune consents to bring Paul down he is in effect promising to do so.

22. The construction changes part way through this verse from indirect to direct speech. Cf. 1.4. The reverse change occurs in vv. 23f.

you have given me this information. Luke uses again the word discussed in v. 15, but here without legal overtones.

23. The tribune feels that the matter is becoming too serious for him to handle; it must go to higher authority. He acts through his **centurions**; normal military practice.

two hundred soldiers. The context shows that infantry are meant. These would determine the speed of the convoy. *Two hundred* would (on paper) correspond to the *two centurions*.

Caesarea, where the governor normally resided. See 10.1. Jerusalem was no place for the trial of an unpopular Jew who was a Roman citizen. **seventy cavalry**. The garrison at Jerusalem was provided with cavalry. **two hundred lancers**. The meaning of this noun is a notorious problem. Literally it means *one who takes something in his right hand*. *Lancers* is the Vulgate translation, and even if it is no more than Jerome's guess it may well be right. An interesting suggestion is that they are *led horses*; between Jerusalem and Antipatris (v. 31) the cavalry would need a change of mount; a led horse is taken in the right hand. See further below on the numbers sent.

The escort adds up to 470 men (500 according to the Western text). If in Jerusalem there was one tribune and correspondingly one cohort this number meant about half the garrison. It has been suggested that the *lancers* were not regular soldiers, but a sort of light-armed police. This is an attractive suggestion, but unfortunately we do not know of any police in Jerusalem except the Temple guard, who would have been a most unsuitable component of an escort guaranteeing Paul's safety. It may be that Luke exaggerated the numbers, or guessed high, though the Palestinian roads were dangerous enough to justify a considerable force.

from the third hour of the night, that is, ready to start at any time thereafter; three hours after sunset; more precisely, 3/12 of the time between sunset and sunrise.

24. The text of vv. 23, 24, (25) is in some confusion; all that need be noted here is a Western addition which explains the tribune's provision of so large a force; he was afraid that if Paul were killed on the way he would be accused of having accepted a bribe to allow this to happen.

to provide beasts. The construction changes from direct to indirect speech; cf. v. 22. *Beast* is usually *ox* or *sheep*; seldom an animal for riding.

to Felix the governor. See *NS* 1.459–66. Antonius Felix, according to Tacitus, Claudius Felix, according to Josephus. He was a freedman, brother of the influential Pallas. His appointment was thus unusual; provinces such as Judaea were usually entrusted to Roman knights. He was appointed in AD 52 or 53; his date of recall is disputed: possibly 55, possibly as late as 60. See on 24.27. He had a bad name as governor; he 'practised every kind of cruelty and lust, wielding the power of a king with all the instincts of a slave' (Tacitus, *Histories* 5.9, LCL translation). This judgement may be somewhat unfair.

25. It is highly improbable that Luke should have been able to obtain access to the letter; but what he writes gives on the whole the sort of report the tribune is bound to have made to his superior.

26. We learn the tribune's name; it may be Luke's invention but need not be. We know (22.28) that he had obtained the citizenship; **Claudius** probably means that he obtained it under the emperor of that name. **Lysias**, a Greek name, suggests Greek origin.

27. The tribune's account differs in some respects from that in ch. 22. This may be no more than careless writing on Luke's part; it may be an attempt by Lysias to give the governor a favourable impression.

when I learned that he was a Roman; equally possible is *because I learned* . . . Hardly possible would be, *I rescued him and subsequently discovered* . . . , which is the story in ch. 22. It looks as if the tribune is 'improving' the story, but it is possible that ch. 22 is mistaken. If Claudius Lysias did not know, or suspect, that Paul was a Roman, why should he have taken such provocative steps to prevent one insignificant Jew from being beaten by his compatriots? In any case the situation was evidently confused and differing accounts are not surprising. The letter makes the points (1) Paul is a Roman citizen and under the procurator's jurisdiction, (2) his rescue was due to Roman power, (3) no Roman offence was committed, (4) the charge is due to internal Jewish party feeling.

28. This verse recalls 22.30.

29. disputes arising out of their Law is not a bad summary of 23.6–9, Law being the authoritative basis of the Jewish religion. The charge of bringing Gentiles into the Temple (21.28) seems at this point to have been dropped; but see 24.19f.

30. The concluding sentence is stilted and awkward; Claudius Lysias passes on the information brought to him by Paul's nephew, adding that he has also ordered the Jews who are accusing Paul to appear before Felix.

31. The letter is concluded and Luke picks up the narrative from v. 24.

so the soldiers took Paul . . . **and brought him by night to Antipatris**. For Antipatris see *NS* 2.167f. The city was founded by Herod the Great in honour of his father, Antipater. It was a Hellenistic city. Its distance from Jerusalem is given by various writers at figures from thirty-seven to forty-five miles – the divergence is due to doubt about the site of Antipatris and to the fact that there were two routes, by Lydda and by Bethel. Whatever estimate is adopted it is very unlikely that the cavalry, with Paul mounted, could reach Antipatris in one night, absolutely impossible that the infantry should have done so. The difficulty is reduced if we suppose that the infantry were intended only to get Paul out of the city and then to return, but v. 32 implies (but does not quite state) that it was from Antipatris that the infantry returned. The details of Luke's circumstantial narrative begin to crumble. He has probably written up a bald statement, perhaps little more than 'Paul was transferred under guard to Caesarea', with less than adequate knowledge of the geography of Palestine.

32. On the next day, after, it seems, one night. **the infantry** (Greek, *they*) **returned to the barracks**. After a reference to the cavalry, who, with Paul, set out on their way to Caesarea, the pronoun *they* must, one would think, refer to the infantry.

33. The military escort fulfilled its mission. From Antipatris to Caesarea was about twenty-five miles. **Delivered** . . . **presented** Luke uses different, appropriate, words for handing over a letter and a person.

34. He . . . inquired of what province Paul was. It seems that the custom of sending an accused person back to his native province was never more than optional, and was not established in the early Principate; a governor might however be glad to avoid a case concerning a Roman citizen involved in Jewish disputes. But Felix, having found that Paul came from Cilicia, decided to try the case himself, possibly because at the time Cilicia had no imperial legate of its own and the legate of Syria would not wish to be troubled with minor cases from Judaea. Felix may have wished to know if Paul came from one of the nearby client kingdoms, in whose affairs it would have been undesirable to interfere.

Cilicia in the early Principate, was a dependency of the province of Syria. It was probably in the early years of Nero that it became an independent province.

35. Herod's praetorium, the palace built by Herod the Great and taken over by the Roman administration. We have no archaeological or other information about it (except that it existed).

XV

PAUL AND THE ROMANS

(24.1 – 26.32)

58. PAUL AND FELIX 24.1–27

**[1] After five days the High Priest Ananias with a number of elders
and a barrister Tertullus, came down; these informed the
governor against Paul. [2] When he was called, Tertullus began his
accusation, saying, 'Since through you we enjoy much peace
and since reforms for this nation are coming about through
your provident foresight, [3] in all ways and in every place we
welcome this, most excellent Felix, with all gratitude. [4] But in
order not to weary you further, I ask you in your forbearance
to hear us briefly. [5] For we found this man a pest, and one who
stirs up riots among all the Jews throughout the world, and a
ringleader of the sect of the Nazoraeans. [6] He also tried to profane
the Temple, and we seized him. [8] From him you will be able yourself, by examining him, to find out about the things of which we
accuse him.' [9] The Jews also joined in this attack, affirming that
these things were so.**

**[10] When the governor motioned to him to speak, Paul
answered, 'Since I know that you have been for many years a
judge of this nation I cheerfully make the defence in my case,
[11] since you can find out that it is not more than twelve days since
I came up to Jerusalem to worship. [12] And neither in the Temple
nor in the synagogues nor anywhere in the city did they find me
arguing with anyone or causing the onset of a crowd, [13] nor can
they prove any of those things of which they now accuse me. [14] I
do confess this to you, that it is in accordance with the Way, which
they call a sect, that I serve our ancestral God, believing all things**

that are according to the Law and the things that are written in the Prophets, [15] having the same hope in God which they also accept that there will be a resurrection of both the righteous and the unrighteous. [16] And so for my part I too exercise myself so as to have continually a blameless conscience towards both God and men. [17] At the end of many years I arrived [here] to bring alms for my nation and offerings. [18] While I was engaged in these sacrifices they found me in the Temple in a state of purity, with no crowd, with no tumult. [19] But some of the Jews from Asia [allege this], who ought to be present before you and bring an accusation, if they have anything against me. [20] Or let these men themselves say what crime they found in me when I stood before the Sanhedrin, [21] unless it be this one thing that I cried out when I stood among them, I am being judged this day before you concerning the resurrection of the dead.'

[22] Felix adjourned [the hearing] since he had an accurate knowledge of the Way, and said, 'When Lysias the tribune comes down I will hear your case and reach a decision.' [23] He charged the centurion that he should be kept safe and have relief from prison regimen, and that he should not prevent any of his friends from doing him service.

[24] After some days Felix arrived with Drusilla his wife, who was a Jewess, and sent for Paul and heard him on faith in Christ [Jesus]. [25] As he discoursed on righteousness, self-control, and the judgement to come Felix became afraid, and answered, 'For the present, go your way; when I have an opportunity I will send for you.' [26] At the same time also he hoped that money would be given him by Paul. For this reason also he sent for him pretty often, and conversed with him. [27] When two years were up Felix was succeeded by Porcius Festus. Wishing to curry favour with the Jews Felix left Paul in prison.

The paragraph falls into two parts: Paul's appearance in court before Felix (vv. 1–23); Paul's private relations with Felix (vv. 24–27).

In the first part the situation has developed beyond 22.30, where Claudius Lysias hoped to use the Sanhedrin as an advisory body. The Jews have now travelled to Caesarea to present their case against Paul. Luke reports speeches made by the Jews' advocate, Tertullus, and by Paul. Both must have said far more than the few verses Luke allows them, but the two short speeches make the essential points, so that this paragraph becomes an important source for the legal issues – at least, as Luke understood them. Tertullus asserts that Paul, a ringleader of the Christian sect, has stirred up unrest among the Jews everywhere, and has attempted to profane the Temple. These Jewish charges lead to the Roman charge of *seditio*, insurrection. Paul replies that he is indeed a Christian, and as a Christian worships the Jewish God and believes everything in the Law and the Prophets; he was responsible for no disturbances in Jerusalem, and as to the rest of the world there are no witnesses to testify; he was in the Temple, but this was to sacrifice and to carry out a charitable mission; he was in a state of purity and there was no tumult. The Jews seem to stress the Roman side of Paul's offence; Paul argues that what is at stake is the understanding of Scripture. The report has been said to constitute a good example of Roman procedure *extra ordinem*; this is true in the sense that questions were raised which fell outside any recognized legal framework, but of *procedure* there is in fact little. Tertullus speaks, Paul speaks, and Felix postpones a decision. The fundamental issue was one on which the court was not competent to pronounce. Was Paul's Christianity a valid, the only valid, form of Judaism, or a perversion of Judaism? He did not intend to provoke riots; his intention was to persuade his fellow Jews of the truth of his belief. But those who thought his opinions not merely wrong but destructive of their religion could not be blamed for a negative reaction, sometimes violently expressed. There was thus a theological dispute, which was a Jewish matter, but it was related to the question of *seditio*, which was a proper concern of a Roman court.

The second part of the paragraph tells of frequent interviews between Paul and Felix, in which the latter's wife Drusilla also took part. Comparisons with the story of Herod Antipas and John the Baptist are worth little. Felix was a problem to Luke. He did not condemn Paul and was therefore a good ruler; he hoped for a bribe and left Paul in prison, and was therefore not good.

The date of Felix's recall (v. 27) is important for Pauline chronology; see the note.

1. After five days. Cf. 23.35; Felix waits for Paul's accusers. *Five* may have some basis in tradition; Luke usually writes *after some* (or *a number of*) *days*. **the High Priest Ananias**; see 23.2. **came down**, from the capital, but also literally. **a barrister Tertullus**. The use of a *barrister*, or *advocate*, was common, but not universal; it probably indicated the importance or complexity of a case. *We seized* *him* (v. 6) has been held to show that Tertullus was himself a Jew, but *the Jews* (v. 5) points in the opposite direction. Use of a barrister may mean that the High Priest and his associates were unable (or unwilling) to use Greek. Some experience in provincial courts was thought useful for young barristers.

2. When he was called. If *he* refers to Tertullus Luke was guilty of a grammatical solecism. This is not impossible, and if Paul was intended one would have expected his name to be used.

Tertullus began his accusation with the customary *captatio benevolentiae*. Josephus expresses a different Jewish estimate of Felix (*Ant.* 20.182).

much peace. There was little peace in Palestine in the time of Felix, though he did put down some bandits. **reforms**: the word was used by the Stoics for *good actions*, but here has its meaning of *reform*, often used in connection with laws. To what reforms Tertullus refers we do not know. **provident foresight**, in Greek one word, which denotes one of the standard virtues of the Hellenistic ruler. It is clear that Tertullus (or Luke?) knows the proper style to use.

It is possible to connect *in all ways and in every place* (v. 3) with the sentence in v. 2, but the sentences seem better balanced if taken as in this translation.

3. we welcome this – the benefits and reforms mentioned in v. 2. **most excellent Felix**. Cf. 23.26.

4. Tertullus continues the polite, ingratiating, manner of his introduction. **not to weary you**. The verb can hardly have its more usual meaning, *to hinder*. In the LXX a cognate word means *wearied*. **forbearance**, a difficult word to translate. It denotes *reasonableness, fairness*, especially perhaps in a judge, who is prepared not to break the laws but to give them an understanding, non-legalist interpretation.

5. For introduces the reason why Felix should give patient attention to what Tertullus says. **we found this man a pest**, literally, *a plague*, or, taking the word as an adjective, *pestilential*. **one who stirs up**, in that he stirs up, **riots**. This was a serious charge, of which a Roman court would be sure to take note, especially as the *riots* were said to take place **throughout the world** – no doubt an exaggeration but see 17.6 as well as the Jerusalem riot. Paul is alleged to be **a ringleader of the sect of the Nazoraeans**. *Ringleader* was originally a military term, one of the front-line troops. For *sect* see on 5.17. *Nazoraean* is applied at 2.22; 3.6; 4.10; 6.14; 22.6; 26.9 to

Jesus, and as used in Acts probably means *who came from Nazareth.* Applied in the plural to Christians it cannot mean this. It is probably derived from the designation of Jesus, so that it means *adherents of the man from Nazareth.* It is however worth while to recall that Epiphanius refers to a pre-Christian Jewish sect with this or a similar name. The Hebrew root *n–ṣ–r* means *to guard* or *to observe*, and it has been suggested that Jesus the Nazoraean was the Chief Observant (of Torah?) and his followers were the Observants. Jesus however does not seem to have lived in such a way as to attract this title, and it is better to think that the title had originally a local meaning and that other interpretations were from time to time drawn from it.

6. He also tried to profane the Temple, by bringing Gentiles into it, 21.28. A Roman court would find this charge relevant because the Romans had accepted the provisions for maintaining the sanctity of the Temple.

7. Some MSS add: *we wished to judge him according to our Law* (in contrast with the Roman law practised in your courts, before you) *but the tribune Lysias came up with great violence and took him out of our hands, with the command that his accusers should come before you.* This presents a Jewish point of view, which was hardly Luke's. This argues in favour of the reading. Or is Luke suggesting that the Jews, changing a riot into a peaceful legal procedure, were misrepresenting the facts? Probably an editor thought that an explicit reference to ch. 21 was called for.

8. From him, that is *From Paul*, if the short text is accepted. If the long text (see on v. 7) is read, *him* will refer to Claudius Lysias. **by examining him** refers to a procedure that would more probably be applied to Paul the suspected criminal than to the responsible officer who arrested him.

9. The Jews is sometimes taken as an indication that Tertullus was not a Jew.

10. Like Tertullus (v. 2) Paul begins with a *captatio benevolentiae*, not unduly straining the truth. **you have been for many years a judge of this nation** may seem to exaggerate, since in senatorial provinces a two-year term was usual, but there is some ground for thinking that Felix had been active in Palestine, as a junior colleague of Cumanus, before his appointment as procurator. **I cheerfully** (some MSS have *more cheerfully*) **make my defence** (cf. 19.33) **in relation to the charge against me** (*my affair*, which was an accusation). The defence is, in effect, that there is no charge to answer.

11. The construction of the verse is obscure, but the general drift is clear. It is not more than twelve days since Paul reached Jerusalem (21.15) – little enough time for the crimes of which he is accused. **I came up to Jerusalem to worship.** This is an incomplete statement of Paul's purpose. He came as the bearer of a gift from the Gentile world (v. 17); probably also with a view to some sort of consultation with the Jerusalem leaders. Luke, as usual, is presenting Paul as a good Jew as well as a good Christian. **not more than twelve days**. None of the attempts that have been made to calculate the twelve days on the basis of what is recorded in Acts can be regarded as successful. The suggestion may be correct that *twelve* was drawn from a source different from that which supplied the narrative from 21.15 onwards; or *twelve* may be a Lucan approximation.

12. nor in the synagogues, conceivably synagogues of the Dispersion, but between **Temple** and **city** it probably means Jerusalem synagogues. **nowhere in the city** is *throughout the city* with a negative. Paul is evidently disclaiming responsibility for the riot in the Temple. He was not **arguing with anyone** – the first step towards making a disturbance.

13. Paul says nothing about the charge of causing world-wide disturbance (a) because no proof was offered and (b) because Felix could try only crimes committed within the area of his judicial authority.

14. I do confess this. *Confess* is not entirely satisfactory. Of the following clauses the first is an admission of what some would count a crime – Paul is a Christian; but the second is an affirmation of innocence. The two however belong together in Luke's regular affirmation: I am a Christian, that is, a good, right-thinking, Jew. **to you** is emphatic, implying: *to them* I assert that I am nothing but a good Jew; *to you*, I don't mind admitting that . . .

it is in accordance with the Way (see on 9.2) . . . **I serve our ancestral God**. Both clauses are important; see above.

which they call a sect, as Tertullus had done (v. 5). The implicit disavowal of *sect* means that Christianity regards itself not as a group or party within the people of God; it *is* the people of God, and its way is the way (the *halakah*) for all Israel.

That Paul does serve *the ancestral God* is proved by the fact that he believes **all things that are according to the Law and the things that are written in the Prophets** (that is, the prophetic books as a division of the OT). Could he have claimed to believe all the things according to the Law? Only if he were allowed to give some of them a new interpretation (see e.g. Rom. 2.29 on circumcision).

15. Not for the first time (cf. 23.6) Paul singles out belief in the resurrection as the central feature of his faith, which it shares with (Pharisaic, not Sadducean) Judaism. It is implied that he ought not to be persecuted for believing what all good Jews believe. On this occasion it is added that the resurrection will be **of both the righteous and the unrighteous**, that is, for judgement. In many passages of the NT the fate of the unrighteous is left unclear because only the righteous are spoken of and only their resurrection is explicitly affirmed. In Judaism there was a great variety of opinion on this matter.

16. I too, as well as my accusers and other Jews, **exercise myself**: the verb was used in the first instance of physical training for various skills and athletic pursuits, but it was easily adapted for moral and intellectual training. Neither the verb nor the cognate noun is used elsewhere in the NT, and the relation between moral discipline and faith is not worked out in Acts, or by Paul in the certainly genuine letters.

a blameless conscience. For Paul's clear conscience see 23.1; also 20.20, 27, 33; also however 1 Cor. 4.4 – a clear conscience is not a ground of justification. *blameless* can be *not stumbling* or *not causing to stumble*. It has the latter meaning at 1 Cor. 10.32, and this seems to be intended here. The meaning is that Paul's intention, the aim of his self-training, is that his conscience shall not accuse him of offending against God or men.

17. At the end of many years. Since when? Not very many years since Acts 15, still fewer from 18.22 (if this implies a visit to Jerusalem). Paul may mean, since he broke off relations with Jerusalem, at his conversion. *Many* is in fact a comparative and may be a true comparative referring to *many* in v. 10: More years than you have been in office.

to bring alms for my nation. We know how important his collection for the poor saints in Jerusalem was for Paul from Rom. 15; 1 Cor. 16; 2 Cor. 8; 9. In Acts there is no reference to it but this. It is surprising that Luke should pass it by in almost complete silence. We must conclude either (1) that Luke was less well informed than one would expect in a fellow traveller; or (2) that he found the collection less interesting and important than Paul did; or (3) that there was some good reason for suppressing it. This could have been that the well-intended gift led only to misunderstanding or misapplication, or that it later formed the basis of a charge of diverting funds that should have been applied to the Temple tax. It is probably right to infer from Luke's silence elsewhere that the present allusion comes from tradition.

and offerings. The word refers to sacrifices. Paul had paid for the sacrifices of the four vow-makers (21.26), but he had not come to Jerusalem for this purpose. There is nothing in Acts to suggest that Paul had this intention, and nothing in the epistles to suggest that he would have been likely to entertain it.

18, 19. While I was engaged in these sacrifices. A variant reading has *Meanwhile*. **they found me in the Temple in a state of purity**. See 21.24, 29. There was **no crowd, no tumult**. Cf. v. 12.

If a full stop is placed at the end of v. 19 **some of the Jews** is left without a verb. Presumably Paul (Luke) intended to say, I was making no disturbance, but certain Jews *have alleged that I was doing so*. They **ought to be present before you and bring an accusation**. This was a legal requirement and failure to fulfil it was a serious offence. Paul has the opportunity of turning the tables on his opponents. A less probable way of dealing with the text is to put a comma at the end of v. 19 and supply a verb out of v. 20. The Jews of Asia ought to be here to present their case; in their absence, *let those Jews now present themselves speak.*

20. For a possible connection with v. 19 see on that verse. It is better to let this verse begin a new sentence. The only charge that the Jews now present can bring with eye-witness testimony relates to my appearance before the Sanhedrin. See 22.30 – 23.10.

21. This verse recalls 23.6. The Jews have nothing to complain of but one cry that Paul uttered, in which he asserted that the real issue in his trial was that of resurrection, thereby associating himself with one part of the Sanhedrin (the Pharisees) and opposing the other (the Sadducees). True, this led to an uproar; but if to be a Pharisee was a crime, half the Sanhedrin were criminals. The argument (certainly Luke's, possibly Paul's) is that the Jews have no case against Paul except in regard to theological opinions, of which Felix would take no cognizance.

22. Felix adjourned the hearing, literally, *adjourned them*. This was standard procedure. Felix has no intention of being drawn into an internal Jewish dispute, or of doing injustice to a man whose only offence lay in what other Jews regarded as unorthodox theology. He

had, Luke says, **an accurate knowledge of** Christianity – **the Way** (see 9.2). No other evidence confirms this. The adjective in Greek is in the comparative degree. This may be elative – *very accurate* – but may be a real comparative: more accurate knowledge than the Jews had, or perhaps better, more accurate knowledge than they thought he had. How had Felix obtained his knowledge? The answer sometimes given, Through Drusilla, has no foundation.

23. that he should be kept safe. It seems that though Paul is not set at liberty there is at least an element of protective custody in Felix's order. Paul is to **have relief**; this means the Latin *custodia libera*. **he should not prevent any of his friends from doing him service**. Literally, *his own people*; this would normally mean *family and friends*, here no doubt *fellow Christians*. For Romans prison was not a punishment but a means of keeping people available for trial or future punishment. Food and comforts brought by friends could make it tolerable.

24. Felix arrived. It is not clear what this means or where Felix's interviews with Paul took place. **with Drusilla his wife**. This was not Drusilla the granddaughter of Cleopatra and Antony (Tacitus, *Histories* 5.9) but Drusilla the sister of Herod Agrippa II (Josephus, *Ant.* 20.141–4). This is shown by the addition, **who was a Jewess**, though the Herods were not fully Jewish.

Felix . . . **heard him on faith in Christ Jesus**. More about the themes discussed follows in v. 25. It seems doubtful whether *faith* here means what it means in the epistles; but see below.

25. righteousness is a theme of central importance in Paul's letters, but here it seems to be used in a different sense. See 10.35 and 17.31, which suggest the double meaning of righteous behaviour in men and righteous judgement in God, who will duly reward those who practise righteousness. The only other use of the word in Acts, at 13.10, harmonizes, in a negative sense, with these meanings. **self-control** occurs at Gal. 5.23 as part of the fruit of the Spirit, elsewhere in the NT only at 2 Peter 1.6 (but cf. 1 Cor. 7.9; 9.25; Titus 1.8 for cognates). In itself the word means *mastery* over something or someone, but, especially from the time of Plato, mastery over oneself, one's pleasures and desires. It is an essentially ethical concept. Righteousness and self-discipline, in which it is not for man to estimate his own achievement, lead to **judgement to come**. Cf. 17.31. It is hardly surprising that Felix was frightened by the thought of judgement, but the words of his response are ambiguous.

Cf. 17.32. Does he mean that he seriously intends to converse further with Paul, or is he making a polite gesture? Verse 26b suggests the former.

As in ch. 17 the theme of judgement is not complemented by any reference to salvation; it may be that one should refer back to v. 4 and give *faith* a more positive content than that verse in itself suggests. Cf. 16.31.

26. The ambiguity noted on v. 25 continues in this verse. Felix **hoped that money would be given him by Paul**; but he also **sent for him pretty often and conversed with him**. It has been argued that Luke here exposes his inadequacy as a writer; it is impossible for the same man to hope for a bribe and to hold serious conversation on faith, righteousness, self-control, and judgement. It is in fact the criticism that shows inadequacy in human understanding. It is possible, and indeed is very common, for men to have mixed motives. Whether this was in fact true of Felix it is impossible to say. Luke may have wished to represent Felix as both the 'good Roman', who protects Paul and takes him seriously, and the 'bad Roman', who panders to the Jews and does not release him.

27. Felix was succeeded by Porcius Festus. Little is known of Festus. He did something to put down the brigands. He was reasonably tolerant with the Jews over a wall they built in the Temple with a view to preventing Agrippa from seeing the sacrifices. He seems to have died in office, perhaps in AD 60. When did he succeed Felix? The Armenian version of Eusebius' *Chronicle* has 54–60, Jerome's has 56–60. When Felix was recalled he was accused by the Jews of misdeeds and would have been punished but for the intercession (with Nero) of his brother Pallas who fell from power early in Nero's principate (AD 54–68). This tends to confirm 54 or 56. *NS* 1.465f. however prefers a later date, AD 60, which gives Festus a very short period in office.

When two years were up. This note of time has often been taken to apply to the time Paul spent in prison under Felix. Grammatically this could be correct; grammatically the words could equally well apply to Felix' procuratorship. If the latter possibility is correct the overall chronology would fit with it well; see *Romans* 4f., and Introduction, p. xli. It has been argued that Luke is interested in Paul rather than in Felix and that it is therefore likely that he is referring to Paul's imprisonment. At this point however he is dealing with the procuratorial succession. Another possibility is that his source referred to the succession, but that Luke understood the reference to be to Paul.

The change of ruler might have seemed a suitable time for Paul's release. But Felix left him in prison, in order to curry favour with the Jews – in which purpose he was not successful (see above on this verse). The Western text gives a different motive, *on account of Drusilla*. As an insertion this might have been intended to account for the mention of Drusilla, in v. 24, more probably perhaps to bring out a parallel with John the Baptist's suffering at the hands of Herodias.

59. PAUL APPEALS TO CAESAR 25.1–12

**1 So Festus arrived in the province and after three days went up
to Jerusalem from Caesarea. 2 The chief priests and the leading
men of the Jews informed him against Paul and begged him,
3 asking a favour against [Paul], that he would send him to
Jerusalem, for they were making an ambush to kill him on the
way. 4 Festus answered that Paul was being kept at Caesarea, but
that he himself would shortly be going [there]. 5 'So', he said, 'let
the eminent men among you come down with me and, if there is
anything wrong in the man, let them accuse him.'**

**6 He spent not more than eight or ten days among them, went
down to Caesarea, and on the next day sat down in the place of
judgement and commanded Paul to be brought. 7 When Paul
arrived the Jews who had come down from Jerusalem surrounded
him bringing many weighty charges, which they were not able to
prove. 8 Paul in his defence said, 'Neither against the Law of the
Jews, nor against Caesar, have I done any wrong.' 9 Festus,
wishing to curry favour with the Jews, said in response to Paul,
'Are you willing to go up to Jerusalem and be tried concerning
these matters there before me?' 10 Paul said, 'I am standing in
Caesar's court, where it is right that I should be tried. I have
done no wrong to the Jews, as you well know. 11 If then I am a
wrongdoer and have done something worthy of death I am not
refusing to die, but if there is nothing in the things of which they
accuse me no one can make a present of me to them. I appeal to
Caesar.' 12 Then Festus spoke with his council and replied, 'You
have appealed to Caesar, to Caesar you shall go.'**

A new governor has taken office in Judaea. He is a man of energy. Three days are enough for him to settle in Caesarea before setting out for his second capital city, Jerusalem, where not more than eight or ten days are needed for a preliminary survey, which includes a request from the Jews to try Paul in Jerusalem. The old plot of assassination (23.12) is revived: Paul will be murdered on the way. Whether because he suspects the plot or on general principles, Festus refuses. He is going to Caesarea; let the Jews do so too that there may be a hearing. There is a hearing; and it is inconclusive. The Jews present their accusations; Paul affirms his innocence. Instead of reaching a decision

Festus asks Paul if he is willing to go to Jerusalem and be tried there. Why does Festus not complete the legal business in Caesarea? The answer given is that he wishes to do the Jews a favour, but this desire is qualified by his question to Paul, which is meaningless if Paul is not free to answer, No, I am not willing to go to Jerusalem. In fact he does so answer, and in doing so demands much more than the second trial in Caesarea that Festus by implication offers him. Paul had as much to fear from acquittal as from condemnation. Released from custody in Caesarea with no Roman soldiery at hand to protect him he would have been an easy victim to the assassin's knife. By appealing to the emperor he took the case not merely out of Jerusalem but out of Judaea and assured himself (as far as there could be any assurance) of a safe passage to Rome.

The story as Luke tells it hangs together. This does not prove that it is historically true. It might be intelligent fiction. Some have argued that the narrative in general is Luke's own work on the basis of the parallels between the 'trial' of Paul and that of Jesus in Luke 23. These parallels however have been exaggerated, and Luke himself does nothing to draw attention to them. The essential question is whether Paul was a Roman citizen (see on 16.37; 22.25) and used his citizenship as a means of having his case transferred from Caesarea to Rome. Given the citizenship, the appeal makes very good sense, and there is little to be said for the view that Paul travelled to Rome as a free man.

1. Festus arrived in the province, or, perhaps, entered upon his provincial office. There is no difference in meaning; each translation implies the other. Little is known of Porcius Festus; see Josephus, *Ant.* 20.185–7. He died in office and was succeeded by Albinus. For the date of his accession see on 24.27. Judaea was a department of the province of Syria; the word *province* is loosely used. The procurator usually resided at Caesarea and **went up** (cf. 11.2, but here the word is used in its literal sense) to Jerusalem when occasion required.

2. The chief priests, plural; cf. 4.23; 5.24, and many passages in the gospels. **the leading men of the Jews**; cf. 28.17, also perhaps v. 5. They **informed him against Paul**. For the verb see 23.15. They also have a request to make.

3. The request is specified: they ask **a favour against Paul** – a favour for themselves, but this is not expressed. If Paul is sent from Caesarea to Jerusalem there will be an opportunity for ambush and assassination, similar to those planned but averted in ch. 23. The language of this verse contains several Lucan features.

4. Festus is not to be hoodwinked but behaves with a proper responsibility towards his prisoner. He is another of Luke's 'good' Roman officials. If the Jews wish to make a case against Paul they must go where he is, that is, to **Caesarea**.

5. Festus' decision changes from indirect to direct speech.

let the eminent men among you. This is the probable meaning; possible but less likely is *those who are able* (*to come*). Festus does not intend that the courtroom shall be cluttered with a large number of Jews, and perhaps suspects an attempt on Paul's life. For the same reason, probably, he wishes the Jews to **come down with me**. The Jews are to accuse Paul **if there is anything wrong in the man**. *Anything wrong* is a mild expression for crime; either Festus is showing proper legal caution, or Luke is presenting Paul in the best possible light.

6. Festus did not stay long among the Jews, but **went down** (cf. *went up* in v. 1) **to Caesarea**. **on the next day**: Festus makes no delay. **the place of judgement**: for the expression see 18.12 (with the note).

7. Luke has given the **many weighty charges** in earlier court scenes and sees no need to repeat them. He is himself certain that there is no truth in them, so that inevitably there was no proof.

8. Paul's defence is no more explicit than the Jewish accusations, and Luke moves rapidly on to the dramatic dénouement in v. 11. He does however make what he clearly regards as the essential points, relating to **the Law of the Jews** and **Caesar** (as the head of Roman authority). Paul (as Luke represents him) has not abandoned the Law, he has not counselled his fellow Jews to abandon the Law; he has revised the conditions for the admission of Gentiles. The Temple offence has been dealt with, both by narrative and by exposing the slender basis of the charge: Jews of Asia – now unavailable as witnesses – had seen Paul with Gentiles in the city and *thought* he had taken them into the Temple (21.28f.; 24.6, 12, 18). As for the offence against Caesar, he was not the Egyptian or any other rebel (21.38). He was a Roman citizen, and a loyal one.

9. Festus wished **to curry favour with the Jews**; evidently then they still wished to try Paul in Jerusalem. It was natural that the new Governor should wish to make a good impression on his notoriously difficult people, and have a theological question dealt with in Jerusalem. Crucial to the understanding of Festus' proposal are the final words, **before me**. Do they mean, *With me as presiding judge*? or simply, *In my presence*? Was Paul to be judged by a Roman magistrate, or would he be in the hands of those who were already determined on his death? Behind this lies the question of Festus' motivation in making his proposal. Such questions rest upon the assumption that we have in this paragraph a factual account and that we ought to be able to find in it, or behind it, the various motives, personal, moral, theological, that made the actors act as they did. But the first (though not the only) question that must be asked is, What does Luke wish to convey in this paragraph? Undoubtedly he wishes to show a representative Christian as innocent on all counts and the victim of malice. Against this, it has been maintained that the proposition ascribed to Festus was either hypocritical (he wished to get rid of Paul and to take money from the Jews) and legally impossible, a literary device on Luke's part to get his hero to Rome. But the trial of a theological issue (assuming Paul's political innocence) might well be held in Jerusalem, and if Festus presided over it Paul would be relatively safe. Both Festus and Paul however might welcome the appeal, the former as relief from a difficult decision, the latter as taking him to his desired destination. There is more to be said both for the historicity of the event and for Festus' integrity than is sometimes recognized.

10. I am standing in Caesar's court, where it is right that I should be tried. Paul's words are given in the MSS in three forms. Two may be translated as given here. The third runs, *Standing in Caesar's court I am standing where it is right that I should be tried.* This is contained in one MS only, but that one is the old Codex Vaticanus, and it may well be right. In Caesarea Paul is in Caesar's court; in Jerusalem he would not be. The fact is that (in Luke's narrative – and, it may be, also in fact) Paul feels safer with Romans than with Jews, who had determined to have his blood. If it is true, as Paul asserts, that I have done no wrong to the Jews, nothing is left but the charge of insurrection, clearly a matter for a Roman court.

Paul can almost call Festus as a witness: **as you well know**. The clause may mean, *As you are coming to know better*. Festus' knowledge of the facts and understanding of the issues is improving as time goes on.

11. Paul is not asking for favours but for justice. If he is guilty he will not attempt to buy off the appropriate penalty. But he must be found guilty by a competent court.

I appeal to Caesar. Paul knows his rights and makes them as secure as possible by appealing over Festus' head to Caesar. Appeal at this time meant not the later *appellatio*, by which a condemned and sentenced person might apply to a higher court to have verdict, or sentence or both changed, but *provocatio*, which was an appeal before trial to a higher court which would then take the whole case, trial, verdict, and sentence, out of the lower court. Henceforward Paul will appear before the Governor only in a fact-finding process, designed to help Festus to draw up the report that he must send to Rome.

12. Festus spoke with his council, the body of assessors who would sit with a Roman judge. It was established custom that the judge should (a) consult his council, and (b) reach his own decision.

There was in fact little to discuss. As a citizen Paul had a right to make his appeal. It is possible but unlikely that Paul was appealing to Caesar in the person of Caesar's appointed representative, Festus, who to avoid a difficulty interpreted Paul's words in a way different from Paul's intention. *If you appeal to Caesar you shall have not me but Caesar himself.*

60. FESTUS AND AGRIPPA 25.13–22

[13] When some days had passed King Agrippa and Bernice came to Caesarea and greeted Festus. [14] As they stayed there many days Festus referred Paul's case to the king, saying, 'A man has been left a prisoner by Felix [15] concerning whom, when I was in Jerusalem, the chief priests and elders of the Jews laid information asking for a sentence against him. [16] I answered them that it was not the Romans' custom to hand over any man before the accused has had his accusers face to face and received the opportunity of making a defence against the charge. [17] So they came here with me and I made no delay but on the next day sat in court and commanded the man to be brought. [18] Concerning him his accusers stood and brought no charge of those evil things that I suspected, [19] but they had disputes with him about their own religion and about a certain Jesus who had died and whom Paul alleged to be alive. [20] For myself, I was at a loss over the inquiry about these things and asked if he would be willing to go to Jerusalem to be tried on these matters. [21] But when Paul appealed to be kept for the Emperor's decision I gave orders that he should be kept until I should send him up to Caesar. [22] Agrippa said to Festus, 'I could wish to hear the man myself.' 'Tomorrow', said Festus, 'you shall hear him.'

It has been held that the episode involving King Agrippa was introduced by Luke into the story of the judicial proceedings against Paul in order to create a parallel with the story of Jesus (Lk. 23.6–12). There is much to be said for this view, but there are differences as well as a parallel between the two passages. The Agrippa passage is far longer (forty-seven verses against seven), and there is more detail. In Acts, Agrippa's sister, Bernice, is present throughout, and has no counterpart in Luke. There are precedents (see on v. 13) for courtesy visits by the royal couple. Luke must himself be responsible for the conversations between Festus and Agrippa; they cannot have been reported. We cannot therefore make anything of the omission of the serious Roman charges of *seditio* and *laesa maiestas*; if they were dropped it will have been because there was no evidence. Festus is presented as another 'good Roman', who intends that Paul shall be treated fairly. This of course is how Luke wishes us to see him, in contrast with the Jews; but there is nothing necessarily unhistorical in his picture.

13. When some days had passed. How long the interval was we do not know. It was more natural to think in terms of days than of years. Festus had not decided how to report on Paul's case. **King Agrippa.** This (Herod) Agrippa was the son of the Herod (Agrippa) of 12.1. See *NS* 1.471–83. He succeeded his uncle, Herod of Chalcis, who died in AD 48. He seems to have died in AD 92 or 93 (according to Photius, AD 100). **Bernice** was his sister. She had been married to Herod of Chalcis, after his death she lived with her brother (provoking a good deal of scandal). There is some evidence that suggests that brother and sister travelled together to pay courtesy visits on neighbouring rulers; so e.g. Josephus, *Life* 49. Her name is more correctly written Berenice. **came to Caesarea and greeted Festus**. Behind the verbs lies a disputed point of Greek grammar, but there is little doubt that this is what Luke meant, though *came to Caesarea in order to greet Festus* is possible.

14. Festus referred Paul's case to the King. The terminology is legal, though the reference is informal. Festus, in need of consultation beyond that which he has had with his assessors (25.12), takes advantage of the friendly visit, and begins to sum up the case so far as it has gone.

15. the chief priests and the elders. See 4.23; 23.14.

laid information. See on 23.15; 25.2.

16. Cf. 25.4f. Festus represents himself as having taken a high moral tone with the Jewish accusers; Luke as usual shows Roman officials in a good light. Roman custom must be observed, but the custom is oddly expressed as not **to hand over any man**. Cf. 25.11; but there is no indirect object. The translation *to favour* (*grant favours to*) *any man* is scarcely possible. **before the accused has had his accusers face to face and received the opportunity of making a defence**. The construction of this clause is classical and the language (except the word *opportunity*) and thought are properly legal – a fact that shows Luke's ability to write in a manner suitable to educated and upper-class speakers, when he wishes to do so.

Festus expresses himself in impressive language, but has been accused of hypocrisy. This seems unjust. If he had wished simply to gratify the Jews (over whom it was his business to rule) he could without danger of reprisals have eliminated Paul. In fact he asked him whether he was willing to be tried in Jerusalem or not, and put no obstacle in the way of his appeal – and journey – to Rome. To some extent this picture may be due to Luke's anti-Jewish and pro-Roman sentiment, but this sentiment had its causes; and Paul remained alive in Caesarea and reached Rome in safety.

17. sat in court. See 18.12; 25.6, 9, 10. The site of the *court* is determined by the presence of the judge.

18. It would be natural to suppose that a man for whom severe punishment was demanded would be accused of serious crime. A Roman official could hardly be expected to understand that to 'deny the root' of Jewish religion was the most serious crime imaginable. Luke is emphasizing Paul's innocence from the Roman point of view. The Jews had however come to a Roman court (though they would have preferred their own) and might be expected to make accusations in terms of Roman law. Yet there was **no charge of those evil things I suspected**.

19. Paul was accused not of crime but of heresy, matters of dispute concerning **their own religion**. The noun is cognate with the adjective used in 17.22; see the note. So far Paul would have agreed with Festus' assessment; he is reported as claiming (and in his epistles did claim) that Christianity was true Judaism, the fulfilment of Judaism. He would also have agreed (though in each case he would have expressed the matter differently) with Festus' second point: the dispute between Paul and the Jews turned upon a certain Jesus who had died but was affirmed by Paul to be alive. Cf. Rom. 10.9: Jesus is Lord; God raised him from the dead. All this can, of course, be no more than Luke's guess at what may have passed between Festus and Agrippa.

20. The drift, and the reference back to 25.9, are clear, but the Greek is, to say the least, unusual. **asked** in the translation is really *said*, which is not normally used to introduce an indirect question. C. F. D. Moule (*Idiom Book*, 154) suggests writing 'more loosely and idiomatically', *I said, would he like . . .* This loose but idiomatic English represents the Greek well, but the Greek, though loose, is not idiomatic.

21. the Emperor's decision. The Greek for *decision* represents the Latin technical term *cognitio*. **I should send him up**, another technical term for the remission of a case to a higher court.

22. I could wish: the Greek imperfect tense; not the best but good literary style, contrasting oddly with the unliterary expressions noted above.

61. FESTUS, AGRIPPA, AND PAUL 25.23 – 26.32

**[23] On the next day, when Agrippa and Bernice came with great
pomp and entered the audience chamber, along with the tribunes
and the leading men of the city, and when Festus had given the
word of command, Paul was brought. [24] Festus said, 'King
Agrippa, and all you gentlemen who are present with us, you
behold this man, concerning whom the whole people of the Jews
petitioned me, both in Jerusalem and here, shouting out that he
ought to live no longer. [25] I however did not see that he had done
anything worthy of death, and when he himself appealed to the
Emperor I decided to send him. [26] I have nothing definite about
him to send in writing to the Emperor; for this reason I have
produced him before you, and especially before you, King
Agrippa, in order that, when examination has taken place, I may
get something that I may write. [27] For it seems to me nonsense to
send a prisoner and not at the same time to signify the charges
against him.'**

**[1] Agrippa said to Paul, 'It is permitted you to give an account
of yourself.' Then Paul stretched out his hand and began his
defence. [2] 'I consider myself fortunate, King Agrippa, that I am
today about to make my defence, concerning all the things of
which I am accused by the Jews, before you, [3] especially since [I
know] that you are familiar with all the customs and disputes
current among the Jews. So I beg you to hear me patiently. [4] All
the Jews know my manner of life from my youth, which was
from the beginning within my own nation and in Jerusalem.
[5] They have known from of old, if they are willing to testify, that
I lived in accordance with the strictest party within our religion,
a Pharisee. [6] And now I am standing trial for the hope of the
promise made by God to our fathers, [7] [the promise] to which our
twelve-tribe people, zealously worshipping [God] night and day,
hope to attain. It is for this hope that I am being accused, O King,
by Jews. [8] Why is it judged incredible with you that God raises
the dead? [9] I myself thought that I ought to do many things
contrary to the name of Jesus the Nazoraean. [10] And this I did in
Jerusalem, and I shut up in prison many of the saints, having
received authority from the chief priests; and when they were
being killed I cast my vote against them. [11] And often in all the**

synagogues I tried by punishing them to make them blaspheme, and being exceedingly mad against them I persecuted them even
to foreign cities. [12] And so as I was travelling to Damascus with
authority and commission from the chief priests, [13] at midday, on
the road, I saw, O King, a light from heaven, beyond the brightness of the sun, shining round me and those who were travelling
with me. [14] We all fell to the ground and I heard a voice saying to
me in the Hebrew language, "Saul, Saul, why are you persecuting
me? It is hard for you to kick against the goad." [15] I said, "Who
art thou, Lord?" The Lord said, "I am Jesus whom you are
persecuting. [16] But get up and stand on your feet. For this is why I
have appeared to you, to appoint you a minister and witness both
of the things that you have seen and of those in which I shall
appear to you, [17] rescuing you from the people and from the
Gentiles, unto whom I now send you, [18] to open their eyes, so that
they may turn from darkness to light and from the authority of
Satan to God, so that they may receive forgiveness of sins and a
lot among those who have been sanctified by faith in me."
[19] Consequently, King Agrippa, I did not prove disobedient to the
heavenly vision, [20] but first to those in Damascus and in Jerusalem,
and in all the land of Judaea and to the Gentiles, I proclaimed
that they should repent and turn to God, doing works worthy of
repentance. [21] Because of these things Jews seized me when I was
in the Temple and tried to make away with me. [22] So, having
obtained the help that comes from God, I stand to this day,
testifying to small and great, saying nothing but the things which
the prophets and Moses said were to happen, [23] that the Christ
was to suffer, and that he first would, on the basis of the
resurrection of the dead, proclaim light to both the people and
the Gentiles.'

[24] While Paul was saying these things in his defence, Festus
said with a loud voice. 'Paul, you are mad; your great learning
is leading you into madness.' [25] Paul said, 'I am not mad, most
excellent Festus, but uttering words of truth and sober— mindedness. [26] For the king, to whom I speak with boldness, knows
about these matters, for I am persuaded that none of them escapes
him; for this was not done in a corner. [27] King Agrippa, do you
believe the prophets? I know that you believe.' [28] Agrippa said to
Paul, 'With little trouble you are trying to persuade me to play
the Christian.' [29] Paul replied, 'I wish to God that, with little

trouble or much, you and all who hear me today would become such as I myself am – apart from these bonds.' [30] The king rose up, and the governor and Bernice and those who were sitting with them. [31] When they had withdrawn they spoke to one another, saying, 'This man is doing nothing worthy of death or imprisonment.' [32] Agrippa said to Festus, 'This man could have been released if he had not appealed to Caesar.'

It is hard to see what trustworthy information Luke can have found about the private meeting between Festus and Agrippa (25.13–22) but the new paragraph purports to relate a more public event. There is no hint that Christians were present, but at least it was not a private conversation. The main feature of the narrative is a long speech by Paul which contains the third account of his conversion. The speech is interrupted by Festus' shout, 'You are mad, Paul'. After a brief conversation between Paul and Agrippa the scene is wound up by the explicit assertion by both rulers that Paul is innocent. There is little in the narrative that provides an opportunity for historical comment. Would a Christian writer, composing freely, introduce into his narrative the assertion that Paul was mad? Yes, he might do so, since as a writer he is obviously free to allow Paul to reply, and even to have the last word. In fact Luke presents here what he takes to be Paul's reply to a charge brought against Christians in his own (Luke's) time, at the same time constructing a climax in his picture of the heroic Paul.

The present account of Paul's conversion differs from the first and second (9.1–19; 22.4–21) in several respects. It has been adapted to its setting; there are touches (for which see the notes below) that should make it appealing and intelligible to a Gentile audience.

Luke undoubtedly wishes to assert in the strongest terms that Paul, though in Roman custody and on his way to trial in Rome, was, and was recognized by competent authorities to be, an innocent man. Whether the opinions expressed in the story by Festus and Agrippa were in fact held by them we have no means of knowing. Paul was probably not displeased with the situation in which he found himself.

23. On the next day takes up *tomorrow* in 25.22. **audience chamber**, a room designed, or used, for the purpose of hearing; often a lecture room. *Audience chamber* guesses at its meaning here; not a *courtroom* – no lower court than the emperor's may try Paul now.

This is a show for the entertainment of Agrippa and Bernice, with an additional practical usefulness for Festus.

Paul was brought. The simple statement contrasts with the show. If (as some have thought) there is snobbery in Luke's account it is a sort of counter-snobbery.

24, 25. These verses sum up the position regarding Paul that has now been reached. The Jewish people as a whole (this seems to be intended) want him dead. Festus however **did not see that he had done anything worthy of death** – perhaps the strongest assertion so far of Paul's innocence (from the Roman point of view).

26. To decide to send Paul to Rome was one thing; to know what to say in the accompanying report was another. Such a report was required (*Digest* 49.6.1). If Festus was convinced that Paul was innocent he could have released him at once; he may however have recognized that it was in Paul's interests to be packed safely off to Rome.

the Emperor (so in v. 25) is here *the Lord* (Greek, *kyrios*). This title was not at first used by the emperors. According to Suetonius (*Augustus* 53) Augustus found the title objectionable, Tiberius (*Tiberius* 27) an insult. From the time of Claudius it began to be used; it became more usual in the time of Domitian. Luke evidently expects it to be immediately understood and to evoke no comment.

27. it seems to me nonsense . . . No doubt it would seem equally unreasonable to the emperor.

1. It is permitted you. The impersonal passive gives a formal touch to the proceedings. **to give an account of yourself**, perhaps *to speak on your own behalf*, but Luke's preposition taken strictly means *about* rather than *for*. **Paul . . . began his defence**. Luke writes as if this were a trial; and so it may well have seemed, to him and especially to Paul. But speaking about himself leads Paul to speak about Christ.

2. I consider myself fortunate. Another *captatio benevolentiae*; cf. 24.2, 10. *Consider* is expressed in a way that suggests that Paul (Luke) is writing in good style. There are however lapses.

the things of which I am accused. It is because of these accusations that Paul stands where he does, and he can hardly speak of them without thinking in terms of a *defence* (v. 1).

3. The *captatio benevolentiae* continues but the attempt at fine style breaks down. Some such supplement as **I know** is needed.

4. All the Jews know my manner of life . . . from the beginning within my own nation and in Jerusalem. The precise meaning of this verse, and its relation with 22.3, raise difficult questions. Are *within my own nation* and *in Jerusalem* distinguished, or could *in Jerusalem* be included within *my own nation*? What does Paul consider his *own nation from the beginning*? Is Paul (Luke) thinking of Jerusalem or of Tarsus? If of Jerusalem, *from the beginning* is to be noted.

5. the strictest party within our religion. See on 5.17. **a Pharisee**. See on 23.6 and cf. Phil. 3.5f. If, as has been suggested, Paul was a Zealot (see *NS* 2.598–606) he (Luke) does not say so here.

6. And now, in contrast with his former manner of life as a Pharisee, yet also in continuity with it, for Paul continues to maintain that his Christianity was true Judaism. **the promise** was **made by God to our fathers**.

I am standing trial in Greek stands with great emphasis at the end of the sentence. For this hope, the core of our national life, I am not praised or respected but – on trial. This rhetorical pattern is repeated in v. 7.

7. The **twelve-tribe people . . . hope to attain** *the promise* (v. 6). Their constant (**night and day**) worship is directed to this end. Paul is making his own contribution to this effort, yet **it is for this hope that I am being accused . . . by Jews**. The contrast already noted in v. 6 is made even more paradoxical. For this *Jewish* hope I am being accused *by Jews*. Of course, Paul is not being blamed for maintaining the Jewish hope but for holding (falsely, in the opinion of his compatriots) that it was fulfilled in Jesus.

8. Why is it judged incredible . . . ? There is no grammatical connection with the preceding sentence, and some think that this verse should be placed between vv. 22 and 23, or that v. 23 should follow v. 8 at this point. There are linguistic points in favour of this re-arrangement, but in substance it is not necessary. For Luke (and Paul) the *hope* was concentrated and fulfilled in resurrection, especially in the resurrection of Jesus; the transition (from v. 7 to v. 8) would not be convincing to a Jew, but to Luke (and Paul) it would be.

with you. *You* is plural, which comes oddly after the vocative singular *O King* of v. 7. Luke probably thinks of the Christian on trial as addressing Jews – and could perhaps have classed Agrippa as one of them (cf. v. 27).

9. This verse looks back to v. 5, vv. 6–8 being a parenthesis. Paul can assert the theme of resurrection in its Christian form (i.e. the beginning of the general resurrection, Christ having been raised as the firstfruits of all who sleep) because (a) he has himself seen the crucified Jesus alive, and (b) this event has transformed him from persecutor to preacher of Christ. It follows that he will now proceed with the story of his conversion, beginning with reference to what he did **contrary to the name of Jesus the Nazoraean**.

10. And this I did in Jerusalem. See 8.3.

having received authority from the chief priests. See 9.1f., where the authority is expressed in letters and is related to Paul's journey to Damascus (v. 12).

when they were being killed I cast my vote against them. Luke writes a little carelessly. While they were being killed it would be too late to vote for or against them. Luke means, When it was a question of the death penalty, I cast my vote . . . It is implied that Paul, having a vote, was an ordained rabbi, that the Sanhedrin followed due legal procedures, and that the Sanhedrin could pass and execute capital sentences (cf. 25.16 and Jn 18.31). It is also implied that a number of Christians (more than Stephen and James) were put to death. This is often questioned, the words ascribed to Paul being treated as 'rhetorical'. But cf. Jn 16.2; Mt. 24.9; Mk 13.12; 2 Cor. 11.24–27. Luke was writing many years after Saul's persecution, but he probably represents at least folk memory of the period.

11. in all the synagogues: cf. 9.2. It is implied that Christians still frequented synagogues; that is, they wished to continue to be Jews though they now believed in Christ. This was probably true of Paul himself, who received five synagogue beatings (2 Cor. 11.24). **I tried . . . to make them** . . . The imperfect of the verb *make* (*compel*) is probably both conative and repetitive (**persecuted** can only be repetitive). **blaspheme**: from a specifically Christian point of view, perhaps by cursing Christ. Cf. 1 Cor. 12.3; also Pliny, *Epistles* 10.96.5 (to curse Christ, which nothing can compel those who are in truth Christians to do).

12. And so, perhaps, *In the course of which activity*. **authority and commission from the chief priests**. Cf. 9.1f. In the ensuing narrative some details found in chs. 9 and 22 are omitted, probably in order to make room (vv. 16–18) for more information about Paul's vocation.

13. In comparison with chs. 9 and 22 there are several verbal changes. In those chapters the fellow travellers are not mentioned at this point.

14. We all fell to the ground. At 9.4; 22.7 only Paul is said to fall; it is not said, however, that the others did not fall. **I heard a voice**. On the case taken with the Greek verb *to hear* see on 22.7. **in the Hebrew** (probably meaning *Aramaic*) **language**; perhaps intended as an apology to the distinguished audience for the barbarian name **Saul**. **It is hard for you to kick against the goad**. There is no parallel in ch. 9 or ch. 22. This is an old Greek proverb, unlikely to have presented itself to Paul's conscious mind at the time of his conversion. The phrase refers not to an inner struggle but to man's inability to withstand God. The proverb here takes up the thought that Paul is resisting, persecuting, Jesus himself in hindering his work. Cf. Euripides, *Bacchae* 795 (kick against the goad, a man against God). There are few Jewish parallels and they are not close; see Psalms of Solomon 16.4. For the view that Luke knew Euripides' *Bacchae* see on 5.39; 16.26.

15. This verse agrees substantially with 9.5; 22.8.

16. Only here (not in chs. 9 and 22) is Paul's commission explicitly given at the time of his conversion. It cannot be said that the version of the story in this chapter is due solely to abbreviation; this could have been done more economically with some such phrase as, 'Later, in the Temple . . .'. Either Luke is deliberately introducing variation in order to keep the reader's attention, or, less probably, he has variant traditions. He may be influenced here by a desire to dispense with Ananias.

But, as at 9.6. You have been persecuting me, *but* henceforth you will . . . **get up and stand on your feet** recalls Ezek. 2.1–3; other prophetic passages less closely, Jer. 1.7; Isa. 35.5; 42.7, 16; 1 Chron. 16.35. **I have appeared to you**. Paul uses the same verb at 1 Cor. 15.8; but **I shall appear to you** at the end of the verse shows that it is not confined to resurrection appearances. **to appoint you**, the verb of 3.20. It is not said that Paul is appointed to be an apostle; see on 14.4, 14, and Introduction, pp. lviii–lx. He is to be a **minister**; for this word see Lk. 1.2. Paul is to be such a *minister of the word*. He is also to be **a witness**. At 13.31f. the apostles are witnesses of the resurrection, and as such appear over against those who like Paul are preachers of the Gospel. His testimony will not be confined to the resurrection; there will be future visions of Christ. In the epistles Paul displays considerable reluctance to speak of visions (2 Cor. 12.1–5; see *2 Corinthians* 34, 250, 305–313).

17. rescuing you. The classical meaning of this verb is *choosing*, but its meaning here is determined by the parallel in Jer. 1.8.

the Gentiles, unto whom I now send you. Cf. 22.21. Naturally the reaction of the Temple crowd is not repeated here.

18. An important verse, which shows how Paul (according to Luke) understood his mission to the Gentile world. Some of the language here is based on the OT, but had probably become something like a 'conversion formula' among Christians; similar language is found at Qumran; see e.g. 1 QS 11.7f. **from darkness to light** is metaphorical, and it is not difficult to specify contrasts in the realms of morals and thought that it would represent, though such contrasts are hardly to be found in Acts. **from the authority of Satan to God** implies that men are held captive by Satan and are released by the Gospel to return to God their Creator. For **forgiveness of sins** see 2.38. **those who have been sanctified** are more frequently in Paul *the saints* (*holy ones*), but cf. 1 Cor. 1.2, as well as Acts 20.32. It is not indicated whether their **lot** (cf. 1.17; 8.21; Col. 1.12) refers to membership of the church in the world, or in the age to come. Both are no doubt intended. Sanctification, and the inheritance that goes with it, are effected **by faith in** Christ.

The various points made in this verse (*to open . . . to turn . . . receive forgiveness . . . a lot among those who have been sanctified*) are not intended as stages within a process but are rather alternative pictorial images of a divine act, almost any one of which could, if developed, stand for the whole. The piling up of images constitutes an impressive if not perfectly clear climax. Cf. Isa. 42.7, 16; Eph. 6.12; James 1.17; Col. 1.12–14; 1 Clement 59.2.

19. I did not prove disobedient. An example of Lucan litotes; cf. 12.18; 15.2; 19.11, 23, 24; 20.12; 21.39; 26.19,26; 27.20; 28.2. The impression given here is one of modesty on Paul's part, but in fact Luke seems to use this form of speech as a form of emphasis. **the heavenly vision**; in fact, the vision of a heavenly being, who commanded (v. 17) and was obeyed. Cf. 2 Cor. 12.1; Gal. 1.15f. Paul himself refers very seldom to visionary experiences.

20. In obedience to the divine commission Paul has carried out what is intended to be understood as (at least in outline and in principle) a universal preaching mission. The sentence however is not clear. The opening phrase sounds at first as if it could include Gentiles, but **and to the Gentiles** seems to prohibit this. There is a difficulty in that according to Gal. 1.22 Paul remained personally unknown to the churches of Judaea. At Rom. 15.19 however he claims to have preached the Gospel from Jerusalem round as far as Illyricum. His hearers are to **repent** (cf. 2.38) and **turn to God** (cf. 3.10), and to do **works worthy of repentance**, that is, they are to prove the sincerity of their repentance by amended lives. A Jewish missionary seeking to convert the heathen to Judaism would have made similar demands.

21. This verse is a sufficiently accurate summary of what is described at length in chs. 21 and 22. **Because of these things**. If *these things* refer to what is said in vv. 16–20 it is a more accurate account than some of the violent attack on Paul. He might or he might not have brought Trophimus into the Temple; he had certainly spent the last few years in taking the Gospel of Messianic salvation to uncircumcised nations outside the boundaries of Israel.

22. Paul now winds up his speech by setting out the religious basis and theological structure of his Christian life and belief.

having obtained the help that comes from God. Greek has (at least) two words for *help*; that which is used here may (in contrast with the other) denote help that comes from without. It is not his own strength that has maintained Paul but that which comes *from God*. **testifying to small and great**, in the market-place and in the procurator's hall.

nothing but the things which . . . The content of Paul's testimony is simply the message of the OT, reinforced by the affirmation that what the OT foretold has now been fulfilled. On this Paul frequently insists; see e.g. 24.14; 28.23.

For the suggestion that v. 8 should be transferred to follow this verse and precede v. 23 see on v. 8.

23. This sentence follows on *testifying* (v. 22); it could follow on v. 8 (literally, *if God raises the dead*); this is not an adequate reason for transposing v. 8.

that the Christ was to suffer. The word (*ei*) here translated *that* most often means *if*. Its use here has evoked various explanations, suggesting its origin in discussion and debate: *If* the OT says . . . These suggestions are unnecessary. The word can bear the meaning *that*, especially after a verb of feeling – though it may hint at the fact that what is being asserted may possibly be denied.

the Christ was to suffer, *was liable to suffering*, a word that occurs nowhere else in the NT but was taken up in the second century (Ignatius and Justin). **on the basis of** is an attempt to combine the local and causative aspects of the Greek preposition.

The Messiah, who suffers and is raised from death, proclaims light to both Jews and Gentiles. Thus the three points are made which, though Paul insists that they are already made by the prophets and Moses, incense the Jews. No OT passages are quoted in support of Paul's assertion. In controversy between Jews and Christians such passages must have been quoted and their interpretation discussed, but this is a debate into which Luke never enters (though a passage such as 17.11 shows that he was aware of it).

24. in his defence. Cf. v. 1; it was not in a properly legal sense a defence because he was not on trial; but what he said would influence the content of the dossier that Festus would send to Rome and therefore had defensive value. Festus was not impressed. **Paul, you are mad.** The story of a crucified and risen Messiah is nonsense (a) because a king would not proceed by way of suffering and death, and (b) because dead men do not rise (see on 17.31). **your great learning**: *many writings* is an alternative possibility (it could refer to OT passages used by Paul but not quoted by Luke; see on v. 23), but it is less probable. **is leading you into madness**. The enthusiastic madness of 1 Cor. 14.23 is not a parallel. The 'philosophic madness' of the inspired wise man (cf. Plato, *Phaedrus* 245a. 249d) is closer but still not correct; in the next verse Paul rebuts the suggestion of madness: he is not what Festus says he is.

25. I am not mad. a firm contradiction, but made courteously, respectfully: **most excellent Festus**. Cf. 23.26: 24.3. I am ... **uttering**. The word is used at 2.4, 14. where it is often said to suggest inspired, even ecstatic speech. This however is what Paul here disclaims. He is speaking **words of truth and sober-mindedness**. *Truth* refers to the objective content of what Paul is saying, *sober-mindedness* to the subjective manner in which he speaks. Paul's words set forth *truth* and they are controlled by sober judgement. For this cf. Rom. 12.3: 2 Cor. 5.13, and Paul's treatment of glossolalia at Corinth.

26. the king . . . knows about these matters. *These matters* might refer to what is written in the OT (cf. vv. 27, 28), but in view of the end of the verse it is better to take them to be the Christian event, the ministry, death, and resurrection of Jesus. Agrippa II was born in AD 27/28 and was therefore not aware of the story of Jesus at first hand: moreover he lived at Claudius' court till AD 50 or later. He did however show considerable concern over Jewish affairs, and may well have heard of the origins of Christianity. **done in a corner** has become an

English idiom, but it was not so used in antiquity, though two or three somewhat distant parallels can be cited.

27. Agrippa, like some other members of his family, though in fact a Gentile, could on occasion represent himself as a Jew in spirit. Paul appeals to his knowledge of and belief in the OT. Reference to his belief in the prophets recalls *these matters* in v. 26, and, contrary to the suggestion made on that verse, might suggest that *these matters* are the prophetic themes of vv. 22f. – or rather, that there is no great difference between the two interpretations. What the prophets foretold is what happened in the story of Jesus. Belief in the prophets is (for Paul – and Luke) not an end in itself but a step on the way to belief in Christ.

28. Agrippa's words to Paul are perhaps the most disputed, as regards their construction and meaning, in Acts. There are several variants.

The active, **You are trying** [these two words represent the tense of the Greek verb] **to persuade me**, is in one MS replaced by the passive, *you are persuaded*. This gives a relatively easy sense: You are persuaded that I know all about Christianity; perhaps you are persuaded that I believe it too. The support could not be scantier, and it is an 'easy' reading; it must almost certainly be rejected. Again, **to play** [in our translation] **the Christian** is, in many MSS, *to become a Christian*. This makes good sense, but it evades a difficulty and the evidence is on the whole late. We must see what can be done with the more difficult reading.

With little trouble translates what would literally be *in little*. With this must be borne in mind Paul's reply in v. 29. **with little trouble or much**, literally, *in little or great*. It is hard to take *great* with *time*, and we should supply *trouble*.

to play the Christian is literally *to make a Christian*. It is not easy to handle the pronouns here, but it is just possible to render *You are trying to persuade me that you have made me, with little trouble* (or, *in little time*) *a Christian*. This has the advantage of harmonizing with v. 29, where Paul wishes all his hearers to become Christians, that is, he wishes to make them Christians. Against this, one would think that if Agrippa had been made a Christian it would scarcely be necessary to persuade him that this had happened.

An alternative interpretation is based on 1 Kings 21.7, where the corresponding words seem to mean *to play the king*. The meaning of the present passage would be, *You are persuading me to play the*

Christian, that is, to act a part for your convenience (by getting me to profess belief in the prophets). This is an attractive suggestion, perhaps the best available, but one over-literal rendering of a Hebrew verb is not enough to establish a Greek idiom.

We must ask whether Agrippa is speaking seriously or ironically – and ask first what Luke wishes us to hear. He perhaps intends to give the same impression of Agrippa that he has given of Felix (p. 372) and of Festus (p. 380). He is the neither wholly good nor wholly bad official, who will at least treat Paul fairly.

29. with little trouble or much. See on v. 28. In Greek the two parts of the phrase are connected by the word normally translated *and*. There is evidence of its occasional use as expressing an alternative. There are however other ways of taking the words: *in small and great* may be used for *wholly, altogether*; or the words may be used in the sense of v. 22 (*to small and great*), that is, *to everyone*. Paul's desire to make Christians applies to the least and to the greatest, to the king himself. Paul wishes for all his hearers the election, the call, and the commission he himself has.

30. those who were sitting with them. The word is used of assessors sitting with the principal judge; here informally, for this is not a trial or a court.

31. When they had withdrawn from the audience chamber (25.23) into a retiring room. It is clear that neither Luke nor any third party heard the conversation that followed. Since this was not a trial there was no formal verdict to announce. If kindly disposed, one or both of the rulers may have had a word with Paul.

32. This, like the saying in v. 31, must have seemed to Luke and his readers very quotable. The appeal has been made, and must go forward; otherwise Paul could have been set free. Acquittal and release would not have been impossible but would have been untactful with regard to both the emperor and the province. It seems too that continuing custody with a free voyage to Rome will have suited Paul very well. At least he was protected from Jewish assassins.

XVI

PAUL REACHES ROME

(27.1 – 28.28)

62. THE SEA VOYAGE 27.1–44

**1 When it was decided that we should set sail for Italy they handed
over Paul and some other prisoners to a centurion called Julius,
of the Augustan Cohort. 2 We embarked on a ship of Adramyttium
which was about to sail to places on the coast of Asia and put out
to sea; the Macedonian Aristarchus, of Thessalonica, was with
us. 3 The next day we put in at Sidon and Julius treated Paul in a
kindly way, allowing him to go to his friends to receive care.
4 Thence we put out to sea and sailed under the lee of Cyprus
because the winds were contrary. 5 We sailed across the open sea
off Cilicia and Pamphylia and put in at Myra in Lycia. 6 There
the centurion found an Alexandrian ship sailing to Italy and
embarked us on it. 7 Sailing slowly for a number of days and barely
getting as far as Cnidus, since the wind did not permit us to
approach we sailed for refuge under the lee of Crete off Salmone.
8 Coasting along it with difficulty we came to a place called Fair
Havens, to which the town of Lasaea is near.**

**9 Since a considerable time had now elapsed and sailing was
already risky because even the Fast was now already past Paul
offered advice, 10 saying to them, 'Men, I see that the voyage is
going to be attended by damage and much loss not only of
the cargo and the ship but also of our lives.' 11 But the centurion
was persuaded by the captain and the owner rather than by
Paul's words. 12 Since the harbour was not suitable for wintering the majority formed the plan of putting out from
there and getting if they could to Phoenix, a harbour of Crete**

**looking into the south west and north west winds, and wintering
there.**

**13 When a gentle south wind sprang up they supposed that
they had achieved their purpose; they set out and coasted
along Crete as close in shore as possible. 14 But before long a
tempestuous wind called Euraquilo flung itself down from the
island. 15 The boat was seized by the wind and was unable to
head into it, so we gave way to it and ran before it. 16 We ran
under the lee of a certain small island called Cauda and were
scarcely able to gain full control of the dinghy. 17 They hauled it
up and made use of auxiliary devices, frapping the ship, and
fearing lest they should be cast upon the Syrtis they dropped
the sea anchor, and so drifted. 18 Since we were severely storm
tossed on the next day they jettisoned [some of the cargo]. 19 On
the third day they threw out with their own hands the ship's gear.
20 For many days neither sun nor stars were to be seen, no small
storm was upon us, and finally all hope of our being saved was
disappearing.**

**21 Since many were going without food Paul then stood in their
midst and said, 'Men, you ought to have listened to me so as not
to have left Crete and incur this damage and loss. 22 And now I
advise you to take heart, for there will be no loss of life of any of
you but only of the ship. 23 For this night there stood by me an
angel of the God whose I am and whom I serve, 24 saying. "Fear
not, Paul, you must stand before Caesar, and see, God has granted
you all those who are sailing with you." 25 So take heart, men; for
I believe God that it will be just as it has been told me. 26 But we
have to be cast on a certain island.'**

**27 When the fourteenth night came and we were being tossed
about in Adria, in the middle of the night the sailors thought that
land was approaching them. 28 They took soundings, and found
twenty fathoms; they moved the boat on a little, sounded again,
and found fifteen fathoms. 29 Fearing lest we should fall upon
rocky places they threw out four anchors from the stern and
wished it were day. 30 The sailors were seeking to escape from the
ship and let down the dinghy into the sea, under the pretence
that they were going to let out anchors from the bow. 31 Paul said
to the centurion and the soldiers, 'Unless these men stay in the
ship you cannot be saved.' 32 Then the soldiers cut the ropes of
the dinghy and let it fall away.**

**33 When it was nearly day Paul exhorted them all to partake of
food, saying, 'Today you are looking to the fourteenth day and
are continuing without food, having taken nothing. 34 Therefore I
urge you to partake of food. For this is for your welfare, for not a
hair will be lost from the head of any of you.' 35 When he had said
this he took a loaf and gave thanks to God before them all; he
broke it and began to eat. 36 They all took heart and themselves
also partook of food. 37 We were in all 276 souls in the ship. 38 When
they were satisfied with food they set about lightening the ship,
casting the food into the sea.**

**39 When day broke they did not recognize the land but
perceived a bay with a beach on which they planned if possible to
run the ship. 40 They detached the anchors and let them slip into
the sea, at the same time loosening the fastenings of the rudders
and raising the foresail to the breeze they held on to the beach.
41 They ran upon a shoal and ran the ship aground. The bow
became fixed and remained firm but the stern began to break up
under the violence of the waves. 42 It was the plan of the soldiers
to kill the prisoners, lest any should swim off and escape. 43 But
the centurion, wishing to get Paul safely through, put a stop to
their intention and commanded those who were able to swim to
throw themselves overboard and come first to land 44 and [then]
the rest, some on planks of wood and some on some of those who
came from the ship. And in this way it came about that all got
safely to land.**

There can be no doubt that whoever was responsible for the substance of this chapter was familiar with the sea and with seafaring, in particular with conditions and places in the Mediterranean and the Adriatic. The question that arises is whether all the nautical details (for which see the notes) belong to a journey actually made by Paul on the way from Caesarea to Rome. Were the references to Paul, to things said and done by him on the voyage, an integral part of the story from the beginning, or were they inserted into an already existing narrative of a voyage and shipwreck that did not originally contain them?

The outline of the story is cast in the first person plural (vv. 1, 2, 3, 4, 5, 6, 7, 8, 15, 16, 18, 20, (26), 27, 29, and 37). That there are verses where Paul is subject or object and is referred to in the third person singular is no proof that either set of verses was inserted. It would be not only untrue but ridiculous to write in vv. 9f., We offered advice . . . If anyone gave this advice it was Paul. The same sort of observation covers the use of the third person plural. It has to be asked whether the Pauline interventions are credible as parts of the story as a whole.

Passages that have been reckoned insertions include vv. 3b, 9–11, 21–26, 31, 33–36, 43c, and it has been alleged that Luke's picture of Paul is false to history, in that he knows only the strong, unshakable darling of God who strides on from triumph to triumph. There is a measure of truth in this as a general observation, though Paul's 'triumphal' progress to Rome was marked by mob violence, imprisonment, attempted assassination, and a narrow escape from drowning. The story has by now become virtually a biography and it is not surprising that the subject of the biography occupies the centre of the stage. There is nothing surprising in the influence of one man of unshakable faith and imperturbable courage. Parallels are as uncommon as such men are, but they exist. A point worth bearing in mind is that Paul makes two predictions of the outcome of the voyage (vv. 10; 24–26). They contradict each other. According to the former, lives will be lost; according to the latter, no lives will be lost. It is very unlikely that Luke simply invented these contradictory predictions. If he did not, he must have received one or possibly both of them from some kind of tradition of Paul's attitude and action on the ship. This need not have been detailed, it may not have been accurate; it has certainly been written up by Luke in the light of his acquaintance with the sea and his estimate of Paul.

Paul is not portrayed as a 'divine man' (see pp. 38, 39). He is not able to control the storm but under its violence behaves with courage and faith. And Luke has no doubt that it was God's will that he should reach Rome.

1. When it was decided must refer to practical arrangements for the journey; the decision that Paul should go to Rome was made earlier. **that we should set sail**. *We* can hardly not mean that the writer accompanied Paul. On the 'We' passages see Introduction, pp. xxxi–xxxiii. Some think Aristarchus (v. 2) to have been the author. **they** (officials of Festus, presumably) **handed over Paul . . . to a centurion called Julius** (of whom nothing more is known than is told here), **of the Augustan Cohort**. There is good epigraphic evidence of the presence of a Cohors Augusta I in Syria in the first century AD.

2. a ship of Adramyttium, its home port; it was probably used for coastwise traffic round the north-eastern corner of the

Mediterranean. The centurion would hope to pick up **on the coast of Asia** a ship sailing further west, perhaps even to Rome.

Paul's only named companion was Aristarchus, see 19.29; 20.4. It has been suggested, with little ground, that he left the party at Myra, intending to continue in the ship as far as Adramyttium on his way home to Thessalonica. He is not heard of again in Acts and we do not know what happened.

3. The next day we put in at Sidon. Luke's word means always *the day after the one last mentioned* (thus at 20.15 it means *the day after tomorrow*). Sidon, a Phoenician port, was a hellenized city; in 24 BC Augustus made it part of Ituraea. There is some evidence of the presence of Jews (*NS* 3.14, 15). If **his friends** were Christian friends, Sidon had been evangelized, we do not know when or by whom. It is possible that *the Friends* had become a technical term for Christians; cf. 3 Jn 15. Paul was allowed **to receive care** from the friends. Luke no doubt thinks of what Ignatius (*Polycarp* 1.2) describes as 'care both physical and spiritual'. Luke evidently thinks of Julius as another 'good' Roman soldier.

4. How long the ship and its passengers stayed in Sidon we do not know. When they left they **sailed under the lee of Cyprus**. Which was the lee side? The reference in v. 5 to Cilicia and Pamphylia makes it practically certain that they sailed on the north side (at 21.3 Paul sailed on the south side). The north side (except for ships trading at Salamis or Paphos) was the natural side for a land-hugging vessel to take. **the winds were contrary**. If they were sailing north west the Etesian winds would be against them, but they would be helped by offshore breezes and a westward current.

5. We sailed across the open sea, the Pamphylian Bight.

The Western text adds that the journey lasted *fifteen days*, which, with contrary winds, might well be correct. The Alexandrian corn ships rarely sailed direct to Rome but often put in at Myra, whence a north wind would take them to Sicily.

6. an Alexandrian ship sailing to Italy would probably be one of the corn fleet. Egypt supplied Rome with a third of the year's corn requirement, and the corn ships were used by official travellers as well as by private persons. Alexandrian sailors had a good reputation.

7, 8. The translation sets out, in what seems the best possible way, a long and somewhat complicated sentence.

Sailing slowly may possibly be a technical term for *beating*. **for a number of days** uses one of Luke's favourite words for a number which he either is not able. or has no wish, to give precisely. **Cnidus** is mentioned here only in the NT. It lay at the extremity of a peninsula of the mainland, north west of Rhodes. Since 129 BC the town had been a free city under Roman rule.

we sailed for refuge under the lee of Crete. The verb was used in v. 4 There is some doubt about the spelling of **Salmone**, also about its precise location; there are two capes and it is uncertain which is referred to. Crete was brought under Roman rule by Q. Metellus in 67 BC: it was united with Cyrenaica and made a senatorial province.

Even the sheltered south side of Crete (usually taken by sailing ships) presented problems to the navigators, and it was not without difficulty that they coasted along it as far as a place called **Fair Havens**. A port bearing this name still exists, and gives protection from northerly and westerly winds. It was about five or six miles from a place that has been identified with **Lasaea**. Apparently the port had little but safety to commend it (v. 12).

According to Titus 1.5 Paul (on some occasion) left Titus in Crete; the epistle presupposes the existence of a fairly developed and numerous church in the island. There is no confirmation of this in the present narrative, and, considerately as Julius treated Paul, he will hardly have permitted him to set about evangelizing the island.

It is often held that v. 8 (or v. 9a) connects with v. 12. vv. 9–11 being a Pauline insertion into a non-Pauline narrative. See p. 401.

9. In Luke's narrative it is clear and understandable that continuation of the voyage was under discussion. **a considerable time** had now elapsed (since they left Caesarea? or Myra?) and Fair Havens was not suitable for wintering. Claudius had taken financial steps to encourage late and risky sailings for the corn fleet. But the danger of sailing was sufficient to constitute a case for staying where they were. In this situation **Paul** intervened. Was he in a position to do so? Perhaps; he was under guard but he was a privileged person, who must be delivered to the emperor. He had not been found guilty of any crime, and it was the Governor's opinion that he was innocent.

the Fast is the Day of Atonement, the only fast in the Jewish calendar. This fell on Tishri 10: Tishri corresponds to the latter part of September and the former part of October. The 10th would come at the end of September or the beginning of October. By this time, sailing was reckoned unsafe. The reference to the Fast has been used as a means of dating the journey. *The Fast* is preceded by a Greek word which might well mean *even* or *too*: *even the Fast* or *the Fast* *too* was past, suggesting that this year the Fast fell exceptionally late. In AD 59 the Fast fell on October 5; it was earlier in 57, 58, 60, 61, 62. From this some have inferred that Paul's journey took place in AD 59. This is an unsafe inference. There is no need to give the Greek word this quasi-superlative force. It was late; even the day usually considered as marking the end of sailing was past. There must have been an uncertain period. One talmudic passage (P. Shabbath 2.5b.25) reckons sailing to be unsafe after the Feast of Tabernacles, Tishri 15.

There is no suggestion that Paul had any interest in observing the Day of Atonement; the Fast appears only as a date in the nautical calendar.

10. Paul addresses the company. Almost everywhere else in Acts **Men** is accompanied by another word, making the address more precise. Here, and in vv. 21, 25, it is alone, probably because there was no single word aptly descriptive of all Paul's fellow travellers. Paul foresees that **the voyage** if persisted in **is going to be attended by damage and much loss not only of the cargo and the ship but also of our lives**. Ship and cargo were lost, but no lives (v. 44). The forecast of vv. 23–26 is more accurate. The contradiction does not suggest absolutely free composition by Luke, who might have explained it by saying that in v. 10 Paul expressed his own human opinion but gave in the later passage a supernatural communication.

11. Julius' favourable treatment of Paul did not extend to a preference for his advice over that of the professionals. **the captain**: literally *the steersman* but the primary and ultimately responsible steersman was the captain of the ship. **the owner**: the meaning is uncertain. The word sometimes means *ship-owner*, and an owner, even if not travelling, would be very interested in the possibility of shipwreck. So would be his acting representative. Not all ships in the corn fleet were in private ownership; in such a case one would think of a *manager*. It is reasonably clear that the two mentioned represented the nautical and financial interests respectively.

Are we dealing here with a small committee? If so, can Paul the prisoner have made a fourth with centurion, captain and owner? Or does Paul address the whole ship's company? It is in fact quite reasonable that the whole company of passengers should expect to have a say in where they were to spend the winter.

12. This verse could be connected with v. 8 or with v. 9a; hence the suggestion that vv. 9–11 are an insertion; see above, p. 400.

The harbour at Fair Havens was inconvenient for wintering. What made it inconvenient is not stated; perhaps insecure anchorage for the ship, perhaps a lack of social amenities for the crew.

So **the majority formed** a **plan**. *The majority* of the whole ship's company? The centurion, captain, and owner against Paul? Certainty is impossible. Julius, an intelligent man, will call together the interested and knowledgeable parties and find out their views. The majority view is that they should not stay at Fair Havens and should not attempt the long voyage to Rome, but should move on **to Phoenix, if they could**.

The precise location of *Phoenix* is disputed. The name occurs in ancient authors and its location there can be established as about fifty miles west of Fair Havens and about thirty-four miles east of the western extremity of Crete. For many years its harbour was identified with that now known as Loutro, which has been described as the best harbour on the relevant part of the south coast of Crete. In the present verse, however, the harbour is described as **looking into the south west and north west winds**, that is, facing west. The harbour of Loutro faces east. In the attempt to support the identification with Loutro violence has often been done to the Greek, but there can be no doubt that the translation given here is what Luke wrote – and meant. The explanation is as follows. The harbour of Loutro is formed by a promontory that projects southward from the coast. It lies on the eastward side of the promontory. On the westward side is another harbour, called today Phineha – almost certainly a modification of the ancient name Phoenix. In the past this has been discounted as a possible harbour because it has no suitable anchorage. It has now however been shown that Crete has suffered considerable geological changes, and archaeological and other evidence puts it beyond reasonable doubt that Phineha, sheltered from the north east wind (which in the end destroyed the ship – v. 14), was the harbour for which Paul's ship was making.

13. a gentle south wind was exactly what the seamen wanted; it would enable them to reach Phoenix without difficulty. The voyage seemed as good as complete before it was begun.

14. a tempestuous wind . . . flung itself down. Adjective and verb are chosen to give an impression of the violence of the storm wind. **down from the island**. The word *island* is not used, but a pronoun. The meaning may be *against it* (the ship); *from it*, that is, *from the island*, suits the meteorological conditions. Sudden and violent off-shore winds are known in the area, and a south wind will sometimes back suddenly to a violent northeaster. It has been suggested that a sudden squall from the mountainous island drove them out into the path of a steady gale which had passed over them when they were close to the shore.

As a recognized (and probably not unfamiliar) phenomenon the wind had a name. **Euraquilo** is a Greek–Latin compound: *Euros* (Greek), south east wind, and *Aquila* (Latin), north wind. Presumably it was a wind blowing somewhat east of north.

15. There was nothing to do but let go and let the ship run before the wind; it was impossible **to head into it**. The Western text adds that *we furled the sails* – no doubt true, whether Luke wrote it or not.

16. We ran under the lee. The word is similar to that used in vv. 4, 7, but with emphasis on speed. *We* are the whole ship's company. **a certain small island called Cauda**. There are many textual variants of the name: Kauda, Klauda, Klaude, Gaude. The reference must be to a small island south of Crete, whose modem name is Gaudes (or Gaudouesi, or Guzzo).

were scarcely able to gain full control of the dinghy. In normal circumstances this would probably be towed but would now be hoisted on board lest in the storm it should be damaged, or damage the ship.

17. They hauled it up, presumably the dinghy. **and made use of auxiliary devices**, literally, *helps*. This may have a general meaning. The sailors (who must be the subject throughout the verse) made use of various unspecified devices in order to reduce danger by increasing control and stability. Or the word may have a specific meaning as a nautical technical term. This is probable, but we do not know what processes or instruments were meant. **frapping the ship** (possibly using the dinghy) by running ropes (possibly the *helps*) round it, at right angles to its axis, in order to prevent its being broken up by the waves. If this was the intention it was in the end unsuccessful. The sailors feared **lest they should be cast upon the Syrtis**. The Greater Syrtis (now the Gulf of Sidra) was the eastern, the Lesser Syrtis (now the Gulf of Gabès) the western, stretch of water between Tunisia, Tripolitania and Cyrenaica. The water was shallow, and the tide caused sandbanks to shift unpredictably. The area was feared and avoided. But would the sailors have feared it so soon? The Syrtes were about 375 miles from Cauda. They took, it seems, an early precaution by dropping **the sea anchor**. The noun used here means *gear, equipment* in general, and *sea anchor* is a – quite probable – guess based on the circumstances. They **drifted** – but they would drift as slowly as possible.

18. The narrative returns briefly to the first person plural since *we* were all storm-tossed, but it immediately reverts to the third person, for it was the crew who, on the next day, jettisoned the cargo. Cf. Jonah 1.5, where the wording is similar. The statement runs literally, *they made a jettisoning, a throwing out*; one guesses that it was the cargo they dispensed with. See v. 19.

19. they, the crew, **threw out with their own hands**. This is very probably the original text. Some MSS have the first person plural, *we* threw out. The thought behind this may be that some piece of tackle (perhaps the main yard) was too heavy for the crew alone, so that *we* too, the passengers, were obliged to help *with our own hands*. *They threw*, however, is probably correct. They threw out **the ship's gear**. The word here is related to but not identical with that taken to mean *the sea anchor* in v. 17. In English, *gear* or *tackle* is a term wide enough in meaning not to be seriously misleading, though it does not give a clear picture of what was done.

20. For many days neither sun nor stars were to be seen – not only heavy cloud cover but loss of the means of navigation. **no small storm**: characteristic Lucan use of litotes, for emphasis. **Finally**, and the continuous imperfect tense **was disappearing**, go a little oddly together. The last stage in distress was the gradual disappearance of **all hope**.

21. Paul deals with this state of hopelessness by practical measures. People on board were short of food, not because there was nothing to eat (it is not till v. 38 that food is thrown overboard) but because it was not being eaten – through preoccupation, fear, and no doubt seasickness. The appeal to take food achieves no success till v. 36. Perhaps it was necessary first to deal with fear.

Paul then stood in their midst. The point of *then* is not clear; it may go with *in their midst* (cf. 17.22) as emphasizing Paul's intervention in a situation of fear and hopelessness.

Men. Cf. v. 10. **you ought to have listened to me**. Paul refers back to the advice he gave at Fair Havens (v. 10). For **damage and loss** see also v. 10. One would be inclined to think Paul's 'I-told-you-so' approach unlikely to win friends (and thus a mark of Lucan fiction?), but in Greek Paul's opening clause is so expressed as to lead to the expectation that it would be followed by some such words as, 'but you did not listen', which Paul omits out of courtesy – an interesting but not entirely convincing suggestion.

The verse contains in Greek several features characteristic of Luke's style. Is it then an insertion into a secular sea story designed to bring it into the story of Paul? Certainly this verse (and indeed the whole of vv. 21–26) makes Paul stand out as a commanding character. But perhaps he was one.

22. Paul is able to give the strongest grounds for renewed courage. **there will be no loss of life . . . but only of the ship**. This prediction differs from that of v. 10; it is given on supernatural authority (vv. 23, 24). For the loss of the ship see v. 41; for the safe arrival of all the travellers see v. 44.

23. For introduces the grounds on which the encouragement Paul offers rests. It derives from an angelic message delivered **this night**, presumably, that is, the night now past, but see on v. 33. In Acts angels appear as carriers of messages and doing other kinds of service. **there stood by me**, a verb often used of supernatural visitations. It has often been observed that such visitations and consequent protection are characteristic of the 'divine man'; it is characteristic of Luke, recognizing this, to point out that, though in some respects Paul may resemble figures represented as 'divine men', he is in fact no such thing. He is the property and the servant of another, who alone can bear the title **God**. **whom I serve**. The same verb (*serve*) is used at Rom. 1.9, which illustrates the kind of service Paul (Luke) has in mind: *whom I serve in the Gospel of his Son*.

24. Fear not, words characteristic of such visitations; cf. 18.9; also Lk. 1.13, 30; 2.10; 5.10. Paul is assured that what is for him the goal of the voyage will be reached: he will **stand before Caesar**.

and see: not translation Greek but an imitation of the LXX – no doubt thought suitable for angels. For Paul to appear before Caesar it is necessary only that he should escape the storm, but as a favour God has granted him (the lives of) all who are sailing with him. It is implied, not quite necessarily, that Paul has prayed for his fellow travellers.

25. So take heart, **men**, takes up *to take heart* in v. 22. Paul believes God, that is, not that he trusts in God, but that he accepts as true the message that God has sent: God will do what he has said he will do. Hence, *Take heart*.

26. There is a qualification of the promise of safety in the storm. The ship will be **cast on a certain island**. The angel did not specify the island and it will not be identified till 28.1. Some think that the prediction of shipwreck must be distinguished from the angel's message, from which it is an inference.

we have to be has been seen as giving a theological interpretation to the whole event. This goes too far, but undoubtedly Luke means to represent the whole course of action as leading Paul, under God's providence, to Rome.

27. The main clause, **the sailors thought**, is given a threefold determination. (a) **When the fourteenth night came**, (b) **we were being tossed about** (a better rendering than *were drifting across*) **in Adria**, and (c) **in the middle of the night**. These give a clear picture. It has been calculated that thirteen or fourteen days would be the time required, in the conditions described, for the passage from Cauda to Malta. There is (it has been maintained) no place other than Malta that satisfies this requirement. See however on 28.1–10. *Adria* in antiquity meant more than is understood today by the Adriatic Sea. It might cover anywhere between Venice and North Africa.

The sailors thought **that land was approaching them**. This is a tolerable way of describing the relative motion of ship and land, but it is somewhat unusual, and this may account for a variant reading which probably (but not quite certainly) means that the sailors thought they heard land *resounding*, or *echoing*, no doubt as it was beaten by the waves (breakers, it has been suggested, on the rocky point of Koura, in the neighbourhood of St Paul's Bay, on Malta). Alternatively, *resound* may be the original reading, *approach* the variant. Fortunately there is no doubt about the general meaning of the verse. The sailors became aware that they were not far from land.

28. Suspicion that the ship was approaching land naturally led the sailors to take **soundings**. **Twenty fathoms** (120 feet) was still fairly deep, but the depth was diminishing. The figures seem to be compatible with data derived from St Paul's Bay, Malta.

29. The rapidly shelving seabed meant that it was imperative to halt the ship's motion or at least to reduce its speed. The sailors were afraid that **we** (the ship and its company, collectively) **should fall upon rocky places**. Accordingly they **threw out four anchors from the stern**. It was usual to anchor by the bows, but since the ship was driving before the wind anchoring *from the stern* would be the best way to check its progress (vv. 15, 17, but cf. v. 30).

30. Having let down anchors from the stern, **the sailors** proposed **to let out anchors from the bow**. It may be supposed that the stern anchors had checked the forward motion of the ship and that the sailors' intention (if it was not that which Luke attributes to them) was to maintain the ship's position in the line of the wind, and so to prevent it from being struck broadside on by the heavy seas. This would make sense, and the sailors would need the dinghy to stretch out the anchor lines. According to Luke, the sailors were deceiving the passengers. Their real intention was to escape from what they regarded as a doomed ship. It has been argued, and may well be true, that in this Luke misrepresented the sailors, who would not have tried to escape in a dark and stormy night in a boat that could have held very few of them. It should be added that if Luke was making a mistake he was probably making a mistake about something that really happened. He would not invent an action and invent also, without letting his reader into the secret, a mistaken interpretation of it.

31. Paul evidently (according to Luke) viewed with dismay what he thought to be the impending departure of the only persons with sailing skills. With them all prospect of safety would disappear. (But could he not as before rely on the divine promise?) It is surprising that he should address the soldiers directly, as well as their commanding officer. And one would have thought that even if some sailors escaped (presumably to the land which the ship seemed to be approaching (v. 28)) enough would have been left, unable to get into the dinghy, to run the ship.

It is worth observing, without prejudice, that what seems improbable in an account of what really happened must also seem improbable in a work of fiction written by an author with any concern for verisimilitude. It may be that Luke's motive was to show (in v. 32) the respect shown to Paul by the soldiers.

32. If the sailors were not to be allowed to escape in the dinghy the simplest, but not necessarily the wisest course, was to get rid of the dinghy. This the soldiers did. It was suspended over the side of the ship (v. 30) and the soldiers cut the ropes and let it fall away. A foolish act, some think; with the dinghy it would have been possible to sit out the gale and row ashore, without losing the ship.

33. This verse, and the following paragraph, might have been introduced by v. 21a. It is surprising that the reference to food should come a second time; it may be that Luke took that verse out of the present section and used it as an introduction to vv. 22–26. Many think vv. 33–36 to be an insertion; see on v. 37.

When it was nearly day Paul exhorted them. A strong case can be made for translating, *Until day was about to break Paul kept on exhorting them.* If this is accepted it is natural to look back to v. 23, *this night*, which may imply that *this night* has not ended at the time Paul is speaking. This could in turn bear on the construction of the chapter, especially if it is thought to include 'Pauline' insertions into an independent sea-voyage story. See pp. 397f.

Paul's exhortation begins with another unusual note of time. **Today you are looking to the fourteenth day**. Cf. v. 27, *the fourteenth night.* It is implied that nights are counted before days. We are approaching the end of the fourteenth night; the fourteenth day is about to dawn. **without food** takes up *going without food* in v. 21.

34. Therefore I urge you. Paul's exhortation is repeated in the first person of direct speech. **this is for your welfare**. The word *welfare* would in appropriate contexts be translated *salvation*, in a religious sense. The ambiguity of the word is of interest in the present context. The promise (**not a hair** . . .) recalls that of v. 22; the expression is proverbial (cf. 1 Sam. 14.45; 2 Sam. 14.11; 1 Kings 1.52; Lk. 12.2 = Mt. 10.30; Lk. 21.18 is important because it is a Lucan insertion).

35, 36. To give weight to his words Paul initiates a meal in words and acts that have important parallels. These may be set out as follows:

He took a loaf: Cf. Lk. 22.19; Lk. 9.16.
gave thanks to God: Cf. Lk. 22.17, 19; Lk. 9.16.
he broke it: Cf. Lk. 22.19; Lk. 9.16.
began to eat: Cf. Lk. 22.15.
gave also to us (added by some MSS): cf. Lk. 22.17, 19; Lk. 9.16.
They . . . **partook of food**: Cf. Lk. 9.17.

Cf. also references to the *breaking of bread* at Lk. 24.30, 35; Acts 2.42, 46; 20.7, 11. As far as language goes, the present passage is more 'eucharistic' than any other in Acts. At the same time the context demands more than a symbolic meal; it satisfies the physical needs of men who for days have been too busy, preoccupied, and fearful to eat. Paul *began to eat* and the rest – *all* of them – followed his example. The Christians did not withdraw to hold a special, still less a secret, rite of their own. **before them all** is clear.

Luke's readers can hardly have failed to note the 'eucharistic' allusions, yet these terms and allusions are all such as are rooted in ordinary Jewish practice – the blessing of God and the breaking of bread. They belong to a time, lasting at least to the date of the composition of Acts, in which the eucharist (understood as a rite including the symbolic eating and drinking of bread and wine to which a theological interpretation is attached) was not yet separated from a fellowship meal in which normal quantities of food and drink were consumed. This is consistent with other references in Acts to the breaking of bread (and with Pauline and other evidence; see *1 Corinthians* 231–5, 261–77; *CMS* 60–76). Other interpretations, especially those that attempt to answer the question, Was this meal a eucharist? with a clear Yes or No, instructive in some respects, as many of them are, fail because they assume something like the clear, developed distinction between an 'ordinary' meal and a 'sacramental' or 'eucharistic' meal, between bread and eucharistic bread.

For the breaking of the loaf see on 2.42 – also for the absence of any reference to wine. Of course the use of wine during a storm at sea would have presented very considerable practical difficulties.

all took part in the meal – except no doubt any actively engaged in navigating the ship.

37. The numbering of those on board follows upon the *all* of v. 36. It is as apt here as after v. 32, where some would put v. 37. Unfortunately the number is textually uncertain. The two main variants are *276* and *about 76*. These have often been explained as due to the reduplication of a Greek letter which could be used as a numeral. The original text was probably 276 – not an impossibly large number. Josephus (*Life* 15) records his own experience of shipwreck (in Adria), as a result of which almost 600 were obliged to swim all night.

38. When they were satisfied with food. This requires a meal for the satisfaction of physical hunger, whatever else it may have signified to (some of) the participants.

the food, perhaps *the wheat* – it was probably a corn ship. To jettison the food was rash unless they were satisfied that they would soon be on land.

39. When day (the longed-for day – v. 29) **broke** they could see land but **did not recognize** it. It is identified in 28.1. What they saw was **a bay with a beach**. This offered a way of escape from the storm. Had the dinghy still been available it might have been used for successive trips to the shore; it was not available (v. 32) and the alternative was **to run the ship** on shore. This they would do **if possible**; less probably, *They were considering whether they could . . .*

40. This verse describes the steps taken by the sailors to achieve the goal planned in v. 39.

They detached. The Greek word, usually *to strip off, to take off*, is used in an unusual sense, but with **the anchors** must mean what is given here in the translation. Greek ships were usually steered by a pair of steering-paddles, which were joined by a kind of yoke. The action described here by Luke is reasonably clear: the anchors were let go and the steering apparatus was dismantled. The wind would drive the ship where they wished to go. To this end they raised **the foresail** and **held on to the beach**.

41. They ran upon: Luke's verb is used of ships falling foul of one another, or being wrecked, often with the sense of something unexpected. So here; their course to the beach was interrupted by **a shoal**, literally, a *place of two seas*. The meaning of this expression is disputed. Some think that the reference is to the two areas of sea that lie on either side of a headland, on which the ship was run. This however is inconsistent with what follows. If the ship had been driven on to a headland all would have been able to disembark on dry land; there would have been no need for swimming. *Shoal* is not inconsistent with the etymology (of *two seas place*); there was sea before and behind the ship. Disembarkation would be through the water in front of the ship and the stern would be exposed to the force of the waves.

the stern began to break up. The verb is in the imperfect tense; the process of breaking up now began and went on – a continuous process. **under the violence of the waves**. There is good textual evidence for the omission of *of the waves*. Whether the words are original or not, this (not *of the impact*; this would have affected the bow, not the stern) must be the intended meaning.

42. It was the plan of the soldiers to kill the prisoners. The plan was sensible enough. The soldiers were responsible for the safe custody of the prisoners (v. 1); see on 12.19; 16.27. For them it was better that the prisoners should die than that they should escape. Where they might swim to is not clear, but no doubt some would have thought the risk of drowning to be worth taking.

43. The centurion thought otherwise. From the beginning he had treated Paul with consideration (v. 3) and now he wished **to get** him

safely through. The verb here is a compound of *to save* with *through*. It may be no more than a strengthened form of the simple verb, or mean *to get him safely through the water to the land*. Or Luke may wish to show that he is not here speaking of *to save* in its Christian, religious sense. The centurion could not save Paul without saving others, or at least giving them an opportunity of saving themselves. Some could swim (from 2 Cor. 11.25 one guesses that Paul could). They (with other passengers) were **to throw themselves overboard and come first to land**.

44. the rest, non-swimmers, would need help. Two groups are distinguished. The first were to go **on planks of wood** – the word can mean almost any piece of timber. Others (clearly distinguished by the Greek construction) were to go on *either* things *or* persons (the relevant word in Greek can be either neuter or masculine/feminine) **from the ship**. It is hard to see the difference between *planks of wood* (which can hardly have come from anywhere but the ship) *and pieces from the ship* (which can hardly have been anything but wooden if they were to serve as floats). It seems best therefore to choose the masculine rather than the neuter gender: some of those who could swim helped those who could not.

As a result, **all got safely to land**.

63. FROM MALTA TO ROME 28.1–16

**1 Having got safely through we then recognized that the island
was called Malta. 2 The local inhabitants showed us no ordinary
kindness, for because of the rain that came on and the cold they
lit a fire and brought us to it. 3 When Paul gathered a bundle of
sticks and put them on the fire a viper came out because of the
heat and fastened on his hand. 4 When the inhabitants saw the
creature hanging from his hand they said to one another, 'No
doubt this man is a murderer; though he escaped from the sea
Justice has not permitted him to live.' 5 He however shook off the
creature into the fire and suffered no harm. 6 They were expecting
that he would swell up or suddenly fall down dead. But as they
went on waiting and saw that nothing amiss was happening to
him they changed their minds and said that he was a god.**

**7 In the neighbourhood of that place there were domains
belonging to the chief man of the island, Publius by name, who
received and entertained us with kindly hospitality for three days.
8 It happened that Publius' father was sick and confined to bed
with fevers and dysentery, Paul went in to him and prayed, laid
his hands on him and cured him. 9 When this happened the others
in the island who had illnesses approached and were healed.
10 They bestowed upon us many honours, and when we left put on
board the things that we needed.**

**11 After three months we set sail in a ship that had wintered on
the island, a ship of Alexandria, ship's sign, The Dioscuri. 12 We
landed at Syracuse and stayed there three days. 13 Casting off from
there we reached Rhegium. After one day a south wind arose and
we came on the second day to Puteoli. 14 There we found brothers
and were invited to stay with them seven days; and in this way
we made our journey to Rome. 15 From there the brothers, having
heard of our affairs, came to meet us as far as Appius' Market
and Three Taverns. When Paul saw them he gave thanks to God
and took heart.**

**16 When we entered Rome Paul was permitted to stay on his
own with the soldier who guarded him.**

The vigorous sea story of ch. 27 winds down quietly into something like domesticity. Paul joins in the necessary task of finding firewood, and in the process is bitten by a snake. The availability of firewood and of snakes raises the question of the identity of the island. Can it have been Malta, or was it Meleda, an island in the Adriatic? The essential points are considered below. The identification cannot be settled by the story of vv. 6–9; not only is its historicity open to question, but no expert naturalist was at hand to describe the snake and to confirm or dispute the islanders' belief that Paul was in danger of death.

Not unnaturally the ignorant islanders suppose that Paul is a god, an opinion Luke does not share. Healings lead to favourable treatment and a generous send-off from the island – at a date earlier than one would have thought desirable (see on v. 11).

The journey from Malta to Rome is given in some detail. The seven days' stay in Puteoli, the two references to Rome (vv. 14, 16), and the mention of both Appius' Market and Three Taverns, are a little surprising but cannot be dismissed out of hand.

In this paragraph the use of *We*, dropped towards the end of ch. 27, is resumed. It occurs in vv. 1, 2, 7, 10, 11, 12, 13, 14, 15, 16, so that it is natural to think of a travel narrative that identified the island and the host who showed hospitality to Paul (and his friends – but not necessarily to the ship's complement of (2)76), but did not contain the wonders of vv. 2–6, 8, 9. It then took Paul to Rome, but perhaps did not contain the references to Appius' Market and Three Taverns. It is probable that the miracles, whatever we make of their historical trustworthiness, were to be found, and were found by Luke, in the tradition, possibly in local tradition. If they were ever used to support a 'divine man' picture of Paul this is discounted by Luke. It is however true that Luke takes the opportunity or underlining some features of his account of Paul: he is capable of working miracles, and he comes through all kinds of dangers and opposition to his goal, Rome. But the delegations from Rome are not described by Luke in triumphalist vein; their effect is to cheer Paul and give him courage for what awaits him. It would have been easy to omit the receptions at Appius' Market and Three Taverns if Luke had wished to suggest (contrary to fact) that Paul had founded the church at Rome. The view may well be correct that we hear little of the Roman Christians because their welcome was not as warm as Luke (and Paul) would have desired. Cf. (if Philippians was written from Rome) Phil. 1.15, 17.

1. Having got safely through (cf. 27.43f.) **we then recognized that the island was called Malta** (Greek, *Melitē*). How they *recognized* the island is not stated; possibly experienced travellers once they were out of the water found that they knew it, perhaps the islanders (v. 2) told them, though in that case *we learned*, or *we were informed*, would have been expected.

The island has usually been taken to be that now known as Malta, but an eighth-century writer thought rather of an island in the Adriatic now known as Meleda, Melite, or Mljet, in antiquity as Cephallenia, and this has been taken up by some modern writers. To go in detail into all the arguments, nautical, topographical and archaeological, that have been adduced on either side is impossible; the most important points will be mentioned in the notes as they arise. Here it may be observed that it seems unlikely that a wind that threatened to drive the ship on to the Syrtes (27.17) should have led to a wreck on the east side of the Adriatic.

Malta had been a Roman island since it had been captured from the Carthaginians in 218 BC. See further on v. 7.

In this verse 'we' is left undefined, and the tension of the narrative drops. It may be that Luke now has a different source.

2. The local inhabitants are in Greek *barbaroi*. In Acts the word is used only here and at v. 4; cf. Rom. 1.14; 1 Cor. 14.11; Col. 3.11. Its primary meaning was linguistic. The 'barbarians' were those who did not speak Greek and whose speech therefore sounded (to a Greek) like a meaningless ba-ba-ba. After the Persian War the word came to mean 'brutal, rude'. Here it evidently retains its linguistic meaning; these *barbaroi* were anything but brutal and rude. The linguistic reference has been used in favour of the identification of the island with Cephallenia. Malta had long been hellenized and romanized. There is however in addition to Greek and Latin inscriptions evidence that local workers spoke Punic. It may be assumed that both in Malta and in Meleda there were uneducated people who could not, and educated people who could, speak Greek (or Latin or both).

The **kindness** (the word is cognate with Julius' *kindly way* in 27.3) was shown in their *lighting* **a fire**, **because of the rain that came on** (it would not make them wetter than the sea had done but would prevent drying) **and the cold**. In Cephallenia the rainfall is greater and the average temperatures are lower than in Malta. Two points, perhaps, for Cephallenia, but men in wet clothes, with a good breeze blowing, would not be sorry to see a fire.

3. Paul, gathering wood for the fire, was bitten by a snake. It appears in the following verses that this did him no harm. Luke plainly regards this as a miracle; he therefore understood the word he uses in its proper sense: the snake was poisonous, **a viper**. He also represents the native inhabitants as sharing his view – a man bitten by one of 'their' snakes should swell up and fall down dead (v. 6). There are, it seems, no poisonous snakes on Malta, whereas on Cephallenia there are many kinds of snake, including the viper. This seems to be a point in favour of Cephallenia as the scene of the incident; alternatively, it means that the story is fictitious, or belongs to another setting – it is at this point that the first person plural ceases (see p. 413). A further possibility is that Malta may in the first century have been richer in snakes than it is now.

4. the inhabitants saw what was happening; **the creature** was **hanging from** Paul's **hand**. They drew a natural conclusion; Paul has deserved death; he has escaped drowning and will therefore be punished by the snake. **Justice has not permitted him to live.** The barbarians may well have personified *Justice* as a divine being. Parallels to the story, thus understood, exist.

5. For the snake; cf. Lk. 10.19 as well as Mk 16.17f.: in the background of both, Ps. 90(91).13.

6. Neither **swell up** nor **nothing amiss** is to be regarded as a medical term. Doctors are not alone in being aware of accidents and illnesses, and of their symptoms. The incident does not support the view either that Luke was a physician or that he intended to represent Paul as a 'divine man'. On the contrary, the latter erroneous opinion was held by barbarians, whom a Greek would not think to be right. See on v. 2.

7. In the neighbourhood of that place, the place of the wreck. It would be possible to translate, *In the estates of that place were estates belonging to . . .*

the chief man of the island, Publius (this Latin name is transliterated into a Greek form) **by name.** *Chief* is literally *first* (in Latin, *primus*); there is evidence for the use of this word as a title in Malta (since the early years of Augustus, with the neighbouring small island of Gozo, governed by a procurator). The First (Man) was probably a local native officer. Cephallenia was a free city, in which Roman interests were looked after by a legate of the governor of Achaea. At about the time of Paul's voyage the legate was Publius Alf. (= Alfius or Alfessus) Primus. It has been suggested (in support of the view that Cephallenia was the island of the shipwreck) that what Luke gives us is a confused recollection of the name Publius Primus. The suggestion is not convincing. The title *First* was used in Malta, whether of a Roman or of a local official, and there is no need to go further. Publius **received and entertained us with kindly hospitality for three days**. *us*: in all probability no longer the ship's company but Paul and his companions. There can be no doubt that this statement, correctly or incorrectly, represents the author of the narrative as a close personal associate of Paul's.

It is not said that Publius (or anyone else on the island) became a Christian.

8. Publius' father was sick and confined to bed with fevers and dysentery. Medical writers sometimes use the word *fever* in the plural; so too do others, so that there is no indication here of the author's profession.

Paul went in to him (presumably into his sick room) **and prayed, laid his hands on him and cured him**. For the connection of prayer with the laying on of hands, see p. 192. Cf. James 5.13f.; also from Qumran 1QapGen 20.28, 29. By his *prayer* Paul shows that he is not a 'divine man' but one who believes in the power and benevolence of the true God.

9. The cure of Publius' father naturally evoked hope in other sick inhabitants of the island; these came to Paul for healing and were cured.

10. They bestowed upon us many honours. The words could mean, *They paid us many fees* (for medical and perhaps other services). Cf. Sirach 38.1. But Paul had not been doing ordinary medical work, and material needs are covered in the next clause, **when we left** they **put on board the things that we needed**.

The story in vv. 7–10 seems to be independent of the sea story in ch. 27; that Paul was a prisoner on his way to trial is not hinted at.

11. After three months gives rise to some difficulty. Paul's voyage began after, presumably not long after, the Day of Atonement (27.7), allowing for all the time references given one would suppose that Malta was reached by the end of October. Three months would elapse by the end of January, a very early date for sailing to be resumed. There were however reasons why a grain ship (see below) should be in a hurry, and the crossing to Rhegium was one that might have been made early. *Three months* is in any case to be regarded as an approximation, or a guess.

we set sail. To how many of the (2)76 (27.37) *we* applies cannot be certain; quite possibly only Paul and his companions (and of course the military guard). Ships were commonly laid up in the winter, and the centurion would probably have little difficulty in finding a ship that had spent the winter in an island port and had room enough to take extra passengers. It was **a ship of Alexandria**, in all probability of the grain fleet, which regularly brought corn from Egypt to Rome. It is unlikely that such a ship would winter in Cephallenia.

ship's sign, The Dioscuri. The sense of these words is clear, though their construction in Greek is not. Ships in antiquity often bore an image of a god or gods, whose name provided the name of the ship. The Dioscuri, Castor and Polydeuces (latinized as Pollux), were a natural choice as patrons of a ship; they were called upon by sailors as helpers in times of need.

12. We landed at Syracuse and stayed there three days. *We* is probably but not necessarily Paul's party. No reason is given for the delay; it was early in the sailing season and an unexpected spell of bad weather is as good a guess as any.

Syracuse was an old-established Greek city on the east coast of Sicily, originally a Corinthian colony. It is roughly twice as far from Cephallenia as from Malta, but neither journey would be impossible.

13. Casting off is a probable, hardly certain, attempt to give meaning to an unusual use of a Greek verb. That it is unusual may be responsible for a variant, *we came round*, a statement easily explained by reference to a map. The ship evidently sailed through the strait of Messina on its way to **Rhegium** and **Puteoli**. *Casting off*, however, is not so difficult as to be impossible and may be accepted.

Of the first day (as far as Rhegium) nothing is recorded; On the next day **a south wind arose**. This was exactly what was needed for a voyage up the west coast of Italy and brought the passengers to Puteoli, a town founded by the Ionian Greeks. It was taken by the Romans in the Second Punic War and became a Roman colony in 194 BC. There had been a Jewish community there since at least 4 BC; see *NS* 3.81, 110f.

14. For the first time since they reached the west the travelling party encountered **brothers**, that is, Christians. The party (expressed in the first person plural) **were invited** (or, *encouraged*) **to stay with them seven days**. A variant reading has, *We were encouraged, having stayed with them seven days*. This alleviates the difficulty of the prisoner's being *invited* as if he were a free man. The difficulty may have produced the variant. The delay of seven days is the more surprising in that, notwithstanding the favourable wind, the journey continued by land.

In this way we made our journey to Rome. These words are often translated, *So we came to Rome*, which suggests arrival at the travellers' destination, which is in fact not reached till v. 16. It has been suggested that here, in v. 14, *Rome* means the *Ager Romanus*, the area directly under Roman administration. The point seems rather to be that this was the last stage of the journey to Rome.

There is no confirmatory evidence for the presence of Christians at Puteoli at this time.

15. The final stage of the journey, from Puteoli to Rome, could be covered by a good walker in five days. Paul and his company were now in contact with the city. **the brothers . . . came to meet us**. The first person plural is still in use. The brothers had **heard of our affairs**, possibly during the seven days of delay in Puteoli. If they had read Romans they would know that Paul was planning a visit but would not know when to expect him.

as far as Appius' Market and Three Taverns. Does this mean two separate deputations – one Jewish, one Gentile perhaps? There is no hint in Acts of anything of this kind. Or did some walk faster, or start earlier, than others? The 43rd milestone (Roman miles) is still extant at Appius' Market (*Appii Forum*). Three Taverns (*Tres Tabernae*) was thirty-three miles from Rome.

There were Christian *brothers* in Rome. It is possible that there were Christians there as early as Acts 18.2 (see the note). It follows that the church in Rome was not founded by Paul, as his epistle itself makes clear. Neither in Acts nor in Romans is there any hint that the church in Rome had been founded by Peter; see however 1 Clement 5.4 and Ignatius, *Romans* 4.3.

16. Verse 16a seems to repeat v. 14b. See on v. 14; but the possibility should also be considered that the apparent doublet is due to Luke's use of more than one source, or to the need for an introduction to the next paragraph, 28.17–28. The party would enter Rome by the Via Appia through the Porta Capena.

Surprisingly there is (in the Old Uncial text, for the Western text see below) no reference to the Roman authorities to whom Paul was being delivered at so much trouble, danger, and expense. The fact is that Luke is allowing the legal proceedings against Paul to drop out of his narrative; the relation of Christianity to Judaism is (to him) a more important theme. But to say that **Paul was permitted** implies an authority who gave permission. He was permitted **to stay on his own**, not in a public prison but in private accommodation (cf. 28.30), in *custodia libera*, not *custodia militaris*. There would be however a **soldier who guarded him**. The custom was for a prisoner to be handed over to two soldiers; they would presumably watch in shifts, hence the singular. If this is correct, it must have been decided, at least provisionally, that Paul was not a threat to public order.

The Western text adds that *the centurion handed over the prisoners to the officer commanding the camp*. This (in Latin, *praefectus castrorum*) is the equivalent of Luke's Greek word, but the *leader of the camp* (*princeps castrorum*) is perhaps more likely to have been in charge. This was the chef administrative officer of the Praetorian Guard. Some MSS add, after *on his own*, *outside the camp* (the Praetorian barracks).

64. PAUL AND THE JEWS IN ROME 28.17–28

**17 After three days Paul called together the leading men among
the Jews. When they assembled he said to them, 'Brothers,
although for my part I had done nothing against the people or
our ancestral customs I was handed over from Jerusalem into
the hands of the Romans as a prisoner. 18 They examined me and
wished to release me because they found in me no capital charge.
19 But because the Jews contradicted this I was compelled to
appeal to Caesar, though not because I had anything of which
to accuse my nation. 20 For this reason therefore I asked to see
you and to address you, for it is for the hope of Israel that I
wear this chain.' 21 They said to him, 'As for us, we have neither
received letters about you from Judaea, nor has any of the
brothers who have come here reported or spoken any ill of you.
22 We should therefore like to hear from you what is in your mind,
for as for this sect it is known to us that it is everywhere spoken
against.'**

**23 They appointed him a day and came to him in large numbers
to his lodging. He gave them an exposition, testifying the kingdom
of God and persuading them about Jesus on the basis both of the
Law of Moses and of the Prophets. This he did from early morning
till evening, 24 and some believed the things he said, others did
not. 25 The gathering broke up without agreement, with Paul
saying one thing. 'Well did the Holy Spirit speak to your fathers
through Isaiah the prophet, 26 saying, "Go to this people and say:
You will hear and hear and not understand, and you will look
and look and will not see. 27 The heart of this people has been
hardened, and they have heard dully, and they have shut their
eyes; lest they should see with their eyes, and hear with their
ears, and understand with their heart, and turn, and I should
heal them." 28 So let it be known to you that this God-given
salvation has been sent to the Gentiles; they will listen.'**

The final narrative piece in Luke's book fulfils the goal frequently alluded to in the course of Acts (1.8; 9.15; 19.21; 23.11; 27.34; see also Lk. 3.6; 24.47). Paul has now reached Rome, and though he must still appear before the emperor's court he is in circumstances favourable to the proclamation of the Gospel. Luke is primarily a narrator, and the end of his book represents the successful achievement of a primary goal, and thereby the victory of the word of God.

Detailed examination of this final scene, however, raises questions and difficulties. Paul had been met on his way (28.15) by delegations of Christians. In the new paragraph they are not mentioned, and *prima facie* v. 22 suggests that they did not exist. It is incorrect to argue that Luke wished to suggest that Paul was the founder of the church in Rome; if he had this intention he must have omitted 28.15. Why is there no further reference to the Roman church? And what is Luke's authority for his account? The brethren came out from Rome to meet *us* so that *we* must have been present in Rome. But in this paragraph there is no hint of Paul's companions. Was Paul rejected by the local Christians, or a substantial number of them? The epistle to the Romans indicates that in the local church there were both Jews and Gentiles (*Romans*, 6, 23). Was one party not pleased by the exposition of the Gospel that they had read and now heard from Paul's lips? According to 1 Clement 5.5 Paul suffered on account of 'envy and strife'; among Christians? Again, we may ask: Why does Acts end at this point? If it is not correct (see p. xxv) that Luke had simply brought his story up to date, why does he not go on to describe Paul's appearance at the imperial court? Either triumphant acquittal or martyrdom would have made a magnificent conclusion. A possible answer is that a true account might have been very unimpressive. A true account might have had to describe Paul's desertion by those who should have stood by him (cf. 2 Tim. 4.16).

There are further problems. For a long time Paul had been regarded as the enemy of Judaism. The Sanhedrin had done their best to destroy him, regarding him (conscientiously and understandably) as an enemy of the people. Is it credible that no whisper of this should have reached the Jewish community in Rome? And is it likely that Jews in Rome should have no first-hand knowledge of or contact with the Christians, some of whom were themselves Jews?

There can be little doubt that Luke (traces of whose style are frequent) composed the paragraph and that there was a good deal he did not know and quite possibly some things that he knew and did not mean to set down. This is not to say that all is fiction. It is significant that Paul meets with the Jews on two occasions (vv. 17–22, 23–28). It would have been easy and natural for a writer composing freely to make of this material one encounter only; the conclusion that may probably be drawn is that Luke found the double meeting in a tradition that he was using. He evidently chose to close his book not with a martyrdom or any other colourful event but with a statement on the Jews, the Gentiles, and the Gospel. As throughout the book, he maintains that the Christian Gospel is the true, fulfilled version of the OT and Judaism. He has now proclaimed the triumph of the Gospel as it reaches Rome, and he shows that what may appear less than triumphant is itself the fulfilment of Scripture. The whole story is in the hands of God, and there Luke is content to leave it.

17. With a minimum of delay (**After three days**) **Paul called together the leading men among the Jews**. There is no reference to Christians; for possible reasons for this see above. The *leading men* could have been synagogue heads. In Rome the Jews were gathered together in a number of synagogues, of which eleven are known by name. For these and their heads see *NS* 3.95–100. Paul, as a prisoner, though well treated, cannot attend the synagogues; their representatives must come to him. Apparently the Jews have returned after their expulsion under Claudius.

Brothers, literally, *Men brothers*. See 2.29; 22.1. The brief summary of events that have led to Paul's presence in Rome does not correspond exactly with the narrative of the preceding chapters. In part as the result of radical abbreviation it appears that Paul's position as a Roman prisoner is due to Jewish legal action. It may be correct to see in **into the hands of the Romans** the influence of the story of Jesus. The passion of the servant of Christ is described in terms drawn from Christ's own.

18. The parallel with the story of Jesus continues. Pilate found Jesus innocent (Lk. 23.4, 15, 22); Roman courts found Paul innocent (23.29; 25.18, 25; 26.31f.). They wished to release Paul because no charge requiring the death penalty existed **in me**.

19. Paul does not conceal the fact that the Jews took a different view of the loyalty to Judaism and *our ancestral customs* (v. 17) that he professes. He denies the intention of bringing any accusation against his own race, though in the preceding sentences he has accused them of an unjustified attack upon himself; it is in Caesar's court that he will not accuse them. Paul's motive is given in a Western addition: *that I might deliver my life from death*.

'The Jews' stand over against Paul; yet he does not accuse them. This distinction and the absence of accusation are both elements in Luke's attitude to Judaism.

20. For this reason. It is not clear to what reason Paul refers. The phrase may look forward (for the sake of Israel's hope) or backward (the reason in v. 19 for Paul's appeal to Caesar). It is best to give the *reason* a somewhat wider explanation than the words themselves demand. It is because my appeal to Caesar puts me in an ambiguous position, in which I am at the same time defending myself against an unwarranted attack from the Jewish side while I am maintaining all that is true and valuable in Judaism, that I must seize, or create, an opportunity of making clear to you exactly what the facts are.

Elsewhere Paul has insisted that the point at issue between himself and his Jewish adversaries is resurrection (23.6; 24.15). It may be that this is what is meant here by **the hope of Israel**. At 26.6, however, and perhaps at 24.15, the meaning of *hope* is different, and it is probable that here *the hope of Israel* is the promise of Messianic salvation. Paul alleges that this hope has been and will be fulfilled in Jesus. This is guaranteed and anticipated by the resurrection of Jesus, but the hope is wider than the personal resurrection of the crucified Messiah. Understood in this way the statement represents fairly enough the issue between Christianity and Judaism.

Paul's present position is vividly expressed: **I wear this chain**. Was this metaphorical? If it was literal, the *Lex Julia*, which forbade the chaining of a citizen, was being contravened. The wording is of course Luke's.

21. The Jews in Rome cannot comment on Paul's relations with the Jews in Jerusalem or on the version of Judaism which he presents. Correspondence with Jerusalem had contained no reference to Paul. This is surprising. If the Sanhedrin had determined to destroy Paul they would surely have enlisted the help of Jews in Rome and would also have warned them against a perverting and disruptive presence. The latter part of the verse however is ambiguous. It may mean that no report at all concerning Paul had reached Rome, or that those who had spoken of him had had no evil to say. On the whole the former seems more likely.

The verse suggests an almost complete cleavage between Jews in Rome and Jews in Palestine, and also between Jews and Christians in Rome. Neither seems probable. It appears to be Luke's intention not to suggest that Paul was the founder of the church in Rome (see above), but to present him as the spokesman of Christianity to the Jews. This is borne out in the following verses. It has been suggested that the Jews now intended to withdraw their accusations against Paul.

This is unlikely, in part because this would have entailed severe penalties.

22. The Jews, having heard nothing of Paul and only little, and that unfavourable, about Christianity, wish to know **what is in your mind**. Cf. the desire of the Areopagites (17.19).

Christianity is described as a **sect** or party within Judaism. For the word; cf. 5.17; 24.5, 14. It is a form of Judaism with its own interpretation of Jewish principles. Luke would hardly have disagreed, though he would insist on openness to Gentiles.

Jewish ignorance of Christianity fits badly with the notion that the expulsion of the Jews from Rome (see on 18.2) was caused by rioting between Jews and Christians. Luke probably wishes to represent Paul not as founding the church in Rome (see on v. 21) but as starting a clean sheet in relation with the Roman Jews.

23. The Jews **came to him in large numbers to his lodging**. *Lodging* might be translated *hospitality*. This is less probable and would make no difference to the sense. If they came to his lodging he was their host; if he entertained them it must have been at his lodging (which he was not free to leave – see v. 17). *In large numbers* could be – *in larger numbers* (*than on the previous occasion*).

Exactly what **testifying the kingdom of God** means is not clear, but elsewhere (e.g. 28.31) Luke appears to use *the kingdom of God* as a summary of the Christian message. The next clause brings out the Christological content and basis of the message; it is proved by the OT. Luke still wishes to portray Paul as an observant Jew, in no way an enemy of the Law.

24. The outcome of Paul's words was mixed; for a similar result, cf. 17.32–34. It is important, in view of the following verses, to note that Luke is at pains not to represent all Jews as unbelieving. He refers first to those who were persuaded by Paul's message.

25. The gathering broke up without agreement, with Paul firing one Parthian shot, quoting a passage (Isa. 6.9f.) used in a number of notable places in the NT (see Mt. 13.14f. = Mk 4.12 = Lk. 8.10; Jn 12.40; Rom. 11.8; cf. Justin, *Trypho* 12.2; 33.1). Belief in the inspiration of the OT is clearly expressed. The words were given through Isaiah but the actual speaker was the Holy Spirit. Cf. CD 4.13, 14.

26. This verse gives the words of Isa. 6.9 substantially as they appear in the LXX, though there are some small variations in order, and variations also in MSS of the LXX.

The prophet is sent to his people with the message that there is no possibility of their understanding what they hear or seeing what they look at. The built-in failure of the message is the content of it. The unbelief of Israel is not an unhappy accident but part of God's intention. The theme is continued in the next verse; see on that verse and on v. 28 for the use Luke (Paul) makes of his quotation.

27. The quotation of Isaiah 6 continues, with small differences between Acts and the LXX. The textual tradition of Isaiah and that of Acts show various assimilations in both directions.

The verse is probably intended by Luke (and was probably intended by Isaiah) as a description of people who had made up their minds not to understand, not to hear, not to see. **they have heard dully** states a fact, **they have shut their eyes** means that the people were themselves to blame for the fact that they did not see. Like v. 26 this verse states that they did not understand, hear, or see, and that this fact does not stand outside God's purpose. The immediate historical consequence of this fact was that the Gospel was taken to the Gentiles – as God intended. Luke is not dealing with the more remote consequence of the ultimate destiny of Israel. He does not see into the situation as clearly as Paul does in Romans 9–11, and he does not recognize (at least, he does not state) the underlying truth that it is only out of disobedience that men can in faith discover mercy (Rom. 11.30–32).

28. This verse makes explicit the intention that has already been given implicitly in vv. 26, 27. If the Jews vacate their place, the Gentiles will fill it. For Luke this is not so much a theological proposition as a statement of fact; he could not fail to observe the fact that the Gentiles were pouring into the church, the Jews were not. This does not mean that Luke considered the mission to Jews (apart from a few individuals) to be now at an end. This is too simple an analysis of Acts. The chief Lucan motif which emerges here is one which runs through his work as a whole. Nothing can or will prevent the spread of the Gospel. The most favoured nation may reject God's offer of salvation; others will take it up. You refuse to listen; they will hear. Luke has his own kind of triumphalism; it is the triumphalism of the word.

this God-given salvation. Luke uses here a form of the word for *salvation* which he does not use elsewhere; perhaps its use in Ps. 66(67).3 is in his mind. **has been sent to the Gentiles**; cf. at the beginning of Paul's mission 13.26: *Brothers, you who belong to the family of Abraham, and those among you who fear God, to us has the message of this salvation been sent.*

XVII

CONCLUSION

(28.(29)–31)

65. CONCLUSION 28.(29)–31

[29] When he had said this the Jews went away, holding much debate among themselves. [30] He stayed a full two years in his own hired house, and received all who came to him, [31] preaching the kingdom of God and teaching the truths concerning the Lord Jesus Christ with all boldness and without hindrance.

In themselves these verses are clear enough. The form of custody in which Paul is kept permits him to receive all who wish to visit him and he continues to preach with freedom and without restraint. The question is why Luke stops when he does. What happened at the end of the 'two years' (v. 30)? It is not surprising that a number of different answers to this question have been given. A good list is given by S. G. Wilson (*Gentiles* 233–6). 1. Luke was writing at the time to which the verses refer. He wrote no more because nothing more had happened. 2. Luke planned to take the story further in a third volume which either was never written or has been lost. 3. Luke did not record Paul's martyrdom because he wished to avoid parallels both with pagan martyrdoms and with the story of Jesus. 4. The martyrdom would have interested neither Luke nor his readers; their concern was with theology, not biography. 5. After two years Paul would automatically be released (see on v. 30). 6. Luke did not wish to encourage a piety of martyrdom. None of these suggestions is satisfactory. Wilson himself makes the points that the readers (in Rome?) already knew the facts and ch. 28 sums up the preceding narratives and their themes. Even these points however do not make a satisfactory answer to the question.

It may be suggested – it cannot be more than conjecture – that the end of the story was omitted because it was not edifying. There are two possibilities which may be to some extent combined. One is that after two years Paul's *custodia libera* was changed into more severe imprisonment; in other words, he was shut up in a dungeon and left to rot. The Roman church may have attempted much or little on his behalf; in the end they gave up. Was it part of Luke's purpose to revive the memory of the forgotten Paul? The second possibility is suggested by 2 Tim. 4.16, which can hardly be pure fiction. There existed a tradition of a desertion of Paul by those who should have stood by him. One possible explanation of the curious fact that after 28.15 there is no reference to the Roman church is that the church was divided and lukewarm in its attitude to Paul. Luke may have thought that his brief concluding note would do better than a description of what happened when the two years of continued evangelism ended in a discreditable failure on the part of Roman Christians.

The two concluding verses were composed by Luke himself. Verse 30 takes up v. 23; *in his own hired house* takes up *to his lodging*; *came to him*, *came to him*; *preaching* and *teaching* take up *gave an exposition* and *persuading*; *the kingdom of God* is repeated; *the truths concerning the Lord Jesus Christ* expands *about Jesus*. The only difference is that in vv. 23f. the audience is wholly Jewish, whereas in v. 30 it includes *all*, which cannot exclude either Jews or Gentiles. This is important, because it shows that 28.26–28 means not that there will no longer be a mission to Jews but that Jewish unbelief is not due to the preacher's failure but is written in Jewish scripture itself.

29. This verse is added by a number of MSS, probably because it was felt that the story begun in 28.23 needed a narrative conclusion. It indicates what Luke probably intended to convey – not the total and final rejection of Judaism but a people divided in their response to the Gospel.

30. a full two years, that is, probably twenty-four months; otherwise *two years* could have meant (by inclusive reckoning) much less.

It was formerly maintained that ancient readers would recognize that an accused person whose accusers did not appear within two years would be released. It is now virtually certain that this view rests on the misdating of a papyrus, which belongs not to the time of

Nero, as was supposed, but to a much later period. The two-year rule was laid down by Justinian, AD 529. Previously however the emperor could have exercised his *imperium* and at the end of two years dismissed the case.

His own hired house is probably correct, but the meaning might be *at his own expense*. **all who came to him** is important to Luke, and his meaning (though not his text) is correctly given by the Western addition, *both Jews and Greeks*.

31. As elsewhere (e.g. 28.23) **the kingdom of God** serves as a general summary of the Christian message, **the truths concerning the Lord Jesus Christ** brings out its Christological content. **preaching** and **teaching** are synonyms and do not denote different operations.

For **boldness** see on 4.13. It has here its primary sense of freedom of speech. **without hinderance** is often used in legal contexts. No one ventured or was able to hinder or prevent.

INDEX